EDUCATIONAL MEASUREMENT AND EVALUATION

second edition

EDUCATIONAL MEASUREMENT AND EVALUATION

JUM C. NUNNALLY

Professor of Psychology, Vanderbilt University

74633

With the collaboration of
NANCY ALMAND ATOR

McGRAW-HILL BOOK COMPANY
*New York   St. Louis   San Francisco   Düsseldorf
Johannesburg   Kuala Lumpur   London   Mexico   Montreal
New Delhi   Panama   Rio de Janeiro   Singapore   Sydney   Toronto*

To my children: Jeffry, Russell, Scott, and Kimberly. They were kind enough to understand that in order for me to write this book I would not be very available as a father and pal during a period of one and a half years.

EDUCATIONAL MEASUREMENT AND EVALUATION

Library of Congress Catalog Card Number 70-37103

07-047553-9

1 2 3 4 5 6 7 8 9 0 KPKP 7 9 8 7 6 5 4 3 2

This book was set in Uranus by University Graphics, Inc., and printed and bound by Kingsport Press, Inc. The designer was Rafael Hernandez; the drawings were done by John Cordes, J. & R. Technical Services, Inc. The editors were Walter Maytham and Ellen Simon. Peter D. Guilmette supervised production.

contents

preface

This is a substantial revision of the first edition of *Educational Measurement and Evaluation*. Because the first edition was well received by students and their professors, the original content coverage and organization have been retained. The intention in writing the first edition was to provide future teachers with an introduction to the most useful theories and technical methods in the field of educational measurement, but in all cases to focus directly on pragmatic issues concerning daily activities in the classroom. In the second edition, that intention has been brought to further fruition by expanding considerably those chapters that are most directly pertinent to the applied use of tests in school situations. This is true of all of Parts II and III, which are concerned with teacher-made tests and standardized achievement tests, respectively. The chapters in these parts have been enlarged in terms of topics covered, references, and illustrations.

All parts of the book have been modernized and, we hope, improved. The statistical appendix (C) has been enlarged to include statistical methods that should prove useful over the years to classroom teachers and others who work directly with educational measurement methods. The test appendix (D) has been considerably expanded and brought up to date. Descriptions are given there both of many traditional tests and of some important new ones that are not covered in most other textbooks. In many places newer tests were substituted for older ones in illustrating principles of educational measurement.

Because there were many things that we wanted to add to the first edition but not much that we could bring ourselves to delete, inevitably the second edition became noticeably longer than the first. The length of the second edition should be about right, however, for a one-semester (or one-quarter) course in educational measurement. Much of the added length is taken up with appendixes and with more extensive explanations and illustrations of the same issues that were covered in the first edition.

In writing this book, I have borrowed heavily from my other books published by McGraw-Hill Book Company: *Tests and Measurements* (1959), *Psychometric Theory* (1967), and *Introduction to Psychological Measurement* (1970). Appreciation is expressed to McGraw-Hill for permitting this wholesale swapping around of materials from book to book.

The lady who has provided me with invaluable assistance in writing other books became a full-fleged collaborator on this one—Mrs. Nancy Almand Ator. Mrs. Connie Lee made many contributions to the manuscript styling and typing. In addition to these two persons, literally scores of others have helped me in many different ways. But to mention one or several would serve only to slight the rest.

Jum C. Nunnally

PART I

BASIC PRINCIPLES
OF MEASUREMENT
AND EVALUATION

chapter 1

WHY USE TESTS?

Mrs. Throckmorton feels both proud and relieved. Her third-grade angels have shouted their way out of the building and are meandering to their night-time homes. "What's on the docket for tomorrow? We have to finish up the spelling bee which was interrupted by lunch. It's too muddy to play out, so we will have to think of something for the children to do inside at recess. If *Weekly Readers* come in tomorrow, we could start on that, and we still haven't finished the mimeographed exercises. Yipes! Tomorrow is the 14th—two hours of achievement testing. I wonder if my children will do better this year in number skills."

Mr. Blair gave his eleventh-grade students back their midsemester examinations in American history. "I don't think they liked it very much, but they got what they deserved. Twice during the month I told them that they needed to study more."

Pete Bronson stayed after class to express great concern about his C+ grade in biology. Pete reminded Mr. Murdock, as he frequently does all his teachers, that he intends to go to medical school in six more years, and he needs good grades. Pete tries to find fault with the coverage and grading of the examination, but Mr. Murdock assures him that the examination was carefully constructed and graded according to the most exacting of standards.

Miss Brown is having a rough time of it. It is her first year out of teachers college, and she has thirty-two of the toughest customers who ever hit second grade. "I get along with most of them most of the time, but I don't understand Jeffrey. He never sits still. Whatever we do, he does something else. Even sitting in a corner by himself, he can keep the whole class in an uproar. I would rather have a full grown hippopotamus wandering freely around the room than have Jeffrey in the class. Maybe if the school psychologist gave him some tests and talked with the parents, we might find some ways to help Jeffrey."

Teachers are by far the greatest users and producers of tests. They swim in a sea of grades, norms, achievement levels, IQs, and school-wide testing programs. Consequently, the teacher who is not familiar with modern theory and methods of testing cannot function at a high level of effectiveness. Our purpose in this book is to bring teachers and prospective teachers up to date on the most effective methods of test construction, standardization, administration, scoring, and interpretation. Since teachers are the prime users of tests, they need to learn to recognize and appreciate the essential features of good tests, and also to recognize and understand the weaknesses and limitations of tests. They need to learn to view the elements of educational testing in a critical and unemotional manner so that they will be able to interpret results realistically and constructively, to both students and parents. Since teachers may be called upon to interpret (and defend) test usage to the public, it is important that they develop a professional attitude toward tests and measurements. Before we go into detail about how tests are developed and used, we should first consider what tests can do for the teacher. This leads to our first principle: *Tests are useful only if they help in making decisions.*

Each use of a test can be traced to a need to make a decision—about a pupil, about a method of instruction, or about a curriculum. The word "decision" must be construed broadly to include all the courses of action that might follow from test scores. If Johnny makes a very low score on the achievement test, the decisions might involve placing him in a remedial section, talking with his parents about his low standing, and encouraging him to work harder. If the best that Pete can do is to make C+ grades in all his courses, he might decide to talk to the guidance counselor about taking some aptitude and interest tests to help him decide on a realistic course to follow after high school graduation. If, on achievement tests, the Wiley School students come out much lower in arithmetic, in terms of national norms, than they do in other subject-matter areas, the decision might be to consider new methods of instruction in the topic. If all the students made very low grades on the American history examination, then perhaps the test did not differentiate well between the levels of ability in the class, or perhaps Mr. Blair did not achieve his objectives of instruction for the unit. He might decide to analyze his test items more carefully or to go back over the material with the class. If it is found that Jeffrey has a very high IQ, the decision might be to provide him with extra material to occupy his overactive mind. When students make poor scores on adjustment inventories, the decision might be to talk with parents, have the students see the school counselor, or consult with a clinical psychologist.

How well a particular test helps in making particular decisions is an indication of how valid it is. Sometimes tests are used which have proved helpful in making numerous decisions. This is the case with intelligence tests, which are useful in making decisions about classroom sectioning, handling of adjustment problems, vocational guidance, and many other matters. Other tests have more narrowly defined functions, such as spelling tests or diagnostic arithmetic tests. Regardless of its potential functions, however, if a test does not effectively aid decision making in a particular situation, then it is not worth the time and effort of administering and scoring. Tests are not, and should not become, ends in themselves; they are means to ends. Using a test should expedite achieving those ends. In this book, we shall talk a great deal about the kinds of decisions which are aided by the use of tests, the ways in which decisions are made, and the means which are used to determine the validity of decisions.

Two of the many schools of thought about the effectiveness of tests are quite wrong. The first holds that tests, particularly personality tests, are both useless and unnecessary intrusions into the sacred privacy of human lives. The second holds that psychological tests are infallible gauges of present abilities and personality characteristics and infallible predictors of future success and adjustment. The truth lies between these two extremes. Although existing tests have their weaknesses, it is safe to say that *tests usually work better than subjective judgments.*

What would the teacher use if tests were not available? On what would he base grades? He probably would do what was done at the turn of the century and base his grades on classroom recitations. The difficulty with these is that they favor the outgoing, glib, self-confident student to the detriment of the less confident, shy, but often more knowledgeable, student. If tests were not available, how would sectioning be accomplished? It would probably be done on the basis of only several days of experience with new students. Even though the teacher often is a talented observer of students, like any other observer he falls prey to typical errors. He has his own idiosyncratic definitions of what constitutes superior abilities—ones which would not be completely shared by other teachers in the same situation. Being human, it is easy for him to confuse likeability with ability and to advance those students who fall into favor.

If the teacher has had only a relatively short period of acquaintance with students, much of his judgment is based on the accidental occurrences in that short time. After three or four months of experience with students, he can make much better estimates of their abilities, but then it is too late. Looking back on his earlier estimates of ability, he can see that he made many mistakes. It takes time to judge people, and if there is not considerable time available, judgments often are quite inaccurate.

In making judgments about students, either about their progress in particular units of instruction or about their over-all abilities, it is difficult to become familiar with an *entire* class. Out of thirty students, six or eight will stand out, either because they are so superior or because they cause so much trouble of one kind or another. The in-between students are like the background of a painting, never attracting much attention, never doing anything either so good or so bad as to receive notice; therefore, it is very difficult for the teacher to make accurate judgments of them.

Without the use of tests, how would teachers judge the effectiveness of new methods of instruction? For example, say that a new method of reading instruction is being employed. After students have undergone the new type of instruction, the only resource available would be to reach subjective conclusions about how well the new method works. Such decisions would be influenced by many things which are unrelated to the issue. Some people are skeptical of anything new and would tend to downgrade new procedures purely because of this. Other people are joyously optimistic about anything new, whether newness means improvement or not. If the new method of instruction is carried out by an unpopular teacher, other teachers are likely to regard the results as dubious, while if it is carried out by a highly respected teacher, others are likely to approve of the results regardless of their intrinsic merits.

The purpose of tests is to help take the personal element and the guesswork out of decisions such as those described above. In such cases, tests have their weaknesses, but they usually are far more effective than the alternative means in meeting most objectives of evaluation. Because there is nothing better to employ, it is not sensible to discuss whether or not tests *should* be used. Rather, the important points to discuss are *how* tests should be used and what procedures can be employed to make tests more effective.

WHAT IS A TEST?

A test is a *standardized situation that provides an individual with a score.* Let us look at the two important words in the definition: "standardized" and "score." By standardized is meant that all the procedures of testing are stated in advance in such a way that all students are tested with the same questions or problems and in the same way. A test is standardized only if two test administrators working independently could obtain the same results with the same group of students. Some of the most essential ingredients of standardization are (1) all students should answer the same questions; (2) instructions should be clear, and the same instructions should be given to all students; (3) no student should be given any advantage not given to all students; and (4) a predetermined system of scoring should uniformly be applied to the answers of all students.

Several examples will suffice to show poor standardization. In administering his own arithmetic test, a teacher fails to tell students that only thirty minutes' time will be allowed. With only ten minutes left, the teacher announces the time limit. Assuming that the test would last an hour, some students have been working slowly, and they do not have enough time left to show what they actually know.

In grading an essay examination, the teacher grades all the questions for one student, then all the questions for the next student, and so on until all tests are graded. At first the teacher has very high standards for grading, but after seeing that none of the papers measure up to his expectations, he becomes more lenient. Obviously, the grades of students depend to a considerable extent on the order in which tests are graded.

An intelligence test is used to help make a decision about the grade placement of a transfer student. The test indicates that the student has an IQ well below average. Unfortunately, the norms for the test were not carefully constructed. A better standardized test would show the student to be of average ability.

Ideally a test should be standardized to the extent that the testing routine can be written down and mailed to Atlanta, Toronto, or London; and the testers in those settings would be able to obtain results identical to those that would be obtained by the persons who originated the test. To the extent to which there are some special subjective elements, either in the test administration or in the scoring, the test is not completely standardized. Standardization is the essence of testing, and without it, it is not proper to use the word "test." Later in the book we will criticize some methods of testing because they lack the essential elements of standardization. The need for standardization in testing is much the same as the need for standardization in the measurement of physical quantities. For measures of length and weight, international standards of measurement are kept in Paris, and measures the world over are calibrated by these. Although we have not yet reached that level of standardization in psychological and educational testing, the effort is the same.

The second important term in the definition of a test is "score." A score means a numerical indication of a student's performance. Why do we need a numerical score rather than simply an adjectival description of how well a student performs, such as "poorly," "pretty good," "very good," etc.? Numerical scores are needed because of the precision which they provide. Such precision allows us to differentiate between the scores of two students, both of whom might be scored as "pretty good." Only when test results are expressed in numerical form is it possible to perform mathematical analyses of the results. Without such mathematics it would not be possible to establish rules for the use of particular tests or to validate the effectiveness of tests in making decisions.

Much of test construction is concerned with our two key words: standardization and scoring. To obtain standardization, a carefully edited set of problems or questions is used. Instructions for taking the test are written out in advance. All necessary materials for taking the test are supplied, and account must even be taken of the fact that some students are sure to break their pencil points in the middle of the test. To maintain standardization, all tests should be given in reasonably comparable environments. For example, standardization would be broken if it were necessary (for some odd reason) for some students to take tests when they were very tired, such as very late in the evening, or for some students to take tests in a highly distracting environment, for example in a room where carpenters are noisily refurbishing the interior. Although common sense would prevent us from making such gross breaches of standardization, more subtle failures to obtain standardized conditions can adversely influence the results of tests. A general rule is that a test is standardized to the extent that results are repeatable by other persons in other settings. This is the same as saying that a test is standardized if it is *reliable*. In Chapter 4 we will discuss at some length the nature of test reliability and the factors that promote reliability.

PHYSICAL AND MENTAL MEASUREMENT

Why is there need to have a book of this kind on mental measurement? In what ways does mental measurement differ from the measurement of lengths of lumber, temperatures of fluids, velocity of atomic particles, heights of blood pressure, and other physical measurement? In terms of purposes there are no differences. Both in the measurement of mental and physical quantities the intention is to assign numbers to objects (with mental measurement the objects are humans) according to specified rules. What differences there are between mental and physical measurements are matters of degree rather than matters of kind. One difference that you often find is that mental measures are more changeable than physical measures. For example, if you measure the length of a piece of lumber now and two years from now, you will find some slight change; however, if you measure the intelligence of a child now and two years from now, the relative amount of change (in terms of practical implications) is likely to be much greater. Some of the personality attributes are even more subject to change over time. To show that such changes are not peculiar to mental measurement, you also find relatively large changes over time in such physical measurements as blood pressure and heart rate.

One of the major differences between most physical and mental measurements is that it is relatively more difficult to interpret some mental measurements. Many physical measurements are so easy to interpret that the question of interpretation is seldom raised. For example, if you were told that a table is 6 feet long, the meaning of rulers and the measurement of length are readily understood without further interpretation. Similarly, with blood pressure: its meaning is relatively clear. This is also the case with some types of mental measurement. For example, if a student performs poorly on a series of arithmetic tests, it points to an obvious deficiency. However, with some types of mental measurements, particularly with measurements of personality characteristics, the meaning of responses is not at all certain. For example, if in an ink blot test the student says that a particular portion of the blot looks like a butterfly, it is not at all clear what the response indicates about him.

In mental measurement, more so than in physical measurement, the proper evaluation of results is a crucial question. Indeed, evaluation of test results with reference to some standard lies at the heart of mental measurement. Evaluation usually implies attaching some label of "good" or "poor" to a measurement. When we measure a boy's height, it usually satisfies our purposes merely to record how tall he is, without any evaluation. Of course, finding out that he is 4 inches taller than most boys in his grade might be regarded as good news for the basketball team, but as bad news in terms of his fitting comfortably into classroom desks. However, even without these evaluations, the recorded height means something to us. On the other hand, when we report that same boy's score on an achievement test, our first question is, "What does it mean?" Just knowing how many items he answered correctly is not enough. We need to know what the score means in relation to some standard before we can make sense of it. How did he score relative to his peers, to his teacher's goals of instruction, and to his ability level?

To obtain answers to questions like these is said to constitute *evaluation* of measurements. Thus, in the title of this book, the words "educational measurement and evaluation" refer to the twin processes of first obtaining measurements and then making sense out of them by comparing them with various standards. The purpose of this book is to explain the many matters that are involved in educational measurement and evaluation.

Because with some types of mental measures there is a need to clarify how results should be interpreted, we speak of "validating" a test. By validating a test we determine how useful an instrument is in making certain kinds of decisions. Because different kinds of tests are intended to help in making different kinds of decisions, a test may be useful or valid for one purpose but totally useless or invalid for others. Consequently, several different types of validation procedures are possible, depending on the nature of the instrument. Chapter 2 will go into detail on methods of test validation.

ADVANTAGES OF MEASUREMENTS

Although the reader probably already appreciates the need for psychological and educational measurement, he may not have considered the specific advantages which such measurements provide. Suppose that a high school teacher is trying to judge the intelligence of a student in order to advise him whether or not to go to college. Even though the teacher may be an excellent judge of such matters, the best that he can do is to describe the student's intelligence in rather gross terms such as "very intelligent" or "highly intelligent." As was mentioned earlier, one of the advantages of measurements is that they allow a more precise, numerical description of how much the student is above or below average.

Mathematical methods cannot be applied to subjective appraisals such as "very high," "below average," etc. Mathematics can be applied to test scores. In this way it is possible to construct norms, make statistical predictions of future performance, and establish statistical rules for making decisions with psychological tests.

Another advantage of measurements over subjective judgments is that measurements allow us to communicate results to others more easily. For example, if a meteorologist had no measurement methods, all that he could report is that on a particular day the wind was "very strong." The phrase "very strong" might be interpreted very differently by different people who hear or read about the results. Because meteorologists have anemometers, they can report that the wind velocity on a particular day was 46 miles per hour. In the same way, it is relatively easy to communicate to others that a student's intelligence is above 99 per cent of those in his age group.

Another advantage, mentioned earlier, is that measurements help to take the subjectivity out of evaluating students. A particular teacher may become very adept at subjectively estimating the capabilities of students and be able to make wise decisions about them. Unfortunately, other teachers may not possess the same subjective skills and may not be able to evaluate students with high accuracy. But if standardized measures were used, all teachers could obtain essentially the same valid results.

A final, and often not fully appreciated, advantage of measurements is that they frequently are much more economical than are *thorough* subjective evaluations. It would take at most one hour for a student to complete a long and thorough spelling test. Although the results would not be a perfect indication of the student's spelling ability, it would probably take the teacher several months of informal observation to reach a comparable level of evaluation of the student's ability in spelling. Similarly, a good intelligence test can be given to high school students in no more than one hour. To obtain equally valid indications of the students' abilities, if ever, it would take even an excellent teacher some months of careful observation. For a relatively short amount of time that tests consume, they are far superior to informal observation and subjective appraisal. Even when teachers have months to observe students, some traits are measured more effectively by mental tests. This is the case, for example, with intelligence tests, which, even though they take relatively short periods of time, are usually considerably more valid than any subjective estimates of intelligence. Regardless of what faults they may have, mental tests are usually cheaper, quicker, and more accurate than subjective appraisals.

MEASUREMENT IN EDUCATION

Most educators agree that developments in psychological and educational testing have gone a long way toward taking the guesswork out of many types of educational decisions. However, there are still many critics of standardized tests. It is easy to find fault with particular tests. Existing tests are far from perfect because there is much still that we do not know about methods of testing. Tests must be constructed on a limited budget and in a limited amount of time. The people who construct them are fallible humans; consequently, some test products are not as good as they should be.

Some say that classroom tests and achievement tests emphasize only trivial details, reward the memorizer, and penalize the more creative student. There is some truth in these and other criticisms, but they are not reasons for *doing away* with tests but rather for constructing and using tests better.

Regardless of how well or how poorly tests are constructed, some would argue that tests are "undemocratic," that they give students feelings of inferiority, force students to be competitive with one another, and result in an unhealthy "valuing" of the child. In the same vein, some argue that standardized achievement tests place a straitjacket on the teacher, causing him to emphasize topics that will appear on the test and hindering his pursuit of ideas that he considers more important.

In connection with nationally standardized tests, some fear that such testing programs will have a Procrustean effect upon schools. Procrustes, in Greek mythology, was a robber who stretched or amputated the limbs of those who fell into his hands to make them conform to the length of his bed! Critics fear that "average" will have the connotation of "normal," with the result that there will be a tendency to try to make everyone average at the expense of neglecting individual differences. A sound understanding of test norms (to be discussed in Chapter 3) would reassure such critics that norms are meant to reflect levels of achievement rather than to dictate what those levels should be.

To disavow the use of tests would represent a head-in-the-sand attitude. Teachers, students, and parents need to know the facts. To ignore the facts only postpones the day of reckoning and keeps all disturbed in the meantime. It is not democratic, or in the long run even kind, to hide the fact that one student has limited abilities or that another has special talents.

We may all be created equal in the sense of human worth, but we are not all equal in terms of abilities and personality characteristics. It would be a great social waste not to help the talented achieve as much as they can, and a great social harm to encourage unsuited students to labor in ventures that will bring failure and discouragement. Taking a frank look at our abilities and personality characteristics is not always pleasant at the moment, but it is necessary for long-range achievement and happiness.

The real question at issue is, "What types of educational decisions do we want to make about students, teachers, and methods of instruction?" If we decide to issue report cards which show graded performance, then tests (usually those composed by the teacher) are the most effective means available for assigning grades. If a school-wide program of counseling is to be instituted, then tests of aptitude and personality are essential. If we want to find new and better methods of instruction, it is necessary to use tests to determine the differential effectiveness of the different approaches.

Tests are valid for specific purposes and for specific groups under specific conditions. It is when these purposes are subverted, and the results interpreted carelessly, that injustice and misunderstanding result. The test itself ought not to be made the scapegoat for the results of invalid use and interpretation. Otherwise, a bad attitude toward all tests can result, which is ultimately a loss to both teacher and student.

Here we shall not try to solve the complex problems of philosophy that underlie American education, but one firm stand will be taken: In making decisions, *the more information, the better.* For example, if something must be done about Jeffrey (the child mentioned earlier, who continually disrupted the class), test results would constitute one useful type of information. Should we not consider his high IQ in the same way that we would take into account poor eyesight or a hearing deficiency? As another example, suppose that Mr. Murdock must explain to a boy's parents why he is being required to repeat the seventh grade. Should not Mr. Murdock consult the results of achievement tests and use these in explaining the problem to the boy's parents? Because the teacher cannot construct a perfect spelling test, should he rely instead on his subjective judgment of students' spelling ability?

Undoubtedly tests provide a useful source of information that is helpful in making educational decisions. The real questions arise when we consider *how* test information will be used, which will be discussed throughout this book. Tests are here to stay, and anyone who seriously advocates their disuse is in the same class as the person who, exasperated with modern motoring, advocates a return to the horse and buggy.

HISTORICAL ORIENTATION TO TESTING

People have always been interested in the assessment of human attributes, but testing, as we know it today, is a phenomenon of the twentieth century. In the Western world, the oral examination reigned supreme for centuries, although the Chinese had a well-developed system of written examinations as early as 1000 B.C. DuBois (1965) writes that achievement or proficiency tests were uniformly applied to all men in the empire who aspired to public office. The candidates were largely self-educated men whose own diligence kept them at their studies for decades, despite the realization that the proportion who would ultimately attain office was exceedingly small. The honor attached to passing the first two levels of examination, and achieving the titles of "Budding Genius" and "Promoted Scholar," was evidently enough to spur them on. The examinations had many of the characteristics of good standardized tests. They were written; all candidates were assigned the same tasks; and each was shut up in a private cell to write his examination. Although even the Chinese were not advanced enough to have devised multiple-choice questions, they evidently were aware of the factors which could affect the reliability of essay test scores. Before being submitted for judging, papers were re-copied by a scribe to ensure the anonymity of the composers.

It was not until the mid-1800s that American educators began seriously to question the validity of the oral method of appraising student progress. Typically, the teacher or a visiting member of the local school committee asked a question of the student. The student responded orally, and an immediate subjective appraisal of the answer was given. Different pupils were asked different questions, so there was no comparability from student to student, and as might be expected, the glib, outgoing student was at an advantage over the shy, less fluent one. Little thought was given to such factors as the reliability or validity of the appraisal. Individual differences in children's performance were usually attributed to laziness, which could be dealt with by means of the hickory stick.

The first recorded instance of written examinations being substituted on a large scale for oral questioning of students occurred in the Boston public schools in 1845 (Caldwell & Courtis, 1924). The examinations, consisting of a large number of essay questions on a variety of topics, were given to refute charges of weaknesses in the schools made by the Secretary of the Massachusetts State Board of Education—Horace Mann. To the surprise of his detractors, the results of the tests proved Mann's criticisms to be justified. Despite the startling results of this survey and the general recognition of the potential value of such a method of examination, it was another fifty years before anything like the Boston survey was again undertaken.

In order to understand the development of educational testing in the twentieth century, we must also consider the growth of measurement in psychology. The two paralleled each other, and developments in both education and psychology were spurred by events in the latter half of the nineteenth century which changed man's way of thinking about himself.

In 1850, psychology was still largely a philosophical discipline and had not yet developed the research methods essential for scientific inquiry into human behavior. One of the most promising milestones in the growth of psychology was the work of Gustav Fechner, during the middle decades of the nineteenth century. At the University of Leipzig, he laid the logical foundation of an area of research known as *psychophysics,* which is the precise and quantitative study of how human judgments are made. He saw in psychophysics "an exact science of the functional relations of the dependency between mind and body" (Guilford, 1954, p. 3). Fechner conducted a long program of research on human judgment in which he performed now classical studies on lifting weights, visual brightness, and the sense of touch. He demonstrated how the logic and methods of science could be used in psychological measurement. This encouraged others to become pioneers in the development of the science of psychology.

Another challenge to man's traditional way of thinking arose with the publication, in 1859, of Darwin's *On the Origin of Species.* Not only did the theory of evolution have a great impact on the philosophical world, but it also had a profound influence on the direction of research in the scientific community. Prior to this time, the predominant view was that man is a static being, having possessed since the day of creation a uniform and unchanging set of physical and mental attributes. Any individual differences were considered "nature's mistakes" in producing the average man. There had been no systematic attempt to study the part which individual differences play in everyday life.

Sir Francis Galton, an adherent of Darwin's theories, became interested in studying individual differences, both physical and psychological, and the hereditariness of individual characteristics. He began the first large-scale testing program to measure many different human attributes at his Anthropometric Laboratory in 1884. Each visitor was charged threepence for having his measurements taken on a variety of physical and sensory tests. In order to analyze the data obtained, Galton made use of statistical methods. His particular need was for a measure of association, or correlation, to detect the amount of resemblance between the individual characteristics of fathers and their sons. Karl Pearson, a colleague of Galton's and a genius in mathematical statistics, derived the statistics of correlation—the procedures which are now widely used in the study of individual differences.

The last two decades of the nineteenth century saw a considerable expansion of studies of individual differences in England and America. The tests were an attempt to measure intelligence, but were largely of a sensory and motor type. Toward the end of the century, it came to be realized that these tests of individual differences were not tapping intelligence. Scores on such tests bore almost no relationship to measures of intellectual achievement, such as school grades, thus refuting the hypothesis that sensory ability is closely related to intelligence and setting the stage for Alfred Binet's breakthrough in the testing of intelligence.

Although Binet, like other psychologists of his time, had worked at constructing tests of sensory and motor abilities, he found that these simpler functions do not measure intelligence as we commonly think of it. Consequently, he abandoned these efforts and decided that it would be more feasible to study the end products of intellectual functioning, than to measure all the simple skills that underlie intelligent behavior.

The advent of modern intelligence tests paralleled important changes in social philosophy. Active concern for the downtrodden, the sick, and the psychologically maladjusted had arisen in France after the French Revolution. This concern for the individual was evidenced in education by the realization that children who fail in school might have problems other than mere laziness. Therefore, the French Minister of Public Instruction commissioned Binet to develop a test for distinguishing the lazy or maladjusted schoolchildren from those who lacked the fundamental capacity to learn. Binet, working in collaboration with Theodore Simon, published the result of his endeavors in 1905. The Binet-Simon Scale was radically different from the tests of Galton and his followers in that it concerned the child's ability to understand and reason with material in his cultural environment.

The United States proved to be extremely fertile ground for the growth of the new ideas which had been originating in Europe. By 1915, the basic principles and techniques of educational and psychological measurement were becoming established. Fundamental statistical methods were known, and some important pioneer work in testing had been done. Advances were seized upon eagerly and utilized by psychologists and educators alike.

In the period between 1900 and 1915, standardized achievement tests in school subjects were being developed, as well as intelligence tests. The need for such tests had been demonstrated by J. M. Rice, who, in 1895, set out upon what was to be a decade of research into the teaching of spelling across the country. Over sixteen thousand pupils were tested, and wide variation was found in achievement from class to class, school to school, and city to city, regardless of such factors as time devoted to study, location of the school, and efficiency of the teacher. Rice's work is significant not only because it demonstrated the need for uniform standards but also because of his scientific approach and his skill in devising measuring instruments.

The entrance of the United States into World War I spurred widespread practical applications of the new principles of testing. As a result of the need for an expedient procedure for appraising and classifying the hundreds of thousands of draftees, the first group test of intelligence, the Army Alpha, was developed. Based on the work done by Arthur Otis, the Alpha was a verbal test for appraising general intelligence. However, the large number of illiterate and foreign-born soldiers made the need for a nonverbal measure apparent, and the first nonlanguage group test of intelligence, the Army Beta, was devised. Nearly two million men were tested with these instruments in 1917 and 1918.

After the war, the Army Alpha and Beta tests were used with many thousands of high school and college students, and the "boom" period in testing had begun. Educational measurement developed rapidly as a result of the increasing interest in educational surveys and appraisals

of school curricula, the recognition of the need for state-wide testing programs, and the establishment of educational journals and professional
organizations through which advances in measurement could be ex-
changed. In 1923, the first standardized achievement battery was published—the Stanford Achievement Test for use in the elementary grades,
a test which has continued to be highly regarded through various revisions
to the present day.

Tests multiplied rapidly in all areas, and were administered widely and
often indiscriminately. The uncritical use of results frequently served as
the basis for unjustified judgments and actions with respect to individuals.
As was inevitable, questioning and doubt about the validity of, and justi-
fications for, this approach to testing arose. The period from 1930 to 1945
was a time of critical appraisal and of taking stock. The emphasis shifted
from measurement of a limited range of skills to evaluation of the whole
range of educational objectives, including interests, attitudes, and appre-
ciations. This expanded range of concern with educational and psychological measurement fit in with the shibboleth of the times—concern for
the "whole child."

During World War II, psychologists were again called upon to devise
tests to aid in the screening and classification of large numbers of men
and women in the armed forces. Testing was more systematic than in
World War I, and test batteries for tapping many aspects of a person's
abilities and aptitudes were developed. Experimental work on tests and
testing programs was begun by psychologists in the armed services, work
which continued to be supported by the Federal government through the
universities after the war.

Today, standardized commercial instruments are available for many
different purposes, which will be discussed in later chapters. It should
be recognized, however, that the historical growth of psychological and
educational measurement has been important not only for commercially
distributed instruments but also for the measurement practices and devices that the teacher employs in the classroom. Many of the principles
that apply to standardized commercially distributed instruments also
apply to the daily practices of teachers in determining to what extent
students are meeting the goals of instruction. These principles will be
discussed throughout this book.

SUMMARY

Teachers top the list of professional groups who need and use educational
and psychological tests. Not only are they the greatest consumers of commercially distributed tests of aptitude, achievement, and others; but also,

because of the thousands of tests that teachers construct for their own students, it is safe to say that they are responsible for at least 75 per cent of all the tests produced in this country each year. For these reasons it is very important for teachers to understand why various types of tests are used and how they can be used to the most advantage.

It was emphasized that tests are useful only if they help in making educational decisions—about students, about classroom activities, about a particular unit of instruction, and about educational practices. To the extent to which a test actually helps in making certain types of decisions, it is said to be *valid* for those purposes. Because the validity of tests must be established rather than taken for granted, various types of studies must be undertaken to show that particular tests are worth using.

A test was defined as a standardized situation that provides each student with a numerical score. All measurement requires standardization, and tests are no exception. If tests were not standardized, the results would depend haphazardly on the persons who administered and scored them. Then it would not be possible to compare scores of different students on the same test, the scores of the same students on different tests, or the scores that students make from year to year. It is important that results are expressed in numerical form in order to make precise comparisons among students and to permit statistical analyses of the results.

The worth of tests is often challenged on two counts. First, it is frequently said that tests cause an unhealthy stratification of children according to their abilities and that tests hamper the teacher in trying to educate children by the methods that he thinks best. These and other bad side effects of using tests certainly occur on occasion, not necessarily because the tests are at fault, but rather because unwise use is sometimes made of them.

The second indictment of tests is that they are not very effective measures of aptitude, achievement, personality, and other characteristics which they attempt to measure. It is easy to find some poor items on even the most carefully constructed test, and it is easy to find whole tests which are not good. Also, there is still much that we do not know about educational measurement, and in some instances admittedly crude measures must be used for want of more valid instruments. However, these potential and real faults should not be used as arguments for doing away with tests; rather, they should act as spurs toward the construction of better instruments. If tests were not available to serve the many purposes that they now serve in schools, the only recourse would be to base decisions on the subjective evaluations of teachers and others. Whenever research comparisons are made between the differential effectiveness of tests and subjective evaluations, tests prove to be cheaper, quicker, and more valid.

SUGGESTED ADDITIONAL READINGS

Cronbach, L. J. *Essentials of psychological testing.* (3rd ed.) New York: Harper & Row, 1970, chaps. 1, 2.

Goodenough, F. L. *Mental testing.* New York: Rinehart, 1949.

Goslin, D. A. *The search for ability: Standardized testing in social perspective.* New York: Russell Sage, 1963, chaps. 2–4.

Goslin, D. A. *Teachers and testing.* New York: Russell Sage, 1967.

Lorge, I. The fundamental nature of measurement. In E. F. Lindquist (Ed.), *Educational measurement.* Washington: American Council on Education, 1951, chap. 14.

Miller, G. A. *Psychology: The science of mental life.* New York: Harper & Row, 1962.

Nunnally, J. C. *Introduction to psychological measurement.* New York: McGraw-Hill, 1970, chaps. 1, 2.

Stanley, J. C. *Measurement in today's schools.* (4th ed.) Englewood Cliffs, N.J.: Prentice-Hall, 1964, chap. 2.

Thorndike, R. L., and Hagen, E. *Measurement and evaluation in psychology and education.* (3rd ed.) New York: Wiley, 1969, chaps. 1, 2.

chapter 2

WHAT IS A VALID TEST?

Just as horses come in different sizes, colors, and shapes and are useful for different purposes, tests differ in appearance and intended usefulness. Just as it would not be possible to judge a race horse by the same standards one would use to judge a dray horse, it is not sensible to apply identical standards to different kinds of tests. In this chapter, we shall discuss the major functions served by tests and the procedures which are used to determine how well tests serve those functions.

If a test serves its intended function well, it is said to be *valid*; if it does not, it is *invalid*. It cannot be too strongly emphasized that a test is valid only for some specifiable functions with specific groups under specific conditions. No test can be said to be valid in a general sense. For example, a teacher might construct an achievement test for use in his class that was quite valid one year but not equally valid the next year because of changes in emphasis and in the instructional material. Whereas a test of motor coordination might be valid for predicting which students will learn to type rapidly, the same test might have little validity for predicting which students will perform well in athletics. Similarly, a particular test might be valid for grouping students with respect to instruction in reading, but have little or no validity in terms of grouping students with respect to instruction in mathematics. Consequently, it is not sensible to place a label on a test saying "generally good" or "generally bad"; it is necessary to label a test as being good for this or that purpose, rather than good in general.

In discussing differences between tests, it is easy to focus on relatively superficial characteristics. For example, the teacher is likely to be concerned with whether tests are of the multiple-choice or essay type. School psychologists discuss intelligence tests in terms of their being verbal or performance. Although these and other such differences in appearance are important (and will be discussed in later chapters), much more important are the three major functions served by tests: *prediction, assessment,* and *trait measurement,* each of which will be discussed in detail in this chapter. To say that a test serves a particular function is to say that it is intended to be useful in making particular kinds of decisions.

When a test is intended primarily to serve a prediction function, its worth or validity depends on the extent to which it is actually successful in estimating performance in some type of real-life situation. An example is a reading-readiness test, which is valid only to the extent that it predicts how well children will perform in first-grade reading activities. An assessment function is successfully served when an instrument directly measures the level of performance in some topic. Whereas the reading-readiness test serves a prediction function, measures of reading achievement serve assessment functions. Scores on reading achievement tests would serve as the criterion against which the predictor instrument would be validated.

Trait measurement is considerably more complicated than assessment and prediction. A prime example of a trait measure is a test of intelligence. Another example of a trait measure is a personality test of the tendency to be dominant rather than submissive in social situations. As will be discussed more fully later, such trait measures cannot be validated entirely by the standards that are applied to either assessment or predictor instruments; rather, what is required is a demonstration of the validity of trait measures through gradual accumulation of data from their use in numerous investigations.

The method of test validation used depends upon the purpose for which the test is intended. As we discuss prediction, assessment, and trait measurement, it will become apparent that a particular test can serve more than one function. For example, an intelligence test can serve as either a predictor or a trait measure. A test in English grammar and composition can serve as either an assessment or a predictor. The legitimate use of any test to perform a certain function depends not upon the name given to the test but upon whether the test has been validated for that function.

THE PREDICTION FUNCTION

One important use of tests is to predict how individuals will behave in certain situations. For example, when tests are used to select students for college, the major purpose is to forecast how well students will do when they actually go to college. If tests are accurate in making these predictions, then they are valid in that sense. Tests are used to make many different predictions in addition to performance in college—performance of stenographers, likelihood of recovering from mental illness, success of pilots in training, tendency for factory workers to have accidents, presence of brain damage, and many others.

In elementary and secondary schools, predictor tests relate importantly to the concept of *readiness.* A primary concern at all levels of education is the readiness of students for succeeding levels of instruction. Whereas, traditionally, a chronological age of six has been acceptable for entrance into first grade, many children could profit from the experience earlier. At the other extreme, even at six years of age, many children are too immature to participate successfully. Tests are valuable in helping to make decisions about the readiness of children for first grade. If such tests accurately forecast how well children will get along in first grade, then they validly serve a prediction function.

The importance of determining readiness extends from kindergarten up through all grades. Readiness tests (much like intelligence tests) are helpful in determining the readiness of students to participate in the first grade. Reading-readiness tests are intended to predict which students will need special help. If ability groupings are used in schools, tests are often used to predict how well students will perform.

When a student transfers from one school to another, the records that accompany him are often difficult to interpret with respect to the new school setting. The two schools may be in quite different localities, differ in the over-all levels of ability of their students, and have important differences in practices and objectives. Tests are often used to predict how well students will perform in new school settings.

In secondary schools, tests are useful in predicting how well students will perform in various aspects of the school program. The test results are helpful in making decisions about the entrance of students into vocational programs, general courses of study, accelerated courses of instruction, honors programs, and others. Near the end of high school, predictor tests are useful in making decisions about vocations and future schooling.

Regardless of what is being predicted, prediction functions are judged in the same way. A test serves a particular prediction function well if it bears a strong statistical relationship to the intended outcome. If a test selects students who subsequently do well in college, it is valid for that purpose. If a test helps obtain more stenographers who succeed on the job, then it is valid for that prediction function. If a test accurately picks out those preschool children who are in need of special training before being introduced to ordinary first-grade fare, then it is serving that prediction function well. In all cases, the prediction function is judged by the strength of the statistical correspondence, or correlation, between a predictor test and the behavior to be predicted.

In order to determine how well an instrument serves a prediction function, it is necessary to have some important behavior to predict. The thing to be predicted is called the *criterion.* For the selection of college students, the criterion would probably be average grades at the end of four years of study. For the selection of stenographers, the criterion might be ratings by supervisors of how well stenographers performed on the job. For the prediction of first-grade performance, the criterion would be grades or ratings made by teachers. In all cases, the criterion stands as a measure of the goodness or badness of some outcome, and the purpose of the predictor is to estimate the outcome. Tests never do a perfect job of predicting outcomes. Consequently, it is necessary to measure the *degree* to which outcomes can be predicted from tests. In Chapter 4 will be discussed the statistical measures which are useful in studying the extent to which tests are predictive of particular criteria.

How do you recognize a good predictor test? Even if you are an expert, you cannot tell for sure by looking at the instrument. Only by conducting a study to determine how well a test actually predicts a criterion can the validity be determined. Sometimes the most unlikely looking test material will prove to be predictive of some criterion. Following is an example:

W#lt*du ———— W#Lt*du

eRT:xCD ———— eRt:xCD

&niOSxc ———— &niOSxc

PaSFk-q ———— paSFk-q

In the above example, the purpose is to place a check mark between each pair of letter groups if they are identical and not to check if one group differs from the other. Just looking at this example you are likely to think that it is only a trivial game. On the face of it nothing important is being measured. However, research has shown that this type of test item tends to measure an ability called *perceptual speed*. Items of this kind are useful in predicting success in clerical work, where it is necessary to quickly recognize mistakes in letters, find names that are out of alphabetical order, and spot particular words in written materials. The test would be useful in advising students about some commercial courses in high school, and it would be useful in counseling students about jobs as secretaries and file clerks.

An employer might rightly question why he should hire people because of their ability to quickly recognize similar and dissimilar groups of letters, such as is required in the type of items shown above. What the employer should be told is that, even if the test may not appear to be important, previous studies have shown that persons selected on the basis of the test (and other such tests) work out well on the job. Six months after workers are on the job, those who scored high on the test are given better ratings by employers than those who scored relatively low on the test.

Sometimes tests which are used to make predictions do have a good deal of intrinsic meaning. Following are some examples.

1. *Indolent* means most nearly the same as
   a. obvious
   b. hard
   c. lazy
   d. untruthful

2. *Up* is to *down* as *friendly* is to
   a. kind
   b. hostile
   c. healthy
   d. obstinate

3. The square root of 121 is
   a. 242
   b. 12.1
   c. 17
   d. 11

4. Add:
   4269
   1954
     62

5. Bill picks 14 apples and gives half of these to his mother. He decides to save 4 apples for his father and to eat the rest. How many apples did Bill eat?

6. An automobile radiator has a capacity of 16 quarts. Presently, it contains 12 quarts of water and 4 quarts of alcohol. How many quarts of fluid would have to be drained and replaced with alcohol to make the mixture half alcohol?

7. The Cathedral of Notre Dame in Paris is an excellent example of
   a. Georgian design
   b. Gothic design
   c. Byzantine design
   d. Romanesque design

The reader will recognize these as examples of items measuring vocabulary, number skills, mathematical reasoning, and general information. Items like these appear on intelligence tests. Such tests provide very useful predictive information to help in making decisions about the readiness of students for each step in the educational process and for special programs of study. Even if some items look important and others look unimportant, when prediction functions are being studied, the real proof of the pudding is in the actual statistical relationships obtained between the tests and their respective performance criteria.

The intuitive appeal of the content of a test relates to what is called *face validity.* That is, the test items look as though they measure something important. Such attractiveness of the items on a predictor test can be important in establishing rapport in the testing situation, but the ultimate standard is how accurately the test actually predicts performance on a criterion measure. A test can give the appearance of measuring something important and then not be useful in predicting anything. As will be discussed more fully later, face validity is much more important for assessment (e.g., achievement tests) than for predictor tests.

The criterion is a necessary aspect of any study of a predictor test. In many studies, determining the criterion presents a larger problem than obtaining good predictors. It must be remembered that while the relationship between test and criterion is a statistical one, the choice of the criterion itself is made on a rational basis. That is, often there is room for disagreement in choosing a criterion, and one must make a good case to justify choosing one criterion over another. Two important criteria are school grades and achievement test scores, both of which reflect the extent to which students have mastered the intellectual objectives of instruction. Both are very sensible criteria, and they are widely used in determining the validity of certain types of predictor tests. However, even school grades and achievement tests frequently do not mirror all the goals of instruction. For example, some of the goals of instruction are to promote intellectual curiosity, motivation for scholarly activities, social adjustment, and the acceptance of widely held social values. We must continuously search for better predictors of traditional criteria of accomplishment in school; at the same time, we must continuously evaluate the extent to which criteria of accomplishment actually consider the important indicants of intellectual development.

The success of a predictor instrument depends entirely upon the extent to which it correlates with some criterion of successful performance. Investigations of the validity of predictor instruments require empirical research in which the predictor instrument is administered at one point in time and criterion measures are obtained later. One example would be administering a test of reading readiness to first graders and measuring reading achievement at the end of the second grade. Another example would be administering a test of college aptitude and obtaining grades made over four years of college. To the extent that the predictor instrument actually forecasted performance on the criterion measure, it could be said to be valid for that type of function. In addition to performing the research required to obtain scores on the predictor test and scores on the criterion measure, it is necessary to make statistical analyses of the degree of relationship between the two types of measures. Essentially, these statistical measures concern *correlational analysis*, which will be discussed in Chapter 4.

THE ASSESSMENT FUNCTION

In contrast to the prediction function, the assessment function concerns a direct measurement of the effectiveness of performance at a particular point in time. An outstanding example of the assessment function is seen when the teacher tests his class for progress in a unit of instruction. When the eighth-grade teacher uses a test in geography, the purpose is to measure directly how well students have met the objectives of instruction in that topic. The purpose of the test is not necessarily to predict anything the student will do in the future, although it would be hoped that grades in the geography class would relate to future performance. Even if it were sensible to judge classroom tests by the prediction function, it would be extremely difficult to determine what such tests should predict and even more difficult to carry out the studies. It is conceivable that a student could do an excellent job in eighth-grade geography yet never take another course in geography, never take another course in which geography was even indirectly involved, and never work at a job where geography was important.

Another example of an assessment function is the use of standardized achievement tests. When standardized achievement tests are given to fourth-grade children, the purpose is to measure directly their over-all performance up to that time. Whereas it was said that items used on predictor tests need bear no obvious relationship to what is to be predicted, items on an assessment instrument should be obviously related to the performance to be measured.

What are some of the essential ingredients of a valid assessment? First, an assessment is always a sampling of the behaviors that connote good or bad performance in a particular situation. On a spelling test it is not possible to include all the words that the student might have encountered. In a test of number skills, only a relatively small sample of all possible problems is included. The notion of sampling is intimately related to assessments. A good assessment is one that covers a representative sample of the important behaviors in a particular situation.

A key term used in our definition of a good assessment is that of *im-*

portant behavior. The items in a good assessment are not randomly drawn from all the things that are seen and heard in the performance situation. Hypothetically, one could write down on slips of paper all the things that were seen and heard with respect to a unit of instruction, including everything in the textbooks and everything that the teacher said. The test questions then could be randomly selected from the total collection of events. If they were randomly selected, the teacher could rightly ask questions such as "Whose picture is on page 96 of the textbook?" "What country were we discussing on April 22?" "What color dress was the teacher wearing last Tuesday?" Of course, such incidental facts would not find their way into any good test. The reason is that a good assessment instrument is restricted to the important aspects of performance.

How do you determine what the important behaviors are in assessment situations? This is necessarily a matter of human values. Classroom testing involves values—values of the particular teacher, values of the school, and values of American education in general. The values which are used to determine the sampling of content for an assessment originate in some individual or some group that has the responsibility for making such decisions. The teacher who tests the students on knowledge of geography has the responsibility to evaluate performance. He determines what behaviors are relatively good and relatively bad, and he tries to tap those behaviors with tests. He includes items of particular kinds because he considers them to be important. Others he excludes because he believes them to be relatively unimportant.

Of course, wherever values exist, differences in values among individuals also exist. Some of the test materials that one teacher would consider important would not be considered important by other teachers. This happens in all types of assessments—in schools, in industry, in military settings, and in other places. Fortunately, in most places where assessments are made there is relatively good agreement about the types of content that should be considered. For example, if three different teachers compose tests for eighth-grade geography classes, although there would be some differences in emphasis, in the main their tests probably would measure much the same thing.

As another example of how assessments necessarily depend on human values, two teachers might have somewhat different goals for instruction in arithmetic. One teacher would tend to stress memorization of arithmetic facts and principles; the other would stress arithmetic concepts. These differences in objectives would lead the two teachers to compose somewhat different examinations for measuring progress in arithmetic.

Because assessments inevitably rest upon human values, it is not meant to imply that teachers do or should compose their examinations without recourse to widely accepted standards. In education some values are held quite widely, and most teachers try to implement those in their instruction as well as in their evaluation of students. For example, nearly all teachers will agree that it is more important for students to grasp general principles about the subject matter rather than to concentrate on the rote memorization of miscellaneous details. Consequently, insofar as possible, most teachers would like to have their examinations relate most prominently to general principles embodied in the subject matter. In education the problem of effective assessment is more a problem of implementation than one of differing values among teachers.

Regardless of how well founded the value system behind classroom instruction and classroom testing, adequate implementation of the values in the form of effective tests requires special efforts and skills. One of the major purposes of this book is to show teachers how to apply their efforts most effectively in constructing classroom tests.

Commercially distributed achievement tests are assessments in the same sense that classroom examinations are, and they depend on the same standards of validity. Prior to the construction of most batteries of achievement tests, groups of educators are consulted about the subject matter emphases that should be employed. For example, before composing a comprehensive achievement test battery to be employed in the eighth grade, groups of educators had to answer such questions as "How much emphasis should be placed on the social sciences?" "Should there be items on geography in the test?" "What maximum level of mathematical training should be assumed?" Working with educators, test constructors are able to arrive at a subject-matter coverage which fits the majority's views. Test specialists are then available to ensure that items are carefully written. Regardless of the elaborateness with which the content is determined and the availability of experts for the construction of achievement tests, they do not differ in principle from the midsemester examination in tenth-grade algebra.

Suppose someone questioned the validity of the tests that you use in your own classroom. How could such arguments be settled? No amount of empirical study would completely answer the questions. No amount of elaborate statistics would provide the key. Questions of validity with assessments inevitably must resort to a rational appeal to the coverage of content areas.

In discussing the validity of particular assessments, some relevant questions are as follows: "Why did you not include questions on the Civil War period in your test?" "Why did your test contain so few items?" "Why did you include more items relating to facts than to applying principles?" To the extent to which a teacher can provide sensible answers to questions like these and others relating to the nature of the content coverage, he gains assurance that good assessments are being made. If the teacher has no good reasons for the content coverage or the mode of presentation of the items, some questions should be raised about the effectiveness of the examination. Trying to answer such questions will often show the teacher that he is not doing a very effective job of implementing his own values about the course or more generally held values about the particular subject matter.

One way to ensure some validity for an assessment is to carefully outline the goals to be implemented in a course of instruction and then to compose examinations relating to that outline. This will help demonstrate, in a direct way, that a broad coverage of important content areas is included in examinations. Examples of such outlines will be discussed in Chapter 5.

From the foregoing discussion, it can be seen that the validity of an assessment depends upon the adequacy with which a body of intellectual content is covered. For this reason, it is frequently said that acceptable assessments require *content validity*. This section of the book has been concerned with the methods whereby the content validity of assessments is determined. Because classroom teachers are usually concerned more directly with assessments than with predictor instruments or trait measures, the remainder of the book will be concerned largely with assessments and with content validity.

MEASUREMENT OF PSYCHOLOGICAL TRAITS

All teachers are familiar with the two test functions which were discussed previously: prediction and assessment. They are familiar with intelligence tests and special aptitude tests used to predict success in various subject-matter areas. Teachers are highly familiar with assessments, not only in the form of standard achievement tests, but also in the form of the many tests they compose for their own students. However, there is another important test function, one with which teachers usually are not very familiar. This is the measurement of psychological traits, or *constructs*, as they are often called. For example, psychologists have many theories about the construct of anxiety and perform many experiments relating to anxiety. One theory is that a moderate amount of anxiety facilitates certain kinds of learning. In order to perform experiments to test such a theory, it is necessary to measure relative amounts of anxiety in students. Many procedures have been suggested for measuring anxiety, including physiological measures of the electrical resistance of the skin, personality inventories, and others. But how do you tell whether any or all of these actually measure anxiety rather than something else?

Can the proposed measures of anxiety be validated by the same standards applied to predictor tests? No, the purpose of the test is not to predict something else, but to measure anxiety then and there. There is no single criterion that can be used to test the test. Can the test of anxiety be validated as an assessment in the same sense in which achievement tests and classroom examinations are judged? No, that standard cannot be applied either. There is no obvious content to be outlined and represented in an examination in the way that this can be done for a course in geography or algebra. The test items do not obviously measure anxiety, and some proof must be given.

Another type of test requiring construct validation would be an inventory used to measure dominance versus submission. The following item is used on such an inventory (Allport & Allport, 1939):

Someone tries to push ahead of you in line. You have been waiting for some time and cannot wait much longer. Suppose the intruder is the same sex as yourself, do you usually:

Remonstrate with the intruder   _____

Call the attention of the man at the ticket window   _____

"Look daggers" at the intruder or make clearly audible comments   _____

Decide not to wait and go away   _____

Do nothing   _____

It would be easy to list hundreds of such test items intended to measure psychological traits. The above is a self-report type of item, but in practice many other types of test materials are used in the attempt to measure psychological traits, including measures of perception, ink blot tests, tests of behavior in group situations, and others.

Trait measures are said to concern constructs and to require *construct validity*. Trait measures are constructs in the sense that they are things that scientists literally put together to account for phenomena in the world. Constructs do not exist as visible events in daily life. Thus, the terms "intelligence" and "anxiety" do not represent simple, observable events in daily life; rather, they represent devices employed to explain many forms of behavior. Such constructs are essential to all areas of science. The construct of gravitation is important for physics; the construct of evolution is important for biology; and the construct of cultural lag is important for anthropology. And so it goes in all areas of science—

the scientist must employ constructs as explanatory devices. Employing such construct names assumes that a very general process is being indexed. Thus, when one employs a particular test in an investigation and refers to the test as a measure of anxiety, what is being assumed is that the test measures a very general tendency to experience anxiety in many situations. Similarly, when one refers to a particular test as an intelligence test, the assumption is that the test measures the tendency to perform intelligently in many situations.

How do you determine the validity of trait measures? Measures of psychological constructs gain meaning only after they have been applied in many different circumstances. In construct validation, a new measure is tested against those variables and situations where everyone will agree that relationships would be expected. If the new test is a valid measure of a psychological construct, then many experimental results could be expected. For example, a valid measure of anxiety should show differences between students diagnosed by school psychologists as being anxious and unselected groups of normal students. Scores on the test should change when students are in anxiety-provoking situations, such as immediately before an important final examination. Many more such relationships would be expected. If the new measure fits in well with these expectations and if it correlates with those variables where correlations are expected and shows differences where differences are expected, then our faith in the validity of the measure is increased.

It would be likely that some of the expected results from construct validation would be obtained and that others would not be obtained. This shows the limits of the validity of the new measure and helps to redefine the measure. For example, after many studies, it might be found that the proposed measure of anxiety does seem to measure anxiety related to possible physical harm, such as in athletic contests. However, it might not measure anxiety provoked in social situations, such as when embarrassing incidents occur in the classroom.

Another example of construct validation has to do with individually administered tests, such as the well-known Stanford-Binet. Confidence in the legitimate use of the term "intelligence" to refer to such tests has been gained from a multitude of sources. First, items were selected which intuitively seemed to concern intelligence, such as general information, knowledge of words, and ability to solve simple problems. Second, only those items were retained for which there was an improvement as a function of age. Because it is generally assumed that intelligence increases with age, at least up to the late teens, the selection of items that correlate with age gives further confidence that intelligence is being measured. Third, items were retained for the final scale only if they all tended to measure the same thing. This provides further evidence that intelligence is being measured because intelligence is thought to be a rather general attribute that pervades many types of intellectual activities. Fourth, and most important, evidence for the legitimate use of the term "intelligence" in relation to existing tests has been obtained from many studies in which such tests were used. It has been found, for example, that such tests relate to success in school settings of all kinds, ratings of intelligence by teachers, success in daily life, and many other things that logically should relate to intelligence. Although no one would claim that existing measures of intelligence perfectly fit the construct, the aforementioned mass of circumstantial evidence encourages continued use of the tests and continued use of the construct name of "intelligence" to refer to what the tests measure.

In essence, construct validation consists of weaving a network of meaningful relations between a new measure and other supposed measures of the same trait. If such relations hold, the new measure then can be trusted in subsequent use. If such relations do not hold, subsequent use of the instrument should be held suspect.

RELATIONS BETWEEN PREDICTION, ASSESSMENT, AND TRAIT MEASUREMENT

It was said that the three functions of measurement—prediction, assessment, and trait measurement—are validated, respectively, by the accuracy of specific forecasts, the completeness of coverage in a content area, and the degree to which expected relationships are obtained in a variety of situations. It should not be thought that these functions are entirely unrelated. Here we shall describe some of the ways in which the three interact.

The three functions of measurement are related in the sense that one instrument may, at one time or another, serve two or even all three of them. For example, a classroom examination in ancient history could be used to make predictions about future performance. The midterm examination in ancient history probably would be an excellent predictor of final grades in ancient history and might also be predictive of future course work, even though it was not specifically constructed for that purpose.

Achievement test batteries are constructed as assessments, and their primary validity depends on the reasonableness of their coverage as judged by teachers and other educators. However, achievement tests are also excellent predictors of future academic achievement. One of the best predictors of performance in college is a comprehensive achievement test given at the end of high school. The important consideration is what function is being exercised for an instrument at a particular time, and the instrument must be validated for that function. If an achievement test is being used, as it usually is, to provide a direct assessment of the progress of pupils, then it must stand as an assessment and be judged accordingly. If in addition it is used to make predictions about future academic or vocational success, then in those instances the achievement test must be validated as a predictor and must show strong correlations with future indices of success.

Although it was said that trait measurement is not the same as the prediction function, in a sense predictions are at the heart of the matter. The difference is that with the prediction function the effectiveness of an instrument stands or falls on one comparison, that between the test and the criterion. In construct validation (trait measurement), rather than there being one specific prediction to be made, a host of predictions is made, no one of which is crucial. Whereas in prediction you can state the validity in terms of one statistical index, in construct validation there is no one measure that can be applied, such as to say that the test is a 70 per cent pure measure of anxiety.

Whereas it was said that the validity of assessments mainly is determined by an appeal to the representativeness of the content coverage, other validation procedures also provide useful information. For example, it is helpful for the teacher to inspect the difficulty of test items. If the teacher intended a particular item to be relatively easy and, in fact, it is found that practically none of the students get the item correct, the teacher would certainly have reason to reconsider the item and how it is stated in the test. It would be helpful when constructing achievement tests to study the amount of improvement which students show throughout a course of training. For example, if an achievement test in high school mathematics is being developed, it would be interesting to see how much improvement there is on the test from before to after. Obviously if students made no better scores after the course of training than before, either the course of instruction or the test was no good. Those items on which the most improvement occurs usually relate more strongly to the actual content of the course. On some types of items a great deal of progress might be shown and on others relatively little progress would be shown. These differences would provide hints to the test constructors in regard to how to improve the achievement test.

Although the types of statistical results mentioned above and others are helpful in constructing assessments, it is important to keep in mind that these are secondary to the use of human judgment to determine the appropriateness of content coverage. Statistical results do not dictate how assessments are composed, but rather they provide clues about how to improve achievement tests and classroom examinations. For example, even if students fail to get a particular type of item correct on the classroom examination, this does not mean that the items necessarily are inappropriate or poorly formulated. It may be the fault of the students, and the teacher may decide to retain the specific type of item on future tests and instruct students to do better in the particular content areas represented. Similarly, it would not be correct to judge achievement test items purely in terms of the relative amounts of change from before to after. If this were the case, then an excellent item would be "What color is your textbook?" Many of the students will not know the answer before the course gets under way, but nearly all of them will know it afterward. Statistical evidence is not the primary basis for the construction of assessments, but it provides many hints about how assessments can be generated and improved.

Whereas it was said that the prediction function does not necessarily depend on the instrument's looking as if it is important (face validity), this does not necessarily mean that test material always is or should be nonsensical in appearance. Although the proof of the pudding is in the statistical relationships which are obtained, it certainly gives one more initial confidence in choosing and studying a predictor if the content appears, intuitively, to be importantly related to what is to be predicted. Selecting and trying out tests to serve a prediction function should never be done randomly. The better you are able to guess initially which predictors will work, the quicker the problem is solved. Consequently, the intuitive appeal of the test content may determine those instruments which are studied for their actual predictive power in particular situations.

SUMMARY

It is never safe to accept a new test at face value until some evidence is obtained to show that it does what it is purported to do. In the same way that it would be foolish to accept a new medicine as a cure for hay fever until some evidence is shown that the medicine actually works, it is unwise to accept so-called measures of intelligence, fourth-grade achievement, neuroticism, and others until the evidence is shown. In school settings, tests are worthwhile (valid) only if they help in making educational decisions. Special investigations must be undertaken to ensure that particular tests actually serve their intended functions well.

Although the types of decisions for which tests potentially provide helpful information are legion, they can be classified into three broad classes or functions. The simplest function to understand is that of prediction, in which the effort is to accurately forecast some important behavior. This function is exercised when tests are used to place underage children in the first grade, when they are used to assign children to different levels within grades, and when they are used to counsel students about college training. Tests used in these ways serve their functions validly only if they actually forecast how well students will perform. Validity is determined by correlating test scores with criteria of performance obtained later.

The second function which tests serve is that of assessment, which concerns the performance of a student in a unit of instruction or the overall progress of a student in school up to a particular point in time. Primary examples of assessments are achievement tests and tests composed by the teacher to measure the progress of his students. Assessments are not validated principally by empirical studies and statistical analyses of results; rather, their validation consists in a careful inspection of the content relative to the comprehensiveness of the coverage.

The third function which tests serve is that of measuring various psychological traits such as anxiety, dominance, intelligence, and others. Such tests are very useful in educational research. Tests intended to measure psychological traits cannot be validated solely by their statistical relationships with criteria (as is the case with predictor instruments) or solely by a study of the content (as with assessments). What must be done is to relate such instruments to numerous other tests and real-life situations in which their respective traits supposedly occur. Essentially, this is a "bootstrap" operation in which the worth of a new measure is determined through many correlations with other measures. Although teachers are seldom directly concerned with developing or administering measures of psychological traits, they need to know something about them in order to interpret the results of educational research and to understand their functions in guidance and counseling.

SUGGESTED ADDITIONAL READINGS

American Educational Research Association and National Council on Measurements Used in Education, Committee on Test Standards. *Technical recommendations for achievement tests.* Washington: National Education Association, 1955.

American Psychological Association. *Technical recommendations for psychological tests and diagnostic techniques.* Washington: American Psychological Association, 1954. (Also in *Psychol. Bull.,* 1954, **51,** No. 2, Part 2.)

Anastasi, A. *Psychological testing.* (3rd ed.) New York: Macmillan, 1968, chaps. 5, 6.

Cureton, E. E. Validity. In E. F. Lindquist (Ed.), *Educational measurement.* Washington: American Council on Education, 1951, chap. 16.

Ebel, R. L. *Measuring educational achievement.* Englewood Cliffs, N.J.: Prentice-Hall, 1965, chap. 12.

Noll, V. H. *Introduction to educational measurement.* (2nd ed.) Boston: Houghton Mifflin, 1965, chap. 4.

Nunnally, J. C. *Psychometric theory.* New York: McGraw-Hill, 1967, chap. 3.

chapter 3

SCORES, NORMS, AND STATISTICS

One of the great advantages of standardized measures is that they supply numerical results—inches of height, number of words correct on spelling tests, and IQs. Because of these numerical results, it is possible to apply many types of mathematical treatments to test scores. Mathematical treatments are very helpful in answering questions like (1) How much has the spelling ability of Sam Parks improved from the beginning to the end of the fourth grade? (2) How well are students at Wiley School progressing in arithmetic relative to the progress shown by students in other schools across the country? (3) How much above average in general intelligence is Sarah Russell? (4) Is Jack Franklin performing as well in school as his abilities permit?

Unfortunately, some teachers in training are afraid of mathematics, and they fail to learn some elementary principles that would greatly facilitate their use and interpretation of test results. This is particularly sad because the mathematical procedures required in educational measurement are simple indeed. It is not possible fully to comprehend how tests are constructed, standardized, used, and interpreted without first understanding some simple mathematical principles concerning scores, norms, and statistics.

The need for mathematical analyses of test results can be illustrated by a typical event in the day of a student. Susie tells her mother that she made 44 in spelling and 18 in arithmetic. The mother is happy about the spelling grade, but worries about Susie's progress in arithmetic. Of course, the mother does not have sufficient information to make such decisions about Susie's progress. If the spelling test had 100 words and the teacher expected students to know the majority of them, then 44 was a very poor score. If the arithmetic test contained only 25 problems, then 18 might have been a very good score.

The direct results of tests are referred to as *raw scores*. For example, such scores would be the number of correct answers on a true-false test and the sum of points obtained on an essay test. Raw scores are seldom directly meaningful until they are compared with standards. The first standard is a statistical one which is obtained by comparing the score of each student with the average score of a group of students. We can compare Susie's score with the scores obtained by other members of her class. If it can be said that Susie's score is above the average score or below the average score, this offers a basis for interpretation. When the actual performance of some group is used as the frame of reference for interpreting test scores, we speak of using *norms* as indices of performance.

The second standard is one of values. Regardless of who is average, above average, or below average, the teacher might decide that, as a group, the students have done poorly or well. He does not base this interpretation on statistics, but on values, goals, or expectations. Perhaps the teacher knows that although a student made a below-average score, he is performing well, considering his limited ability. As another example, a teacher may be displeased rather than pleased by finding that his students are moderately above average in reading skills as compared with national norms. Because he is teaching a special class of supposedly gifted students, he expected them to score even higher on the average than they did. These types of interpretations are based on subjective standards rather than on the more objective statistical norms. Both standards for interpretation are important. In this chapter, we shall consider normative standards and how they are derived; in Chapter 7, we shall discuss other factors which go into teachers' evaluations.

MEASURES OF AVERAGE PERFORMANCE

Much of what happens in the classroom depends on what the "average" student can and does do. In many ways the average student is king, because he sets the pace for the whole class; and it is only by comparison with his performance that the extremes of good and poor performance can be recognized. Also, the goals of instruction largely are judged by how well the average student progresses. For these reasons, it is important for teachers to learn some principles regarding the calculation and interpretation of measures of average performance.

The word "average" has several meanings. As a prelude to discussing them, let us look at some typical raw scores, the scores of eleven students on an arithmetic and a spelling test. By looking at the two sets of scores, the experienced teacher would have an approximate idea of how well the group as a whole performed (the "average") and how widely the students varied in performance (the "dispersion"). Rather than rely solely on a subjective evaluation of the results, there are some simple measures which

	Arithmetic	Spelling
Johnny	22	48
Fred	12	52
Mary	14	49
Bill	12	51
Kim	14	55
Susan	14	52
Michael	17	50
Sharon	19	62
Harry	11	56
Patricia	15	52
Eric	20	75

can be used to index the average performance and the dispersion of performance. Not only are the measures more precise than a subjective evaluation of the results would be, but they also have an additional advantage: they greatly facilitate the communication of results to other persons. If Mrs. Wilkins wants to show other teachers how much better one section of ancient history performs than another, one way to do this would be to show both lists of test scores. More to the point, and much easier to understand, would be to show the precise average scores in the two sections. Similarly, in communicating test results to students, parents, and others, communication is facilitated by saying that a particular score is "above average" or "much above average." Even better is to state the percentage of students which Susie surpasses on a particular test.

Just as there is more than one way to skin a cat, there is more than one measure of average performance and more than one measure of dispersion in performance. First, we will look at some of the measures of average performance and discuss their relative advantages and disadvantages. Later we will discuss measures of dispersion.

Before discussing measures of average performance, it is important to distinguish between *score points* and *scores*. Score points are all possible numerical values on the test continuum. If, for example, the test consists of 100 multiple-choice items, the range of possible score points is from zero to 100. Scores are the actual numerical results obtained from a particular group of students. There are two reasons why it is important to distinguish scores from score points. First, with sets of test results scores usually are obtained for only some of the possible score points. In the example above, even though there may be a score point of 100, it might be the case that no student would score at that point. When there are many items in the test and only a few students are tested, inevitably there are many more score points than are represented by actual scores at those points. The second reason why it is important to keep the distinction in mind is that score points include all numerical values including fractional values, but usually it is the case that raw scores are expressible only in whole numbers. In measuring average performance, it often is found that the average is a fractional number like 41.26. If, as is usually the case, it is possible only to receive scores expressed as whole numbers (e.g., 41 or 42, but nothing in between), then the average must be thought of as a score point rather than an actual score. Keeping in mind the distinction between scores and score points will facilitate an understanding of the material in this and subsequent chapters.

MODE.   The measure of average performance which is the easiest to compute, and in many ways the easiest to understand, is the *mode.* Quite simply, the mode is the most frequently occurring score. In the arithmetic test, the most frequently occurring score is 14, with three students (Mary, Kim, and Susan) achieving that score. The mode is 52 on the spelling test. Although the mode is sometimes a useful measure, it has several faults, particularly when it is determined on as few students as are in most classes. The mode is a relatively "unstable" measure; i.e., it changes considerably when different groups are tested. If a teacher used the mode as the preferred measure of average performance and if he applied the same test to several different classes, he would find rather marked shifts in the mode due purely to the happenstance of some brighter pupils being in one rather than another class. Even if the same, or a very similar, test is administered to the same class on two occasions, the mode is likely to change by relatively large amounts — more so than the two measures which subsequently will be discussed.

Another fault of the mode is that it is indeterminate when two scores occur with equal frequency. Suppose that on the arithmetic test three students had scored 13, and three had scored 14, and no other score occurred more than twice. Then which is the mode, 13 or 14? We might cut this Gordian knot by saying that the mode is 13.5. More likely what would happen would be that scores as divergent as 12 and 16 would be competing as the mode with equally high frequencies. Then it is relatively meaningless to talk about the mode and not much help to talk about modes in the plural.

As if these faults were not enough, the mode is a poor starting point for the development of other statistics, e.g., measures of dispersion. One standard which is employed in selecting measures is that of mathematical convenience. It often is much easier to develop additional mathematical procedures when starting from one measure than from another. By this standard the mode is a rather poor measure.

For the same reason that it is valuable to know the bad signs as well as the positive features in purchasing a horse, it is helpful to know some of the potential faults of statistical measures. Only by understanding the faults of some measures is it possible to appreciate the advantages of others.

MEDIAN.   Another measure of average performance (central tendency) is the score point (unlike the mode, not necessarily an actual score) which divides the students into two equal groups, where 50 per cent score higher and 50 per cent score lower. This is called the *median.* If a student scores above the median, it can be said that he is in the top 50 per cent. If he scores below the median, he is in the bottom 50 per cent. The median is easily interpreted and easily communicated to others.

To determine the median, start by ranking the pupils, writing at the top of the page the name of the student who makes the highest score, next the second highest score, and so on to the student who makes the poorest score. There usually will be many ties; e.g., Johnny will score the highest with 26 and thus be ranked 1, and three students will come next with identical scores of 25. Rank the ties arbitrarily, giving ranks of 2, 3, 4 to the three in whatever order they appear. In this way every student will receive a rank, and the ranks will run from first to last, the last being ranked 11 or 30, or however many students took the test.

If an odd number of students took the test, the median can be defined as the score made by the middle person. If there are eleven students and their scores are ranked, the median is the score obtained by the student ranked sixth (five students above and five below). If there is an even number of students, the median falls (theoretically) halfway between two scores. If there are ten students and the one ranked fifth has a score of 18 and the one ranked sixth has a score of 17, the median can be stated as 17.5.

The approach to determining the median described above is somewhat disrupted by the extent to which there are tied scores at the median. To illustrate the difficulty, suppose that five students score 18 or higher, five score 17, and one student scores 16. Then by the rule stated above, the median is said to be 17, but this is rather misleading. According to the strict definition of the median, 50 per cent of the students are supposed to score less. In this instance, if a student had a score of 17, he would be at the median, which implies that about 50 per cent of the students score lower. In fact, only one student scores lower. This is a very unusual circumstance, but to a lesser degree the same type of problem occurs in most instances in which the median is used. More typically, 47 per cent of the students would score 18 or higher, 38 per cent would score 16 or lower, and 15 per cent would score 17. By the rule stated above, the median would be said to be 17, but actually there are more (47 per cent) above than below (38 per cent).

When there are tied scores at the median, as there nearly always are in practice, the median is not uniquely defined and must be estimated. One method of estimating the median was stated above. A more precise way is to *interpolate*, i.e., in the example above to obtain a hypothetical figure somewhere between 17 and 18, such as 17.2 or 17.4. A method for so interpolating is discussed in Appendix C-5. Although it is useful to make such interpolations in large-scale test development projects, it is seldom worth the effort in determining the median for classroom examinations. For most practical purposes, the rule stated above will suffice. To reiterate, rank the students, and if an odd number of students is tested, find the middle ranked student and designate his score as the median; if an even number is tested, find who has the lowest score in the top 50 per cent and designate his score as the median. According to the rule, the median is 14 on the arithmetic test. Of the eleven students, five make scores higher than 14 and the remaining six make scores of 14 or lower. On the spelling test the median is 52, with three students scoring at the median.

Teachers will find the median a useful index of central tendency. Its advantages are that it is easy to compute when there are no more than twenty or thirty students, and it is relatively easy to explain to others. The disadvantages are that, if many students are tested and exact estimates are needed, the median is "messy" to compute; and as is the case with the mode, it does not offer as much mathematical convenience as the measure which will be discussed next.

MEAN.   A measure of central tendency is available which can be easily computed and easily understood and can be used in many mathematical developments. The *mean* is obtained by adding all the scores on a test and dividing the sum by the number of students tested. The sum of scores on the arithmetic test is 170. Dividing this by 11 (the number of students) gives a mean of 15.45. In the same way a mean of 54.73 is found for the spelling test.

The mean is the measure that we most frequently think of when the word "average" is used. If there are many items on the test and many students taking the test (say at least twenty of each), the mean, median, and the mode usually are very much the same. In the arithmetic test the mean, median, and mode are, respectively, 15.45, 14, and 14. On the spelling test they are 54.73, 52, and 52.

If the mean has a fault, it is that it is strongly influenced by extreme scores. The story is told of the census taker who sought to find the average wealth in a very small town. He found seven persons penniless and one person worth 10 million dollars. By studiously computing the mean, the census taker came to the conclusion that the "average" person was a millionaire. In a less dramatic way, an extreme score had a marked effect on the mean of the spelling scores. Eric's score of 75 is so divergent from the others that it pulled the mean upward making it 2.45 score points higher than the mode and the median. Fortunately, such extreme scores are unusual. When they occur, the median usually is preferable to the mean as a measure of central tendency.

The mean is the preferred measure of central tendency to be used in most situations. Where there are very extreme scores or where expediency is an important consideration, the median can be used instead.

DEVIATION SCORES.   After the mean is obtained, the performance of each student can be described in terms of his relative position above or below the mean. On the arithmetic test, Eric is 4.55 score points above the mean, and Patricia is .45 score points below the mean, which indicates that Eric is above average and Patricia is below average. Scores stated in reference to the mean are called *deviation scores,* which are obtained by subtracting the mean from each of the raw scores. A positive deviation score indicates that the student is above average; a negative deviation score indicates that the student is below average. The full set of deviation scores on the arithmetic and spelling tests (the raw scores of which were listed earlier) are as follows:

Arithmetic deviation scores	Spelling deviation scores
6.55	−6.73
−3.45	−2.73
−1.45	−5.73
−3.45	−3.73
−1.45	.27
−1.45	−2.73
1.55	−4.73
3.55	7.27
−4.45	1.27
− .45	−2.73
4.45	20.27

Deviation scores are useful, in themselves, as a quick method for determining how much scores vary about the mean; but they are also very important as the basis for measures of dispersion, to be discussed next.

MEASURES OF DISPERSION

An understanding of measures concerning the spread, or dispersion, of scores about the mean is as important as an understanding of measures of average performance. In neighboring schools, two fourth-grade classes could show the same average performance on an achievement test and yet differ importantly in their dispersions of scores. In one class scores could be packed tightly about the mean with no very high or low scores. In the other, scores could range from those to be expected of students several grades higher to those of students who are functioning at the second-grade level. Of course, such differences in dispersion would have many implications for sectioning of students according to levels of ability and many implications for daily classroom practices.

Before we can meaningfully interpret particular deviation scores, we must learn how widely scores are scattered above and below the mean. A deviation score of 2.00 would represent superior performance if all the scores are closely packed about the mean. But if there are deviation scores as high as 100 and as low as −100, a deviation score of 2.00 would indicate near average performance. Consequently, we need a measure of the spread, or dispersion, of scores about the mean to help interpret particular deviations. As was true of the "average," there are various measures of dispersion that can be used. Two of the most useful ones will be discussed.

RANGE.   One very simple index of dispersion, the *range,* is obtained by subtracting the lowest score from the highest score. The highest score on the arithmetic test is 22 and the lowest is 11, giving a range of 11. The range of scores on the spelling test is 27, indicating that the dispersion of scores is greater in spelling than arithmetic.

The range is a quickly obtained and often used index of dispersion. The major fault of the range is that it depends on only two scores, the highest and the lowest. Consequently, it is rather unstable. If Eric had not taken the spelling test, the range would have been only 14 instead of 27. In other words, if by chance Eric had been in another school or another section at the same school, the teacher would have come to a very different conclusion about the dispersion of scores on the test. Another fault of the range is that it does not offer a good starting point for the development of other statistics. The range is recommended as a measure of dispersion only when expediency is important and there are no very extreme scores. When time permits its calculation, a much better measure of dispersion is the *standard deviation.*

STANDARD DEVIATION.   The standard deviation offers the best all-around measure of dispersion. It serves very well to summarize how widely the scores of students are distributed about the mean score point. By comparing the deviation score of each student with the standard deviation, one can judge the extent to which a student is above or below average.

The first step in developing the standard deviation is to square each of the deviation scores. Then these are summed, and the sum is divided by the number of students. The resulting measure is called the *variance*. The variance is a very useful measure of dispersion in the employment of inferential statistics, such as would be used in testing the statistical significance of differences in the average achievement test scores of students in the fourth grade of three different schools. However, for the interpretation of the test scores of individual students, the square root of the variance is a much more useful measure of dispersion. The square root of the variance is called the *standard deviation* (SD). The variance and SD for the arithmetic and spelling tests are obtained as follows:

	Arithmetic squared deviations	Spelling squared deviations
	42.90	45.26
	11.90	7.45
	2.10	32.83
	11.90	13.91
	2.10	.07
	2.10	7.45
	2.40	22.37
	12.60	52.85
	19.80	1.61
	.20	7.45
	20.70	410.87
Sum of squares	128.70	602.12
Variance (sum of squares/11)	11.70	54.74
SD (square root of variance)	3.42	7.40

The variance is the mean squared deviation score; the SD is the square root of the variance. The reason why it is more convenient to work with the SD rather than the variance will become clearer in a moment when the normal distribution is discussed. For the meantime, the important point is that the SD is a very useful measure of dispersion. When the SD is relatively large, scores scatter widely about the mean; conversely, when the SD is relatively small, students do not vary widely in performance.

Figure 3-1 illustrates two distributions of test scores that differ markedly in terms of standard deviations, although the mean score is the same for both distributions. Distribution A shows the scores on a reading achievement test of students who differ widely in terms of ability. Some students make very low scores, and some students make very high scores. Distribution B shows the scores of students who do not differ very much in ability. All scores are clustered rather tightly about the mean, and consequently there is very little difference between the student with the highest score and the student with the lowest score. Thus, in order to interpret properly an individual student's score by normative standards, we need to know not only the group mean but also the standard deviation of the scores in that group.

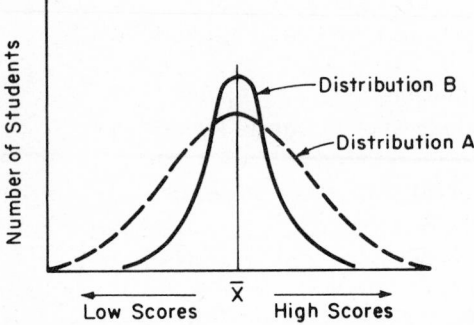

Figure 3-1. Comparison of two distributions of achievement test scores in reading. One distribution (A) has a large standard deviation, and the other distribution (B) has a small standard deviation.

There are numerous shortcut formulas for obtaining the SD. If an automatic calculator is available, the SD can be computed directly from raw scores without having to compute deviation scores. Formulas for this and other computational approaches for obtaining the SD are described in Appendix C-8. All the formulas give the same result.

Like the mean, the SD is sensitive to very extreme scores. For example, it was seen that the squared deviation score for Eric in spelling (the last in the list) was 410.87, which served to greatly enlarge the standard deviation. As was mentioned previously, it is fortunate that such extreme deviations are unusual; the SD is thus a meaningful measure of dispersion in most practical work.

TRANSFORMATIONS OF THE MEAN AND STANDARD DEVIATION

In developing the norms for a commercially distributed test, it is often convenient to transform raw scores to a new set of scores having a particular mean and standard deviation. One such transformation is to fix the mean at 50 and the standard deviation at 10. The advantage of using a set mean and standard deviation is that it facilitates the interpretation of particular scores. Such transformations help circumvent the problems in comparing scores on tests that differ with respect to mean and standard deviation. For example, if the records of a transfer student show that in the fourth grade he made a score of 420 on achievement test X, how does this compare with the norms on achievement test Y used in the new school? This would be easier to answer if norms on both tests had been converted to distributions having the same mean and standard deviation.

Transformations of score distributions are helpful to teachers in comparing results from different classroom examinations, for example, the results from four tests of arithmetic administered over a period of eight months. The tests might have differed considerably in terms of difficulty of problems and number of problems. These differences would make for differences in means and standard deviations. Converting the scores from the four tests to distributions having the same mean and standard deviation would greatly facilitate interpretations of the results. Another advantage of such conversions is that it permits us to work with nice round numbers rather than with awkward numbers.

How conversions of scores are made can be illustrated with a spelling test which, when administered to a large group of students, has a mean of 30 (words correctly spelled) and a standard deviation of 5. To convert scores to a distribution with a mean of 50 and a standard deviation of 10, the first step would be to multiply all scores by 2. The resulting scores will have a mean of 60 and a standard deviation of 10. Then by subtracting 10 from all scores, a distribution is obtained with a mean of 50 and a standard deviation of 10. These calculations illustrate two rules in transforming distributions. First, if all scores are multiplied by a number, the mean and standard deviation are multiplied by that number. Second, if a number is either added to or subtracted from all scores, the mean is either increased or decreased by the amount of that number, but the standard deviation is unchanged. In Appendix C-10 a convenient formula is described for transforming scores to a new distribution having any desired mean and standard deviation.

SCORE DISTRIBUTIONS

In addition to computing the measures discussed so far in this chapter, it often facilitates the interpretation of test results to make a graphic presentation of the scores. This will provide a useful picture of the total results. The first step is to obtain a *frequency distribution*, which is simply a count of the number of students who made each score. Frequency distributions for the arithmetic and spelling tests are as follows:

Arithmetic		Spelling	
Score	Frequency	Score	Frequency
22	1	75	1
21	0		
20	1		
19	1	62	1
18	0		
17	1		
16	0	56	1
15	1	55	1
14	3	54	0
13	0	53	0
12	2	52	3
11	1	51	1
		50	1
		49	1
		48	1

The two frequency distributions are presented graphically in Figure 3-2. The vertical bar above each score indicates the number of students making that score. The bars show that on the arithmetic test only two score points have frequencies greater than one: the score point of 12 has a frequency of 2, and the score point of 14 has a frequency of 3. Two pieces of information are obtained immediately by looking at frequency distributions—the mode and the range. The mode is represented by the tallest bar, 14 on arithmetic and 52 on spelling. The lowest and highest scores can be immediately seen (11 and 22, respectively, on the arithmetic test). The difference between these, 11 for the arithmetic test, is the range.

Although the eleven scores on each of the two tests are sufficient to indicate how frequency distributions are formed and interpreted, the real importance of the frequency distribution comes into play when many

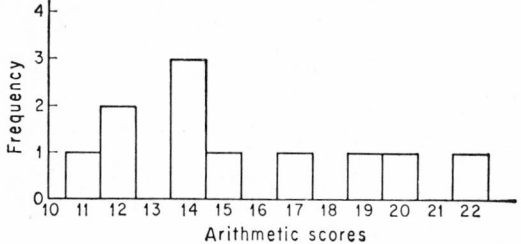

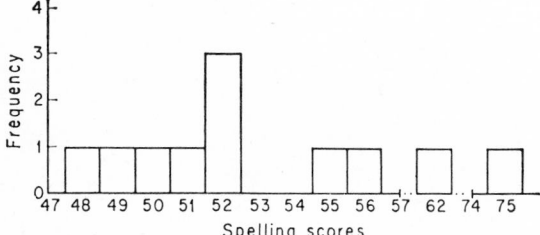

Figure 3-2. Frequency distributions for arithmetic and spelling tests.

scores are being analyzed. Suppose we had the scores of 200 students on the arithmetic test. The resulting frequency distribution would probably look much like that in Figure 3-3. The frequency distribution shows, for example, that ten students made scores of 12 and that twenty students made scores of 18. The mode is 16, and the range is 13 (10 to 23).

In addition to providing a handy pictorial representation of scores, the frequency distribution is valuable because such distributions tend to resemble a particular mathematical distribution, known as the *normal distribution,* which has many interesting properties. Although exceptions are to be found, distributions obtained when many students are tested tend to have much the same appearance. The highest frequencies are usually found in the middle of the distribution, in the zone of scores from 15 to 17 in Figure 3-3. The farther one goes from the middle, the less frequently scores occur. At the extremes, or "tails," of the distribution, frequencies are very small. In Figure 3-3, only two students score 10, and only two score 23. Distributions of test scores tend to be *symmetrical;* i.e., score frequencies tend to fall off at the same rate to the right and left of the mean. Moreover, the rate at which frequencies lessen when going in either direction from the mean is fairly predictable from the normal distribution. Because of the importance of the normal distribution in

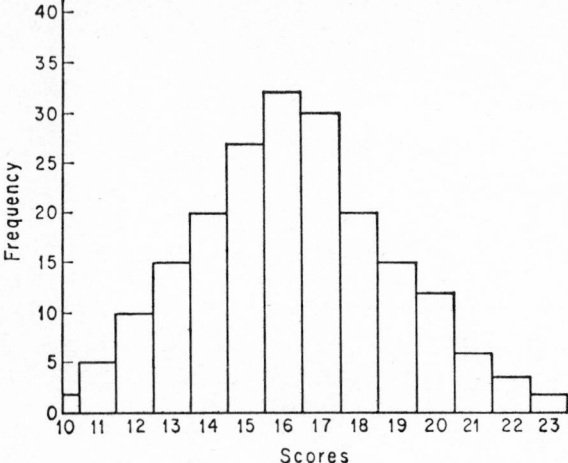

Figure 3-3. Hypothetical frequency distribution of arithmetic scores for 200 students.

analyzing and interpreting test scores, further explanations and examples will be given. (Teachers should understand that the characteristics which have been described—symmetry and decreasing frequencies in general resemblance to the normal distribution—usually occur only when many scores are being analyzed. When only a few scores are being analyzed, distributions can, and usually do, depart widely from these ideal properties.)

NORMAL DISTRIBUTION.   The normal distribution was discovered in connection with games of chance, where, for example, one problem is to estimate the frequencies with which certain coin tosses occur. Suppose, for example, that 10 coins are tossed on a table. What are the odds that 8 of them will be heads? If 10 coins were tossed 1,000 times, in how many tosses would all 10 be heads? What would occur more frequently, 8 heads and 2 tails or 7 heads and 3 tails? The normal distribution was derived in connection with questions such as these. It is a mathematical formula which estimates the frequency with which chance events occur.

The normal distribution formula relates to the situation in which 10 coins are tossed many times, say, 1,024 times, to choose a statistically convenient number. The expected distribution of results is shown in Table 3-1. The distribution of results shows, as intuition would suggest, that the most frequently occurring result would be 5 heads and 5 tails, occurring 252 times. On the extremes, 10 heads would be expected only once. The frequency distribution is shown graphically in Figure 3-4. Note the general resemblance to the distribution of arithmetic scores shown in Figure 3-3.

Table 3-1 Expected occurrences of heads and tails for 10 coins tossed 1,024 times

Frequency	1	10	45	120	210	252	210	120	45	10	1
Heads	0	1	2	3	4	5	6	7	8	9	10
Tails	10	9	8	7	6	5	4	3	2	1	0

Suppose that each toss had employed 100 coins instead of 10. Then the graph would contain 101 bars, covering the range from zero to 100 heads. Because of the larger number of bars, the graph would look less jagged; i.e., the "steps" on the graph would be much narrower. If the number of coins were increased to 1,000, the steps would be so small as to be hardly visible, and the frequency distribution would begin to look

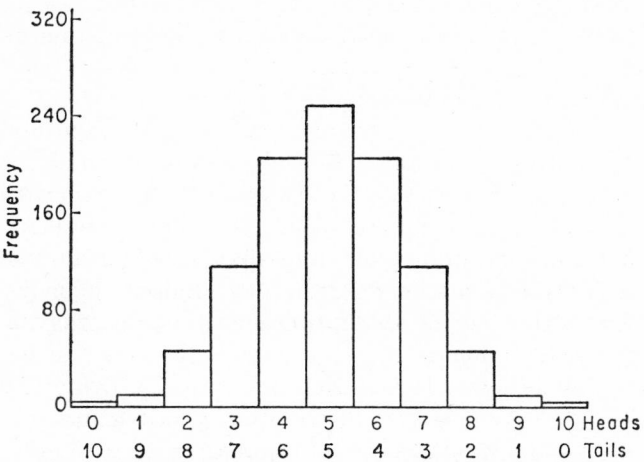

Figure 3-4. Graph of expected occurrences of heads and tails for 10 coins tossed 1,024 times.

like a smooth curve rather than a set of steps. Challenging the imagination further, what would the frequency distribution look like if there were an *infinite* number of coins tossed an infinite number of times? The normal distribution tells us what to expect, which is shown by the smooth curve in Figure 3-5.

If the normal distribution applied only to games of chance, it would be of little interest to us here. The reason why the normal distribution is so important is that test scores often distribute themselves much like the normal distribution. In that case, each test item is the counterpart of one coin, and each toss is the counterpart of one student. For example, if a well-constructed spelling test containing ten words were administered to 1,024 students, the results might approximate the frequency distribution

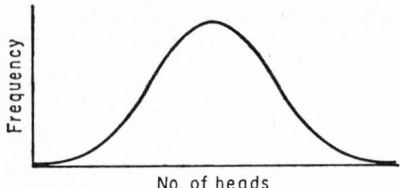

Figure 3-5. Smooth curve showing expectancies of heads for a large number of coins tossed many times.

shown in Figure 3-4. Zero heads would correspond to getting none of the spelling words correct, and ten heads would correspond to getting all the words correct. For reasons too technical to discuss here, the distribution of test scores obtained in practice probably would be slightly different from that shown in Figure 3-4, but if the test were well constructed (in accordance with principles which will be discussed in later chapters), the difference between the shape of the distribution of test scores and that obtained from coin-tossing experiments would be relatively slight.

Instead of only a ten-item test, imagine that the test contains an infinite number of items and is administered to an infinite number of students. Then the results would tend to approximate the bell-shaped curve (normal distribution) shown in Figure 3-5. Of course, infinity is only a useful fiction, but the normal distribution is often well approximated when the test contains 30 items or more and is administered to 100 students or more. Because of the resemblance between many distributions of test scores and the hypothetical normal distribution, it is possible to borrow some of the very useful mathematical results that follow from the normal distribution.

Many different human attributes are distributed approximately in accordance with the normal distribution. One of the first persons to make systematic studies of individual differences was a Belgian statistician named Adolph Quetelet. Quetelet undertook to gather a considerable amount of information about European populations. He collected information on the number of children in families, the number of children born in different years, and the physical characteristics of people. He found that many of these characteristics distribute themselves in a shape much like the normal distribution. For example, he found that the chest measurements of soldiers were distributed like the normal distribution. Since the time when Quetelet conducted his research, in the early nineteenth century, many other studies have confirmed the finding that most human attributes are distributed approximately in accordance with the normal distribution. Indeed, it is the exception to find human attributes which are not distributed, at least roughly, in accordance with the normal distribution.

There is nothing magical about the normal distribution and no necessary reason why test scores should be so distributed. But because the normal distribution is an intuitively appealing way to think about test scores, and because having an approximately normal distribution opens the door to many useful mathematical procedures, we often construct tests in such a way as to ensure approximately such a distribution of scores. Having an approximately normal distribution is much more important when the need is to distinguish sharply between the abilities of children, as in standardized achievement testing, than when the aim is to measure whether or not children have mastered a particular unit of instruction. In all measures of human ability and achievement, however, one usually obtains a distribution of scores that at least approximately resembles the normal distribution.

In practice it is not necessary to be compulsively concerned about the normal distribution. All that is necessary in order to use the procedures which depend on the normal distribution is to look at the frequency distribution and see whether the resemblance is reasonably close. For all practical purposes, a distribution of test scores can be considered a reasonable approximation to the normal distribution if the bulk of the scores cluster about the mean, if the distribution is not markedly lopsided, and if scores trail off about the mean in a way that generally resembles the curve shown in Figure 3-5.

In spite of the usefulness of the normal distribution in analyzing the results of tests, it should be clearly understood that having a normal distribution is not necessarily an indication that the test is valid in any of the three senses in which test validity was discussed in Chapter 2. Remember that coin tossing would provide a good approximation of the normal distribution, and, although students sometimes accuse us of using it, tossing coins would not provide a valid test.

STANDARD SCORES.   One important property of a score distribution is its standard deviation. As was shown previously, the standard deviations for the arithmetic and spelling distributions are 3.42 and 7.40, respectively. Using the standard formula, a standard deviation could be obtained for the 200 arithmetic scores shown in Figure 3-3 and even for the distribution of "heads" shown in Figure 3-4. When the distribution of scores is approximately normal, the standard deviation has a very useful property: it indicates the percentages of students who lie in various regions of the distribution.

Previously it was said that it is difficult to interpret raw scores and that one of the ways to make scores more interpretable is to convert them to deviation scores (by subtracting the mean raw score from each raw score). It is difficult to interpret deviation scores, however, until the dispersion of scores is considered. One way to do this is to compare each deviation score with the standard deviation, in other words, to use the standard deviation as a unit of measurement. Scores analyzed in this way are called *standard scores* and are obtained by dividing each deviation score by the standard deviation of the particular distribution as follows:

$$\text{Standard score} = \frac{\text{deviation score}}{\text{standard deviation}}$$

Applying the formula to Johnny's arithmetic score we find:

$$\text{Standard score} = \frac{22 - 15.45}{3.42}$$

$$= \frac{6.55}{3.42}$$

$$= 1.9$$

On the spelling test, Johnny's standard score is:

$$\text{Standard score} = \frac{48 - 54.73}{7.40}$$

$$= \frac{-6.73}{7.40}$$

$$= -.9$$

Johnny is almost two standard deviations above the mean on arithmetic and almost one standard deviation below the mean on spelling. Some computational procedures for obtaining standard scores are presented in Appendix C.

The reason why the normal distribution is important is that if the distribution of test scores resembles the normal distribution, standard scores on the test can be easily interpreted. In that case, it is very easy to determine the approximate number of students who score above or below any specified number of standard deviations above or below the mean. A complete table showing the percentages of students lying in various regions of the normal distribution is given in Appendix B. A less detailed breakdown is shown in Figure 3-6. The figure shows, for example, that only about 2 per cent of the students score above two standard deviations— have standard scores of 2.0 or higher. Because Johnny has a standard score in arithmetic of 1.9, most of the students score lower. (The exact interpretation of the percentage of students who score lower would

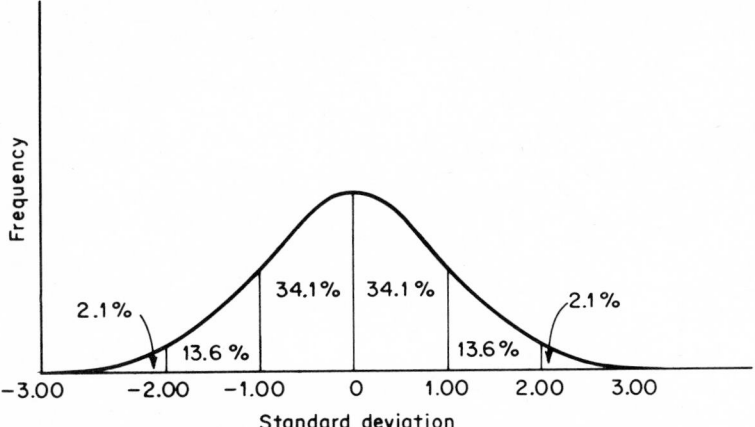

Figure 3-6. Percentages of subjects in various regions of the normal distribution. (The percentages add up to 99.6 instead of 100 because a fraction of 1 per cent of the cases lie above and below three standard deviations.)

require testing many more than eleven students. In the small number of students in this example, Johnny actually has the highest score in arithmetic.)

As Figure 3-6 shows, practically none of the students have standard scores below -3.0. Going upward, about 2 per cent score less than -2.0 standard scores, 16 percent less than -1.0, 50 per cent less than .0 (below the mean), 84 per cent less than 1.0, and 98 per cent less than 2.0. When there are at least thirty test items and 100 students, such interpretations of standard scores are fairly accurate. Even when there are fewer items and students, say, twenty items and thirty students, the normal distribution provides a useful approximation of the percentages of students scoring above and below selected points on the score continuum.

Standard scores (or transformations of them) are widely used in commercially distributed tests, such as intelligence tests. Because these tests usually have many items and are administered to thousands of students, and because distributions closely approximate the normal distribution, standard scores can be interpreted rather exactly.

As was mentioned previously, it frequently aids in the interpretation of test results to convert the distribution to one having a desired mean and standard deviation. Essentially, this is what is done in converting scores from raw (or deviation) scores to standard scores. Expressed as standard scores, all distributions have the same mean, which is zero; all distributions have the same standard deviation, which is 1.0. The value of using this transformation, rather than some other transformation, is that it ties in directly with the normal distribution and provides an easy guide to the numbers of students scoring above or below selected points on the test continuum.

TRANSFORMED STANDARD SCORES. Although standard scores are directly useful to anyone who is familiar with educational measurement, people who are naive in this respect have some difficulty in interpreting standard scores. For example, a standard score of zero is often misinterpreted as meaning zero instead of average performance on the test. Some people find it difficult to understand negative standard scores, those below the mean. For these reasons, standard scores are often transformed to a distribution having a desired mean and standard deviation. One such distribution (mentioned earlier) is obtained when standard scores are transformed to a new distribution having a mean of 50 and a standard deviation of 10. A handy formula for making such transformations is presented in Appendix C-10.

NONNORMAL DISTRIBUTIONS. Although approximately normal distributions are found in most areas of educational measurement, there are some important exceptions. A very drastic exception is shown in Figure 3-7. The figure shows the number of acts of truancy in a particular school during one year. Most of the students committed no acts of truancy. Consequently, the number of students above the zero point is much higher than the number above subsequent points. A relatively small number of students committed one act of truancy, and lesser numbers of students committed more numerous acts of truancy. Only one or two students in the whole school committed as many as five acts of truancy. Obviously, distributions like that in Figure 3-7 are far removed from the normal distribution, and it would be highly erroneous to employ statistics relating

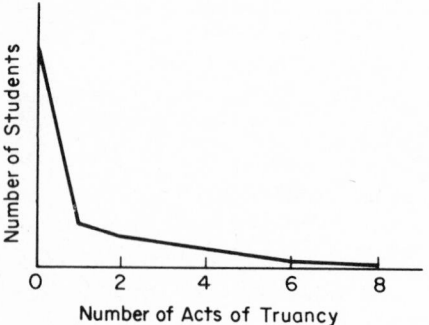

Figure 3-7. Example of a nonnormal distribution.

to the normal distribution in such cases. It would be extremely rare indeed to see a distribution like that in Figure 3-7 for any types of test scores—aptitude tests, achievement tests, intelligence tests, personality tests, or any others.

One frequently finds distributions of test scores that deviate substantially from the normal distribution; however, they seldom deviate as extremely as the distribution shown in Figure 3-7. Two such distributions are illustrated in Figure 3-8. Each distribution has a much longer "tail" on one end than on the other. Such distributions are said to be *skewed*.

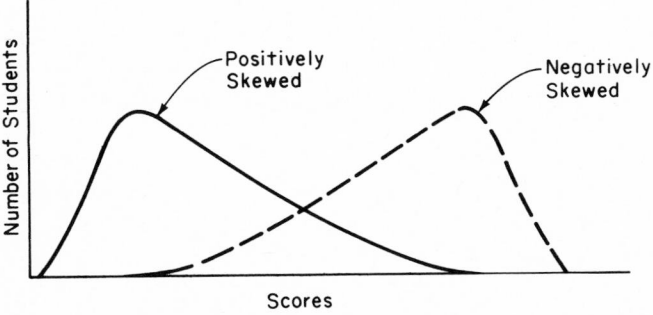

Figure 3-8.   Comparison of a positively skewed distribution of test scores with a negatively skewed distribution.

If the longer tail is toward the higher-score end of the continuum, then the distribution is said to be *positively* skewed. In contrast, if the longer tail is toward the lower-score end of the continuum, the distribution is said to be *negatively* skewed. In a positively skewed distribution, most of the students make low scores, and a few students make very high scores. In a negatively skewed distribution, most students make very high scores, and a few students make very low scores. For reasons which will be discussed more fully in Chapter 6, a positively skewed distribution is obtained from a test that is very difficult for the average student, and a negatively skewed distribution is obtained from a test that is very easy for the average student. For example, if on a teacher-made test it is found that the distribution is highly skewed positively, this means that the test was rather difficult for the class as a whole. Even though there is some skewness in most educational measures, it is usually present to such a small extent that the percentages of students in different regions of the distribution still remain approximately the same as in the normal distribution, and thus statistics relating to the normal distribution still apply.

SCORES BASED ON RANKS

There are two principal methods of converting raw scores to more interpretable units. One has been discussed extensively in the preceding pages. In summary, it consists of transforming raw-score distributions to distributions with prescribed means and standard deviations, e.g., standard scores. The second method is based on ranks. As will be shown, the methods are complementary, and ultimately they provide much the same information.

One of the simplest methods of transforming raw scores to more meaningful units—and in many ways the most sensible—is to rank raw scores from highest to lowest. In this connection, imagine that we are studying the scores made by twenty students on a thirty-item test. The student who gets the most answers correct is given a rank of 1, the student who gets the next most answers correct is given a rank of 2, and so on. When tied scores occur, students are given the average rank. For example, if three students make identical raw scores and are tied for second, each student receives the average of ranks 2, 3, and 4, which is 3. If two students are tied for rank 4, they would each receive the average of ranks 4 and 5, which is 4.5. Following is a list of ranks for an arithmetic test:

Student	Raw Score	Rank
Kim	29	1
Fred	27	2.5
Mary	27	2.5
Bill	26	4
Sarah	24	5
Lewis	21	7
Martin	21	7
Jean	21	7
Patricia	20	9
Walter	18	10
Susan	17	12
Russell	17	12
Scott	17	12
Keith	16	14
Janet	15	15.5
Betty	15	15.5
Ronald	14	17
Lee	12	18
Caroline	10	19
Cecil	8	20

When dealing with the scores for a test administered to only one class, ranks are in many ways the most desirable units of scoring. They are easy to obtain, and they are easily communicated to others.

PERCENTILES.   When many students are being studied, and when comparisons are being made among students in different localities, it is useful to make a transformation of ranks to what are called *percentile ranks.* A percentile rank is simply the percentage of students who fall below a particular score. Thus if 95 per cent of the students score lower than Fred, Fred is said to be at the 95th percentile. If only 20 per cent of the students score lower than Mary, she is at the 20th percentile.

Percentiles are very much like the ranks that would be obtained in a group of exactly 100 students, except that in using ranks we customarily give the highest score a rank of 1. If instead we gave the lowest score a rank of 1 and the highest score a rank of 100, these would be almost identical with percentiles. The slight difference is that percentiles are defined as the percentage of students who score lower than a particular score. Thus, the person with rank 100 would receive a percentile score of 99, because 99 per cent of the students are lower. Also, the student with rank 1 would receive a percentile score of 0 because none of the students score lower. However, the difference is so slight that it is useful to think of percentiles as representing ranks when (1) exactly 100 scores are being studied and (2) the largest rank (100) is given to the student with the highest test score and the smallest rank (1) is given to the student with the lowest test score.

If there are no tied scores, percentiles are obtained by finding the percentages of students below each raw score. For example, if in studying 200 test scores, Fred makes a score of 76, no other student makes a score of exactly 76, and 160 students make scores of less than 76, then Fred is at the 80th percentile (160 divided by 200, and the result multiplied by 100).

Because there nearly always will be tied scores, a slight modification of the method described above must be used to obtain percentiles. Why such a modification of procedures is necessary is illustrated by the situation in which 35 per cent of the students score higher than Fred, 50 per cent score lower than Fred, and 15 per cent (including Fred) make exactly the same score. In that case it would be misleading to say that Fred is at the 50th percentile, because, in fact, only 35 per cent of the students score higher. This ambiguity can be remedied by considering half of the students who make the same score as Fred as scoring higher and half of the students as scoring lower. Then the first step in obtaining percentiles is to find the number of students who score below a particular raw score plus half of the number of students who make the particular raw score.

The total is divided by the number of students in the study, and the results are multiplied by 100. For example, if 20 students score higher than 44, 70 students score lower than 44, and 10 students score exactly 44, then 44 corresponds to a percentile of 75. By this method percentiles can be calculated for all scores, regardless of ties in raw scores.

The following are the percentile scores for two students on the subtests of a reading achievement test:

Subtest	Fred Worth	Jack Spain
Word knowledge	90	48
Reading comprehension	83	22
Reading speed	38	81

The percentiles are in relation to national norms for students in the sixth grade. Fred's score is at the 90th percentile on word knowledge, and therefore 90 per cent of the students in the national sample scored lower than Fred did. Fred's score is above 83 per cent of the national sample in reading comprehension, but above only 38 per cent in reading speed. These percentile scores suggest that Fred has the capacity to learn to read more rapidly and still maintain a relatively high level of comprehension. Jack Spain is at the 48th percentile on word knowledge, very close to the average of score obtained from the national sample. His reading comprehension score is at only the 22nd percentile, which contrasts strongly with his reading speed percentile of 81. This pattern of scores suggests that Jack moves too quickly through written material without fully comprehending what he reads. These examples demonstrate how percentiles are interpreted in school situations.

Percentiles and standard scores supply much the same information. It will be remembered from previous sections that when certain conditions hold, standard scores indicate the percentages of students who fall in various score regions. For example, approximately 98 per cent of the students will have standard scores less than 2.0; approximately 84 per cent of the students will have standard scores less than 1.0; and so on, for the other regions of the normal distribution. One of the major pieces of information obtained from standard scores is the percentages of students making scores above and below particular points on the test continuum. Because of the ease with which standard scores can be converted to percentages of students in various score regions, one can obtain percentiles by converting all raw scores to standard scores and then transforming these to percentiles, using the table in Appendix B. This will offer an approximation of the percentiles obtained by the more direct method described previously. The approximation will usually be good if (1) the distribution of raw scores is approximately normal, (2) there are many test items (at least thirty), and (3) at least one hundred students are being studied.

One must be careful not to confuse percentile scores with percentage-correct scores. Regarding the latter, it is sometimes useful to think in terms of the percentage of items that students get correct. However, as should be obvious, percentage-correct scores do not directly tell anything about students' standings with respect to one another. If an easy test is being used, a student can get 75 per cent of the items correct and yet be in the bottom quarter of his class and thus have a percentile score of less than 25. If a hard test is being used, a student can have a percentage-correct score of only 50, and yet be at the 90th percentile in his class.

Since test scores tend to be distributed normally, there are many more raw scores, and ties in raw scores, in the middle of the distribution than at the extremes. Consequently, when percentiles are computed, differences in raw scores near the middle of the distribution tend to be exaggerated, whereas differences in raw scores near the extremes tend to be minimized. In Figure 3-9, the distortion of distances between scores can be seen clearly. A wider range of raw scores falls below the 10th percentile than falls between the 10th and 20th percentiles. As one goes closer to the middle of the distribution, the range of test scores included between percentile points becomes even more restricted. A student falling at the 95th percentile is farther away from a person at the 85th percentile in score points than a student at the 55th percentile is from one

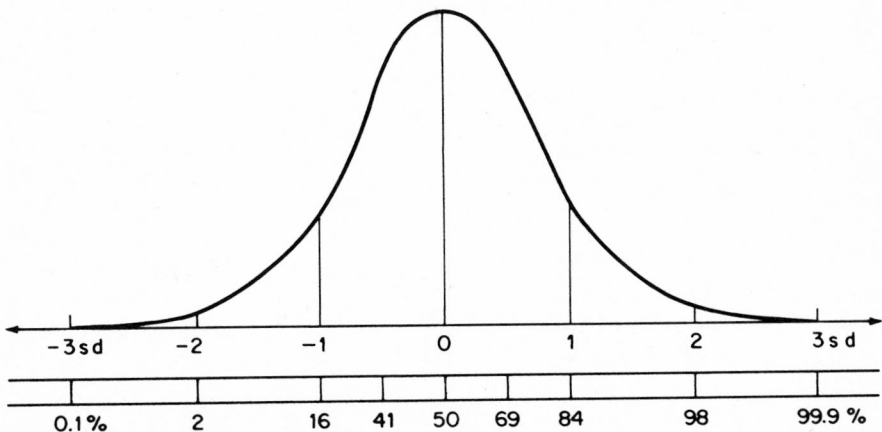

Figure 3-9. Percentile equivalents for a normal distribution.

at the 45th percentile. Thus, in interpreting percentile scores, one should keep in mind that percentiles show an individual's relative position in the normative sample, but not the amount of difference between scores. Another point to remember is that it is usually not wise to average percentiles obtained on two tests. Rather, it is better to average raw scores or standard scores, and then convert the averages to percentiles.

NORMS

Two types of scores have been discussed so far: those based on ranking, such as percentiles, and those based on the normal distribution, such as standard scores. Both of these were illustrated with relatively small groups of students in classroom settings. Comparisons between students in individual classes are very important. They help determine grades, sectioning, and plans of study and help settle other problems of day-to-day instruction. In addition, it is often necessary to compare scores with standards that are somewhat external to the performance of the particular students. Earlier it was said that one such standard is what the teacher expects of his pupils. Regardless of who is above and below the mean, and by how many standard deviations, the teacher may decide that all the students are doing poorly or doing well. The teacher's standards will be discussed in Chapter 7.

Another important type of standard is the performance of larger groups of students, possibly including students in other classes at the same school and students from other schools and other cities. Scores obtained from such large groups of students are called *norms*.

The teacher can see that Johnny made a high score in spelling relative to the other students in the class. It is easy to jump to the conclusion that Johnny is a good speller in the absolute sense, that he could hold his own with students anywhere. This can be determined only by comparing Johnny's spelling ability with that shown by much wider groups of students.

How does the teacher evaluate how well his class as a whole is doing? Are they learning to spell well, or are they doing poorly? Although the teacher's past experience and expectations are important, normative comparisons also are very helpful. By comparing the average performance in the class with the average performance in other schools and other cities, the teacher would have a better idea of how well his class was progressing.

The first step in obtaining norms for a test is to define a normative population. What population is defined depends on the interpretations that need to be made of scores. This may be all the children in the United States (the normative population for most intelligence tests), all the children in a particular school system (which would offer one basis for interpreting achievement tests), or all the children in the fourth grade at Woodlawn Elementary School (which would be useful in making decisions about pupils in the local setting).

The construction and use of norms is not nearly as simple as it appears at first glance, and there are some definite pitfalls to be avoided. The use of norms will be discussed at a number of points in the following chapters. In this chapter we will discuss some of the types of scores with which norms usually are expressed.

PERCENTILE NORMS. Norms can be expressed by percentiles in much the same way that the teacher converts the scores of his students to percentiles. When using large-scale norms, however, the teacher compares the performance of particular students with the performance of the normative group. In developing percentile norms for commercially distributed tests, the test author gathers responses from many children (usually more than 1,000 and sometimes as many as 40,000). He then translates raw scores into percentile equivalents. The percentile equivalents are published in the manual of instructions for the test. An example is as follows:

Raw score	Percentile
140–142	99
138–139	98
137	97
136	96
. . .	. . .
14	1
12–13	0

If Johnny makes a score of 140, 141, or 142, he is at the 99th percentile, having scored higher than 99 per cent of those in the normative group. If he scores either 138 or 139, he is at the 98th percentile. Scores of 137 and 136 are, respectively, at the 97th and 96th percentiles. Percentile equivalents are not shown for percentiles of 95 through 2. A score of 14 would represent the 1st percentile, with only 1 per cent of the group standing lower.

STANDARD-SCORE NORMS. Norms are often expressed as either standard scores or transformed standard scores. The performance of particular pupils is then compared with the mean score in the normative group and with the standard deviation found in the normative group. Nearly all commercially distributed tests have tables available to translate raw scores directly into standard scores and/or transformed standard scores, so that it would not be necessary to go to the trouble of actually subtracting the mean from Johnny's score and dividing this by the standard deviation. Following is an example employing both standard scores and norms transformed to a distribution having a mean of 50 and a standard deviation of 10:

Raw Score	Standard Score	Transformed Score
148	3.3	83
147	3.2	82
. . .	. . .	
85	.1	51
84 (mean)	.0	50
83	− .1	49
. . .	. . .	
21	−3.2	18
22	−3.3	17

AGE NORMS. It sometimes is desirable to express norms in terms of children's ages. One such set of age norms could be obtained by testing the vocabulary of children at all ages from four to twelve. For this purpose, a list of 100 words varying in difficulty could be used. The mean score could be obtained for each age group separately. A graphic plot of these would resemble that shown in Figure 3-10. The figure shows, for example, that the average seven-year-old child has a larger vocabulary than the average six-year-old, as would be expected.

Age norms would prove useful in interpreting the vocabulary scores of particular pupils. Suppose that a child is seven years old and makes a vocabulary score of 25 (correctly identifies or supplies the meaning of twenty-five words in the list). The mean score for seven-year-olds in the normative group is 30, which indicates that the particular pupil is somewhat below average for his age level. To determine how much below average, we can find the age group which corresponds to a score of 25. Although there is no age group whose mean score is exactly 25, we can work as though the curve were continuous throughout all age levels and determine the fractional age group corresponding to that score. Reading from Figure 3-10, it is seen that an age group of approximately 6.5 corresponds to a score of 25. It can be said that the seven-year-old child has a vocabulary approximately that of the average 6½-

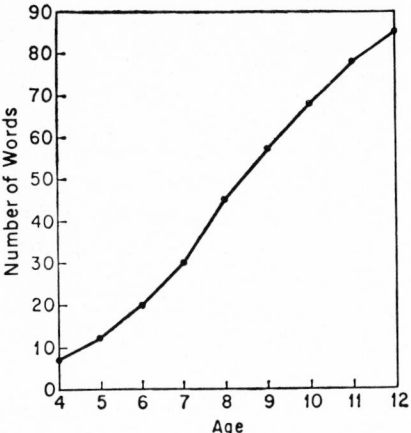

Figure 3-10. Mean vocabulary scores of children at each age from four to twelve years.

year-old. Age norms fit in well with the way in which we customarily think about the progress of children, and they are therefore very useful in the interpretation of test scores.

Educational age. Age norms are often employed with commercially distributed achievement tests which cover most of the subjects taught in school. After the test is administered to a broad sample (normative group), average scores can be found for each age level. Then in all future uses of the test, scores of particular pupils can be compared with the age norms. If a nine-year-old child achieves an age score of only 7, this means that he is considerably behind his age group. Such an age score is often referred to as the *educational age* (EA) of the pupil. If some cautions are heeded (ones which will be discussed later in this chapter), the EA offers one way of interpreting the progress of students.

Mental age. Age norms are employed with some of the commercially distributed intelligence tests. By comparing a child's score with age norms, it can be determined whether he is more or less "intelligent" than the average child of his age. A score which is compared in this way with age norms is referred to as a *mental age*. If a six-year-old performs as well as the average seven-year-old child, he is said to have a mental age of seven. Although there are some definite dangers in interpreting mental ages (which will be discussed later), they have been used quite widely, and if not overinterpreted, they offer a useful way of understanding the mental ability of pupils.

GRADE NORMS. Norms which are very similar to age norms can be obtained by finding the mean scores for children at various grade levels. If a standard spelling test were given to children in the fourth through eighth grades, the means could be plotted by grades, much as they were plotted by ages in Figure 3-10. Comparing scores with grade norms gives the teacher an indication of how well pupils are progressing.

Age and grade norms are usually obtained at the end of the school year, for example, by testing children who are finishing the fourth, fifth, etc., grades. Age norms usually are very similar to grade norms, and it is difficult to argue that one type of norm is generally better than the other. The advantage of grade norms is that comparisons are made among children who have had the same amount, if not precisely the same kind, of education. The relative disadvantage of grade norms is that they tend to penalize accelerated pupils and overestimate the progress of retarded pupils. If a pupil has just been double promoted, he may appear only average in comparison with his classmates, who are a year older; but he would still appear superior with respect to children of his own age (using age norms rather than grade norms). Also, because children sometimes differ by as much as eight months or more of age within grades, there is some inequity in the use of grade norms. When possible, it is helpful to convert students' scores to both age norms and grade norms to utilize the slightly different kinds of information which they supply.

QUOTIENT SCORES AS NORMS. With a number of the norms discussed previously, there are two indices involved: educational age and chronological age, mental age and chronological age, grade equivalent and actual grade, and others. It is tempting to divide one component into the other and obtain a quotient of performance. This has proved so popular that a number of such quotient scores have been widely used. Although in a later section it will be shown that such quotient scores have very serious faults, and better indices are available, the quotient scores have been too widely used to be ignored here.

The most popular quotient score is the *intelligence quotient* (IQ), which is obtained as follows:

$$IQ = \frac{MA}{CA} \times 100$$

In this formula, MA stands for mental age and CA stands for chronological age. The formula shows, for example, that if an eight-year-old child does as well on an intelligence test as the average ten-year-old, he has an IQ of 125. An IQ of 100 is precisely average; above 100 means above average, and below 100 means below average.

Similar to the IQ, an *educational quotient* (EQ) can be obtained by dividing educational age by chronological age and multiplying the result by 100. Whereas the IQ is intended to represent the relative intelligence of the child, the EQ is intended to represent his relative progress in school.

An even more complex quotient score can be obtained by dividing EA by MA (or EQ by IQ), which is called the *accomplishment quotient* (AQ). This supposedly represents the extent to which the student is working up to capacity. However, for reasons which will be discussed in the next section, the AQ is so riddled with conceptual pitfalls and statistical artifacts as to be nearly worthless.

As will be discussed more fully in Chapter 12 and elsewhere in the book, these days the IQ and EQ are usually computed either as transformed standard scores or as percentiles with respect to each age level, rather than as a ratio of mental age or educational age to chronological age. This approach prevents the aforementioned difficulties with respect to the use of quotient scores from cropping up.

CAUTIONS IN THE USE OF NORMS

Norms, expressed in the forms discussed in the previous section, are completely essential to anyone who works with tests. Unless the weak points and potential pitfalls in the use of norms are understood, however, some very poor interpretations can be made of test results. In order not to interrupt the explanation of how various norms are obtained, extensive criticisms were not made of the various types of normative scores. Criticisms and cautions will be given in this section.

SAMPLING.   A potential fault of any set of norms relates to the way in which the normative group is obtained. The normative group is supposed to be *representative* of some defined population. As was said previously, the population may be all the children in the United States, all the children in a particular school district, or all the children in a particular school, depending on the ways in which the norms are to be used. To obtain representativeness, it must be ensured that the normative group is *unbiased* and that sufficient numbers of students are tested.

A normative group (in statistical language, a *sample*) is unbiased if every child in the designated population has an equal chance of being selected for testing. One of the surest ways to guarantee that a sample is unbiased is to select children randomly, i.e., draw names out of a hat. Random samples can be drawn when norms are constructed locally, but for regional and national norms, approximate procedures must be employed. These approximate procedures involve selecting a sample of children to be representative of the region or the country as a whole. Such factors as community size, socioeconomic balance, public-parochial school balance, and many others are taken into account in selecting the sample used in establishing norms. If carefully done, these approximate sampling procedures can lead to representative results. Criticisms by experts of sampling procedures used in the standardization of tests are usually found in the research literature. (Some of the most prominent sources for such criticisms are listed in Chapter 17.)

In addition to being unbiased, a sample must contain sufficient numbers of children. If, for example, there were only twenty children in the sample (normative group), luck might have it that as a group they would be much above average or much below average. Norms obtained from so small a group would provide a very poor basis for the interpretation of scores. In comparison to such norms, a child who is really average might appear either superior or much below average. The only definite rule that can be given in choosing the number of students to test is "the more the merrier." To obtain national norms, it is wise to include at least several thousand students in the sample. If norms are to be obtained from a particular school district and there are 20,000 students in the district, it would be wise to test at least 1,000 students (and, as was said previously, these should be selected by a random, or approximately random, procedure).

If in a test manual it is indicated that the sample was biased (e.g., only children in Chicago were tested), or only a relatively small sample was employed, the reported norms should be held suspect. Because of these potential errors of sampling, it is often found that a child will make rather different scores on two tests, purely because of the non-representativeness of one or both of the samples used to obtain norms. For this, and for numerous other reasons to be discussed later, *it is always much safer to average the normative scores obtained from two different tests than to depend on the results from one test alone.* This rule cannot be overemphasized.

Often a school system will find it advantageous to develop local norms for use with certain tests. Local norms which have been carefully constructed can supplement the test-manual norms, which may be inappropriate or inadequate for the local setting. Since national norms average out the differences in performance of widely varying groups, they cannot be truly representative of many of those groups considered separately.

Some schools find, then, that local norms are more appropriate than national norms for their own testing purposes, such as predicting achievement in special programs of study or grouping students for instruction. In addition to allowing for evaluation of the performance of individual pupils in terms of the local score distribution, local norms can facilitate comparison of results on different tests used in the local school system. It must be remembered, however, that when local norms are constructed, they are applicable only to the local setting and do not permit comparison with schools outside the local area. Only with national or regional norms is this type of comparison possible.

UNRELIABILITY.   Regardless of how carefully norms are obtained, a child's score should not be taken as a final and exact indication of his performance. Any particular score depends to some extent on pure luck, the luck being either good or bad depending on the child, the test, and the day on which he is tested. If a child scores at the 70th percentile on a particular test on a particular day, it is wrong to think of this as an exact indication of his ability; rather, one should consider his score to be somewhere close to the 70th percentile, maybe higher or maybe lower. The chance factors (unreliability) that are present in all test scores give the above rule added support: The results from two different tests given on different days are better than the results of one test.

NORMATIVE SCORES.   Both percentiles and standard scores (or transformed standard scores) are excellent ways in which to express norms. Both indicate where the child stands relative to children in the normative group, and both are easy to interpret. Uses of grade norms and age norms do not introduce new types of scores, but rather they determine the normative groups over which percentiles and standard scores are to be computed. In this way, for example, percentile scores for a test are determined with respect to children in the sixth grade, or standard scores are determined with respect to eight-year-olds.

In contrast to percentiles and standard scores, the quotient scores described previously definitely are not recommended. One of their largest faults is that the same quotient seldom has the same meaning from grade to grade or age to age. This is because in order for quotients to have the same meaning at different levels (ages or grades), it is necessary for quotient scores to have the same standard deviations at different levels. For example, suppose that a five-year-old and a ten-year-old both have EQs of 120. It is easy to jump to the conclusion that they are equally advanced with respect to their educational accomplishment. This is a correct conclusion only if the standard deviations of EQs are the same for five-year-olds and ten-year-olds. Suppose that the standard deviation for five-year-olds is 10. Then the five-year-old child is two standard deviations above his age group, approximately at the 98th percentile. In contrast, suppose that the standard deviation of EQs for ten-year-olds is 20 instead of 10. Then the ten-year-old child is only one standard deviation above his age group, approximately at the 84th percentile.

In constructing and standardizing a test, it is nearly impossible to equate standard deviations of quotient scores at different age and grade levels. Consequently, misinterpretations are sometimes made of particular quotient scores. Also, quotient scores on different tests often have different meanings because of differences in standard deviations. If one child manifests an IQ of 125 on a test and another child manifests an IQ of 130 on another test, it may be the case that the first child actually would have a higher score expressed as either percentiles or standard scores. Far better than to use either the EQ or the IQ (as obtained from quotient scores) is to express school performance and intelligence as percentiles and/or standard scores. (On the more recently developed intelligence tests, the so-called IQ is really a transformed standard score rather than a ratio of MA to CA. This improvement will be discussed more fully in Chapter 12.) Because of the many difficulties with the EQ and the IQ when they are expressed as quotient scores, it should be obvious that the AQ (which is the quotient of EQ over IQ) is even more unreliable and difficult to interpret.

SCORE PROFILES

In many instances, educational measurement concerns batteries of tests rather than only one test. This is the case with over-all measures of achievement which contain subtests relating to reading achievement, mathematical skills, science, and other topics. Chapter 11 will discuss multifactor aptitude batteries which contain tests relating to verbal aptitude, reasoning, perceptual ability, memory abilities, and other attributes. Batteries of personality tests containing measures of sociability, dominance, and other personality characteristics will be discussed in Chapter 16. In other areas of measurement, one frequently encounters batteries of related tests rather than only one general measure.

It facilitates interpretations of test batteries to depict scores in the form of a graph. Such graphs are referred to as *profiles*. Figure 3-11 shows the scores of two persons on six subtests of a sixth-grade achievement test battery. The raw score for each person on each test was com-

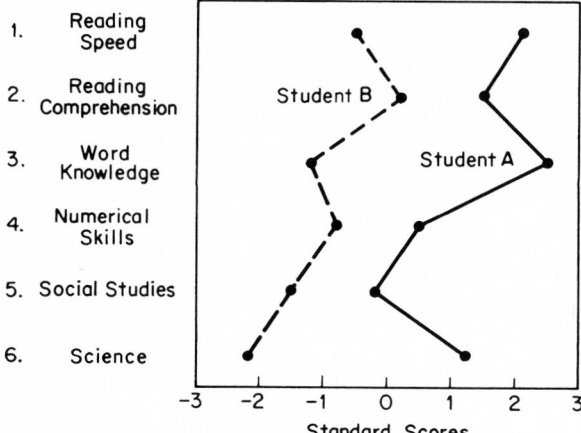

1. Reading Speed
2. Reading Comprehension
3. Word Knowledge
4. Numerical Skills
5. Social Studies
6. Science

Standard Scores

Figure 3-11. Profiles of achievement test scores for two students.

pared with national norms expressed as standard scores. Thus, student A has a standard score on reading speed of slightly more than 2.0. Similarly, student B has a standard score of less than −2.0 on science. The other points depict the standard scores of the two students on the remaining tests.

Another score profile is presented in Figure 3-12, which shows the scores on a battery of four personality tests for one student. A comparison of Figures 3-11 and 3-12 will illustrate some principles regarding score profiles. First, score profiles are useful not only for the interpretation of tests of ability but also for measures of interests, values, personality traits, and other human attributes. Second, one has a choice of plotting profiles in terms of standard scores (or transformed standard scores) or percentiles. As was mentioned previously in this chapter, both types of scores supply essentially the same information for interpreting test scores. Third, one has a choice of many different styles of charts for portraying profiles. One can use lines connecting points, as in Figure 3-11, or bar graphs, as in Figure 3-12, and there are numerous other possibilities. Choices among these pictographic approaches should be made in terms of clarity of presentation and artistic considerations.

CHARACTERISTICS OF PROFILES. There are three major types of information in score profiles. First, there is the *level,* which is the average score for a person over all the tests represented in the profile. In Figure 3-11, student A obviously has a higher average score over all six tests than student B. It makes sense to compute the level of an individual's

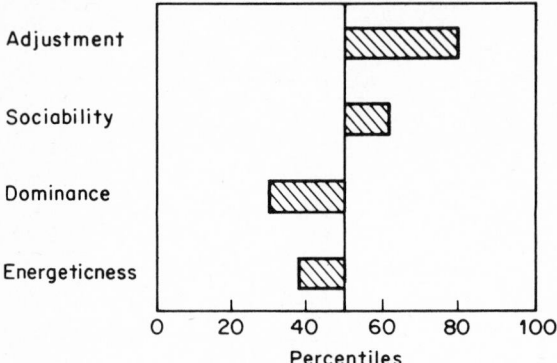

Figure 3-12.   Profile of personality traits for one student.

profile only if all tests in the profile add up to some common characteristic. It would make sense to obtain levels (average scores) for the two
students in Figure 3-11, which would represent over-all achievement
for them. In contrast, it would not make much sense to average the scores
in Figure 3-12 because how would one interpret the average score on
multifactor batteries concerning personality, interests, and values?
Only for measures of various types of abilities, such as aptitude tests
and achievement tests, do measures of level usually make good sense.
With other types of measures, it is usually the case that no sensible
interpretation can be made of the average profile score.

The second type of information in a profile is the *scatter,* or *dispersion.*
The scatter concerns the extent to which an individual varies considerably in scores over the tests in a profile, rather than obtaining much
the same scores on all tests. A good measure of the dispersion would be
the standard deviation of scores for one person over the different tests
in a profile. For example, in Figure 3-11 one could compute a measure
of the scatter for student A by taking his six scores and placing them
in one of the formulas for computing the standard deviation, discussed
earlier in this chapter. As is true of measures of level, measures of scatter
are usually interpretable only with various types of tests of ability, and
not with measures of personality, interests, and values. An exception
would be a case in which the subtests of a battery of personality tests
all relate to much the same thing, as in a battery concerned with the
tendency to have various types of mental disturbance. In tests of ability,
the degree of scatter indicates the extent to which the student is uneven
in his aptitudes or levels of achievement. Two students could have identical levels and thus the same average ability, but one student could
vary widely in terms of abilities, and the other could be relatively uniform.

The third, and most important, type of information in a score profile is the *shape*. The shape concerns the particular places in which the individual has high or low scores. The shape is determined simply by rank ordering the subtests for a student from the one on which he scores the highest to the one on which he scores the lowest. For example, in Figure 3-11 it can be seen that student A scored highest in word knowledge and lowest in social studies. The proper rankings of the four remaining tests can also be seen. If some cautions (which are to be discussed in the next section) are applied, the profile shape provides very useful information about abilities, personality characteristics, and other attributes of students. For example, the relatively low score made by student A in social studies suggests that he is not working up to capacity in that area. If all the students in a particular class or particular school have similarly low scores in social studies, this suggests that it is not the students' fault but the fault of the curriculum. Student B's relatively high reading comprehension score suggests that if he were supplied with the proper reading materials, he might improve his low score in social studies and his very low score in science. In these and other ways, the ups and downs of profile points for individual students, and for whole groups of students, provide many suggestions regarding classroom practices, guidance work, educational research, and curriculum management.

INTERPRETATION OF PROFILES. A number of cautions must be heeded before the information in score profiles can be interpreted meaningfully. First, it should be obvious that the physical appearance, or shape, of the profile does not mean anything in and of itself. It does not mean anything psychometrically if a profile resembles a saw, the man in the moon, or anything else. It should be obvious that such resemblances to real things would be altered markedly by rearranging the order in which the tests appear in the profile. It is usually the case that the order in which tests appear is largely arbitrary.

As a second caution, it should also be obvious that the different tests in score profiles are seldom equally important for the situations in which profiles are used. In Figure 3-11, for example, reading comprehension is usually considered more important than social studies or science. In multifactor batteries of aptitude tests, measures of verbal ability are usually more important than measures of memory or perceptual abilities in selecting high school students for college. In educational research, it is usually the case that some personality traits in score profiles are more important in relation to educational activities than other personality attributes.

A not-so-obvious caution is that it is very risky to interpret small differences in profile points for any student. For example, in Figure 3-11 it would probably be quite safe to conclude that student B is substantially higher in reading comprehension than in science, but it would be very risky to conclude that he is higher in numerical skills than in word knowledge. There is a chance factor in the scores obtained on any test. These chance factors are said to influence the test reliability, a matter which will be discussed in detail in Chapter 4.

The influence of chance factors on score profiles can be envisioned in the circumstance in which student B is given a second battery of tests designed to measure the six attributes depicted in Figure 3-11. Then one could plot two profiles for student B, one for the first battery of tests and one for the second battery of tests. It would be extremely unlikely that the two profiles would be identical, and indeed when one considers the limited reliability of most available tests, one would expect some substantial differences between the two profiles. For reasons which will be discussed in Chapter 4 and elsewhere in this book, some tests are much more reliable than others, and consequently the degree of difference between the two profiles for student B would depend on how well the two test batteries were constructed. With even the best of test batteries, however, the two profiles would tell somewhat different stories. For that reason, one should make confident interpretations only of rather large differences in profile points and write very small differences off as probably due to the unreliability of the tests. The establishment of standards for interpreting differences in profile points will be discussed in more detail in Chapter 4. In Appendix C are discussed some statistical formulas and technical principles for deciding how large differences in profile points must be before they can be interpreted safely.

THE TEACHER'S USE OF NORMS AND STATISTICS

What will the teacher use in interpreting the results of the midsemester examination in ancient history? He probably will not employ any of the elaborate methods of analysis which have been mentioned, such as converting scores to percentiles and standard scores. He usually does not have the time, and even if he did, there probably would not be enough test items or students to make such statistical results meaningful. He might go to the trouble of computing the mean and the standard deviation.

Teachers are sometimes called on to analyze the results from tests given to large segments of a student body, such as a final examination in mathematics given to over one hundred students in a half dozen or more sections. In such cases, it would be appropriate and worth the effort to compute percentiles and/or standard scores.

Teachers frequently read research reports regarding educational practices. Also, many teachers participate directly in educational research. It would not be possible to fully understand research reports without understanding some simple principles concerning scores, norms, and statistics.

The principal need for a knowledge of scores and norms is in interpreting the results from commercially distributed tests of achievement, intelligence, personality, interests, and other factors. There, the teacher will see percentiles, transformed standard scores, educational quotients, and others. If he does not understand these, the teacher can make some very bad mistakes in interpreting test results. To enhance that understanding has been the major purpose of this chapter.

SUMMARY

Raw scores obtained on commercially distributed tests, teacher-made tests, and others are not directly meaningful until they are compared with two types of standards. The first type of standard is what the teacher expects of his students, a discussion of which is reserved for later chapters. A second type of standard is obtained by comparing the scores of students with those of other students. This chapter was devoted largely to discussing the procedures that are useful in applying this second type of standard.

In order to understand how well students do with respect to one another, the first need is a measure of central tendency. It was said that the arithmetic mean is the preferred measure of central tendency in most situations. Second, it is necessary to obtain a measure of the spread, or dispersion, of scores. The standard deviation was shown to be very useful for that purpose. Because most distributions of test scores resemble the normal distribution, many useful properties of the normal distribution can be borrowed. Two important advantages of converting raw scores to standard scores are that it (1) provides a simple way of averaging the scores obtained from different tests and (2) provides an estimate of the percentages of students who lie in various regions of the test continuum.

Complementary to the use of standard scores is the ranking of students' raw scores and the conversion of these to percentiles. Both standard scores and percentiles indicate how well students perform with respect to their classmates or larger groups of students.

For studying the results of their own tests, teachers will seldom find it necessary to compute means, standard scores, percentiles, and other such statistics. However, in order to compare the progress of their students with that of larger groups of students—throughout a school system, a geographic region, or the nation as a whole—it is necessary for teachers to use such transformations of raw scores and to understand some simple principles concerning scores, norms, and statistics.

SUGGESTED ADDITIONAL READINGS

Anastasi, A. *Psychological testing.* (3rd ed.) New York: Macmillan, 1968, chap. 3.

Blommers, P., and Lindquist, E. F. *Elementary statistical methods in psychology and education.* Boston: Houghton Mifflin, 1960.

Flanagan, J. C. Units, scores, and norms. In E. F. Lindquist (Ed.), *Educational measurement.* Washington: American Council on Education, 1951, chap. 17.

Garrett, H. E. *Elementary statistics.* (2nd ed.) New York: McKay, 1962.

Lyman, H. B. *Test scores and what they mean.* Englewood Cliffs, N.J.: Prentice-Hall, 1963, chaps. 4–7.

Seashore, H. G. Methods of expressing test scores. *Test Service Bull.,* No. 48. New York: Psychological Corporation, 1955.

chapter 4

CORRELATION
AND RELIABILITY

One of the most important features of any test is its *reliability.* A test is reliable if it provides highly precise indications of students' standings with respect to one another; if a test is not highly reliable, a zone of uncertainty must be considered in interpreting particular scores. For example, if on a highly reliable achievement test it is found that a student stands at the 80th percentile, this can, with some confidence, be taken as a rather exact indication of his standing. If the test were not highly reliable, then the score would have to be interpreted with caution, and the possibility would have to be considered that the student's real standing was either considerably higher or considerably lower than that shown by the test. Obviously, it is desirable for all educational tests to have a high degree of precision (be highly reliable); therefore, test reliability is one of the most important topics to be discussed in this book.

It is not possible fully to understand test reliability until some basic principles of correlational analysis are grasped. Correlational analysis is used to determine the extent to which people are ordered alike on two measures. For example, if students in a classroom receive almost identical IQs on two intelligence tests, then the tests correlate very highly. In contrast, if the standard scores that students make on a spelling test are almost totally unrelated to the standard scores that they make on a mathematics test, then the two tests have a very low correlation. The statistical measure for determining the extent to which persons are ordered alike on two measures is called the *correlation coefficient.* The correlation coefficient is useful for many purposes, for example, in determining the extent to which a predictor test accurately forecasts a criterion variable. As another example, the correlation coefficient is useful in determining the extent to which a test item measures much the same thing as other items on a particular test. These and other uses of the correlation coefficient will be discussed throughout the remainder of the book. Correlational analysis is being introduced in this chapter because it is particularly relevant to the measurement of test reliability. Although, as will be seen, there are a number of different ways of measuring test reliability, they all concern correlational analysis.

Test reliability concerns the extent to which test results are repeatable. As was mentioned previously, some luck is involved in the results obtained on any particular test given on any particular day; thus some students score lower than they should, and other students score higher than they should. To the extent that particular results are due to luck, different scores should be obtained on different occasions. By administering the same test on two occasions or by administering two similar tests on two occasions, the extent to which luck (measurement error) influences scores can be determined. If the test results were due entirely to chance (say, if coins were tossed to determine grades on both occasions), there would be practically no relationship between the two tests. If instead two long, carefully standardized tests (say, spelling tests) were used, luck would not be an important factor, and high correspondence would be found between the two tests. The correlation coefficient is used to measure the amount of correspondence, and when it is used in this way, it is called the *reliability coefficient*.

CORRELATIONAL ANALYSIS

Before discussing the particular relevance of correlational analysis to the measurement of test reliability, let us go into a more general discussion of correlation.

Mr. Martin is comparing the results of the first test in American history with the results of the second test. He wants to know how well the two sets of scores correspond. He can see that many of the students have done relatively as well or as poorly. John made the top score on the first test, and he is near the top on the second. Poor Jimmy was on the bottom of the heap both times. But here is an exception: Joan was only average on the first test, but she is near the top on the second. Fred really fell down. He was above average on the first test, and now he is barely above Jimmy. Because of the number of students in the class, and because in some cases agreement is good and in other cases scores changed markedly, it is difficult to summarize the over-all degree of correspondence between the two sets of scores. In this case, Mr. Martin would find correlational analysis very helpful.

COMPUTATION. In determining the amount of correspondence between the two sets of scores, Mr. Martin quickly grasps one of the fundamentals: The absolute size of the scores on the two occasions is irrelevant. There were twice as many questions on the second test; therefore, scores are generally larger on the second occasion. Jimmy got twenty-two multiple-choice items correct on the first test and forty-six on the second test, but he was at the bottom of the list both times. The most important consideration is the relative ordering on the two tests. Consequently, to understand the correspondence, it would help if all the scores were converted to ranks or to some other type of relative scores, such as percentiles or standard scores. It happens that it is mathematically most convenient to start with standard scores, as shown in Table 4-1. The two sets of standard scores show, for example, that student A made the highest score on the first test and next to the highest score on the second test. Student E was exactly at the mean on the first test and above the mean (.59 SDs) on the second test.

Table 4-1   Hypothetical standard scores for students on two tests

Student	First Test Standard Scores	Second Test Standard Scores
A	1.55	1.18
B	1.16	1.77
C	.77	.59
D	.39	−1.18
E	.00	.59
F	−.39	−.59
G	−.77	−.59
H	−1.16	−.59
I	−1.55	−1.18

To illustrate the correlation problem further, in Figure 4-1 a graphic comparison is made of the two sets of scores. Here it can be seen that there is a strong correspondence between the two tests. The points tend to group about the *best-fit* line, which is shown in the figure. The best-fit line is the line drawn through the origin of the graph about which the points scatter the least. (How such best-fit lines are obtained is explained in Appendix C-2.) Most of the points in Figure 4-1 fall on or near the line, but there are definite exceptions. The correlation coefficient concerns the extent to which the points are tightly packed about the best-fit line. If the points are tightly packed about the best-fit line, then the correlation is high. In contrast, if they tend to scatter very widely about the best-fit line, then the correlation is low.

After standard scores are obtained, it is very easy to compute the correlation coefficient (symbolized as r). First, multiply the two standard scores for each student. Add these and divide by the number of students.

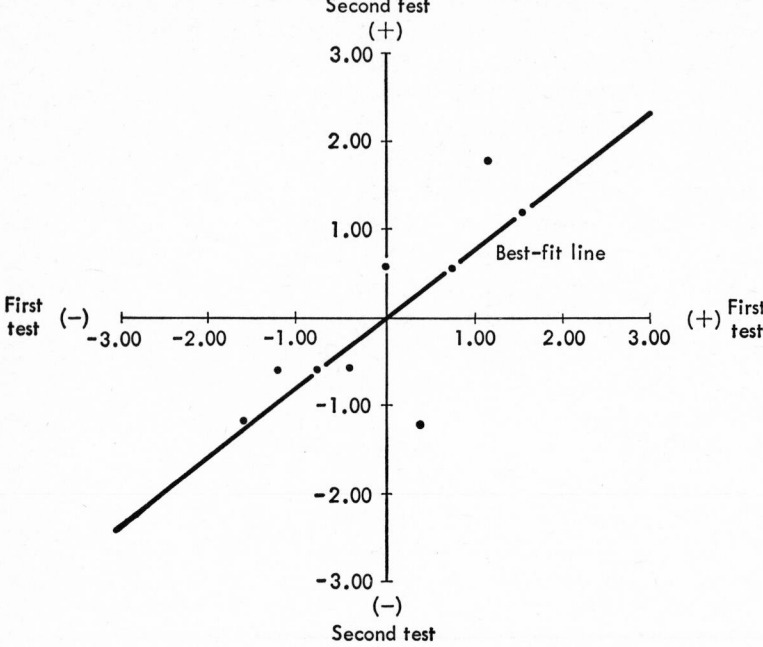

Figure 4-1.   Comparison of standard scores on two tests for ancient history.

The result is r, the correlation coefficient. The computational steps are shown as follows:

$$
\begin{aligned}
1.55 &\times 1.18 = 1.83 \\
1.16 &\times 1.77 = 2.05 \\
.77 &\times .59 = .45 \\
.39 &\times -1.18 = -.46 \\
.00 &\times .59 = .00 \\
-.39 &\times -.59 = .23 \\
-.77 &\times -.59 = .45 \\
-1.16 &\times -.59 = .68 \\
-1.55 &\times -1.18 = \underline{1.83} \\
&\text{Sum} = 7.06
\end{aligned}
$$

$$
r = \frac{\text{sum}}{\text{no. of students}}
$$

$$
= \frac{7.06}{9}
$$

$$
= .78
$$

The correlation coefficient r is the average produce of standard scores. For this reason, it is often referred to as the *product-moment* correlation coefficient ("moment" meaning standard score in this case). In practice, it would be excessively laborious to first obtain standard scores before computing the correlation. Consequently, numerous formulas are available for computing the coefficient from either raw scores or deviation scores. Several of these are described in Appendix C-2. It should be emphasized that there is only one product-moment correlation coefficient corresponding to any set of paired scores. The different formulas one sees in texts on statistics and testing are different computational approaches to the same value. All the product-moment formulas supply the same result.

INTERPRETATION.   Is a correlation of .78 good or bad? What is a good relationship depends on the situation in which the correlation coefficient is being used. Correlations range from 1.00 through zero to —1.00. A correlation of 1.00 means a perfect positive relationship—students are rank-ordered in exactly the same way on both tests. Correlations between zero and 1.00 indicate varying degrees of correspondence. A correlation of zero means that there is only a chance relationship between the two tests. Some of the students who score high on the first test score high on the second, and others score low on the second. A zero correlation means that the first test supplies no information at all as to how well students will do on the second test. As good an estimate can be made by tossing coins for each student.

A negative correlation means that there is an inverse relationship between the two tests. Students who rank high on the first test tend to rank low on the second test and vice versa for students who rank low on the first test. A good example of a negative correlation would be between school grades and days absent from school. Generally it would be expected that students who were absent a considerable number of days would, on the average, make somewhat lower grades than those who seldom were absent. A correlation of —1.00 means a perfect inverse relationship. Correlations between zero and —1.00 indicate varying degrees of inverse relationship.

One way to think about the meaning of the correlation coefficient is in terms of the amount of "scatter" shown when the two sets of scores are presented graphically, as in Figure 4-1. Although it was convenient to use the scores of only nine students to illustrate the correlation problem, actually it would be rather meaningless to apply correlational analysis to so small a group. In most important correlational problems there are at least one hundred students involved and in some studies more than one thousand. In a graphic presentation, the two scores of each student are represented by a point. Because the points tend to "scatter" over the graph, the graphic presentation is referred to as a *scatter diagram.*

Figure 4-2 shows a typical scatter diagram relating the scores on an English achievement test to scores on a mathematics achievement test. If there were a perfect correlation between the two tests, all the points would fall exactly on the best-fit line (see Appendix C-2), and there would be no scatter about the line. The more the scatter, the less the correlation between the two tests. Figure 4-2 shows the amount of scatter when the correlation is .67. Even though it is a relatively high correlation in terms of what is often found, it can be seen that some students are real exceptions to the general trend of correspondence. Some students do very well in English and only average in mathematics. Some are only average in English and superior in mathematics.

The wider the scatter of the points about the best-fit line, the lower the correlation. When the points tend to pack tightly about the line,

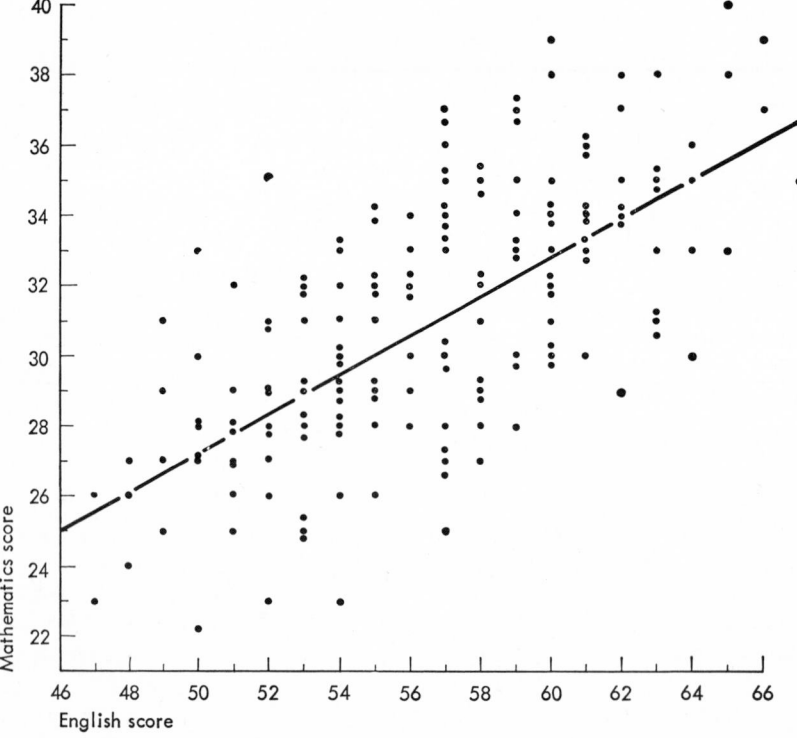

Figure 4-2.   Scatter diagram of scores on English and mathematics achievement tests.

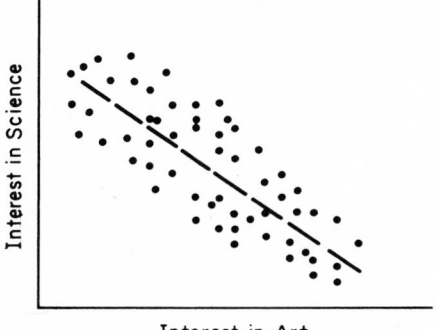

Figure 4-3. Illustration of a negative correlation.

the correlation is high. When the points scatter all over the graph and there is no visible trend of correspondence, the correlation is near zero.

A negative correlation has the same implications regarding amount of scatter as a positive correlation of the same size. The only difference is that the best-fit line slants downward, going from left to right on the graph, rather than upward, as when a positive correlation is present. A negative correlation is illustrated in Figure 4-3. The figure shows the relationship between a measure of interest in art and a measure of interest in science. Because the two types of interests tend to be somewhat antithetical, the correlation is negative. That is, the higher the interest in science, the lower the interest in art, and vice versa.

In many cases, the sign of the correlation is arbitrarily determined by the way in which tests are scored. If, for example, the number of errors is scored in spelling and the number of correct answers is scored in mathematics, a negative correlation is to be expected. Then, by reframing the problem as one of relating accuracy in spelling (rather than errors) to accuracy in mathematics, the sign of the correlation can be reversed; e.g., a correlation of —.72 would become .72.

In addition to serving as a very useful index of correspondence, correlational analysis provides a number of other important statistics. The best-fit line, which summarizes the trend of relationship, has already been mentioned. In addition, estimates can be made of the amount of error entailed in forecasting scores on one test from scores on another. Some statistics relating to correlational analysis are discussed in Appendix C-2.

The correlation coefficient is used for many purposes in addition to that of measuring the correspondence between two tests. One important use is that of determining the predictive validity of aptitude tests. In a typical problem, the test is used to select students for an accelerated program of study in high school. Because the test is being used to serve a prediction function, the validity with which that function is served is determined by correlating test results with a criterion, which in this case would probably be grade-point averages earned in the special curriculum. Of course, it would be necessary to wait one or more years after the test was administered in order to obtain the grade-point averages. Each student then has a pair of scores, one on the predictor test and a grade-point average. The correlation formulas (either the one given previously in the text or the ones given in Appendix C-2) can be applied.

A very important use of correlational analysis in studies of predictive validity is with respect to college aptitude tests. Each year, millions of high school students are required to take such college aptitude tests as part of the admissions requirements of colleges and universities. Being predictor tests, their validity depends upon the extent to which test scores are predictive of over-all grades earned later in higher education. Most typically, what is done is to correlate test scores with grade-point averages earned over four years of college.

Table 4-2 displays some typical correlations between predictor tests and various criteria of academic achievement. For example, the high correlation of .84 between the Academic Promise Test and the Stanford Achievement Test is what is typically found between a measure of scholastic aptitude and a comprehensive measure of achievement in the elementary grades.

Another important use of the correlation coefficient is in educational research. As a simple example, it might be desired to study the correspondence between muscular coordination and intelligence. Scores from a coordination test could be correlated with scores from an intelligence test. Another example would be to correlate school grades with amount of time students study. Thousands of such correlations have been computed in order to learn about the educational process.

Returning now to the primary question of "What is a good correlation?" the best guide is to compare correlations with those which usually are obtained when carefully composed tests are used. Correlations between tests given at different times in the same class, e.g., American history, would be expected to be at least .50 but probably not higher than .80. Correlations between achievement test results and intelligence test scores run about .75 or higher. Two forms of a carefully constructed, commercially distributed test (such as two forms of an intelligence test) would probably correlate at or above .90.

Table 4-2   Sample predictive validity coefficients

Test	Criterion	Coefficient
Academic Promise Test for grade 6	Stanford Achievement Test score (battery median)	.84
Differential Aptitude Test—Verbal Reasoning Test (administered in grade 2)	College grade-point average	.52
Lee-Clark Reading Readiness Test	Teacher ratings of ability to read at end of year	.51
Metropolitan Readiness Test	Stanford Achievement Test—primary battery: Word reading score Arithmetic	.63 .67
School and College Ability Test—total score for grade 5	Grade-point average— grade 5	.68

Correlations between predictor tests and their criteria usually are lower than those reported above. A typical reading-readiness test given to entering first-grade students would be expected to correlate about .60 with reading achievement grades at the end of the first grade. Intelligence tests and comprehensive achievement tests used to select students for honors programs and other accelerated curricula in high schools would be expected to correlate around .70 with over-all grade-point averages. Scholastic aptitude tests used to select students for college would be expected to correlate around .55 with grade averages in college. Personality tests tend to correlate less well with school criteria than ability tests do. For example, the test constructor would probably be very happy to find a correlation of .30 between a test of social adjustment and school grades or teachers' ratings of adjustment.

Correlations found in educational research tend to be even smaller than those found in measuring predictive validity. For example, one would expect only rather low correlations, if any, between muscular coordination and intelligence and between grades and amount of time spent in study. Such variables are quite complex, and it is unreasonable to expect high correlations among them. The major question at issue is whether there is a perceptible correlation. In this context, correlations as low as .20 often are quite interesting, and correlations as high as .30 or .40 are sometimes considered major findings.

Definite exceptions are sometimes encountered to the rules above—correlations of near zero between two tests in ancient history, predictive validity as high as .80, and correlations in educational research much higher than those quoted. But these are exceptions, and the fact that they are recognized as exceptions when they occur is owing to the sizes of correlations which typically are found.

Returning finally to Mr. Martin, we can tell him that a correlation of .78 between his two tests represents a relatively high degree of correspondence. The correlation is as high, or higher, than that typically found in such situations.

CAUTIONS IN USING CORRELATION. The correlation coefficient is not necessarily a measure of *causation.* For example, there is a positive correlation between the number of books in homes and the grades of students. It would be wrong to conclude from this that students make better grades *because* books are in the home. In well-to-do homes there are more books, typewriters, baths, golf clubs—more everything. Poor students would probably not make better grades (or not much better) if books were placed in their homes, and good students would not lower their grades appreciably if the books were removed from their homes. But even if correlations do not necessarily measure causation, they provide many clues to causative connections (using the word "cause" to mean necessary and sufficient antecedent conditions, e.g., to bring about good grades).

Like any other statistic, the correlation coefficient computed on a particular set of scores is only an *estimate* of the "real" correlation. Suppose, for example, that you want to learn the correlation between the height and weight of all eighth-grade students in the United States. You would probably not measure the height and weight of that many students. Instead you would probably measure a sample of them, say 5,000 students from schools across the country. The correlation found in the sample is of no importance in its own right. It is important only to the extent that it is an accurate estimate of the correlation that would be found if all the eighth graders were measured and the correlation computed.

Previously it was said that the two important characteristics of any sample is that it be unbiased and that sufficient numbers of students be involved. If the sample is unbiased, the precision with which the sample correlation estimates the real (population) correlation varies with the number of students involved. Correlations based on 100 students provide more accurate estimates than those based on 10 students. Correlations based on 1,000 students would provide much better estimates. When the sample is as large as 10,000, estimates are so accurate as to be exactly correct for all practical purposes.

Any particular correlation should not be considered as an exact point but rather as a range extending above and below the sample value. If, for example, a correlation of .50 is found in a sample of 100 students, the proper view is that the real correlation lies in a region centering on .50, perhaps being as high as .70 or as low as .30. Such a region is referred to as a *confidence band,* a region in which we feel confident that the real (population) correlation lies. For this purpose, a 95 per cent confidence band is often employed, which means essentially that the odds are 95 out of 100 that the population correlation is somewhere within the band.

An example will help show how confidence bands are used. With a sample of 100 and a sample correlation of .50, the band extends from .34 to .63. Another way of saying it is that the odds are 95 out of 100 that the real value lies somewhere between .34 and .63. As the sample size is increased, the confidence band shrinks, which is another way of saying that we can have more confidence in correlations obtained from larger samples.

What happens if the confidence band covers zero? For example, with a sample of 20 and a correlation of .25, the 95 per cent confidence band extends from —.22 to .62, which means that the population correlation might be zero or even negative. When the confidence band covers zero, there is no reason to believe that the population correlation is other than zero. To demonstrate that the correlation is other than zero would require a larger sample. In many correlational studies, the sample is small, and the confidence band is so large that the results are inconclusive.

The reader who has not studied statistics will, of course, not understand the intricacies of how confidence bands are generated. This is not the important consideration here. The important points are to think of correlations obtained from samples as representing bands rather than exact points and to compute such bands using formulas presented in statistical texts. The reader who has a special interest in the sampling error of correlation coefficients should consult the statistics texts listed in the Suggested Additional Readings. Some elementary concepts are discussed in Appendix C-6.

Confidence bands for interpreting correlation coefficients should not be confused with confidence bands for interpreting particular test scores. The former concern the sampling of people; the latter concern the amount of measurement error we would expect to occur in using a test, i.e., the reliability of the test. This has been a brief discussion of confidence bands for correlation coefficients. Confidence bands for interpreting test scores of individuals will be discussed later in this chapter.

RELIABILITY OF MEASUREMENTS

As was mentioned previously, some luck or chance is involved in all test scores. To the extent to which such chance factors predominate, a test is said to be unreliable. Conversely, when the influence of chance factors is slight, a test is said to be highly reliable. The chance element in test scores is referred to as *measurement error*. Measurement error is always bad in the sense that it tends to obscure the actual abilities of students. We cannot observe measurement error directly, but we can indirectly observe its effect, which is to make measurements inconsistent from occasion to occasion. That is, if a particular student happens to be lucky on a particular day on a particular test, he is not likely to be so lucky on another day taking another test. Similarly, the student who is somewhat unlucky on the first occasion is not likely to have such bad luck the second time. Consequently, by comparing the scores made on two occasions and measuring the relative degree of consistency, we can indirectly determine the amount of measurement error involved in the particular type of instrument.

It should be obvious that if measures are completely inconsistent, then they are worthless. For example, if Mr. Martin were to give two final examinations in American history rather than one and if these were separated by an interval of several days, the correlation between the two tests would indicate the reliability. If the two tests correlate zero or near zero, then something is definitely wrong. Susie Smith would have received an A if the first test had been counted but a C if the second test had been counted instead. In contrast, Bill Jones would have failed the course if the first test had been counted but would have received a B if the second test had been counted. Then either one, or more likely both, of the tests are completely dominated by measurement error and are, consequently, worthless. Using either of the tests would be no better than flipping coins to determine grades.

A zero correlation between two such classroom tests practically never occurs in practice, but it is often the case that two such tests do not correlate highly, meaning that a sizable portion of measurement error is present. As was mentioned previously, reliability coefficients obtained from many of the carefully constructed, commercially distributed tests are .90 or higher. Although such careful test construction efforts are not possible for most classroom tests, it would be expected to find reliability coefficients for final examinations to be at least as high as .75, and preferably higher than .85. To the extent to which reliability coefficients are lower, say, as low as .50, it means that a very poor test is being used. Some of the sources of such measurement error will be discussed in a later section.

TRUE SCORES.   In discussing test reliability, it is useful to think in terms of hypothetical *true scores,* the scores that people would make if tests were perfectly reliable, if no chance factors were involved. There is no direct way to measure such true scores, but an approximation is available. If we administered many similar forms of a test on many different days, the average score would closely approximate an individual's true score. Over these many occasions, chance factors would tend to average out. The more test scores averaged for an individual, the less would be the measurement error. This is why it was said previously that two tests are better than one, and three or four, or even more, tests would be better still, if it were not for the practical difficulties involved in employing so many tests.

The scores obtained on the different occasions would tend to range about the true score, luck having it that, on some days and on some forms, the student would score higher than his true score, and on other days and other forms, the student would score lower than his true score. Because all such errors tend to be normally distributed, the expectation is that the obtained scores would be normally distributed about the true score, which is illustrated in Figure 4-4.

Figure 4-4 shows the hypothetical true scores and distributions of obtained scores for two students. Student A has a relatively high true score, and student B has a relatively low true score. Of course, it would be totally

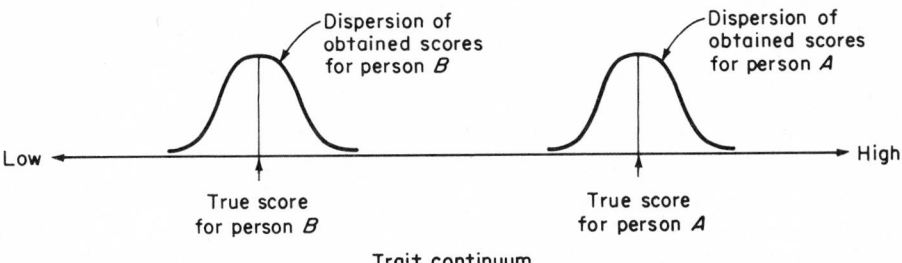

Figure 4-4.   True scores and distributions of obtained scores for two persons.

impractical to give enough alternate forms to demonstrate the normal distributions of obtained scores indicated in the figure. However, the normal distributions are approximately what would be expected. In the figure, the normal distributions of obtained scores are shown to be the same width; i.e., they have the same standard deviation. The standard deviation of the distribution of obtained scores is a direct measure of the amount of measurement error or unreliability present. If the standard deviation is large, the measure is relatively unreliable. Conversely, if the standard deviation is small, the measure is relatively reliable. Although it is possible, and sometimes likely, that the standard deviations of obtained scores would be different for different students, in most practical work it is assumed that all the standard deviations of errors are approximately the same. Consequently, a typical standard deviation is used to describe the errors likely to be shown by all students. This typical measure of error is referred to as the *standard error of measurement.* When the reliability is low, the standard error of measurement is large, and vice versa when the reliability is high. In a perfectly reliable test, the standard error of measurement would be zero. Obviously a large standard error of measurement is "bad" because it reduces the precision with which the test can be used for any purpose. Although there is no direct way to compute the standard error of measurement, there is an indirect way to estimate it, which will be discussed later in this chapter.

INTERPRETATION OF OBTAINED SCORES. A score obtained on a particular test on a particular day should not be considered as an exact point, but rather it should be thought of as representing a zone in which the student's true ability lies. That is, if a particular student scores at the 60th percentile, it is wrong to conclude that this is his exact standing. It is more appropriate to say that his true score lies somewhat near the 60th percentile, how near depending on the reliability of the test. Some methods for determining the reliability will be discussed in a later section. If the reliability is low and, consequently, the standard error of measurement is large, then a very broad band must be considered. In that case, the student's true score might actually be as high as the 90th percentile or much below the 50th percentile. When the reliability is high and the standard error of measurement is small, a much narrower band of error needs to be considered. Then, we can confidently interpret the student's true score as lying somewhere in a band ranging from, say, near the 50th percentile to near the 70th percentile. Even in the most reliable test, there is a band of error that must be considered.

A very important point to comprehend, one that is much misunderstood, is that scores obtained on any particular test, on any particular day, are somewhat biased. High scores are too high, and low scores are too low. In looking at the results of any particular test, we are not only witnessing the abilities of the students, we are witnessing the relative amounts of luck that they had. As a group, those who made very high scores are not only high in ability, but they were also somewhat lucky on that particular occasion. Conversely, as a group, the students who made very low scores are not only low in ability, but they also had some bad luck. If an alternate form of the test is administered on another day, the students who scored very high the first time will, as a group, come down somewhat. The students who scored very low the first time will, as a group, come up somewhat. This effect is referred to as *regression toward the mean*; i.e., the people who were very far from the mean on the first occasion, either very much above or very much below, will, as groups, tend to regress, or move toward, the average value. A moment's reflection will show that there is nothing else that could happen. If a student is at the 99th percentile on the first occasion, he cannot possibly score any higher, relative to his classmates, on an alternate form administered on another day. He can either remain at his high level or score lower. Similarly, a student who is at the zero percentile on the first occasion cannot go any lower the second time. He can either move upward in his standing or remain at the bottom of the heap. This tendency to regress toward the mean occurs to some extent for students at all levels. Students who score at the 90th percentile will, as a group, tend to score slightly lower on the second occasion, and similarly for people at the 80th, 70th, and 60th percentiles. Students who score below the mean at the 10th, 20th, 30th, and 40th percentiles will, as groups, tend to move up toward the mean on the second occasion.

The principle of regression toward the mean does not necessarily occur for each person. One student who scores at the 90th percentile on the first occasion may actually go up on the second occasion to, say, the 95th percentile. A student who scores at the 10th percentile on the first occasion may actually go down. However, it should be obvious that there is not as much room for the former student to go up on the second occasion, and not as much room for the latter student to go down on the second occasion. All scores above the mean tend to be somewhat biased upward; i.e., they are probably higher than they should be. Scores below the mean tend to be biased downward.

In percentile terms, or in terms of standard scores, the further an obtained score is from the mean, the more it is likely to be biased. For example, if we took a rather extreme group of students, say, all those who score exactly at the 90th percentile, the odds are that their average score on an alternate form would place them at, say, the 80th percentile, depending on the reliability of the test. In contrast, a much less extreme group, for instance, all those lying at the 70th percentile, would, in percentile units, regress less toward the mean on the second occasion. For example, we might find that, as a group, they would show an average percentile of 65 on the second occasion, regressing toward the mean by only half as much as the more extreme group.

The less reliable the test, the more scores tend to be biased. For example, if test scores were determined by flipping coins on the first occasion and the alternate form consisted of flipping coins on another day, the first set of scores would be completely biased. Even if coins were used to determine scores, some students would lie at the 90th percentile, others at the 80th, and so on. For students who were at the 90th percentile on the first occasion, the best bet is that, as a group, they will average out at the 50th percentile on the second occasion, there being no reason for them to score either above or below average on this chance test. The more reliable the test, the less scores tend to be biased.

Regardless of how high or low the reliability, some element of bias is present. Only the scores of students who score exactly at the mean are completely unbiased. There is no reason to believe that they would, as a group, go either upward or downward on the second occasion. Scores which are relatively close to the mean embody relatively little bias. On most of the well-constructed, commercially distributed tests, where the reliability is high, the bias is slight. Between the 20th and 80th percentiles, the bias is so slight that it can be ignored for all practical purposes. Beyond those extremes, the bias is not inconsiderable and should be taken into account in interpreting test scores.

There are two ways to take the bias into account in interpreting test results. First, statistical corrections can be made for the probable bias. Methods for doing this are discussed in Appendix C-4. More important for the teacher is to remember that extreme test scores tend to be biased, even on the best commercially distributed tests, and to take this into account when interpreting test scores. For example, after an achievement test is administered to fourth graders, the teacher should remember the probable bias of extreme scores and make interpretations accordingly. If she sees that Johnny is at the 4th percentile on the test, she should say to herself, he is probably doing poorly, but the odds are that he has slightly more ability than indicated on the test. (As was mentioned previously, there is some likelihood that Johnny has even less ability than indicated, but the odds are that his real ability is slightly higher than shown on the test.) Conversely, if Susie has a score at the 98th percentile on the achievement test, the teacher should say, Susie is a very bright child, but she probably is not quite as bright as indicated by the score.

People who do not understand the bias inherent in extreme scores, or fail to take the bias into account, make some very poor interpretations of test results. For example, suppose that Mr. Martin performs an experiment with the students who score very low on an achievement test. Suppose that he takes all the students who score at or below the 20th percentile, gives them a month of special instruction, and then administers an alternate form of the achievement test. (Such alternate forms are available for many commercially distributed tests.) Whereas on the first test the average percentile was 10, on the second test the average percentile is 20. Mr. Martin takes the result as evidence that his special instruction was highly effective. Because of the bias inherent in extreme scores, *this is a completely erroneous conclusion.* Owing to the tendency of extreme scores to regress toward the mean on another occasion, the special group of students would probably have gone from an average 10th percentile to an average 20th percentile purely because of measurement error, without the opportunity for special instruction.

As another example of how misinterpretations can be made by failing to take measurement-error bias into account, suppose all students entering the fourth grade are given a comprehensive reading test at the beginning of the school year and an alternate form of the test at the end of the year. In comparing scores on the two occasions, the teacher might be surprised to find that two-thirds of the students who made very high scores on the first test tend to make lower scores on the second test, and two-thirds of the students who made very low scores on the first test tend to make higher scores on the second test. It is tempting for the teacher to relate this finding to the educational process and to the particular fourth-grade curriculum, but it would be completely erroneous to do so. One such erroneous conclusion would be that brighter children tend to get duller, and duller children tend to get brighter as they both grow older. However, such regression toward the mean is completely to be expected, regardless of what happens in the interval between the two tests. It is caused by the chance factors in test scores and not by the intervening instruction.

Teachers may be somewhat bewildered by the seemingly complex statistics which are used to assess the amount of bias and the relative error which is inherent in all test scores. (Those who are interested in some of the related statistics will find them discussed in Appendix C-4.) However, the statistical arguments are not the important points for the teacher to understand. First, it is important to realize that extreme scores tend to be biased and to remember this when interpreting particular test results. Secondly, even after the bias is taken into account, it must be remembered that there is a band of error surrounding all test scores, and the width of the band depends on the reliability of the test. Many of the manuals for commercially distributed tests provide excellent discussions of the amount of error to be expected. They supply useful rules of thumb for gauging the zones in which it is safe to interpret test results.

Teachers are not likely to perform complex studies of reliability or make elaborate statistical estimates of the effect of measurement error on classroom examinations. However, they can remember what measurement error tends to do to test scores and try to take this into account in looking at particular test results.

EFFECT ON VALIDITY.   In the previous section we discussed the effect of measurement error, or unreliability, on test scores. In this section we will discuss the effect of measurement error on predictive validity. In Chapter 2 it was said that when a test is intended to serve a prediction function, validity is determined by the correlation between the test and its intended criterion. Examples of tests used in prediction are (1) tests of general intelligence used to decide on the admission of a 5½ year old child to the first grade, (2) tests of reading readiness to help plan the instruction of students in primary grades, (3) comprehensive achievement tests to help in assigning students to special courses of study in high school, and (4) scholastic aptitude tests to help in counseling students about college training. To the extent to which such predictor tests have large amounts of measurement error, they provide poor forecasts of how students actually will perform in particular courses of study. For these

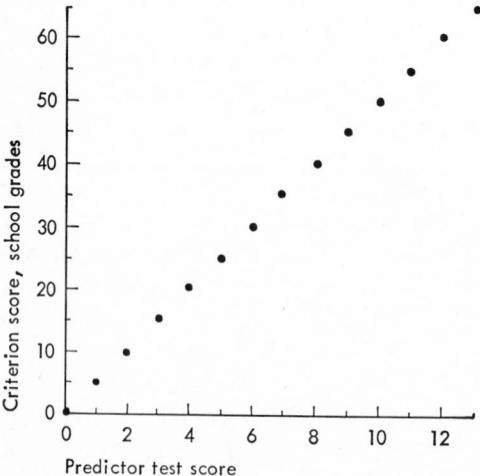

Figure 4-5.   Relationship between a predictor test and its criterion before measurement error is added.

reasons, it is important for teachers to understand the effect of measurement error on predictive validity.

Measurement error, or unreliability, always works to obscure or, as we say, *attenuate* any type of scientific lawfulness. Whatever "real" lawfulness there is in nature will appear blurred if relatively unreliable measures are used to chart that lawfulness. When dealing with predictor tests, this means that, to the extent to which the test has much measurement error, it cannot do a good job of predicting a criterion. Measurement error tends to attenuate correlations; i.e., it makes them closer to zero. An example may help to show how this works.

Figure 4-5 shows a hypothetical relationship between a predictor test and its criterion. As would be the case only in hypothetical circumstances, the test predicts its criterion perfectly, and all the scores lie on a straight line. Let us see what happens when some measurement error is introduced into the test scores. What we will do is flip a coin for each score in turn. If it turns up heads, we will add three points to the score; and if it is tails, the score will be left as it is. Flipping the coin for each of the test scores in turn, we find the following:

Original Score	Coin Flip	New Score
0	H	3
1	T	1
2	H	5
3	H	6
4	H	7
5	T	5
6	T	6
7	H	10
8	H	11
9	H	12
10	T	10
11	T	11
12	H	15
13	T	13

In Figure 4-6, the new scores with the included error component are plotted against the criterion. The criterion scores have not, of course, been changed by the random additions to the predictor test scores. In Figure 4-6 it can be seen that there is no longer a perfect correlation. The effect of adding error to the scores is to lower the correlation. Since we

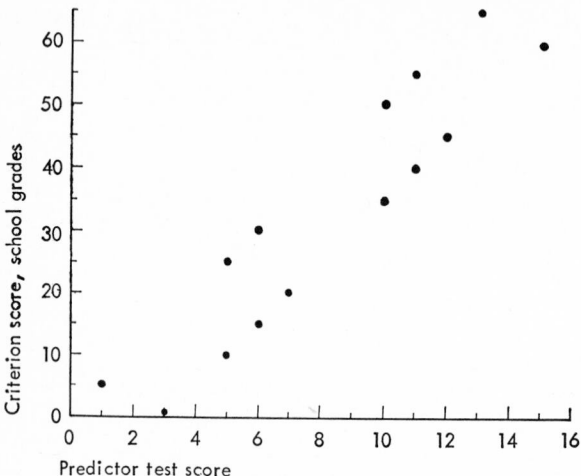

Figure 4-6.　Relationship between a predictor test and its criterion after measurement error is added.

started off with a perfect relationship, there is no way for the relationship to change except to a lower correlation. The important point is that the addition of random error will tend to lower the correlation no matter what it was originally. If we had pictured a scatter plot with a correlation of .50, the random addition of score points would have tended to make the correlation nearer zero. Likewise, if we had a correlation of —.50, the random addition of score points would have tended to make the correlation nearer zero.

With as few scores as those shown in the example above, it is possible that the random changes in scores would either leave a correlation unchanged or could, in a very rare circumstance, make the correlation higher. However, the odds are against anything but a lowering of the correlation, and if the number of students is as large as one hundred, it can be predicted not only that the correlation will be lower but with fair accuracy just how much it will be lower.

Measurement error in educational tests works very much the same as the chance component introduced by the coin flips. Because unreliability tends to lower all correlations, it will lower the correlation of a predictor test with its criterion and thus lower the validity of the test.

The relationship between test reliability and test validity should be carefully considered, but reliability does not necessarily ensure high validity. Reliability concerns the consistency of what is measured, regardless of whether what is measured is good or valid in any sense. For example, we might use the weights of children to predict school grades.

Whereas, weight might be determined very precisely and be quite accurately repeatable, weights of children would serve as a very poor predictor of school grades and thus not be valid. For another example, grades in American history could be determined by measuring how far students could throw their textbooks. Such tosses would probably prove to be highly reliable. That is, if we asked them to toss their textbooks on another occasion, or to toss another textbook, the two "tests" would probably correlate highly and thus be highly reliable. It is not necessary to belabor the point that tossing textbooks would not provide a valid assessment of knowledge of history.

Even if reliability does not ensure validity, reliability does place a limit on the extent to which a test is valid for any purpose. In order to have high validity, it is absolutely necessary to have relatively high reliability. High reliability is a necessary, but not sufficient, condition for high validity. If the reliability is zero, or not much above zero, then the test is invalid, regardless of the type of validity intended (those discussed in Chapter 2). Consequently, as a prelude to determining the validity of tests (achievement tests, aptitude tests, measures of psychological traits), it is important to first determine the reliability. If the reliability is low, it must be raised (by ways to be discussed in a following section) before the test can possibly achieve the desired validity.

Statistical estimates can be made of the effect of unreliability on predictive validity. For example, suppose that you have a predictor test which has a reliability of .70 and in its present form correlates .30 with its criterion. When the reliability is increased, the predictive validity will increase, which means that the correlation will be higher than .30. Formulas are available for estimating how much predictive validity will be increased by an increase in reliability. These are discussed in Appendix C-1. With the previous example, if the reliability is increased from .70 to .90, the estimate is that the predictive validity will increase from .30 to .34. Although it is easiest to demonstrate the effect of unreliability on the validity of predictor tests, this is not the type of test with which teachers are most concerned. They are more concerned with the results of achievement tests and day-to-day classroom examinations. Even though it is not as easy to demonstrate, reliability has the same effect on instruments of this kind. If two alternate forms of a classroom examination or two alternate forms of an achievement test do not correlate highly, and thus are said to be relatively unreliable, they cannot be highly valid as assessments. If the reliability of assessments is not greater than, say, .60, then they cannot be valid measures of school performance. Only if the reliability is above .80, and preferably above .90, is it possible for tests to be highly valid assessments of performance. When teachers fail to heed some of the cautions which will be mentioned later in this chapter, and in other chapters, their tests often are far less reliable then they should be, and often so unreliable as to be nearly worthless assessments of performance.

SOURCES OF UNRELIABILITY

It was stated that any random influence on test scores would cause unreliability. There are many ways in which this can happen in practice. Some of the most prominent sources of unreliability are discussed in the following sections.

ERRORS DUE TO DAY-TO-DAY FLUCTUATIONS.   One source of measurement error in most tests is the day-to-day fluctuations in the individual which lower or raise scores. Changes in mood, physical well-being, happenings in the home, and many other events contribute to inconsistencies in test scores from one occasion to another. The abilities and personality characteristics of children change somewhat from day to day. Added to the rather enduring pattern of abilities and personal features which characterize the child, he has his definite ups and downs. This is seen most markedly when the child is ill or has had a very bad time with Mom and Dad before coming to school. On the positive side, a child will be on top of the world one day, very alert, amiable, and mentally sharp. On the day on which a test is given, the child who is "up" is lucky, and the child who is "down" is unlucky, and these relative amounts of luck are reflected in test scores. Consequently, the test given on one occasion is not totally reliable. The results are influenced by the happenstance of events occurring during the previous twenty-four hours or the previous several days.

The extent to which such day-to-day fluctuations in the child result in unreliability of test scores depends on the type of test. In some types of personality tests, the influence can be relatively strong. For example, if the test contains items like "Do most people like you?" and "Are you as smart as most of your friends?" the child who is in a bad mood on a particular day is likely to make a rather different score from what he would make on another day, in another mood. In contrast, most tests of ability, such as intelligence tests, achievement tests, and classroom examinations, are influenced to some extent by day-to-day fluctuations in the child, but not nearly to the same extent as some of the personality tests.

Although one should be alert to the day-to-day changes in the individual that contribute to measurement error, most teachers and students probably overemphasize the extent to which such errors are present in test scores. Teachers frequently hear students say that they would have done much better on a particular examination if they had not been suffering from a bad cold or had not stayed up late because of an athletic event. Such changes in general well-being do not have nearly as much impact on test scores as is commonly thought. Even though a student is not up to par on a particular day, he usually can muster sufficient energy to show what he knows on classroom examinations, achievement tests, and aptitude tests. (The effects of fatigue, motivation, and other such day-to-day contingencies upon test scores are discussed in detail in Nunnally, 1967, chap. 15.)

ERRORS DUE TO THE SAMPLING OF CONTENT. In Chapter 2, it was said that assessments depend on a sampling of the important content in a course or larger unit of instruction. For example, in a final examination, a teacher tries to pose questions which range broadly across important material included in the lectures, the text, the supplementary reading, and other sources. Even so, there is an element of chance involved in what questions are included in the test. Every student has had the feeling that he was lucky on a particular test, that of the many topics in the course, the instructor happened to ask about things which he knew. Another student, with the same level of understanding about the whole course material, may have been unlucky, in that he happened not to know about the particular questions. If the teacher were to start over and compose another examination, the luck of these students might be reversed, and their scores might be somewhat different.

As in all sampling problems, the more questions there are, the less unreliability will come from the sampling of questions. If the test contains only 10 questions, luck will probably have a greater influence on test scores than if 100 questions are used instead. Stretching this point of view to the extreme, as larger and larger numbers of questions are included, the instructor would approach including everything important, and it no longer would be only a sample. Although there is a practical limit to the length of tests, generally speaking, longer tests are more reliable than shorter tests. For this and for other reasons, it is often said that *a long test is a good test.* Even though one can easily think of exceptions to this rule, e.g., 1,000 questions concerning the Civil War as a measure of over-all knowledge of American history, the saying has a great deal of merit.

The major source of error in most psychological measures relates to the sampling of content. Although the other sources of measurement error that are discussed in this section are important, the unreliability inherent in most tests is due to the fact that they are not long enough and not broadly representative enough of the content in a particular unit of instruction, an area of achievement, or an aptitude trait. Nothing helps to promote the precision (reliability) of a measuring instrument as much as having a relatively large number of items that diversely represent the content in a particular topic.

ERRORS IN SCORING TESTS.   On multiple-choice tests, the errors in scoring are purely mechanical. If the test is scored by hand, it is possible to accidentally score some correct answers as incorrect, and vice versa. Also, errors can be made in counting up the number of correct and incorrect answers for each student. If tests are machine-scored, an improperly functioning machine can add a considerable amount of measurement error to test scores.

The errors in scoring an essay examination are more subtle in character, but they also generate unreliability. Whereas errors in scoring are relatively minor in multiple-choice tests, they are very prominent in the subjective grading of essay examinations. If three different persons teach the fourth grade in a particular school, they will probably have at least slightly different ideas about what kinds of answers merit good and poor marks. Consequently, the grade that a student gets is partly dependent on the happenstance of which teacher he has.

In addition to differences in grading standards, there is an element of measurement error built into the individual teacher. If a teacher regrades a set of essay examinations after a period of time and there are no identifying marks to indicate what the earlier grades were, the grades will be somewhat different the second time. Even within one grading session, the teacher often changes his standards as he marks the test. He might have a strict standard at first, but as he goes through the papers and sees that none of them measure up, he is likely to become more lenient. Consequently, the grade that the student obtains is partly dependent on the chance appearance of his test in the order in which they are graded. Some ways of improving the reliability of essay examinations will be discussed in Chapter 7.

ERRORS DUE TO GUESSING.   Errors due to guessing occur in examinations where the student is asked to identify the correct answer from two or more choices. For example, in a true-false examination, a student who knew nothing at all about the subject matter would be able to guess approximately half of the answers, even if he went to the extreme of flipping a coin. If, instead of using true-false alternatives, a student is asked to choose the correct alternative among four, guessing is not as prominent, but it still plays a part. What students typically do is go through an examination marking the answers of which they are relatively sure, and then go back to those about which they are uncertain. If (following a rule which will be recommended in Chapter 7) all students attempt all items, some students are bound to make wild guesses on at least some of the questions. Even so, there is some probability that the student will choose the correct alternative. Another student who may be equally well or poorly informed about the subject matter may choose the wrong alternative purely by chance. Two students both may guess at a test item, and both may be incorrect, but for different reasons. One student may have known nothing about the issue and taken a wild guess, while the other student may have been knowledgeable enough to rule out all but two alternatives. One student knew more about the topic than the other student, but this difference is not reflected in the answers given to the question, which contributes to measurement error. Therefore, the guessing that occurs on multiple-choice tests acts as another form of measurement error. If students were asked to take the same test over and their memory of the previous testing was erased, it is likely that they would guess differently, and their scores on the two occasions would not be exactly the same.

A free-response (fill-in) test, one in which the student supplies the correct answer, is theoretically more reliable than a multiple-choice test. However, there are few subject matters which can be cast in the free-response form, the requirement being that there be only one word or term which represents the correct answer. Consequently, the fact that some measurement error is due to guessing on identification-type questions is not a sufficient reason for doing away with true-false and multiple-choice forms. The important consideration is that the measurement error due to guessing is less influential as the number of alternative answers for each question is increased. On a true-false test, purely by chance the odds are fifty-fifty of getting the correct answer. If ten alternative answers are used instead, the odds are only one out of ten of getting the correct answer, and chance has less influence on the test results. If the subject matter permits, a test will be more reliable if four or five alternatives are used for each item instead of only two or three.

Because of the difficulties in composing tests and the limited amount of time available for testing, some compromise must be reached between the need to have many items and many alternative answers for each item. That is why standardized tests have sought a compromise solution by using about four or five alternatives, with as many items as time will permit.

ERRORS DUE TO TEST STANDARDIZATION. Standardization is the essence of testing. A test is said to be standardized when the rules for taking the test are made sufficiently clear that all children are given essentially the same task. When a test is made easier for some children, and more difficult for others, or when the rules for taking the test are not made clear, some measurement error is introduced into test scores. To ensure that tests are well standardized, test manuals for most commercially distributed instruments spell out the rules in some detail. If it is to be a timed test, the exact amount of time is stated, and this should be followed religiously. When one teacher allows his students a few extra minutes, it makes the over-all use of the test somewhat unreliable.

Before the test begins, students should be told whether or not they should attempt all items, even those about which they are unsure, and if, after answering the last question, they are permitted to go back and check answers given earlier. If special materials are required in taking the test, such as special pencils, rulers, or other equipment, these should be placed on desks before the testing begins. If students are allowed to ask questions during the test, it must be decided what kinds of questions will be answered and how students are to submit their questions.

In addition to being a collection of questions, each test embodies a set of rules and procedures which must be followed carefully. This is so not only for well-constructed, commercially distributed tests, but also for classroom examinations. The rules should be thought out in advance by the teacher and applied uniformly to all students. In particular, it is important to write out the test instructions in advance, which are then either read by students or given orally by the teacher. These should make all the testing procedures and rules absolutely clear. Some suggestions for writing test instructions will be given in Chapter 5. If the rules and procedures are not made absolutely clear, or are not uniformly enforced by the teacher, some students will be given an advantage, and others will be given a disadvantage. This inevitably results in measurement error.

ERRORS DUE TO LONG-RANGE INSTABILITY. Previously it was said that day-to-day fluctuations in the individual's performance constitute a source of unreliability. Another consideration is whether scores remain stable over long periods of time. Would an eight-year-old child demonstrate the same IQ that he obtained when he was six? Would adults show the same scores on interest tests that they obtained when they were in their early teens?

Scores on some types of tests tend to remain fairly stable over periods of one or more years. Scores on other types of tests tend to change markedly during such periods of time. Whether or not long-range stability is expected depends on the type of test and the way in which tests are used. Scores on intelligence tests are expected to remain stable over relatively long periods of time. If a child's IQ goes up or down by as much as 15 points over a period of two years, it makes the test very difficult to use. On the other hand, there are measures which are expected to change in relatively short periods of time. If an experiment is being conducted to alter the attitudes of a group of students toward some political issue, it is expected that a test of attitudes given after the experiment will show differences from a test given before the experiment. Changes are expected on tests measuring interests in recreational activities. Nine-year-old children play at different games than six-year-olds, and twelve-year-olds have even different recreational activities. Consequently, no one expects the interest pattern shown at one age to remain stable over periods of years.

There are two important considerations regarding the long-range stability of scores. First, the investigation of long-range stability is an important research area in its own right. For example, studies have been made of the growth and decline of intelligence, and long-range investigations have been made of the stability of interests over periods of ten and twenty years. Some of these developmental studies will be mentioned in later chapters. The second important point is that, if scores are actually used over long periods of time to make decisions about students, then any instability over those periods of time acts like the other sources of measurement error to make the test results unreliable. For example, if an intelligence test is given to children in the second grade and the results are used to make decisions about students three and four years later, it is essential that the test results be stable over that period of time.

Suppose that in the second grade Susie manifests an IQ of 125. Three years later in the fifth grade, the earlier test result is used as one of the bases for assigning Susie to a special instruction section. But instead of using the earlier test result, suppose that Susie were retested, and this time she shows an IQ of only 110. It should be obvious that the more recent test result would be more representative of Susie's actual abilities at the time, and to have used the test result obtained earlier would have been incorrect.

If scores are used over a period of time as an indication of an individual's standing and the scores are found to be unstable over that period of time, the instability usually generates unreliability in the same sense in which the other sources of error contribute to unreliability. The important consideration is that it is generally unsafe to use test scores over long periods of time, say over more than one year's time. It is far wiser to retest periodically, although such constant testing can be a real drain on school resources. Wherever possible, it is wisest to administer some of the major instruments at least every other year. Otherwise individuals are likely to change considerably, and test results will be outmoded and inaccurate. Theoretically, the best time to administer tests is immediately before decisions are to be made. Although this ideal seldom can be carried out in practice, it is wise to remember that test results usually become largely antiquated after a period of several years.

ESTIMATING THE RELIABILITY

In the previous section we discussed a number of kinds of "gremlins" that cause test scores to be unreliable. The effect is much like that of tossing coins or dice to introduce an element of pure chance into test results. Such measurement error is bad because it introduces a zone of uncertainty about particular scores, and it obscures the relationship between any test and its criterion. Consequently, one of the very important steps in constructing a commercially distributed test is to study the reliability. Such studies consist of learning the consistency with which scores are maintained on alternate forms of the test over various intervals of time. The extent to which two such sets of scores correlate is called the *reliability coefficient.* Previously, it was said that for commercially distributed tests it is expected that the reliability coefficient will be at least as high as .80, and preferably .90 or higher.

Theoretically, one could argue that there are many different reliability coefficients for each test, corresponding to measures of the various sources of error discussed previously. However, in practice the usual effort is to obtain the reliability coefficient in such a way that it measures as many of the potential sources of error as possible. This will show the maximum influence that chance factors could have, and if, in spite of these, a test still produces consistent results, we can feel relatively sure that measurement error has only a slight influence. First will be discussed a relatively ideal way to measure reliability, and then some useful approximations will be discussed.

ALTERNATE-FORM RELIABILITY.   The most comprehensive measure of reliability is obtained by correlating the scores which students make on two alternate forms of the same test. For many of the commercially distributed tests there are two or more forms which are intended to measure the same thing. For example, to measure spelling achievement, the test publisher will construct two tests, each containing fifty words. These might then be referred to as forms A and B of the fourth-grade spelling achievement test. Care is taken to make sure that both lists contain a wide variety of words and that both lists are at approximately the same level of difficulty. Test experts employ some specialized statistical procedures to select items for alternate forms which help ensure that they measure much the same thing. Such alternate forms are useful, not only to measure reliability, but also to help solve numerous practical problems. For example, if form A is given at the beginning of the year, form B can be given at the end of the year to measure the over-all improvement of the group. Alternate forms are also useful in case something goes wrong in the first testing and another form must be used.

The correlation between two such alternate forms offers an excellent measure of reliability. Preferably, the two forms should be administered to the same students with at least a two-week interval. This will allow for the day-to-day fluctuations in the student which constitute a primary source of unreliability. If the two forms were administered on the same day, or only one or two days apart, this would not allow sufficient time to tap the normal ups and downs in students' performance. Although in a situation where two forms were administered on the same day, the reliability coefficient would not mirror errors due to day-to-day fluctuations, the reliability coefficient would reflect errors due to the sampling of content, guessing on multiple-choice tests, and some of the other sources of unreliability.

In addition to serving as a check on short-range fluctuations in ability, the alternate-form method does a good job of assessing the other components of reliability. It provides a good check on errors due to the sampling of content. When it is possible to draw two samples of content, such as the two lists of spelling words, and students make much the same scores on both, it is an indication that both tests involve relatively little error due to the sampling of content. If the test is not well standardized in the sense that the instructions are unclear, or the rules of testing are not explicit, this would result in different scores on the two tests. If multiple-choice tests are used and guessing introduces a component of unreliability, this can also be determined by correlating the two alternate forms. If the purpose is to study long-range stability, a number of alternate forms can be administered over a period of years.

The alternate-form method of measuring reliability is the ideal because it measures more of the sources of reliability and measures them better than any other method which is used. If it were not for practical difficulties, the alternate-form method of measuring reliability would be used in most instances. This is the measure of reliability which usually is, and should be, reported in the manuals for commercially distributed tests.

The alternate-form measure of reliability is not used in some studies because of the practical difficulties in constructing two forms. It is often difficult to make up one good test, and it is almost twice as difficult to make up two. Even if alternate forms are available, it is sometimes excessively time consuming, or very difficult, to get people back for a second testing. This usually is not the case in schools, where students are more readily available for a second testing. But the difficulty does often occur in industry and in military settings, where men often only are available for testing on one or two days and then must leave for other jobs and assignments. Because of practical difficulties, the following approximate measures of reliability are often employed.

RETEST METHOD. Rather than administer two alternate forms of a test, the same test can be given on two occasions. The correlation between two such repeated administrations of a test is called the *retest* measure of reliability.

The important advantage of the retest method is that it precludes the time and effort necessary to construct alternate forms. However, there are two important disadvantages in using the retest method. The first is that because the content on both occasions is the same, the obtained reliability coefficient will reflect none of the error due to the sampling of content. The second disadvantage is that the individual's memory of the answers he gave on the first test administration is quite likely to influence the answers he gives on the second test administration. He is even likely to make the same kinds of guesses and tend to perpetuate the same relative amount of good or bad luck that he had on the first test administration. Memory works to make the two sets of test scores correlate highly; consequently, the reliability coefficient is usually an overestimate when determined by the retest method. For example, if the retest measure of reliability is found to be .90, it would ordinarily be the case that an alternate-form measure would be less, say, .85 or .80. Memory is less influential as the interval between testings is increased. But during the two weeks to one month in which it is advisable to complete both testings, memory is likely to be a strong factor; thus, the retest method will often provide a substantial overestimate of what would be obtained from the alternate-form method.

There are two related major exceptions to the foregoing criticisms of the retest method of determining reliability. The first is in the incidence where content sampling is not a major problem—where the sampling is so extensive that there is very little room left for errors due to content sampling. This would be the case, for example, if in a study of students' preferences for geometrical designs, one had the students make ratings of 300 designs that varied in terms of complexity, symmetry, and other characteristics. Such an extensive sampling of content would leave little room for error in relation to content sampling. Consequently, if students were retested on the same material after a period of about two weeks, the retest coefficient would not suffer badly from failure to include explicit measures of errors due to content sampling.

Another exception to the foregoing criticisms of the retest method of measuring reliability is in the situation where memory has very little effect on test results. This would be the case, for example, in a test of over-all athletic ability, which might contain measures of running speed, jumping, and numerous exercises. If one repeated such measures after several weeks, there is no reason to believe that "memory" would markedly influence results on the second measurement. Content sampling and memory of results are important mainly where classroom examinations, achievement tests, and aptitude tests are concerned. With such tests, the retest method of determining reliability usually fails to tap some of the more important sources of error, and thus it provides an overestimate of the actual reliability.

SUBDIVIDED TEST METHOD.   Instead of making up two alternate forms, a compromise procedure is to obtain part scores for different sections within the same test when it is administered on one occasion only. The most popular of such procedures, referred to as the *split-half method,* consists in giving the student one score on all the even-numbered questions in the examination and another score on all the odd-numbered questions. The two halves of the same test can then be thought of as approximations of alternate forms. Scores from the two halves can be correlated to obtain an estimate of the reliability, after which a statistical correction must be made to estimate the reliability of the whole test, not just of the half tests. (The correction is presented and discussed in Appendix C-7.)

Practical considerations have caused the subdivided test methods to be used as extensively as they have. In many situations, either it is too expensive to compose alternate forms, or it is not possible to obtain the same students for a second test administration. However, there are some definite cautions that should be heeded in the use of the subdivided test method. Although the method determines some of the error due to the sampling of content, it does not do this as well as the alternate-form method. In constructing any one test, it is usually the case that the individual biases the content toward certain aspects of the subject matter rather than others; e.g., he may select arithmetic items that relate more to numerical operations than to the solution of word problems. If the same individual attempted to construct an alternate form, he probably would vary the content somewhat from his first test. Even more to the point, if another individual constructed a test for the same purpose, the content he selected would be even more different. Consequently, the correlation of alternate forms is usually somewhat lower than that which would be expected from the correlation of half tests.

Because both halves of the test are given at the same time, the sub-divided test method shows none of the error due to instability over time. For the foregoing reasons, the subdivided test method usually gives an overestimate of the reliability. In Table 4-3 it can be seen that the alternate-form reliability coefficients are lower than those coefficients obtained by the subdivided test method.

Table 4-3   Reliability coefficients for subtests of the Iowa Tests of Basic Skills, grade 3

Subtest	Alternate Form	Split half
Vocabulary	.82	.89
Reading	.84	.90
Language	.92	.96
Work-Study	.81	.89
Arithmetic	.85	.89

It is particularly misleading to use the subdivided test method on a highly speeded test, for example, one in which students are asked to complete as many simple arithmetic problems as possible in a short period of time. If the problems are very simple, it is a test of how fast the students work. Each student is likely to get most of the problems correct as far as he goes, and students will differ mainly in terms of how far along they are in the problems when time is called. This works to make the students' scores very much alike on the split halves. The odd and even scores will be alike on most of the items up to the point at which time is called because most of them will be correct. Also, the odd and even items will be alike beyond that point because they would all be either incorrect or not answered. The split-half reliability estimate obtained on a purely speeded test, such as the one illustrated above, would be completely meaningless. Fortunately, there are very few tests which are purely concerned with speed. Most tests have some time limit primarily as a practical means of getting the test completed, but time, as such, often has only a trivial influence on scores. However, we should always be wary of split-half reliability estimates based on highly speeded tests.

There are numerous other variants of the split-half method. For example, one improvement on the approach described above is to administer the odd and even halves on different occasions, say on occasions separated by two weeks or more. When this is done, the resulting correlation will reflect the day-to-day fluctuations which constitute a prominent source of unreliability. The reliability coefficient obtained in this way should closely approximate that from the alternate-form method. (The same statistical correction mentioned above, see Appendix C-7, also would need to be used in this instance.)

INTERNAL-CONSISTENCY RELIABILITY.   As was mentioned in the preceding section, there are many different ways to subdivide a test, the most popular of which is to use odd and even items. Another way of subdividing would be to place items one through twenty in one half and items twenty-one through forty in another half. And still another approach would be to place the first three items in one half, the next three items in the other half, and so on. A conceptual problem arises in that reliability coefficients obtained from these different ways of subdividing the test would not all be the same. For example, it is quite likely that the correlation between odd and even items would be considerably higher than the correlation between the first and second halves of the test. To circumvent these inconsistent estimates of the reliability, statistical measures are available which estimate the reliabilities that would be obtained from all possible ways of subdividing the test. These statistics operate on the amount of overlap, or correlation, among the individual test items. One of the most popular of these formulas, Kuder-Richardson formula 20, is discussed in Appendix C-3.

Teachers will probably find the internal-consistency estimates of reliability far too complex to use with classroom tests. But since these formulas are often cited in test manuals, it is essential for teachers to understand what they estimate. Because these formulas work within the items on one test administration, they provide no indication of one very important source of unreliability—fluctuation in performance from day to day. What these formulas do is to provide a conservative estimate of the subdivided test type of reliability. The internal-consistency formulas are the preferred procedures when the retest method is not advisable and when alternate forms are not available.

USES OF INFORMATION ABOUT RELIABILITY

Previous sections in this chapter have presented general principles concerning the estimation of test reliability and the effects of measurement error on test scores. This section will consider the use of statistics concerning reliability in the daily practice of employing educational and psychological measures.

STANDARD ERROR OF MEASUREMENT. Previously, it was stated that the amount of measurement error in a test due to unreliability can be indicated by the standard error of measurement. The standard error of measurement is defined as the standard deviation of the distribution of scores that would be obtained if an individual took many comparable forms of the same test. Because it obviously is not feasible to administer enough forms of a test to obtain the standard error of measurement directly, some method of estimating that statistic is needed. A method of estimation can be obtained by making the assumption that the standard error of measurement would be essentially the same for all students if it were actually possible to administer many forms of the same test. When, as in the usual case, only two alternate forms are applied, each person has two scores. If a reliability study were conducted with 300 students, then one would have 300 pairs of scores. More importantly, one would have 300 differences between the scores on the two tests. One can make a frequency distribution of these differences in the same way that one can for any set of scores. The standard deviation of this distribution of differences is then an estimate of the standard error of measurement. In other words, what one does in estimating the standard error of measurement in the previous example is to compute the standard deviation of 300 difference scores rather than the standard deviation of 300 scores obtained for one individual on that many alternate forms of a test. The standard error of measurement obtained from a distribution of difference scores is then a type of average standard error of measurement that would be obtained by actually computing a standard error of measurement for each individual and averaging those statistics over many students.

Rather than go to the labors of actually obtaining a distribution of difference scores as discussed previously, one can estimate the standard error of measurement (SEM) more easily with the following formula:

$$SEM = SD \sqrt{1 - r_{11}}$$

where SD = standard deviation of the test
r_{11} = reliability coefficient of the test

Exactly the same results would be obtained by using the above formula as would be obtained by actually computing the standard deviation of a set of difference scores for two alternate forms of a test. The mathematical derivation of the above formula is presented in detail in Nunnally, 1967.

The formula for the standard error of measurement can be illustrated in the situation where the standard deviation of a test is 10 and the reliability coefficient is .91:

$$
\begin{aligned}
\text{SEM} &= 10 \sqrt{1 - .91} \\
&= 10 \sqrt{.09} \\
&= 10 \times .3 \\
&= 3
\end{aligned}
$$

Note that the standard error of measurement is always a fraction of the standard deviation of the test in question. If the test were completely unreliable, the standard error of measurement would be identical to the standard deviation of the test. That is what one would expect from a perfectly unreliable test because the observed distribution of test scores would be a distribution of measurement errors only.

Figure 4-7 shows the ratio of the standard error of measurement to the standard deviation for different levels of test reliability. Note that unless the reliability is high, the standard error of measurement is appreciably large in comparison to the standard deviation of test scores. Even with a reliability of .70, the standard error of measurement is

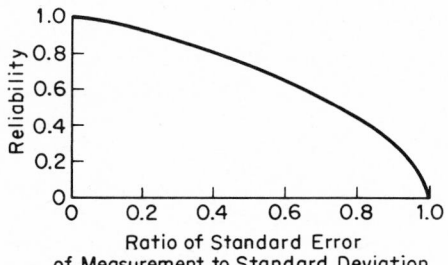

Figure 4-7. Relation between the size of the reliability coefficient and the size of the standard error of measurement.

approximately half as large as the standard deviation. Only when the reliability is above .85 does the standard error of measurement become small in comparison to the standard deviation.

CONFIDENCE BANDS. Although teachers are not likely to compute standard errors of measurement and related statistics, they need to understand the standard error of measurement in order properly to interpret scores obtained by students on standardized tests. The standard error of measurement can be used like any other standard deviation. That is, it is assumed that 68 per cent of the scores a person would obtain on many alternative forms of a test would fall within plus or minus one standard error of measurement about the mean. The mean in this case (see Figure 4-4) would be the individual's true score. Thus, we can say that the chances are two to one (68 per cent to 32 per cent) that the obtained score will fall between plus or minus one standard error of measurement on either side of his true score. Expressed another way, we would say that the odds are that an obtained score, which is farther than one standard error of measurement away from the true score, would be expected to occur only about one time out of three. If a student has a true-score IQ of 100, then we would expect that 68 per cent of the time his scores on comparable forms of an intelligence test would fall within plus or minus one standard error of measurement of 100.

In actual practice, we do not know a person's true score, but there is a procedure for estimating it, which is given in Appendix C-4. The formulas for estimating true scores and for obtaining the standard error of measurement of a test can be used together to arrive at *confidence bands* for interpreting individual test scores. That is, we find a range or band of scores into which the obtained score falls and in which we can say, with some degree of confidence, that the true score is located. Consequently, we do not feel secure if the probability is any higher than one in twenty that the true score is outside the confidence band on either side. Another way of saying this is to say that a confidence band is chosen such that we can feel 95 per cent certain that the true score lies somewhere within the band. A confidence band, in that case, is obtained by going approximately two standard errors of measurement above the estimated true score and two standard errors of measurement below the estimated true score. For example, if the estimated true score is 9 and the standard error of measurement is 3, then the confidence band would extend from a deviation score of 3 to a deviation score of 15. Then one could say that the odds are only one in twenty that an individual would obtain a score of less than 3 or more than 15 if he were administered many alternative forms of a test. Most importantly, the confidence band indicates the zone in which it is safe to interpret an individual score. For example, if on an intelligence test the confidence band for an individual extends from 115 to 130, it is safe to conclude that the individual is not a genius, but that he probably is enough above average to perform successfully in college.

A set of confidence bands for the subtests of a comprehensive achievement test battery is shown in Figure 4-8. Note that the bands are asymmetrical about the obtained scores, which are indicated by the dots. Many textbooks on psychological measurement, and many test manuals, make the mistake of arranging such confidence bands symmetrically about obtained scores. As was mentioned previously, the bands should be placed symmetrically about the estimated *true* scores. In Figure 4-8, the only confidence band that is perfectly symmetrical about the obtained score is that for reading speed. Since the student obtained a score that was exactly at the mean, the obtained score and the estimated true score are identical.

In Figure 4-8, the longer side of each confidence band extends toward the mean. Because the student is well above the mean in numerical skills, the side of the confidence band extending toward the mean is considerably larger than that extending away from the mean. In contrast, because the student scores well below average in social studies, the side of the confidence band pointing toward the mean is larger than that pointing toward lower standard scores.

It should be noticed in Figure 4-8 that the confidence bands for different tests vary in size. This is because the tests vary in terms of re-

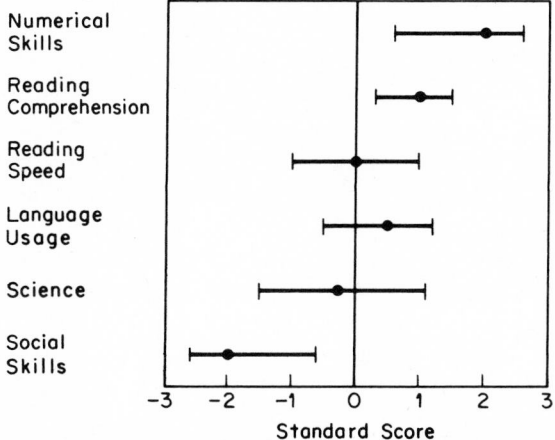

Figure 4-8. Obtained scores and confidence bands for a student on a battery of achievement tests.

liability. The test for reading comprehension has a high reliability, and therefore the confidence band is small. In contrast, the test for science has a relatively low reliability, and therefore the confidence band is relatively large.

A set of confidence bands like that in Figure 4-8 is very useful in interpreting test results for students. Confidence bands lend caution in making overly precise interpretations of obtained scores, and they indicate the range within which it is safe to make interpretations. Illustrative sets of such confidence bands are presented in many test manuals in terms of standard scores, transformed standard scores, and percentiles.

It would be too laborious for teachers to construct confidence bands for all their students on achievement tests and classroom examinations. However, the illustrative sets of confidence bands that appear in test manuals provide the teacher with some guidelines as to how precisely scores at various levels can be interpreted. Also, with the advent of computers for scoring and analyzing test results, the results of more and more commercially distributed tests will be provided to teachers in the form of profile sheets and confidence bands for each student on tests of achievement, aptitude, interest, and other attributes.

RELIABILITY OF DIFFERENCE SCORES. Teachers frequently are called upon to interpret differences between scores on tests. In the case where a student scores at the 90th percentile in reading comprehension and at the 70th percentile in numerical skills, the teacher might conclude that the student is much better in reading than in arithmetic and adjust the plan of study for that student accordingly. However, one must be cautious about interpreting such differences in scores before taking any form of action. An important principle to be grasped is that difference scores tend to be less reliable than the individual scores. This is because a difference score contains two sources of measurement error, one from each of the two tests. Formulas for determining the reliability of difference scores are presented and discussed in Appendix C. More important, here, is an understanding of the nature of the problem.

An analogy may help to illustrate the principle that difference scores tend to be less reliable than individual scores. If a student is unsure exactly when Christmas vacation begins and unsure exactly when it ends, then he is even less sure of how long it lasts. Similarly, if one is somewhat unsure of the precise score for a student on one test and somewhat unsure of the precise score on another test, one is even less sure of the precise difference in scores that would be obtained if no measurement error were present.

When problems arise concerning the interpretation of difference scores, the formulas presented in Appendix C should be applied. However, usually there is nothing that the teacher particularly needs to do about this matter except to be somewhat cautious in interpreting differences in scores. If reliabilities for both tests are high, say, both above .90, then difference scores are almost as reliable as individual scores. In contrast, if reliabilities are no higher than .70, then most apparent differences between scores are due entirely to unreliability of the measuring instruments rather than to any real differences in abilities or other traits.

EFFECTS OF DISPERSION ON RELIABILITY. A particular reliability coefficient is meaningful only if it is computed on a sample of students that is typical of the population of students with which the test will be used. The reliability coefficient is a correlation coefficient, and thus its size depends on the standard deviation of ability in the sample being investigated. If the sample is more homogeneous than the population in which the test will be used, the reliability will be underestimated. In contrast, if the standard deviation is larger than that in the population in which the test will be used, the reliability will be overestimated. The former would be the case if one correlated alternate forms of a reading comprehension test after administering the tests only to students in "above-average" school districts. Such schools would tend to have only students with average or above-average ability in reading, and consequently the correlation between alternate forms would be less than if a more diverse collection of students were used in the study of reliability. The latter circumstance would occur if the reliability study contained children from the fourth, fifth, and sixth grades. Because the purpose of using the tests is to make interpretations *within* grades, the use of a more diverse sample of students would lead to an overestimate of the test reliability.

In studying test manuals, it is important to see whether reliability coefficients are based on representative samples of students, rather than on samples that are either overly homogeneous or overly heterogeneous. In particular, if the test manual does not state in detail the nature of the sample on which statistics relating to reliability were determined, one should be very suspicious of the test and the company that produced it.

INCREASING THE RELIABILITY

Rather than worry about unreliability after it has occurred, it is much more important to eliminate as many sources of measurement error as possible when the test is being constructed. For some of the sources of error mentioned previously, definite steps can be taken to lower measurement error. As was mentioned, the measurement error due to guessing can be lowered by using a larger number of alternatives for each question. The test can be more highly standardized by carefully composing the test instructions, ensuring that all necessary information for taking the test is supplied to students, and religiously following the rules for administration and scoring. Unreliability due to the sampling of content can be lowered to some extent by carefully spreading the test questions across the important content in the course. Errors in scoring on objective tests can be greatly decreased by the simple expedient of checking one's scoring. Errors in scoring essay examinations can be greatly decreased by following some of the rules given in Chapter 7.

INCREASING THE NUMBER OF ITEMS. After all efforts have been made to improve test standardization, the reliability can be raised by making the test longer. The increased length will act to reduce the errors due to guessing, the errors due to sampling of content, and some of the accidental factors in the testing session which tend to increase or decrease scores. As tests are made longer and longer, these sources of measurement error tend to average out and permit a more reliable result. This is why it was previously said that, other things being equal, a long test is a good test.

RESIDUAL SOURCES OF ERROR. In spite of the tester's best efforts, there will remain some measurement error, and there will be considerably more in some types of tests than in others. Nothing can be done to completely remove the measurement error related to day-to-day and year-to-year fluctuations in the individual. The individual is simply not completely the same from day to day, nor from year to year, and no amount of test construction or statistical manipulation will make him so.

SUMMARY

Essentially, the correlation coefficient indicates the extent to which two instruments measure the same thing. In educational research the correlation coefficient primarily is useful for (1) determining the extent to which a predictor test forecasts a criterion and (2) determining the reliability of tests.

There is some error, or chance, involved in the results from even the best tests; and in some tests the amount of error is so large as to render them nearly worthless. Some of the major sources of measurement error are (1) fluctuations in the student from day to day, (2) poor sampling of content, (3) chance factors that enter into the scoring of tests, (4) guessing on multiple-choice tests, and (5) poor standardization of tests.

Measurement error has several undesirable effects. First, it tends to "blur" the relationships between predictor tests and their criteria, making correlations lower than if the measurement error were not present. Second, it tends to bias scores, high scores being somewhat too high and low scores being somewhat too low. Third, it makes it necessary to consider scores as lying in zones on the test continuum rather than representing precise points.

The ideal way to determine the reliability is to correlate two alternate forms of the same test administered approximately two weeks apart. If the correlation is high, it means that very little measurement error is present in using the instrument; but if the correlation is very low, it means that chance factors are so large as to make the instrument untrustworthy. When two alternate forms are not available, or for some reason cannot be applied, approximate methods are available for estimating reliability. Seldom will teachers find occasion to make elaborate studies of reliability, but because investigations of reliability are reported for most commercially distributed tests of achievement, aptitude, personality, and others, it is important for teachers to understand the nature of the problem.

More important than to measure the amount of measurement error that is present in tests is to eliminate as many sources of unreliability as possible when instruments are being constructed. Definite steps can be taken to lessen many sources of unreliability. The ultimate limit on the reliability of tests is set by the tendency for people to change in their abilities and personality characteristics over time. Two important lessons to be learned from a discussion of test reliability are (1) a long test almost always is more reliable than a shorter test, and (2) the average score obtained on two tests of the same attribute administered on different days is more reliable than the result from only one test.

SUGGESTED ADDITIONAL READINGS

Anastasi, A. *Psychological testing.* (3rd ed.) New York: Macmillan, 1968, chap. 4.

Ebel, R. L. *Measuring educational achievement.* Englewood Cliffs, N.J.: Prentice-Hall, 1965, chap. 10.

Garrett, H. E. *Elementary statistics.* (2nd ed.) New York: McKay, 1962, chap. 7.

Guilford, J. P. *Fundamental statistics in psychology and education*. (4th ed.) New York: McGraw-Hill, 1965.

Nunnally, J. C. *Psychometric theory*. New York: McGraw-Hill, 1967, chaps. 6, 7.

Nunnally, J. C. *Introduction to psychological measurement*. New York: McGraw-Hill, 1970, chap. 5.

Thorndike, R. L. Reliability. In E. F. Lindquist (Ed.), *Educational measurement*. Washington: American Council on Education, 1951, chap. 15.

PART II

CONSTRUCTION AND USE OF TEACHER-MADE TESTS

In terms of sheer numbers, students see many more teacher-made tests than any other kind. Regardless of how well commercially distributed tests of achievement and aptitude are constructed and used in schools, if teachers did not do a good job of composing and applying classroom tests, our educational system would be in chaos.

Because of the differences in curricula among schools and school systems, and because of the differences in emphases among teachers, it usually is not possible to test accomplishment in individual units of instruction with commercially distributed tests. Even if it were possible, it would be prohibitively expensive for most schools. Consequently, teachers must construct their own tests; and if test scores and the decisions based upon them are to have any meaning, the tests must be as well constructed as possible, commensurate with the time and energy teachers can spare from their many other duties.

Some concepts, facts, and techniques are essential to learn before constructing tests. To explain these is one of the major purposes of this book. In addition to being a "learnable" body of knowledge, test construction is, in part, an art which cannot be acquired solely from textbooks. Like any other art, it must be learned from much practice, and particularly from working with those who have already mastered the art. When teachers first start to construct tests, their products are usually poor, and they get better (if ever) only after much experience. To help structure that experience, the following three chapters will discuss some of the basic principles in the construction and use of teacher-made tests.

chapter 5

PLANNING THE TEST

Max Marshall is a bright and shining new face on the staff of Central High. He is young enough to be the son, and maybe even the grandson, of some of the older hands there; and they have given him a tough task: teaching four sections of general science. His first month at Central has been marked with a number of casualties: sixteen test tubes were broken, three students burned their fingers on bunsen burners, one girl ruined a dress with a splotch of acid, and, finally, to climax it all, the last laboratory demonstration in electrical resistance knocked out all the lights on the second floor for a whole afternoon. As if these troubles were not enough, Max encounters a new obstacle. Looking through the textbook, he sees that the first quarter of the subject soon will be covered, and consequently, it will be a good time to examine students on what they have learned. Max has been so busy keeping test tubes clean and keeping one chapter ahead of his young Einsteins that he had almost forgotten about tests.

The rest of the afternoon Max worries about how to test his students, and he is not as fast on his feet as he usually is in preventing the acid from spilling and the sparks from flying. As Max remembers from his course in educational measurement and as he can see now, he should have planned his test much earlier in the semester and preferably even before the semester began.

Good tests do not simply happen as a product of last-minute inspiration. Good tests are planned in detail well in advance, and the plan for the test is closely interrelated with the over-all goals of the course, the classroom instruction, the readings in the text, and the laboratory exercises.

Numerous questions occur to Max: What type of test item should I use? How much of the text should the test cover? How long should the test be? Should the test cover only the text and classroom discussions, or should it also cover the laboratory work? How many tests will I have this semester? Will semester grades be based only on the tests, or should I count the laboratory exercises and class projects? Because Max has not thought out these questions much earlier, it will be rather difficult for him to coordinate his tests with the instruction and with the other means of evaluating over-all performance. Because he did not explain the schedule of testing, and the nature and scope, to students at the beginning of the semester, they are confused as to how to divide up their time, what to emphasize and what to deemphasize, and what the standards are for successful performance in the course. That evening Max fishes out his textbook on educational measurement from beneath unpacked fishing gear, trading stamps, and past issues of *National Geographic*. According to the chapter on "Planning the Test," and as Max now remembers, the purpose of a test is to supply a number of types of information.

INFORMATION SUPPLIED BY CLASSROOM TESTS

The construction, administration, and scoring of tests are some of the most difficult and time-consuming chores of teaching. Many teachers who otherwise do excellent jobs fail miserably when it comes to preparing and using tests. In a popularity contest, tests would rank somewhere below castor oil in the affection of students. If tests hold difficulties for teachers and are unpleasant to students, why then do we use them? We use them because we have to. They supply some very important information that would be difficult, if not impossible, to obtain by any other means.

INFORMATION FOR THE TEACHER.   Tests primarily are helpful to teachers in determining the extent to which students are meeting the objectives of a unit of instruction. Such objectives always do (or at least should) exist either explicitly stated in a course outline or held in the teacher's head. For example, in teaching number skills some of the goals are to have students master principles concerning the use of dollar signs, carrying in addition, and dealing with remainders in division. Both teacher and students live by these objectives. Only to the extent that the average student meets them can the teacher feel satisfaction with the instruction as a whole, and the progress of individual students is judged largely by how well they perform with respect to the objectives. Tests are very helpful because they supply one of the most important sources of information as to how well students are meeting the objectives of a unit of instruction.

One of the primary reasons for using tests is to let the teacher know how each student is doing. Otherwise he cannot make intelligent decisions about promoting and failing students, sectioning, providing special help to students in difficulty, and producing stimulating material for students who are moving ahead of the group. To provide information to help in making such decisions, it is necessary for the test to represent a comprehensive sample of the important material in the course. If the test is slanted toward some particular aspect of the subject matter, to the detriment of other important areas, then it would serve as a poor basis for making decisions. If the test concerns only trivial aspects of the subject matter rather than more important ones, decisions based upon it would be faulty.

In addition to providing information about the progress of particular students, the test supplies information about how the class as a whole is progressing. If the average performance is much worse than the teacher had expected, this might indicate either that the teacher had expected far too much of the students or that the program of instruction was not working well.

In a sense tests provide the teacher with some clues about what he actually teaches, what he emphasizes, and what he values. If the teacher will look carefully at the content of his tests, he will see what types of subject matter emphases he considers important. The teacher may not realize what values he has with respect to various aspects of the subject matter until he sees what he actually places in his own tests. Because the emphases in the course should be consciously followed by the teacher, and because they should be imparted to students, this information should be available quite early in the term. This is why we said previously that Max Marshall made a mistake by waiting until immediately before testing time to give careful consideration to the construction of a test.

The results from a test provide the teacher with some indications of what he actually has taught and how well the text and special exercises have covered the subject matter. If students do much better on some types of questions in the test than on others, this is an indication of how well they are being instructed in the various aspects of the subject matter. For example, if in a test of number skills, students do much better with multiplication problems than with division problems, this gives the teacher some clues about the adequacy of the over-all instruction.

INFORMATION FOR STUDENTS.   In addition to the information supplied to teachers, tests also supply very valuable information to students; and whether or not they profess to like taking tests, the information they obtain is invaluable. Students often are quite unsure about how well they are doing in a unit of instruction. Few of the A students think they are failing, and few of the failing students think that they are doing

A work. But within wide latitudes students often are quite unsure of their actual standing. Students who receive good grades on a test will be encouraged to continue the work habits and methods of study that brought them success. Students who do poorly on tests are warned to work harder, work differently, and seek help from others. Over a period of years students slowly learn the kinds of things they can do well and the kinds of things at which they usually do poorly. Such information is invaluable to the student in planning his future.

Tests also provide students with information about what the teacher values and actually intends to stress in the unit of instruction. No amount of hallowed words by the teacher will convince students. They craftily wait to see what he puts on the examination, and henceforth they study the kinds of things which he has emphasized. If a teacher's test in tenth-grade algebra usually contains numerous problems on linear equations and few, if any, on quadratic equations, students will soon catch on and emphasize the former rather than the latter type of problem in their study. If in a course in American history the teacher emphasizes the events relating to the Civil War in his test, students will catch on and so concentrate on this in their readings. After a teacher has been at a school for some time, older students pass along to younger students the lore about what a particular teacher emphasizes in his tests. Such information which students receive from taking tests can be either helpful or detrimental, depending on the quality of the test. As will be discussed in more detail later in the chapter, teachers should carefully think out what they value about a unit of instruction and what they intend to point up in the instruction. If these emphases are made prominent in tests, then this communicates to the students in a very concrete way the emphases which the teacher values. If, on the other hand, the teacher verbalizes one set of standards for emphasis in the subject matter and includes different kinds of items and questions on the test, then the teacher is fooling himself, and students are moved to study what often are trivial aspects of the course, e.g., the memorization of names, places, and dates in a course on American history.

INFORMATION FOR PARENTS.   Test results also supply very valuable information to parents regarding how well their sons and daughters are doing in particular subjects. Parents often are surprised when they find out how well or how poorly their children are progressing. Students at least have some basis of comparison: they are in the classroom, know how often they succeed and fail with particular kinds of exercises, and see how well other students do. But parents are lacking these guideposts, and they often are very poor judges of the progress of their children. Teachers sometimes fail to see how difficult it is for parents to judge the progress of their children. The teacher who has taught the fourth grade for three or four years has seen many children of approximately the same age and witnessed their efforts to learn standard materials. If a child is unable to read a passage in a standard text or to perform adequately on certain types of number skills, the expert eye of the teacher soon catches the difficulty. But teachers often fail to realize that parents may have only one child, and if more than one, they probably have only one in the fourth grade. All that the parent can rely on is some vague recollection of how he did when he was in the fourth grade or what his friend's little girl did when she was in the fourth grade. Even those who have several children and watch them progress through school often forget how well each performed at each level. Consequently, tests provide very useful information to parents as to how well their children are doing in school.

Teachers find test results much easier to discuss with parents than any other type of evaluation. If, in conferring with a parent, the teacher tells Billy's mother that he is having great trouble in spelling, it is much easier to communicate this information to the parent if some of Billy's spelling-test results are available. If no tests are available, the parent is likely to be skeptical; she is likely to say to herself, "Billy spells as well as most other children," or "I think he spells well." But when the parent sees that Billy has consistently scored near the bottom of his class in spelling, and when she sees that he gets no more than four or five words correct out of a list of twenty, this usually is convincing.

Information supplied by classroom tests helps the parent to help the child. The over-all progress of the child over a period of years provides information that helps the parent in planning for the future. The child who does only mediocre or poor work throughout the elementary and high school grades is a very poor bet for college, and student and parents should be warned about this years in advance. On the other hand, the student who always does A work probably has the energy and the capability to go far, and if parents know this in advance, they can plan and save to help the child go on for more schooling.

Information from tests helps parents to structure the child's study at home. Working on the assumption that the child has been doing very well in school, the parents may have been quite lax about insisting that he do his homework and about checking it. After parents learn that the student is doing poorly, either over-all or in special areas of instruction, this provides information as to how the child can be helped at home.

INFORMATION FOR COUNSELING AND EDUCATIONAL RESEARCH.
In addition to the information supplied to teachers, students, and parents, many other persons will obtain information from teacher-made tests and the grades that depend in part upon them. The permanent records of students will be inspected and used by many people. For example, one of the important things for the high school counselor to consider in providing career guidance to a student would be the grades made in specific units of instruction (which are based in large measure on results from teacher-made tests). If the student's record shows that he has made very good grades in mathematics and science topics, and if his grades agree with tests of aptitudes and interests, the counselor might inform the student that his abilities and interests are such that he probably would succeed in and enjoy life as a chemist, physicist, or engineer. Principals and teachers use student records to make decisions about grade placement, remedial instruction, counseling, and many other things.

Grades made by students in particular units of instruction are useful in many different types of educational research. For example, consider an experiment conducted on the usefulness of a new type of phonographic recording for instruction in French. In twenty classes in a number of high schools, a random half of the students are provided the usual instruction, while the other half are given the new method of instruction. An achievement test is constructed by a committee of French teachers and is administered to all the students. Comparisons can then be made of the scores obtained by students in the two groups. If students who received the new form of instruction perform much better than those who did not, it would indicate that changing the curriculum to include the new method of teaching French would be worthwhile.

Scores made on teacher-made tests and grades based in part upon them continue to have an important impact on students after they leave high school. Most colleges these days are selective regarding the students they will admit, and selection is usually based more on grades made in high school than on any other factor. Teacher-made tests, and the grades based upon them, are also important to those students who do not go on to higher education. A high school graduate seeking employment as a stenographer will probably find that prospective employers want to see a transcript of her high school grades. If the grades are good in English, typing, business administration, and other courses relevant to stenographic work, this will go a long way toward persuading the employer to hire the young applicant.

From the foregoing discussion, it can be seen that teacher-made tests, and grades based largely upon them, are important for many, many purposes. Thus, it is the teacher's duty to do the very best job he can in composing tests to make them as reliable and as valid as possible. In Chapter 4 we discussed some ways of improving test reliability; others will be mentioned in later chapters. In this chapter we shall be discussing the procedures for ensuring the validity of classroom tests.

OUTLINE OF OBJECTIVES

Except in the case of the exercises in law and order that we teachers sometimes force upon our students, everything that happens in a unit of instruction should be aimed at having all students achieve a set of specified objectives or goals. Schooling is not an end in itself, and all good teachers recognize that schooling would be largely a waste of time if the individual did not continue to think and learn on his own long after he graduates. As teachers, we spend most of our time developing intellectual and social skills in our students—obvious skills like those required in spelling, arithmetic, and typing and subtle skills like those necessary for making an excellent speech at a businessmen's luncheon, detecting fine differences in two renditions of a Beethoven sonata, and sensing the course leading to the invention of a new type of water-purification system. As teachers, our goals of instruction focus on the future— on the near future when we teach foundation skills needed to progress from one level to the next, and on the distant future when we try to develop abilities necessary for successful performance in higher education and in vocations. Of course, as teachers, we are not always sure of the types of performance at one level of instruction that contribute to success at higher levels of instruction and in life pursuits. However, we do have definite values regarding what is important for students to learn in various units of instruction; these values are based on educational research, the opinions of experts, and our personal judgments. As much as possible, those values should determine the nature of the instruction, broadly speaking. Also, as much as possible, teacher-made tests should measure the extent to which those values have been implemented.

The validity of achievement tests in general, whether constructed by an individual teacher for use in his own classroom or by commercial test specialists for use across the country, is determined by evaluating how well a test represents the curricular content. To have content validity, a test should contain items which adequately sample the areas of subject matter and the abilities which a course of instruction has aimed to develop. The first step toward ensuring the content validity of a test is to formulate *realistic, precise,* and *measurable* objectives of instruction.

All too often we find stated objectives expressed in terms that are useless when it comes to actually constructing a test. Rather than stating objectives in such vague terms as "instilling an appreciation for the American form of government," we should strive to list in precise terms the major concepts, facts, and skills that the teacher hopes to impart during the course of study. By stating objectives in precise terms, specific with regard to the course content, the teacher is building a blueprint for later test construction. Objectives such as "familiarity with the strengths and weaknesses of the republican form of government" or "familiarity with the differences between the republican form of government and a monarchy" are relatively precise and straightforwardly measured. Each objective suggests specific test items for measuring achievement in the unit of instruction.

Having well-thought-out written objectives to serve as a blueprint for test construction can help in overcoming many of the common faults of classroom tests, e.g., overemphasis on trivial details and inadequate, uneven coverage of instruction material. Formulating a comprehensive set of objectives for a unit of instruction helps ensure that instruction and evaluation will be coordinated. Failure to construct tests which validly reflect course objectives cheats both the student and the teacher. The student is cheated because his course grade does not adequately reflect his level of achievement. The teacher is cheated because he fails to obtain adequate feedback about the effect of the over-all instruction on individual students and the class as a whole.

In the following pages, we shall discuss how outlines of objectives are formulated. Many educators have devoted a great deal of time and effort to developing systems for classifying objectives of instruction. (See Bloom, 1956; Gerberich, 1956; Krathwohl, Bloom, & Masia, 1964; Smith & Tyler, 1942.) Teachers may wish to delve into these discussions for themselves in order to obtain more insight into the many kinds of educational outcomes which may be measured. For classroom testing purposes, many of these schemes will seem unrealistically laborious and detailed. Such complex and highly specific outlines are most realistic and, indeed, desirable for use by curriculum planning committees and those constructing standardized tests for wide use. However, the fact that such elaborate and time-consuming systems of objectives are impracticable for the average classroom teacher should not cause him to abandon altogether the effort to construct thorough outlines of objectives. The construction of such outlines should serve both to increase the quality of instruction and to promote the content validity of teacher-made tests.

TYPES OF OBJECTIVES.   In the same sense that there are many different ways to classify fish in the sea and shells on the shore, there are many different ways to classify objectives of instruction. A major way in which different sets of objectives of instruction differ from one another is in terms of the relative generality versus the specificity of the objectives. For example, at the most general level, all educational processes are concerned to a greater or lesser degree with (1) intellectual functions, (2) habits, and (3) values. Intellectual functions are involved in knowing and thinking, such as in knowing the proper spelling of the word "severe" and being able to think out the proper solution to a problem in trigonometry. Habits concern such matters as the use at home of information obtained in a unit of instruction on health care, employing a dictionary to learn the meaning of unfamiliar words, using a comma before the conjunction in a compound sentence, keeping up to date on current events, and unplugging electronic appliances before working on them. Values concern such matters as believing in free speech for everyone, appreciating a wide variety of art forms, being willing to respect the advice of experts in various fields, appreciating "good" literature, desiring to be a good citizen, showing respect for school authority, and demonstrating concern for the plight of American Indians.

The aforementioned three very general objectives of instruction can be broken down into subgoals. For example, the very general concept of values can be broken down into attitudes, interests, and others. However, it would not be worth the space here to break the categories of habits and values down into more specific objectives because, in this chapter, we shall be concerned primarily with intellectual functions. When one speaks of tests, one thinks mainly of the intellectual functions. Assessments of habits and values are based either on teachers' observations and ratings or on measuring instruments that usually are not referred to as "tests." How such measurements are made will be discussed in later chapters. In this chapter we shall be concerned with tests in the stricter meaning of the term and with how teacher-made tests are used to measure the degree to which students are meeting the intellectual objectives of a unit of instruction.

TYPES OF INTELLECTUAL OBJECTIVES.   There are various ways of breaking down intellectual objectives into meaningful subdivisions, one of which is as follows:

1. Memory for facts
2. Understanding of simple principles

3.   Understanding of complex principles
4.   Use of principles to evaluate proposed solutions to problems
5.   Use of principles to solve problems
6.   Inventive extension of old principles to the development of new principles

The six levels of intellectual functioning posed above range from the simple memorization of content details to the creative building of new knowledge on the basis of old knowledge. The differences between the six levels are a matter of degree rather than kind.

Test questions that represent the six levels are as follows:

1.   Name the planets in our solar system.

2.   Explain why we have night and day.

3.   Explain how the moon causes the ocean tides.

4.   An astronomer wants to demonstrate that the earth revolves around the sun rather than vice versa. He plans to prove this by taking two photographs of a portion of the heavens, six months apart. Decide whether or not this procedure will prove the astronomer's point and explain your decision.

5.   Using Newton's second law of motion (the cause of acceleration is an unbalanced force), explain how a satellite can be kept in orbit around the earth.

6.   Imagine that you are working on plans for the first space station on the moon. Outline some of the distinctive aspects of living and working on the moon. Consider how a person would have to adjust to living in such an alien environment, both practically and psychologically. Consider the advantages of making astronomical observations from the moon. Outline how you would design the space station to take into account the distinctive aspects of this situation.

If teachers had their way, students would become proficient at all six levels of intellectual functioning in each subject-matter area. Regardless of how much some students gripe about it and how often specialists in education gibe teachers about the matter, at the lowest level it is absolutely necessary for the student to master some simple facts before he can acquire any higher understanding of subject matters, and the mastery of such facts should be examined in a good teacher-made test. The problem is that many teachers devote too much time in their instruction to the memorization of such simple content detail, and most of their test items concern such simple facts. Of course, such practices are to be deplored, and it does not hurt the reader to hear that said one more time here. At the other extreme, some teachers have a proper respect for creativity among their students, they encourage it in their students, and they take account of it in evaluating students' progress. (Some methods for encouraging creativity and measuring it are discussed in Chapter 14.) However, although creative thinking can and should be encouraged in the classroom, most of the time must be taken up with the encouragement of somewhat lower levels of intellectual development. Also, because creative thoughts tend to spring from many forms of background knowledge (as in the sample item above concerning the design of a space station on the moon) rather than from the activities in a specific unit of instruction, it is very difficult to employ items concerning creativity to measure either the effectiveness of a particular unit of instruction or the attainment of students in that unit. As will be discussed in more detail in Chapter 14, creativity should be both encouraged and measured, but in terms of fairness to students and taking into consideration the practicalities of measurement and evaluation, most teacher-made tests should confine themselves largely to the first five levels of intellectual functioning described above.

Levels 2 and 3 of intellectual functioning are distinguished purely in terms of degree, and using twenty-seven levels would have been as sensible as using only two. Levels 2 and 3 differ from level 1 in that they require the generalization of a statement of fact into instances of its occurrence, ones that have not been memorized from textbooks or lectures. In other words, levels 2 and 3 require the student to see principles at work in various ways, rather than just to memorize them. Of course, memorization is necessary as a first step, but both in the instruction and in the measurement of students' progress, it is important to test for the ability to employ principles in understanding natural phenomena. All the levels above level 3 are concerned with the evaluation or production of new knowledge, at least new as far as the student is concerned when the problem is presented. At level 4, a proposed solution to a problem is given to the student, and on the basis of his knowledge of the subject matter he is required to evaluate the quality of that proposed solution. At level 5, the student is given only the problem and is required to produce a solution on his own. In a sense, this is a somewhat higher level of intellectual functioning than that involving judgment of the quality of other people's proposed solutions. At the highest level of all, the level of creativity, the problem is not highly structured, and the student has no proposed solutions. Rather, the student is posed with a very general issue, such as what life on the moon will be like, and is required to invent good ideas on his own.

Teachers should be highly concerned with all the foregoing six levels

Table 5-1 Distribution and relationships of content and objectives for a test in high school biology *(Adapted from Noll, 1965, by permission of author and publisher.)*

Content	Objectives						Total
	I. To Achieve Knowledge and Understanding of		II. To Achieve Skill in			III. To Develop Scientific Attitudes of	
	A. Biological Facts and Concepts, 25%	B. Biological Principles, 25%	A. Interpretation of Graphs, Charts, Data, Maps, Tables, etc., 15%	B. Problem Solving, 20%	C. Use of Biological Information in the Appraisal of Real Situations, 10%	A. Suspended Judgment, Open-mindedness, Sensitivity to Problems and to Cause-and-effect Relationships, 5%	
Methodology of science, 5%		1		1	1	2	5%
Characteristics common to living organisms, cellular structure and functioning, molecular biology, 15%	5	4	1	3	2		15%
Kinds of living things and their groupings, 5%	1	1	1	1	1		5%
Nature of processes essential to the life of individual organisms: food manufacture, cir-							

							Total
...culation, excretion, coordination, and adjustment, 25%	7	6	5	4	2	1	25%
Processes associated with continuance of species, reproduction, and heredity, 25%	6	6	4	6	2	1	25%
History of life on earth, theories of evolution, 5%	1	2	1	1		1	5%
Interrelationships: ecological, harmful organisms, parasites, disease, beneficial organisms, conservation, 20%							20%
Total	5	5	3	4	2	1	100%
	25%	25%	15%	20%	10%	5%	

of intellectual functioning, both in their instructional activities and in the measurement of student progress. It is difficult to say what proportion of the time should be spent in encouraging the development of these various levels of intellectual functioning and equally difficult to say what proportion of test items should be chosen to represent each level. The important point to remember here is that teachers should keep all levels of intellectual functioning in mind as they compose their outlines of objectives, and they should compose test items to measure how well students have succeeded in achieving those objectives.

GOALS IN PARTICULAR SUBJECT MATTERS. The foregoing paragraphs considered very general goals of instruction, ones that apply quite widely to different types of subject matter. It is necessary to translate these more general goals into content-related goals when considering particular subject matters. An example is presented in Table 5-1, which shows the content objectives for a unit of instruction in high school biology. The percentages in the left-hand column show the planned emphasis in the total instruction. The percentages shown at the top of the table indicate the amount of emphasis that should be placed on evaluating the progress of students with tests and other methods of appraisal. Such an outline would be useful both in guiding the instruction and in formulating teacher-made tests. Of course, an outline such as that shown in Table 5-1 represents an ideal. One cannot proportion instruction into exact percentages, and it usually proves very difficult to proportion test items exactly as one would like. However, an outline of content objectives, such as that in Table 5-1, is very helpful to the teacher in planning instruction and in formulating teacher-made tests. An outline is analogous to a health regimen concerning diet, exercise, and other habits: We do not always follow it precisely from day to day, but when we do not, the regimen at least serves to remind us of what we should be doing. So it is with good outlines of content objectives. We may not always follow them in minute detail, but still they serve as very useful guides to action, both in determining the instruction and in formulating effective methods of evaluating the progress of students with respect to the objectives.

Because of the importance of outlines of objectives, the following sections will illustrate, in detail, outlines for three school topics. It is recognized that to a large extent teachers do and should rely on excellent objectives set forth in curriculum guides and teacher's manuals. In many cases they may not find it necessary to construct outlines of objectives for course content, but instead can rely on precisely formulated objectives provided by a textbook publisher. Even though such outlines are widely available, teachers should not fail to be aware of the principles which guide the construction of good outlines of objectives. Knowledge of these principles is as important in evaluating the usefulness of objectives formulated by others as it is in constructing one's own outline. Often, after viewing a published outline of objectives with a critical eye, a teacher may be able to redefine his own objectives in more precise, measurable terms.

OUTLINE OF CONTENT OBJECTIVES FOR MATHEMATICS

Below is an outline of objectives for the fall term of instruction in mathematics for fourth-grade students. The outline portrays the types of knowledge and skills that the teacher hopes to develop in his students during the unit of instruction:

A. Addition
1. Two-, three-, and four-row problems
2. Problems requiring, and others not requiring, carrying
3. Decimal points and dollar signs

B. Subtraction
1. Three-, four-, five-, and six-column problems
2. Problems requiring borrowing
3. Decimal points and dollar signs

C. Multiplication
1. Memorization of multiplication table through 12 times 12
2. Multipliers of one, two, three, and four digits
3. Multipliers of 10, 20, 100, 200, etc.
4. Problems requiring carrying
5. Decimals and dollar signs

D. Division
1. Divisors of one, two, and three digits
2. Quotients without, and others with, remainders
3. Decimals in divisors and/or dividend

E. Word problems
1. Requiring only one operation, e.g., division
2. Requiring two operations in sequence, e.g., first division, then subtraction
3. Requiring answers in fractions

The reason that such an outline should be composed early in the term is that it will prove useful not only in generating tests but also in guiding the instruction. Inevitably it is the case that, near to the time when a test is to be administered, the teacher will see that parts of the outline have not been sufficiently covered, e.g., that few or no word problems have been studied which required two operations in sequence. The teacher must then use the remaining days of classwork to ensure that the outlined subject matter has been adequately covered before the test is administered.

The way to compose a test is to write *good* items for each section and each subsection of the outline. How to write good items will be discussed in detail in the next chapter. Here we will be more concerned with the outline and with illustrating how outlines can be translated into tests. Some sample items are as follows:

For section *C*, subsection 4:

$$
286 \qquad 9284 \qquad 529
$$
$$
\times\,48 \qquad \times\,36 \qquad \times\,311
$$

For section *D*, subsection 1:

$$
3\,\overline{\smash{)}\,6921} \qquad 15\,\overline{\smash{)}\,810} \qquad 222\,\overline{\smash{)}\,9102}
$$

For section *E*, subsection 2:

Billy picked 24 apples and gave half of these to his mother. From his remaining half, he gave 4 apples to a friend. How many apples did Billy have left for himself?

In the above outline of fourth-grade math, there is a total of five sections. These five sections contain a total of seventeen subsections (three in each, except multiplication, which has five). If the teacher composed only one item relating to each subsection, the test would contain seventeen items. However, many of the subsections relate to two or more items, e.g., subsection 1 under "Division": "Divisors of one, two, and three digits." Consequently, to cover all the subsections completely, the test would have to contain three or four times as many items as seventeen, which might be too many for the children to complete in the time available.

The emphasis placed on the various subsections is determined in two ways. First, the importance which the teacher attaches to the different sections and subsections will partly determine the emphasis and the number of related items which are composed. In the example above, the teacher would probably place the most emphasis on word problems (section E) because, typically, this is one of the areas of concentration at the fourth-grade level. Consequently, the teacher would decide to compose nine items for section E—three for each of the subsections. In contrast to the emphasis placed on word problems, some other sections and subsections may be given relatively slight emphasis. If the class as a whole is doing well in math, it would be a waste of time to compose items relating to some of the simpler types of problems, e.g., multiplication problems that do not require carrying and addition problems with only two rows of numbers. For these and other relatively unimportant parts of the outline, few or no items would be composed.

The outline for fourth-grade mathematics can be looked at in terms of the six levels of understanding described previously. Sections A to D in the outline would concern mainly levels 1 and 2 in the hierarchy of intellectual objectives, i.e., memory for facts and understanding of simple principles. Higher levels of understanding could be tested with respect to section E of the outline for mathematics (word problems). With respect to that section, the teacher could compose items that concern higher levels of understanding, the evaluation of proposed solutions for problems, and the solution of problems that require relatively high levels of understanding for the age group. However, in the instruction of elementary core topics like math, the teacher necessarily must devote most of his time to instilling simple facts and simple principles. Thus, it is only proper that teacher-made tests for the topic concern primarily computational problems and relatively simple word problems.

The levels of understanding that are emphasized in the objectives of instruction and in teacher-made tests are, to a large extent, determined by the capabilities of the particular group of students. Previously it was mentioned that because of their age and intellectual background, it is not usually feasible to place major emphasis on high levels of understanding for most students in fourth-grade mathematics. As students mature in the elementary grades and throughout higher levels of education, the emphasis can and should shift toward the higher levels of understanding, and less emphasis should be placed on the grasping of facts and simple principles. Also, at any one age level, students in different schools vary widely in their ability to achieve at the higher levels of understanding. Teachers in culturally disadvantaged neighborhoods usually find that most of their time is devoted to the simple fundamentals, and although it should still be the goal to push all students as far as possible up the ladder of levels of understanding, it frequently is all or more than we can do to impart factual information and induce an understanding of simple principles. In contrast, students in more fortunate cultural circumstances frequently can rush through the lower levels of understanding and spend most of their time attempting to achieve higher levels of understanding. Such differences between schools are important in terms of the emphasis placed on various types of material in outlines of goals of instruction and in the formulation of teacher-made tests.

In addition to the purposeful placing of emphases, the number of items composed for different parts of the outline are (or rather should be) allotted on a random basis. The outline of math above is relatively simple, and it would be possible to cover all the parts in one relatively long test. When more complex outlines are required, as would be the case with eighth-grade geography and high school physics, it is not possible to cover adequately even the important subsections of the outline in the test. Consequently, the teacher must compose more items for some parts of the outline than for others. This is all right as long as these "random" emphases do not in fact slant the test much more toward one part of the subject matter than to others, e.g., many items on multiplication and none on division. If teachers consistently slant tests toward certain portions of the subject matter, students will catch on and correspondingly slant their study.

Such random choosing of items is best accomplished if the teacher has a large store of items available, obtained from tests given in previous years. If these are placed on file cards (which have many advantages), all those relating to particular sections of the outline, e.g., word problems, can be shuffled and the desired number dealt out. This would approach true randomness, which, because the test requires content validity, is good. Teachers who are new at instructing a particular subject will probably not have a large store of items available. Then it is very helpful if the new teachers can borrow stocks of items from other teachers who have had considerable experience in dealing with the subject matter.

If teachers do not have their own stock of items and cannot borrow them from other teachers, they must try to be as "random" as possible in the final selection of items (keeping in mind that the number of such items allotted to major sections is primarily determined by the judged importance of the sections). There is no way to tell a person how to "be random," but essentially what is meant is to scatter the items around throughout all possible problems and questions. After tests are composed, it often is easy to see that the items are overly slanted toward one or more aspects of the subject matter, e.g., too many questions about electricity in the science examination and too few questions about agricultural regions in the geography examination.

One precaution against overly slanting the test toward particular features of the subject matter is to ask fellow teachers to look through the intended test and to make suggestions for additions and changes. It often is easier for our friends to notice such overemphases. Fellow teachers should also be consulted for many other problems in composing reliable, comprehensive tests. Admittedly this sometimes is a painful experience for beginning teachers, but it is necessary for the growth of professional skills. To further illustrate the development and use of subject-matter outlines, in the following sections outlines of objectives will be shown and discussed for eighth-grade geography and for high school physics.

OUTLINE FOR EIGHTH-GRADE GEOGRAPHY

Fourth-grade arithmetic was chosen as the topic for the first illustration because, comparatively speaking, arithmetic is easy to outline and easy to test. There are some definite divisions of the subject matter, and it is relatively easy to compose problems relating to these subdivisions. Here we will consider a subject matter, geography, which is not quite so easy to outline and which is more difficult to adequately test. In the example imagine that the teacher is planning a two-month period of instruction relating to the continent of Africa, and at the end of that time he intends to compose a test.

A. Principal racial, ethnic, and religious groups
  1. Names of groups
  2. Principal region each occupies
  3. Relative social and economic positions
  4. Conflicts and changing relations

B. Major topographic and climatic regions: North Africa, Sahara region, tropical rain forest, temperate Southern Africa
  1. Names of countries in each region
  2. Types of rivers, lakes, and rainfall
  3. Elevation, topography, types of soil
  4. Density and nature of populations
  5. Indigenous animals and plants

C. Agriculture
  1. Major products of different regions
  2. Products that "grow wild"
  3. Methods of cultivation and merchandising
  4. New products and methods being introduced

D. Commerce and industry
    1. Degree of self-sufficiency
    2. Transportation
    3. Prominent mineral resources
    4. Typical industrial products
    5. Major exports and imports

E. Political subdivisions
    1. Names of major countries
    2. Different forms of government
    3. Movements toward self-government
    4. Political alliances
    5. Problems of new nations

For the arithmetic test, it was relatively obvious what types of problems should be used. For the test of geography, a much wider selection of topics and item forms is available. Following are some types of items that could be used to turn the outline into a good test.

For section A, subsection 3:
One of the most primitive groups of people in Africa is the
a. South African Boer
b. Pygmy
c. Watusi
d. Egyptian
e. Berber

For section D, subsection 3:
Southern Africa leads the world in the mining of
a. coal
b. iron ore
c. silver
d. diamonds
e. bauxite

For section D, subsection 5:
Name five principal export commodities from Africa.

For section B, subsection 2:
The longest river in the world is in Africa. It empties into the Mediterranean Sea. Its name is the _____.

For section D, subsection 2:
The camel is used for transportation in certain regions of Africa. State three physical features of the camel that make him ideal for transportation in desert regions.

For parts of sections *A*, *B*, *C*, and *D*:

Describe the typical village farm in Central Africa. Include in your description

a. the crops often grown
b. methods of farming
c. trading of farm products
d. types of homes and buildings for animals
e. danger from wild animals
f. education, work, and play of children

For various parts of the outline as a whole:

What do you see as some of the major problems facing the young nations in Africa? Among other things, consider education of the people, experience in self-government, natural resources, and relations between the new nations and former colonial powers.

As can be seen from the example above, there are many different types of items that could be used for the test of geography. The merits of these and other types of items will be discussed in the next chapter. However, before getting to that subject matter it should be understood quite early in the book that any of these types of items and most of those that will be discussed in the next chapter can be made into good tests. The essential consideration is that items be carefully thought out and carefully composed regardless of their specific forms.

Another teacher might have composed a somewhat different outline from that above and composed different items with respect to the outline, but that is not the important point. The important point is that there should be a comprehensive outline and that the outline should be skillfully translated into a broadly representative collection of test items.

In the following section one more example will be given of an outline for constructing a classroom test; then in the subsequent sections of this chapter some general principles will be stated for constructing teacher-made tests.

OUTLINE OF OBJECTIVES FOR HIGH SCHOOL PHYSICS

A. Measurement in physics
    1. Types: length, mass, volume, density, and time
    2. English and metric systems
    3. International standards
    4. Accuracy of measurement

B. Forces in liquids
   1. Relations between force and pressure
   2. Influence of gravity and depth on pressure
   3. Archimedes' principle
   4. Pascal's law
   5. Underwater vessels and equipment
   6. City water supply

C. Forces in gases
   1. Relations of gases to fluids
   2. Air pressure
   3. Siphons and pumps
   4. Composition of atmosphere
   5. Biological effects of air and air pressure
   6. Weather and weather forecasting
   7. Boyles' law
   8. Principles of flight

D. Laws of motion
   1. Vector and scalar quantities
   2. Components of force
   3. Balanced and unbalanced forces
   4. Relations among speed, time, and distance
   5. Newton's laws of motion
   6. Gravitation
   7. Laws of freely falling bodies
   8. The pendulum

In addition to using these subject-matter classifications, the teacher decided to compose items to test three types of knowledge: (1) knowledge of simple facts and definitions, (2) understanding physical laws, and (3) applications in daily life. Examples of items which would fit the outline are as follows:

For section A, subsection 2:
   The major advantage of the metric over the English system of measurement is the
   a. higher accuracy of measuring very small objects
   b. inexpensiveness
   c. ease of changing from one unit to another
   d. familiarity of the average American with the metric system

For section B, subsection 2:
   Force on a submerged object is

a.   exerted equally in all directions
b.   is exerted more on the bottom
c.   is exerted more on the top
d.   is exerted in proportion to the density of the object
e.   is exerted in proportion to the weight of the object

For section *B*, subsection 3:
Why does oil float on water?

For section *C*, subsection 4:
More than three-fourths of the earth's atmosphere is composed of _____?

For section *C*, subsection 8:
Why are rockets able to go much higher than balloons?

For section *D*, subsection 2:
An airplane is headed due north at an airspeed of 200 miles per hour. A wind is blowing from west to east at 30 miles per hour. Diagram the component and resulting forces. What are the approximate ground speed and direction of flight of the plane? In order to arrive at a city directly north of his point of take-off, how would the pilot have to alter his course?

For section *D*, subsection 5:
Describe Newton's three laws of motion. Illustrate each with how the ball behaves in a game of baseball.

SPECIAL PROBLEMS

Even if someone gave Max Marshall an excellent outline of course content and an excellent set of test items to match, there would still be a number of questions in his mind as to how the final test should go. Following are some of the major issues that he might encounter.

TIMING THE TEST.   Nearly all tests have a time limit, if for no other reason than to get the testing over so that other activities can begin. If students are told that they can take as much time as they like, typically what will happen is that half the students will complete the test in thirty or forty minutes, most of the rest will finish within an hour, and a few will go on interminably. Since the total time of testing is determined by the last individual who voluntarily quits, giving an unlimited amount of time often means that the total testing time lasts far longer than is intended. On nearly all tests a finite, if generous, amount of time is allotted, and all students are required to stop at that point. Most teachers are chary of using highly speeded tests, in which speed per se rather than a deeper understanding is the major thing being tested. Consequently, we are prone to give students more time than they actually need on tests. Studies have shown that unless time limits are quite restrictive, more restrictive than would usually be the case, that speed per se has relatively little influence on results. A good working rule is to try to set a time limit such that 90 per cent of the students will feel that they have ample time. The other 10 per cent probably would feel that they were rushed even if they were given much more than the amount allotted.

In setting the time limit for the test, the teacher must compromise two standards. In order to make the test a comprehensive coverage of the subject matter, and thus to make it reliable, it is necessary to include as many items as possible. On the other hand, in order to prevent the inclusion of too many items, and thus rush students excessively, it is necessary to put a ceiling on the number of items that is used. Several rules may be helpful in judging what would be the ideal compromise. On multiple-choice tests where, say, there are five alternatives for each item, students in the higher elementary grades and in high school can usually complete at least forty items in a period of fifty minutes without being excessively rushed. If instead of multiple-choice items, essay items are used in which each answer is restricted to no more than one-half page, most students can easily complete six or more such items in a period of fifty minutes. Of course, where an extensive amount of writing is required, children below the fifth or sixth grade would need to proceed more slowly. It usually would be the case that forty multiple-choice items or six half-page essay items would provide reasonably comprehensive coverage of one month's or six week's content in most subjects.

PHYSICAL SETTING.   To say that tests should be given in quiet, well-lit rooms where students have ample space is to offer the type of aphorism that will make readers yawn. However, in practice teachers are often the worst offenders of the rule. While students are busily taking tests, teachers (at least inexperienced ones) are often guilty of pencil tapping, foot thumping, pacing back and forth between the window and the door like caged lions, noisily opening and closing desk drawers, and indulging in stage whispers with visiting fellow teachers. Students are quite attuned to what teachers do and say, and nothing is so distracting as for the teacher to move or make a noise. In most situations it is best for teachers to remain at their desks and stay alert to the need to answer students' questions. If it is necessary to move about the room, this should be done as quietly as possible.

In addition to the obvious rules that anyone would employ about the setting for testing, the time of day is important. Indeed one could make the argument that there is no good time for testing. When children first arrive in the morning, they are still waking up, after recess they are too tired, before lunch too grouchy, after lunch too sleepy, and near the end of the school day too itchy. Seriously, it is wise to test during those periods when children are at their best and neither so hungry nor so full, so restless nor so tired as to not be able to manifest their best performance. Although it is not always possible to stick to such an ideal schedule, the hours between nine and eleven and one and two are usually the best times for testing.

ANNOUNCING TESTS.   With a look of fiendish delight, Miss Gail said "I gave my biology class a pop quiz this morning." Although all teachers can appreciate the pop quiz as one of the few remaining ways of hitting back now that corporal punishment is going out of fashion, Miss Gail was probably not doing the best thing for her students. The bulk of the argument is on the side of announcing tests well in advance and preferably even giving students a complete schedule of testing at the beginning of the term. (This rule is more applicable to students in junior and senior high school. Students in the lower elementary grades would either forget or not particularly care when tests were to be given.)

The announcement of tests is part of the general principle that, many other things being equal, instruction is most effective when students are as well informed as possible about the course, the teacher's intentions, the merits of different types of study, the relative emphases to be placed on different aspects of subject matter, and the standards of grading that will be applied. Not to announce tests is not to provide students with information which they need. Although the pop quiz can, in part, be justified on the grounds that it tends to keep students "on the ball" who otherwise would wait until the last minute to study, there are better arguments for fully informing students about the time of testing. Even the most conscientious student must plan his work in terms of a schedule of testing.

Unannounced tests are frequently useful in spot-checking the progress of students in a unit of instruction. For example, during a particular unit a teacher may feel that either students are not applying themselves as well as they should or something is wrong with the over-all instruction. Consequently, that night the teacher composes an examination consisting of six short-answer essay questions concerning highly central topics in the unit. Results of the test confirm the teacher's suspicions, which in turn induces him to have a talk with the class about their study habits, their attitude toward the instructional material, and any aspects of the unit which may be confusing.

Two principles should be obeyed in employing unannounced tests, as

in the foregoing example. First, they should be applied only to meet un-
expected problems that arise in the course of the instruction, rather than
administered as a frequent practice. Pop tests are usually disturbing to
students and troublesome for teachers to prepare, and consequently they
should be employed only when a particular need arises. Second, such
unannounced tests should not be employed as part of determining the
final grade. Aside from the fact that students regard them as unfair, such
tests are generally so short as to be quite unreliable and are not composed
with the care that should go into the preparation of a test used to appraise
student progress. It should be pointed out to the students that although
the test grades will not be used in determining their final grades, they
should regard their test grades as indicative of how well they are absorbing the material in the unit. The teacher, of course, will gain information
on how well the class as a whole is performing. Such information can be
particularly useful in deciding whether or not some review is indicated
or whether the students can move on to more advanced material without
much difficulty.

FINAL DETAILS.   A good test consists not only of a set of items but also
of a set of rules and procedures that must be made clear to students in
advance. The test instructions constitute a very important part of the
procedure. Not only should the instructions be stated clearly to all the
students, but often it is advisable to go through sample test items with
the students before they begin. This practice is particularly recommended
for students in the primary grades and when the test contains types of test
items with which the students may not be familiar. For example, often
students need to be reminded that on multiple-choice items they are to
choose the *best* alternative even though other alternatives may be partially
correct. Students should be told in advance if special materials are required in the testing. In this regard, students should be told whether or
not it is to be an "open-book" exam, whether scratch paper will be needed,
and whether rulers and other mechanical aids will be required.

When no more than twenty or thirty students are to be tested in one
class, final preparations for testing are usually not elaborate. In contrast,
if relatively large numbers of students are to be tested either simultaneously or in successive groups, it is very important to plan the testing routine
carefully. This would be the case when, for example, either a teacher-
made test or a commercially distributed test is being administered to all
the children in the sixth grade in a large school. One of the best ways to
ensure that the testing routine is complete is to *role-play* the testing. This
is done by conducting a mock testing in which fellow teachers serve as
students. The teachers who will administer the test go through all the

testing routine, starting with seating instructions and ending with the collection of finished examinations. The "students" follow the directions of the test administrators and take notes on places where the test administration can be improved. After the mock administration, all the participants join in a discussion of the testing routine and make suggestions for improvements.

Such a role playing of the test administration inevitably produces a wealth of ideas for improving the testing routine. The following are typical of the suggestions that would be obtained: (1) Place the tests and answer sheets on the individual desks beforehand rather than take the time to pass out these materials after the students are seated, (2) place a large clock in the front of the room so that the students can see how much time has elapsed, (3) clarify the instructions regarding whether or not students can go back through the test and answer questions that they omitted the first time around, (4) obtain a supply of sharpened pencils for those whose pencil points will inevitably break, (5) tell the students to leave their test booklets and answer sheets at the rear of the room as they file out rather than bringing them to the head of the room, (6) more fully explain to the students how the special answer sheet is to be used, and (7) inform the students that they can use the backsides of pages in their test booklets as scratch paper. By role playing the test administration, teachers will get many ideas for improving the final testing.

A REALISTIC OUTLOOK ON TEST CONSTRUCTION

A point that will be made many times throughout this book is that it would be silly for us to recommend the use of overelaborate, highly time-consuming procedures of test construction, administration, and interpretation. Of course, teachers have thousands of things to do in addition to the construction and use of tests. The major purpose of this book is to show teachers how they can best exert their energies in the construction and use of tests, but this must necessarily be done in a relatively small portion of the teacher's time. Consequently, it would be foolish to recommend the development of extremely detailed and complex outlines of subject matter or the use of very long and involved tests.

One can envision a hierarchy in terms of the amount of time and effort that one can expect to spend in the formulation of objectives of instruction and the construction of tests to measure progress of students with respect to those objectives. At the highest level, a great deal of time and effort in that regard is invested in the development of each commercially distributed test of achievement, such as a comprehensive battery of achievement tests for the sixth grade. Months are spent on outlining the objectives, checking them with subject-matter experts and classroom teachers, and transforming the objectives into an excellent examination. Subsequently, much research is conducted on how well the test actually works. Chapter 8 will consider in detail the procedures involved in the development of standardized achievement tests.

At the bottom of the hierarchy in terms of what can realistically be expected in the development of tests is the teacher-made test which will be used on only one occasion with one class of students. Although the teacher should do the best that he can with the time and energy that he has available, it is unreasonable to expect each test to be a paragon of educational measurement. In between the aforementioned two extremes is the locally standardized achievement test. Frequently it is the case that no commercially distributed test is available which fits a particular unit of instruction. This might be the case, for example, with a unit of instruction on health education in the school system of a city. All the schools in the city cover the same topic. The teachers who conduct these units employ a common curriculum guide, use the same textbook, and share other instructional materials in common. The unit of instruction is specifically tailored to the values of the particular school system. Because no existing commercially distributed test fits the specific unit of instruction, the teachers in charge of the unit of instruction decide to develop their own. With periodic modifications, they plan to employ the instrument each year as a final examination in the unit of instruction. Because of the importance of the instrument, a committee is appointed to construct a standardized test to be used locally. A detailed outline of objectives is drawn up, and the test is carefully constructed and standardized according to the principles discussed in this chapter and those which will be discussed in later chapters.

Because of the practical difficulties involved, it is unrealistic to expect each teacher-made test to be a paragon of test construction, and both teachers and students often tend to take the results of any one test too seriously. Much more important than the results of any one test is the cumulative record of a student in a particular subject matter. If, for example, from the fifth through the eighth grades a student has a great deal of difficulty in mathematical topics, the deficiency in mathematics is well documented, and appropriate actions can be taken. For a teacher to reach important conclusions about students on the basis of only one teacher-made test would be as unwise as for a prospector to abandon his claim because the first shovelful was not brimming with gold.

SUMMARY

Good tests do not arise from sudden inspiration or from last-minute desperation; rather, they must be planned in advance. The major aspect of planning a test is to outline the objectives of a unit of instruction. In most commercially distributed achievement tests, a great deal of care is spent in constructing the outline of content. Although teachers will not have the time to lavish such care on the planning of their own tests, they can at least jot down the major areas of content to be covered. Actually, the small amount of time spent in constructing an outline will be repaid by the relative speed with which items can be constructed once the outline is available as a guide.

In addition to promoting the representativeness of tests, the outline also provides the teacher with some insights about what he teaches and what he values with respect to the subject matter. After looking at their own outlines, it is often easy for teachers to see that either they are not emphasizing important material in their instruction or they are including inappropriate items in their tests.

SUGGESTED ADDITIONAL READINGS

Bloom, B. S. (Ed.) *Taxonomy of educational objectives. Handbook I: Cognitive domain.* New York: Longmans, 1956.

French, W. *Behavioral goals of general education in high school.* New York: Russell Sage, 1957.

Furst, E. J. *Constructing evaluation instruments.* New York: McKay, 1958, chaps. 1–6.

Kearney, N. C. *Elementary school objectives.* New York: Russell Sage, 1953.

Krathwohl, D. R., Bloom, B. S., and Masia, B. B. *Taxonomy of educational objectives. The classification of educational goals. Handbook II: Affective domain.* New York: McKay, 1964.

Michaelis, J., Grossman, R., and Scott, L. *New designs for the elementary school curriculum.* New York: McGraw-Hill, 1967.

Noll, V. H. *Introduction to educational measurement.* (2nd ed.) Boston: Houghton Mifflin, 1965, chap. 5.

Ragan, W. B. *Modern elementary curriculum.* (3rd ed.) New York: Holt, 1966.

Thorndike, R. L., and Hagen, E. *Measurement and evaluation in psychology and education.* (3rd ed.) New York: Wiley, 1969, chap. 3.

chapter 6

TEST ITEMS

The basic unit of test construction is the *item*, the individual "thing" that is scored. Because total test scores are obtained by adding up the item scores, it should be obvious that the total test can be no better than the items of which it is composed. Items take on very different appearances in different types of tests—true-false, multiple-choice, identification, short-answer essay, problems, and many others.

In spite of the obvious importance of test items, the inability to compose good items is the major reason why some teachers do a poor job of evaluating the progress of students. One cardinal fault of many sets of test items is that they are not broadly representative of the important content in a particular unit of instruction. Either they are overly slanted toward one or another aspect of the content, or even if they are broadly representative, they tap only trivial information, e.g., memory for miscellaneous facts. How to avoid these pitfalls was discussed in the previous chapter, where it was said that the best way to ensure a broad representation of the important content is to start with an outline of the concepts to be covered in a unit of instruction.

Even if the teacher has done an excellent job of outlining the unit of instruction, the test which he composes may be very poor. The outline represents an *intention* to construct a good test; but without the patience and skill to translate it into valid items, the outline itself is only camouflage for poor evaluations of students.

It takes patience to construct good tests because, like most important tasks, test construction is a time-consuming pursuit. Because teachers have many, many other things to do besides construct tests, it would be unrealistic to expect weeks of effort to be devoted to each test or to expect each to be a masterpiece of educational measurement. However, some teachers, even some of those who otherwise do an excellent job of teaching, devote a disproportionately small amount of time to the construction of tests. Either they are cavalier enough to assume that tests are unimportant or vain enough to think that a good test can be composed in a few minutes' time.

The skill of writing test items springs from two interrelated components.

First, there is a great deal of technical information available on the effectiveness of different types of test items. Some of the most important rules for constructing items will be described in this chapter. If these are not obeyed, it is very doubtful that teachers will construct good tests.

In addition to learning and using the technical details of item writing, another ingredient is essential: journalistic skill. Item writing is partly an art, in the same sense that golf, bridge, painting, and writing books are arts. No art can be learned entirely from a book, but successful performance (writing test items) is usually built on a foundation of technical information (rules for writing items).

The art of item writing must be acquired from classroom experience. Most teachers learn to write better items after several years of practice; although, in this respect, some teachers defy the time-honored principle that practice makes perfect. Teachers who save copies of tests often can look back to earlier years and see that many of their items were inappropriate, ambiguous, trivial, too difficult, or too easy.

Over a period of years teachers obtain information about the effectiveness of their tests from a number of sources. The test results themselves offer one important type of information. If students do better or worse than expected on the whole test, or if students do better on some parts of the test than others, these offer hints for composing better items. (Some simple statistical procedures to facilitate the analysis of test results will be mentioned later in the chapter.)

The reactions of students constitute another important type of information. Although students generally are not known to like tests, they become pretty fair judges of the adequacy of examinations. By listening to their complaints and, surprisingly, the praise they sometimes give, the teacher learns to construct better tests.

Probably the most important source of information is obtained from one's fellow teachers. Items that we think are models of clarity may appear ambiguous to our friends. Whereas we may think that our tests are not too long, other teachers may use only half as many items for a one-hour test. Whereas we may think that we are employing ingenious items, other teachers may have even better ideas. A free exchange with fellow teachers is one of the most effective ways to help polish the art of writing test items.

ESSAY AND OBJECTIVE EXAMINATIONS

In the essay examination the student is given a few questions to which he responds in some detail. A typical essay item is:

Discuss the Bill of Rights, considering (1) its place in the Constitution, (2) the people in Congress who supported it, (3) its purpose, and (4) how it grew out of sections in the constitutions of various states.

Relating to the same subject matter, an objective item would be:

The major reason for enacting the Bill of Rights was to
a. free the slaves in the South
b. ensure the freedom of individuals
c. establish law enforcement agencies for the protection of citizens
d. ensure that all adults could vote in national elections
e. prevent illegal seizure of property

Because the essay and the objective item form the backbone of most teacher-made tests, it is important to discuss in detail their characteristics and their relative advantages.

The "objective" examination is so-called because the scoring procedure can be completely stated in advance of testing. On each item the student tries to select the correct answer (usually only one) from a prescribed list, or he supplies the one term, name, or date which answers the question. It should be realized that such examinations are "objective" only in the sense that the rules for scoring are absolutely clear. It may be, and it often happens, that the teacher is wrong and has designated an incorrect response as being correct. Nevertheless, in the objective examination the teacher makes it clear what he considers to be correct answers, which offers the basis for forthright discussions with students and teachers about the test items. In contrast, on essay examinations teachers sometimes have such difficulty in determining their own standards for grading that it makes it hard to communicate with students and teachers, and an important type of information is lost which might help in constructing better examinations in the future.

The results of essay examinations tend to be subjective in that, in many cases, the teacher's evaluation is based on a personal judgment about the quality of the answer rather than on any objective features that can be listed. Of course, the distinction between objective tests and essay tests is usually a matter of degree. With some essay questions, the teacher can list most of the points that the student should cover in his answer. In addition to the crucial difference in scoring between the essay and objective types of items, there are other important distinctions. In a so-called objective item, the student typically is not required to produce an answer all on his own; rather, he is required to recognize the correct answer by one method or another. In contrast, on essay items the student is not given choices from among which to choose the correct answer; rather, he must supply the answers on his own.

Because it usually takes less than a minute for the average student to answer each item, it is possible to include many items in the objective test (more than forty in fifty minutes, without "pushing" students). In contrast, on most essay tests, many fewer items usually are employed. The advantage of having more items is that it permits a much wider sampling of the content. (For this reason, later it will be recommended that the teacher use many short-answer essay questions rather than only three or four long-answer questions.)

Previously, it was said that one way to increase test reliability is to increase the number of items. For the sake of reliability, the more items, the better, because a test is only a sample of what the student knows, and unless it is an extensive sample, the test may do a very poor job of assessing knowledge. On essay tests containing only a few long-answer questions, a student often has the feeling that he was lucky that the teacher happened to choose questions with which he was familiar. Another student with the same level of ability might not have been as lucky. One of the purposes of a good test is to take the element of chance out of classroom evaluation, and this cannot be done unless the test items broadly sample the important content. From the standpoint of content sampling, objective tests and essay tests with many short-answer questions have decided advantages over essay tests that contain only several long-answer questions.

Objective examinations are often said to (1) get at only the memory for simple facts and trivial details, (2) provide no opportunity to see how well students organize their thoughts, and (3) measure none of the students' critical and creative abilities. These are legitimate criticisms of the ways in which objective tests often are constructed, but they are not necessary faults of objective tests. Much depends on the skill of the test constructor. The truly skillful item writer can test almost anything with objective items. Examples of how this can be done will be shown later. The reason why so many teacher-made objective tests do not get at more important parts of the content is that the teacher does not have the skill and/or the time to compose an excellent test.

Do essay examinations provide an opportunity for students to show how well they can organize their thoughts? If well constructed, they can, but often this potential advantage of essay examinations is not fully realized. In long-answer questions, students often are not provided with sufficient guides as to how they should answer. For example, in the question, "What happened to art during the renaissance?" so many different lines of attack could be made that even the brilliant student is apt not to produce the type of answer which the teacher wants. Students often must become mind readers to figure out what the teacher wants. Consequently, they write a hodgepodge of things to ensure that they have covered the topic.

Long-answer essay items give a distinct advantage to the student who writes well, even if he does not know a great deal about the subject matter. If he writes in a clear hand, uses fancy words, and weaves his words into elegant sentences, it is hard for the teacher not to be influenced when assigning grades. Another student who has an illegible scrawl, misspells words, and makes grammatical errors may actually know more about the topic; but even if the topic is biology or physics, teachers are loathe to give such students good marks on tests. These and other potential factors which can affect the validity of scoring essay items have been documented by Marshall (1967) and Scannell and Marshall (1966). Because composition errors so often influence grades on essay tests, teachers should shy away from using long-answer essay items for testing in subjects other than English, such as science, geography, and health, particularly at the elementary and junior high school levels. While good writing form always should be encouraged, test performance should be evaluated only in terms of the specific course objectives being measured. Where those course objectives do not include teaching grammar and composition, a teacher should be careful not to prejudice his tests against those students who may know the material but do not express themselves easily and clearly in prose.

Do essay questions really get at the student's understanding of subject matter? They can, but in practice they often do not. When we ask students to explain, analyze, and criticize, what we too often are asking is that they recite the facts stated in the text or lectures. For example, when we ask students in an essay question to "explain" the events leading up to the First World War, what we often mean is to recite the sequence of events as it is presented in the text, e.g., the Serajevo assassination.

The objective test often is criticized because it provides students with no opportunity to learn to express themselves in writing, which is, of course, correct. Does the usual essay examination help students to learn to express themselves in writing? It can if examination questions properly structure the types of answers that should be given and if students are given ample time to respond. However, students often are so hurried on essay examinations, and so mindful of the need to write a lot, that they seldom turn out elegant prose. Because of this, some have suggested that the prevalence of essay examinations has contributed to sloppy writing. Of course, it is very important that students learn to write well, but the essay examination is probably not the place to learn. Much better is to assign project reports, themes, and term papers. In these, the student has the time to carefully compose his ideas, to write well, and to manifest his real critical abilities. Such out-of-class papers constitute a very important addition to classroom tests.

Do you usually get very different results from essay and objective tests? Suppose, for example, that you give your students an essay test and an objective test, both of which are intended to cover the same material. Would they correlate highly? They usually do. Within the limits that measurement error permits, two such tests usually correlate quite highly. A study conducted by the College Entrance Examination Board (Godshalk, Swineford, & Coffman, 1966) resulted in the finding that this relationship between essay and objective tests holds even for a test of correctness and effectiveness of expression. The objective tests predicted scores on an extended and carefully judged series of essays almost as well as the stability of the essay score would permit. A writing sample added very little new information about the pupils. Consequently, even if intuition suggests that the two types of tests should produce markedly different results, the research evidence makes it obvious that the two usually are not very different in practice.

The worst potential fault of the essay examination, particularly the long-answer kind, is unreliability of scoring. If two teachers grade the same essay questions, they might disagree markedly about some of the responses. One teacher would give a paper C, and the other would give an A. One teacher would give failing grades to half the class, and the other would give a high proportion of A's and B's. Even if a teacher regrades a set of questions after a month's time (and there are no indications of the previous mark awarded), he will disagree somewhat with his prior gradings of some of the papers. A number of studies have been conducted which document the unreliability of scoring essay questions (Coffman & Kurfman, 1968; Diederich, 1961; Eells, 1930). Fortunately, there is usually enough consistency in the grading of essay examinations so that the accumulated average of a student over a semester, and particularly over the years, comes to represent a fairly reliable evaluation. But we should not fool ourselves about the results of only one essay test as it typically is constructed, administered, and scored: The results often are not highly reliable.

To prevent the dire warnings above from leaving readers with the feeling that all examinations are no good (objective tests completely trivial, and essay tests completely unreliable), let us summarize a few important points. Above were discussed the faults that often occur in classroom tests. Tests can be made much better than they usually are. If the items are ingeniously constructed, objective tests can measure almost anything, including the higher levels of understanding that were discussed in Chapter 5. Essay tests can also be oriented toward higher levels of understanding, and if some of the rules stated later in Chapter 7 are followed, they can be made highly reliable. Both objective and essay tests, and many different types of each, *can* be excellent methods of evaluation if they are carefully constructed.

The decision whether to use objective or essay exams, and which particular type, often depends on practical considerations: the number of students to be tested, the particular subject matter, the preferences and skills of the teacher, and the grade level of the students. The practical advantage of the objective test over the essay test grows with the number of students to be tested. It takes much longer to construct a good objective examination than to construct a good essay examination, but it takes much less time to score the objective examination. If there are only ten students in the class, it usually takes less total time to construct and score an essay test. When there are as many as twenty students in the class, it is usually timesaving to employ an objective test. If the number of students is as large as forty, the savings in time is immense. (Procedures for scoring objective tests will be discussed in Chapter 7.)

Some subject matters are easier to test with objective exams, and others are easier to test with essay exams. For example, tests in topics such as geography, history, and physics are easily cast in the objective form. Others, such as tests in English composition and foreign languages, are usually more easily composed in the essay form, but even these subjects can be tested with objective items by the experienced item writer.

It was said above that almost anything can be tested with objective items, but this does not mean that inexperienced teachers necessarily can do that. Test-construction experts, such as those who construct commercially distributed achievement tests, are usually quite gifted at turning important content into good objective exams. It usually requires considerably more skill to compose good objective tests than to compose good essay tests. Consequently, until a teacher gains experiences in constructing objective items and/or if he feels that he is not sufficiently skilled to compose good objective tests, he is quite right in relying mainly on essay forms. It is usually wise for the teacher to follow his own judgment and use the types of items with which he feels most comfortable and then, gradually, to use a larger variety of item types.

Better than using objective or essay items exclusively is to combine the two, either in the same test or in different tests. One procedure is to reserve half of the testing time for objective items and the remainder for short-answer essay questions. When the results from such tests are combined with the results of out-of-class themes, reports, and term papers, as well as informal observation and appraisal, the total material often provides an excellent basis for evaluating the progress of students.

TYPES OF OBJECTIVE ITEMS

In a sense, there are as many kinds of objective items as there are flowers in the fields, but fortunately they can be classified into a few basic types. The most prominent types are discussed below.

TRUE-FALSE.   Perhaps the most familiar type of objective item is the true-false, in which the student is presented with a statement to be marked as either true or false. A simple example is:

   T   F   Oil is one of the principal exports of Venezuela.

The popularity of the true-false item is probably due to the ease with which such items can be composed. It is usually easy to make up many such items in a relatively short period of time. However, the true-false item has several serious faults, and it is not recommended for general use.

One of these faults is that grades on true-false items are greatly influenced by guessing. Even if a student knew nothing about the subject matter, he could get approximately half of the items on a true-false test correct by flipping a coin. What this means in practice is that about half of the items are wasted. If the true-false test contains sixty items, it is unlikely that many students will get more than thirty wrong because they could get thirty correct purely by guessing. This means that the score range is limited and the test is not discriminating between the levels of student accomplishment as well as it could.

In addition to the restriction of range, the large amount of guessing that can occur introduces a considerable amount of unreliability. Teachers should be warned that they cannot get rid of the measurement error due to guessing by applying the numerous correction formulas which have been proposed, e.g., number right minus number wrong. Not only are these formulas (to be discussed in Chapter 7) of doubtful accuracy, but they do nothing to remove the measurement error which is introduced. The only way to lower the measurement error due to guessing is to make the true-false test very long—more than sixty items.

Another serious fault of true-false items is that it is usually very difficult to make statements that are either absolutely true or absolutely false. In the example above, it is absolutely true that oil is the major export of Venezuela, but let us look at two items in which the absolute truth is in doubt.

T   F   The major problem of nations in Africa is to develop more industry.

Although it is agreed that creating new industry is one important problem, the discerning student may rightly contend that it is not the most important one. He might argue that more essential is to develop political stability.

T   F   Regardless of how loud they are, all sounds travel at the same speed.

In one sense the statement is true: loudness does not influence the speed of sound. For that reason the knowledgeable student might be inclined to mark "true." But to do so would ignore the fact that the speed of sound is influenced by temperature and the medium in which it travels. If he takes this aspect of the statement into account, he would mark "false." To respond correctly, the student has to guess what the teacher has in mind.

There are few subject matters in which absolutely true or false statements can be made. Even then it is often necessary for teachers to supply considerable detail in the statements to ensure that students are not misled. Consequently, a *good* true-false test is often more time consuming to construct than a multiple-choice form.

An item type similar to the true-false form is one that presents two statements from which the student is to pick the one that is *more* correct:

_____ The speed of sound is directly proportional to the loudness.
_____ The speed of sound is not influenced by loudness.

This is a much better item than the previous one. Here the student can clearly see that the central issue is the effect of loudness. Although this type of item avoids some of the ambiguity of the true-false form, it does not reduce the effect of guessing.

A third major fault of true-false items is that they introduce unwanted test-taking habits. Some students typically mark many answers "true" no matter what test they are taking and regardless of how much they know. Other students have a habit of marking "false." These general tendencies are compounded with guesses about what proportion of true and false answers the teacher typically uses. Students usually assume that most teachers have a near balance of true and false answers, which is not a bad assumption. Students often learn that a particular teacher usually employs many more true or many more false items. These test-taking habits, assumptions about the usual balance of true and false items, and guesses about the proclivities of particular teachers can serve only to lower the effectiveness of the tests.

Although the true-false item is not generally recommended for use in teacher-made tests, if the teacher chooses to use this type of item, there are some rules that should be heeded:

1.   Limit each statement to a single idea.   Do not try to trip up the student by using unnecessarily complex sentences, especially ones which contain both true and false elements. A poor item of this nature would be:

>   T   F   The number of representatives in the United States House of Representatives is determined by the population of the respective states, and the number of senators is specified in the constitution of each state.

It would be better to make two items:

>   T   F   The number of representatives in the United States House of Representatives is determined by the population of the respective states.

>   T   F   The number of senators in the United States Senate is specified in the constitution of each state.

2.   Avoid the use of specific determiners.   Words such as "all," "never," "no," and "always" are more likely to be found in statements that are false rather than true. Students soon come to realize this fact and thus can make an "educated guess" that the statement is false without much further thought about the item. By the same token, students usually come to realize that very cautiously worded statements employing such words as "frequently," "usually," "generally," and "most of the time" are likely to be true. Thus, it is better practice to avoid the use of specific determiners.

3.   Make sure that statements are unequivocally true or false.   An ambiguously worded statement is more likely to be frustrating to the knowledgeable student than to the less knowledgeable student. A poor item would be:

>   T   F   Craters on the moon were caused by meteors.

The well-informed student would wonder whether the statement should be marked "true" because some craters were caused by meteors or "false" because craters were also caused by volcanic activity on the moon. Statements should be composed so that someone knowledgeable in the field would be able to judge them as unequivocally true or false. The above item could be better phrased as:

    T   F   One cause of craters on the moon was the impact of meteors.

4. Avoid the use of negative statements.   Studies (Wason, 1961; Zern, 1967) have shown that more errors are made in response to negatively phrased items and that more time is required to answer a negatively phrased item than a positively phrased item. Some students may not notice the use of the negative, while others may become frustrated at having to deal with the semantic tangle of the negative statement. A negatively phrased item which may be false presents an even greater difficulty for the student. Consider the following example:

    T   F   The right to bear arms is not one of the guarantees of the Bill of Rights.

Since the object of the item is to test the student's knowledge of the Bill of Rights rather than his understanding of semantics, couching the item in negative terms introduces a potential source of error. Much better would be:

    T   F   The right to bear arms is one of the guarantees of the Bill of Rights.

5. Try to use an approximately equal number of true and false statements.   If students know that a teacher has included an approximately equal balance of true and false items, there ought to be less of a tendency for them to develop test-taking habits of marking either most items true or most items false.

FILL-IN.   In the fill-in (or completion) item, the student supplies the one term, name, or date which either completes a st tement or answers a question. Two examples are:

The Constitution requires that a member of the United States House of Representatives be at least _____ years old.

How long must an individual be a citizen before he is eligible to become a member of the United States House of Representatives? _____

The fill-in type of item is midway between the objective and essay forms. One might say that the fill-in item is actually a short, short essay item because rather than choosing from among given alternatives, the student must supply the correct answer. The fill-in item is included among the objective types because, as it is treated here, only one or more terms must be supplied, which can be stated in advance of testing. The fill-in type of item, while not a recognition item, bears much kinship with recognition items because (1) each item concerns a very limited issue, (2) the rules for scoring can be explicitly stated in advance, and (3) many of them can be administered in a relatively short period of time.

The fill-in type of item is most useful when knowledge of many simple names, dates, and facts is to be tested. If the part to be filled in requires several terms and/or sentences, the fill-in item is usually inappropriate. Relating to this principle, the author once encountered the quintessence of ambiguity in a fill-in item on a test for a driver's license:

Most automobile accidents are caused by _____, _____, and _____.

In a puckish mood, the author filled in "men," "women," and "children." Although these were not at all the answers the examiners had in mind, they had to admit that they pretty well covered the field.

Even when there is only one term to be filled in and the teacher has in mind an unambiguously correct response, the phrasing of the statement might confuse the student. Several principles will be given for unambiguously phrasing fill-in items:

1.   As a rule, use only one or two blank spaces.   When more than two blanks are used, as in the item above, ambiguity is much more likely to be a problem. An item calling for more than three blanks may, of course, be used legitimately if it is constructed with caution. An example of the legitimate use of multiple blanks is:

The three elements which are essential for combustion are _____, _____, and _____.

2.   Make sure that only one term will sensibly complete the statement or answer the question.   A poor example is:

Venezuela is located _____.

In addition to the intended answer of "in South America," equally reasonable would be "far from us," "North of Brazil," and (for the fun of it) "with difficulty." Better would be:

Venezuela is located on the continent of _____.

Another example of a fill-in item in which numerous responses would be correct is:

Oxygen is essential for _____.

Equally good responses would be "combustion," "breathing," and "submarine crews." Better would be:

Which one of the gases in the atmosphere is essential for combustion? _____.

The two examples above are rather obvious instances in which the intended response is ambiguous. In more subtle ways, teachers often mislead students in regard to which answer should be inserted. The usual fault is that teachers fail to add sufficient detail to pinpoint the correct answer. After the test is administered, teachers often learn from the responses of students that more than one answer could probably be inserted, and, in this way, they gradually learn how to write less ambiguous fill-in items.

3.   Leave only important terms blank.   A poor example is:

In 1492 Columbus _____ America.

Obviously better would be:

Columbus discovered America in the year _____.

4.   Place the blank space near the end of the sentence.   When the blank space is at the end of the sentence, the task is made easier for the student in that he is given the problem first, rather than having to work backward to it. A poor item is:

The _____ is authorized by the United States Constitution to try all cases of impeachment.

Better would be:

> The United States Constitution states that all cases of impeachment will be tried by the _____.

Not only does placing the blank at the end of the sentence aid the student, but it also can simplify the scoring procedure for the teacher.

5.   Avoid repeating textbook phrasing word for word.   Lifting sentences word for word from the textbook to use as fill-in items encourages too much reliance by the student on rote memorization.

6.   Avoid grammatical cues to the correct answer.   Examples of poor items are:

> The United States Constitution allows each state _____ senators.
>
> A type of plant which completes its life cycle in one year is known as an
>
> _____.

Better would be:

> The United States Constitution allows each state _____ senator(s).
>
> A type of plant which completes its life cycle in one year is known as a (an)
>
> _____.

The fill-in item has only a modest place in most test-construction problems. To summarize the major drawbacks: (1) Not many subject matters concern simple facts of the kind that usually are required for fill-in items, (2) to rely solely on fill-in items would make it very difficult to test for higher levels of understanding, and (3) even when such items are appropriate, it is difficult to phrase them with sufficient clarity so that students will not be confused.

MATCHING.   In the matching item, students are presented with two lists of names, facts, or principles. A simple example is as follows:

_____ discovered the Pacific Ocean	a. Marquette
_____ first sailed around the world	b. Pizarro
_____ first explored Mexico	c. Balboa
_____ conquered Peru	d. Hudson
	e. Magellan
	f. Cortez
	g. Ponce de Leon

Students are asked to write in the blank space the letter corresponding to the option on the right which matches the item on the left. The major advantage of the matching item is that a considerable amount of material can be presented in a short space. The matching-type item has definite advantages if some simple rules are followed:

1. The list of options should be at least 50 per cent longer than the list of items. If the two lists are of the same length, guessing plays a prominent part in matching items. If, in the example above, there were only four names on the right and a student knew three correct matches, he would get the fourth one "free." If there were only five names on the right, he would have a fifty-fifty chance of correctly matching the fourth item, even if he flipped a coin. Consequently, the list of options should be considerably longer to lessen the influence of guessing.

2. The list of items should contain no more than about eight entries to be identified. When lists are longer than this, students get lost in scanning the two lists and may make incorrect matchings purely because of clerical errors. Also, as the length of the lists is increased beyond the maximum recommended, the time required to complete the matching goes up markedly.

3. When a matching item consists of a word or phrase having many associations to be paired with a more specific word or phrase, the more specific term should be placed in the stem column. In effect, the stem column asks a question, and the option column provides the answer. Thus it is more sensible to ask who the first Secretary of State was than to present the name of Thomas Jefferson and ask the student to guess which of his many accomplishments has been placed in the list of options. If possible, it is best for the stem entry to suggest one correct answer. The amount of time needed to complete a matching exercise can be reduced by following the principle suggested here, since the student need search for only one specific answer in the option column.

4. All the entries in each list should relate to the same central theme. In the example above, it would have been poor practice to put "George Washington" in the list of names because he clearly belongs in a different era and relates to different historical events. For the same reason, it would have been wrong to include in the list of activities "signed the Declaration of Independence" or "invented the microscope." If such implausible entries are placed in either list, students may be able to rule them out as being applicable; thus, the item is made easier than the teacher intended it to be. Conversely, the teacher should avoid making a matching exercise a potpourri of dissimilar topics. Each exercise should have a central theme. For example, the one given above deals with explorations and discoveries of the sixteenth century. In a unit test over a few weeks' worth of material, the tendency to combine dissimilar items into a matching exercise might not be so great, but on a test at the end of the term in general science, for example, there might be the tendency to construct an exercise such as the following:

_____ fungus	a. thermometer
_____ simple machine	b. tuberculosis
_____ measures of air pressure	c. chlorophyll
_____ prism	d. athlete's foot
_____ detected by X-rays	e. heat conduction
_____ simplest type of matter	f. refraction
_____ photosynthesis	g. lever
_____ tides	h. legume
	i. barometer
	j. element
	k. moon
	l. erosion

Such a heterogeneous exercise as the one above makes it difficult for the student to form a mental set about what things are being matched. In addition, a homogeneous matching exercise usually requires finer discriminations on the part of the student.

5.   The test instructions should clearly state how matching is to be performed.   Students should be told whether they are to locate something an individual did, facts that relate to principles, definitions of terms, or whatever else is at issue. In particular, students should be told whether more than one match is to be made for each entry and/or whether an entry on one list can be matched with more than one entry in the other list. Generally, it is better to avoid both of these practices and to require that only one match be made for each entry. If double matching, as described above, is permitted, the student is placed in a quandary similar to that which he faces in true-false tests. Not only must he decide which entry matches best, in a relative sense, but he must also make decisions about absolute matching. This would not be a great drawback with material as simple as that used in the example above. However, when the entries concern terms and definitions, facts and related principles, and other such complex material, it is unwise to assume that entries can be stated in sufficient detail and clarity to make absolute matching possible.

Customarily, the matching item is used when there are many simple facts, dates, names, and definitions to be remembered. However, the matching item can serve to test more important and more complex mental processes. An example for measuring the application of principles is:

Event	Principle
_____ rocket flight	a. Archimedes' principle
_____ book on a shelf	b. friction
_____ weight of an object	c. siphoning
under water	d. potential energy
_____ warming the hands by	e. magnetism
rubbing them together	f. equal and opposite
	reaction

In order to match the items correctly, students must understand the principles and see their relevance to events in daily life. Many more examples could be given in which carefully composed matching items can measure high levels of intellectual functioning.

MULTIPLE-CHOICE.   By far the most popular type of objective item is that in which the student is required to choose one alternative response to a problem or question. A simple example is:

Balboa's major discovery was
 a.   the coast of North America
 b.   the Pacific Ocean
 c.   a new route from Europe to the Far East
 d.   the Inca civilization

Multiple-choice items either begin with an incomplete sentence, as in the example above, or with a question such as "What was Balboa's major discovery?" Both of these will be referred to as "the problem."

It does not greatly matter whether the problem is stated in the form of an incomplete sentence or a question. Most experienced item writers prefer the incomplete sentence because (1) it can save space both in the problem and in the alternatives, and (2) if well constructed, it permits a smooth and rapid transition from reading the problem to seeking the correct alternative. The potential disadvantage of the incomplete statement is that, if the teacher is not careful, some of the alternatives may be phrased in such a way that they do not follow grammatically or would make awkward sentences. Examples of these will be given later. Also, it usually is found that students below the sixth-grade level more easily comprehend items expressed as questions rather than as incomplete sentences. The versatility of the multiple-choice item permits the testing of many aspects of learning, some of the most prominent of which are as follows (to save space, only the correct response will be given for each item):

1. *Definitions:*
   The soft coal mined in Alabama and adjoining states is called
     bituminous

2. *Facts:*
   At sea level in an open container, the boiling point of water is
     $212°$ F

3. *Cause:*
   One important cause of feeblemindedness is
     heredity

4. *Association:*
   Tornadoes most frequently occur when
     warm and cold air masses collide

5. *Evaluation:*
   In hilly country one of the most effective ways to prevent erosion is
     contour plowing

6. *Purpose:*
   The purpose of the Bill of Rights is to
     guarantee the freedom of individuals

7. *Application of principle:*
   The law that "for every action there is an equal and opposite reaction"
   explains why
     rocket motors can supply thrust above the atmosphere

8. *Implication:*
   The switch in consumer spending from goods to services hinders
     the continued growth of industry

9. *Reasoning:*

   Ten books are placed on one end of a lever, and two books on the other
   end. To make the two books balance the ten books, the fulcrum must be
   between the center and the ten books

10. *Interpretation:*

    Soda pop fizzes because it contains
    carbon dioxide gas

11. *Skills:*

    John bought a notebook for 75 cents and a box of pencils for 29 cents.
    He gave the clerk $2. How much change should he get back?
    96 cents

These are only some of the many kinds of learning that can be tested
with multiple-choice items. Not only are they very versatile, but multiple-
choice items are also relatively free of some of the ills that beset other
types of objective items. Unlike true-false items, multiple-choice items
do not require that one alternative be absolutely correct. With multiple-
choice items, the requirement is that one of the alternatives be markedly
better than the others. Multiple-choice items are relatively immune to
test-taking habits. Because students must choose one response for each
item, there is no opportunity for them to manifest their proclivities for
saying "true" or "false" in general. Also, multiple-choice tests are not
influenced by students' hunches as to how many "true" responses are on
the test. Because there usually are four or five alternatives on multiple-
choice items, they are not influenced by guessing to the same extent that
true-false items are. On a true-false item, the odds of obtaining the correct
answer by chance alone are fifty-fifty. If there are five alternatives on a
multiple-choice item, the odds are only one in five of obtaining the correct
answer by chance alone. These differences in probability make an important difference in the extent to which the two types of items are beset
with measurement error.

Multiple-choice items are not subject to the same amount of ambiguity
as fill-in items. Also, because multiple-choice items rest on the principle
of selecting the best alternative rather than supplying one which is absolutely correct, the problem need not be specified as elaborately as is often
required with fill-in items.

Although, as was said previously, the matching item can be used for
many purposes, it is usually easier to test more complex aspects of learning
with multiple-choice items. If the things to be matched are long and involved, the matching item becomes tedious to read, and students often

get lost in the maze of comparisons. This difficulty is lessened in the multiple-choice form.

Unless teachers feel much more comfortable with other types of objective items and/or they feel that the particular subject matter requires other types of objective items, it is strongly recommended that the multiple-choice item be employed for most objective tests. The many virtues of the multiple-choice item have caused professional item writers to rely upon it almost exclusively for use in commercially distributed achievement and intelligence tests. Because of their wide use and importance, the following section will go into considerable detail on the rules for writing good multiple-choice items.

RULES FOR WRITING MUTIPLE-CHOICE ITEMS

On the basis of the experience that test constructors have had and the research that has been performed, a list of rules has been formulated for the construction of multiple-choice items. The most important rules will be discussed in this section. Most of the items which will be used to illustrate the rules will concern mainly the knowledge of content details, rather than higher levels of mental functioning with respect to various subject matters. This has been done in order not to distract the reader from the description and illustration of the rules. However, the rules which will be stated apply with equal force to the various types of items that measure the more complex products of learning, and they also hold with respect to the numerous other examples of the measurement of high-level mental functioning that will be given later.

1.   The problem should clearly point to the theme of the correct alternative answer.   The multiple-choice item should not merely present a collection of unrelated facts or ideas, one of which is true and the others false. Instead, a clear question should be posed by the problem which can be reasonably answered by one, and only one, of the alternative responses.

VIOLATION:

In southern Africa
  a.   mining of diamonds is one of the most important industries
  b.   tropical rain forests abound
  c.   camel caravans carry trade goods
  d.   economic development is hindered by a lack of modern transportation

When the problem begins with such a vague statement as "In southern Africa," many different responses could follow. The problem might as well have been stated "Which one of the following things is true of southern Africa?" Unless the one "true" and the remaining "false" alternatives are stated very precisely, which often requires them to be very long, then the intended correct alternative does not logically follow from the problem. In the example above, the teacher intended alternative *a* (mining diamonds) to be correct, but because of the failure to establish the theme of the intended response, students could also make a good case for alternative *d*.

IMPROVED:

    Southern Africa leads the world in the mining of
    a.   bauxite
    b.   diamonds
    c.   iron ore
    d.   coal

Here the problem clearly focuses on mining products; the qualification "leads the world" further specifies the correct alternative; and the response "diamonds" is definitely better than the others.

2.   Incorrect alternatives should be plausibly related to the problem. In some items the incorrect alternatives are so completely unrelated to the problem that, even if the student knows very little about the problem, he can rule out all but the correct alternative.

VIOLATION:

    The vessel which carries oxygenated blood from the heart to the body is called the
    a.   trapezius muscle
    b.   forebrain
    c.   patella tendon
    d.   ascending aorta

Even if a student knows little about the circulatory system, he probably knows that muscles, tendons, and parts of the brain are not blood vessels. Consequently, he rules out all but alternative *d*.

IMPROVED:

The vessel which carries oxygenated blood from the heart to the body is called the
a. vena cava
b. pulmonary artery
c. femoral artery
d. ascending aorta

In the improved version, unless the student knows the major veins and arteries, he cannot rule out the incorrect alternatives.

When constructing multiple-choice items which involve arithmetic operations, it is particularly important that the incorrect alternatives be plausibly related to the problem. Typically, the distractors are solutions which would be obtained by following an erroneous procedure, e.g., subtracting instead of adding.

The rule in composing alternative answers is that, *to the student who knows the answer, only one alternative is plausible; to the student who does not know the answer, all the alternatives look equally plausible.* To achieve this ideal state, teachers must keep a fine balance between (1) making incorrect alternatives so obviously incorrect and/or unrelated to the problem that nearly all students will mark the correct alternative and (2) ensuring that one alternative is actually more correct than the others.

3. Correct alternatives should not be consistently different in appearance from incorrect alternatives. Only knowledge of subject matter should provide clues about the correct alternative.

VIOLATION:

a. $424°$ F
b. $282°$ F
c. $212°$ F at sea level, in an open container
d. $98°$ F

It was not necessary to include the problem in order to point the reader to the correct answer. Alternative *c* is so much longer and more detailed than the others that it is a dead give-away.

IMPROVED:

The boiling point of water at sea level, in an open container, is
a. $424°$ F

    b.   282° F
    c.   212° F
    d.   98° F

The violation above was a rather obvious example of making the correct alternative look different from the others. In a less obvious way teachers often make the correct alternative look different. This is often done by (1) making correct alternatives consistently longer than incorrect alternatives and (2) using extra qualifications and more detailed specifications for the correct alternative. The best way to avoid these two faults is to include all necessary qualifications and specifications in the problem, for instance, in the example above to include in the problem "at sea level, in an open container."

In some items it is difficult to prevent the correct alternative from being longer and more highly specified than the incorrect alternatives. This will not necessarily provide unwanted clues to students if the correct alternative is not *consistently* different in appearance. To balance out such clues to students, in some items some of the incorrect alternatives should be longer and more highly specified.

If the teacher has time to perform a little experiment, he can determine to what extent the appearance of alternatives is providing clues to students. This is done by presenting students with the sets of alternative responses but deleting the problems, as was done in the example above. If students can guess the correct responses without even seeing the problems, the teacher is not making correct and incorrect alternatives uniform in appearance.

4. Alternatives should be randomly ordered for each item. Teachers often unwittingly place the correct alternative more frequently in the middle of the list rather than in either the first or last positions. Or, if on one item the correct alternative is in the *a* position, teachers are prone to place the correct alternative for the next item in the last position.

By far the best method of ordering alternatives is to do it randomly. Many books on statistics (e.g., Lordahl, 1967) contain tables of random numbers which can be used to order the alternatives randomly for each item. A table of random numbers is typically one in which the numbers 0 to 9 have been generated randomly so that each number has an equal probability of being selected on each "draw." To use a table of random numbers to order the alternatives on a test item, we would first assign the numbers 1 to 5 to the five alternatives for the item (the correct answer and four distractors). We would then arbitrarily select a point in the table of random numbers and go through the table in some predetermined way, such as down the columns or across the rows. The order in which the numbers 1 to 5 are encountered determines the order in which the corresponding alternatives are to be arranged under the stem for that item. When duplicates or nonapplicable numbers are encountered, they are merely disregarded. We would continue through the table obtaining an order for each of the remaining items in the same manner.

While a table of random numbers, either taken from a book on statistics or generated by the school system's computer, is the best way to obtain truly random orders, there are other methods which teachers may employ. For example, a city telephone directory could be used in the same way as a table of random numbers. When any such random procedure is used, students cannot accurately detect patterns in the ordering of alternatives.

5. Avoid irrelevant sources of difficulty in the statement of the problem or in the alternatives.   Items are supposed to be made difficult because of the particular subject matter and not because of irrelevant sources of difficulty.

VIOLATION:

Hitler's first major transgression of the Versailles concordat was
a.   invading Poland
b.   occupying Bavaria
c.   occupying the Rhineland
d.   invading Austria

In the example above, irrelevant difficulty is introduced by the "fancy" words "transgression" and "concordat." Even a student who knew a great deal about the subject matter might mark the item incorrectly, purely because of the unnecessarily difficult words. It might be said that such an item would be more a test of vocabulary than of history.

IMPROVED:

Hitler first disobeyed the Versailles treaty when he ordered German troops to

In some cases teachers want to test the ability to use technical terms, such as those to be found in biology, chemistry, and physics. However, if difficult words are employed, they should be ones that are directly appropriate to the subject matter. If, for example, in a calculus problem, several French words were used, a student would have to understand the French words before he could possibly solve the problem, no matter how well he understood calculus. Usually it is wise to keep the terminology as simple as possible. When it is desired to test for word knowledge in general, or knowledge of the technical terms in a particular field, specific parts of the test should be reserved for that purpose.

6.   Avoid including material in the problem which is unrelated to the theme of the intended response.   The problem should be stated in sufficient detail to orient the student to the desired response. However, if superfluous details are inserted in the problem, they will serve to confuse students.

VIOLATION:

John, who is a handsome boy and makes good grades in high school, has an IQ of 105. His intelligence would be classified as
a.   superior
b.   genius
c.   average
d.   below average

The clause "who is a handsome boy and makes good grades in high school" is completely superfluous and misleading. If the teacher wanted to test for an understanding of how intelligence tests are used to classify students, the problem would be better phrased as follows:

IMPROVED:

John has an IQ of 105. His intelligence would be classified as

When stated in that way, alternative *c* (average) is clearly correct. The danger of including superfluous material is that it may mislead the knowledgeable student into marking one of the incorrect responses. In the example above, the phrase "makes good grades" might set the knowledgeable student to wondering if the IQ were a good index of John's true ability and cause him to mark alternative *a* (superior). In general it is wise to include only those details that are necessary to "aim" the student toward the intended response.

7.   Do not employ alternatives which say "none of the above," "both a and c above," "all of the above," etc.

VIOLATION:

The purpose of the Bill of Rights was to
a.   free the slaves
b.   give everyone the right to vote
c.   ensure the freedom of individuals
d.   none of the above

If "none of the above" were not included as an alternative, alternative *c* clearly would be the best answer. With "none of the above" included as an alternative, knowledgeable students are placed in a dilemma: they must decide whether or not "ensure the freedom of the individual" is absolutely correct. The clever student might think of other reasons why the Bill of Rights was enacted, e.g., to prevent the central government from becoming too powerful. Consequently, a student might mark "none of the above" because he knows so much rather than because he knows so little. The use of "*a* and *c* above" would pose even worse dilemmas for students. Although the Bill of Rights does not directly mention slavery, it has definite implications for human bondage. Consequently, the knowledgeable student must ask himself, "What does the teacher want?"

The use of "none of the above" and other such alternatives changes the basis for answering from one of seeking the *most* correct alternative to one of seeking one or more alternatives that are *absolutely* correct. This introduces all the difficulties found in true-false items. The use of "none of the above" and other such alternatives is definitely not recommended.

8.   Avoid grammatical cues and sentence structures that give away the correct alternative.

VIOLATION:

A feather and a rock would fall at the same speed in a
   a.   atmosphere
   b.   vacuum
   c.   any fluid
   d.   gases

To get the correct answer, students need know nothing about physics. It cannot be "atmosphere" or "any fluid," because the problem ends in "a." Since the sentence cannot (grammatically) end in "a gases," alternative *d* is ruled out.

Fortunately, such extreme ineptness is probably never found in teacher-made items, but to a lesser extent grammatical cues often help students to rule out some of the incorrect alternatives. This is most often the case when some of the alternatives break no obvious rules of grammar but simply would make awkward sentences.

9.   Use negatives sparingly in problem statements.   In some items the only sensible course is to have students look for an alternative that does not apply or does not follow from a principle. If done sparingly, some use of the negative is understandable. The difficulty with using negatives is

that it is somewhat confusing to students, who are more used to seeking correct answers rather than incorrect ones. Also, in phrases such as "Which one of the following men was not . . .," students are prone to misread it as "was" rather than as "was not" and thus mark the alternative which appears most correct rather than the one which appears most incorrect. Also, it is more difficult for students to think in terms of "degrees of incorrectness" than in "degrees of correctness."

When possible it is better to give positive rather than negative expressions of problems. When negatives must be used, make sure that the negative word or phrase is underlined or in some other way made clearly evident to students. By all means avoid the use of double negatives— negatives in both the problem and in some of the alternatives.

10.   Each item should be independent of every other item.   There are two aspects of writing test items to which this rule relates. On the one hand, there is the rather obvious point that a problem as stated in one item should not give away the answer to another item.

VIOLATION:

The green material in the leaves of plants which works with carbon dioxide and water in photosynthesis is
a.   resin
b.   chlorophyll
c.   stomate
d.   chlorine

To carry on photosynthesis, a plant removes which gas from the air?
a.   oxygen
b.   nitrogen
c.   carbon dioxide
d.   water vapor

The converse of the problem of giving away the answer to an item is that of having the correct answer to one item depend upon correctly responding to a previous item.

VIOLATION:

The nutrient which the body uses to obtain most of its energy and heat consists of
a.   carbohydrates
b.   fats
c.   proteins
d.   minerals

A food which provides us with this nutrient is
a. fish
b. cheese
c. cake
d. salt

After a test has been constructed, it is a good idea to read it over very carefully to be sure that the principle of independence of items has not been violated inadvertently.

11.   Alternatives within an item should not overlap or be synonymous with one another.   Alternatives within an item which overlap or are synonyms can either cause the item to be unnecessarily confusing (if the correct answer is one of the overlapping alternatives) or result in effectively reducing the number of alternatives (if the synonymous alternatives are among the distractors).

VIOLATION:

The vitamin which is useful in preventing scurvy is
a. vitamin K
b. thiamin
c. niacin
d. vitamin C
e. vitamin B_1

A student who knew that thiamin is another name for vitamin B_1 could eliminate both alternatives at once.

An effort should also be made not to repeat the same or similar alternatives too often within a test. If a certain word or phrase reappears frequently, the test-wise student soon comes to realize that it probably is not the correct answer most of the time it appears.

12.   Ensure that item content relates to important aspects of the subject matter.   The final and most significant rule is to ensure that something worthwhile is being measured. No matter how faithfully teachers apply the other rules of item construction, if their items concern only trivial facts, nothing can be done to save the test.

In all units of instruction, it is important to test for the memory and understanding of some names, dates, terms, and simple facts. However, it must be ensured that such simple facts are truly necessary as a foundation for deeper understanding. Students cannot understand the functions of the heart unless they remember "left ventricle," "right ventricle," etc.

Students must remember the multiplication table, or they will be constantly troubled in more complex mathematical problems later. Students must remember simple rules of grammar before they can go on to more complicated forms of composition. In these instances, it is proper to test for the memory of simple facts. In many cases, teachers relate an inordinate proportion of their test items to the memory of simple names and facts, either because they actually value this type of knowledge or because they are not skilled enough to construct better tests.

As was discussed in detail in Chapter 5, a good outline of objectives for a unit of instruction will help guide the teacher toward the inclusion of important materials in classroom examinations. When looking at the outline of objectives, the teacher will be encouraged to include items regarding relatively high levels of understanding rather than items that concern only simple content details.

As has already been said and demonstrated in a number of places in this book, objective test items can test many facets of understanding in addition to memory of details. Examples have been given (and others will be given later) of objective test items that can measure numerous forms of understanding, including (1) implications of facts, (2) relations between concepts, (3) practical applications of principles, (4) deductions, and (5) critical reactions. Although it takes patience and skill to measure "higher" forms of knowledge with objective test items, it can be done.

CONSTRUCTION OF ESSAY ITEMS

In essay items, students supply their own answers in their own ways. If well constructed, essay items can be used to measure the students' ability to deal with subject matter at a high level of understanding, to organize their thoughts, and to express themselves in writing. To help ensure that these important aspects of learning are actually measured, the following rules should be heeded:

1.   Employ a relatively large number of short-answer items rather than a relatively smaller number of long-answer items.   Long-answer questions are prone to a number of faults. Students often get quite lost in their own answers, tend to repeat themselves, and are not sure when they have said enough. Teachers get lost in reading page after page of response to one question, forget what the student said earlier, and have difficulty in forming a reliable impression of the quality of the response. In long-answer questions, it is very difficult to aim the student toward the types of responses which the teacher wants.

Long-answer essay items often turn into a speed-writing contest, in which students try to write as much as possible and in which teachers are often unduly influenced by the sheer length of the response. On long-answer questions, the highly verbal student has a distinct advantage even if he is not highly knowledgeable about the subject matter.

Another disadvantage of the long-answer item is that only a small number of items can be used in the test because of the limited amount of time that is available for most classroom examinations. This usually results in a very poor sampling of the total subject matter to be covered by the test, and consequently chance (measurement error) plays a large part in the results.

Far better than to use a relatively small number of long-answer questions is to use a larger number of short-answer questions. By the latter is meant a question that is answered in no more than one-half page (8 by 11 inches). If well constructed, the advantages of short-answer questions are (1) students are more easily "aimed" at the correct response, (2) speed of writing is not strongly influential, (3) teachers have more concrete standards for grading, and (4) the questions can be ranged broadly across the subject matter.

To ensure that students actually restrict themselves to a limited amount of space, teachers should inform students of the amount of page space that can be used for each question. One way to do this is to inform students that questions 1 and 2 must be answered on the first page, 3 and 4 on the second page, and so on until the end of the test. Even better, if duplicating services and sufficient paper are available, the questions can be reproduced with lines drawn on the paper to indicate the areas within which answers must be given.

2. Provide enough detail in the question to accurately aim students toward the correct response. One of the major faults of many essay items is that they pose such global and/or ambiguous questions that even an expert in the field could not provide the teacher with an A answer. Rather than being a simple rule of test construction which any teacher can easily heed, the accurate "aiming" of essay questions is a major part of the art and skill of test construction. Because of the importance of the problem, a number of examples will be given of "violations" and "improved" versions:

VIOLATION:

What happened to art during the Renaissance?

The question is so vague and open-ended that almost any answer could follow.

IMPROVED:

> Describe the changes in art during the Renaissance, considering *(a)* stylization, *(b)* portrayal of the human figure, *(c)* use of color, and *(d)* sources of support for artists.

VIOLATION:

> Why was the Bill of Rights enacted?

Here again, the question is so vague that almost any answer could follow, including "because it was a good idea."

IMPROVED:

> Describe the political and popular support given to the enactment of the Bill of Rights. In your answer, discuss *(a)* the types of rights covered, *(b)* the relations of the bill to similar provisions in state constitutions, and *(c)* the part James Madison played in the enactment of the bill.

In the improved version, students have a much better idea of what the teacher wants.

VIOLATION:

> What are Newton's laws of motion?

This question obviously lacks the needed amount of specification to aim students accurately toward the correct response. Although the teacher included the question on the test for the purpose of finding out whether the students understand Newton's laws of motion, the question, as presently phrased, asks only for a listing of the laws of motion.

IMPROVED:

> Describe each of Newton's three laws of motion. Illustrate each with the action of the ball in a game of baseball.

The major reason why so many essay items fail to aim students accurately is that teachers do not supply the specifics of what is meant. In constructing items, it takes only a few more minutes to supply the detailed specifications.

Even when the detailed specifications are given, in some types of questions it is difficult to aim students accurately. In such cases, a number of techniques prove helpful. One of these is to provide the student with a "hint," or an example of the type of response which is being sought:

In a right triangle, the side opposite divided by the hypotenuse forms a ratio called the *sine* of the angle. There are six basic ratios in trigonometry. State the names and formulas for each of the other five.

A good rule to remember in writing essay questions is that they should be phrased in such a way that a person who is knowledgeable about the topic but who is not a member of the class would be able to answer the questions accurately. A student may know the subject matter well yet not score well on a test because he does not share the terminology and language habits of the teacher. This, in effect, tests how well a student can read the teacher's mind and only adds to the subjectivity and unreliability of the essay test.

3. Require all students to answer the same questions. Unless all students answer the same questions, the test is not really standardized, and it is very difficult to make accurate comparisons between students. One way in which this rule is violated is to give students a choice of questions. For example, the teacher might give eight questions and let each student choose four. Some teachers argue for the use of this procedure, because, as they say, it allows a student to appear at his best. However, the purpose of a test is not to see how well the student can do if he is allowed to pick his own questions, but rather to determine how proficient he is when tackling a representative list of questions.

If students choose their own questions, it is difficult to make comparisons among students. Conceivably two students could choose entirely different questions, and there would be no concrete basis for comparison. Also, to let students choose their own questions places too much of a burden on the student's judgment of his own areas of competence. The student may think that he knows more about the battles of the Civil War than about the Reconstruction period and choose the question relating to the former topic, while, in fact, if he had written on the Reconstruction period, he might have received a better grade. Teachers have different standards for grading different questions. On some questions, teachers are satisfied if students know the bare bones of the issue. On other questions teachers expect students to have detailed knowledge. It is very difficult for students to gauge these differences in standards accurately, and when given a choice, they sometimes choose questions on which they will do poorly.

One reason why teachers sometimes give a choice of questions is that they think they are being "nice" to students. Students like to have a choice of questions. They like any procedure which appears to let them *control* the testing situation in such a way as to get a good grade. The student's worst fear is that he will be "trapped" by a question, or questions, which he does not understand. Consequently, he feels that being given a choice offers an escape hatch.

If students know that they will be offered a choice of questions on the test, there is less motivation to cover all the material. They are lax in their coverage because they reason that, if permitted a choice, they should be able to find some questions which they can answer. All these things considered, it is definitely unwise to give students a choice of questions.

4. Do not require too much writing for the time available. Teachers sometimes require much more writing than most students can complete in the time available. This is done by giving either a few very-long-answer questions or many short-answer questions. When too much writing is required, the test turns into a speed-writing contest. If a student is only average in his ability to write rapidly, he might make only an average grade even if he is quite knowledgeable about the topic.

To judge the amount of writing which should be required of students, teachers should first specify the total amount of page space which will be permitted. This amount of space should then be apportioned among the questions which will be used. A good rule to follow is to require no more than two full pages of writing in fifty minutes from sixth-grade students. A half page of writing can be added for each grade above the sixth. Eighth graders can usually complete three pages of essay answers in fifty minutes, tenth graders can complete four pages, and twelfth graders can usually complete five pages. Although the rule is only approximate, being too lenient for some students and some topics and too strict for other students and other topics, it offers a starting point for gauging the amount of writing that can reasonably be required.

We have refrained from giving any recommendations on the amount of writing to be expected from students below the sixth grade because there is some question as to whether or not essay tests should be used with children in the lower elementary grades. In employing essay items for a test in a topic other than English composition, the teacher is assuming that the class as a whole is competent enough in language skills to be able to answer the questions, that is, that the students have had enough practice in expressing themselves in writing so that even though their grammar, punctuation, and spelling may not be perfect, those who know the material will be able to express themselves intelligibly in writing. The grade in which the children may be able to answer essay questions undoubtedly varies from community to community and from school to school. Thus, the teacher himself must be the judge of whether or not he can reasonably expect that the answers to essay items will be a valid reflection of the students' knowledge about the topic. As was said before, a teacher should always strive to encourage good writing habits among his students, but the proper time to acquire composition skills is not during an essay test. The most appropriate use of essay tests in the lower grades, then, is for testing language and composition skills.

5.   **Phrase questions in such a way that they encourage the demonstration of relatively high levels of understanding.**   We started off this section by stating that the special virtue of essay tests is that they can be used to measure a student's ability to organize material and to deal with the subject matter at a high level of understanding. Whether or not essay questions do perform this function depends on whether or not they are phrased in such a way as to actually encourage answers at this level. Essay questions should require the student to summarize major developments in the topic, to explore relationships, to explain how principles apply to novel situations, or to compare and contrast. If an essay question requires the student not to deal with the material in a new way but merely to regurgitate facts from books or notes, then the material could be tested more reliably and imaginatively with objective items.

ITEM ANALYSIS

So far in this chapter, we have talked about procedures that will usually result in good tests. In applying these rules, it is necessary for teachers to use their own judgment as to how well items will actually work. Although such judgment is the primary basis for all good teacher-made tests, a discussion of some empirical procedures and results will be helpful.

   Some simple statistical analyses of the results of a test administration will provide some clues regarding which items should be chosen for new tests and which items need to be either revised or discarded. Item-analysis results can also be an aid to teachers in discovering which teaching methods have been most effective and which need improvement. Earlier it was suggested that teachers file test items individually on index cards. When test items are filed in this way, it is a simple matter to enter the results of item analysis on each card for future reference.

EASINESS.   On objective tests, one of the most useful statistics is the percentage of students who get each item correct, which is called the *easiness percentage*. What is called the easiness percentage here is frequently referred to as the *item difficulty*. However, this is a misnomer because the higher the percentage, the easier the item is, rather than the more difficult it is. The easiness percentage is found quite simply by tallying the number of students who get the item correct and dividing this by the total number of students taking the test. Sample results are as follows:

Item number	Easiness percentage
1	55
2	34
3	92
4	45
5	12
6	69

Of course, in such a study there would be many more than the six sample items shown above. The study shows that some of the items are easy: 92 per cent get item 3 correct, and 69 per cent get item 6 correct. Other items are difficult: only 12 per cent get item 5 correct.

It is important to compute such easiness percentages because extremely easy or extremely difficult items add little information. In a statistical sense, the ideal item is one with a 50 per cent easiness rating because such an item provides the maximum number of discriminations. This rule holds only with a free-response item, such as a fill-in item, where guessing has no influence on the easiness percentage. As will be discussed below, in multiple-choice items, where guessing plays a part, the most discriminating items usually have an easiness percentage above 50.

When an item is either very easy or very hard, it serves only to differentiate a relatively few students from the others. Item 3 above serves only to differentiate 92 per cent who pass the item from 8 per cent who do not.

Teachers may wonder how a test composed entirely of 50 per cent easiness items could differentiate truly bright students and truly dull students from the average. The reason that such items can effectively differentiate at all points on the score continuum is that on each item a somewhat *different* 50 per cent would get the item correct. Only if items measured exactly the same thing would the same 50 per cent get all the items correct. Because the 50 per cent would be composed of somewhat different students on each item, there is ample room for one student to get all the items correct and for another student to get none of the items correct. A complete, and highly reliable, distribution of scores can be obtained by using items all of 50 per cent easiness.

Although teachers do not need to go to the extreme of seeking items all of which are at or quite near 50 per cent easiness, it usually is well to beware of items at the two extremes. They will not hurt the test, but they will take up room that could be given to more differentiating items. A good rule to follow is to use few items that are either above 80 per cent or below 20 per cent. Items which have been found to have easiness percentages above 80 or below 20 often can be restructured in ways that will make them more discriminating. After finding the easiness percentages for items on a test, it is fruitful to go back through and carefully examine items that were too difficult or too easy. Analyzing test items in this way provides useful feedback to teachers on how to construct more discriminating test items.

Of course, the objectives of a particular unit of instruction and the nature of the subject matter should have precedence over statistical considerations in the development of test items. Some topics are inherently either easy or difficult for students as a whole, but teachers will not want to avoid such topics entirely. Teachers may even give tests before teaching a certain unit to determine how much students already know about a topic. For example, a spelling pretest might be given early in the year to provide some information as to the general level of spelling ability in the class. On diagnostic tests such as these, a teacher would want to include questions which covered the whole range of easiness percentages, but determining easiness percentages from the results of the diagnostic test itself would be meaningless.

In constructing a test, some rather easy items should be included to give the below-average but deserving student a sense of accomplishment, and some rather difficult items should be included to show students that they still have much to learn about the topic. However, even items intended to serve these purposes usually need not be beyond the 20 to 80 per cent zone of easiness. Typically, easier items would be included at the beginning of the test to get the students off to an optimistic start, while the more difficult items would be placed near the end to prevent students from spending an undue amount of time on difficult items early in the testing period.

When a test consists of objective items rather than free-response items, the items should be somewhat easier than indicated in the rule given above. Why this is so can be illustrated with the true-false item. A true-false item with an easiness percentage of 50 would be one on which all students apparently guessed at the correct answer. If on a multiple-choice item there are four alternative answers, 25 per cent of the students would get the correct answer by blind guessing. In that case, one obviously would not want to follow the aforementioned rule of accepting items with easiness percentages as low as 20. To do so would require the inclusion of items to which none of the students knew the correct answer. When guessing enters the picture, as it does with all objective items, it becomes extremely difficult to say what would be an ideal easiness percentage (many other things being equal), and, similarly, it is very difficult to state the precise range of easiness percentages from which items should be selected for subsequent tests. Some approximate general rules are as follows: For a true-false test, select the items in the range between an easiness percentage of 60 and an easiness percentage of 95. For a multiple-choice item with three alternatives, select items in the easiness range between 45 and 90. For a multiple-choice item with four or more alternatives, select items in the easiness range between 35 and 85. (A further discussion of this issue may be found in Nunnally, 1967, pp. 250–254.)

Analyses of item easiness can also be made of scores given on essay questions. For this purpose, imagine that the teacher has assigned numerical grades to the individual answers of 5 to 1, corresponding to letter grades of A, B, C, D, and F. If the teacher has a collection of grades given to questions used in previous classes, he can compute the average easiness of each essay question. This is done by adding all the grades for the question and dividing by the number of students answering the question. In much the same way that extreme items are weeded out of objective tests, extremely easy or extremely difficult items can be weeded out of essay tests. Using the grading scheme presented above, these would be items with average scores higher than 4.0 or lower than 2.0. Just as extreme items on objective tests provide little information about students, extremely easy or extremely difficult essay items fail to produce a sufficient "spread" of scores.

In addition to the aforementioned uses of easiness percentages to weed out unfit test items, easiness percentages also provide teachers with information about how well students are meeting the objectives in a unit of instruction. This information is so easy for teachers to obtain that it is a pity if they do not avail themselves of it. After the easiness percentages have been computed, the items are rank ordered from easiest to most difficult. This is facilitated if test questions have been typed on file cards and the easiness percentages entered on each card. The cards can then be lined up on a table. By looking down the list, the teacher obtains a visual image of what proved easy for students and what proved difficult. For example, in a high school course in physics, such an analysis of easiness percentages might make it apparent that students had little difficulty in correctly answering questions on laws of motion, but did very poorly on questions concerning hydrodynamics. This would cause the teacher to think about the different amount of interest shown by students in the two topics, the classroom lectures, coverage in the textbook, and auxiliary instructional materials. Similarly, in measuring the progress of students in any other topic, a simple inspection of easiness percentages will tell the teacher much about the differential progress of students in different aspects of the subject matter and will provide many suggestions about the adequacy of various aspects of the total instructional program.

DISTRIBUTION OF ANSWERS TO ALTERNATIVES. On multiple-choice items it is useful to compute the percentage of students who mark each alternative. (For the easiness score, only the percentage marking the correct alternative is required.) An example is as follows:

Southern Africa leads the world in the mining of:
Per cent

2	a.	coal
16	b.	bauxite
54	c.	diamonds
28	d.	iron ore

The first thing to note about the distribution of preferences for alternatives above is that, statistically speaking, this is a "good" item in the sense that about half (54 per cent) of the students choose the correct answer. In addition to learning about the easiness percentage, the distribution of preferences provides two other important types of information. First, it can be seen whether or not some of the incorrect alternatives are give-aways. If so, they should be discarded and replaced by more plausible alternatives in future uses of the item. Such is the case with alternative a above which is marked by only 2 per cent of the students.

It is difficult to give a complete rule for the weeding out of give-away alternatives, because the standard would fluctuate with the number of alternative answers being used. One useful standard regardless of the number of alternatives is to replace those that do not receive at least 5 per cent of the marks. Another standard, which is more complex to obtain but which takes into account the number of alternatives, is found by subtracting the percentage of persons who get the item correct from 100 and dividing the result by twice the number of incorrect alternatives. In the example above, 54 per cent get the answer correct, leaving 46 per cent who miss the correct answer. Dividing 46 by 6 (there being three incorrect alternatives) gives a figure of approximately 8 per cent. This figure equals one-half the average per cent given to the three incorrect alternatives. Another way of saying this is that if the alternative does not reach the specified level, it is less than half as distracting as the average of the incorrect alternatives. If an incorrect alternative does not reach this level, it is not serving sufficiently as a distractor and should be replaced by a more plausible alternative. In the example above, only alternative *a* ("coal") would be replaced using the rule.

The second important type of information provided by the distribution of percentages is the likelihood that some items are ambiguous. Following is an example:

Southern Africa leads the world in the mining of:

Per cent

42	*a.*	cobalt
11	*b.*	bauxite
38	*c.*	diamonds
9	*d.*	iron ore

Because "coal" proved to be too poor a distractor, the teacher replaced it with "cobalt," which in subsequent use of the item proved to be an even more popular response than the intended correct alternative ("diamonds"). Whenever more students mark one of the intended incorrect alternatives than mark the intended correct alternative, the teacher should carefully inspect the item for sources of ambiguity. When this happens, students often have a good reason for their "incorrect" choice. In the example above, the 42 per cent who marked "cobalt" might say that they were including the Congo as part of Southern Africa, and unless the text or classroom instruction has specifically ruled out this identification, then "cobalt" is as good an answer as "diamonds."

Although some would defend the use of highly popular incorrect alternatives as providing good misleads, it is usually the case that such items really entail some ambiguity which is serving to "trap" even very knowledgeable students. In general it is unwise to retain incorrect alternatives that are more popular than the designated correct alternative.

DISCRIMINATION.   Another important method of analyzing test results is to determine the extent to which each item "goes along with," or measures the same thing as, the total test in which it is included. There are several ways to do this, one of the most simple of which is described as follows. First, find the top 25 per cent of students in terms of *total test scores*. Next find the bottom 25 per cent. If scores are available on 100 students, this would represent the top 25 and the bottom 25 in terms of total test scores. Next, for each item determine the percentages of students in the top and the bottom groups who get the item correct. Finally, subtract the percentage for the bottom group from the percentage for the top group. The resulting measure is a very important index of the extent to which each item contributes to the total test. Some sample results are shown in the following table:

Item	Per Cent of Bottom Group	Per Cent of Top Group	Difference (Discrimination Index)
1	24	72	48
2	48	32	−16
3	54	56	2
4	16	39	23
5	18	84	66
6	38	65	27

The important measure above is the difference in percentages shown in the right-hand column. Other things being equal, the larger the difference, the better the item. It should be obvious that if on a particular item the bottom group does as well, or almost as well, as the top group, the item is doing little or nothing to distinguish the bright from the dull. Such percentages of difference are almost always positive, an exception being item 2 above where 48 per cent of the bottom group gets the item correct and only 32 per cent of the top group gets the item correct. When the difference is negative, it usually means that the teacher has not chosen the correct alternative or that the item is ambiguous, particularly for students who know the most.

If the difference is small, the item is adding little to the total test. In general, it is wise to be suspicious of items for which the difference is not at least 20 percentage points. Only items 2 and 3 above fail to achieve that standard. It is exceptional to find items that discriminate as effectively as item 5 above (66 per cent difference).

There are several reasons why an item may fail to discriminate top from bottom students, among which are (1) ambiguity of wording, (2) extreme easiness percentage, either extremely easy or extremely difficult, and (3) incorrect designation of the "right" answer by the teacher. If any of these are the case, the teacher would want either to delete or to revise the item for subsequent use. However, there is a fourth possibility, one which is not easy to detect: the item may pertain to an important, but rather isolated, aspect of the subject matter. This might be the case if the item related to a specific assignment which was not covered in the lectures or text. Students who read the assignment would tend to get the item correct; students who did not read the assignment would tend to get the item incorrect. The tendency to get the item correct might then be relatively unrelated to general knowledge of the subject matter. This is particularly likely to happen when the teacher has not clearly indicated that the special assignment would be covered in the test. If this is the case, the teacher, after inspecting the item, might decide that there is nothing wrong with it and that it should be retained on future tests. Instead of deleting the item, the teacher would make the assignment clearer to students.

Although there are special cases, such as the one described above, in which teachers may rightly retain nondiscriminating items, such items should usually be held suspect. It is very comforting to know that an item does serve to discriminate top from bottom students. If an item does not discriminate, the teacher should take a long, hard look at it before deciding to retain it in future tests.

Teachers will usually not have the time to compute indices of discrimination for most of their tests. Such computational labors would probably be reserved for very important tests which are used with many students. It would be worth the trouble to compute indices of discrimination for an important final examination which is routinely used with several sections and on which many of the same items will be used from year to year.

Indices of discrimination (either the index described above or ones that provide similar results) are routinely used in the construction of commercially distributed tests. Because on such tests each item is carefully selected, it is important to determine to what extent it discriminates top from bottom students.

In addition to the index of discrimination presented previously, there are numerous other statistical indices concerning the extent to which individual test items tend to measure the same thing as a test as a whole. The most popular statistical index used with commercially distributed tests is the *item-total correlation*. Each student has a score on each item (e.g., pass or fail on identification items) and a score on the test as a whole. Correlation coefficients can be computed in that circumstance, using formulas presented in Chapter 4. Because commercial firms which construct standardized tests have computers available, it is an easy matter to compute such correlations. However, they supply essentially the same information as that supplied by the simple discrimination index, discussed earlier.

If, as is frequently the case these days, a school system has computers available, then it is entirely feasible for teachers to obtain indices of discrimination for items. If such computational equipment is not available, teachers usually will not have the time to compute indices of item discrimination for most of their tests. However, even if they do not frequently calculate such statistics themselves, it is very important for teachers to understand the information that they provide. Although all measures that require content validity (commercially distributed achievement tests as well as teacher-made tests) are based mainly on rational objectives rather than statistical findings, some types of statistical findings are very helpful. The most helpful type of statistical finding is some type of index of discrimination for each item, showing the extent to which it tends to measure the same thing as the test as a whole. Whereas the test as a whole may not be a perfect gauge of achievement, logically it is a much better gauge than any item taken separately. Therefore, one should be suspicious of items that correlate very little with test scores as a whole, and one should be encouraged when finding an item that correlates well with the total test scores. After all rational steps have been applied to the construction of good commercially distributed achievement tests, it is nearly always the case that indices of item discrimination (usually item-total correlations) are computed. The results of this analysis are usually reported in test manuals, and for this reason it is important for teachers to be able to interpret statistical indices of item discrimination.

CAUTIONS IN ITEM ANALYSIS.   One of the most important cautions is to pay little attention to statistical results unless they are based on relatively large numbers of students. All the indices discussed in this section are quite erratic when based on only a small number of students. A good rule to follow is to take such statistical results seriously only if they are based on at least forty, and preferably one hundred, students. If no more than ten or twenty students are involved, the results depend greatly on chance. With that small a group of students, very different results would probably be obtained if the items were administered to another group of students. The "forty rule" means that there should be at least forty students tested to obtain the easiness percentage and the distribution of percentages for alternatives on multiple-choice items; for the index of discrimination, there should be at least twenty students in the top and twenty students in the bottom group, requiring that at least eighty students be tested in all.

A prominent exception to the foregoing rules regarding numbers of students required to make statistical results meaningful concerns the rank ordering of items in terms of their easiness percentages. Previously, it was mentioned that an inspection of such a rank ordering frequently indicates areas of content in which students are having difficulty and other areas of content in which students are performing well. Because in this instance one is looking at a whole pattern of easiness percentages rather than at the easiness percentage for each item taken separately, the rank ordering of easiness percentages would be meaningful with even as few as fifteen or twenty students.

A second important caution is that statistical results are useful only if the instruction and the text remain much the same. Obviously, if an item pertains to sections which were covered in an old text but not in a new one, the item will not serve as well in future tests as it has in the past. Also, if classroom instruction or outside assignments have been markedly changed, the statistical results obtained from students previously tested will supply misleading information about how items are likely to work in future tests.

A third and final caution is that teachers should realize the important but limited extent to which statistical procedures alone can guide them in constructing good tests. Statistical results provide many hints and clues, particularly regarding possible faults in items. However, unless the original collection of items was carefully constructed in such a way as to broadly sample the important content, no amount of statistical analysis can turn a poorly conceived, badly written collection of items into a good test. Statistical procedures are most helpful in adding a final polish to a basically good group of items.

SUMMARY

Items are the building blocks for tests. Unless the individual items are good, the total test cannot possibly be good. Writing good test items is an art which many teachers seem never to learn. Their major faults are (1) they fail to include important content in test items, and (2) they use poor journalistic style in composing items. For the former, it is important for teachers to think out carefully what they consider to be the important content, to outline the content, and to translate the outline into a good test. For the latter, teachers need to obey some of the rules for writing items which were discussed in the chapter and to gradually sharpen their journalistic skill through much practice in composing tests. However, learning rules for writing items and practicing writing items are not sufficient to achieve a high level of skill in test construction. In addition, it is necessary to gather information from students and fellow teachers about the adequacy of one's test items and sometimes to perform statistical analyses of the items within tests.

There are many different types of test items—essay and objective, and numerous kinds of each. It was emphasized that most of these types of items can be translated into excellent tests *if* they are skillfully composed. Skillful writing of items is far more important than the particular type of item which is used. It was recommended that a good combination of materials to use over a school term for evaluation are (1) some short-answer essay questions, (2) some multiple-choice questions, and (3) themes, projects, and class reports. Taken together, these should provide an excellent basis for evaluating the progress of students.

SUGGESTED ADDITIONAL READINGS

Ebel, R. L. Writing the test item. In E. F. Lindquist (Ed.), *Educational measurement.* Washington: American Council on Education, 1951, chap. 7.

Gerberich, J. R. *Specimen objective test items.* New York: Longmans, 1956.

Stalnaker, J. M. The essay type of examination. In E. F. Lindquist (Ed.), *Educational measurement.* Washington: American Council on Education, 1951, chap. 13.

Stanley, J. C. *Measurement in today's schools.* (4th ed.) Englewood Cliffs, N.J.: Prentice-Hall, 1964, chaps. 6–8.

Thorndike, R. L., and Hagen, E. *Measurement and evaluation in psychology and education.* (3rd ed.) New York: Wiley, 1969, chaps. 3, 4.

Vaughn, K. W. Planning the objective test. In E. F. Lindquist (Ed.), *Educational measurement.* Washington: American Council on Education, 1951, chap. 6.

chapter 7

SCORING, GRADING, AND REPORTING

In Chapter 5 we left Max Marshall pondering what type of test to give to his students in general science. Belatedly, he followed our advice and composed an outline of the important content to be covered in the test. Then, while paying heed to the rules for writing good test items described in Chapter 6, he composed a test consisting of twenty multiple-choice items and four half-page essay questions. The testing session went well. None of the students seemed overjoyed with the test, but, on the other hand, no students complained bitterly about "confusing questions," "material not in the book," or "not enough time."

Now Max has the papers back at his desk. What does he do now? First, he must turn the results into numerical form in such a way as to show which students performed "better" and which performed "worse." Second, he must *evaluate* the results, give meaning to them with respect to his own standards, the standards of the school, and the standards of outside educational agencies. Third, if the scores are to supply needed information to students, parents, the school, and others, they must be reported in a manner that accurately communicates how well students performed. The purpose of this chapter is to discuss these three important steps required to transform raw test results into meaningful units of discourse.

SCORING OBJECTIVE TESTS

Scoring objective tests is purely a mechanical problem which requires no special skill. If it is truly an objective test, a scoring key is available stating the correct answer for each item. Scoring consists of checking the student's response to each item to see if it is correct.

The simplest, and usually the most sensible, way to obtain a total score for each student is to count up the number of correct answers. This would be, respectively, the number of true-false or multiple-choice items marked correctly, the number of correct matchings in matching items, and the number of correct terms supplied in fill-in items.

WEIGHTING. Some teachers would argue that it is not wise to obtain total scores by simply counting the number of correct responses. Their reasoning is that some of the items are more important than others and, consequently, should be counted more (weighted more) than others. Is there much to be gained from "weighting" items, such as to count correct responses to some items 1, and others 2, and still others 3? For two reasons, very little usually is gained by weighting items. The first reason is that it is very difficult to decide which items should receive which weights. Two teachers asked to make such weightings might disagree markedly. When there is no very sensible basis for weighting, the most sensible rule is to weight all items the same, which results in simply counting the number of correct responses throughout the test.

The second reason why little is to be gained from weighting is that it makes only minute changes in relative standings of students. A student who scored near the top of the class on an unweighted scoring would remain near the top of his class on a weighted scoring of the same test. The relative influence of weighting is affected by the length of the test. If there were only five items on the tests, "weights" might have a relatively marked influence on the comparative standings of students. With as many as ten items, weighting would have some influence, but not much. If there were as many as twenty items on the test (and there almost always are), weighting would have practically no influence on relative standings. For these reasons, it usually is wise to obtain test scores by simply counting the number of correct answers.

SPECIAL ANSWER SHEETS. It greatly facilitates the scoring of objective tests if students are provided with special answer sheets on which to mark responses. It usually is found that students in the fourth and higher grades have little difficulty in using answer sheets. Either answer sheets can be purchased from commercial firms, or with only a small amount of effort, they can be typed and reproduced in the school. A sample is as follows:

Item	Correct answer	Item	Correct answer
1	a b c d e	21	a b c d e
2	a b c d e	22	a b c d e
3	a b c d e	23	a b c d e
4	a b c d e	24	a b c d e
. . .	. . .	. . .	. . .
20	a b c d e	40	a b c d e

Students are told to mark out (with ordinary pencil) the letter correspond-ing to the correct alternative for each item. By using both the front and back sides of each page, more than one hundred answers can be obtained. In addition, spaces can be provided for name, section, age, and other pertinent information.

When special answer sheets are used, tests can be scored quickly with the aid of a stencil. A stencil is made by taking a copy of the answer sheet and cutting out the letter corresponding to the correct alternative for each item. This is most easily done by using one of the paper punches which are especially constructed for this purpose.

When the stencil is placed over an answer sheet, the teacher can see which items have not been marked correctly. Each incorrectly answered item can be marked (through the hole in the stencil) with a colored pencil. The student's total score is obtained by counting up the number of colored pencil marks and subtracting that from the total number of test items. The colored pencil marks will serve to indicate to students both the items which they missed and the correct answers to those items. Of course each answer sheet should be scanned before using the stencil to ascertain whether or not there have been any irregularities in marking answers (such as marking out *all* the alternatives rather than only one). Also, it is always wise to do the scoring twice for all students as a check for clerical errors.

A special answer sheet is useful not only in scoring examinations but also for other purposes. The answer sheet should be returned to the student along with a copy of the test. This gives him the opportunity to learn which items he answered correctly and which he answered incor-rectly. The teacher can then collect the copies of the test itself as a means of preventing circulation of objective test items among students. The answer sheets for important examinations can be kept in students' files to be used for item analysis. Also, the answer sheets provide the teacher with diagnostic information about difficulties that particular students may be having and about the progress they are showing with respect to those difficulties. The special answer sheets are useful not only for the informal research that the teacher himself conducts on the effectiveness of his own examinations but also for more formal research conducted by specialists in educational research. For example, an expert in educational measurement might wish to make comparisons in a number of school systems of the types of items that students typically miss on certain kinds of examinations. For all the foregoing reasons, it is good practice to employ special answer sheets with objective examinations.

CORRECTIONS FOR GUESSING.   As was said previously, and will be reaffirmed here, corrections for guessing should not be made. Such corrections apply only if students are allowed to mark as many items as they choose. It is far better to require all students to mark every item, even if they feel that they are only making wild guesses. When all students mark all items, the correction-for-guessing formulas do not change the relative standings of pupils. The top student, before the correction was made, would remain at the top afterward; the bottom student would stay on the bottom; and all students would retain their rank-order positions.

It is only when students are instructed to omit those items about which they are uncertain that using the correction formula changes their ranking. If students are allowed to mark different numbers of items, sheer guessing will penalize some. Teachers have tried to rectify this inequity by applying numerous so-called correction formulas. Most of these formulas are quite illogical, e.g., subtracting the number wrong from the number right on multiple-choice examinations. Even those formulas which are logical from a statistical standpoint (see Nunnally, 1967, pp. 575–593) depend heavily on two faulty assumptions when employed with teacher-made tests and standardized achievement tests. First, they assume that either a student is 100 per cent certain when he makes a correct response or he guesses blindly. Any person who has taken tests knows that this is a very faulty assumption. Very seldom is a student absolutely sure that he is correct, even if he makes the correct response, and although a student may know very little about the subject matter covered by the item, seldom does he guess blindly.

The second faulty assumption underlying the use of so-called correction formulas for guessing is that students understand admonitions not to guess and understand the nature of correction formulas. When told not to guess, some students will be extremely conservative and leave items blank unless they are absolutely sure of the correct response. Other students will mark an alternative even if they are only halfway sure. That this is the case can be seen from the fact that even with admonitions not to guess, students vary widely in the number of incorrect answers. Obviously, if students really understood statements regarding the control of guessing, they will differ from one another only in the number of items that they responded to, and there would be no incorrect answers. Readers of this book already know that the aforementioned circumstance does not hold. There are large and consistent individual differences in the tendency to answer multiple-choice items when unsure of the correct answer. Waters (1967) found that the number of items omitted did increase as the penalty for wrong answers increased, but the students with the more severe scoring penalties still did not omit as many as they should have to achieve the highest score. The formula that is used most widely as a correction for guessing (Nunnally, 1967, p. 578) is difficult for some teachers to understand thoroughly. How, then, can we expect students to understand the implications of such correction formulas for their own behavior during an examination? The student is told that a correction formula will be applied, but what does this mean to him? Will two or three items marked incorrectly spell doom for him, or would it be better to "take a flyer" here and there in order to make the best possible score? It is far better to require all students to mark all items. Then each student has at least an equal opportunity to be lucky, and no correction formulas are needed.

Some teachers object to having students attempt to answer every item because, they say, it encourages guessing and sloppy thinking in all schoolwork. Even though it is doubtful that this simple practice has such a profound effect on students, good counterarguments can be given. It can be argued that if students attempt to answer every item, they are at least actively trying and not giving up in defeat. Even "guessing" in this way forces the student to think about the item and to try to make a good guess. This often motivates him to look up the matter in the text, which he might not have done if he had given up at first glance and not marked the item at all. Also, even when the student guesses incorrectly, it means more to him to see the red mark on the returned test answer sheet than to see no mark at all, which would be the case if he merely omitted the item.

In large measure, learning consists of trying, finding out that you are wrong, studying or thinking more, and trying again. To start the learning process, even a wild guess is psychologically better than no attempt at all. For these reasons, even if we were not forced into the practice because of the inequities that would otherwise result, it would probably be better pedagogical practice to require all students to mark all items.

SCORING ESSAY ITEMS

It is much more difficult and time-consuming to turn essay responses into numerical form than to do this with objective items. Also, many special pitfalls must be avoided which do not arise when scoring objective items. Some of the most important rules for scoring essay tests are the following:

Before scoring, outline the major points to be considered in each question. Both objective and essay questions should reflect the objectives of a unit of instruction. In framing questions and in scoring the responses, teachers should ask themselves questions such as the following: (1) What are the important facts and concepts covered in this unit? (2) What skills should have been developed? (3) What implications should students be able to see for events in everyday life? Such questions are most easily answered by referring to an explicit outline of objectives for a unit of instruction, such as was discussed in Chapter 5.

When a teacher composes an essay question, he should have in mind an ideal answer. If he has the time, it is helpful to write out the ideal answer as a basis of comparison for students' answers. At least he should write down some of the major points he wishes to see included. When scoring responses, however, he should not go entirely by his preconceptions of what constitutes a good answer. First, he should read through all, or at least some, of the students' answers. Students often make excellent points which the teacher had not considered. Also, because of some ambiguity in the questions, students often take a different slant from that which the teacher had in mind. If, in looking back at the question, the different direction is defensible, the teacher should be flexible enough to score on the basis of *how well* it was followed in the answers.

Reading through all or some of the answers as a prelude to scoring a particular question has another advantage: It will help the teacher to formulate a realistic base line. It is often the case that before reading some of the responses, the teacher's expectations are far too high. After seeing that a question is much more difficult than he had thought, he is likely to be more lenient.

Do not allow factors other than knowledge of content to influence the score.   Earlier, it was mentioned how extraneous factors can influence the grading of essay questions. For example, Scannell and Marshall (1966) have shown that a test with errors in composition is graded lower than one with good composition, even though raters were instructed to ignore such errors. Factors such as composition, spelling, and handwriting are particularly likely to influence scoring if a teacher has not been scrupulous about preparing an outline of points to look for in each answer and adhering to it. In contrast to occasions on which such things as composition errors inadvertently influence a score, teachers sometimes decide purposely to take off points from a student's score because of composition or spelling errors. Such a practice serves only to lower the validity of the essay test. A score on a general science test, for example, should reflect only how well the student has met the objectives of the unit in general science and should not be confounded by factors extraneous to those objectives. Of course, such an admonition does not suggest that the teacher should not feel free to make notes and suggestions to the student on the quality of his composition and spelling. In elementary school classes, where one teacher is responsible for teaching and grading all academic subjects, it may even be desirable to give a second mark to the student reflecting the quality of his composition. If students have been made responsible for learning to spell words germane to the subject matter, the teacher may want to give a special mark to indicate achievement in that area of competence. However, the score on the test itself should reflect performance only on the specific objectives being tested.

Develop a numerical scale for use with all questions.   One method of scoring an essay test is to affix a letter grade to each question. Although it is useful for teachers and students to think in terms of letter grades, it is also useful to have a corresponding numerical scale for the scoring of each essay item. This will permit teachers to add up scores on individual items to obtain a total test score.

It is not extremely important how many points the teacher adopts for his numerical scale—whether it has four or seven steps, for example. The important considerations for teachers are to define the meanings of the points and to develop a scale with which they feel comfortable in continued use. Most teachers find that using fewer than five points (scoring 1, 2, 3, or 4 for each question) does not provide fine-enough distinctions. At the other extreme, most teachers get lost using more than seven or eight points. The most widely used practice is to employ a five-point scale, with 5 corresponding to A, 4 to B, and so on, to 1 for F. A more complete specification of the meaning of the scoring system is as shown in Table 7-1. The numerical scale (either the one given above or the one that the teacher develops on his own) is applied to each answer. Total

Table 7-1   Meaning of scores on a five-point scale assigned to answers on essay tests

Score	Letter Grade	Meaning
5	A	Excellent answer. Student supplied nearly all the pertinent information and showed very good judgment and understanding.
4	B	Basically good answer, but either lacks some important information or does not exhibit excellent judgment and understanding.
3	C	A very ordinary answer—"nothing to brag about." Supplies only part of the required information and exhibits little real understanding of the problem.
2	D	Poor answer—"a shame the student doesn't know more." Only one or two ideas related to the problem and those not understood.
1	F	Clear failure. Nothing, or almost nothing, related to the question and/or completely confused about ideas presented. "Either he doesn't study at all or, if so, he should never have been promoted last year."

scores on the test are obtained by adding up the numerical scores given to the separate questions. Although the final numerical total test scores may be far from perfect, they are usually good enough for the types of analyses that must be performed upon them.

Weight each item approximately in relation to the page-length limit for answers. Whereas it was recommended that teachers not employ differential weights for the items on objective tests, it is usually wise to employ differential weights for the questions on essay tests. Although there is no foolproof way of determining such weights, the most sensible procedure is to weight them, at least approximately, in terms of the amount of page space allotted for each answer. When a teacher allows one-half page for one question and a whole page for another, it is reasonable to assume that he considers one question to be twice as important as the other. Consequently, they should be given different weights in determining total scores.

Weighting by page length is simple to accomplish. For example, suppose that the test contains 2 one-page questions and 6 half-page questions. First the numerical scale is employed with each answer. Because it is assumed that the responses on the one-page questions should be weighted twice as much as those on the half-page questions, each numerical score on the former is multiplied by 2. The numerical scores on the half-page answers are left as they are. The two weighted and the six unweighted scores are then summed. The sum is divided by the total number of *units*, which equals the number of unweighted answers, plus 2 times the number of answers weighted 2, plus 3 times the number of answers weighted 3, and so on. In the example above the sum of weighted plus unweighted numerical scores would be divided by 10. This system of handling scores places the total score in the same scale units as that used for each separate question.

If teachers do not place page-space restrictions on answers (they should) and/or if the page-space allotment is approximately the same for all questions, then there is no need to apply differential weights. In that case, total scores should be obtained by summing all the scores given to separate questions and dividing by the number of questions.

Keep test responses as anonymous as possible. One of the largest pitfalls in scoring essay tests is that teachers usually are influenced considerably by the knowledge of the student's name. No matter how fair and objective we try to be, we make marked differentiations among students. We are convinced that some are very well informed and others very uninformed, and often we are quite wrong. One purpose of tests is to take some of the guesswork out of evaluation, and this cannot be done if we mix our evaluation of the test responses with our over-all impression of the student. If we think the student is very bright, we are prone to excuse his poor answers on the grounds that "he really understands the subject." Also, we are likely to let our impression sway us when grading the paper of a student we do not esteem. In that case we are prone to get hypercritical, seeing faults in answers that we would somehow overlook with our good students.

If test responses are not kept anonymous, another source of bias comes from our personal likes and dislikes for students. Any teacher who says that he uniformly likes all his students is either a saint or a liar. Most of us get secret urges to flunk the noisy scoundrel in the third row and give an A to the darling little girl who brings presents and stays after school to help clean up the debris. Sometimes we show reverse prejudice by giving good grades to a student purely because we are so on guard not to show prejudice. One of the good things about tests is that they protect us from our own biases about particular students. This is easily achieved with objective tests. With essay tests it can only be achieved if responses are scored in ignorance of which student wrote which answer.

One of the best ways to keep responses anonymous is to start by writing numbers on cards, or slips of paper, using as many cards as there are students. The cards are then shuffled and passed out to students. Students are instructed to write their names on the cards. Then students are told that they are not to place their names anywhere on the test responses but to write their number on the responses. At the end of the testing period students can drop their cards in an envelope. With this method, the teacher can score papers without knowing (for sure) which student gave which answer; and after the scoring is completed, the envelope can be opened to see who made what over-all score.

The only flaw in the above procedure is that teachers often inadvertently recognize the author of an exam by his characteristic style of writing or by some other clue. Nothing can be done to prevent this happening occasionally. However, we are seldom perfectly sure of the student. We may say to ourselves, "This writing is so bad it must have come from Billy, but it may be Jack or Linda." This introduces a sufficient amount of uncertainty to keep our biases from exerting their full force.

Although the "cloak and dagger" atmosphere can be carried too far, any effort at anonymity is better than none. Even if students place their names on their papers, some anonymity can be obtained. After grading the first question, with the name clearly visible, the responses can be folded over to hide the name. Then, when coming back to grade other questions, the teacher can hide the names from himself. Any effort at keeping names hidden will cut down on the influence of personal bias, and also, it generally will make students feel that they are being treated fairly.

Score all the answers to one question before going on to the next.   It is definitely unwise to score in sequence all the test responses for one student then move on to score all the answers for the next student. One thing wrong with this approach is that the scoring of a previous answer will influence the scoring of subsequent answers. After scoring the first answer, we might become peeved because the student made such a poor showing. If we then go immediately to his second answer, we are prone to be hypercritical. Scoring in sequence destroys the *independence* of grading. If questions are not scored independently, the reliability will be lowered.

Another fault with grading in sequence for each student's responses is that it makes it difficult to keep standards in mind. The teacher may forget some of the points which he wanted covered.

Teachers usually shift their standards somewhat when reading through many answers. For a while they will be tough and then later they will become more lenient in their scoring. If all a student's answers are graded in sequence, the student might be unlucky enough to catch the teacher in a tough mood. Consequently, on all his answers the student is treated severely. A student whose paper is scored later might be lucky enough to find the teacher in a more lenient mood and would receive good scores on all his answers.

By far the best approach is to score all the responses to question 1, then score all the responses to question 2, and so on to the end of the test. Before starting to score all the responses to one question, it is wise to shuffle the papers. This will prevent students from always appearing near the end or near the start of the order of scoring.

Score the papers over a period of time rather than all at once.   It is usually unwise to score all the papers in one long sitting if for no other reason than that the scorer becomes too tired and too confused in the mass of words to do an adequate job. Even a fifteen-minute break will allow the head to clear and give pause to reflect on the standards which are being applied. After scoring papers for several hours, it is easy to become grouchy and to take the meanness out on students. When the papers are set aside for awhile, the teacher might say to himself, "What should I expect—they are only seventh-grade kids, and I am scoring like they were college students."

If possible, have two independent scorings made of the test.   The reliability of the test will be raised considerably if the teacher will score the papers twice, preferably with several days intervening. If this is done, scores for students on the first occasion should not be recorded on their papers but should be written on a separate sheet. The sight of the scores given on the first occasion will markedly influence the second scoring, which is another example of the failure to maintain independence of scoring.

When teachers perform two independent scorings of the same papers, they usually are surprised at the differences in scores on the two occasions. Seldom does a 1 score change to a 6 or even a 2 to a 5, but many changes of one and two points are noted. The average of the two sets of scores is usually much better than either of the two separately. If teachers had the time (they usually do not), it would greatly increase the reliability of essay tests to perform two scorings. However, teachers sometimes find the time to make two gradings of very important tests, such as an important final examination in high school.

Even better than to have two scorings by the same teacher is to have the papers scored by two teachers. This will go even further to remove idiosyncracies in scoring. The average scores given by the two teachers will usually be much more reliable than either teacher's scores considered separately. Although it is difficult to find a fellow teacher who is sufficiently familiar with the topic and who can spare the time, two scorers are much better than one. For very important essay examinations, such as those used to award scholarships or comprehensive examinations in graduate schools, it is customary to use a number of scorers, often as many as six. The average scores obtained from the group of scorers are usually highly reliable.

Provide students with detailed information about their responses to each question.   Although it takes somewhat more time to do this, it greatly helps the student to receive comments on questions in addition to a numerical score. Without such comments, the student is likely to say to himself, "Why did I make a low score on this question? I thought I had the answer cold." If, in addition to measuring progress in a unit of instruction, an examination is meant to promote future learning, then the student needs more than a score on each question and an over-all test grade. Thus the teacher should make comments such as, "You placed too much emphasis on public opinion rather than on the role of political parties," "Lack of atmosphere on the moon also results in lack of sound," or "Even though it lives in the water, a whale is not a fish." Making such comments gives the teacher an excellent opportunity to communicate directly with each student about his understanding of the subject matter. Also, such comments frequently prove helpful later in discussing test results with students. If he does not make such comments, it is necessary for the teacher to read back over entire responses to questions and to try to remember what his major reasons were for giving a particular score. Also, marginal comments by the teacher frequently save the student from having to inquire about aspects of grading.

EVALUATION BY GRADING

After the objective or essay test is scored, how are the results to be interpreted? Raw scores on objective tests have little meaning without comparison to *standards*. On a forty-item test, is a score of 25 good or bad? It might be either, depending on the standards being used. Scores on essay tests are usually more directly meaningful. If a numerical scale is used, such as the one discussed previously, the average score for a student over the test items has some intrinsic meaning. If on a five-point scale a student has an average score of 4.5, this means that his answers were judged to be generally quite good. In contrast, an average score of 1.8 would be considered rather poor. But it is still not possible to interpret such scores completely until some standards are applied. Suppose, for example, that all the students made high averages; would the average of 4.5 still be considered excellent?

Before test results can be interpreted and communicated to others, they must be *evaluated*. That is, some statement must be made regarding what is good and what is poor performance. One important type of evaluation is called *grading*, which is one step removed from scoring. Grading consists in using labels, symbols, and verbal descriptions to indicate the quality of performance corresponding to particular scores. Forms of evaluation other than grading will be discussed in a later section. Because grading constitutes an additional step, in the previous two sections a careful effort was made to speak of scoring rather than grading.

Students need to learn how well they performed on tests. They will not be satisfied to learn only that they got thirty-four items correct on an objective test or that they achieved an average of 3.8 on an essay test. They want to know whether their scores are good or bad. Periodically teachers must make over-all evaluations of students for (1) their own information, (2) informing students of their progress, (3) reporting to parents, and (4) helping to make many decisions within the school. To make such evaluations, teachers must grade individual tests, exercises, and assignments and then combine these into an over-all appraisal. First a basis must be adopted for evaluating individual tests and exercises, and then a way must be found to combine them. The former is the far more difficult problem. Once an acceptable philosophy has been adopted for evaluating individual tasks, the problem of combining grades is not insurmountable. It must first be decided *what* is to be evaluated and then, *how* it is to be done. *What* will be considered in this section; *how* will be discussed in the next section. Following are some of the various approaches to what is evaluated.

PERSONAL PREFERENCES.   Too often evaluation and grades are partly based on how well the teacher likes students. Of course, this is very poor practice, and every precaution should be taken to eliminate personal biases in making evaluations. Carefully composed and wisely used tests go a long way toward removing personal preferences for students as a basis for evaluation.

EFFORT.   It is tempting to evaluate students in terms of how hard they are trying. Of course, we are all concerned with getting students to do their best. If grades are based largely on effort, however, it will make it very difficult to communicate with others. Then parents, the student, and teachers are not sure what a good grade means. Does it mean that the student knows a great deal, or does it mean that he is showing much more effort than progress?

Teachers should take notice of how hard the student is working and try to communicate this information to others. But it is better not to compound this with grading. Rather, it would be better to make a separate rating of "effort" and include this in over-all evaluations of students.

ATTITUDES.   It is often said that one of the major purposes of education is to create desirable attitudes, and part of our classroom effort is aimed at that purpose. Some of the "good" attitudes that we try to engender are liking to read, respect for scholars, and flexibility of opinions. Should such attitudes be included in evaluations? If so, they should be rated separately and not be considered in formulating grades. If teachers attempt to rate attitudes, they should be aware of how difficult that is to do. Teachers frequently do not know students nearly as well as they think they do, and ratings of attitudes often are quite unreliable. Two teachers asked to make the same ratings might form very different impressions.

Better than to try to single out individual students with respect to their attitudes is to try to gear the over-all instruction toward creating desirable attitudes in *all* children. When the attitudes of students are poor, it is more often the case that teachers and schools deserve low grades for not doing a better job. Such attitudes vary greatly from class to class depending on the skills and personal qualities of the teachers.

Information about attitudes, amount of effort, and other dispositions toward schoolwork can be communicated separately from course grades. One way to do this is in conferences between teachers and parents. Another way is to have separate ratings on report cards of children's behavioral tendencies in the classroom. These and other behavioral dispositions in the classroom will be discussed more fully later in this chapter and in future chapters.

INDIVIDUAL STANDARDS.   Some teachers argue that it would be fairer to grade each student with respect to his capabilities. They rightly point out that a student who would receive a C grade with respect to brighter students may be doing as much as he is capable, and to continually give him low grades will tend to discourage his efforts. This is a good point, one that will be discussed more fully in a later section; but it is quite confusing to try to base grades on individual standards. First, it is extremely difficult to decide what a student is capable of doing. Teachers' impressions in this regard are not sufficiently valid. We might try to use intelligence tests for this purpose, but that has numerous pitfalls also, some of which are: (1) Intelligence tests are not intended to be perfect measures of the ability to perform well in school, (2) much of the apparent difference between intelligence test performance and performance in school is due to sheer measurement error rather than to real differences in performance, and (3) to make such comparisons and to reach conclusions about the causes of differences requires specialized training not had by most teachers. For these reasons it is best not to try to evaluate students and grade them on the basis of individual standards.

Of course, this does not mean that teachers should fail to recognize extreme differences in the capabilities of students when they occur. The child who is very slow to learn should be encouraged to make whatever progress he can. The child who is obviously extremely bright should be challenged to perform at a high level. Other than in the case of such extremes, however, the teacher should go very slowly in passing judgment on students' capabilities and on how well those capabilities are being transformed into progress in the classroom.

USE OF KNOWLEDGE.   One of the purposes of instruction is to get students to use what they learn in the classroom. Should usage be one of the standards for assigning grades? The best answer is "generally no." There are two good reasons why. In most subject matters, it is nearly impossible to measure how well students use their knowledge. In some subjects this can be done to a limited extent. For example, it is possible to determine whether or not students practice good spelling and punctuation in all their schoolwork. However, for most other subject matters this would be nearly impossible. For example, how would one determine how well students are "using" geography, history, or biology?

Even if it were possible to measure usage of knowledge, it probably would be unfair to let this influence grades. Suppose that a student *knows* but chooses not to *use.* Is this not his own business, and would it not be rather repressive to punish him for exercising his own choice? A student may do exceedingly well in English composition; but in writing personal letters he might misspell, commit grammatical errors, and use inelegant expressions. Although teachers do try to influence students (hopefully for the better), in the final analysis, what students do with their knowledge is their own business.

ACHIEVEMENT.   By far the most sensible basis for grading is in terms of actual achievement. A grade should convey to others how competent the student is with respect to the subject matter. By *achievement* is meant not only the memory for details but, insofar as they can be and are measured, the many additional objectives of acquisition of skills and application of principles. If a student receives a good grade in fifth-grade arithmetic, this should imply that he can perform arithmetic operations well, that he understands arithmetic concepts, and that he can solve a variety of word problems. Specifically, the grade should mean that the student is ready for sixth-grade arithmetic and will probably perform well there. Although in many ways it may seem cold and impersonal, and it certainly leaves much to be said about the student, the primary basis of grading should be knowledge of subject matter. When this is the case, everyone concerned will understand what the grade means.

Of course, intellectual goals are only some of the goals that are important in education. Equally important are to broaden the horizons of all students, to imbue all students with a love of learning, and to help all students search for self-fulfillment. In spite of the importance of these and other goals, they should not be mixed in with other considerations in the assignment of grades. Somewhere, in some form, students, parents, and others need to know how well students actually are achieving in particular topics. This cannot be accurately communicated if grades are complexly determined from aptitude, attitude, effort, and actual achievement. Grades (as on report cards) should reflect actual accomplishment. The other important goals of education should also be reflected in evaluations. Some of these evaluations can be included in report cards (e.g., ratings of effort and attitudes); others can be communicated to students and parents during discussions.

HOW TO EVALUATE

After deciding (at least the author has) to use actual achievement as the primary basis for assigning grades, we need to make some further decisions about how that is to be done. Below are described some standards by which achievement on individual classroom examinations can be evaluated. A later section will consider methods for combining results from different examinations, exercises, and reports into over-all term grades.

ARBITRARY PERCENTAGES.   A time-honored but questionable standard is to say that 90 is A, 80 is B, 70 is C, etc. One might rightly inquire "90 what?" If such standards are literally applied to objective tests, they result in very poor testing practices. In that case, it would be necessary to include many very easy items in the test to ensure that the average student got well over 70 per cent correct. In the previous chapter it was said that it is very poor practice to include either many very easy or many very difficult items in a test.

On essay tests, the 90, 80, etc., standard is merely a device for communicating the teacher's impressions of the quality of the work. In this sense it is much like the numerical scale discussed previously. However, the standards are usually not made explicit, and both teachers and students are sometimes confused in regard to what is meant by 78.

On objective tests the arbitrary 90, 80, etc., standard is completely inappropriate and should not be used. On essay tests the arbitrary standard is more ambiguous and less directly useful than the type of numerical scale discussed previously.

RANK IN CLASS.   One way to grade students and report progress is simply to state how well each did with respect to the others in the class. This can be done with ranks, e.g., third from the top out of twenty-four students, or, better, with percentiles and/or standard scores. When this approach is followed, students actually are not graded at all. Grades imply values, statements of what is "good" and what is "bad." The 90th percentile does not necessarily mean "good," but without further information, most of us would take it to mean that.

When differences between students are small, ranking can do more to distort students' achievement than to clarify it. The distance between ranks is not equal, and therefore merely knowing a student's rank tells one nothing about how far away he is from the next higher-ranked student in score points. Thus, the student who is ranked fifth may be only fractions of a point (in the case of class average) away from the one who is ranked first, and more than five points away from the one who is ranked sixth.

Indeed, if the class is rather homogeneous in ability, there may be a very small spread of scores from the first- to the last-ranked, whereas in a more heterogeneous group of students, the range of scores would be much larger. Where rank in class is employed to report student progress, teachers should make every effort to see that differences in rank representing only negligible differences in student achievement are not misinterpreted.

RANK GRADES.   One way to assign grades is automatically to give percentages of A's, B's, etc., corresponding to the ranks or percentiles of students. One of the most popular such schemes is as follows:

Grade	Per cent of students
A	Top 10
B	20
C	40
D	20
F	Bottom 10

When this type of grading is used, the exact percentages vary from teacher to teacher, from level to level within a school, and from school to school. This method is referred to by students as *grading on the curve*, which means that grades are automatically determined by positions of students with respect to one another.

Is this a good method of grading? In its strictest form, no. Before we criticize this method of grading, let us look more carefully at what was meant in the last sentence by "in its strictest form." If a teacher adopts a uniform curve which he applies year after year, then the method has serious faults.

The worst fault of the method is that it does not, and cannot, take account of the over-all level of performance in the class. The class as a whole may be very dull or very bright, or may be doing very well or very poorly, but still (if the curve is slavishly followed) the same number of A's and F's will be given. A student who might have done well in one class does poorly because he is in another. This criticism is much more applicable to high school and college courses, where the levels of aptitude and effort often vary markedly from section to section of courses and from term to term. However, even in the elementary grades some inequity is encountered. A student who goes to school in an upper-middle-class area has much stiffer competition than the student who goes to school in a working-class neighborhood. Sometimes the competition is so keen that a child who would be considered an A student in most schools consistently gets C's in his rarefied school environment.

Another fault of slavishly grading on the curve is that it tends to create bad attitudes among students. The student soon realizes that he is in direct competition with his classmates. Consequently, he is tempted to hope that his friends do as poorly as possible so that his efforts will look good in comparison. In this environment, "curve busters" (students who consistently make high scores on tests) usually are envied but are not always well liked.

Strictly grading on the curve makes a farce of efforts to help and encourage particular students. Because, if the scheme is strictly adhered to, some 10 per cent, or some other fixed percentage, *must* fail. All the teacher can do by helping and encouraging one student is to boost him out of the lower 10 per cent, which automatically drops another student into the failing zone.

Strict adherence to the curve takes no account of differences among teachers. Some teachers encourage and excite their students to work and learn far beyond what they would have done with another teacher. Then is it still fair to adhere strictly to a set percentage of grades in each category?

Another major fault of rank grades is that teachers use *different* curves. Some typically give about 20 per cent of the students A's, and others give only 5. Some teachers seldom give F's, and others typically give more than 15 per cent. If all teachers used the same curve, at least the resulting grades would have uniform meaning, in which case they would serve only as a rough shorthand for the student's rank in class. Because teachers use such different curves, it makes it difficult to interpret particular grades.

ABSOLUTE STANDARDS.   Most of us would like to think that we have absolute standards, that we can, and do, judge the knowledge of students without recourse to any other standards. We can be heard saying "That is an A paper," and "That paper deserves an F." Although the use of absolute standards is, in many ways, the ideal way to evaluate students, let us look at some of the difficulties which currently are encountered in trying to put that into practice.

Even those teachers who say that they use absolute standards usually pay heed to the curve. Suppose that a teacher follows his absolute standards in grading either an objective or an essay test, and after the grading is completed, he finds that, by his grading, all the students would fail. Would he really give F's to all his students? Even though there are some hardy (or foolhardy) exceptions, most teachers would change their standards before posting grades. At all levels of instruction, including that in graduate schools, it is hard to avoid some pressure to give the "usual" numbers of A's, B's, and C's. When teachers depart markedly and consistently from the "usual," there often are subtle, and sometimes not so subtle, pressures to bring grading in line with that of others in the school setting. Perhaps this pressure is not good, and perhaps teachers should not succumb to it, but it is there nevertheless.

Another problem in developing absolute standards is that of formulating reasonable bases for the standards. Older instructors often act as though years of teaching alone is sufficient for the mysterious accumulation of wise and just standards. If you question teachers about their "absolute standards," you usually get rather fuzzy, and often rather defensive, replies.

Absolute standards are easier to set at some levels of training and in some types of courses than at other levels of training and in other types of courses. In general, the higher the grade level, the easier it is to apply absolute standards. To a large extent, colleges and universities can set their own standards and adhere to them rather strictly. Either students meet the standards or they go elsewhere. Even further along, in graduate and professional schools, professors have rather firm standards about what constitutes adequate performance, and they can enforce their standards with little regard for how well the group as a whole performs.

Even at lower educational levels, in some types of courses it is possible to set rather absolute standards. This would be true in some of the vocational courses in high school. For example, the teacher knows that if the student cannot type thirty words per minute correctly, he is not going to make out as a typist. Consequently, the teacher can allot grades with little regard for how many A's, B's, and C's are given. The same is true of other vocational courses. However, for most courses in high school, and nearly all those in elementary school, it is very difficult to establish absolute standards.

The discussion in this section is not meant to deride the idea of absolute standards, for the idea is in fact quite appealing. What is meant to be conveyed is that (1) even those teachers who say they use absolute standards usually employ other criteria as well, (2) in school settings it is very difficult to stick to one's own absolute standards, and (3) it is often quite difficult to provide a reasonable basis for the absolute standards which are used.

COMPROMISE PROCEDURES.   Admittedly, the use of grades as a form of evaluation presently poses many knotty problems, and there are legitimate differences of opinion about what should be done. One solution is not to use grades at all and, instead, to rely on other forms of evaluation, some of which will be discussed in a later section.

The question of whether or not to use grades, and if so, how, depends on a number of considerations. One relevant consideration is the use that will be made of evaluations. For example, teachers may want to use letter grades for their own information but not report these to students and parents.

Another consideration is the level and type of course. As was mentioned previously, absolute standards can be applied more easily at upper levels of education, and particularly in certain types of courses. In other types of courses and at lower levels of instruction, rank in class usually must be given strong consideration.

At most levels, and in most cases, when grades are determined and reported to students and parents, they usually are *jointly compounded of rank in class and absolute standards.* Most teachers try to use absolute standards only, but they temper this somewhat by how well the group as a whole performs.

REPORTING GRADES

As was mentioned in the previous section, the use of grades depends in part on the person(s) for whom the information is intended. Following are some of the most prominent uses of grades.

TEACHERS.   One of the most prominent uses of tests is to supply teachers with information as to how well students are doing. Without this information they will have difficulty in managing the instruction and in gearing it to the particular needs of students. If tests served no other purpose than to help teachers make day-to-day decisions, they would still be well worth the effort.

When evaluation is used to supply information to teachers, many of the complex problems which were mentioned previously do not crop up. First, the teacher needs to know rank in class in order to give special help to those who need it most. Second, the teacher needs to form at least an approximate notion of how well the class as a whole is progressing. He can do this either by forming an impression of the over-all test results or (better) by trying to adhere to absolute standards in allotting grades. The latter would mean taking seriously the average grade given on essay questions and the average number of items correctly answered on objective tests. This is usually sufficient to give the teacher a good impression of how well the class as a whole is performing. Third, tests provide teachers with diagnostic information about how well students are progressing with respect to different aspects of the over-all instruction. As was discussed in Chapter 6, this information can be obtained by an inspection of the easiness percentage for items. This method enables teachers to locate the stumbling blocks that students are encountering in meeting the objectives in a unit of instruction, which can lead the teacher to make constructive changes in the over-all presentation.

STUDENTS.   The problem is more difficult when considering how to report evaluations to students. Because reporting letter grades to students does often discourage those who are less capable, and because it often motivates students to strive for good grades as an end in itself, some have proposed that grades should not be reported to students. One proposed alternative is to let students evaluate their own progress. Although this appeals to our democratic urges, it simply does not work. Students are often grossly ignorant of how well they are doing until, by one means or another, the teacher evaluates their work. Even college students often are surprised when they learn how well or how poorly they are doing in particular courses.

Students need to learn how well they are doing, and by some method or another, they have to be told by the teacher. In doing this, rank in class alone is probably not the most useful thing to report. Similarly, grades based directly on rank in class (grading on the curve) are little better than the ranks themselves. Probably the best compromise is (as was advocated previously) to use letter grades based partly on rank in class and partly on absolute standards. This will allow the flexibility that is often needed to (1) show the students as a group that they are doing relatively well or relatively poorly, (2) show students that they are performing very differently, or very much the same, and (3) indicate to individual students how well the teacher thinks they are progressing regardless of their rank in class. Admittedly, using letter grades in this way to report progress to students has some drawbacks, but at the present time no better compromise solution is available.

The skilled teacher has many opportunities to supplement letter grades with less "cold" types of communication. He can let less capable students know that he likes them even if they never do A work; he can (when it is true) compliment them on their nonintellectual achievements; and he can encourage them to work for their own self-enhancement. Similarly, the teacher can let bright students know that even though they stand near the top of the class, they can do much better. In these ways, he can try to bring out the best in every student and emphasize learning for its own sake, regardless of grades.

PARENTS.   Probably the most difficult problem arises when reporting evaluations to parents. It is often the case that students are more willing to accept their victories and defeats than are the parents. It is very hard for many parents to accept the fact that C work is the best that their child can do, and other parents are disturbed if their child occasionally drops from A to B. Some have suggested that parents themselves should evaluate the progress of their children without other forms of evaluation being used. If students are often poor judges of their own progress, parents are notoriously poor judges of how well their children are performing. If this were the only form of evaluation available to parents, they usually would be grossly ignorant of how well their children were doing in school, and they would be in a poor position to help their children in school or help plan for their future schooling.

Although the old-fashioned report card has many faults, no one has yet found a way to do away with it. Some of the bad attitudes which report cards can engender are widely known and have been mentioned in previous sections. Among other things, report cards (1) engender too much concern for differences between students, rather than for a common educational experience for all students; (2) suggest that grades constitute a stamp of moral worth on the child, irrespective of intellectual performance in other areas of study and irrespective of nonintellectual traits; and (3) tend to cause students and parents to be motivated toward obtaining high grades for their own sake, regardless of how well the student actually is maturing intellectually and socially. Perhaps rather than do away with report cards, it would be well to modify them in such a way as to reduce some of the bad effects and retain the necessary communication of how well students are progressing in school.

One way to convey evaluations is in relation to grade level of work. A much used procedure is to report "working at grade level," "working below grade level," or "working above grade level." The three-category scale is applied separately to different topics. This method of reporting progress has some advantages over the traditional A, B, C, etc., system, particularly in the elementary grades. It is a less personal system and more accurately reports the standing of the student. At the elementary levels, grade-level progress is easily understood by parents and others. However, in the upper elementary grades and in high school it is probably wise to use the A, B, C system instead. Grade level has little meaning in high school. For example, in a course like physics, which is offered only in high school and for which there are no preceding courses, grade-level progress makes little sense. Also, by the time the student reaches high school, he has formulated a reasonably good idea of his capabilities and is not as "hurt" by poor grades. By this stage of training, finer distinctions are more necessary in evaluation, e.g., to help students and parents decide whether or not application for college training should be made.

In using report cards, it is good to include a number of types of information in addition to grades. Ratings can be made of effort, social behavior, work habits, attitudes, and other factors. Although, as has been mentioned a number of times, such ratings have their limitations, they do provide a means of communicating about students who are quite extreme in some respect, e.g., the child who is highly withdrawn and shy. Teachers, parents, and others who study the information from report cards should be aware that ratings of behavioral dispositions are only modestly reliable at best. Any parent who has watched his child move through the levels of schooling has witnessed the unevenness with which children are rated each year in behavioral dispositions, such as cooperation, respect for others, and appropriate use of time in class. A child will be rated consistently as highly cooperative by teachers in grades 1 to 5, for example, but for some reason the sixth-grade teacher rates him as most uncooperative. As in all forms of educational measurement, what we should look for is consistency in patterns of ratings over the years. If there is a consistent pattern of rating a negative behavioral disposition by numerous teachers at numerous grade levels, then the problem is obvious and should be dealt with. However, a negative rating by one teacher alone at only one grade level should be taken with a large grain of salt. Teachers and parents should adopt a wait-and-see attitude about how well the student performs in the future.

A number of practices have been recommended to supplement the use of report cards. Unfortunately, they all add many more hours of work to already overworked teachers. One suggestion is that teachers write letters discussing the progress of individual students. This is sometimes advisable, and feasible, for a few exceptional students—exceptional either because they are having a great deal of trouble or because they are making excellent progress. However, if teachers had to write letters periodically to all parents, this would be a very time-consuming activity. Also, unless such letters are carefully composed, parents will read between the lines things that were not intended, and it would be better if they had received no communication.

One good way to supplement report cards is with parent-teacher visits, preferably in the school. If the teacher is skillful at communicating with parents, he can create a great deal of understanding and goodwill in a short discussion. In such discussions, however, teachers frequently do far too much talking and far too little listening. Parents have much to learn from teachers, but teachers also have much to learn from parents. In this regard, consider the case of a boy with a moderately high IQ who is being a general nuisance in class and is making C- grades. In a discussion of the problem with the boy's mother (typically, fathers are difficult to find for such conferences), a new teacher, or an older one who never learned any better, might make the mistake of analyzing in great detail why the boy is behaving as he is. Instead, the teacher should restrain his penchant for psychoanalysis of children's learning difficulties and simply present the problem to the parent in a matter-of-fact and understanding manner. By keeping his mouth shut in the ensuing few minutes, the teacher gains the goodwill of the mother, permits the mother to express some pent-up concerns about the family atmosphere, and learns something important that he would not otherwise have known: Even though the boy is bright in comparison with his classmates, the father has such high expectations of him that the boy has given up and is showing his frustration in many ways.

COMBINING SCORES

The final grade in a unit of instruction is usually derived from a number of tests, out-of-class reports, and exercises. Consequently, it is necessary to develop sensible methods for effectively combining the different sets of scores. Elaborate statistical methods (some of them straight out of Rube Goldberg) have been recommended for combining scores. These will not be described because (1) the reader would drown in the statistical elaborations, (2) practically no teachers (including the author) would ever go to the trouble to use them, and (3) they are no more logical than some simpler methods. Instead, some easily applied methods of combining scores which are quite adequate will be described.

COMBINING OBJECTIVE TESTS.   If the final grade is based entirely on the results from several objective tests, by far the most reasonable practice is to add all the raw scores from the several tests. If, for example, there are two tests with forty items each and a final examination with eighty items, the maximum possible total score is 160. A student with scores of 25, 30, and 65, respectively, on the three tests would receive an over-all score of 120. Because the tests differ in length, it might be questioned why the different tests should not be weighted accordingly. The answer is that, because scores will tend to disperse themselves more on the longer tests, simply adding all scores automatically gives each test an approximately correct weight.

If the final grade consists only of rank in class, this can be easily obtained from the summed scores. Students can be ranked from top to bottom with respect to summed scores, and if it is desired, the ranks can be converted to percentiles. If in addition to rank in class, it is desired to compute rank grades, the curve can be determined directly from the ranks by giving the top specified percentage A, the next specified percentage B, and so on.

If final grades are meant to reflect absolute standards as well as rank in class, it is necessary to define the scores that correspond to each grade level. That is, on a forty-item test, the teacher must say how high a score will be required for an A, a B, etc. When the teacher first tries to formulate such standards, it will seem like sheer guesswork. After some experience with objective tests, teachers become more confident about their standards. Some guidelines can be given to the new teacher.

At one extreme it is unreasonable to expect even very bright students to get *all*, or even nearly all, the items correct. Most teacher-made tests have at least several relatively ambiguous items which would lead even experts to give "wrong" answers. Even without this consideration, it is not expected that any student will completely master a subject matter. Consequently, the A level is usually set at 85 or 90 per cent of the items correct. At the other extreme, students often should be given a failing grade even when they get some of the items correct. Even the most inept, lazy student will usually do better than could be obtained from sheer guessing alone. Consequently, the minimum level for a passing grade is usually set at about 40 or 45 per cent of the items correct. (In this connection, remember that, purely by guessing, students could get some of the items correct, the number being inversely proportional to the number of alternative answers for each item.) In between these two extremes it is hard to be precise in designating grade levels, and probably not worth the trouble to be highly precise. What is usually done is to divide up the number of items between the failing zone and the A zone into three approximately equal parts and designate these as the B, C, and D zones, respectively. One such scheme for allocating grades in terms of absolute standards (illustrated with a forty-item test having five alternatives for each item) is as follows:

Number of Items Correct	Per Cent Correct	Grade
34 or more	85	A
29–33	72	B
24–28	60	C
19–23	48	D
18 or less	45	F

The scheme above is purely illustrative and is not intended as a standard to be used in general. However, it is interesting to note that if comparisons are made among the standards used by different teachers, they tend not to vary greatly from the scheme shown above.

In using a grading scheme such as the one shown above, students should be informed that the scheme strictly applies only to the final summed scores, after the several tests are combined. That is, after scores from the several tests are summed, the teacher gives A's to students who get 85 per cent of the items correct on all tests combined, and so on for the other grade levels. Basing grades on the percentage of items correct on final summed scores will save the teacher from getting into many knotty problems about how to combine the letter grades from the separate tests.

In using grade standards such as the one illustrated above, teachers should be aware of the effect of regression toward the mean. In looking at the results of the first test, teachers and students are often fooled into believing that approximately the same percentage of students will get A's at the end of the term as appeared on the test, that the same percentage will fail, and that approximately the same percentages will be in the other grade categories. This definitely is not the case. The reason that it is not the case is that the group which gets A's on the second test, and other tests, will not be quite the same as the group which made A's on the first test. Also, the students who fail the second test will, as a group, be somewhat different from the group who failed the first test. Some sample results will help illustrate the effect of regression toward the mean. In this case imagine that three tests are given, that a fixed percentage of students make grades in each letter category on each test, and that the three tests are summed to determine final grades.

Per Cent of Items Correct	Per Cent of Students on Each Test	Per Cent of Students on Summed Tests
85–100 (A)	10	4
72–84 (B)	20	18
60–71 (C)	40	56
48–59 (D)	20	18
0–45 (F)	10	4

As the results above show, even though 10 per cent of the students reach the A level on each of the separate tests, only 4 per cent *consistently* score high enough to reach the A level on the summed scores. At the other extreme, 10 per cent fail on each separate test, but only 4 per cent consistently score so low that they receive a final grade of F.

The lesson that should be learned from the illustration above is that in order to have a proper balance of final grades, the teacher probably will want to give more extreme grades on individual tests than he would want to give for the final grades in a unit of instruction. On individual tests, teachers should be relatively lenient in giving A's and B's and relatively severe in giving D's and F's. Many of the students who receive extreme grades in either direction on the separate tests will end up with averages nearer the middle of the grade range. In trying to establish absolute standards (and this discussion illustrates some of the difficulties in so doing), the teacher should think in terms of what grades should be given for consistent performance at particular levels.

COMBINING ESSAY TESTS.   If the final grade is based solely on essay tests, it is not very difficult to combine the results from separate tests. Whereas it was recommended that the teacher simply average the results of objective tests, the results of essay tests should usually be weighted before averaging. The most sensible way to weight is in proportion to the amount of page space allotted for answers on each test. If four tests are given during the term, three requiring three pages of answers and a final exam requiring six pages of answers, the final test should be counted twice as much as the others. The tests are averaged in exactly the same way as one averages the numerical scores given to the separate questions within one test. In this case, the numerical scores for the 3 three-page tests would be summed, and to this would be added twice the numerical score obtained on the six-page test. The total should then be divided by 5 in order to place the final scores on the same scale used to grade each of the separate tests.

Regression toward the mean occurs in combining the numerical scores from essay tests in exactly the same way as it does on objective tests. Consequently, teachers should grade more toward the extremes on separate tests than they would if only one test were given all term.

Even if separate questions are graded on a scale with 5 corresponding to A, 4 to B, 3 to C, 2 to D, and 1 to F, this still does not tell the teacher exactly how to allot grades on the basis of summed test results. It is not reasonable to expect the A student to get all 5s, nor would the F student be exempted from failing merely because he got scores higher than 1 on several questions. One approximate scheme for translating average numerical scores on separate tests into letter grades is as follows:

Letter grade	Score average
A	4.5 or more
B	4.0–4.4
C	3.0–3.9
D	2.0–2.9
F	1.9 or less

The grading scheme can be applied both to the separate tests and to the final weighted average.

COMBINING RESULTS FROM DIFFERENT TYPES OF TESTS.   More difficult problems are encountered when trying to combine the results of essay and objective tests, and combining both of these with reports and themes. Probably the most feasible approach (within the limits of time and energy that can be expected of teachers) is to try to reduce all the different types of scores to the type of numerical scale recommended for grading essay questions—5 for A, 4 for B, etc. The grading scale can be directly applied to lab reports, themes, term papers, and other such materials that are used in addition to tests for determining final grades.

It is somewhat more difficult to generate a thoroughly logical scheme for transforming results of objective tests to the five-point scale in order to facilitate combining with other indices. A reasonable approximation is to transform objective test results by giving the student a score on the five-point scale approximately corresponding to the letter-grade equivalent made on the objective test. Using this method to compare the scheme shown previously for grading objective tests and that shown for grading essay tests, we see that the following transformations would be made:

Per Cent of Items Correct on Objective Test	Corresponding Score on Five-point Scale	Letter-grade Equivalent
85	4.5	A
72	4.2	B
60	3.0	C
48	2.0	D
45	1.9	F

If more than one objective test is used during the term, it would be best to make the transformation on summed scores rather than on scores obtained from the separate tests. Then, if a student got 85 per cent of all the objective items correct, this would be transformed to an equivalent of 4.5 on the five-point scale. A student who got 48 per cent of the objective items correct would receive an equivalent score of 2.0. Unfortunately, this method of transforming results of objective tests runs into a snag when, as will surely happen, students get "odd" percentages of the items correct, e.g., 87 per cent and 64 per cent. In these cases the only thing that can be done is to make an interpolation of the objective test results to the nearest equivalent on the five-point scale. Either teachers should try to make the best interpolation "by eye" or do some simple arithmetic. A method for doing this is described in Appendix C-9.

After all types of tests and exercises have been transformed to the five-point scale (or some other type of scale which the teacher prefers), it is much easier to combine results and arrive at a final grade. In deciding on the weights to be applied to the different sources of evaluation, teachers have to rely mainly on their own judgment. One clue is the amount of class time used for each type of test. For example, if two hours during the term were used for objective tests and four hours were used for essay tests, this might suggest that the essay tests should be counted twice as much. In weighting laboratory reports, themes, and other exercises, teachers have to rely almost solely on their judgment regarding the relative weights that should be given. A typical set of results is as follows:

Average Scaled Scores				
Objective Tests	Essay Tests	Reports	Final Average	Grade
3.4	3.0	3.8	3.4	C
4.6	4.3	4.0	4.3	B
2.1	1.6	1.4	1.7	F

In the example above, the three sources of evaluation were weighted equally to simplify the illustration. The first student receives a total average of 3.4, which is in the C zone; the second student receives an average of 4.3, which is in the B zone; and the third student receives an average of 1.7, which is in the failing zone.

If the purpose of combining measures is to obtain rank in class, this can be obtained from the final averages. If rank grades are given, the predetermined percentages can be obtained from the ranks, and these can be converted to letter grades. If teachers want to give literal interpretations of their absolute standards, they can assign letter grades corresponding to the five-point scale, as was done in the example above. But, because of the difficulties in formulating absolute standards and the difficulties of implementing these in the form of test scores, most teachers temper the absolute results with some consideration for how well the group as a whole performed. If after seeing that students as a group do poorly, and if, after considering the matter, the teacher thinks that he has been too rough in his grading, he would want to be somewhat more lenient. Conversely, he might decide to be a little tougher before assigning final grades. When teachers take such considerations into account (and nearly all do), the standards are considered as zones of uncertainty rather than as exact points. If a student receives a final average of 4.8, he obviously has performed so well that he deserves an A. But a student whose final average is 4.5 might be given an A or a B depending on how well the group as a whole performs. Similarly, a student with a final average of 1.8 might receive either an F or a D depending on the performance of the total group.

What usually happens when trying to implement absolute standards is that the standards help greatly to *reduce* the uncertainty regarding what grades should be given. But they do not entirely remove the uncertainty, because teachers inevitably temper their standards by (1) how well the group as a whole performs, (2) afterthoughts about how easy or difficult the tests were, and (3) what other teachers considered to be "usual" standards for grading.

A REALISTIC OUTLOOK ON EVALUATION

In discussing how tests should be composed, scored, and evaluated, it is easy to be carried away into assuming that all teachers are highly expert in these matters and that they can devote full time to them. Because these assumptions are obviously incorrect, it is proper for us to realistically analyze the place and scope of testing and evaluation in everyday classroom instruction.

In a sense it is easy to take one's own evaluations of students too seriously. Our tests are not perfect; our gradings of them are not infallible. We combine grades from separate tests and reports in ways that are not without some elements of subjective bias, and during the short periods in which we instruct students, they are growing and changing.

Of course, in one sense, teachers should be very *serious* about evaluations. They should construct the best tests that they can, grade them as fairly as possible, and try to report in such a way as to do the most good for everyone concerned. However, teachers should be modest and frank enough to realize, that, even with the best efforts, evaluations provide only a somewhat blurred image of something (the student) which is growing and changing.

Teachers, students, and parents should learn to take the results from one test, and even the final grades from a whole term, with a large grain of salt. Such grades should be considered as only highly tentative indications of the student's basic abilities, his application to schoolwork, and his attitudes toward learning. Bad grades during one term may correctly spell trouble for the future; or they may equally well mean that the teacher was biased in grading the student, that the tests were poorly constructed, that the teacher has unreasonably tough standards for grading, or that the student is going through a "phase" which he will outgrow later.

Considering the potential weaknesses of all forms of educational evaluation, there are two principles that teachers should hold firmly in mind. First, it is relatively safe to make "strong" evaluations and, if necessary, to communicate these to parents and others only for the students at the extreme ends of the distribution of individual differences. One can feel relatively sure of the evaluation placed on students who always get A's. At the other extreme, the student who constantly fails in some or most of the school topics is obviously in real trouble. It is important to give special help to students at both extremes, often as much as, or more so, for the very bright as for the very dull or very maladjusted child. When evaluations are constantly extreme, it is safe to take the results seriously in managing day-to-day classroom activities, in reporting progress to the school, and in discussing the student's progress with parents and others. For the 90 per cent of the children who do not fall into the extreme categories, it is wise to go very slowly in making strong evaluations to parents and others or in taking strong actions based on those evaluations.

Second, until abilities become more crystallized in the later years of high school and until an accumulated record of evaluations is available, it is wise to maintain a wait-and-see posture with nearly all students. Time is on the side of more accurate evaluation, and since in the early elementary grades there is usually no rush to make important decisions about most students, it is wise to wait and see what time will show.

Unless students in the elementary grades are obviously extreme in some way, it is better not to arouse either undue pessimism or excessive pride in students and parents. For the great bulk of in-between students, it is best, until considerable experience indicates otherwise, to say to ourselves that "this is a normal, healthy child, apparently doing satisfactory work in school."

SUMMARY

After a test has been constructed and administered according to the principles set down in Chapters 5 and 6, an important aspect of the testing process still remains. If teacher-made tests are to convey usable information with regard to student achievement, care must be exercised to see that the message is not lost through improper methods of scoring, grading, or combining scores from different tests.

While scoring objective tests is a purely mechanical problem, which can be made even simpler by the use of special answer sheets, scoring essay items is a process which can be full of pitfalls. In scoring objective tests, the teacher merely counts up the number of correct answers. It was strongly recommended that corrections for guessing not be used because of the faultiness of their underlying assumptions. In scoring essay tests, on the other hand, each answer must be read and reread carefully, with an outline of points to look for close at hand and with admonitions kept firmly in mind not to let factors such as composition errors, identity of the writer, fatigue, or the teacher's own mood influence the score assigned to each answer.

Separate from merely scoring test questions is the process of evaluating test results. Grading is one form of evaluation in which labels, symbols, and verbal descriptions are used to indicate the quality of performance corresponding to particular test scores. The grading process is the point at which standards enter the picture. The most sensible basis for grading is in terms of actual achievement. A grade on a test should represent how well the student has answered the questions, and a grade in a particular course should reflect his competency with respect to course content. Factors such as attitude, effort, and use of knowledge are best communicated separately through special ratings and parent-teacher conferences. There are many methods for assigning grades, among them arbitrary percentages, rank in class, rank grades, and absolute standards. Most grades are usually determined by a combination of rank in class and absolute standards; however, the level and type of course and the use to be made of grades are the primary factors influencing which method of grading is used.

When assigning grades for achievement over a period of time, such as a semester, it is necessary to combine scores received on a number of tests and other assignments. Approaches for accomplishing this for objective tests, essay tests, and a mixture of different types of tests were discussed. An important factor to consider in combining scores is regression toward the mean. Therefore, in order to achieve a more realistic balance of final grades, teachers will probably need to grade individual tests more stringently than they would if only one test were given for the entire term. How the different sources of evaluation should be weighted is usually left to the teacher's own judgment, with amount of class time devoted to each source being an important consideration.

Finally, teachers should keep in mind that even when all possible precautions are taken in grading students, many sources of unreliability still remain. Thus, it is best to make strong evaluations only about students whose performance is consistently very good or very poor and to adopt a wait-and-see policy with the majority of students.

SUGGESTED ADDITIONAL READINGS

Stanley, J. C. *Measurement in today's schools.* (4th ed.) Englewood Cliffs, N.J.: Prentice-Hall, 1964, chap. 11.

Strang, R. *How to report pupil progress.* Chicago: Science Research, 1955.

Thomas, R. M. *Judging student progress.* (Rev. ed.) New York: Longmans, 1960.

Thorndike, R. L., and Hagen, E. *Measurement and evaluation in psychology and education.* (3rd ed.) New York: Wiley, 1969, chap. 17.

Wood, D. A. *Test construction.* Columbus, Ohio: Merrill, 1960, chap. 8.

Wrinkle, W. L. *Improving marking and reporting practices in elementary and secondary schools.* New York: Rinehart, 1956.

PART III

STANDARDIZED ACHIEVEMENT TESTS

In terms of sheer numbers, standardized achievement tests outrank all other commercially distributed educational and psychological tests. In terms of impact on the classroom, standardized achievement tests are second in importance only to tests which the teacher himself develops for use with his own students.

The word "standardized" means that the tests are carefully constructed by experts for use throughout the country. Directions for administration, scoring, and interpretation are made explicit; and norms are provided which make possible direct comparisons between students of different ages and between students in different schools and localities. Some of the purposes, principles, and methods for constructing and using achievement tests will be discussed in Chapter 8.

One primary distinction among achievement tests is that between comprehensive tests and tests for individual topics. Comprehensive tests contain subtests for all, or most, of the important topics taught at particular grade levels. For example, a comprehensive test for the sixth-grade level typically would contain subtests for reading, language, arithmetic, science, social studies, and others. Individual achievement tests are aimed only at parts of the total subject matter, such as reading only, geography only, or chemistry only.

Another distinction among achievement tests is that between *survey* tests and *diagnostic* tests. Survey tests are intended to measure *how much* students know; diagnostic tests are intended to "look inside" the student's performance in such a way as to provide clues about work habits and particular faults. As will be discussed more fully later, the distinction is more a matter of degree than of kind. The diagnostic measures are all tests of separate topics rather than comprehensive batteries. They are restricted almost exclusively to reading and arithmetic. Comprehensive achievement tests will be discussed in Chapter 9; survey and diagnostic measures for separate topics will be discussed in Chapter 10.

chapter 8

CONSTRUCTION AND USE OF STANDARDIZED ACHIEVEMENT TESTS

Miss Martin is near the end of her first year of teaching, and she is rather proud of the progress shown by her fourth-grade children. Now, early in May, it is time for her students to take a comprehensive achievement test. She has heard a lot about the tests from other teachers and has learned that the tests are considered quite important in the school. She hopes that her students will perform well and that the tests will confirm her judgments about the relative standings of her students with respect to one another. "Will the tests show that my students as a group have done well in the fourth grade? Will they confirm my opinion that Bill Harris is an outstanding student and that Ann Blackman should be held back in the fourth grade? Will the new approach that I used in the teaching of number skills 'pay off' on the tests?"

PURPOSE OF ACHIEVEMENT TESTS. The purpose of achievement tests is to measure progress in school up to a particular point in time. The purpose of a comprehensive battery given at the end of the fourth grade is to determine how well students have mastered school topics such as reading, number skills, spelling, grammatical usage, and social studies. Standardized achievement tests are natural outgrowths of teacher-made tests. They share the same standards of validity, and they are both aimed directly at school-learned information and skills. The most important differences between standardized achievement tests and teacher-made tests are as follows:

1. Coverage.   Standardized achievement tests usually cover much more material than that in most teacher-made tests. This is true of comprehensive achievement test batteries, but it is not necessarily true of achievement tests for special topics, for example, an achievement test in high school chemistry, which might be quite similar in terms of breadth and amount of detail to teacher-made tests for the same topic. Typically, a teacher-made test is intended to measure progress in learning number skills over a one-month period or progress in American history over a school semester, for example. Whereas an achievement test would have a section dealing with the Civil War in general, a teacher-made test might concern much more highly specialized aspects of the war, such as the activities of Indian tribes in a particular locality. Comprehensive achievement batteries measure progress in all, or most, important topics up to a particular point in time. The teacher-made test often provides more detailed information about how well the student has mastered a particular topic; the achievement test provides a picture of the student's over-all educational development.

2.   Objectives.   In addition to having broader coverage, the content in achievement tests tends to differ somewhat from that in the teacher-made test. The teacher-made test is specifically aimed at local objectives, those of the teacher and the school as a whole. Achievement tests are based on the core educational objectives shared by educators across the country. Consequently, some materials on the achievement test may not be considered very important by a particular teacher, and some of the types of material that he considers important may be given little, if any, coverage in the achievement test. Rather than this imposing a conflict of objectives, if properly understood the partial difference in objectives means that achievement tests provide a valuable supplementary source of information to teachers and whole schools.

3.   Construction.   One of the most important differences between achievement tests and teacher-made tests is in terms of the relative care and expense given to the two types of tests. It would be foolish not to frankly recognize that few teachers are truly expert in matters relating to educational measurement and that they have only a limited amount of time to construct and use tests. In contrast, commercially distributed achievement tests are constructed by experts, who may take as long as several years to develop a new test. Because of the resources available, very careful plans can be made for the content of the tests, much time can be devoted to the construction of items, and elaborate empirical investigations can be made of the quality of individual items and whole tests. Teachers should not be so foolishly proud as to ignore the fact that, item per item, standardized achievement tests usually are much more carefully constructed than are teacher-made tests.

4.   Norms.   One of the major advantages of achievement tests is that they provide norms for comparing individual students, classes, and whole schools with the school progress shown by students in schools across the country and with students in individual states and geographical regions. Such norms are obtained as part of standardizing the tests. Teachers seldom have such norms available for their own tests. Typically, they test only twenty or thirty students, and the most they can do is to compare students with one another or with the scores made by students in previous years on similar tests. Norms are useful in making many comparisons, such as comparing the mathematical achievement of students in all the high schools within a city, comparing the level of reading ability of children in one school system with that of children in the country as a whole, and comparing a student's levels of attainment in number skills at the completion of the fourth and fifth grades. It is in helping to make such comparisons that standardized achievement tests have their particular advantage over teacher-made tests.

5.   Uses.   Because of differences in scope, content, construction, and normative data, teacher-made tests and standardized achievement tests are intended to supply somewhat different kinds of information for use in making educational decisions. It is unfortunately the case that some teachers regard standardized tests as "competitors" to their own tests and informal observations of pupils. Actually, the two types of measures are intended to serve largely different functions. There are some areas of overlap, e.g., diagnosing the particular difficulties that a student has in mathematics, but these are small compared with the relatively unique advantages of each. The particular uses of achievement tests will be spelled out in detail later in the chapter. To set the stage for those detailed discussions, the following sections will allude to some of the more important uses of achievement tests.

The differential usefulness of the two types of tests—standardized achievement tests and teacher-made tests—lies in the kinds of valid comparisons that can be made with them. The teacher-made test, if well constructed, is usually more valid for evaluating how well a class as a whole and students individually are meeting the objectives of a particular unit of instruction. These types of comparisons are best made with teacher-made tests, rather than with standardized achievement tests, because the well-constructed teacher-made test is more closely tailored to local objectives. For example, a major objective in a particular school system might be the development of core skills in reading and mathematics, with lesser emphasis on content areas such as science and social studies. Thus, even though a comprehensive measure of achievement might indicate that students in that particular school system were performing at the national average with respect to reading and mathematics, the students might not be meeting the local objectives in these areas. Similarly, even though the comprehensive battery might show that students were well behind the national average in terms of the various content areas (e.g., science), this may be no different from what the school system expected in light of the local curriculum emphases. For these and other reasons, teacher-made tests, if well constructed, are most appropriate for evaluating students as a group and comparing them with one another in relation to local objectives. Consequently, teacher-made tests are potentially more valid for making decisions regarding the progress of students in school, as is evidenced in the special treatment of students in day-to-day instruction, communications to students and parents, decisions about grade placement, and other matters concerning the progress of individual students. Standardized achievement tests do provide important auxiliary information for making all the aforementioned types of decisions, but when it comes to evaluating students as a group and individually with respect to local objectives, the well-constructed teacher-made test is logically the more appropriate instrument. Of course, so many teacher-made tests are poorly conceived and constructed that this potential usefulness is frequently subverted.

In contrast to the types of comparisons best made with teacher-made tests, let us consider now the types of comparisons best made with nationally standardized achievement tests. One of these is the comparison of students' performance in a particular unit of instruction locally with that of students in the national standardization sample. For example, Fred Lawrence might make a very high grade on teacher-made tests for fifth-grade mathematics, and thus in terms of local standards he appears to be quite bright in math. However, it might be found on a nationally standardized achievement test that Fred is indeed above average, but not nearly as much above average in comparison with students nationally as might be supposed on the basis of teacher-made tests alone.

A second type of comparison that necessarily must be made with nationally standardized achievement tests is a comparison of students' progress in a unit of instruction having locally held objectives with their performance on a nationally standardized test constructed with broadly accepted objectives for that unit of instruction. As will be seen more fully later, nationally standardized achievement tests grow out of a consensus among experts regarding objectives for progress in reading, mathematics, science, and other topics. It is only reasonable to expect that these objectives, arrived at from a consensus, will differ somewhat from local objectives. Although it is improper to argue that one or the other set of objectives is wrong and the other is right, differences in those regards should be instructive to teachers, and such differences can be determined only by the types of comparisons that can be made with nationally standardized achievement tests.

A third type of comparison for which nationally standardized achievement tests are better suited is a comparison of a student's progress from one year to the next. Although some informal comparisons in that regard can be made with teacher-made tests, strict comparisons require that highly comparable tests be used at each grade level. This requires that the tests be developed from the same set of objectives, that the item types be very much the same, that the tests be highly reliable, and that scores be interpretable in terms of a meaningful normative group. These characteristics are very seldom found in teacher-made tests. In mathematics, for example, teachers at various grade levels typically have slightly different objectives, employ somewhat different types of tests, combine scores from various tests in different ways, and differ in other ways in their assessments of student progress. Although such differences in practices usually are not so gross as to make comparisons from year to year utterly meaningless, they rule out the possibility of making the relatively fine comparisons which can be made with nationally standardized achievement tests. It would be possible with a nationally standardized test to arrive validly at the conclusion that a particular student has increased his standing in mathematics by about twenty percentile points over a period of three years.

As can be seen from the above discussion, the relative usefulness of teacher-made tests and nationally standardized achievement tests depends on the types of comparisons that must be made. Part II of this book was concerned with the types of comparisons that are best made with teacher-made tests and the principles that underlie the construction of these tests. Part III of this book is concerned with the types of comparisons that are best made with nationally standardized achievement tests and the principles that underlie the planning and development of valid measures of that kind.

VALIDITY OF ACHIEVEMENT TESTS. In Chapter 2, three kinds of validity were described, depending on the functions which particular instruments are intended to serve: *prediction*, *assessment*, and *trait measurement*. Standardized achievement tests are primary examples of assessments. Their validity depends on exactly the same standards as do teacher-made tests. Assessments are valid if their content is *representative* of a particular unit of instruction or an over-all course of training.

The validity of predictors and trait measures rests largely on empirical and statistical procedures, the former on the correlation of a test or test battery with a criterion, and the latter on a complex of correlations with numerous measures. To study these two types of validity, experiments must be undertaken and statistical analyses made of the results.

As was mentioned previously, some empirical and statistical procedures are helpful in validating achievement tests, but those are not the primary standards. It is inevitably the case that the validity of achievement tests and teacher-made tests rests on "rational" considerations. Only by the exercise of expert judgment can it be told whether or not an achievement test faithfully adheres to the goals of instruction. Because of the availability of experts and other resources, it usually is possible to guarantee a higher level of content representativeness in standardized achievement tests than in teacher-made tests. This is accomplished by carefully planning the content of standardized achievement tests in conjunction with a representative cross section of educators, composing items of a kind that are most likely to measure important aspects of learning, and by systematically gathering opinions from teachers about the quality of the tests. How these steps are undertaken will be described in a later section of this chapter.

APTITUDE AND ACHIEVEMENT.   An issue that has been raised previously in this book, and must be raised again, is that of the difference between aptitude and achievement. Ideally, aptitude is the capacity to learn, a forecast of how much students *can* achieve under favorable conditions. Achievement is how much students *have* learned up to a particular point in time. Another way of saying it is that aptitude tests are meant to be predictive of future achievement, and achievement tests are meant to assess the actual level of attainment.

It is easy to see that presently we have no way of measuring aptitude entirely apart from past achievement, and, indeed,. the two are logically semi-inseparable. We have no way of "looking inside" people to gauge their intelligence and special aptitudes. Rather, we must judge aptitude by how well people have mastered their cultural environments up to particular points in time. Consequently, many of the items on aptitude tests, e.g., tests of intelligence, are similar to items on tests of achievement. For example, vocabulary tests usually are present in both types of measures. Also, however one conceives of aptitude, it is reasonable to believe that it is influenced by the richness of past schooling and other experiences. If, in some sense, two children are born with the same level of aptitude, their aptitudes should be changed by what occurs during the years of maturation.

Aptitude tests are frequently criticized because the results are influenced to some extent by the type of environment in which the child has been reared. For example, children in culturally impoverished environments make lower scores on intelligence tests than children who are reared in more fortunate circumstances. This and other forms of evidence regarding the effects of environment on one's achievement on aptitude tests have been used as a basis for criticism of the employment of aptitude tests for any purpose, e.g., selecting students for college. What the critics of such tests fail to realize, however, is that even if scores are determined partially by previous environment at any particular point in time, they frequently do make valid predictions of performance at the next step in educational development. Numerous experiments have been undertaken to enrich the environments of culturally impoverished children. Typically, these investigations report that average aptitude test scores (e.g., on intelligence tests) increase appreciably. By some perverted line of reasoning, this finding has been taken to imply that aptitude tests are not good measures of actual aptitudes. If anything, the finding shows just the opposite—that aptitude tests are sensitive to changes in the individual's intellectual capacity at any particular point in time. When such capacity is altered, aptitude tests are the first and best method for detecting the change. The obtained scores are still the most predictive indices available about how well students will perform in intellectual endeavors in the immediate future. Most properly, aptitude should be thought of as aptitude for the *next step* in education, rather than as some innate and unchanging characteristic of the student.

In spite of the theoretical and practical difficulties of measuring aptitude somewhat apart from achievement, the distinction is too well rooted in common sense to be discarded. When Bill is taunted by one of his friends about his dog's inability to perform tricks, Bill says "He ain't dumb; he just ain't had no education." At a simple level, this is recognition of the difference between what an organism might accomplish under favorable conditions and what it has accomplished. The same type of distinction is made by teachers every day. We hear this when a teacher says, "If he wanted to, he could make all A's." It is heard in another form when a teacher says, "He actually has less ability than one would judge from his grades; he is knocking himself out to keep up with the class"; and it is heard in still another form when a teacher says, "He is not failing because of lack of ability, but because of his disturbed personality."

The distinction between aptitude and achievement is too important and too well founded in practical experience to be ignored. Admittedly, teachers are prone to overemphasize the distinction between the two. Seldom does the student with high aptitude make poor grades even if he is under adverse conditions in the classroom and at home. Conversely, seldom does the "slow learner" begin to make excellent grades after even the best of individual attention. However, moderate, and sometimes even marked, differences are found between measures of aptitude and achievement; and when they are, they are of real diagnostic importance. For this reason, it is important to do the best job possible of measuring aptitude somewhat apart from achievement. In this part of the book will be discussed principles relating to the measurement of achievement; in Part IV of the book will be discussed principles relating to the measurement of aptitudes.

CONSTRUCTION OF ACHIEVEMENT TESTS

The principles and methods for constructing standardized achievement tests are essentially the same as those described in Part II for the construction of teacher-made tests. First, the purposes of the instrument must be clearly decided. Second, a detailed outline is made of the content to be included. The statement of purposes and the outline of content are discussed wih educational experts and with classroom teachers. Such discussions usually result in clarifications and changes in both the statement of purposes and the outline of content. Next, items are composed for each part of the outline of content, and these are inspected by numerous persons for their clarity, representativeness, and importance. In this process, some items are discarded, some modified, and others added. The items are then administered to large numbers of (usually more than a thousand) students. Item analyses are then made along the lines discussed in Chapter 7. The items that meet the necessary statistical requirements are used to form the actual test. The test is then administered to thousands of children across the country who form a representative sample of all those students with whom the instrument will be used, e.g., a sample of fourth-grade children. Statistical analyses are then made to obtain norms for the country as a whole and for separate geographic regions, states, and local school systems. The norms usually are reported in several different forms, including percentiles, standard scores, transformed standard scores, grade equivalents, age equivalents, and others. Finally, after all these things have been done, manuals must be carefully written for the administration, scoring, and interpretation of the test. The test is then ready to be placed "on the market." From the foregoing, it is obvious that the construction of a new standardized measure of achievement requires a great deal of time, money, research, and expert attention.

OUTLINE OF CONTENT. The outlining of content for achievement tests does not differ in principle from that used by the teacher in composing his own examinations. However, in practice there are several features that usually distinguish the two. First, the outline of content for achievement tests is usually much more carefully constructed than that for teacher-made tests. Second, because the coverage is broader in achievement tests, the outline must also be more extensive. Third, whereas the outline used by the individual teacher for his examination is usually determined by himself alone, the outline for a commercial achievement test must be cooperatively derived by educational experts, educational administrators, and teachers. The following outline of content for the reading, language usage, and arithmetic sections of the Iowa Tests of Basic Skills, for grades 3 to 9 (Lindquist & Hieronymous, 1964), illustrates the care and detail required of content specifications for standardized achievement tests. It should be pointed out here that the Iowa tests utilize a multilevel format in which test questions for all grades are printed in one test booklet but in which the pupils in each grade begin and stop at different points. Thus, there is an overlap of items in the successive grades. Some of the skills outlined in the following summary are dropped out as one goes into the items for the higher grades, and other skills are added at the appropriate levels.

    I.   Reading comprehension
        A.   Details
            1.   To recognize and understand important facts and details
            2.   To recognize and understand implied facts and relationships
            3.   To deduce the meaning of words or phrases from context
        B.   Purpose
            1.   To detect the main purpose of a paragraph or selection
            2.   To recognize the main idea or topic of a paragraph or selection
        C.   Organization
            1.   To recognize common elements or parallel topics in incidents or paragraphs
            2.   To recognize proper time sequence
        D.   Evaluation
            1.   To develop generalizations from a selection
            2.   To recognize the writer's viewpoint, attitude, or intention
            3.   To recognize the mood or tone of a selection
            4.   To recognize outstanding qualities of style or structure

II. Language usage
    A. Use of pronouns
        1. Case form
        2. Agreement with antecedent
        3. Order of first-person pronouns in compound constructions
        4. Miscellaneous forms commonly confused
    B. Use of verbs
        1. The past tense
        2. The past participle
        3. Agreement of subject and verb
        4. Miscellaneous forms incorrectly used
    C. Use of adjectives and adverbs
        1. Forms commonly confused
        2. Articles
        3. Comparative and superlative forms
        4. Miscellaneous modifying forms
    D. Avoidance of double negatives
    E. Avoidance of redundancies
    F. Homonyms commonly confused
    G. Miscellaneous word forms
III. Arithmetic concepts
    A. Currency
        1. Reading and writing amounts
        2. Counting
        3. Relative values of coins
        4. Making change
    B. Decimals
        1. Reading and writing
        2. Relative sizes
        3. Rounding
        4. Fraction, decimal, and per cent equivalents
        5. Fundamental operations
    C. Equations
    D. Fractions
        1. Part of a whole and part of a group
        2. Relative sizes
        3. Reducing terms
        4. Fundamental operations
    E. Geometry
        1. Parallel and perpendicular lines
        2. Recognizing kinds of geometric figures
        3. Angles and triangles

    4.   Dimensions, perimeters, and areas of polygons
    5.   Parts and areas of circles
    6.   Use of protractor and compass

F. Measurement
    1.   Quantity
    2.   Time
    3.   Temperature
    4.   Weight and length (use of ruler and precision)
    5.   Area and volume
    6.   Liquid and dry capacity
    7.   Fundamental operations with compound denominate numbers

G. Numerals and number systems
    1.   Counting
    2.   Ordinals
    3.   Place value and zero as a place holder
    4.   Roman numerals
    5.   Odd and even numbers
    6.   Positive and negative numbers

H. Per cents
I. Ratio and proportion
J. Whole numbers
    1.   Reading and writing
    2.   Relative sizes
    3.   Rounding
    4.   Partition and measurement
    5.   Averaging
    6.   Fundamental operations

A CASE HISTORY OF ACHIEVEMENT TEST CONSTRUCTION. After the outline is completed come the many labors of manufacturing and standardizing the completed instrument. To illustrate how this is done, selected parts will be quoted[1] from the Directions for Administration, Metropolitan Achievement Tests for grades 3 and 4 (Durost, 1960).

Curriculum research. The Metropolitan series attempts to measure those outcomes of instruction which, according to authoritative judgment and consensus of current practice, are the important goals of present elementary instruction. To ascertain what these goals or outcomes are, subject by subject and grade by

[1]The quoted material is presented by permission of Harcourt, Brace, & World Inc. Some sections of the quoted material have been omitted and other parts have been slightly altered in order to conform to the style and purpose of this book.

grade, the authors reviewed expert pronouncements concerning the goals of elementary education, current research on the nature of essential skills, such as reading and the work-study skills, representative courses of study, and several widely used textbook series in the various branches. From these sources, they developed a detailed outline or blueprint for each test at each level, specifying the objective and, where appropriate, the content areas or topics to be covered and indicating the proportionate emphasis to be devoted to each objective or outcome as well as the desired distribution of the test content among various areas.

Experimental editions. After the specifications had been formulated, test items were prepared, edited, and in many cases reviewed by one or more subject-matter specialists. Considerable research was undertaken on matters of item type, appropriateness of directions, time limits, and related issues. Whenever there was any question about the appropriateness of a proposed new type of item, its suitability was experimentally verified before its adoption in the experimental forms. A total of approximately fourteen thousand items were developed 30 to 40 per cent more material than was ultimately to be used in the final forms.

Tryout programs. The experimental forms were administered in a series of carefully planned programs to pupils in nine school systems. These school systems constituted a varied group of communities, widely divergent with respect to type of pupil population, type of community, textbooks in use, and other characteristics presumably related to achievement status.

Item analysis. The per cent of pupils answering correctly was computed for every item, separately for boys and girls for each grade in which the item was administered. For most subtests, an item discrimination index was also computed, indicating how effectively the item distinguished between pupils scoring high and low.

On the basis of the actual performance of the items in the tryout, final forms of the various tests were developed that are of appropriate difficulty, both with respect to average difficulty and range of difficulty and that discriminate as effectively as possible both among pupils in successsive grades and among pupils of varying ability within each grade. The selection of items was carried on so as to produce equivalent final forms, each conforming to the original specifications established for the test.

Teacher evaluation. All teachers who administered the experimental forms of the test were asked to comment on, and criticize, these forms particularly with respect to appropriateness of the content for grades in which administered, clarity of directions, clarity of the test questions themselves, and general pupil and teacher reaction.

In addition to the steps described in the quoted material above, numerous other labors were required to produce the final battery of achievement tests. The final forms were administered to over 500,000 pupils for the purposes of obtaining norms. These included students from 225 school systems in 49 states. For each grade level, raw scores were transformed to grade norms, percentiles, standard scores, and transformed standard scores. Finally, investigations were made of test reliability. Split-half reliability correlations were separately computed for each grade level in each of several school systems. Reliabilities were found to be generally good, averaging about .90. After the study of reliability was completed, tests and test manuals were prepared for publication. Since their publication in 1959, The Metropolitan Achievement Tests have been widely used. Some other good achievement tests are described in Chapters 9 and 10, and a more extensive list is given in Appendix D.

MAJOR USES OF ACHIEVEMENT TESTS

Standardized achievement tests provide such a wealth of information about students that it would be impractical to describe all their uses. In his report on practices and attitudes regarding the use of standardized tests in schools, Goslin (1967) includes data pertaining to the reported frequencies of using standardized achievement tests (and other types of tests) for specific purposes. Table 8-1 shows these actual frequencies for elementary schools. Readers may find it interesting to refer to this table in relation to the following discussion of some of the major types of educational decisions that are aided by the use of achievement tests.

GRADE PLACEMENT.   Whenever there are questions about the assignment of students to particular grade levels, achievement tests provide very useful information. Whether a particular student should be placed in the fourth or fifth grade, for example, depends upon what we know about him. If the student has been enrolled in a particular school for at least half a year, the decision should be based mainly on teacher-made tests and the impressions of the teacher and others in the school setting. Questions regarding promotion should depend largely on teacher-made tests because those tests are (or at least should be) more directly representative of local objectives than standardized achievement tests. In questions of retaining students in a grade, however, standardized achievement tests provide important auxiliary information. In the case, for example, where a teacher is of the opinion that a student should be held back in the fourth grade rather than forced to make an uphill fight of it in the fifth grade, the results from standardized achievement tests would provide

Table 8-1 Percentage of time various uses are reported for each type of test in 714 elementary schools* *(Adapted from Goslin, 1967.)*

Uses of Tests	Reading Readiness	Individual Intelligence	Group Intelligence	Reading Achievement	Arithmetic Achievement	Achievement Battery	Other Tests	Nonstandardized Reading Tests	Total
Homogeneous grouping	60.8†	30.6	38.8	42.2	29.2	39.4	52.3	46.1	40.8
Counseling children	12.0	29.5	32.0	21.1	21.9	34.0	23.9	20.0	28.2
Grading	5.9	2.5	4.7	8.1	12.0	9.1	1.1	11.9	7.7
Evaluating the curriculum	16.9	4.6	13.9	31.9	37.3	33.1	26.1	16.9	27.6
Evaluating teachers	.8	.3	1.4	1.2	3.0	4.2	—	4.7	2.7
Diagnosing learning difficulties	55.1	70.5	59.6	77.5	78.1	78.8	79.5	77.5	71.7
Counseling parents	21.2	58.7	34.5	20.6	18.8	30.4	36.4	20.5	29.4
Other uses	7.3	17.5	9.3	5.7	4.7	3.8	13.6	5.3	6.5
Average number of uses reported	(1.8)	(2.05)	(1.95)	(2.09)	(2.06)	(2.42)	(2.37)	(2.04)	(2.15)
Total number of tests given	(508)	(325)	(1,821)	(752)	(233)	(2,738)	(88)	(922)	(7,387)

*Principals could list up to four main uses for each test; consequently, percentages do not add to 100. The data are organized by test; that is, principals reported main uses for every test regularly given in their schools.

†The largest percentage figure in each column is italicized to indicate the most frequently reported use for that particular test.

important supporting information. If they confirmed the results from teacher-made tests and the teacher's impressions, this would give added assurance to the teacher that the decision was a wise one, and the evidence from achievement tests would help parents and others understand why the decision was necessary.

Achievement tests are particularly helpful in deciding on the grade level for transfer students. The student coming from another school in another locality might have been fed a very different kind of educational fare from what he will receive in his new school. The over-all ability levels of students in the two schools might differ greatly, and the emphases in instruction might be very different. The grades that students bring with them are of some help in assigning transfer students to grade levels, but they leave many questions unanswered. Although the student may have received instruction in social studies, do the two schools mean the same thing by "social studies"? Although the student may have received passing grades in his previous school, does the previous school have different standards than the new school? Standardized achievement tests help answer such questions.

Regardless of where the student previously attended school, he probably will have the results of achievement tests on his records. These scores can be interpreted directly in the new school setting. Even if the previous school employed a different achievement test battery from that used in the new school, the needed comparisons can be made. If the tests administered in the previous school show that the student stands at the 55th percentile in reading achievement compared with national norms, this can be compared directly with the average reading score obtained by students at the new school. In this way, it can be told whether or not a student is likely to perform satisfactorily at a particular grade level.

Of course, whenever a student transfers from one geographic area and type of environment to another, initial grade placement should be highly tentative, and the teacher and others should be alert regarding the need for readjustment after a period of several months or one semester. During this time, the teacher will have an opportunity to apply his own tests and gather other information about the extent to which the student is properly placed at a grade level commensurate with local goals of instruction. Until this information has been collected, and even after it has, the results of standardized achievement tests provide useful information regarding the most appropriate grade placement for a transfer student.

GROUPING FOR INSTRUCTION.   Another important use of achievement tests is in grouping children for instruction. One approach is to group children within a grade into several levels, or tracks, in terms of over-all ability. The members of each group work together, are provided instruction tailored to their supposed level of over-all ability, and are given readings and exercises that may differ from those given to students at other levels. Of course there is considerable controversy about whether or not ability grouping should be done; but if it is done, standardized achievement tests are helpful in making the necessary decisions. For grouping students in the first three grades, intelligence tests are somewhat better than achievement tests. This is because (1) at that level school topics are not sufficiently broad to tap a student's potential for later schoolwork, (2) successful performance in the first several grades is dependent to some extent on "incidental" abilities, such as is evidenced in the rote memorization of multiplication tables, (3) some children do not "settle down" in their schoolwork until they have passed the primary grades, and (4) achievement in the first several grades is dependent to some extent on whether or not students attended kindergarten and on whether or not parents have undertaken some preschool "coaching" of their children. Although intelligence tests do not entirely circumvent these sources of error in forecasting the long-range accomplishments of students in school topics, at the primary level they are somewhat broader and less dependent on incidental factors than are achievement tests.

Beginning with about the fourth grade, achievement tests start to surpass intelligence tests in terms of importance in making ability groupings. After that point, intelligence tests still provide useful supplementary information, but standardized achievement tests become the mainstays for making decisions about ability groupings. Also, at every level, course grades and opinions of teachers are important sources of information for use in assigning pupils to the proper sections.

The disadvantages of grouping students according to over-all levels of ability, or into different tracks of instruction, probably outweigh the advantages. The potential advantages of such over-all groupings are (1) they provide students at all levels with an opportunity to proceed at their own pace, being neither dragged along by the very bright nor held back by the slow learners; (2) they provide an opportunity for semi-individualized instruction by means of special instructional materials for each group; and (3) they simplify the work of the teacher, to some extent, by allowing him to employ pedagogical procedures that are appropriate to each level without having to worry about boring some students or going over the heads of others. However, the disadvantages of grouping students in terms of over-all levels of ability and of placing them in different tracks of instruction are even more imposing. First, the student is somewhat branded by the procedure, and he, his friends, and others usually catch on to the implications of his particular group assignment. This disadvantage is avoided, to some extent, by a flexible outlook on the part of the teacher regarding shifting a student from group to group as new evidence is amassed about him and as he grows and changes. A second, and more telling, argument against grouping students in terms of over-all ability is that any grouping of students should take account of particular intellectual talents and shortcomings. As will be discussed more fully in Chapter 11, measures of over-all ability (e.g., intelligence tests) provide a great deal of information about students, but they also leave a great deal unsaid. Two students could have the same over-all level of ability, but differ considerably in terms of their particular talents. One could be excellent in the use and understanding of language and only average in mathematics, and the other could be just the opposite. If the teacher employed groupings in terms of over-all ability, these two students would end up in the same group or track. Then one student would be well ahead of his ability group in terms of language arts but behind in terms of mathematical ability, and the other would be just the opposite.

Grouping for instruction is more defensible and more effective when it is based on competence in particular areas of learning, rather than on over-all ability. In particular, different groupings for instruction should be used in reading and in mathematics, and still other groupings prove useful for other topics. Such groupings are directly related to the daily needs of instruction, they do not permanently brand the student in terms of intellectual quality, and they can be changed easily from month to month and year to year. Such grouping is aided considerably by the results from nationally standardized achievement tests. The part played by achievement tests is particularly prominent at the beginning of the school year, when the teacher has had very little experience with the students. To take a very simple example, the fourth-grade teacher could use the evidence from achievement tests in establishing five groups of six students each for work in reading and three groups of ten students each for work in mathematics. During the school year, students could be shifted around from group to group on the basis of manifest competence in reading and mathematics.

The ultimate in grouping students is nongraded instruction, a practice which is being given considerable attention these days and which is being implemented to some degree in many school systems across the country. In the truly nongraded school, the individual student is the focus of the curriculum, and grouping by any arbitrary criterion, be it age or ability level, is the antithesis of the nongraded program. Children do work in groups with other children, but groupings are very flexible and may be changed whenever the teachers feel that such a change will be beneficial. A student is placed in a group for a particular type of instruction, e.g., math, not because he is a certain age or in a particular grade but because he has the same skill needs as other students in the group. He moves on to the next level of instruction in an academic subject when he gives promise of being able to perform well at that level. Standardized achievement tests are extremely helpful in determining what skills children already have and where they should be placed in the curriculum.

If a school makes wide use of nongraded instruction, more reliance will have to be placed on standardized achievement tests than otherwise would be the case. Although there are obvious advantages to employing nongraded instruction, there is a major disadvantage in that systematic observations of, and comparisons between, students at each level are difficult to make. Carried to the extreme, nongraded instruction could result in a student's moving about so much from group to group and teacher to teacher that it would be very difficult to obtain a clear idea of how well he performs over-all in relation to his classmates. For example, if a particular student performs below average in an advanced group in mathematics, what does that say about how well he performs with respect to the average student at his age level? The foregoing is not meant as a major criticism of the use of nongraded instructional groupings of students, for they have obvious advantages. What is intended to be emphasized here is that if such nongraded instruction is employed, heavier reliance must be placed on nationally standardized achievement tests than would otherwise be the case. Such tests are extremely helpful in assigning students to groups, and because of the lack of a clearer local frame of reference, they are very useful in measuring the over-all progress of students in school.

PLANNING DAILY INSTRUCTION.   If standardized achievement tests served no other purpose, they would still be of value to the individual teacher in planning the day-to-day instruction of his students. Each year, teachers receive a new class in which each student is largely an unknown. How well have the students mastered their previous training? As a group, what are their strong points and their weak points? Which students need special attention? If comprehensive achievement tests were administered late in the previous school year or at the beginning of the new year, the results will go a long way toward providing the teacher with the information he needs to deal effectively with the class as a whole and with individual students. Without this information, teachers would have to spend much of the time during the first month or two of school trying to size up the previous accomplishments and capabilities of their new students. By then, much valuable time would have been lost, the class as a whole might have been set on improper courses of study, and the problems of particular students would not have been fully understood.

Following are several examples of how results of achievement tests help in planning day-to-day activities in the classroom. For some time the teacher noted that Jack Whitmore apparently had some difficulties in reading, but it was difficult to tell exactly what the problem was. Some clues were obtained on a special achievement test for reading skills. Jack performed well in the section of the test concerning word knowledge, and average in the section on reading comprehension; but in the section on rate of reading it was found that he read very slowly. During the next week the teacher could see that Jack was very timid about reading aloud in front of other students and that he spent much time in looking up from his page to see how fellow students were reacting. Perhaps timidity about "performing" in front of others had generated bad habits in reading. For the next two months, the teacher did not ask Jack to read aloud. Instead he was asked to read silently and then tell the teacher what he read. Also, the teacher made special efforts to be understanding of Jack's shyness. With these and other remedial practices, Jack's reading speed gradually increased to the normal rate.

Mrs. Long is teaching the fourth grade in a new consolidated elementary school that draws students from districts that each formerly had small schools. Mrs. Long worries that her new students will differ markedly from one another in terms of the quality of their previous training. Inspection of achievement test results confirm her suspicions. Most of the children apparently are up to grade level in achievement, but six students who all came from the same small school are performing far below grade level. Mrs. Long decides that for the first several months she will start those six children on third-grade-level readings and exercises and then see whether, in time, they can catch up with the class as a whole.

The teacher is assisted in the aforementioned and other uses of achievement tests in planning daily instruction by the computerized services for scoring and by the statistical analyses that are provided by most companies that distribute nationally standardized achievement tests. By studying scores on individual subtests as well as the item-analysis information usually provided, teachers can gain clues about specific types of problems common to most members of the class. For example, the teacher may discover that most members of the class had trouble with problems involving fractions, that almost everyone did poorly on the language items involving punctuation, or that on the study-skills test, members of the class did well in every area except map reading. The teacher's manuals distributed with most major standardized commercial achievement tests often contain suggestions about the best way to utilize the statistical analysis of test results provided by the scoring service. An example of how such information would be useful is as follows.

In looking over the report for a test concerning capitalization and punctuation, the teacher finds that his class does even better than the national norms group in using commas but that they could use some more drill in capitalization. For some tests (e.g., the SRA series), item reports for individual students are also available upon request. When achievement testing is done at the end of the school year, these reports may be particularly useful in providing a picture of the specific strengths and weaknesses of the members of the newly formed classes at the beginning of the next school year.

EVALUATING SCHOOL OBJECTIVES AND CURRICULA. In addition to being useful in planning daily instruction, standardized achievement tests are also very useful in planning the curriculum throughout a school or throughout a school system. There is so much ferment these days, in education as well as in everything else, that change is more to be expected than sameness. Each year one sees new topics introduced in the schools, new groupings of subject matters, new types of instructional materials, and new ways of teaching particular topics advocated. With all this pressure toward the adoption of new educational methods, some guideposts are needed for evaluating the effectiveness of both old and new methods. Nationally standardized achievement tests are invaluable for that purpose.

An example of the use of achievement tests in curriculum planning is provided in the case of a school system which had been rather slow to adopt textbooks and instructional methods geared to the "modern math." The new approach to mathematics was being introduced throughout the school system at the sixth-grade level, but not any earlier. It was decided to try out textbooks and instructional methods geared to the new approach at the fourth- and fifth-grade levels. At the end of the school year, students were administered an achievement test in mathematics which emphasized the modern math. Statistical analyses were then made by the testing company of scores in three schools in grades 4 and 5. The average score was somewhat lower than had been obtained in the previous year on achievement tests oriented toward traditional instruction in mathematics: the mean had dropped from the 55th percentile to the 45th percentile. However, it was decided that this was not a great loss in comparison to the advantages of getting in tune with the new approach to mathematics instruction. The testing service also provided easiness percentages for each item for students in the three schools. An analysis of these easiness percentages by teachers involved in the instructional program provided many hints about the difficulties that students were having with particular aspects of the new program of instruction in mathematics.

Another example of how nationally standardized achievement tests can be used in curriculum planning can be seen in the case of Wiley School. Wiley School was very proud of its efforts to introduce science topics into the curriculum. Intensive treatment of science topics had been planned for the sixth and seventh grades. The first year the new program was tried, the teachers were shocked to find that their sixth-grade students' performance on the science section of a comprehensive achievement test was only average. However, after looking carefully at the test items and at the responses of their students to the test, the teachers could see the problem. The science section of the test contained a broad collection of items on biology, physics, astronomy, geology, and other subjects. In the curriculum, it had been planned to emphasize the life sciences in the sixth grade and the physical sciences in the seventh grade. Consequently, the teachers decided not to worry about the apparent average performance and to wait and see how well the students performed after they had been introduced to the physical sciences in the seventh grade. By the end of the seventh grade, the students' scores on the science section of the achievement test had gone up markedly, which reinforced the school in its decision to maintain its new approach to teaching science.

GUIDANCE. It should be obvious that the results of standardized achievement tests are very helpful in dealing with students who have problems of one kind or another. In conjunction with course grades, achievement tests provide a measure of how well students have progressed in their schoolwork up to a particular point in time. Let us look at two problems in which the results of achievement tests would be helpful.

Scott Kendall is in trouble in the fourth grade. He is overactive and undisciplined. His teacher feels that Scott is actually learning very little, and she recommends to the guidance counselor that Scott be given remedial instruction. One of the first things the guidance counselor does is to look at Scott's scores obtained on comprehensive achievement tests in the first three grades. Surprisingly enough, he is well above the average of his classmates in all topics. Discussions with Scott's previous teachers show that he has always been hard to handle. However, Scott does not need remedial instruction. Even though he does not cooperate, and apparently does not study, he is managing to do rather well in school topics. The guidance counselor decides that, rather than provide remedial instruction, discussions will be held with Scott's parents in which suggestions will be made about providing some controls over Scott's obstreperous conduct.

The results of standardized testing are particularly useful for guidance at the high school level. Goslin (1967) reports that in high schools, the emphasis is generally on using test results for guidance in helping the individual student plan for his future career or schooling. Take the case of Bill Rogers, who is a high school student in Minneapolis. He graduates at the end of the school year, and he is considering applying for admission to the University of Minnesota. He is concerned because his high school grades are only average, and he wonders whether or not he has what it takes to perform well in college. What Bill does not fully understand is that he is in an above-average high school in a very well-to-do neighborhood. The high school counselor shows Bill that in comparison with students across the country, he stands at the 90th percentile on a previously administered achievement test. The counselor makes an even more important comparison for Bill. He shows Bill a table in which the grade averages of students at the University of Minnesota are compared with the achievement test scores which they made earlier in high school. This comparison makes it easy for Bill to see that he has the potential for performing very well at the university. Obviously, if the achievement test scores had not been available and if Bill had made his decision on the basis of grades alone, he might have been discouraged from going to the university.

EVALUATION OF INSTRUCTION.   Some teachers are leery of achievement tests because they view them as tests of teaching ability. For example, if it is found that students do poorly on an achievement test in biology compared with students in neighboring schools, this suggests that the biology teacher is not doing a very good job. For a number of reasons, it is doubtful that school administrators should systematically use the results of achievement tests to evaluate individual teachers.

Obviously, the threat of "exposure" can be quite frightening to teachers and can lead to poor educational practices. If a high premium is placed on the results of achievement tests, teachers are prone to emphasize in their instruction those skills and kinds of knowledge measured by the tests. This tends to prevent teachers from spending time on matters not directly represented in the tests, reduce the teacher's interest in promoting character and good attitudes toward learning, and make teachers reluctant to experiment with promising new approaches to instruction.

Even if it were not for the poor attitudes engendered by the practice, the use of achievement tests to evaluate teachers often is on shaky ground. How well a class performs is directly related to the aptitude of the students. In some schools most of the students score *above average* in comparison to national norms. In other schools most of the students score *below average*. Obviously, the teacher cannot be given the credit, or suffer the blame, for the initial levels of aptitude of his students.

Achievement tests measure not only how much students have learned in a particular school year but also how much they have learned in all their prior schooling. Consequently, teachers are not solely responsible for the scores their students make in any one year. For example, if the third-grade teacher gives very poor instruction in number skills, this will carry over to the fourth grade and be evidenced to some extent on an achievement test administered at the end of the year.

After the factors discussed above have been considered, it cannot be denied that the individual teacher plays an important part in determining how well his students do on achievement tests. Although it is not recommended that achievement tests generally be used by school administrators to evaluate teachers, it is very helpful for teachers to know how well their students perform. In fact, the full value of administering standardized achievement tests will not be realized unless teachers feel free to take an objective look at the results, rather than feeling the need to defend themselves and their methods. A nonthreatening attitude on the part of the school administration is most constructive toward this end, allowing teachers to use the results from achievement tests, but not to be threatened by them or made to tailor their instruction entirely to what the tests measure. For example, it would help a teacher to know that his students perform relatively much better in reading than in grammatical usage. The teacher may have purposefully deemphasized the learning of grammatical usage and, perhaps for a good reason, may decide to continue that practice in the future. However, teachers should be fully aware of their relative emphases and should either continue their present practices or make changes on a rational rather than a hit-or-miss basis. If the threat is removed, achievement test results provide teachers with valuable information for judging their over-all and differential effects on students and for planning their instruction with future classes.

RESEARCH.   Much educational research would be all but impossible to conduct without the availability of standardized achievement tests. This is so both for the informal research that whole schools and individual teachers conduct on their educational practices and for the more formal research undertaken by psychologists and educational research specialists. Two examples will suffice to illustrate such uses.

In a particular school district, parents are alarmed by the apparently poor caliber of the schools. A movement is started to provide more money for the schools, to obtain better school administrators, and to upgrade the caliber of the teachers. Numerous steps are taken to improve the schools. Several years later everyone wonders whether or not the measures have worked. How can the question be answered? At first thought, one might study the grades of students before and after the change, but it would be misleading to do that. Because of tightening up of standards, many individual students, and students on the average, may be receiving *poorer* grades after the change than before. Only by the use of standardized achievement tests can it be told whether or not the changes have worked. If, in comparison to national norms, students as a group stand higher after the changes than before, there is good reason to believe that the changes have been beneficial.

In a more formal investigation, psychologists are studying the effectiveness of a new approach to teaching mathematics to fifth-grade children. The new approach minimizes rote memorization of mathematical procedures and, instead, relies heavily on imparting some of the central "ideas" required to understand mathematics. The new approach is tried in ten schools. Some sections of the fifth grade in each school use the new method, and others employ traditional methods. Now it most be determined whether or not the new method is actually an improvement. This could not be determined by comparing the teacher-made tests and term grades in the two types of instruction, because the two types of instruction have been concerned with largely different material. The only sensible way to make the comparison is with a standardized achievement test, either one that is regularly employed in schools or one that is specifically designed for the research project.

SUMMARY

The use of standardized achievement tests has become so commonplace in elementary and secondary schools that we seldom stop to consider what their properties are and why they are used. Standardized achievement tests share a number of properties with teacher-made tests. Principally, both are concerned with school-learned concepts and skills, and both depend on content representativeness for validity. Standardized achievement tests tend to differ from most teacher-made tests in that (1) their content coverage is broader and less detailed with respect to some aspects of subject matter, (2) they are intended to measure over-all progress in school rather than progress only in particular units of instruction or only in particular subjects, and (3) they usually are much more carefully constructed and standardized than is possible for most teacher-made tests.

The construction of a new achievement test is a large-scale undertaking, which may require several years and consume many thousands of dollars. Some of the major steps that must be taken are (1) consultation with teachers and subject-matter specialists to determine the goals of the instrument, (2) composition of a detailed outline of the content to be included, (3) writing and rewriting of hundreds of test items, (4) large-scale tryout and statistical analysis of items, (5) construction of final forms, (6) administration of tests to thousands of students to obtain norms, and finally (7) composition of testing manuals.

Rather than being competitive with each other, teacher-made tests and comprehensive achievement tests have their special advantages in shaping educational decisions, and they share in the making of some kinds of decisions. Teacher-made tests are usually better for (1) determining how well students perform in particular units of instruction, e.g., trigonometry, (2) determining course grades, (3) structuring day-to-day activity in the classroom, and (4) determining how well local objectives are being met in the instruction. Achievement tests have an advantage in making certain types of comparisons, such as (1) comparisons of students' progress from year to year, (2) comparisons of performance in different schools and in different localities, (3) comparisons of students' performance with that of students across the country, and (4) the comparisons that are required in educational research. Teacher-made tests and standardized achievement tests share in the making of many types of educational decisions, particularly those regarding grade placement, grouping for instruction, planning daily instruction, and handling any type of problem student.

SUGGESTED ADDITIONAL READINGS

American Educational Research Association and National Council on Measurements Used in Education, Committee on Test Standards. *Technical recommendations for achievement tests.* Washington: National Education Association, 1955.

Bean, K. L. *Construction of educational and personnel tests.* New York: McGraw-Hill, 1953.

Goslin, D. A. *Teachers and testing.* New York: Russell Sage, 1967.

Thorndike, R. L., and Hagen, E. *Measurement and evaluation in psychology and education.* (3rd ed.) New York: Wiley, 1969, chap. 9.

Wood, D. A. *Test construction.* Columbus, Ohio: Merrill, 1960.

chapter 9

COMPREHENSIVE ACHIEVEMENT TESTS

Comprehensive achievement tests are the mainstay of school-wide testing programs. They provide the best evidence available regarding the over-all educational progress of students up to particular points in time. Their results are sufficiently valuable that if the school can afford it, comprehensive achievement tests should be administered each year to all students.

The comprehensive achievement tests of today are far better than their predecessors of thirty or more years ago. Earlier tests tended to be narrow in content, emphasized primarily rote memory and simple skills, and were standardized as the result of only meager research. Some of today's tests represent mammoth undertakings, and they go a long way toward measuring the truly important goals of education. In this chapter we shall look at the typical content of comprehensive tests, see examples of different kinds of tests employed at different grade levels, and discuss some general principles for the effective use of the instruments.

CONTENT OF COMPREHENSIVE TESTS

Comprehensive achievement tests differ from grade level to grade level principally in terms of (1) the broadness of their coverage and (2) the level of understanding which they measure. Regarding the former, comprehensive tests tend to incorporate an increasingly wider range of content as one goes from tests appropriate to the primary grades to those appropriate to the last two years of high school. The increasing breadth of subject matter covered is illustrated in Table 9-1, which shows the number and kinds of subtests employed in the Metropolitan Achievement Tests (Durost, 1960) at different grade levels. Whereas only four kinds of content are included in the primary I test, thirteen kinds of content are included in the advanced test. The progressive broadening of content in comprehensive tests is intended to keep pace with the actual scope of classroom

Table 9-1   Content of Metropolitan Achievement Tests

Subtests	Grade Level				
	Primary I (First Grade)	Primary II (Second Grade)	Elementary (3–4)	Intermediate (5–6)	Advanced (7–9)
Word knowledge	x	x	x	x	x
Word discrimination	x	x	x		
Reading	x	x	x	x	x
Arithmetic:					
Concepts and skills	x	x			
Problem solving			x	x	x
Computation			x	x	x
Spelling		x	x	x	x
Language:					
Usage			x	x	x
Punctuation and cap.			x	x	x
Parts of speech and grammar				x	x
Kinds of sentences					x
Language study skills				x	x
Social studies information				x	x
Social studies study skills				x	x
Science				x	x

instruction. Admittedly, during the first several primary grades the content is largely restricted to reading and simple arithmetic skills. In contrast, by the end of high school, students have studied so many different topics that a truly comprehensive test must be very long (often requiring over six hours to administer) and must contain many different types of content.

At numerous places so far in this book, the point has been made that achievement tests depend upon content validity, which requires essentially that the content and the method of testing the content meet with the approval of educational researchers, subject-matter experts, classroom teachers, and other persons who participate in establishing goals of instruction. The broadening range of content at higher grade levels is commensurate with the requirements for content validity of achievement tests. At the primary level, the goals of instruction focus on the basic skills and are considerably narrower with respect to content coverage than they are in later grades.

In varying degrees, today's tests tend to stress *understanding* rather than rote memorization only. Items depending upon rote memory alone would have to do with such things as remembering the date of the signing of the Declaration of Independence, remembering that 4 times 8 is 32, and remembering how to spell the word "business." In Chapter 5 six levels of understanding were discussed, ranging from a knowledge of simple facts, on the lower end, to the creative use of principles relating to subject matters, on the higher end. In that connection, a student might memorize Newton's laws of motion without really understanding them in any broad way. He would evidence a higher level of understanding, for example, by using the laws to explain natural events, e.g., why satellites remain in orbit. It is important to measure goals of instruction at all levels of understanding. However, the major commercially distributed achievement test batteries vary to some extent in terms of the level of understanding at which most of the test materials are aimed.

Although rote memorization is not the major goal of the educational process, at even the highest levels of education some definitions and facts must be memorized before understanding is possible. This is particularly true in the primary grades, where so much simple material must be mastered. For this reason, comprehensive achievement tests for the primary grades tend to contain a considerable amount of simple rules and facts relating to reading, language, and arithmetic. After the primary grades, broader understanding becomes increasingly important up through high school and beyond.

At all levels, it is important for comprehensive achievement tests to employ a balance of material concerning different levels of knowledge. First, some comprehension of simple facts, definitions, and rules is important at all levels. Second, understanding of restricted generalizations is important in each subject matter, e.g., biology or civics. That is, if students have mastered particular topics, they should be able to successfully employ related principles, e.g., as mentioned previously, to reason why satellites remain in orbit. Third, at the higher levels of understanding, students should learn to see relations between diverse events and give critical reactions to arguments.

Of course, it is relatively easy to test for rote memory and for simple levels of understanding, but it is a real challenge to measure higher levels of understanding effectively. Examples were given previously of how various types of understanding can be measured, and some of the available comprehensive achievement tests do an admirable job in that respect.

As an example from one test concerning the understanding of literature, the student is provided with a segment from a play and is asked to respond to items concerning inferences about events that occurred prior to the scene, intentions of the actors, and purposes of the author in the casting of characters. As another example, the understanding of the scientific method of inquiry is tested with items which present an everyday occurrence or observation and require the student to select which deductions may reasonably be made or which approach to use in finding the answer to the problem. As a third example, to test the understanding of numerical concepts, the student is presented with the number 348 and is asked, "What does the 3 stand for?" Other types of items for measuring various levels of understanding will be illustrated in the following sections.

WORD KNOWLEDGE.   Most of the comprehensive achievement tests have a subtest concerning the meaning of words. Of course, a knowledge of individual words is a prerequisite to all learning, and it is one of the essential things to measure at each grade level. Word knowledge is relatively easy to measure with objective test items, there being many different types of items to use. Most widely used is the straightforward, multiple-choice definitional form:

Ample means most nearly the same as
a.   scarce   c.   sufficient
b.   holy   d.   lovable

Also frequently used is the "opposites" form:

Ample means the opposite of
a.   meager   c.   kind
b.   hard   d.   full

For the primary grades, items frequently employ pictures:

a.   horse   c.   rabbit
b.   cow   d.   cat

Some tests combine word knowledge with reading comprehension and provide one over-all score for the two. It is probably wiser to score the two separately. Some students who know the meanings of individual words have difficulty in determining the meaning of whole sentences and paragraphs. Also, some students manage to get the gist of connected discourse, but fail to understand the meanings of some of the individual words.

READING COMPREHENSION. All the comprehensive tests employ basically the same type of item for the measurement of reading. Students are presented with connected passages, varying in length from 12 to 500 or more words. The material is either an excerpt from a story or a description of some event. After reading the material, the student is asked questions about what was read. An example from a first-grade test (Metropolitan Achievement Test) is as follows:

> I can fly.   *a.*   a girl
> I can sing.   *b.*   a bird
> I have a nest.   *c.*   a dog
> Who am I?

A more advanced paragraph (Metropolitan Achievement Test) is as follows:

> Frank has a good hobby. He collects stamps. He has stamps from many different places. Of course, he has many United States stamps. He saves them from letters he gets from his Aunt Carrie in Texas and his Cousin Jack in Ohio. But Frank also has stamps from foreign countries.
>
> Frank's Aunt Carrie lives in
> *a.*   Ohio   *c.*   New York
> *b.*   Africa   *d.*   Texas
>
> In this story, the word *saves* means
> *a.*   rescues   *c.*   keeps
> *b.*   protects   *d.*   prevents

The items on reading comprehension tests vary from those requiring the comprehension of simple facts to those requiring inferences and critical reactions. An example of a paragraph which tests for a higher degree of comprehension is as follows:

> For several months Mr. Williams has heard a strange noise in his automobile. One day he takes it to a repair shop. The repairman inspects the engine and says that a small part must be replaced. The repairman says that he is not sure

when he will find time to make the repairs. Because Mr. Williams will not need the automobile for several days, he leaves it with the repairman. Two days later he returns and finds that the automobile has not yet been repaired. The repairman says, "I will fix it for you now." Fifteen minutes later the work is completed. Then the repairman gives Mr. Williams a bill for $20; $5 is for the part replaced, and $15 is for installing the part. Mr. Williams is quite angry at the size of the bill, and he argues with the repairman that too much has been charged.

Mr. Williams is angry because
a.   the repairman waited two days before making the repairs
b.   the repairman is rude
c.   the work is poorly done
d.   too much is charged for installing the part

Mr. Williams can avoid such arguments in the future by
a.   asking in advance how much repairs will cost
b.   driving his automobile more carefully to prevent breakdowns
c.   taking his automobile to a repair shop the minute that he hears a strange noise
d.   trying different repairmen until he finds one that he likes

LANGUAGE SKILLS. Most of the comprehensive achievement tests have sections dealing with language skills. The available tests vary somewhat in coverage, but generally they include material on spelling, punctuation, capitalization, case, and other elements of grammatical usage.

Spelling is tested in various ways. The teacher of children in the primary grades is usually provided with a list to read to them. The students write the words as the teacher pronounces them. Objective types of items are used to measure achievement in spelling in the higher grades. An example of a commonly used type of item follows:

Read each group of words. One word in each group may be misspelled, or there may be no mistakes in that group at all. When you find a mistake, mark the word that is misspelled. If there are no mistakes in spelling in a group of words, mark letter e.

a.   skate
b.   dead
c.   peaple
d.   ready
e.   no mistakes

Numerous objective-type item forms are also used to measure other aspects of language skills. Following are examples of items used to measure various facets of language skills.

Punctuation.   Following is a sample item from the Iowa Tests of Basic Skills.[1] The student is to look for mistakes in the test exercises. When he finds a mistake, he is to indicate on the answer sheet which line in the item contains the mistake.

1. Danny would like

2. very much, to ride

3. in a police car.

4. (No mistakes)

Capitalization.   The Stanford Achievement Test uses a procedure similar to the following for testing knowledge of capitalization rules. A selection is present in which all capitalization has been left out as well as all punctuation marks. The student is to indicate for each numbered word whether or not it should be capitalized. (The selection presented here is not actually from the Stanford test, but has been designed by the author to illustrate this type of test item.)

       1   2   3
becky and *john* are going on a *world* tour with their parents mr. and *mrs.* carr
            4   5   6   7
will be leaving in *june* and the *carr* children will join them later in *europe both*
                   8   9
children have been studying the *history* and geography of each *country* they
        10
will visit although *english* is spoken by many people in the countries they will
            11
visit particularly in the major cities such as *paris* and tokyo they still want to
       12   13
learn a little *french* japanese and spanish even if only to say *please* and thank
      14
you to the *natives* of each country

---

[1] Reproduced by permission of Houghton Mifflin Company.

Language usage. The following is a sample item from the Iowa Tests of Basic Skills,[2] and is designed to test whether or not students know how to use words properly in sentences. They are to mark the sentence which contains a mistake; if there is no mistake, they mark number 4.

1. We are ready to begin.
2. Our dog bit the mailman.
3. It ain't your turn.
4. (No mistakes)

The Stanford Achievement Test,[3] on the other hand, tests language usage in a different way, as the following sample item illustrates:

Joe $\begin{array}{l}1 \text{ set} \\ 2 \text{ sat}\end{array}$ in the chair.

The student also has the option of indicating whether or not he thinks neither choice is correct, as would be the case with the next sample item.

Sally $\begin{array}{l}1 \text{ ain't} \\ 2 \text{ aren't}\end{array}$ here.

Objective test items do a very good job of measuring most aspects of language skills. For example, objective tests of punctuation and spelling correlate highly with essay tests of the same skills. Where the available comprehensive achievement tests fail to measure language skills is in the actual composition of written material. This illustrates what has been said several times previously: comprehensive achievement tests measure most, but not all, of the important skills and knowledge. Teachers must rely on their own exercises and tests to assess the ability to compose written material.

ARITHMETIC. All the comprehensive achievement tests have sections dealing with arithmetic. The tests differ from one another in their relative emphasis on computation, arithmetic reasoning, and arithmetic concepts. Examples of computational items are:

Add: 189   Subtract: 581
     264   289

[2]Reproduced by permission of Houghton Mifflin Company.
[3]Reproduced by permission of Harcourt, Brace & World.

$5\overline{)\;215}$ = a. 31   b. 41   c. 43   d. 4.1
2.5 × 8 = a. 28   b. 2   c. 14   d. 20

In arithmetic reasoning items students are required to reason out the solutions to problems:

Billy sells magazines in his neighborhood. He sells 14 each week, and he makes 5 cents on each. If he wants to earn $1 each week, how many *more* magazines must he sell?
a.   6   b.   14   c.   24   d.   3

The scale of a map reads that 1 inch equals 60 miles. How many inches long would be a line on the map to show a distance of 40 miles?
a.   ¾ in.   b.   ⅔ in.   c.   1½ in.   d.   ½ in.

Arithmetic concepts concern relations among arithmetic operations and relations between computational procedures and events in daily life. The following items illustrate the measurement of arithmetic concepts:

Which one of the following months comes before June?
a.   April   b.   August   c.   July   d.   November

Jack has saved 425 pennies. This equals:
a. $425   b.   4.25 cents   c. $42.50   d. $4.25

Which one of the following lines is closest to 1 inch?
a.   _____
b.   _____
c.   _____
d.   _____

Which number is closest to 400?
a.   399   b.   395   c.   420   d.   402

How many hours are there between eight o'clock in the morning and eight o'clock at night?
a.   8   b.   12   c.   10   d.   16

Numerator is a word used in
a.   addition   b.   subtraction   c.   multiplication   d.   division

Over the years the emphasis in achievement tests has shifted from computation to arithmetic reasoning and arithmetic concepts. Most teachers will agree that this is a healthy change. Computation is important, but not as important as understanding the meaning of arithmetic operations and knowing how to use arithmetic operations to solve problems. Some computation is required in most items concerning arithmetic reasoning and arithmetic concepts. To prevent these items from measuring only computational skills, the computations are kept simple. You will notice in the items above used to illustrate arithmetic reasoning and arithmetic concepts that some computations are required, but these are very simple computations. More complex computations should be reserved for those items specifically intended to measure computational skills.

One caution that must be observed in constructing arithmetic items is that only very simple words and sentences should be used to state problems. Otherwise, as often happens, the test concerns reading skills and vocabulary more than the understanding of arithmetic.

STUDY SKILLS. It has often been said that one of the major purposes of formal schooling is to teach people how to learn on their own. In the classroom much time is spent in developing study skills. Students learn where to find information in reference sources, how to interpret charts and maps, and many other study skills. Because of the growing realization that study skills are important aspects of classroom learning, most of the comprehensive achievement tests now include related sections. Either the items are interspersed in subtests dealing with content areas, such as social studies and science, or they are made into separate subtests.

In a typical item relating to study skills, the test shows a graph depicting the amount of rainfall in a half-dozen cities. Multiple-choice questions are posed such as "Which city had the greatest average rainfall?" "Which city had the lowest average rainfall?" and "What was the average rainfall of Chicago?" In another item, a road map is shown which covers parts of four counties. Multiple-choice questions are posed such as "The most mountainous road is _____," "Newton and Clancy are joined by _____," and "The largest town on the map is _____." Another type of exercise might involve requiring the student to organize the most important items from a paragraph into an outline.

Typical items concerning where to find information and how to interpret reference sources are:

Where would the part played by the United States Marines in the Second World War be located?
a. information almanac
b. history book
c. dictionary
d. atlas

A dictionary would indicate the accented syllable in *primary* as:

a. pri′ma·ry
b. *pri* ma·ry
c. PRI ma·ry
d. pri*ma·ry

CONTENT AREAS.   Word knowledge, reading comprehension, language skills, arithmetic, and study skills are the core topics in elementary schools and, to a large extent, throughout all higher levels of education. Of course, in addition to the core topics, students study other subjects, including history, geography, biology, physics, and many others. These are referred to as *content areas.* Should the content areas be represented on comprehensive achievement tests? The question is difficult to answer at the present time, which is evidenced by the fact that about half of the available tests do include sections relating to content areas, and half do not.

Good arguments can be made both for and against the inclusion of such materials. The most obvious argument for including content areas is that achievement tests are then more representative of the total school curriculum. There are two good negative arguments. The first is that content areas are secondary to the core topics, i.e., reading comprehension and arithmetic reasoning, and that it would be an imprudent use of space in achievement tests to include them. This argument holds with particular force during the first four or five grades of elementary school. In rebuttal to this, it can be said that whereas the core topics are admittedly the most important parts of education, the content areas are also important. The second negative argument is a practical one. Because of the diversity of material included in the content areas and because of the different coverages in different schools, it is difficult to construct truly representative measures of these topics. It is hard to disclaim this argument entirely. For example, in former years most comprehensive tests included sections on literature; but it was found that reading materials varied so much from locality to locality that it was almost impossible to assemble a representative collection of test items. A compromise is to include material relating to those content areas that are covered in most schools. For example, it is rather universal to teach American history, elementary facts of human biology, the essentials of astronomy, and some simple physical principles. These can be made the basis of subtests for content areas.

The inclusion of material relating to content areas in comprehensive achievement tests varies with the grade level. During the first four grades of elementary school, the overriding emphasis is on the core topics, and not enough content areas are covered to justify their inclusion on achievement tests. Beginning with about the fifth grade, more attention is given to the content areas, and some of the achievement tests for that level, and higher levels, have subtests covering them. From the ninth to the twelfth grades, the curriculum is highly oriented toward content areas, so much so that it is difficult for comprehensive tests to provide a sufficiently broad coverage. At these levels, comprehensive tests can be augmented by tests for special topics, e.g., natural science. Tests for special topics will be discussed in Chapter 10. For thumbnail descriptions of many of the achievement test batteries available commercially, the reader is referred to Appendix D. The purpose of the chapters concerning standardized tests is not to provide a catalogue of available tests, but rather to convey general principles regarding educational measurement. When there is a concrete problem in the selection of achievement tests, the relevant section of Appendix D should be consulted. Sources of information which give more detailed discussions of the tests listed in Appendix D will be described in Chapter 17.

Those tests which include content areas group the items into two broad categories: social studies and science. The social studies tests are usually comprised of material from history, civics, and geography. Typical items for a social studies test for the fifth and sixth grades are illustrated by the following, from the Stanford Achievement Test, Intermediate II Battery:[4]

Money to pay the cost of a new public school comes from:
1. dues
2. taxes
3. stamps
4. mints

People who live on an American desert and have no irrigation probably will raise:
1. corn
2. sheep
3. fresh vegetables
4. cotton

What did the New England farmer in colonial times do with most of his farm products?
1. sent them to England
2. used them to feed his family
3. sold them for cash
4. fed them to animals

[4]Reproduced by permission of Harcourt Brace Jovanovich.

Content subtests for science typically contain a mixture of items from chemistry, physics, biology, botany, and astronomy. Typical items for the high school level are illustrated by the following, from the Tests of Academic Progress[5] for grades 9 to 12:

Space ships taking off from Earth must travel at great speeds to overcome:
1. air resistance
2. the pull of Earth's gravity
3. Earth's magnetic field
4. the electrical field in space

Which of the following is *not* a part of the central nervous system:
1. Cerebrum
2. Cerebellum
3. Spinal cord
4. Autonomic ganglion

Which tissue conducts water from plant roots to the stems and leaves:
1. Cortex
2. Xylem
3. Cambium
4. Phloem

Because the difficulty of selecting commercial achievement tests for content areas which meet the instructional goals of particular school systems, it is sometimes better for a school system to construct and standardize special tests on the content areas at the local level. If the local schools feel strongly that it is important to test content areas such as literature, social studies, or Spanish in a school-wide testing program, then they may select a test-construction committee to study the local objectives and teaching materials in depth. This committee would then go about constructing and trying out test items. The test would be standardized in much the same way that commercial tests are standardized, and local norms would be collected. The resulting tests covering content areas would then be much more useful in measuring local student progress and evaluating local curricula than commercial tests on the same areas that did not truly match local objectives or curricula.

Although, in principle, locally constructed achievement tests could be more appropriate in measuring progress in content areas than nationally standardized tests, that potential advantage is seldom realized in practice. That is because many school systems do not have experts in test construc-

[5]Reproduced by permission of Houghton Mifflin Company.

tion and/or sufficient funds for the project. Consequently, by far the most frequent practice is to select from among the available commercially distributed instruments for measuring progress in content areas.

PRINCIPLES FOR USING COMPREHENSIVE ACHIEVEMENT TESTS

Most of the important principles for using achievement tests were discussed in the previous chapter; however, a few special points need to be considered. These are discussed in the following sections.

WHEN TO ADMINISTER.   There are two important questions to be considered here. The first is how frequently achievement tests should be administered during the elementary and high school years. If a school can afford the time and expense, it would be worthwhile to administer comprehensive tests every year from the first grade through high school. If it were possible to use achievement tests at only one point between the first grade and the senior year of high school, the best point probably would be at the end of the fourth grade. By that time, the student has enough schooling behind him so that achievement tests give a good representation of school performance. Also, at that point, most of the student's formal schooling is ahead of him, and there is ample time to make corrective changes. If achievement tests could be administered at only three points during a student's schooling, the best times would probably be in the second, fourth, and sixth grades. Some school systems employ comprehensive achievement tests only for the elementary grades. With some logic, they argue that the diversity of topics studied in high school is not given sufficient coverage on comprehensive achievement tests and that there is little point in giving the tests at the high school level because by that time much of the good or bad has already been done. The author reiterates his stand that if the school can afford it, it is wise to give comprehensive achievement tests every year.

Much of the value of standardized comprehensive achievement tests is lost to the school, as well as to the student, if such tests are administered routinely only to one or two grades each year. If tests are administered only at the beginning of the fourth grade, for example, then only the fourth-grade teachers derive benefit from the item-analysis data and from use of the scores for the purposes of grouping for instruction or planning remedial work. In addition, the extent to which test results can be used for systematic analysis of student progress in meeting local objectives is also severely limited. In fact, it might well be said that the less often a school system employs standardized comprehensive achievement tests, the more limited is the actual usefulness of the test results.

The second question to answer is that of the time of year in which achievement tests should be administered. In answering this question, one thing is sure: a test should be administered at the time stipulated in the test manual for the particular test. If the manual says that the test is to be administered in the month of May, it should be administered at that time. Otherwise, the test norms will not apply to the particular group of students. If students have several more months of schooling than those on whom the test was standardized, they will appear to perform better than their actual abilities warrant.

Still left unanswered is the question of the best time of year for administering achievement tests. One school of thought says that achievement tests should be administered at the beginning of the school year, and the other school of thought says that they should be administered at the end of the school year. There are good arguments for both points of view. The major argument for administering the tests at the beginning of the school year is that this supplies the teacher with up-to-date information about the strong and weak points of each student. The major argument for administering tests at the end of the school year is that this supplies information needed for decisions about sectioning of students at the beginning of the fall term. Because of the increasing use of summer school for both good and poor students, achievement tests administered near the end of the school year provide valuable information for structuring activities in the summer.

From the foregoing discussion, it can be seen that it is largely a toss-up as to whether it is generally better to administer comprehensive achievement tests at the beginning or the end of the school year. There is a slight advantage for one rather than the other approach, depending upon the major uses made of such tests in particular school settings. If the major uses of the test are in terms of grouping students for instruction, providing special instruction to particular students, and in general setting the tone of instruction, there is a slight advantage to having tests administered at the beginning of the school year. The test results are somewhat more representative of students' actual standings at that time than test results obtained before the start of summer vacation. If, instead, comprehensive achievement tests are being used largely for research on pedagogical practices or curriculum evaluation, there would obviously be a slight advantage to administering tests at the end of the school year. In both cases, the advantage lies in testing very close to the time at which assessments are to be made of students, rather than several months earlier or several months later. In sum, then, whether to test at the beginning or the end of the school year depends mainly upon local considerations rather than on general principles of testing. However, the person who has to make such decisions in the local setting can be comforted by the fact that results typically are not very different when obtained by either of the two approaches.

HOW TO ADMINISTER ACHIEVEMENT TESTS. When comprehensive achievement tests were new, it was the custom to have them administered by an "expert," e.g., a school psychologist. Now that achievement tests are used so widely and so frequently, the practice has changed to having teachers administer achievement tests to their own students. Goslin (1967) reports that 73.6 per cent of public elementary school teachers and 23.5 per cent of public secondary school teachers in his survey were routinely responsible for administering standardized achievement tests. (The lower percentage for high school teachers undoubtedly reflects the fact that not only are fewer comprehensive achievement tests routinely given in high schools, but also secondary school guidance counselors are more often available to administer group tests.) The testing procedures for most of the widely used achievement tests are simplified to the point where any conscientious teacher can adequately administer them. Test manuals are usually quite explicit about how to administer the instruments. For example, in the teacher's manual for the Iowa Tests of Basic Skills, detailed instructions are presented on the questions of seating arrangements, use of pencils for the test, time schedules, distributing and collecting the test materials, preparing the pupils for the test, and the manner in which the various types of answer sheets are to be marked. Explicit instructions to be read to the students at each step in the testing procedure are also provided. Of course, teachers should follow instructions to the letter and not deviate from the standard procedures. To the extent that teachers in any way give their students advantages (or disadvantages) in using the tests, they destroy the standardized testing situation and, thus, the effectiveness of the instruments.

SELECTION OF ACHIEVEMENT TESTS. Although comprehensive achievement tests tend to differ from one another in ways described earlier in the chapter, in one sense they are all alike: all the major, commercially distributed tests are carefully constructed and standardized. The one dimension on which they vary importantly is on the extent to which they measure general educational development rather than mastery of special topics. Some of the tests (particularly the STEP) employ many items that do not relate directly to any particular topics, but rather they concern the extent to which students can deal effectively with concepts. There are very good arguments for employing materials of these kinds, because, to a large extent, the over-all goal of education is to produce the thinking, reasoning man. On the other hand, there is need to know how well students have mastered particular topics such as grammatical usage, history, and geography. It would be easy to advise that both types of instruments be used, but schools are already fully burdened with the cost and time required to use achievement tests.

Actually, concept-oriented and topic-oriented tests are probably not so different as they appear on the surface. Although the author knows of no study to support his claim, it is probably so that the two types of measures would correlate .80 or higher. However, the small difference is important. It may be that concept-oriented achievement tests are somewhat better for predicting success in future schooling and for success outside of school. Also, they may provide useful information about how well the over-all goals of instruction are being met. However, for most of the uses of achievement tests discussed in the previous chapter, conventional, topic-oriented achievement tests probably are best.

Some factors to consider in selecting an achievement test battery from among the many fine ones commercially available are (1) over-all validity; (2) ease of administration, scoring, and interpretation; and (3) economy. In an attempt to objectify the test-selection procedure, a number of writers have suggested systems for weighting the various factors and selecting a test on the basis of the number of points it accrues. Such schemes generally are not only unworkable but also undesirable, since they fail to take into account the individual circumstances of the schools in which the test is to be employed. Factors which usually would not be highly important might be decisive for some schools.

The validity of the test with regard to local objectives of instruction is certainly the most important point to consider, for unless a test is valid for the purpose for which it is intended, there is no point in considering any of the other factors. However, even if a test is valid, if it is not sufficiently easy to administer and interpret, then it probably will have to be rejected. Although some orientation sessions for teachers conducted by various types of experts (e.g., school psychologists) are frequently feasible, it is not practicable to give extensive training in the fine points of administering tests under standardized conditions to all the teachers who would be involved in a school-wide testing program. Instead, the teacher's manual must be quite explicit and straightforward with respect to the details of administering the instrument and scoring test forms if they are scored in the school. Economy might be an unusually important factor if a school has a severely limited budget for testing, and thus the cost of the testing program will have more weight than it might in another school.

Following is an outline of questions which must be considered in selecting an achievement test battery. The answers to these questions for any particular test may best be obtained by referring to a specimen set of the test itself. (Specimen sets are available at a small cost from the publisher of the test. They generally consist of a copy of the test; the different answer sheets which may be used; a copy of the manual for administration, scoring, and interpretation; a technical manual; and any additional materials, such as a class record sheet.) In Chapter 17 additional sources of information for evaluating the usefulness of commercially available tests of all kinds will be discussed. Some of the following questions can be answered by referring to these sources; however, the test itself should also be carefully studied before selecting a comprehensive measure of achievement.

1.   Validity
    a.   How does the content of the test relate to local curricula and objectives of instruction?
    b.   In constructing the test, were ample precautions taken to ensure representativeness of content and/or skills?
2.   Ease of administration
    a.   Are the instructions for administration spelled out clearly?
    b.   Are there gaps in instructions where unreliability could creep in as a result of variations in test administration?
    c.   Are procedures for timing the different parts of the test realistic and clearly noted?
    d.   Are there instructions for handling testing problems which may arise, such as students who are absent on testing day or students who must be retested for some reason?
3.   Ease of scoring
    a.   What options for scoring the test are available?
    b.   Is there a scoring service? If so, what test results are provided routinely, and what additional information may be requested, e.g., item-analysis data?
    c.   Are instructions for hand scoring adequate and easy to follow?
4.   Ease of interpretation
    a.   What norms are provided?
    b.   Are norms billed as "national" truly representative; i.e., were proper sampling procedures followed?
    c.   Are the norms which are provided suitable for the local purposes of testing?
    d.   Does the teacher's manual contain adequate information for interpreting test results correctly, or does the manual assume too high a level of statistical sophistication?

  e. Are aids provided for interpreting scores to parents and students?

  f. Is enough information provided for making the maximum use of all the test results and additional data which may be obtained?

5. Reliability

  a. Is equivalent-form reliability at least above .80, and preferably above .90?

  b. Are test-retest or internal-consistency reliability coefficients reported? Are they generally above .80?

  c. If interpretations are to be made of subtest or part scores, are they generally reliable?

6. Economy

  a. What is the test cost per pupil?

  b. May test booklets be reused? How durable are they?

  c. What is the cost of the scoring services which are desired?

In selecting a test battery for use at more than one grade level, it is wise to examine carefully the test content and technical data for each level, rather than relying upon only one level to tell the story for all grade levels. The final choice of an achievement test battery rests on the composite picture formed after one has considered carefully all the available information about the test and the situation in which it is to be used.

SUMMARY

The purpose of comprehensive achievement tests is to measure the over-all progress of students in school up to a particular point in time. Many of the items on comprehensive achievement tests look much like those that the teacher employs for his own examinations. The two types of tests differ mainly in that (1) comprehensive achievement tests are more concerned with over-all progress, whereas teacher-made tests are more concerned with progress in particular areas of study over relatively short periods of time; (2) large-scale norms are available on achievement tests that permit the comparison of individual students with students across the country; and (3) comprehensive achievement tests are constructed with much more care than is possible for most teacher-made tests.

Corresponding to the increasing complexity of what is taught, the content of comprehensive achievement tests grows more complex in moving from the primary grades up through high school. At the primary level, the major emphasis is on reading comprehension and simple arithmetic skills. At succeeding levels, a broader array of arithmetic content is included, and materials are incorporated to measure language skills and study skills. Beginning at about the fifth-grade level, some of the tests incorporate material relating to content areas. Typically this material is incorporated in two sections respectively concerning science and social studies.

Only about eight comprehensive achievement tests are widely employed in American schools. The major difference among them is that some employ items relating to content areas and others restrict themselves to the core topics and skills. As was described in the chapter, there are good arguments both for and against the inclusion of material relating to content areas. Aside from this major difference, the tests are distinguished from one another by minor differences in content and types of items employed. All the available commercially distributed instruments are excellent, and it is difficult to choose among them.

SUGGESTED ADDITIONAL READINGS

American Educational Research Association and National Council on Measurements Used in Education, Committee on Test Standards. *Technical recommendations for achievement tests.* Washington: National Education Association, 1955.

Anastasi, A. *Psychological testing.* (3rd ed.) New York: Macmillan, 1968, chap. 15.

Noll, V. H. *Introduction to educational measurement.* (2nd ed.) Boston: Houghton Mifflin, 1965, chaps. 8, 9.

Thorndike, R. L., and Hagen, E. *Measurement and evaluation in psychology and education.* (3rd ed.) New York: Wiley, 1969, chap. 9.

chapter 10

ACHIEVEMENT TESTS FOR SPECIAL TOPICS

The previous chapter discussed comprehensive achievement test batteries which are intended to survey broadly accomplishment in school at various levels of education, going from the primary grades up through high school. It was said that for most purposes, it is preferable to employ a comprehensive battery rather than a hodgepodge of tests for separate topics, such as reading, mathematics, social studies, science, and others. There are some instances, however, in which achievement tests for special topics provide important additional information, besides that derived from such survey batteries of achievement tests. Such tests for special topics and their uses will be discussed in this chapter.

Previously, a distinction was made between two kinds of tests for special topics: *survey* tests and *diagnostic* tests. The purpose of the survey test is to tell *how much* the student knows about a particular topic; the purpose of the diagnostic test is to provide some insights into the student's work habits and the special faults in his approach to a topic. In practice, it is difficult to draw fine distinctions between the two or neatly to categorize some instruments as survey tests and others as diagnostic tests. Any test that divides the content into a number of parts provides some diagnostic information. Also, because of the appealing sound of the word, many tests are labeled "diagnostic" that really supply little diagnostic information. Actually, the extent to which a test provides an over-all indication of a student's standing (such as in reading ability) or diagnostic information (such as a profile concerning strengths and weaknesses in various abilities relating to reading) is a matter of degree. At one extreme are the subtests for special topics in comprehensive achievement batteries which yield a single score for performance in each topic, e.g., mathematics. At the other extreme lie the individually administered tests for special topics which provide an opportunity for the teacher to document a student's strengths and weaknesses within topics, such as reading and arithmetic. These individually administered tests more truly earn the name "diagnostic" than the subtests for special topics that appear on comprehensive achievement test batteries. In between the two extremes are some of the group-administered tests for special topics. Although they are administered to a group of students as a whole and can be machine-scored, they do provide considerable diagnostic information about different strengths and weaknesses in relation to particular subject matters.

Group tests for special topics are not different in principle from the subtests on comprehensive measures of achievement. For example, a group test for reading will contain much the same types of materials included in the reading subtest of a comprehensive measure. The major difference is that group tests for special topics usually cover the area in more detail than would be possible in comprehensive measures. For example, an achievement test only for reading skills would contain more items and cover more aspects of reading than would be possible in comprehensive tests, which must cover several different topics. A second difference is that many of the tests for special topics, particularly those for the high school levels, measure achievement in special areas that are either not covered at all or only lightly covered in comprehensive measures. This is the case for tests in special areas like economics, trigonometry, chemistry, and physics.

In a sense, some tests for special topics are competitive with comprehensive tests. That is, rather than use a comprehensive achievement test at the fourth-grade level, separate tests could be employed for reading, arithmetic, language skills, and others. Unless there is some good reason for employing tests for special topics, a hodgepodge of separate tests should not be substituted for a comprehensive measure. Much to the credit of the comprehensive batteries is the fact that all subtests are constructed according to the same general principles, and they are all standardized on the same students. Consequently, it is much safer to make comparisons among the scores on different subtests of the same comprehensive measure than it would be to make comparisons among different tests for special topics, e.g., tests for reading and arithmetic constructed by different test publishers.

In some situations there are good reasons for employing achievement tests for special topics. One is to obtain more detailed information about a child who does poorly on a particular subtest of a comprehensive measure. For example, if a child does poorly on the reading subtest of one of the comprehensive achievement tests, some additional information might be obtained by administering one of the special tests for reading. Another good reason for employing tests for special topics is to measure achievement in those special areas of study in high school that are not well covered on comprehensive measures. For example, if a school wants to know how well students are performing in chemistry, rather than just in science generally, it would be necessary to employ a special test for chemistry. Such special tests also are useful for counseling students who plan higher education. For example, if a student is planning to study engineering in college, it would be very helpful to know how well the student performs on special tests for mathematics, physics, and chemistry. Other combinations of special tests would be useful for advising students on their future courses of study.

Group tests for special topics are also very useful in educational research, for example, in a program of research on new methods of teaching reading. In such a case, it would be important to determine not only the over-all progress in the topic but also progress in relation to separate skills, such as word recognition, reading comprehension, reading speed, and other aspects of reading ability. For such investigations, group tests for special topics are frequently preferable to the survey-type reading subtests that are included with comprehensive achievement test batteries.

Many different kinds of special tests are commercially distributed. To give some idea of the range of tests available, one can find tests of achievement in Hebrew, trigonometry, agriculture, handwriting, industrial arts, and driver education. (Sources for these and other achievement tests will be cited in Chapter 17. Some of the most widely used tests for special topics are discussed in Appendix D.) In this chapter, group-administered tests for special topics for use at the elementary school level will be discussed first. Second will be discussed individually administered tests that provide diagnostic information on individual topics at the elementary level. Third, group-administered tests for special topics that are useful in secondary schools will be discussed.

GROUP TESTS: ELEMENTARY LEVEL

READING SKILLS.   Numerous special tests are available for reading. In principle, these are very much like the reading subtests of comprehensive measures. Typically, they require students to read paragraphs and answer questions about what they have read. Also, they contain sections on word and sentence meaning. Many of them measure speed of reading, which is not measured in most comprehensive tests. The major difference between special tests for reading and subtests for reading included in comprehensive measures is that the former tend to be longer and to test more aspects of reading ability.

An example of a group test for children in the primary grades that supplies considerable diagnostic information is the Primary Reading

Profiles (Stroud, Hieronymus, & McKee, 1967). Level 2 of the test is designed to be used at the end of the second-grade reading program or at the beginning of the third grade. Following are brief descriptions of the five subtests and sample items relating to each subtest.[1]

Test 1.   Aptitude for reading.   This is a listening test in which the teacher reads a brief passage and then asks the students to answer a question relating to what has been read by choosing one of three pictures. The purpose of the test is to measure a pupil's level of mental maturity, or mental readiness, for reading. The test items emphasize general listening vocabulary, attention span, following directions, reasoning, general information, and listening comprehension. The test score is meant to indicate the level of reading achievement which can reasonably be expected from each pupil. An example of one of these test items is as follows: The pupil has before him the three pictures shown below. The teacher reads this passage: "Some things we purchase by the dozen. Some things we purchase in pairs. Fill in the little oval under the picture of something that we purchase by the pound."

Test 2.   Auditory association.   The purpose of this test is to measure a pupil's ability to distinguish between different consonant sounds and to associate sounds with letter symbols. The pupil is presented with five pictures of things familiar to second graders and with four printed words. About half of the words on the test are considered to be familiar to children at this level. Below is shown a sample of one of these item groups. The children are instructed to determine which picture shows an object beginning with the sound of the letters underlined at the beginning of the printed word. For example, the correct picture to be associated with the word "chief" is the one of the chair. The ability measured by this test is important in enabling a student to read words whose meanings he knows when he hears them but which he does not recognize on sight.

[1]Reproduced by permission of Houghton Mifflin Company.

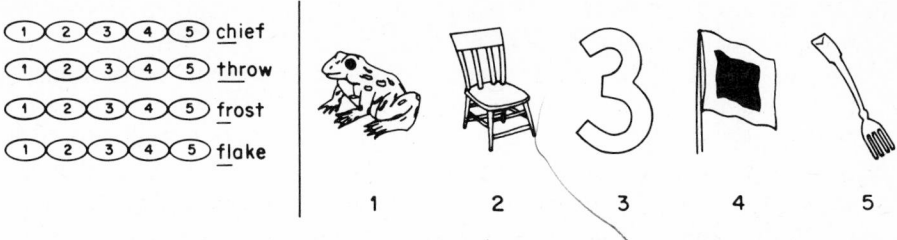

```
①②③④⑤ chief
①②③④⑤ throw
①②③④⑤ frost
①②③④⑤ flake
```

1   2   3   4   5

Test 3.   Word recognition.   This test is designed to measure the pupil's ability to recognize printed word forms. The student is presented with a group of four words. The teacher pronounces one of the words, and the child must mark the one that has been pronounced. An example of one of the groups of words follows:

carpet
market
carport
caper

Test 4.   Word attack.   In this test, the pupil reads a number of short passages to himself. One word has been omitted in each passage, and the pupil is instructed to mark one of the four words following the passage which best fits the meaning of the story. The omitted words are within the speaking and listening vocabularies of children at this level, but probably are not yet part of their reading vocabulary. The purpose of this test is to determine how well the pupil can use contextual and auditory cues to determine the meaning of strange words. Following is an example of an item from this test:

Jack said to Dot, "You cannot find your ball over there. It did not go that way. It went in a different _____."

lost   direction   grounds   dinner

Test 5.   Reading comprehension.   This test is designed to measure how well a pupil interprets and comprehends what he reads. There are two parts to the test. In Part A, the pupil reads simple questions to which he answers either "yes" or "no." An example would be:

Are most fairy stories really true?

In Part B, the pupil reads two rather lengthy stories and then answers a series of questions about what he read.

Special tests for reading skills are employed mainly (1) if comprehensive achievement tests are not used at most age levels to measure progress in that important topic and (2) even if comprehensive tests are used frequently to obtain additional information about students who perform poorly on the reading sections of comprehensive measures. Also, because some of the special tests tend to provide more diagnostic information than can be obtained from the reading subtests on comprehensive measures, group-administered special tests are useful in many forms of research, such as in research on remedial instruction for students who are having difficulty learning to read.

MATHEMATICS. Group-administered separate tests for mathematics are used less frequently in elementary grades than separate tests for reading. The reason for this is that most comprehensive tests provide an adequate coverage of mathematics at the elementary levels, and there is less need for special tests. However, for the same reasons cited above for employing special reading tests, some of the special tests for mathematics also have important uses. This is particularly true of those group-administered tests which concentrate on a number of aspects of mathematical ability—those which can be spoken of more properly as being diagnostic in nature.

An example of a separate test of arithmetic that supplies considerable diagnostic information is the Stanford Diagnostic Arithmetic Test. Following are descriptions of the subtests for Level II (grades 4.5 to 8.5):

1. Number concepts
   a. Number systems and operations
   b. Decimal-place value
2. Computation
   a. Addition and subtraction
   b. Multiplication
   c. Division
3. Common fractions
   a. Understanding
   b. Computation
4. Decimal fractions and per cents
5. Number facts
   a. Addition
   b. Subtraction
   c. Multiplication

   d.   Division
   e.   Carrying

USE OF GROUP-ADMINISTERED DIAGNOSTIC TESTS. The group-administered diagnostic tests for reading and mathematics at the elementary school level share a number of characteristics. First, the employment of such tests constitutes an additional investment in time and money over that involved in routinely administering comprehensive achievement test batteries to students. For that reason, they should be employed only when the additional time and expense are justified, rather than as a routine part of the school testing program. The major purpose is to obtain diagnostic information about those students who are having problems with reading or arithmetic as manifested in classroom performance and/or on the subtests of a comprehensive achievement test. Such special tests for individual topics are also frequently worth the time and expense for many research purposes, both for informal investigations relating to curriculum development and for formal research performed by educational measurement experts.

   A second principle relating to the use of group diagnostic tests is that they require more expertise on the part of the individual who must interpret the scores than would be the case with a comprehensive battery. The teacher who interprets the scores must first of all be very familiar with the individual skills being tested by the diagnostic instrument, and should have had considerable experience and training in teaching those skills. Otherwise, he might not understand some of the fine differences in the meanings of subtest scores on the diagnostic measure.

   The interpretation of scores on diagnostic tests is also made more complicated by the fact that the teacher must be quite cautious in interpreting anything other than large differences between subtest scores. That is, one must understand the principles concerning the reliability of differences in scores which were discussed in Chapter 4. Unless reliabilities of the individual subtests are high and correlations between subtests are only moderately high, most observed differences in subtest scores will be due purely to measurement error and consequently will yield no diagnostic information at all. The problems that arise in interpreting differences in subtest scores may be illustrated by the reliabilities and intercorrelations of the subtests on the Primary Reading Profiles, Level 2, which are shown in Table 10-1. In some cases, correlations between subtests are so high that it would be extremely hazardous to give serious consideration to anything other than very extreme differences in subtest scores. This is the case for differences between tests 4 and 5, which correlate .81. The correlation between the two tests is

Table 10-1   Intercorrelations between subtests for the Primary Reading Profiles, Level 2
(Adapted from Stroud, Hieronymus, & McKee, 1967, p. 23.)

Test	1	2	3	4	5	Composite, 3, 4, 5*
1. Aptitude for reading	—	.48	.43	.50	.47	.50
2. Auditory association		—	.76	.69	.65	.77
3. Word recognition			—	.77	.74	.93
4. Word attack				—	.81	.92
5. Reading comprehension					—	.91
Reliabilities	.73	.95	.95	.92	.91	.97

*The composite score for tests 3, 4, and 5 is said to be an over-all measure of reading achievement, emphasizing the ability to read with understanding.

almost as high as their reliabilities—.92 and .91, respectively. Technical considerations and mathematical formulas relating to interpretations of differences in subtest scores in score profiles are discussed in Appendix C. The important point to grasp here is that one should give careful consideration to reliabilities of subtests and correlations between them before interpreting differences in subtest scores too strongly.

A third principle to consider in relation to the use of individual tests for special topics is that although the tests which are available provide subtest scores for different aspects of reading and mathematics, they differ regarding the constituent abilities which are measured. For example, some reading tests, such as the Stanford Diagnostic Reading Test, emphasize phonic aspects of reading achievement, whereas other tests, e.g., the Primary Reading Profiles, place more emphasis on measuring reading comprehension. (Some of the major group-administered diagnostic tests for reading and mathematics are described in Appendix D.) Because of the differences in emphasis among the available group tests, each school should choose carefully those tests which conform most closely to its teaching approaches and to local curriculum requirements.

INDIVIDUAL DIAGNOSTIC ACHIEVEMENT TESTS FOR ELEMENTARY SCHOOL

Of course, teachers spend much of their time trying to diagnose the work habits and particular difficulties of their students. Mrs. Brown notes that one student makes many reversal errors in reading, tending to substitute "was" for "saw" and "no" for "on," for example. Another student typically accents the first syllables of words even when that is not correct, e.g., de'·light, ad'·mit, and se'·cure. A third student typically confuses certain letters of the alphabet, e.g., *m* and *n*, *b* and *d*.

In arithmetic, the teacher notes that one student makes errors in calculating time because he operates as though there were twenty rather than twenty-four hours in the day. When asked how long it is from eight o'clock in the morning to eight o'clock at night, he responds with "ten hours." In multiplication, another student typically misaligns successive rows. A third student repeatedly makes the same type of error in counting off decimal places in division.

Being able to diagnose characteristic errors provides the teacher with valuable information in tailoring instruction to the needs of each student. Diagnostic achievement tests represent extensions of what teachers try to do every day in diagnosing the particular difficulties of students. The tests provide exercises and problems that maximize the possibilities for making errors and exhibiting poor work habits, and they provide techniques for observing and scoring what the student does.

As was mentioned previously, diagnostic tests are limited to reading and arithmetic. Representative diagnostic tests in these areas will be described in the following sections.

READING. One of the most widely used diagnostic reading tests is the Gray's Oral Reading Paragraphs (Gray, 1915). The test consists of twelve short paragraphs, graded in difficulty from those appropriate to the first grade to those appropriate to the eighth grade. The nature of the test can best be illustrated by quoting sections from the directions for scoring:[2]

> Each pupil should be tested individually in a quiet place, free from distraction, and where other pupils to be tested will not hear the reading.
>
> Hand the pupil a copy of the standardized paragraphs and give the following directions: "I should like for you to read some of these paragraphs for me. Begin with the first paragraph when I say 'Begin.' Stop at the end of each paragraph until I say 'Next.' If you should find some hard words, read them as best you can without help and continue reading." Pupils above the fourth grade should begin with paragraph 4, but are to be given full credit for the first three paragraphs, the same as if they had read them without any errors. However, if two or more errors are made in paragraph 4, ask the pupil to read the preceding paragraphs also. In case pupils in the first two grades hesitate several seconds on a difficult word, pronounce it for the pupil and mark it as mispronounced.

[2]Material quoted by permission of the Bobbs-Merrill Company.

While the pupil is reading, record: (*a*) the time required to read each paragraph, and (*b*) the errors made.

(*a*) Note the exact second at which the pupil begins and completes the reading of a paragraph. Record the number of seconds required in the margin to the right of the paragraph.

(*b*) The following paragraph illustrates the character of the errors and the method of recording them.

> The sun pierced into my large windows. It was the opening of October, and the sky was of a dazzling blue. I looked out of my window and down the street. The white houses of the long, straight street were almost painful to the eyes. The clear atmosphere allowed full play to the sun's brightness.

If a word is wholly mispronounced, underline it as in the case of "atmosphere." If a portion of a word is mispronounced, mark appropriately as indicated above: "pierced" pronounced in two syllables, sounding long *a* in "dazzling," omitting the *s* in "houses" or the *al* from "almost," or the *r* in "straight." Omitted words are marked as in the case of "of" and "and"; substitutions as in the case of "may" for "my"; insertions as in the case of "clear"; and repetitions as in the case of "to the sun's." Two or more words should be repeated to count as a repetition.

It is very difficult to record the exact nature of each error. Do this as nearly as you can. In all cases where you are unable to define clearly the specific character of the error, underline the word or portion of the word mispronounced. Be sure you put down a mark for each error. In case you are not sure that an error was made, give the pupil the benefit of the doubt. If the pupil has a slight foreign accent, distinguish carefully between this difficulty and real errors. Each pupil should be allowed to continue reading until he makes 7 errors in each of 2 paragraphs.

In addition to indicating particular kinds of errors that students make in reading, the test provides a system for converting total numbers of errors into grade-equivalent scores. However, as will be discussed more fully later in the chapter, such norms should be regarded with considerable suspicion.

ARITHMETIC. Typical of the diagnostic tests for arithmetic is the Diagnostic Chart for Fundamental Processes in Arithmetic (Buswell & John, 1925). The student is presented with a series of graded problems in addition, subtraction, multiplication, and division. He is asked to "talk-out" the solution to each problem. Items are scored both for correctness of solution and for the types of work habits exhibited. The work habits shown by each student are indicated on a chart, which is shown in Figure 10-1. Selected passages from the test manual[3] will illustrate the purpose and nature of the test:

A standardized test in arithmetic will indicate whether a pupil is doing satisfactory or unsatisfactory work for a given school grade. It enables the teacher to identify those pupils who need special attention. However, the marked limitation of such a test is that it does not tell why the pupil fails nor how he has made errors. Before the teacher can give effective help to a failing pupil, she must know exactly what the pupil does to cause his failure. She must understand the methods that he uses. These methods of work are so varied and complex that efficient teaching requires a systematic and organized scheme of diagnosing them. To illustrate some of the varied ways in which pupils work, the following examples are given.

In adding a column of figures, the most common method is to proceed regularly either up or down the column. However, many pupils do not do this, but instead, they skip around in an apparently random fashion. One boy explained his method of adding by saying that he did not like to add and therefore he always added the most difficult numbers first in order to be through with them. Consequently, he added all of the nines, then all of the eights, then all of the sevens, and so on down to zero. Needless to say, in this amount of skipping around in the column, he overlooked some of the numbers entirely, and, consequently, got a wrong answer. Other children tried to make as many easy combinations as possible, for example, a 4 and 6, regardless of whether the 4 and 6 appeared together or at opposite extremes of the column. While grouping numbers appears to have some advantages for skilled accountants, observation of children's work indicates that such attempts at grouping more frequently result in failure than in success.

Another type of procedure in adding is illustrated by the work of a girl in the sixth grade. She had never learned her combinations sufficiently well, consequently she constantly resorted to counting in order to get the proper answer. For example, in adding 7 and 9 she worked as follows: "Well, 7 plus 4 is 11, 7 plus 5 is 12, 7 plus 6 is 13, *7 plus 8 is 14,* 7 plus 9 is 15." She made an error, due to skipping the combination 7 plus 7, but she failed to notice it. Throughout her work she continuously added in this fashion. Needless to say, she can never do effective work in addition until these extravagant and time-

---

[3]The quoted material is presented with the permission of the Bobbs-Merrill Company. For the sake of brevity, the quoted material leaves out some passages and sections from the test manual.

Teacher's Diagnosis

for pupil *13*

TEACHER'S DIAGNOSTIC CHART
FOR
INDIVIDUAL DIFFICULTIES
FUNDAMENTAL PROCESSES IN ARITHMETIC   Printed in U. S. A.
Prepared by G. T. Buswell and Lenore John

THE TEST DIVISION OF THE BOBBS-MERRILL COMPANY, INC.
SUBSIDIARY OF HOWARD W. SAMS & CO., INC.
4300 WEST 62nd STREET · INDIANAPOLIS 6, INDIANA

Name *John Dix*   School *Lincoln*   Grade *IV* Age *10* IQ *98*

Date of Diagnosis:_____ Add. *4-7-25*; Subt._____; Mult._____; Div._____

Teacher's preliminary diagnosis *Slow and inaccurate in fundamental operations*

ADDITION: (Place a check before each habit observed in the pupil's work)

- X a1 Errors in combinations
- X a2 Counting
- ____ a3 Added carried number last
- X a4 Forgot to add carried number
- ____ a5 Repeated work after partly done
- ____ a6 Added carried number irregularly
- ____ a7 Wrote number to be carried
- ____ a8 Irregular procedure in column
- X a9 Carried wrong number
- ____ a10 Grouped two or more numbers
- ____ a11 Splits numbers into parts
- X a12 Used wrong fundamental operation
- ____ a13 Lost place in column
- ____ a14 Depended on visualization

- ____ a15 Disregarded column position
- ____ a16 Omitted one or more digits
- ____ a17 Errors in reading numbers
- ____ a18 Dropped back one or more tens
- X a19 Derived unknown combination from familiar one
- ____ a20 Disregarded one column
- X a21 Error in writing answer
- ____ a22 Skipped one or more decades
- ____ a23 Carrying when there was nothing to carry
- ____ a24 Used scratch paper
- ____ a25 Added in pairs, giving last sum as answer
- ____ a26 Added same digit in two columns
- ____ a27 Wrote carried number in answer
- ____ a28 Added same number twice

Habits not listed above_____

(Write observation notes on pupil's work in space opposite examples)

(1) 5 2 / 7	6 3 / 9	*Correct*	(5) $6+2=12$ $3+4=12$		*multiplied instead of added. (Habit #12)*
(2) 2 9 / 11	8 4 / 13	*Error in combination (Habit #1)*	(6) 52 13 / 65	40 39 / 79	*Correct*
(3) 12 2 / 14	13 5 / 18	*"13 and 5 are—10 and 5 are 15, 11 and 5 are 16, 12 and 5 are 17, 13 and 5 are 18." (Habit #19)*	(7) 78 71 / 149	46 92 / 38	*"6 and 2 are 8, 9 and 4 are 13." Error in writing answer, omitted the "1" in 13. (Habit #21)*
(4) 19 2 / 11	17 9 / 71	*"9+2 is 11, bring down the 1." (Habit #4) "7 and 9 is 16, 6 and 1 is 7" Carried wrong number (Habit #9)*	(8) 3 5 8 2 / 18	8 7 9 7 / 31	*Counted on fingers. Said, "8 and 7 are 15, and 9 are—16, 17, 18, 19, 20, 21, 22, 23, 24, and 7 are, — 25, 26, 27, 28, 29, 30, 31." Touched one finger for each count. (Habit #2)*

Figure 10-1.   Sample page from the Diagnostic Chart for Fundamental Processes in Arithmetic.

consuming methods are eliminated. The teacher thought that she was merely a slow adder and had no idea of the method she was following, although she was in the sixth grade and passed the following year into junior high school, where the teaching of addition would probably never be mentioned again.

Still a different type of case was a child who did approximately one-half of the examples wrong in a test of addition. In analyzing her work it was found that in every case the error was due to one cause, namely, lack of knowledge of how to carry. Obviously, the proper treatment of this case is specific teaching of how to carry rather than simply the application of more drill in addition.

DIRECTIONS FOR DIAGNOSIS

INDIVIDUAL WORK.   It is recommended that the Diagnostic Chart be used with all pupils who are doing unsatisfactory work in arithmetic. The most economic method is to make a list of the pupils whose work is to be analyzed and then to proceed systematically with the diagnosis, giving the other children in the group practice exercises or seat work until the diagnoses are finished. The diagnosis should be made individually and should cover only one of the four fundamental operations at a given time. For example, after practice exercises or seat work has been assigned to the class, the teacher should select the child to be diagnosed and sit down with him at her desk or at a table in the corner of the room. She should make the child feel as much at home as possible, since the success of the diagnosis depends upon how intimately the teacher becomes acquainted with the details of the pupil's method of work. Since the causes of failure in arithmetic are generally due to poor methods of work, successful teaching depends, first of all, upon finding out just what methods are used.

PROCEDURE.   After the teacher and the pupil are seated at the table where the work is to be done, the pupil should be provided with a Work Sheet and the teacher with the Diagnostic Chart. The blank spaces at the top of the Chart, giving the pupil's name, age, grade, etc., should be carefully filled in before proceeding with the diagnosis. The teacher should then direct the child to proceed with the examples in the operation to be observed, as for example, addition. She should tell the child to work the examples in the way that he ordinarily does and to write the answers in his usual manner. He should be told that the teacher wishes to know just *how* he gets his answers and, for this reason, that he is to do as much of his work as he can aloud. Tell him "to do all of his thinking aloud." A careful explanation by the teacher, together with an illustration by her, is ordinarily sufficient to indicate to the child exactly what is wanted, and after the first example or two, the child usually proceeds in a very natural fashion.

Since the success of this type of diagnosis depends upon discovering how the child works in his *normal* manner, the teacher should *not* make any attempt in the diagnostic process to suggest ways of working or to correct the pupil's bad habits of working. This should be done later. In the diagnosis the aim is to find out just how the pupil works when he is working independently. The child should be made to feel as natural as possible, and a cordial relationship between the teacher and the child during this period is necessary.

As the child works, the teacher should check on the Diagnostic Chart the types of habits which occur, at the same time recording the child's procedure in the space opposite the examples on the teacher's chart. The most satisfactory way to do this is to make a record of the habits observed in the exact words of the pupils, at least for the first few times. If the habit appears later with other examples, it is sufficient to refer back to the earlier procedure. The results of the diagnosis should be that the teacher has a clearer knowledge of the specific habits which are responsible for the pupil's poor work.

DISTINCTION BETWEEN DIAGNOSIS AND TESTING.   One particular distinction between the method of diagnosis and the method of testing should be pointed out. After a test is given the final score is computed, which indicates the grade of work which the pupil is doing. Ordinarily, attention centers simply in the score which is used for purposes of classification. In the method of diagnosis there is no final score. The procedure is not used for purposes of classification, but rather for purposes of teaching. Consequently, the desired result is a very clear understanding on the part of the teacher of *just how the pupil does his work* in order that more effective teaching may follow. Since this is the case, the teacher should not be satisfied simply with making the diagnosis and checking the items, but rather, she should study carefully the characteristics of the pupil's work and formulate in her own mind the most appropriate methods of teaching for such a pupil.

The manual lists numerous work habits and provides examples of each. Some illustrative examples are:

Forgot to add carried number.
Example: 268   The error here is due to neglecting to carry. The subject said,
            961   "8 and 1 is 9; 6 and 6 are 12; 9 and 2 is 11."
          ―――――
          1,129

In subtraction did not allow for having borrowed.
Example: 528   "4 from 8 equals 4; 6 from 12 equals 6; *bring down the 5.*"
            64
          ―――――
           564

In multiplication made error in position of partial products.
Example: 97   A pupil placed the second product directly under the first
            12   in this example.
          ―――――
           194
            97
          ―――――
           291

USE OF INDIVIDUAL DIAGNOSTIC TESTS. Some points about the use of individually administered diagnostic tests should be obvious from the examples shown above. First, such tests ordinarily are given only to children who are having trouble with either reading or arithmetic. They are too time-consuming to apply routinely to all students. Second, diagnostic tests require more skill on the part of the teacher than is the case with survey achievement tests. In order skillfully to present the materials to students and to mark errors accurately as the student goes along, a considerable amount of practice is required. Also, the success of the diagnostic testing session depends, to a considerable extent, on the teacher's personality and his ability to handle children. If the student is afraid of the teacher or if the teacher is not sufficiently skillful to obtain cooperation from shy or hostile students, the diagnostic testing session will be of little avail.

An inherent difficulty of diagnostic tests is that they try to measure so many things at once. To measure adequately all the components of reading, for example, would require a very long and involved instrument. Few diagnostic instruments contain the amount and breadth of material required to measure adequately all the constituent skills involved, an exception being the Diagnostic Chart for Fundamental Processes in Arithmetic, described previously.

One important caution in using individual diagnostic tests is that none of the available instruments have been standardized on a representative cross section of students in this country. (However, some of the group-administered diagnostic tests do have excellent norms.) Consequently, those instruments which deal with scores in the form of grade equivalents and other types of norms are quite misleading. As was said in the material quoted from the manual for the Diagnostic Chart for Fundamental Processes in Arithmetic, numbers of correct and incorrect answers are not what is important on diagnostic instruments, but rather how the student approaches the task. Although most of the available diagnostic instruments are far from perfect, they do provide useful supplements to teachers' informal diagnoses of the work habits of students.

ACHIEVEMENT TESTS FOR SPECIAL TOPICS IN SECONDARY EDUCATION

As was discussed in Chapter 9, comprehensive achievement test batteries are available for the secondary school level as well as the elementary school level. However, the reader may recall that batteries for use in high school emphasize tests of content areas rather than basic skills.

An example of one such battery is the Tests of Academic Progress, which include six survey subtests: social studies, composition, science, reading, mathematics, and literature. Because the tests included in such batteries tend to cover content in a rather broad, general way, schools often employ special tests for particular topics, such as American history or chemistry. In addition, there are many special tests for academic subjects not included on comprehensive test batteries, such as psychology or Spanish.

In contrast to the situation at the elementary school level, none of the tests for special topics at the secondary school level are individually administered instruments. All the major instruments are group tests and employ objective test items (mainly multiple-choice items). Whereas tests at the elementary school level tend to be diagnostic in the sense that they dissect a subject matter into a number of constituent abilities, tests employed at the high school level are diagnostic in that they measure performance in individual units of instruction, such as economics and physics. Tests for special topics at the secondary level differ from one another in terms of the extent to which they are broadly gauged with respect to subject matters, rather than oriented toward more specific units of instruction. For example, one can obtain tests of over-all achievement in mathematics, or one can obtain tests for special topics in mathematics, such as algebra and trigonometry. The characteristics of achievement tests for special topics at the secondary school level are illustrated by the following sample items from a variety of tests.

COOPERATIVE ENGLISH EXPRESSION TEST.[4] In Part I of this test, the student is to demonstrate his ability to recognize and select a word or phrase which precisely conveys the intended meaning of a sentence. Two sample items are as follows:

1. Because literature was not considered an honorable calling, (   ) literary compositions were fairly common in the seventeenth century.
   a. anonymous
   b. fictitious
   c. disguised
   d. confidential

2. Holding his umbrella against the wind, (   ).
   a. the old gentleman stubbornly pressed on to the park to feed the pigeons
   b. the old gentleman pressed on to the park stubbornly to feed the pigeons

    c. the old gentleman who had stubbornly pressed on to the park fed the
        pigeons
    d. the pigeons received food from the old gentleman who was so stubborn
        that he pressed on to the park to feed them.

In Part II, the student is to decide whether there are errors of capitalization, punctuation, spelling, or usage in one of three lines of a sentence. No sentence has more than one line with errors, and some sentences do not have any errors. Two sample items are as follows:

1. *a.* Fewer votes were cast than
    b. had been predicted by even
    c. the most pessimistic of forecasters.

2. *a.* He got a taxicab more quickly than he had anticipated
    b. thus he thought that he had plenty of time to reach
    c. the restaurant where the conference was to be held.

CRARY AMERICAN HISTORY TEST[5]

Matching:

a. developments in radio		1. Edison
b. atomic energy research		
c. combine thresher		2. Marconi
d. incandescent lighting		
e. mass production		3. Urey
f. wireless telegraphy		
g. radar development		4. Fleming
h. penicillin research		

ANDERSON CHEMISTRY TEST.[6]   In the first sample item below, the pupil is to select the term which does not belong in the group with the other four terms:

    a. nitrogen
    b. magnesium
    c. tin
    d. antimony
    e. bismuth

[5]Reproduced by permission of Harcourt Brace Jovanovich, Inc.
[6]*Ibid.*

In the following two questions, the pupil is to give, first, the result of an action or occurrence and, next, the chemical principle which best explains the occurrence:

A storekeeper placed some calcium chloride between his sash and storm window during a severe cold spell. What happened?
a.   The windows became more heavily frosted than the near-by windows.
b.   The substance became dry and powder-like.
c.   The calcium chloride evaporated.
d.   The windows remained almost free of frost.
e.   Nothing happened.

Which one of the following statements gives the principle that best explains the answer to the previous question?
a.   Many gases such as water vapor and carbon dioxide can be solidified.
b.   Many chemical reactions depend upon the lack of, or presence of, moisture.
c.   Many solids such as dry ice and iodine pass directly from a solid to a gaseous state.
d.   Many substances readily lose their water of hydration or crystallization on exposure to air.
e.   Many substances have the property of absorbing moisture from air or other substances.

COOPERATIVE GENERAL ACHIEVEMENT TEST FOR NATURAL SCIENCE[7]

The rate at which an automobile increases in speed after starting is called its
a.   velocity
b.   acceleration
c.   momentum
d.   kinetic energy
e.   inertia

Silvering the inner surfaces of a vacuum (thermos) bottle decreases heat loss by
a.   air leakage
b.   conduction
c.   vaporization

[7]From *Cooperative General Achievement Test II, Natural Science*. Copyright © 1953 by Educational Testing Service. Reproduced by permission.

     d.   convection

     e.   radiation

DUNNING PHYSICS TEST[8]

1.   The sun appears to rise earlier than it actually does. This is due to the earth's atmosphere causing the light waves to be—

     a.   diffused

     b.   reflected

     c.   dispersed

     d.   polarized

     e.   refracted

2.   The phenomenon that best supports the hypothesis that light is a form of transverse wave motion is called—

     a.   polarization

     b.   refraction

     c.   interference

     d.   reflection

     e.   dispersion

SHAYCOFT PLANE GEOMETRY TEST.[9] Each of the questions below consists of a set of measurements applying to a triangle ($\triangle$ *ABC*). The pupil is to decide whether it is possible to construct a triangle with these measurements. He answers by choosing one of the following phrases:

     a.   No such triangle exists.

     b.   All such triangles are congruent.

     c.   All such triangles are similar, but not necessarily congruent.

     d.   Exactly two distinct triangles *(neither congruent nor similar)* can be constructed with these characteristics.

     e.   More than two distinct triangles *(neither congruent nor similar)* can be constructed with these characteristics.

       1. $\angle A = 30°$, $\angle B = 60$, $\angle C = 30°$

       2. $\angle A = 30°$, $\angle B = 60$, $\angle C = 90°$

       3. $AB = AC = BC = 6$ in., $\angle C = 90°$

       4. $AC = BC = 10$ in., $\angle A = \angle B = 30°$

       5. $AB = 6$ in., $\angle A = 150°$

[8]Reproduced by permission of Harcourt, Brace & World, Inc.

[9]Reproduced by permission of Harcourt, Brace & World, Inc.

SEATTLE ALGEBRA TEST [10]

Part A. Vocabulary

In 3 a^2c, the c is
a.   a term
b.   a binomial
c.   an exponent
d.   a factor
e.   a numerical coefficient

Part B. Fundamental processes

$(-2)(-2)(-2)$ equals
a. -8
b. -6
c. $+6$
d. $+8$
e.   none of the above

Part C. Equations

If $\frac{x}{2} = 6$, then x equals
a.   3
b.   4
c.   8
d.   12
e.   none of the above

Part D. Algebraic representation and problems.   The pupil is to decide which of the given algebraic expressions or equations is correct for each problem.

If n represents an odd number, the next higher consecutive odd number is
a. $2n$
b. $n + 1$
c. $n + 2$
d. $n + 3$
e. n^2

[10]Reproduced by permission of Harcourt Brace Jovanovich, Inc.

KWALWASSER TEST OF MUSIC INFORMATION AND APPRECIATION.[11]   In the first series of items below, the student is given the names of famous musical compositions, and he is to write the name of the composer of each.

1. March Slav _____

2. To a Wild Rose _____

3. The Unfinished Symphony _____

4. Liebestraum _____

True-false

1. (   ) The viola is an alto horn.

2. (   ) Violins are frequently employed in brass bands.

3. (   ) The first violin section is seated to the left of the conductor.

4. (   ) The harpsichord is one of the predecessors of the piano.

COOPERATIVE SPANISH TEST[12]

1.   Este verano no podré hacer el viaje a España por falta de
     a. dinero
     b. humo
     c. naranjas
     d. miedo
     e. preguntas

2.   Se parece Vd. mucho a su hermano aunque
     a. él es más joven.
     b. no le he visto.
     c. es Vd. el hijo único.
     d. hoy es lunes.
     e. Vd. no hace nada.

USES OF TESTS FOR SPECIAL TOPICS IN SECONDARY EDUCATION.
Tests for special topics in secondary education have many of the same possible uses as those for special topics at the elementary level, and in

[11]Reproduced by permission of the Bureau of Educational Research and Service, State University of Iowa.
[12]From *Cooperative Spanish Test*, Elementary Form P. Copyright © 1939 by Educational Testing Service. Reproduced by permission.

their usefulness they overlap the employment of coordinated achievement test batteries. Some of the important uses are in (1) understanding the difficulties of students who are having problems in schooling over-all or in particular topics, (2) assigning students to particular courses of instruction, (3) providing information that is important for curriculum development and planning, and (4) serving to measure the results of many different kinds of educational research. In addition to serving these and other functions, some of the tests for special topics at the secondary school level provide information that is directly relevant to planning instructional activities and evaluating the progress of students in particular units of instruction. This is particularly the case for the end-of-term examinations that are available for many topics in high school, such as the tests illustrated previously for English, history, science, mathematics, and languages. Whereas in previous chapters it was argued that the evaluation of student progress in particular units of instruction should rest mainly on local objectives as manifested in teacher-made tests at the secondary school level, it makes good sense to rely more heavily for these purposes on standardized achievement tests. At the high school level, there is less variance among schools in terms of the goals of instruction in many topics. For example, whereas at the elementary school level school districts may differ considerably in their approaches to the instruction of reading or arithmetic, at the secondary school level schools across the country tend to share largely the same goals with respect to particular units of instruction, such as physics and trigonometry. At the high school level, teachers are inclined to be influenced in their approach to instruction and in the content coverage by the goals of instruction advocated by subject-matter experts and by the approaches taken by outstanding textbooks and auxiliary instructional materials. For these reasons, it is proper for teachers to employ end-of-term standardized achievement tests for information in making decisions about instructional activities and in evaluating the progress of students.

SUMMARY

This chapter discussed special achievement tests for individual topics—special in the sense that they are employed by themselves rather than as part of a comprehensive battery of achievement tests. If there were no special advantages to using tests of this kind, their being administered separately would be a serious disadvantage. One of the major advantages cited for comprehensive achievement test batteries is that because the subtests are constructed and standardized in the same manner, it is both more convenient and more logical to make comparisons between differences in subtest scores. Consequently, unless one of the special tests offers an advantage over the subtests of comprehensive test batteries, it would be much better to employ a comprehensive test battery rather than a hodgepodge of special tests. The major advantage of tests for special topics is that they can measure more thoroughly and reliably the many different aspects of achievement in a particular topic than the subtest of a comprehensive battery.

Tests for special topics frequently are useful in (1) learning about the difficulties of particular students in various topics, (2) sectioning and other types of placement of students in courses and curricula, (3) planning over-all instruction, (4) tailoring instruction to the needs of each student, and (5) performing educational research, broadly speaking. Of course, employing such special tests requires additional expense and personnel time. Also, administration and interpretation of some of the special tests require more expertise on the part of teachers than is the case with comprehensive test batteries.

Tests for special topics are useful only to the extent that they are *diagnostic,* in the sense that they pick apart achievement in particular subject-matter areas. The available tests vary in the extent to which they provide considerable diagnostic information, and they also vary in terms of the aspects that are stressed. Consequently, before accepting particular tests, teachers, school administrators, and others need to inspect the instruments, study the test manuals, and read the research literature concerning the instruments.

In this chapter, tests for particular topics were subdivided in two ways. First, a distinction was made between group-administered tests and individually administered tests. Second, a distinction was made concerning the instruments available at the elementary level and at the secondary level. At the elementary level, special tests are restricted almost entirely to reading and arithmetic, for which one has a choice of individual tests or group tests. The major advantage of individual tests over group tests is that they provide an opportunity to study in considerable detail the work habits of particular students. The relative disadvantages of the individual tests are (1) they require more time and expertise to administer and interpret, and (2) because they attempt to measure so many things, they are usually less well standardized than the group-administered measures.

At the secondary school level, only group-administered tests for special topics are available. At this level, the emphasis is on testing for achievement in particular subject-matter areas, rather than on obtaining diagnostic information about the core skills of reading and mathematics. At the secondary school level, a wide variety of excellent instruments is available, covering almost all subject matters that are taught in American schools.

SUGGESTED ADDITIONAL READINGS

Gerberich, J. R., Greene, H. A., and Jorgensen, A. N. *Measurement and evaluation in the modern school.* New York: McKay, 1962, chaps. 15–25.

Noll, V. H. *Introduction to educational measurement.* (2nd ed.) Boston: Houghton Mifflin, 1965, chaps. 8, 9.

PART IV

PREDICTION AND TRAIT MEASUREMENT: HUMAN ABILITIES

Parts II and III of the book were concerned, respectively, with teacher-made tests and achievement tests, both of which are outstanding examples of *assessments*. In Chapter 2 it was said that, in addition to the assessment function, two other important functions are served by tests: *prediction* and *trait measurement*. Although teachers are not as involved with these as they are with assessment instruments, they should know enough about them to interpret the results of commercially distributed instruments used as predictors and research results concerning trait measures. Both Parts IV and V will be concerned with prediction and trait measurement, Part IV with human abilities, and Part V with interests, attitudes, and personality characteristics.

How do you distinguish between ability and nonability (personality, attitudes, interests) measures? In some places the line is quite blurred and the two kinds of measures blend, but for most kinds of tests with which we deal, some important distinctions can be made. Ability tests concern how *well* an individual *can* perform. Typically students are asked to solve twenty arithmetic problems in a short time, memorize a list of words, or comprehend the meanings of paragraphs. The student is keyed to do the best that he can, and what constitutes success and what constitutes failure are clearly understood.

How would the tests mentioned above differ from tests containing items like, "Do you usually lead the discussion in group situations?" "What does this ink blot look like to you?" "Which would you prefer to have as a neighbor: an Englishman or a Frenchman?" "What would you rather do: make a speech or keep records for a club?" The first two items are typical of those that have been used in personality tests, the third is typical of items appearing in measures of attitudes, and the fourth is typical of items appearing on interest tests.

In this latter type of item there are no obvious right and wrong answers.

Tests cannot be scored in such a way as to report to the student how many correct answers he gave. Items of this kind (nonability items) are intended to determine how the individual *typically* behaves: his typical behavior with respect to other people (which is part of what we call personality), his typical preferences for other people (attitudes), and his typical choice of activities (interests). It is best said then that the nonability tests concern *typical behavior*.

To make a distinction between tests of ability and tests of typical behavior is more than mere hair splitting. Different kinds of problems arise when constructing, using, interpreting, and validating the two kinds of instruments. For example, on ability tests, the test administrator must guard against cheating. If a student peeks in the text or at another student's paper, he might obtain the correct answer. But because there are no correct answers in measures of typical behavior, cheating, as such, is not an important problem. Instead, the student is likely to "fake," to give answers which sound good even if they do not typify his behavior.

Another difference between the two types of measures is that it has proved much easier to find valid predictors among ability tests rather than among measures of typical behavior. For example, ability tests have been used successfully for many years to select college students, but valid personality tests for the selection of college students are still not available.

It has proved much easier to obtain "construct validity" for ability-type instruments than for measures of typical behavior, one index of which is the correlation between different proposed measures of the same trait. For example, different tests of intelligence tend to correlate highly, so highly that it is hard to choose among them; in contrast, different measures of some of the personality characteristics, e.g., "rigidity," correlate so low with one another as to raise serious questions about their validity. The distinctions above between measures of ability and measures of typical behavior will be further explained in Parts V and VI.

The measures to be discussed in Part IV mainly are important in helping to make decisions about the "readiness" of students for particular types of educational activities. Typical decisions concerning readiness are those involved in (1) admitting an underage child to kindergarten, (2) placing a slow learner in a special remedial class, (3) permitting a high school student to enter a special accelerated program of study, and (4) advising a student about entrance into college. To the extent to which tests of human ability actually aid in making such decisions about readiness, they perform a very valuable service.

chapter 11

FACTORS OF ABILITY

Ted Bronson was the smartest student that Miss Brown had ever had in the fourth grade. Now he has moved on to the fifth, and Miss Brown wonders how he is doing in Mrs. Martin's class. At lunch Mrs. Martin says that Ted is indeed bright but not quite as bright as Billy Bernstein. In conversations such as this, we frequently fail to ask an important question: Are they bright in the same ways? We too frequently assume that there is only one factor (dimension or yardstick) of intelligence, and after students have been ordered along it, there is nothing to say about their capabilities.

In contrast to the way in which we teachers are prone to make a simple ordering of students with respect to over-all ability, athletic coaches are more discriminating when talking about members of their track teams. If you ask the coach at Woodlawn High if Russell Husek is "a good athlete," a typical response would be, "Well, he is very good at short-distance running, hundred-yard dash, and other sprints, but he does not do so well on the longer runs; also he is a pretty good pole vaulter." Describing another member of the team, the coach might say that he is excellent in all the jumps—broad jump, high jump, and pole vault, but lacks the wind to make a good runner.

In previous chapters the word "intelligence" has been used with some misgivings because it suggests that there is only one general ability, rather than different types of ability. If intelligence is perfectly general, the person who can do one type of intellectual problem well can do all other kinds of problems well, and the person who does poorly on one type of problem will do poorly on all others. If abilities are perfectly general, the child who easily learns to solve arithmetic problems will have the same facility in learning spelling, geography, and other subject matters. Another possibility is that human abilities are completely "specific," that there are no correlations among different intellectual tasks. Then, if we know that a particular child is very adept at learning arithmetic, that offers no basis at all for predicting how well he will do in spelling or geography. Taking the case further, if abilities are completely specific and unrelated to one another, the child who can add numbers very quickly might be slower than the average child in doing multiplication.

Human abilities are neither completely general nor completely specific. The real story lies between these two extremes. In this chapter we shall discuss the history of the problem, related research, and some of the different abilities which underlie human intellect.

FACULTY PSYCHOLOGY.   In the early nineteenth century the belief was prevalent that human behavior was determined by a large number of separate capacities, or faculties, as they were called. There were proposed faculties of attention, memory, reasoning, will power, esthetic appreciation, and many others. It was the early belief that each faculty resided in a particular brain location, and that "bumps on the head" were prognostic of the strength of particular faculties. Although the anatomical theories were soon discarded, the belief in a large number of specific human faculties lingered throughout the remainder of the nineteenth century. Faculty psychology represented the extreme of the point of view that human abilities are highly specific.

BINET AND GENERAL INTELLIGENCE.   In France at the turn of the century, Alfred Binet (Binet & Simon, 1905) studied the measurement of intelligence. At first he worked in line with the faculty school and sought to measure intelligence through many simple physical and behavioral indices. Some of his "tests" concerned suggestibility, size of the cranium, tactile discrimination, graphology, and even palmistry. Like the others who were trying to measure human abilities, he found that these simple functions do not measure intelligence, as we commonly think of it.

Binet abandoned these efforts and, instead, adopted a "global" conception of intelligence. For practical purposes, he thought that it would not be possible to measure all the simple skills that underlie intelligent behavior. Instead, it would be more feasible to study the end products of intellectual functioning. In other words, rather than go back and try to find out why some people behave more intelligently than others, Binet sought to measure the extent to which individuals could deal intelligently with their present environments. He defined intelligence as "the tendency to take and maintain a definite direction; the capacity to make adaptations for the purpose of obtaining a desired end; and the power of auto-criticism."

Working with Simon, Binet developed the first practical test of general ability (or intelligence, as it is usually called). The first test consisted of thirty items which concerned, variously, following simple directions, defining words, constructing sentences, and making judgments about the correct behavior in real-life situations. The Binet-Simon scale has gone through a number of revisions since that time. The scale set the tone for most measures of intelligence to follow, and even our modern measures of general ability bear many resemblances to those early efforts.

An important point to note about the Binet-Simon scale, and all measures of general ability to follow, is that the child is provided with only one score. Because each child receives only one score, it is tacitly assumed that intelligence is general, or, in other words, that only one factor is involved in the test items. If there are, say, two kinds of intelligence involved in the test, the use of only one score is somewhat misleading. Two children could make the same score, not because they are alike with respect to their abilities, but because one child is high in one of the factors and low in the other, and vice versa for the other child. The same assumption of the generality of human abilities is involved in all the tests of general ability (intelligence tests) which have followed from Binet's early work. Binet's test, and all those to follow, represents the extreme opposite point of view from that of the faculty school—that intelligence is perfectly general and that one over-all index is all that is required to indicate a child's intellectual standing.

FACTOR ANALYSIS

Rather than argue over whether intelligence is general or is divided up into many specific abilities, we can employ experimental and statistical procedures which will help answer the question. Many different kinds of tests can be given to students, and correlation coefficients can be obtained for all possible pairs of them. As was mentioned in Chapter 4, the correlation coefficient indicates the extent to which two tests measure the same thing. If many different kinds of mental tests were given to a large number of students and the correlations between them were very high, it would be evidence that intelligence is completely general. In other words, all the tests tend to measure the same thing. On the other hand, if the correlations between the tests were all zero, it would show that each test measures something different from what is measured by the others, and this would be evidence that intelligence is completely specific to the tasks involved.

A look at some correlation coefficients will show how the question of the generality of intellectual functions is solved. Table 11-1 shows the intercorrelations of six tests. The tests are labeled A through F. The table shows all possible intercorrelations between the tests. For example, the table shows that tests A and B have a low correlation, .19 to be exact. There is a high correlation between tests A and C, .64. Test D correlates only .21 with test A. The highest correlation of test D with any other test is .67, with test F. In the table, the blank spaces in parentheses are at points showing the correlations of tests with themselves. Of course, any tests correlates perfectly with itself, at least regarding the particular set of scores obtained on any one occasion. What conclusion should be drawn from the correlations presented in Table 11-1? Do the tests all measure the same thing, or do they each measure different traits? Some of the correlations are quite high; for example, there is a correlation of .72 between test A and test E. Other correlations are close to zero.

A rearrangement of the order in which tests appear in the table will help clarify the question regarding the amount of overlap between tests. In Table 11-2, the order of appearance of the tests has been rearranged to show those tests which tend to correlate highly with one another. When the correlations are presented in this way, it can be seen that tests A, E, and C tend to correlate highly with one another, as do tests D, B, and F. Correlations between the two groups of tests are very low. Lines are drawn in the table to demonstrate the tendency of the tests to divide up into two groups. What we have found is that there are two different types of tests, each of which is said to form a *cluster*, or *factor*. Tests A, E, and C relate to one factor, and any student who does very well on one of these tests is likely to do well on all of them. Tests D, B, and F form another factor, and any student who does very well on one of them is likely to do well on the others. However, if a student does well on the tests representative of one cluster, or factor, this provides little information as to how well he will do on the other. In this example, tests A, E, and C all concern verbal comprehension: vocabulary, grades in English, and scores on a reading comprehension test. Tests D, B, and F deal with addition, multiplication, and the solution of algebraic problems, respectively. The second factor concerns the ability to perform arithmetic operations.

Studying correlation tables, such as the two just discussed, allows us to determine how many clusters, or factors, are involved in intellectual tasks. The example presented above is a very simple one: only two factors are involved, and those are quite easily seen by inspecting the correlation

Table 11-1   Intercorrelations of six tests

	A	B	C	D	E	F
A	( )	.19	.64	.21	.72	.05
B	.19	( )	.22	.64	.12	.55
C	.64	.22	( )	.14	.56	.28
D	.21	.64	.14	( )	.28	.67
E	.72	.12	.56	.28	( )	.11
F	.05	.55	.28	.67	.11	( )

Table 11-2   Rearrangement of correlations from Table 11-1

	A	E	C	D	B	F
A	( )	.72	.64	.21	.19	.05
E	.72	( )	.56	.28	.12	.11
C	.64	.56	( )	.14	.22	.28
D	.21	.28	.14	( )	.64	.67
B	.19	.12	.22	.64	( )	.55
F	.05	.11	.28	.67	.55	( )

table. If the correlational results were always so straightforward and studies contained no more than six tests, it would not be necessary to apply more refined procedures to the results. However, results are seldom as neat as those presented above, and instead of studying only six tests at a time, we often study as many as fifty or more tests in one table. In those instances it is no longer feasible simply to look at the correlation table and rearrange the ordering of the tests in such a way as to show the dominant clusters. Instead, it is necessary to apply some mathematical procedures which identify the major factors and indicate the extent to which each test belongs to each factor. The mathematical procedures which are so applied are referred to as *factor analysis*.

For many purposes, the best way of obtaining factors is by simply averaging or summing scores over tests that form a cluster, like the clusters that can be seen in Table 11-2. For example, if a person has standard scores on the three verbal tests of 1.4, 1.1, and 1.5, respectively, these could be summed to provide a score of 4.0 on the verbal factor. The same would be done for the standard scores of each person in the investigation. A second factor could be obtained by summing scores over the three tests in Table 11-2 that concern arithmetic abilities. The factor scores could then be converted to standard scores or to some type of scores that would facilitate interpretations. Also, the factor scores could be used in future correlational studies in basic research or applied work, e.g., correlating scores on the verbal factor with grades in school.

A factor is nothing more than a set of scores obtained by combining scores over individual tests. In the foregoing example, a very simple type of combination of tests was described, that of simply summing scores over three tests. In actual work with factor analysis, it is frequently necessary to employ much more complex combinations of scores. This is necessary because (1) factor analyses frequently concern huge tables showing the correlations between fifty or more tests and (2) the clusters of related tests are not nearly as neatly divisible as they are in Table 11-2. The sheer complexity of the tables of correlations requires the use of some complex methods of mathematical analysis to determine factors and to determine the types of combinations of tests required to measure those factors. However, the basic principles in all forms of factor analysis are the same. Whether by complex or simple means, one first locates groups of tests that tend to measure the same thing, and then one obtains scores on the factors by combining scores on tests that relate to the factors.

In addition to obtaining factors, it is also informative to correlate the scores on each test with the scores of each factor. Because all persons in the investigation have scores on all tests and all factors, it is a simple matter to perform the necessary calculations.

Table 11-3 presents the correlations of the six tests from Table 11-2, with the two factors obtained by summing scores on the two clusters of tests. Such correlations of tests with factors are called *factor loadings*. The loading of test A on factor 1 is .90, and the loading of that test on factor 2 is .17. Factor loadings help one to understand the nature of each factor, and they indicate which tests are better measures of each factor.

Table 11-3   Loadings
of six tests on two
factors

	Factors	
	1	2
Test		
A	.90	.17
E	.87	.20
C	.84	.25
D	.24	.89
B	.20	.85
F	.17	.86

During the last half century, many different factor-analytic studies have been performed not only on tests of human ability, but also on measures of personality, interests, attitudes, and many other kinds of individual differences. Each factor-analytic study represents a very large undertaking. First, it is necessary to compose all the tests that will be used, and as was said previously, these may number more than 50. Then the entire group of tests must be given to a large number of persons, preferably more than 300. After the tests are scored, all possible correlations must be computed between them, resulting in tables of the kind shown above. Then the mathematical procedures of factor analysis must be applied. The end result is a number of factors showing the dominant clusters among the tests. The factors that have been found in each area of individual differences are said to constitute a *structure,* or, as one might say, a map describing the common tendencies among tests.

FACTORS OF ABILITY

The many factor analyses performed during the last half century have provided the answer to the question of the relative generality or specificity of human abilities. The results show that neither extreme point of view is correct and that a middle ground must be adopted. Arguing for the generality of abilities is the now well-established fact that correlations between tests of ability are almost always positive, even if small in some cases. For example, tests as disparate in appearance as those of vocabulary, memory of digits, and mechanical information all correlate positively, if no higher than .20 or .30. It would be rare, indeed, to find one type of human ability that correlated negatively with another. If that were found, it would indicate that, statistically speaking, people who performed well on one task would tend to perform poorly on another. Human abilities all tend to go together, even though in some cases the statistical relationships are very weak. These findings offer partial confirmation of the generalist point of view as represented by Binet and those who followed in his footsteps.

Factor-analytic results have also provided confirmation for the multifactor point of view. In addition to the tendency of all tests of human ability to correlate positively with one another, there are definite clusterings of the tests as shown by the correlations which have been obtained. For example, all tests involving the ability to understand words, such as tests of reading comprehension and vocabulary, tend to have high correlations with one another, averaging .60 or more. Similarly, all tests involving numerical computations, such as addition, subtraction, multiplication, and finding square roots, tend to correlate highly with one another and thus form another cluster, or factor. Correlations between the two kinds of tests are positive, typically averaging .30 or higher, but correlations between the members of the two clusters are not nearly so high as the correlations within the clusters. This indicates that the members of each cluster tend to hang together and measure something that is partially separate from what is measured by the other cluster, or factor.

Factor-analytic studies have shown that there are dozens, and perhaps even hundreds, of such clusters, or factors. However, most of these factors are concerned with highly specialized activities. For example, one such highly specialized factor concerns the effect of certain types of visual illusions on perceptual judgment; another concerns the ability to memorize digits presented in serial order. A great deal more research needs to be done before it will be possible to say which of these factors are important and in which situations. Some factors have proved useful in predicting success in school, in industry, and in military settings, but the bulk of them have been used insufficiently to determine their importance. A great deal of research has been done on the factors that make for success in school at all levels, and it has been found that only a few of the factors are very important. The following sections will describe some of the most important factors, including those which are important for schoolwork and for vocational activities.

VERBAL FACTORS

The most important factors relating to schoolwork concern the abilities to understand, use, and deal with written and spoken language. As is true of all the types of factors which will be discussed, there are many possible verbal factors that can be found by exhaustively analyzing many different types of verbal tests. However, only two of these seem to be very important for schoolwork. They are verbal comprehension and verbal fluency, which will be discussed in turn.

VERBAL COMPREHENSION.   The most important verbal factor concerns the ability to understand written and spoken language. Verbal comprehension represents most of what we refer to as "reading skill." Although the factor extends far beyond sheer vocabulary, a vocabulary test provides a good measure of verbal comprehension.

Typical items:

1. Which one of the following words means most nearly the same as *salutation?*
    a. offering
    b. greeting
    c. discussion
    d. appeasement

2. Which one of the following words is most nearly the opposite of *languid?*
    a. unemotional
    b. sad
    c. energetic
    d. healthy

VERBAL FLUENCY. Verbal fluency concerns the ability to produce words and sentences rapidly. It can be thought of as the rate-of-production aspect of verbal ability, in contrast to verbal comprehension, which concerns the depth of understanding of verbal material.

Typical items:

1. Write as many names of foods as you can in the next two minutes.

   _____

   _____

   _____

2. In each of the following rows, write three words that mean almost the same as the given word.

   small   _____   _____   _____

   helpful   _____   _____   _____

   kind   _____   _____   _____

Verbal comprehension comes into play when rather complex words, sentences, and paragraphs are being dealt with. Verbal fluency comes into play when the verbal material is relatively simple and when fluidity of expression is at issue. The two types of abilities are somewhat correlated. Correlations of about .40 or .50 are typically found between the tests used to measure verbal comprehension and those used to measure verbal fluency. On the other hand, the two types of abilities are far from perfectly correlated. A child may understand what he reads very well but have difficulty in explaining it because of his lack of verbal fluency. Similarly, the talkative child who produces a torrent of words in ordinary conversation does not always have a depth of comprehension to match. Teachers are sometimes fooled by the child who is quite facile in expression but who does rather poorly when he is required to read and understand material or to analyze poetry or essays.

NUMERICAL FACILITY

One very clear factor of numerical facility has been found in many different studies. It concerns the speed and accuracy of solving arithmetic problems of all kinds—addition, subtraction, multiplication, division, finding square roots, and others.

Typical items:

$$\begin{array}{r} 246 \\ +943 \\ \hline \end{array} \quad \begin{array}{r} 8{,}754 \\ -\ 381 \\ \hline \end{array} \qquad 16 \times 22 = \underline{\hspace{2cm}} \qquad 284/4 = \underline{\hspace{2cm}}$$

In addition to items that obviously concern arithmetic computations, the factor also extends to almost any type of task in which quantitative operations are involved, such as the following items, for example:

1. Which one of the following numbers is closest to 8.2?
    a. 8.1
    b. 8.3
    c. 8.18
    d. 8.23

2. Which one of the following numbers is most nearly the same as the square root of 15?
    a. 225
    b. 4
    c. 5
    d. 1.5

3. Which one of the following would be the largest *positive* amount?
    a. -10×-10
    b. -5×-5
    c. 10×-10
    d. 9×9

It should be clearly understood that not all problems containing numbers measure numerical facility. Numbers also appear in many of the reasoning tests, which will be discussed in the next section, but mainly such problems do not concern numerical facility. The numerical facility factor comes into play when some complex (for the age group) numerical solutions must be obtained. If the numbers involved are very simple and are included only as a way of providing a useful method of expressing the solution to a problem, numerical facility as such may be very unimportant. This distinction will be made clearer in the discussion of reasoning factors.

Tests of numerical facility usually show moderate (about .40) correlations with measures of verbal ability. As was mentioned previously, all measures of human ability tend to correlate positively with one another, but numerical facility has a far from perfect relationship with other factors of ability. Numerical facility is not the same as mathematical reasoning, which is involved in simple algebraic problems. Although algebraic problems require some numerical computations, these are usually relatively simple. Instead, algebraic problems relate more prominently to the reasoning factors, which will be discussed below. The fact that a child is very good in number skills in the elementary grades does not mean that he is likely to be good later in mathematical subject matter, such as algebra, geometry, and trigonometry.

REASONING FACTORS

Although many different studies of reasoning tests have been performed, the factors involved are still somewhat unclear. Reasoning is a complex domain in which the abilities involved tend to blend in different ways in different tests, making it hard to separate the reasoning factors from one another and to find good measures of any of them. The most clearly determined factors are discussed below.

GENERAL REASONING.   The most common and most commonly found factor of reasoning is concerned with the ability to invent solutions to problems. Arithmetical reasoning problems are most characteristic of the factor.

Typical items:

1.   If a machine produces bolts at the rate of two each 15 minutes, how many bolts does the machine produce in three hours?
2.   How would you get exactly 7 quarts of water from a stream if you had one 5-quart container and one 3-quart container?

As was mentioned previously, even though such simple algebraic problems involve numbers, the main ability being measured is not that of numerical computation. In order to solve the problems, the student must invent a solution and grasp some principle by which each can be solved.

The general reasoning factor also appears in items concerning serial completion, in which the subject is required to supply the next entry in a patterned series of letters or digits. Two examples are as follows:

zzyyxxw _____
2132435465 _____

There is an element of discovery in all the tests that measure the factor of general reasoning—the discovery of some principle whereby a correct solution is obtained.

DEDUCTION.   The deduction factor is concerned with the drawing of conclusions, as in logical syllogisms. In this type of reasoning there is nothing in particular to be discovered or invented, the ability being concerned with evaluating the implications of an argument.

Typical items:

1. John is younger than Fred. Bill is older than Fred. Therefore, Bill is _____ than John.

2. A student has 10 marbles. No one else in his class has 10 marbles. This means that:
   a. No one else in the class has marbles.
   b. All the other students have fewer than 10 marbles.
   c. Some of the students have fewer than 10 marbles.
   d. Some of the students have more than 10 marbles.
   e. Only one student has exactly 10 marbles.

Whereas the factor of general reasoning is represented by a very wide variety of items concerning the solution of problems, the deduction factor is more narrowly concerned with only those items pertaining to logical syllogisms.

SEEING RELATIONSHIPS.   A third factor of reasoning involves the ability to see the relationship between two things or ideas and to use the relationship to find other things or ideas. This factor is best represented by verbal analogies and design analogies.

Typical items:

Ship is to *sail* as *automobile* is to
   a. ship
   b. seat
   c. motor
   d. wind
   e. driver

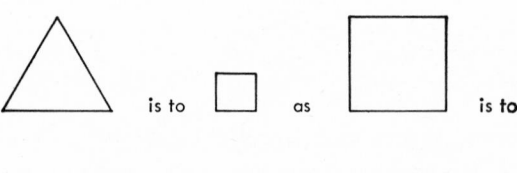

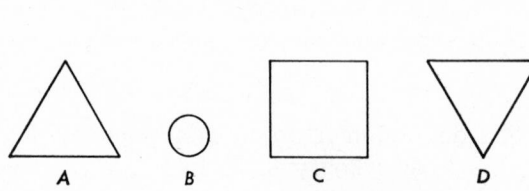

| A | B | C | D |

Some items concerning reasoning abilities represent a blend of the factor of seeing relationships and the factor of general reasoning. This is the case, for example, with the series-completion items illustrated previously.

MEMORY FACTORS

As is true of the other areas of human ability that we have discussed, there is more than one type of memory. Some of the better-established factors of memory are discussed below.

ROTE MEMORY.   The best-established factor of memory concerns the ability to remember simple associations where meaning is of little or no importance.

Typical item:

> The person is given a list of names, each of which is paired with a number. He is given a minute or so to memorize which number goes with which name. Then he is told to turn the page. The next page contains the list of names without the numbers. He is instructed to write the proper numbers next to the names. (Other items which concern rote memory are of the same general kind, involving, for example, pairing colors with words, initials with last names, and letters with geometric forms.)

MEANINGFUL MEMORY.   There is substantial evidence to indicate that there is a factor involved in the retention of meaningful relationships which is separable from rote memory. The factor of meaningful memory appears when the student is requested to memorize sentences, meaningfully related words, and lines of poetry.

Typical items:

1. The student is asked to read and to try to remember a list of sentences like the following:

    John repaired the wagon by welding the broken axle.

    The list of sentences is taken away, and the student is then given the same sentences with one or more of the words deleted from each, like the following:

    John repaired the wagon by welding the broken _____.

2. The student is shown a list of meaningfully related pairs of words such as the following:

dog—bark
shoe—leather
hard—candy
small—box

The list is taken away, and the student is presented with only one member of each pair as follows:

dog   _____
shoe   _____
hard   _____
small _____

There is evidence for several other memory factors. A number of investigators have reported a memory span factor concerning the ability to recall perfectly for immediate reproduction a series of unrelated items. A typical item would be to read a series of five to a dozen digits and ask the student to give the digits back in their exact order. There is some evidence for a visual memory factor in which the ability to grasp the relationships within a picture or pattern is important. A typical item would consist of showing an individual a landscape picture and asking him to remember the details. Then the picture would be taken away, and the student would be asked questions like "How many sheep were in the picture?" "What was the boy handing to the man?" "Where was the swing located?" The visual memory factor might be related to the ability to remember faces and witnessed events.

SPATIAL FACTORS

SPATIAL ORIENTATION. This factor concerns the ability to detect accurately the spatial arrangement of objects with respect to one's own body. The factor would be necessary in deciphering pictures taken from a maneuvering airplane. If the plane is simultaneously turning and climbing, the landscape looks very different from the normal view. The individual who can accurately detect what maneuver the airplane is going through from looking at only a picture of the landscape from that vantage point has good spatial orientation. The factor appears most prominently when the spatial problems are presented under "speeded" conditions.

Typical items:[1]

---

[1]1958, Thelma Gwinn Thurstone. Reprinted by permission of the publisher, Science Research Associates, Inc.

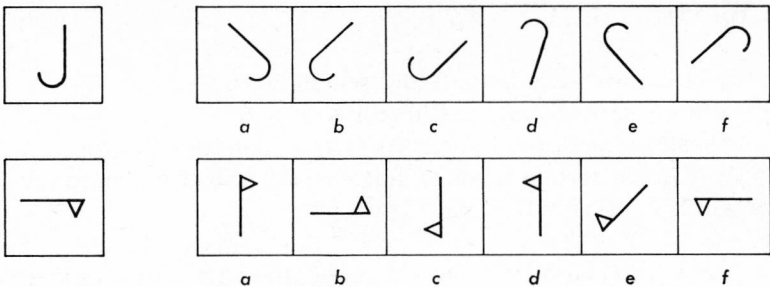

Every alternative that could be obtained by a
rotation of the first figure is to be marked.

SPATIAL VISUALIZATION. This second spatial factor differs in a
subtle manner from spatial orientation. It is present when the student is
required to imagine or *visualize* how an object would look if its spatial
position were changed. Although there is good statistical support for both
of these factors, there has been considerable difficulty in understanding
the underlying processes. Spatial orientation seems to require either an
actual or imagined adjustment of one's own body. In spatial visualization
the student cannot solve the problem by a bodily adjustment; instead,
the student must conceive of how an object would look if its spatial position were markedly changed. In contrast to spatial orientation, spatial
visualization is best tested under relatively "unspeeded" conditions.

Typical item:

The person is shown a folded piece of paper with a number of holes punched
in it. He is asked to choose from a number of unfolded pieces of paper the one
that would be the same as the first.

Other examples of items concerning spatial visualization are shown in
Figure 11-1.

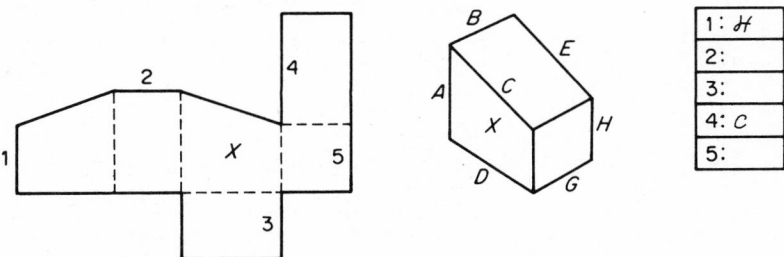

Figure 11-1. Sample item from the Surface Development Test. The subject's task is to
visualize how a piece of paper will be folded to make an object. He is asked to indicate
which lettered edge of the object on the right corresponds to each numbered edge of the
piece of paper at the left. (From *Surface Development Test.* Copyright © 1962 by Educational Testing Service. Reproduced by permission.)

PERCEPTUAL FACTORS

A number of factors have been found which concern the ability to detect visual patterns and to see relationships within and between patterns. Some of these factors are apparently of only limited importance, such as the ability to judge certain types of illusions. Several of the more important factors will be described.

PERCEPTUAL SPEED. This factor is concerned with the rapid recognition of perceptual details and particularly with the recognition of similarities and differences between visual patterns.
Typical items:

1. The person is shown a complex geometrical form and is asked to choose from a number of other forms the one that is the same as the first.

2. The person is told to make a check mark by each pair of letter groupings if they are identical and to make no mark beside groups that are different.
   x'#·Iq ——————X'#·IQ
   a&30(k ——————a&3(oK
   —ro-/w —————— —ro-/w

(Fifty to several hundred pairs would be used, depending on the time allowed.)

PERCEPTUAL CLOSURE. This factor concerns the perception of objects from limited cues. The word "closure" means a sudden awareness of an obscure object or relationship. Perceptual speed requires only the recognition of a perceptual form. Perceptual closure requires the "putting together" of a perceptual form when only part of it is presented.
Typical items:[2]

[2] Adapted from Thurstone (1944).

In the items on the left, the individual is required to recognize the incomplete words. In the items on the right, he is required to recognize the number or letter that is partially outlined.

FLEXIBILITY OF CLOSURE. There is evidence for a flexibility-of-closure factor in problems which require the subject to detect a perceptual pattern which is embedded in a distracting or competing pattern. This factor is found in such items as the hidden-picture games that are printed in newspapers and some children's magazines. For example, a picture that looks like a normal landscape at first glance is found, after careful scrutiny, to contain a number of faces hidden in the trees and rocks. In order to see the faces, it is necessary to resist or "break down" the perception of the object in which the faces are embedded.

Typical items:[3]

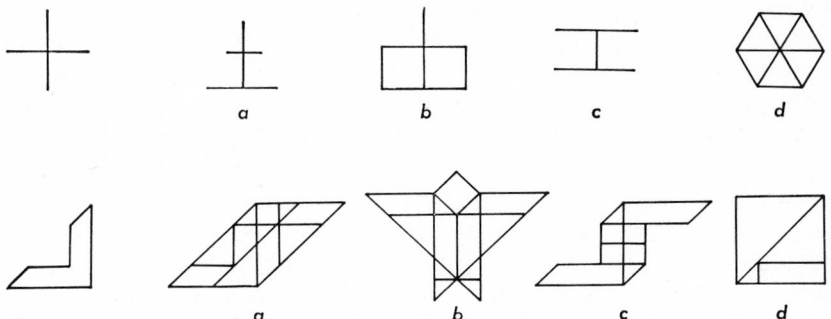

In each of the two items, the figure on the left is embedded in one or more of the four alternative figures on the right.

IMPORTANCE OF FACTORS IN DAILY LIFE

During the last thirty years, factor-analytic studies of human abilities have pushed far ahead. In the early 1940s, many psychologists were developing tests for the armed forces. Tests were developed for so many special types of aptitudes, and with respect to so many types of training programs, that excellent opportunities were provided to extend what was known about factors of human ability. Up through 1950, it could be reported that there were over forty well-established factors of ability. (These are described in detail in J. W. French, 1951.) The number of factors of intellect has continued to grow since the time of French's survey, and now one could argue that there are between fifty and one

[3]Reproduced by permission of Science Research Associates, Inc.

hundred factors, depending on how cautiously one interprets the evidence.

Eventually, what will be needed for an understanding of the importance of factors in daily life is a correlation of those factors with individual differences manifested in real-life situations. Presently, we do not know to what extent some factors of human ability extend beyond the "laboratory" to the things that people do every day. Are those factors of any importance for making change on a bus, recalling phone numbers, or giving a talk to the PTA? Of course, it is not possible to measure performance in a multitude of real-life situations, but at least it would be possible to conduct informal surveys of what people do in daily life. Persons who are familiar with the known factors of human ability could literally follow people around and watch the things that they do, and any task that possibly concerned one of the known factors could be noted. Also, it would be useful to list important tasks that apparently do not relate to any known factors of human ability. Although such an ecological investigation of the importance of factors in daily life might be extremely difficult in many real-life situations, such investigations would be feasible in many types of school settings. For example, teachers could be asked to make subjective analyses of the factors that seem to be important in various activities in the schoolroom. A systematic content analysis of that kind would produce many suggestions regarding statistical investigations of predictive validity and many suggestions regarding efforts to measure important new factors of ability. Gradually, in this way, a classification scheme could be developed for areas in real life that need to be explained by factors of ability, and studies could be made of the correlations between laboratory tests and daily behavior. It may sound rather farfetched, now, to talk of such developments, but issues relating to human abilities are sufficiently important to merit the efforts. In this process, we shall certainly find much "chaff" among presently known factors of human abilities, but the remaining "wheat" will stimulate further basic investigation.

GUILFORD'S CONCEPT OF THE STRUCTURE OF INTELLECT

For over two decades, J. P. Guilford and his colleagues have collected mountains of data with respect to factors of intellect, and Guilford has made notable contributions to methods of analysis; more importantly, however, he has done more than anyone else to develop a systematic point of view about the nature of the factors of intellect (see Guilford, 1967).

One of Guilford's major contributions has been the development of a classification scheme (or taxonomy) for factors of human intelligence. He refers to this as the *structure of intellect,* which is depicted in Figure 11-2. The classification scheme implies that all forms of intellectual functioning can be categorized with respect to subdivisions of three

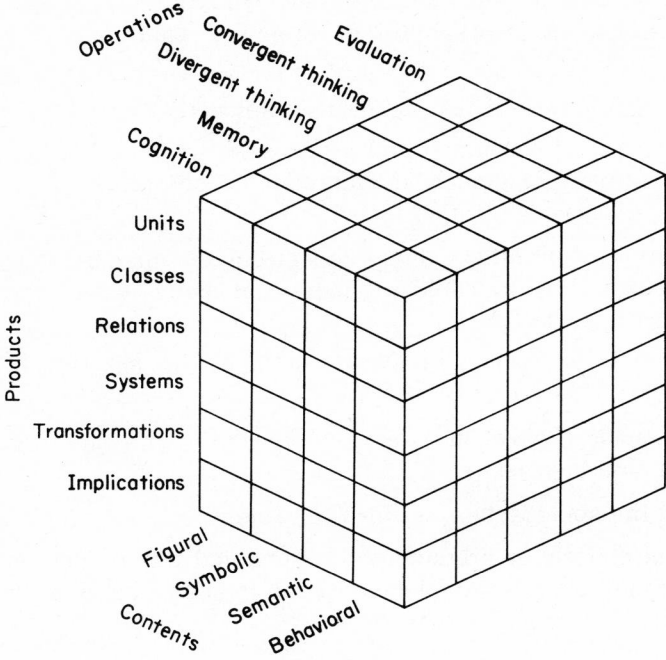

Figure 11-2. A cubical model representing the structure of intellect. *(Adapted from Guilford, 1967.)*

major characteristics. Following is a brief summary of the intellectual traits which Guilford has included in his scheme:

Operations concern the psychological process that is apparently involved in any test.

Cognition refers to "knowing," examples of which are knowing the meaning of the word "tangible" and knowing the product of 12 and 12.

Memory involves simply the operation of retaining information that is briefly presented, such as recalling a phone number heard on the radio.

Divergent production consists of producing a variety of ideas that lead in different directions, such as thinking of unusual uses for common objects.

Convergent production concerns finding either the only solution or the best solution to a stated problem, such as for a problem involving arithmetical reasoning.

Evaluation has to do with reaching decisions about the accuracy, goodness, suitability, or workability of proposed solutions to a problem.

Content concerns the nature of test materials employed.

Figural material has been illustrated previously with respect to items concerning figural analogies, spatial relations, spatial visualization, perceptual closure, and others.

Symbolic content is exemplified in items concerning the unscrambling of scrambled words and the rapid production of many words that begin with a particular letter.

Semantic content is present in items that concern the meaning of verbal material.

Behavioral content is present in tests in which the appropriateness of some overt action is at issue.

Products concern the specific task set for the subject.

Units refer to the finding or producing of a specified thing, such as correctly unscrambling a scrambled word or naming the objects in items concerning perceptual closure.

Classes concern items which require the subject either to place things in their proper groupings or to recognize proper groupings.

Relations are exemplified by items involving verbal analogies and figural analogies.

Systems concern items in which the subject must grasp some principle by which a number of objects are related.

Transformations concern appropriate changes of various kinds and would be involved, for example, in items that measure the factor of spatial visualization.

Implications concern items which require the subject to extrapolate from the given facts to some conclusion, such as an item in which he is asked to state what some of the implications would be if the world population were reduced by one-half during the next 100 years.

MULTIFACTOR BATTERIES

Instead of employing only tests of general ability, it would be possible to employ multifactor batteries containing tests for some of the important factors discussed in previous sections of this chapter. There are two reasons why multifactor batteries are not used more often than they are in school settings. First, as was mentioned previously, in the elementary grades abilities of students tend to be more general, and one general test, such as those which will be discussed in the next chapter, goes a long way toward indicating the student's ability. The second reason is that a thorough multifactor battery is very difficult to construct and is expensive and time-consuming to apply. In order to measure a factor, such as the general reasoning factor, it is necessary to have at least two tests relating to the factor. If the battery contains measures of as many as six factors, this makes for a total of twelve tests. Because each test would require a minimum of twenty or thirty minutes, the total battery would consume a great deal of time. Scoring and interpretation also would require considerable time on the part of teachers and school counselors. When more funds are available for testing, and when better multifactor batteries are made for the elementary grades, we can expect a wider use of such tests at these early levels. At the present time, few uses are made of multifactor batteries until the high school level.

In the following section will be described a multifactor battery that is frequently used with high school students. For each type of test to be discussed in this and the following chapters, one or several examples will be presented. To prevent the book from becoming a dreary catalogue of tests and their individual characteristics, no effort will be made to give a comprehensive review of all the good tests in each area. For example, there are at least a dozen good group tests of intelligence, and to describe them all would make for very dull reading. In addition to the examples which will be described in the text, other good tests relating to each area of measurement will be described in Appendix D.

THE DIFFERENTIAL APTITUDE TESTS. The Differential Aptitude Tests (DAT) were developed by the Psychological Corporation, principally for use in the vocational and educational guidance of high school students (Bennett, Seashore, & Wesman, 1966). Although the tests were intended for use with students in grades 8 to 12, they have a sufficient range of item difficulty to be used with most adult groups. The tests were not developed directly out of factor-analytic work, but were composed in such a way as to incorporate some of the major findings from factor analysis.

The subtests of the DAT, together with the sample items, are as follows:[4]

1. Verbal reasoning. The items consist of verbal analogies in which the reasoning component, rather than the difficulty of words, is emphasized. The test is more concerned with reasoning factors than with verbal comprehension:

_____ is to one as second is to _____
A.   two—middle
B.   first—fire
C.   queen—hill
D.   first—two
E.   rain—fire

_____ is to night as breakfast is to _____
A.   supper—corner
B.   gentle—morning
C.   door—corner
D.   flow—enjoy
E.   supper—morning

Each of the 50 sentences in this test has the first word and the last word left out. Pick out words which will fill the blanks so that the sentence will be true and sensible.

2. Numerical ability. The test covers a wide range of numerical computations. It should be a good measure of the numerical facility factor previously described.

Add 13	A	14		Subtract 30	A	15
12	B	25		20	B	26
	C	16			C	16
	D	59			D	8
	E	none of these			E	none of these

Choose the correct answer.

3. Abstract reasoning. This test differs from the verbal reasoning test in that all the problems deal with abstract patterns.

[4]Sample items reproduced by permission. Copyright 1947, 1961, The Psychological Corporation, New York. All rights reserved.

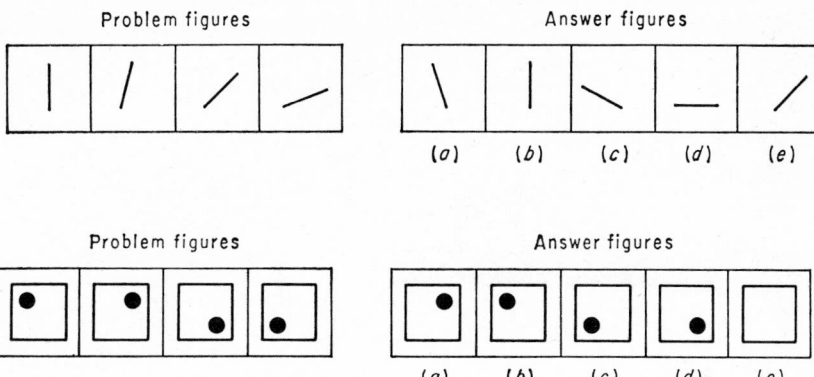

Each row consists of four figures that are called Problem Figures, and five called Answer Figures. The four Problem Figures make a series. You are to find which one of the Answer Figures would be the next, or fifth one, in the series.

4. Spatial relations. The test items concern the individual's ability to imagine how objects would look if they were rotated in space and to visualize a three-dimensional object from a two-dimensional pattern.

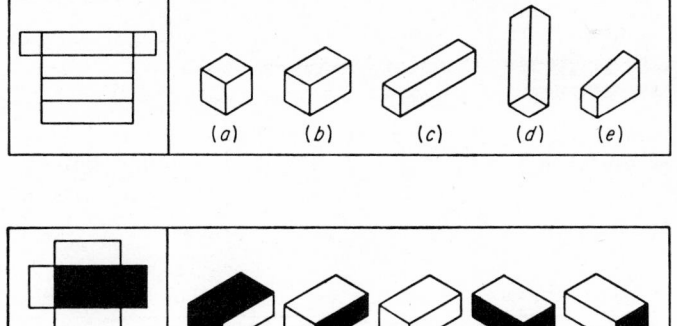

The test consists of 40 patterns which can be folded into figures. For each pattern, five figures are shown. You are to decide which of these figures can be made from the pattern shown.

5. Mechanical reasoning. The test items consist of pictures which portray mechanical problems. The student is asked questions about each picture.

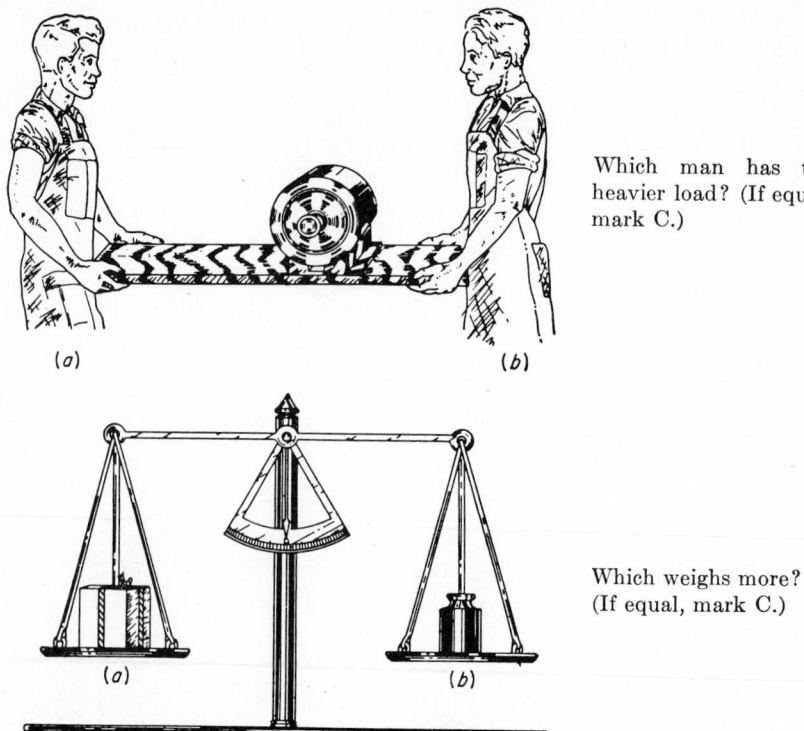

Which man has the heavier load? (If equal, mark C.)

(a) (b)

Which weighs more? (If equal, mark C.)

(a) (b)

6.   Clerical speed and accuracy.   The test is modeled closely after the perceptual speed factor. The student is required to find identical sets of numbers and figures.

TEST ITEMS					
V.	AB	AC	AD	AE	AF
W.	aA	aB	BA	Ba	Bb
X.	A7	7A	B7	7B	AB
Y.	Aa	Ba	bA	BA	bB
Z.	3A	3B	33	B3	BB

SAMPLE OF ANSWER SHEET					
V	AC	AE	AF	**AB**	AD
W	BA	Ba	**Bb**	aA	aB
X	**7B**	B7	AB	7A	A7
Y	Aa	**bA**	bB	Ba	BA
Z	BB	3B	B3	3A	**33**

Each test item consists of five letter and number combinations. You are to look at the one combination that is underlined, and find the same combination on the answer sheet. (The examples above are all correctly done.)

7. Language usage.   This test is more concerned with acquired knowledge, or achievement, than with a specific aptitude. The two parts of the test concern spelling ability and the ability to distinguish between good and bad grammar, punctuation, and word usage.

Part I: Spelling
W. man
X. gurl
Y. catt
Z. dog
   Indicate whether or not each word is spelled correctly.

Part II: Grammar
Ain't we / going to / the office / next week?
   A   B   C   D

   The test consists of a series of sentences, each divided into four parts, lettered A, B, C, and D. You are to look at each sentence and decide which part has an error in grammar, punctuation, or spelling. Some sentences have no error in any part. If there is no error in a sentence, fill in the space under the letter E on the answer sheet.

Although the DAT tests were not derived directly from factor analysis, the tests represent a collection of reasonably independent measures which range broadly over those factors most directly related to school achievement. The tests were constructed primarily for school programs, and it is doubtful that they would meet with the same level of success in other testing situations. The correlations between the tests vary considerably, ranging from .06 to as high as .67. The intercorrelations run about .50 on the average. Although it is desirable to have lower correlations, they are not so high as to prevent the battery from functioning as a measure of differential aptitudes.

The reliabilities of the tests are generally high, ranging from .85 to .93 for all except the mechanical comprehension test. The reliability for men on the mechanical comprehension test is sufficiently high, with a mean coefficient of .85, but the reliability for women is only .71.

A particular point in favor of the DAT is the large amount of research that went into the standardization and validation of the instrument. The norms are based on the testing of 47,000 students in grades 8 to 12 in schools scattered widely over the United States. Because sizable sex differences were found on some the the tests, separate norms are given for boys and girls.

Thousands of correlations between DAT scores and various criteria have been computed. Some correlations between test scores and school grades are shown in Table 11-4. A follow-up study was undertaken of students two years after they completed high school. The results are shown in Table 11-5, in which scores for the total group are broken down in terms of subsequent occupation or college specialty. A second follow-up of the same students was conducted seven years after they completed high school, and the results of the later follow-up reinforced the conclusions of the earlier study. That is, characteristics of high school students, as measured by the DAT, do seem to be related to their subsequent occupational and educational careers. Table 11-6 reports percentiles for occupations in which twenty or more participants in the seven-year follow-up were engaged. Research of this kind provides a firmer basis for the use of the DAT in vocational counseling. The DAT is a model of careful test design, practicality, thoroughness of research, and frankness of reporting. Other test batteries for the measurement of differential abilities are described in Appendix D.

Table 11-4   Median correlations of DAT scores with school grades* *(From Bennett, Seashore, & Wesman, 1966.)*

Test	English	Math	Science	Social Studies, History	Language	Commercial Courses
VR	49(55)	38(41)	45(54)	46(52)	44(48)	37(42)
NA	47(52)	50(53)	44(51)	46(52)	42(40)	44(49)
AR	38(45)	39(54)	38(42)	34(40)	24(26)	24(40)
SR	29(31)	28(32)	34(34)	27(33)	22(18)	21(28)
MR	16(28)	23(26)	29(28)	16(27)	15(19)	11(22)
CSA	27(28)	20(20)	24(25)	24(28)	13(19)	28(25)
Lang.:						
Spell.	45(48)	27(32)	36(40)	38(45)	49(48)	34(45)
Gram.	50(55)	38(40)	44(48)	48(50)	50(49)	39(49)

*Decimal points omitted. The first correlation coefficient in each column entry is for boys; the entries in parentheses are for girls.

USES OF MULTIFACTOR TEST BATTERIES

In spite of the overwhelming evidence indicating that there are numerous factors of ability, multifactor test batteries still are not used widely. Instead, in most situations only a measure of general ability is employed, or only two tests are employed (these typically being a measure of verbal

Table 11-5 **Percentile equivalents of average scores on the DAT for men in various educational and occupational groups** (Adapted from Bennett, Seashore, & Wesman, 1966. Reproduced by permission of The Psychological Corporation.)

Group	No.	Percentiles							
		VR	NA	AR	SR	MR	CSA	Spell.	Sent.
Degree-seeking students:									
Premedical	24	88	86	81	72	77	77	90	90
Science (biology, chemistry, and mathematics)	25	81	85	60	67	68	74	81	72
Engineering (includes architectural)	70	80	86	80	81	82	67	68	74
Liberal arts (includes prelaw)	68	79	75	78	61	64	75	78	81
Business administration	64	72	73	61	63	60	71	67	68
Education (includes physical education)	25	68	66	58	57	48	68	67	66
Various: predental, agricultural, etc.	30	64	67	74	60	73	59	55	64
Non-degree-seeking students in two-year schools:									
Business, technical, fine arts, etc.	43	63	62	71	72	68	60	54	61
Employed:									
Salesmen	23	56	53	53	52	57	44	50	49
Clerks: general office work	55	45	42	52	44	41	41	52	53
Mechanical, electrical, and building trades	66	34	41	46	49	56	44	28	29
Various skilled: butcher, baker, etc.	26	47	37	43	41	49	51	52	45
Various unskilled: truck driver, laborer, etc.	85	35	30	36	42	49	37	35	36
Military service	129	46	42	46	51	50	49	46	41
Unclassified:									
No consistent work or school record	58	53	48	51	54	54	46	47	52

Table 11-6 Percentile equivalents of average scores on the DAT (Forms A and B) for students tested in 1947 in relation to occupational field in 1955 (Bennett, Seashore, & Wesman, 1966, pp. 5–44. Reproduced by permission of The Psychological Corporation.)

Group	N	Percentiles							
		VR	NA	AR	SR	MR	CSA	Spell.	Sent.
Men:									
Engineers	22	84	89	86	81	86	74	79	81
Draftsmen	21	47	47	50	67	53	61	44	51
Technicians	49	42	45	45	48	53	51	37	34
Businessmen	21	57	58	54	36	45	64	58	55
Salesmen	39	56	49	58	50	52	55	55	49
Clerks	46	39	41	46	50	43	45	47	46
Supervisors—foremen	21	43	44	43	52	46	69	48	35
Factory workers	37	43	27	34	52	54	28	29	32
Building tradesmen	21	32	33	45	50	38	43	35	27
Laborers	24	38	21	28	29	35	32	36	25
Students (current)	107	76	74	72	62	63	68	72	76
Military personnel	132	67	67	63	64	64	58	64	66
Women:									
Teachers	49	81	84	81	74	71	73	72	82
Nurses	28	78	75	73	77	64	58	70	66
Stenographers	126	58	56	54	52	52	61	67	56
Clerks	198	46	45	48	48	49	52	46	40
Housewives	277	57	50	55	59	58	52	54	52

comprehension, such as verbal analogies, and a measure of general reasoning, usually with items concerning arithmetical reasoning). The present limited use of multifactor batteries is due partly to the fact that they are more expensive, more time-consuming to administer, and more difficult to interpret than tests of general ability (intelligence tests). Also, multifactor batteries are not used more frequently because of a "cultural lag" in many applied settings regarding the nature of human abilities and the potential uses for such batteries of tests. In addition, much more research needs to be done in the development of truly effective batteries for measuring the more important factors. In the following sections, the major factors that are important in the settings in which multifactor batteries might be useful will be discussed.

EDUCATION.   After looking at the factors presented in previous sections and considering that these are only some of the many factors that have been found, the reader is likely to have the discomforting feeling that the schoolchild is fragmented into many different pieces, which are hard to put together in a living image. Fortunately, the problem is not quite that complex. Some of the factors which have been cited, and most of the many which have not been cited, are of relatively little importance for the teacher in the classroom. Although a great deal more research needs to be done before we can say with confidence how factors of ability grow, change, and interact with success in daily life, there are some guideposts that can be used.

Verbal comprehension is by far the most important factor to consider in relation to schoolwork. Schoolwork consists mainly of words—printed and spoken. The child reads his assignments, learns the meaning of new words, gives verbal replies to questions by the teacher, talks to his friends in relation to group projects, and writes paragraph descriptions of recent events. The school setting is a highly verbal world, and unless the child has an understanding of words and how words go together in sentences, paragraphs, and books, he is crippled. It may be that, depending on his vocation, he will not be so dependent on verbal comprehension in later life, but in the school setting it is all-important. The first four or five grades of elementary school are almost synonymous with the development of verbal comprehension. Because it is of such central importance, a good test of vocabulary or reading comprehension is the best indicator of scholastic aptitude as shown in the primary grades. If a child is very high in verbal comprehension and only average in some of the other important factors (which is a rare occurrence), he still will probably do well in schoolwork. His lack of ability in other areas, such as in the areas of reasoning factors, may hinder him in higher education and in vocational pursuits, but because of the centrality of verbal comprehension for schoolwork, he will probably manage to make good grades, at least at the elementary school level.

Verbal fluency provides the student with a special advantage. He can talk fluently, and he makes a good impression on others. As was mentioned previously, although, statistically speaking, verbal comprehension and verbal fluency tend to go together, there are some real exceptions. Consequently, the teacher should be on guard not to mistake sheer fluency for the deeper understanding of words and written material. Verbal fluency allows an individual to "sell himself," and because it is not always matched by a high level on other important factors of ability, an individual who is high on verbal fluency often oversells himself, to the subsequent disappointment of teachers in school situations and employers and co-workers later in life.

The numerical facility factor is important mainly for some topics in the elementary grades. Children must learn to add and subtract, divide, obtain square roots, and develop other numerical skills. Nothing is more frustrating to a teacher than to have a child who consistently flounders in numerical skills. Although there is some correlation between numerical facility and other important factors, such as verbal comprehension and the reasoning factors, such correlations tend to be relatively low. Consequently, a child can have difficulty in numerical skills and still be superior with respect to more important factors of ability. When the deficiency in numerical skills is very extreme, as in the case of an eighth-grade child who still cannot add and subtract, it probably indicates an over-all deficiency in intellectual abilities. Except for these extremes, facility in numerical computation is a nice thing to possess, but is not intimately related to eventual achievement in most careers. Even some of the better mathematicians (whose abilities depend more on the reasoning factors) are only average at numerical computations.

The reasoning factors are, of course, all-important for high-level vocational and professional activities later in life. They also play some part in success in school situations, more so in high school and college than in the elementary grades. The reasoning factors are directly involved in learning mathematics (not numerical skills) in the form of simple algebraic problems in the higher levels of elementary school and in learning mathematical topics presented in high school and in college. In school situations, the reasoning factors come into play mainly when the student is required to do something on his own, such as write an essay on world government. In such instances, the child who can invent solutions to problems, see logical consequences, and see parallels between historical trends and what is going on now has a distinct advantage.

Memory factors come into play mainly when there are many simple facts, dates, and names to be mastered. The memory abilities are not intimately related to the "higher" abilities—verbal comprehension and the reasoning factors. A child can be quite intelligent in other ways and have great difficulty in memorizing simple facts and details. Memory is apparently strongly influenced by the desire to memorize and the patience to work at it. As is true of nearly all the ability factors, when the deficiency is quite extreme, e.g., in the case of a twelve-year-old child who is unable to memorize the multiplication tables, it suggests an over-all deficiency. Otherwise, memory factors are not highly prognostic of eventual high-level success in college and beyond. Memory plays a very important part in the first several grades at the primary level. Much of the child's time is consumed with memorizing the alphabet, sounds relating to alphabetical letters, the sequence of numbers, names, and simple facts. Although verbal comprehension also plays an important part in the first several grades, the important part played by memory factors often obscures the true ability of some children and causes the teacher to overestimate the ability of others. Some children who perform poorly when details must be memorized manifest a superior ability in later schoolwork.

Nearly all children (excepting some true mental deficients) can be taught to memorize the essential details in schoolwork. First, it would be better if teachers discouraged memorizing for its own sake, e.g., memorizing long lists of names, places, and dates. This does not constitute true intellectual accomplishment, and the child will soon forget most of what he has memorized. Second, where memorization is essential for subsequent understanding, e.g., memorization of the multiplication tables, the ability of all students to memorize material can be greatly increased by the gifted teacher who turns memorizing into pleasant games rather than dull activities.

The spatial and perceptual factors play only a modest part in successful performance in elementary and secondary school. Spatial factors are somewhat important for secondary mathematics, for special mathematics courses in high school (e.g., geometry and trigonometry), and, to some extent, for physics. Perceptual factors are largely auxiliary skills that help students to only a small extent, e.g., in proofreading an English theme for spelling errors. Spatial and perceptual factors come into play when students are out of school engaging in professional and vocational pursuits. Airplane pilots must have spatial orientation; visualization is essential to the draftsman; and perceptual speed is important for file clerks. Tests of spatial and perceptual abilities are quite useful in batteries employed in high school for vocational counseling.

The need to test for many different factors of ability, rather than for general ability only, varies directly with the school level. In the primary grades only several of the factors we have discussed are important, mainly verbal comprehension. Later in elementary school some of the other factors play an important part: deduction, seeing relations, word fluency, and others. In high school some specialized topics, such as typing and mechanical drawing, bring into play some of the more specialized perceptual and spatial factors which were of relatively little importance earlier.

As the student goes into college and eventually enters a vocation or profession, an even wider array of factors must be taken into account.

The school-day world of the child is comparatively simple. He must possess verbal comprehension, some reasoning ability, and at least a modicum of skill in verbal fluency and the memory factors. If he has these, he will succeed. In contrast, vocational and professional skills are quite complex and in many instances may depend on esoteric factors which we seldom consider and which are presently very difficult to measure. Because of the changing intellectual requirements, it can be said that abilities are actually more general in children than in adults. The intellectual demands made on children are more general in that they relate to only several of the factors which we have discussed, and, in a sense, intellectual functions are more general in children. Apparently the many specialized factors which are found in factor-analytic studies, e.g., spatial visualization, are due to the special interests that the individual acquires and the experiences he has as he matures. Because children in the elementary grades have not been exposed to so many varied activities, differences in related skills are not important factors. The greater generality of intellectual functions in children and the generality of requirements at the elementary levels make it feasible to test for general ability without losing a great deal of information. Because only a few of the factors are very important in the elementary grades, and because these tend to correlate with one another, it makes some sense to add them all together in one test of general ability.

What has been said and shown about the factors of intellect has two important implications for teachers. First, as human abilities grow more complex during the high school years, it is important to give measures of some of the most significant factors rather than to test for general ability only. Such measures will prove useful in advising students about future schooling and vocations. Second, the factor-analytic results provide a lesson that abilities, even in the primary grades, are not perfectly general. Students are not uniformly good or poor at all the kinds of tasks that are presented, and every now and then we see a child who is quite uneven in his abilities, e.g., very high in the memory factors but very poor in verbal comprehension. In addition to making over-all measures and appraisals of students' abilities, teachers should be on guard to look at the differential abilities of each student. Some students are simply better at certain kinds of intellectual tasks than at others, and there is nothing "wrong" when this occurs. Because a student is very high in several intellectual dimensions, e.g., the verbal dimensions, teachers often wrongly conclude that he should be very high in others, such as general reasoning. Some unevenness in levels of ability is to be expected of all students. Consequently, rather than ask the oversimplified question of how bright Ted Bronson is, it would be more meaningful to ask how high he is in verbal comprehension, what his level of verbal fluency is, how he does on rote memorization, and how well he performs in numerical computation. To have to consider these somewhat different dimensions of intellectual activity, rather than talk about one over-all dimension of intelligence, complicates our work considerably, but it brings us closer to a faithful map of human ability.

VOCATIONS.   Multifactor test batteries come into their own in advising people about, and selecting them for, particular vocations. Whereas only several factors are highly important for most schoolwork, and a measure of general ability goes a long way toward tapping those factors, different vocations frequently require quite different factors of ability. Consequently, multifactor batteries are used widely in vocational counseling in high school, college, governmental counseling services, and other places. Also, multifactor batteries are used widely for selecting persons for particular jobs in industry and governmental agencies, e.g., television repairmen and secretaries for governmental offices; for placing men in different training programs in the armed forces, e.g., programs in mechanics, radar maintenance, and control-tower operation; and for selecting people for certain types of advanced training in universities, e.g., dentistry. The differential aptitude batteries discussed in Appendix D are frequently employed with respect to the foregoing kinds of selection. Also, because different vocations frequently require different factors of ability, numerous special batteries have been constructed for particular uses. This is the case, for example, with the selection of students in dentistry, where some of the motor abilities, particularly finger dexterity, are important. This is also the case with respect to the placement of men in different forms of technical training in the Air Force, where spatial, perceptual, and motor abilities differ in their importance for different specialties.

BASIC RESEARCH.   It is reasonable to predict that eventually multifactor batteries will be used frequently in educational research, but at the present time they are not being used very much for that purpose. Studies of the learning of motor skills provide an interesting example, e.g., a task requiring an unusual type of two-hand coordination. By correlating measures of performance after different amounts of practice with scores on a multifactor battery administered prior to training, it has been possible to determine the importance of different factors at different levels of training.

There are many places in which well-constructed multifactor batteries of tests would prove very useful in educational research. For example, there is much interest in improving the readiness of culturally impoverished preschool children for entrance into kindergarten and the first grade. Various forms of intellectual stimulation have been employed for that purpose, including challenging the child with many simple and enjoyable puzzles and games which require various cognitive skills. Frequently employed in such investigations are intelligence tests. Although such tests provide very useful over-all indications of improvement in intellectual capacities, they fail to document the particular ways in which programs of cultural enrichment affect children. Multifactor batteries of tests could cast considerable light on this topic.

Another area of research in which multifactor batteries would be quite useful is in the investigation of the development of human abilities. Although not enough research has been done on the topic, the research so far with multifactor batteries indicates that the rates of maturation of different types of abilities vary considerably. For example, children in the middle elementary grades perform about as well in some of the factors concerning spatial abilities, perceptual abilities, and memory as students in the later grades of high school. In sharp contrast, there are wide gulfs in the abilities of these two age groups in terms of some of the verbal factors (particularly verbal comprehension) and some of the reasoning factors. Such differences in growth rates of separable abilities in children are extremely important for educational theory and practice, but not nearly enough is known about these matters.

There are many other places in which multifactor batteries would be helpful in educational research. It can be expected that as sufficient research funds are made available for constructing and employing such instruments widely, and as steady improvements are made in the quality of existing batteries, teachers and educational researchers will become more aware of the characteristics and virtues of multifactor test batteries.

SUMMARY

There has been a historic controversy about human abilities, concerning whether they are perfectly general, as is implied by the use of measures of general intelligence, or whether, instead, there are separable factors of intellect. There is something to say for both points of view. Most tests of ability correlate positively, even if some of the correlations are negligible. This is evidence for the generality of ability. However, modern methods of factor analysis have clearly shown that the patterns of correlations between tests lead inescapably to the conclusion that there are numerous separable, but not entirely independent, factors of human ability.

The problem now is not one of finding new factors of human ability, but rather one of separating the wheat from the chaff among the many factors that have already been found. There are standards for deciding the importance of factors. One important standard is that the factor should relate to a broad range of item content, as the factor of verbal comprehension does. A second standard is that some, but not necessarily all, factors should demonstrate the ability to predict successful performance in applied situations. A third standard is that the factor should relate to mathematical models concerning human abilities. A fourth standard, perhaps the most important one, is that factors should demonstrate their importance in controlled experiments in psychology, e.g., in experiments on learning, motivation, perception, and physiological processes. Despite the fact that many, many factors have reared their heads in statistical analyses of correlations between tests, only a handful of those factors have proved their importance with respect to the aforementioned standards.

Except during the last two years of high school, not much use is made of multifactor test batteries for three reasons. First, as is true of so many measurement methods in education, existing multifactor batteries are far short of perfection. Second, those batteries which are available are somewhat tedious to use and interpret. Third, at least for the first four or five grades of elementary school, success in schoolwork depends very heavily on only one factor of intellect—verbal comprehension; consequently, one test which is heavily concerned with verbal comprehension goes a long way toward serving the need. Because tests of general intelligence lean heavily on verbal comprehension, they serve very well in this regard. However, as better multifactor batteries are constructed and as educators become better acquainted with their advantages, more use will probably be made of the batteries.

A discussion of the generality of intellect should provide several important lessons to teachers. Intelligence is not perfectly general, and teachers should look for the ups and downs in abilities within each student. While a student may be quite capable over-all, there may be areas of scholastic activity in which he is only average, or even well below average. On the other hand, a student who appears to be below average, in general, may be well above average in some scholastic activities. Another lesson that teachers should learn is that it is easy to pay too much attention to some factors of intellect that have very little to do with long-range success in school and in later work. This is particularly so for some of the memory factors and for the numerical facility factor. Although these relate to how well children master some of the simple skills in elementary school, they have little to do with how well students perform later in school, and even less to do with high-level accomplishment in life. Whereas teachers frequently pay too much attention to some factors of ability, they frequently neglect factors that prove to be all-important at high levels of educational and professional activity. That is the case for some of the reasoning factors which were discussed and illustrated in this chapter.

Although much still needs to be done to perfect multifactor test batteries, potentially they offer many advantages over a measure of general intelligence alone. Multifactor batteries can be useful in (1) determining the readiness of students at different age levels for different types of instructional activities, (2) providing counseling and remedial instruction for students who are having difficulty in various school topics, (3) advising high school students about choices of vocations and higher education, and (4) increasing the explanatory power of many forms of educational research.

SUGGESTED ADDITIONAL READINGS

Anastasi, A. *Psychological testing.* (3rd ed.) New York: Macmillan, 1968, chaps. 13–15.

Cronbach, L. J. *Essentials of psychological testing.* (3rd ed.) New York: Harper & Row, 1970, chaps. 7, 9.

Guilford, J. P. Factorial angles to psychology. *Psychol. Rev.,* 1961, **68,** 1–20.

Guilford, J. P. *The nature of human intelligence.* New York: McGraw-Hill, 1967.

Nunnally, J. C. *Psychometric theory.* New York: McGraw-Hill, 1967, chap. 12.

Spearman, C. E. *The abilities of man.* New York: Macmillan, 1927.

chapter 12

TESTS OF GENERAL ABILITY

Parents, mostly mothers, are making the supreme sacrifice in behalf of togetherness with their sons by attending the monthly cub scout pack meeting. While there is a lull in the ceremonies in preparation for awarding badges, insignia, and many special citations, mothers are talking, as they often are, about their children. Mrs. Crankston wonders if the school is doing enough for "gifted children." Her Charlie has been tested by a psychologist and, so she says, "has a high IQ, but they are not giving him any special instruction at Belmont." At the mention of "IQ," the other mothers assume a look of awe, as though something sacred had been broached.

No other product of psychology has had the same impact on the public as have "intelligence tests." Their results are too often reported as though they were infallible guides to all that is wise and good. Such tests do serve many purposes well, but only if they are expertly administered, and only if they are interpreted in the light of the limitations of the tests, the personality of the child, and the special abilities which the child possesses. The purpose of this chapter is to explain the composition, use, and proper interpretation of "intelligence tests."

The term "intelligence tests" has been placed in quotes, and used with some misgiving, because it implies more than can be expected from any test. Consequently, the first issue to be discussed will be that of what the so-called "intelligence tests" actually contain.

THE CONTENT OF "INTELLIGENCE TESTS"

In the previous chapter, it was shown that there are a number of semiindependent kinds, or factors, of intelligence, and it was said that it is somewhat misleading to lump all these together in one over-all measure. That is what the intelligence tests do—they sample from the content of a number of factors of intellect. In other words, they seek to measure how intelligent a person is, in general (or on the average), without specifying the particular ways in which he is more or less capable. Because they sample content from a number of factors, it is more appropriate to refer to them as measures of general ability, rather than to use the more grandiose term "intelligence tests."

For several reasons, tests of general ability have been very useful in the past, and will probably continue to be for some time to come, in spite of the fact that they measure a conglomerate of separable mental functions. Sheer expediency is one reason why it has been necessary to rely heavily on measures of general ability. It is very difficult to construct the extensive batteries which are needed to measure even a few of the more important factors described in the previous chapter. Such batteries are expensive for schools to use and time consuming to administer. Even after the scores on multifactor batteries have been obtained, they usually are very difficult for most persons to interpret.

Another reason why it is defensible to use measures of general ability is that they are not as conglomerate as might be thought. Rather than spreading their content evenly over many different factors, they tend to concentrate on only several of the more important factors. In particular, they tend to concentrate on the factors of verbal comprehension, general reasoning, seeing relationships, and numerical facility. To a lesser extent, they sample items from memory, perceptual, and spatial factors. The factors which predominate in most tests of general ability are the ones that intuitively "look" important, and as studies have shown, they are the ones that are most important in schoolwork. These factors also tend to correlate well with one another. For these reasons, tests of general ability primarily measure some of the more "important" factors, rather than an entirely illogical hodgepodge of mental functions.

The factor content of most tests of general ability was not specifically planned. Rather, each test constructor selected items that looked like they measured "intelligence." In later factor-analytic studies, it was found that most tests tend to measure the same factors, and, consequently, most of them correlate highly with one another. Some examples of the types of items that tend to predominate in measures of general ability are shown as follows:

VOCABULARY:

Indignant means most nearly the same as
a. poor
b. lazy
c. angry
d. spiteful

VERBAL RELATIONS:

Ship is to sail as automobile is to _____.

VERBAL MEANING:

What is the meaning of the saying "penny-wise and pound-foolish"?

FIGURAL RELATIONS:

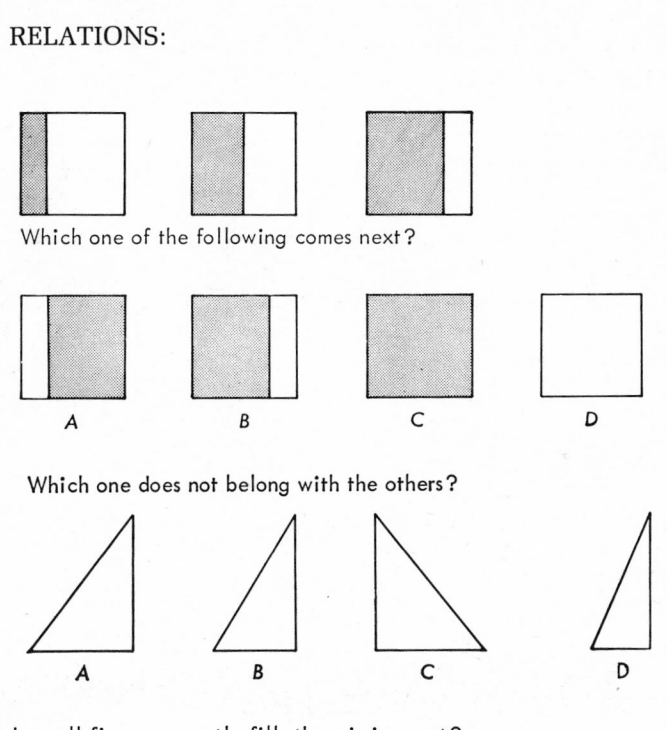

Which one of the following comes next?

A   B   C   D

Which one does not belong with the others?

A   B   C   D

Which small figure correctly fills the missing part?

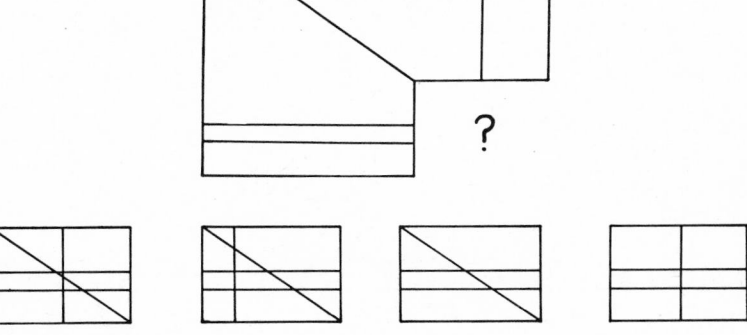

PRACTICAL JUDGMENT:

Suppose that you are walking by yourself and you see a house on fire. No one else sees the fire. What should you do?

ABSURDITIES:

Billy's mother said "You are going to be late for school." To make sure that he got there on time, he set the hands on the kitchen clock back one hour. What is foolish about that?

OBJECT ASSEMBLY:

Put the pieces together to make a square.

ARITHMETIC REASONING:

A boy has 12 apples. He gives half of these to his mother, and half of the rest to a friend. How many apples does he have left for himself?
a. 8 b. 2 c. 4 d. 3

GENERAL REASONING:

A boy goes to a stream with one 2-quart bucket and one 3-quart bucket. How can he arrange it so that he will take back exactly 4 quarts of water?

GENERAL INFORMATION:

What time is it when the minute hand is pointing straight up and the hour hand is pointing straight down?

What is the smallest state in the United States?

ACHIEVEMENT AND APTITUDE

Teacher-made tests and standardized achievement tests are intended to measure how much a student *has* learned in school. Tests of general ability are intended to measure how much the student *can* learn in the future if ideal conditions prevail. Another way of saying it is that tests of general ability are intended to measure the *capacity* to learn rather than, as with achievement tests, how much has been learned up to a particular point in time.

The distinction between aptitude and achievement is commonplace in daily life. We say such things as "If he wanted to, he could be an excellent student." "Even though he has only limited ability, he makes good grades by studying night and day." "His real ability is hidden by the poor schools which he previously attended."

It would indeed be helpful if we had pure measures of aptitude. They would be particularly helpful in spotting children who would do much better in school if they were given better training or if their personal and home environments could be improved. Unfortunately, this goal is only partially accomplished by the currently available measures of general ability. At the present time we do not know how to measure aptitude other than by measuring what the child can accomplish at a particular point in time. There is no way to "get inside" of the child to obtain a pure measure of how much he could accomplish in ideal situations. Rather, what the tests of general ability tend to do is measure relatively *abstract* ability, ability that is not as dependent on specific types of school instruction as is required by achievement tests.

A child probably would not be able to answer questions about the mineral resources of Africa or about the United States Constitution unless he has had good instruction in those topics in school and unless he has made a concentrated effort to study the materials. Such questions are closely bound to the quality of instruction and the energetic study of the student. In contrast, some of the types of items used on tests of general ability are not highly related to the richness of the student's school and home environment. For example, the figural relations items shown previously do not obviously relate to anything that is learned in the home or in school.

The value of most tests of general ability is that they contain items not as directly related to school and home environment as are those found on most achievement tests. The effort in measures of general ability is to use questions that any intelligent person could answer from his daily experience rather than ones that require specific types of instruction. This is true even of items measuring vocabulary and general information. Efforts are usually made to employ largely words and facts that could be learned by any intelligent person.

Even with the best of efforts, it presently is not possible to measure aptitude completely apart from achievement. The same factors that make for achievement in school also, to a large extent, make for success on tests of general ability. The two types of tests usually correlate highly, around .70, with the exact size of the relationship depending on the type of school and the year in school. The difference is more a matter of degree than a matter of kind. Achievement tests are relatively *more* concerned with present accomplishment; aptitude tests are relatively *more* concerned with abstract ability.

When students' scores are compared on achievement tests and tests of general ability, the differences usually are not large, and many of the apparent differences are due only to measurement error. However, when such differences are quite large, they provide important diagnostic information about students. It is in these instances that the major usefulness of tests of general ability is shown.

INDIVIDUAL VERSUS GROUP TESTS

Tests can be given to each individual separately, or a group of individuals can be tested at one time. Although this is a consideration for tests of all kinds, it is a particularly important issue in the use of general intelligence tests. The multifactor batteries are almost always group tests. There is considerable competition between individual and group tests of general intelligence. Numerous articles have appeared in the psychological literature arguing about whether group or individual tests should be used with particular age groups.

INDIVIDUAL TESTS.   The first practical general intelligence test, the Binet-Simon scale, was administered individually. This was necessary because the subjects were young children. The individual test requires a highly experienced examiner. Most individuals who are highly qualified to administer and interpret individual tests of intelligence have advanced degrees in psychology or education. To become proficient in the use of such examinations requires many hours of practice testing under the supervision of an experienced tester. The examiner is, in essence, a part of the standardized testing procedure, and he must standardize his own treatment of the child to conform to established methods.

Many of the items on individual tests cannot be scored unambiguously as right or wrong. Instead, there may be a number of acceptable responses, and different scores are often required to indicate the degree of correctness. The better-established individual tests go to considerable lengths to specify just what will be considered a correct response and how much credit should be given for a response. The examiner must follow the established scoring procedures meticulously and not permit his subjective judgment of a child to influence the test results. Any idiosyncrasies in scoring will make the test less reliable.

GROUP TESTS.   The first practical group tests of general intelligence were developed for the armed forces during the First World War. Because of the number of men to be tested, a quick and economical measurement device was required, and the individual test was unsuited for that purpose.

Most group tests are sufficiently self-explanatory so that the test examiner need have little or no specialized knowledge of testing procedures. The test forms are simply passed out to subjects; either they are allowed to work at their chosen rate, or the examiner directs the subjects when to start and stop.

COMPARISON OF INDIVIDUAL AND GROUP TESTS. Although the following rules are not precisely correct for all group and individual tests, they are sufficiently general to offer a reasonable basis for choosing between the two kinds of tests in most situations.

1. Individual tests are required with young children. Starting at the earliest age, there are no group tests that can be used with infants. Each infant must be examined separately, and any effort at standardization of procedures is difficult. With preschool children, it is usually necessary to use individual tests. Young children either cannot read at all or lack the reading ability to take the self-explanatory group forms. As an additional factor, young children are highly distractible, and it is all that the expert examiner can do to keep one child working at the test materials. Young children are often not motivated to do well on tests, and it is only through the examiner's careful, but standardized, encouragement that a meaningful measure can be obtained.

2. Group tests are more frequently used for testing "normal" adults. When working with most teen-age and adult groups, the well-standardized group tests are as effective as the individual tests. Although the evidence is clear that individual tests are better predictors for young children and that group tests do as well with adolescents or older persons, it is not certain which kind of test is generally more valid with the in-between age group.

Adolescents and older persons are usually motivated and attentive enough to manifest a meaningful score on a group test. Also, they probably are less embarrassed by the group testing situation than they would be in the face-to-face individual testing situation.

Because group tests tend to be equally as valid as individual tests when administered to adults, they are much to be preferred in most practical work. Group tests are much less expensive and time consuming. It takes no more time to administer and score twenty group tests than it does to administer and score one individual test.

3. Individual tests are often useful in clinical settings. The school psychologist often can learn considerably more from the individual test than the subject's score would indicate. The child who appears dull in the classroom may be only hard of hearing. Another child may do poorly in schoolwork because he wants to do poorly, giving wrong answers when he knows what is correct. The older adult may appear to be demented because he is discouraged and withdrawn. These things probably would not be found in group testing situations, but an experienced clinician can often use the individual testing situation to diagnose why an individual is performing poorly.

VERBAL VERSUS PERFORMANCE TESTS

There has been some confusion about the difference between "verbal" tests and "performance" tests, and the distinction is itself somewhat misleading. The following outline of verbal components in tests is offered as a basis for discussing test content:

VERBAL REQUIREMENTS:

1. Understand spoken language
2. Understand written language
3. Speak language
4. Write language
5. Verbal comprehension factor

There are many different combinations of these requirements in particular tests. A test may require the first four items, but deal with language at so simple a level that very little ability in verbal comprehension is required to obtain a high score. It is possible to make up a test in which almost none of the five aspects is required. This can be done by giving the test instructions in pantomine and using test materials that require neither written nor spoken responses. It is also possible to compose a test in which none of the first four aspects is present and the fifth aspect, verbal comprehension, is a cardinal requirement. If the test requires the child to manipulate abstract symbols or to deal with pictures, this will tap, in part, the verbal comprehension factor. Each test should be examined in terms of its combination of verbal requirements rather than simply classified as "verbal" or "nonverbal."

Another distinction can be made among tests in terms of the way in which responses are made:

NATURE OF RESPONSE:

1. Symbolic response. The subject indicates the correct answer either through the use of language or by marking one of a number of choices. The symbolic response might be made with respect to objects rather than printed materials, although this is usually not done.
2. Manipulative response (performance). The subject is required to handle objects in such a way as to complete a specified product.

The product may be anything from a completely finished piece of machinery to the arrangement of a set of blocks.

Some items are not clearly differentiated in terms of the two kinds of responses. For example, in maze tracing, the child is required to coordinate the pencil and move to the goal—the response is as symbolic as it is manipulative.

It has been the custom to call instruments "performance" tests if they deemphasize language requirements, employ three-dimensional materials, and require manipulative responses. Because of these components, the performance tests usually measure motor coordination, speed, and perceptual and spatial factors. Instruments are usually referred to as "verbal" tests if they are printed forms, emphasize verbal comprehension, and require symbolic responses. Because of the ease with which certain kinds of test materials can be placed on printed forms, the verbal tests tend to measure verbal comprehension, numerical computation, and the reasoning factors. There is no clear-cut separation between the factors found in verbal and performance tests, but there is a tendency for different factors to arise in the two kinds of materials.

In addition to the two extreme types of measures, one extreme type heavily involved in verbal requirements and the other extreme type almost exclusively manipulative, there is a third important type of test, which is variously referred to as "nonlanguage," "culture-free," and "culture-fair." In this third type of test, the student is required neither to use and understand language nor to manipulate three-dimensional objects. Rather, the test items consist of symbolic responses (multiple choice) to relationships among figures and designs. Typical of such items are the examples given earlier of items involving figural relations. These tests have a very important place. They avoid complete dependence on verbal ability, and they apparently measure more important intellectual functions than performance tests do. Such instruments are useful for both applied work and for research in relation to individuals who are disadvantaged on highly verbal measures of intelligence, such as (1) the deaf; (2) recent immigrants to this country and their children; (3) children reared in subcultures that are out of the mainstream of culture in this country, such as those on Indian reservations; (4) children reared in culturally impoverished environments, such as some low-income rural settings; and (5) poor readers.

The following sections will describe some typical group and individual tests of general ability. Representative tests will be described for different age groups. As is the rule throughout this book, no effort will be made to present an exhaustive (and, consequently, unreadable) list of all the good measures available. Mention is made of other good tests of general ability in Appendix D. After representative tests are described, some of the major research findings about general ability will be discussed, and some recommendations will be given for the use of tests of general ability in elementary and secondary schools.

THE BINET TEST AND ITS FOLLOWERS

As will be recalled from the previous chapter, Alfred Binet pioneered in the theory and practice of measuring general ability. His immediate practical problem was to construct tests to be used with "problem children" in French elementary schools. Among those children who were failing in school, some method was needed for distinguishing those who lacked the capacity to learn from those who might profit by special instruction. Binet's point of view was that for practical purposes, it would not be feasible to measure intelligence in terms of the many constituent factors involved, but, rather, that it would be necessary to measure general ability by its end products. Consequently, in his tests, Binet emphasized the ability to make correct judgments, the ability to solve problems, and the ability to understand words and written material.

Working with Theodore Simon, in 1905, Binet (Binet & Simon, 1905) produced the first crude measure of general ability. The test consisted of thirty items, graded in difficulty. The first fifteen items in the list are presented as follows:

1. Follow a lighted match with head and eyes.
2. Grasp a cube placed on the palm.
3. Grasp a cube held in line of vision.
4. Make a choice between pieces of wood and chocolate.
5. Unwrap chocolate from paper.
6. Execute simple orders.
7. Touch head, nose, ear, cap, key, and string.
8. Point to objects which experimenter names in picture.
9. Name objects pointed out in a picture.
10. Judge which of two lines is the longer.
11. Repeat immediately three digits read by examiner.
12. Judge which of two weights is heavier.
13. Solve problems that embody novel, ambiguous, or contradictory solutions.
14. Define house, horse, fork, and mamma.
15. Repeat sentence of fifteen words after a single hearing.

The list of problems was tried out on about 50 children, and provisional norms were established. It was found that the first five items could be passed by idiots and normal two-year-olds. Most three-year-olds could go no further than about the ninth item. Most five-year-olds could go no further than about the fourteenth item.

The first test obviously was only a rough beginning to the measurement of general ability, but it constituted a very important first step. Binet's conceptions of how general ability should be measured and the types of items which should be used have dominated most tests of general ability to this day.

Binet later made revisions of his test, employed more items, gathered responses from larger groups of children, and developed more dependable norms. However, the center of activity in the development and use of measures of intelligence soon shifted to America. During the first decade of this century, the Binet-Simon tests became very popular in this country. Instruments of this kind were needed in the care of the feebleminded, in educational research, and in understanding juvenile delinquency. Several translations into English were made of the scales, and efforts were made to broaden and further standardize the tests.

THE TERMAN AND MERRILL REVISIONS.   The most extensive revisions of the Binet-Simon scales were made first by Lewis Terman in 1916 and then by Terman and Maud Merrill in 1937 and 1960. Because their work was done at Stanford University, their revisions were named Stanford-Binet tests. Their work has so extensively revised and extended Binet's tests that it is only out of respect to Binet that the current form of the test still bears his name. The major improvements which have been made are (1) to try out a large number of items, (2) the use of statistical analysis to obtain the most effective items, (3) careful writing of instructions for administration and scoring, and (4) gathering of representative norms from large numbers of children and adults. Since the 1916 revision, the Stanford-Binet series of tests has been used very widely in this country and has been translated into many other languages.

CONSTRUCTION OF THE STANFORD-BINET TESTS.   The   Stanford-Binet contains six subtests and one alternate (in case something goes wrong in the testing) at half-year intervals from two to five years of age, at yearly intervals from five to fourteen, and at four levels of adult performance. (At the "average adult" level there are eight rather than six subtests.) The items at each level were carefully selected according to three principles. First, all items were selected because they "looked" as if they measured "intelligence" (see previous examples). Second, all items retained for the scale should correlate highly with chronological age. Although we may argue about what constitutes "intelligence," all will agree that it grows with the child. Of course, age differentiation is not the *only* desirable standard for selecting such items. The length of the foot also grows with age, but it goes without saying that no one would consider that a measure of intelligence. With respect to the standard of age differentiation, a suitable item for the seven-year subtest would be one where few of the six-year-olds get the correct answer, over half of the seven-year-olds get the correct answer, and most of the eight-year-olds get the correct answer. Needless to say, it is very difficult to find items that meet the standard.

The third standard which was applied to the items was that of homogeneity. For this standard, each item was correlated with the total test, which gives an index of how well the individual items measure the same thing as the whole test. This is a sensible standard in constructing a measure of general ability, because even though the total test may not be a perfect measure, it is logically a better measure than any item taken separately. By applying these procedures, the final collection of items (1) consists of problems that intuitively relate to general ability, (2) differentiates well between adjacent age groups, and (3) is relatively homogenous in content.

THE 1960 REVISION.   The most recent revision of the Stanford-Binet (Terman & Merrill, 1960) consisted largely of recombining and making minor changes in items used in previous forms. The 1937 revision consisted of two alternate forms, called Forms L and M, respectively. Having an alternate form available made it possible to retest children after short periods of time without having the results affected by memory. However, little use was made of Form M. Consequently, in the 1960 revision, the best items were selected from both the older Forms L and M, and the present form is referred to as L-M. Items from the 1937 forms which were out of date were either revised or eliminated. These items were primarily ones involving pictorial material showing familiar articles such as telephones and appliances that had undergone radical changes in the intervening years. Other items were relocated among the age levels because of altered difficulty levels. That is, as a result of cultural changes, some items could be presented at a younger age than was possible in the 1937 standardization sample. Because the new revision was compounded from items from the 1937 test, all the research findings and interpretive data which had accumulated for the earlier test could be brought to bear on the new instrument.

CONTENT OF THE STANFORD-BINET. The present test bears many of the earmarks of the original Binet test. A knowledge of words and the comprehension of written material play a predominant part in the scale, particularly at the upper age levels. Although a number of performance items appear at earlier age levels, these primarily concern the child's recognition and use of common objects. A few items concerning spatial and perceptual abilities are found at different age levels. Many of the items relate to one or more of the reasoning factors discussed in the previous chapter. Three types of memory items appear at one or more age levels, including serial memory of digits, paragraph memory, and memory of geometric designs. To illustrate the nature of the scale, the items at four different age levels are described as follows:

TWO-YEAR LEVEL:

1. *Three-hole form board.* The child is shown a form board containing a cut-out square, circle, and triangle. The pieces are removed, and the child is asked to put them in their places. The child receives credit if all three objects are put in place.
2. *Delayed response.* The child is shown three small boxes and a toy cat. The examiner says, "Look, I am going to hide the kitty and see if you can find it." While the child is watching, the toy cat is placed under the middle box. Then a screen is placed in front of the boxes for about ten seconds. When the screen is withdrawn, the child is asked to choose the box containing the cat. The procedure is repeated, putting the cat under the box on the right and then under the box on the left. The child is given credit if two out of three first selections are correct.
3. *Identifying parts of body.* The child is shown a large paper doll and is asked to point to parts of the body. ("Show me the dolly's hair," etc.) Credit is received for correctly pointing out three of the parts.
4. *Block building.* A box of blocks is placed before the child. The examiner builds a tower of four blocks and asks the child to do the same. Credit is received if the child makes a tower of at least four blocks.
5. *Picture vocabulary.* The child is shown eighteen cards containing pictures of common objects. With each picture he is asked, "What is this?" Credit is given if the child names at least two of the objects.
6. *Word combinations.* The examiner notes the spontaneous speech of the child during the test. Credit is given if the child uses at least a two-word combination, such as "see kitty."

SIX-YEAR LEVEL:

1. *Vocabulary.* The child is asked the meaning of words from a graded list of forty-five terms. Credit is given for five correct definitions. (The same list of words is used throughout all higher age levels.)
2. *Differences.* The child is asked to tell the difference between three pairs of words, e.g., a bird and a dog. Credit is given for making at least two correct responses out of three.
3. *Mutilated pictures.* The child is shown five pictures in which an object has a missing part, e.g., a wagon with only three wheels, and asked to say what is missing in each. Credit is given for getting as many as four of the problems correct.
4. *Number concepts.* Twelve blocks are put in front of the child. He is asked to give different numbers of the blocks to the examiner. Credit is given for selecting three correct numbers of blocks out of four trials.
5. *Opposite analogies.* "A table is made of wood; a window of _____." Credit is given for at least three out of four correct responses.
6. *Maze tracing.* The child is shown three designs, each of which shows two ways for a person to get home. One route is longer than the other. The child is asked to trace the shorter route. Credit is given for two correct responses out of three.

TEN-YEAR LEVEL:

1. *Vocabulary.* The child is asked to define words from the standard list. Credit is given for eleven or more correct definitions.
2. *Block counting.* The student is shown pictures of piles of blocks. Some of the blocks are directly visible, and others are stacked behind and beneath the visible blocks. The student is asked how many blocks are in each pile. Credit is given for correct responses to at least eight of the eleven pictures.
3. *Abstract words.* "What do we mean by _____?" e.g., "curiosity." Credit is given for correctly interpreting at least two of the four words presented.
4. *Finding reasons.* The child is asked to explain why two social rules are necessary, e.g., "Give two reasons why children should not be too noisy in school." Credit is given for supplying two reasons.
5. *Word naming.* The child is asked to name as many words as he can in two minutes. Credit is given for twenty-eight words or more.

6. *Repeating six digits.*   Six digits such as 4, 8, 2, 1, 6, 3 are read
    at one-second intervals. The child is asked to repeat the digits in
    their exact order. Credit is given if one or more complete series
    out of three are recalled correctly.

AVERAGE ADULT LEVEL (AGE 15 AND OLDER)

1. *Vocabulary.*   The subject is asked for definitions of words in the
    standard list. Credit is given if twenty or more are defined.
2. *Ingenuity.*   Three problems are given. An example is: a boy is sent
    to the river to get exactly 3 pints of water, and he has only a 7-pint
    container and a 4-pint container. How can he measure the water?
    Credit is given if two problems are solved.
3. *Differences between abstract words.*   The subject is asked to
    distinguish between three pairs of associated words, e.g., poverty
    and misery. Credit is given if two or more of the distinctions are
    correct.
4. *Arithmetical reasoning.*   The subject is asked to solve three prob-
    lems; e.g., "If two pencils cost 5 cents, how many pencils can you
    buy for 50 cents?" Credit is given for two or more correct solutions.
5. *Proverbs.*   The subject is asked to explain the meaning of three
    proverbs, e.g., "A burnt child dreads the fire." Credit is given for
    two or more correct interpretations.
6. *Orientation.*   Questions are asked which require the understand-
    ing of compass directions, e.g., "Which direction would you have
    to face so your right hand would be toward the North?" Credit is
    given for correctly answering at least four of the five questions.
7. *Essential differences.*   "What is the principal difference between
    _____?" e.g., "work and play." Credit is given for
    correctly answering at least two of the three questions.
8. *Abstract words.*   "What do we mean by _____?" e.g.,
    "generosity." Credit is given for correctly interpreting at least four
    of the five words presented.

ADMINISTRATION OF THE STANFORD-BINET.   The test materials include a box of performance items (beads, toys, pictures, etc.), test blanks
on which the child's responses are recorded, and a manual of instructions. Some of the test materials are shown in Figure 12-1. As was mentioned previously, the administration of an individual test of this kind
requires a highly trained examiner, and no faith should be placed in the
scores obtained by an amateur tester. The test usually can be given in a
period of fifty to seventy-five minutes.

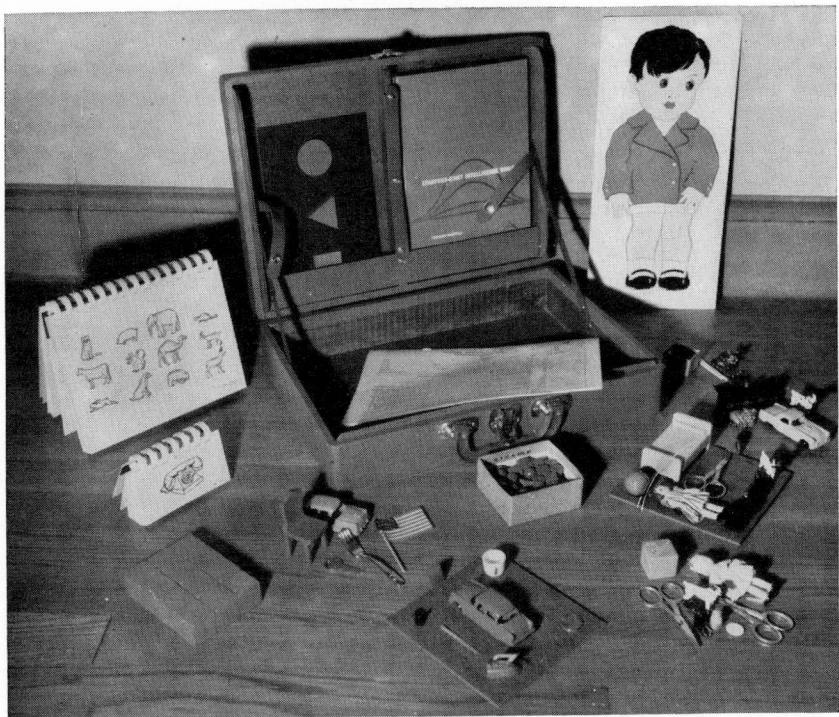

Figure 12-1. Some of the test materials used with the Stanford-Binet. *(Reproduced by permission of Houghton Mifflin Company.)*

No individual is administered all the items. Instead, the individual is started slightly lower in the age scale than he is expected to reach. For example, a typical procedure would be to start a seven-year-old off on the five-year-level questions. The child is then taken up through all the age levels as far as he can go.

In previous forms of the Stanford-Binet, IQ was obtained by dividing mental age by chronological age. As was described in Chapter 3, such quotient scores are fraught with statistical and conceptual difficulties. Consequently, an important innovation in the 1960 revision of the Stanford-Binet was the provision of tables for transforming mental age scores into deviation IQs. The deviation IQs are simply transformed standard scores, with a mean of 100 and a standard deviation of 16 for each age level. The substitution of the deviation IQ for the formerly used ratio IQ overcomes the difficulties of using quotient scores, discussed in Chapter 3, most notably the lack of comparability of scores from level to level or from test to test. The deviation IQ makes it possible to make such comparisons more confidently.

EVALUATION OF THE STANFORD-BINET. The primary purpose of the Stanford-Binet is to provide information helpful in making decisions about programs of instruction for students who are exceptional in some way with respect to their intellectual development, such as decisions about (1) the entrance of an underaged child into the first grade, (2) remedial instruction for a fourth grader who is having considerable difficulty in learning to read well, or (3) counseling for a junior high school student with severe emotional problems. The evidence is that it serves that purpose very well. Some of the salient features of the test are as follows:

1. Construction. The test was very carefully constructed and standardized. A particularly good feature of the test is the care that went into providing detailed instructions for scoring each item.

2. Reliability. Very careful research was undertaken to determine the reliability of the Stanford-Binet IQ at different age levels. An equivalent-form reliability estimate was made separately for each age. Correlations were found between the scores obtained on Form L and Form M administered to the same subjects within one week's time. In general, the findings show that the Stanford-Binet is a highly reliable scale, with most of the reliability coefficients equal to or greater than .90. Scores tend to be more reliable for persons in their teens than they do for young children. The studies also show that low scores are somewhat more reliable than high scores in each age range. In other words, a bit more faith can be placed in the precision of a very low score than in a very high score.

3. Predictive efficiency. The test has shown itself to be a good predictor of different criteria, particularly of school grades. In general, the findings have been that Stanford-Binet IQs correlate in the neighborhood of .70 with elementary school grades, .60 with high school grades, and .50 with college grades. (The decline in validity is probably due to the progressively decreasing dispersion of intellectual ability.) The following correlations (Bond, 1940) were found between Form L IQ and high school achievement test scores. The number of students ranges from 78 to 200.

Reading comprehension	.73	Spelling	.46
Reading speed	.43	History	.59
English usage	.59	Geometry	.48
Literature acquaintance	.60	Biology	.54

4. Testing of adults. On both subjective and empirical grounds, there is reason to believe that the Stanford-Binet is a better test for children than adults (age sixteen and over). One reason for this is that the concept of general intelligence is more meaningful with children than adults. This point will be discussed later in the chapter. The Stanford-Binet does not have a high enough "ceiling" to measure the ability of normal or superior adults, or even superior adolescents. That is, the range of difficulty at the adult level is not sufficient to tap the ability of highly gifted individuals. Because no persons over eighteen years of age were included in the standardization sample, the norms for adults are suspect.

5. Clinical utility. Presumably, a test like the Stanford-Binet should be judged, in the long run, by the success with which it predicts different criteria. Many of the uses, however, to which this and other general intelligence tests are put are so subtle as to make direct empirical validation difficult. For example, the test might be used to decide what type of psychotherapy should be used with a disturbed child. Because of the difficulty in measuring therapeutic success and the difficulty in deciding the importance of "intelligence" for the outcome, it is hard to determine how well the test works in the situation. In many situations only the clinical impression of how well the test performs a particular job can at present be used as an indication of "validity." Judging from the wide acceptance of the test in clinical settings, it is apparent that the Stanford-Binet is judged to be as valuable or more valuable than any other test for use with children.

THE WECHSLER SCALES

The two Wechsler scales are competitive with the Stanford-Binet as individually administered tests of general ability. Unlike the Stanford-Binet, there are separate Wechsler scales for adults and children, which will be described in turn.

WAIS. Wechsler began his work on the measurement of general ability with the development of an adult test. The test frequently is used with students aged fifteen and older. The presently used form is called the Wechsler Adult Intelligence Scale (Wechsler, 1955). The adult scale was intended to differ from the Stanford-Binet in the following respects:

1. The test items were to be more appropriate for adults, and representative norms for adults were to be obtained.

2. Age levels were to be discarded in favor of a number of subtests which all subjects would take.
3. Separate sets of verbal and performance tests were to be constructed allowing for both a verbal and performance IQ.
4. The IQ was to be determined by a transformation of standard scores rather than through the use of mental age scores.

The WAIS consists of eleven subtests, which are described as follows:

VERBAL SCALE:

1. *General information.* The subject is asked twenty-five questions concerning a wide variety of facts. The questions are not intended to tap academic training or specialized branches of knowledge. They are meant to cover the kinds of information that any alert individual can learn from his cultural contacts.
2. *General comprehension.* The test contains ten items concerning why certain social rules are necessary and how everyday problems are solved.
3. *Arithmetical reasoning.* Ten problems of the kind that would be typically encountered in elementary school arithmetic are given. Both speed and correctness of response are scored.
4. *Similarities.* The subject is asked to tell what is similar about twelve pairs of terms. This subtest is very similar to material found on the Stanford-Binet.
5. *Digit span.* This is the familiar memory for digits which also appears at different levels of the Stanford-Binet. From three to nine digits are read to the subject, and he is asked to repeat them in their exact order. In the second part of the test, the subject is asked to repeat the digit series backward.
6. *Vocabulary.* Forty words of increasing difficulty are presented. The subject is asked what each word means.

PERFORMANCE SCALE:

7. *Digit symbol.* This is an adaptation of the familiar coding test. The subject is given a sheet of paper on which nine symbols are paired with nine numbers. Farther down on the page, a jumbled list of the numbers is given, and the subject is asked to write in the matching symbols.
8. *Picture completion.* The subject is shown fifteen incomplete

pictures and asked to describe the missing part in each. This is also very much like material found on the Stanford-Binet.

9. *Block design.* The subject is shown a set of small blocks. Surfaces of the blocks are painted white, red, and red and white. The subject is presented with a picture of a design and asked to reproduce it with the blocks. Seven designs are given in turn. Both speed and accuracy are scored.

10. *Picture arrangement.* The subject is handed a set of pictures and asked to arrange them in an order that tells a story. Six sets of pictures are given. Both speed and accuracy are scored.

11. *Object assembly.* The subject is asked to put together three jigsaw puzzles. Each puzzle pictures some part of the human body. Both speed and accuracy are scored.

WISC. A separate scale is available for children, which is called the Wechsler Intelligence Scale for Children (Wechsler, 1949). The WISC is used for students aged seven to fifteen, and the WAIS is used for all older age groups. The WISC is very similar to the WAIS, the major difference being that the WISC contains material more appropriate for, and more interesting to, younger people. The subtests of the WISC are as follows:

Verbal scale	Performance scale
1. General information	6. Picture completion
2. General comprehension	7. Picture arrangement
3. Arithmetic	8. Block design
4. Similarities	9. Object assembly
5. Vocabulary	10. Coding (or mazes)
Alternate: digit span	

On the verbal scale, digit span is given as an alternate if, for some reason, one of the other tests is not usable. On the performance scale (see Figure 12-2) the examiner has the choice of using either coding or mazes. The coding test on the WISC is similar to the digit symbol test on the WAIS. The maze test is the only one that does not appear on the adult form. It consists of eight paper-and-pencil mazes of increasing difficulty, performance being scored in terms of both time and number of errors.

IQs on the WISC are determined in the same general manner as on the adult test. As in the adult form, IQs can be obtained separately for total scale, verbal scale, and performance scale. All IQs are simply transformed standard scores, with a mean of 100 and a standard deviation of 15.

Figure 12-2. Child being administered performance materials from the Wechsler Intelligence Scale for Children. *(Courtesy of The Psychological Corporation.)*

The manual states the percentage of children that fall at different IQ levels, with a verbal description of what particular scores mean (see Table 12-1).

Table 12-1   Classification of IQs on the WISC *(Reproduced by permission. Copyright, 1949, The Psychological Corporation, New York. All rights reserved.)*

Description	IQ Ranges	Per Cent of Children
Very superior	130 and above	2.2
Superior	120–129	6.7
Bright	110–119	16.1
Average	90–109	50.0
Dull normal	80–89	16.1
Borderline	70–79	6.7
Mental defective	69 and below	2.2

WPPSI. For a number of years, those who used the Wechsler scales felt the need for a separate intelligence scale that would more adequately appraise the abilities of the preschool child. Although the WISC can be used with children as young as five years, it was felt that the period from four to six years constitutes a well-defined landmark in the young child's mental development and that a scale specifically designed for use with this age group was therefore desirable. In response to this need, the Wechsler Preschool and Primary Scale of Intelligence (WPPSI) was published in 1963 for use with children aged 4 to 6½ years.

While similar to the WISC in form and content, the WPPSI is a separate and distinct scale which takes into account the special problems of testing the child in this age group. The majority of the eleven subtests on the WPPSI are simply modifications of WISC subtests; however, three subtests are unique to the WPPSI. These three new subtests (Sentences, Animal House, and Geometric Design) replace Digit Span, Picture Arrangement, Object Assembly, and Coding on the WISC, which could not be adapted to the WPPSI.

Like the WISC subtests, each of the subtests on the WPPSI may be treated separately as measuring different abilities, or they may be combined into a composite score as a measure of over-all intellectual ability. Both the method of computing the IQ and the evaluation scores of different levels (Wechsler, 1967) are the same as for the WISC.

EVALUATION OF THE WECHSLER SCALES. Most of the good things that can be said about the Stanford-Binet apply equally well to the Wechsler scales. In fact, the two types of tests correlate so highly at most age levels that it is illogical to argue which is "better" in general. Although there are some advantages of one type of test over the other for particular purposes, the choice of whether to use one rather than the other type of scale often boils down to the personal preferences of the test user. Some of the salient features of the Wechsler scales are as follows:

1. Administration. Although, like the Stanford-Binet, the Wechsler scales are individually administered, they are somewhat easier to administer than the Stanford-Binet. The full WAIS or WISC usually can be administered in no more than one hour.

2. Standardization. The manual provides relatively detailed instructions for scoring each test. The norms were based on representative samples of children and adults. The care that went into the construction of norms is illustrated by the normative samples used for the WISC.

One hundred boys and one hundred girls were tested at each age level, giving a total of 2,200 children in the standardization sample. A strenuous effort was made to choose a representative cross section of white children in the United States. The sample was drawn from eighty-five communities in eleven states. The distribution of subjects closely resembled that of the country at large in terms of urban-rural proportion, geographical area, and parental occupation. The WISC standardization sample is as representative as that used in almost any current measure of general ability.

3. Reliability. The Wechsler scales are highly reliable; that is, the pure chance factors influencing test results are quite small. Because no alternate forms are available, split-half reliability estimates were used at various age levels. The results at various ages indicate an over-all reliability for the total scale of about .95, which, to say the least, is quite good.

4. Performance scale. The performance items on the Wechsler tests constitute an advantage over the Stanford-Binet for certain purposes. For most students, the more "verbal" types of items, such as appear throughout the Stanford-Binet and on the verbal scales of the Wechsler tests, are more predictive of achievement in school. However, for certain types of "unusual" children, the performance items on the Wechsler scale are quite helpful. They are helpful for children with various types of language problems, with the deaf, and with children who have been reared in other countries. They also are useful with children who have led "impoverished" lives of a kind that would markedly hinder their performance on more verbal tests. Although the verbal and performance scales correlate highly, when a child shows very different scores on the two types of scales, it is of real diagnostic importance.

5. Testing adults. Most will agree that the WAIS is better than the Stanford-Binet for testing most adults, particularly those adults who are well above average in general ability. The WAIS has items which are more appropriate for adults and more interesting to them, and the test has a higher "ceiling" than the Stanford-Binet.

6. Predictive efficiency. Although not as much research has been done with the Wechsler scales to predict school achievement and vocational success, the available evidence indicates that the scales will do approximately as well as the Stanford-Binet. Respectable correlations have been found with both grades in school and indices of vocational accomplishment.

7. **Clinical utility.** As is true of the Stanford-Binet, many of the uses of the Wechsler by educational and psychological specialists are so subtle as to make direct appraisal quite difficult, and it is necessary to rely on impressions of how well the tests work. Evidently, the Wechsler scales are thought to be very useful in making decisions about problem students.

GROUP TESTS OF GENERAL ABILITY

Like the individual tests of general intelligence, the group tests are usually composed of items measuring verbal comprehension, numerical computation, and various mixtures of the reasoning factors. Although the tests differ from one another in appearance, and sometimes in their factor composition, they tend to correlate highly with one another. Where both types of tests can be applied, the group tests correlate highly with the individual tests, such as the WAIS. We see the interesting result that people working rather independently of one another in the composition of intelligence tests ended up with rather similar measures. Where the group tests differ from one another is in their practical advantages. Some are longer and thus more reliable than others. Some have obtained norms in a careful and representative manner; others have only scant or misleading information on norms. Some have either higher or lower "ceilings," making them more useful with one or the other extreme of ability. Considerable research has been done with some of the tests, and only face validity can be claimed for others.

The Binet and Wechsler scales dominate the field of individual tests of general intelligence. Among group measures, neither one nor several tests have dominated the field. The tests which will be discussed here are only examples of the measures available. Other group tests of intelligence are described in Appendix D.

GROUP TESTS FOR YOUNG CHILDREN. The youngest children with whom it has proved feasible to use group tests are those at the five- and six-year levels. Only small groups of approximately a dozen children can be tested in this way, and even then the examiner must exercise considerable skill to obtain the necessary cooperation and attention. Tests at this age level cannot employ written language, and the child cannot be expected to write his own responses. Test instructions must be given orally and supported by illustrations and gestures.

One of the most widely used tests for young children is the Pintner-Cunningham Primary Test (Pintner, Cunningham, & Durost, 1966), which has been in use for over thirty years. The test is available in two equivalent forms, A and B. Each form is composed of seven subtests, which are added together to obtain one score. (Illustrative items are shown in Figure 12-3.)

Equivalent-form reliabilities are found to be generally high for groups of kindergarten and first-grade children, ranging from .83 to .89. Correlations between the Pintner-Cunningham and the Stanford-Binet are usually about .80. In a group of 260 first-grade children, the Pintner-Cunningham correlated .63 with scores on a reading test.

Test 1. Mark the things that mother uses when she sews her apron

Test 2. Mark the prettiest girl

Test 3. Mark the two things that belong together

Test 7. Look at how each picture is drawn; make another one like it in the dots

Figure 12-3. Illustrative items from Form A of the Pintner-Cunningham Primary Test. *(Reproduced by permission of Harcourt Brace Jovanovich, Inc.)*

GROUP TESTS FOR THE ELEMENTARY AND HIGH SCHOOL LEVELS.

As children progress through the elementary school grades, more and more written material can be employed in tests. One of the best available series is the Lorge-Thorndike Intelligence Tests, multilevel edition (Lorge, Thorndike, & Hagen, 1964). The Lorge-Thorndike (L-T) will be examined in some detail as an illustration of the nature of group tests.

The L-T consists of both verbal and nonverbal batteries of tests of "abstract intelligence" for use with pupils in the third grade through the first year of college (which means that the highest level would be suitable for most adults). Although tests which rely on verbal items traditionally have been the best predictors of scholastic achievement, the authors of the L-T recognized that there are many testing situations in which an individual's responses to a purely verbal test would distort rather than clarify any conclusions about his true ability. Such individuals include those, mentioned previously, who are handicapped in some way with regard to verbal material, e.g., those for whom English is a second language and those who are poor readers. In order to provide reliable measures of abstract intelligence in such situations, the L-T follows the thinking of those who construct culture-fair tests and provides for routinely obtaining a nonverbal IQ as well as a verbal IQ score. Where a significant difference is found between the two scores, the information can be valuable for gaining insights into the pupil's difficulties with verbal material.

For both the verbal and nonverbal batteries, the authors felt that items which tap aspects of the ability to reason would be the most appropriate for measuring abstract intelligence. Consequently, the items deal with symbolic relationships. In answering most of the items, the student is expected to find a principle and then apply it.

The verbal battery consists of five subtests and has a working time of thirty-five minutes. The nonverbal battery, which is to be administered in a separate testing session, contains three subtests and requires approximately twenty-seven minutes of working time. Sample items from each subtest are given below:[1]

Verbal battery

VOCABULARY:

Choose the word that has the same or most nearly the same meaning as *loud*:
A. quick B. noisy C. hard D. heavy E. weak

[1] Reproduced by permission of Houghton Mifflin Company.

SENTENCE COMPLETION:

Choose the one word that will make the best, the truest, and the most sensible complete sentence.

Hot weather comes in the:
A. fall B. night C. summer D. winter E. snow

ARITHMETIC REASONING:

Mrs. Jones bought a pound of potatoes for 10¢ and a pound of spinach for 15¢. How much did she spend?
A. 5¢ B. 10¢ C. 15¢ D. 20¢ E. none of these

VERBAL CLASSIFICATION:

Figure out how the stem words are alike and then choose the one among the alternatives that belongs with them.
rose, daisy, violet: A. red B. garden C. sweet D. grow E. lily

VERBAL ANALOGIES:

Look at the first two stem words and determine how they are related to each other; then choose from the alternatives the word related to the third stem word in the same way.
laugh—happy: cry—_____ A. wonder B. sad C. hide D. lost E. rough

Nonverbal battery

FIGURE CLASSIFICATION:

The pupil is to figure out in what way drawings in a series are alike. Then he is to select from the alternatives the drawing which goes with the series. The drawings are all of geometric forms or abstract figures.

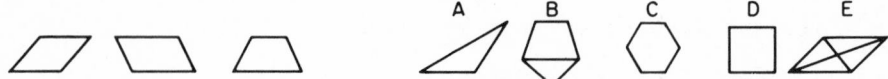

NUMBER SERIES:

A series of numbers or letters is presented in a certain order. The pupil is to determine the rule by which they are arranged and then select the next number or letter in the series.

1 3 5 7 9 _____: A. 10 B. 11 C. 12 D. 13 E. 14

FIGURE ANALOGIES:

The pupil is to determine how the first two drawings in the stem are related. He is then to select a drawing which is related to the third drawing in the stem in the same way. Some of the drawings for the first two levels are of real things; the remainder are geometric forms.

An important feature of the L-T is the multilevel format, which represents an effort to provide the most effectively discriminating items for each grade. An inherent weakness of separate-level tests, in which each level covers a range of grades, is that the spread of item difficulties cannot be truly optimal for most grades. For example, if one level is to be used with students in the fourth through the sixth grades, some items would tend to be too difficult for students in the fourth grade, and too easy for many students in the sixth grade. Such a situation serves only as a source of unreliability. In an individual testing situation, such as with the Stanford-Binet, the examiner can adjust the difficulty level of the items to test adequately the range of ability for each individual. In group tests, this typically is not possible without going to a different level and administering a wholly different set of items. It then becomes questionable whether or not scores thus obtained can be validly interpreted.

In the L-T, the eight different but overlapping scales (A to H) are presented in a single booklet. By varying the starting and stopping points on each subtest, each level can be made to contain 80 per cent of its items in common with the previous and subsequent levels. Thus, the L-T provides for flexibility in moving from one level to another to obtain the optimum level of item difficulty and to provide for scores maximally comparable from level to level. For example, Level C is recommended for use with the sixth grade, generally; however, educationally advanced groups may use Level C in the fifth grade, while educationally retarded groups may use that level as late as the seventh grade.

Some of the other salient features of the L-T are summarized as follows:

1. Norms.   In addition to deviation IQ norms, age, grade, and percentile norms are also provided for both batteries. Procedures for obtaining representative national norms were excellent. Over 180,000 children in 42 states were tested, and it appears that the utmost care was taken to set and adhere to high standards for sampling. Norms for the L-T were based on the same samples used in the norming of the concurrent editions of two achievement tests, the Iowa Tests of Basic Skills (ITBS) for the third through the eighth grades and the Tests of Academic Progress (TAP) for the ninth through the twelfth grades, thus making it possible to obtain comparable intelligence and achievement test scores.

2. Reliability.   The coefficients reported for the L-T are quite high over-all. For the verbal battery, alternate-form coefficients range from .83 to .94, while those for the nonverbal battery range from .80 to .92. Odd-even reliability coefficients are all in the .90s for both batteries.

3. Validity.   Apart from the author's assertion that items which deal with the relationships between abstract and general concepts are the most appropriate for measuring intelligence, most of the evidence for the validity of the L-T rests upon correlations with other intelligence tests and with tests of educational achievement. On the whole, these data are impressive. A correlation of the Stanford-Binet IQ with the L-T verbal IQ was reported to be .79 in one study. In another study, the WISC total IQ correlated .80 with the L-T nonverbal IQ and .78 with the verbal IQ. Correlations between the L-T and the two achievement batteries normed concurrently with it are also high. Correlations between the achievement score and the verbal battery run in the .80s, on the average. For the nonverbal battery, the coefficients run somewhat lower, in the .60s and .70s.

4. Correlation of verbal and nonverbal batteries.   The correlation between the two batteries ranges from about .65 to .75 in different grade groups, so there clearly is much in common between what is measured in the two series. However, the intercorrelations are sufficiently lower than the reliabilities of the two batteries, so that a difference of fifteen points or more in the two IQs does have some stability and significance. The reliability of the difference is around .70.

In summary it may be said that the L-T is a very flexible and reliable instrument for assessing intelligence in the school setting. The data would seem to indicate that a general factor of cognitive ability does underlie what is measured in all the subtests and that the tests do serve quite well in predicting scholastic achievement. The inclusion of the nonverbal battery represents a noteworthy union of two traditional points of view regarding group tests of intelligence.

GENERAL INTELLIGENCE TESTS FOR INFANTS AND PRESCHOOL CHILDREN

A separate section has been reserved here for the discussion of infant and preschool tests because of the special problems that are involved. One of the pioneers in the testing of infants was Arnold Gesell. For over twenty years, he and his colleagues performed longitudinal studies of child development. A group of 107 infants was systematically observed at four, six, and eight weeks and at every four-week interval to fifty-six weeks. The children were studied again at eighteen months and at the ages of two, three, four, five, and six years. On the basis of these observations the Gesell Developmental Schedules were prepared (Gesell & Amatruda, 1949). They are intended to measure the following attributes:

1. *Motor behavior.* How well the child can hold his balance, coordinate, stand, walk, and manipulate objects.
2. *Adaptive behavior.* How well the child can solve the problems of his small world: obtain objects, remove obstacles, solve puzzles, and react to stimuli.
3. *Language behavior.* How well the child can communicate, using the word in its broadest meaning, including the use of gestures and primitive words, to the later development of real language.
4. *Personal-social behavior.* How well the child learns habits of personal care such as toilet training, dressing, and feeding himself. At a later age consideration is given to how the child manages himself in social situations and in play activity.

During the first year of life, when the Gesell scales would supposedly have their unique value, most of the observations have to be made about motor behavior. The four-week-old infant cannot, of course, talk or follow oral instructions of any kind. The most that can be done at the infant stage is to watch the child's spontaneous movements and note how he reacts to various stimuli. At 1.4 months the average child can coordinate his eyes on an object held before him. At 3 months he will make reaching movements for an object. At 5.5 months he will make reaching movements for an object and will react differently to strangers from the way he does to his parents. (See Figure 12-4 for illustrative test materials.) Other tests for infants are the Cattell Infant Intelligence Scale (Cattell, 1947), the Bayley Scales of Infant Development (Bayley, 1968), and the Northwestern Infant Intelligence Tests (Gilliland, 1949).

Figure 12-4. Test materials used with the Gesell Developmental Schedules. *(Courtesy of The Psychological Corporation.)*

ANALYSIS OF INFANT TESTS. Tests for infants are difficult to standardize, administer, and score. They are, of course, all individual measures. Infant tests are less reliable than tests for older children. The reliability is considerably lower during the first six months than afterward. Several studies of different tests have found reliabilities around

.65 for testing during the first six months. After six months, the reliabilities move up to respectable figures in the .80 to .90 range. Except for the first weeks and months, the infant tests do measure something consistently. The question is, what do they measure? A real difficulty in validating infant scales is that there are almost no criteria available until the child enters school. A customary procedure has been to correlate infant tests with scores made several years later on more established intelligence tests, like the Stanford-Binet. Studies have shown that infant tests given at the age of one year or less correlate about zero with intelligence tests given five, ten, and fifteen years later to the same persons. It is obvious that infant tests do not measure intelligence as it is customarily measured in older children. The key to this dilemma seems to be that the infant scales primarily measure motor and sensory abilities, and the research on reliability shows that there is some consistency in the development of these attributes. It is quite likely that the infant tests would predict motor and sensory skills later in life, but interestingly enough, almost nothing has been done to test this hypothesis.

Whereas infant intelligence tests are not very informative regarding the future mental performance of most children, they have been found to have some predictive value in differentiating between normal and brain-damaged, or retarded, children. In the case of severely retarded children, sensorimotor performance does relate to later intellectual development. However, even in the case of retarded children, the results of infant intelligence tests alone are not sufficient for a conclusive diagnosis. The tests must be supplemented with careful clinical observations (Escalona, 1954).

PRESCHOOL TESTS.   Between the ages of two and five the developing intellectual processes become accessible to psychological tests. After the child develops speech, can manipulate objects, and becomes acquainted with the world about him, he can be tested with some of the materials that are customarily used in intelligence tests. However, many of the difficulties in test standardization and administration still remain. The test materials must be largely pictorial or consist of performance problems.

The difficulty in testing infants is that they usually do little one way or the other to indicate their intellectual abilities. Children between the ages of two and five do too much. They are so active and distractible that it is difficult to carry on any formal testing procedures. Many children in this age group are shy with strangers and will give little if any cooperation to the examiner. They often are not highly motivated to impress the examiner or themselves with how well they can perform. Consequently, the test must be posed as an interesting game to the child, and much depends on the examiner's skill

One of the most prominent tests for young children is the Minnesota Preschool Scale (Goodenough & Van Wagenen, 1940). There are twenty-six subtests, incorporating twelve practice items and ninety-seven test items. Some of the items are as follows (see Figure 12-5 for an illustration of some of the testing materials):

1.   Pointing to parts of the body on a doll
2.   Telling what a picture is about
3.   Naming colors
4.   Digit span
5.   Naming objects from memory
6.   Vocabulary
7.   Copying simple geometrical designs
8.   Block building
9.   Jigsaw puzzle
10. Indicating missing part in pictures

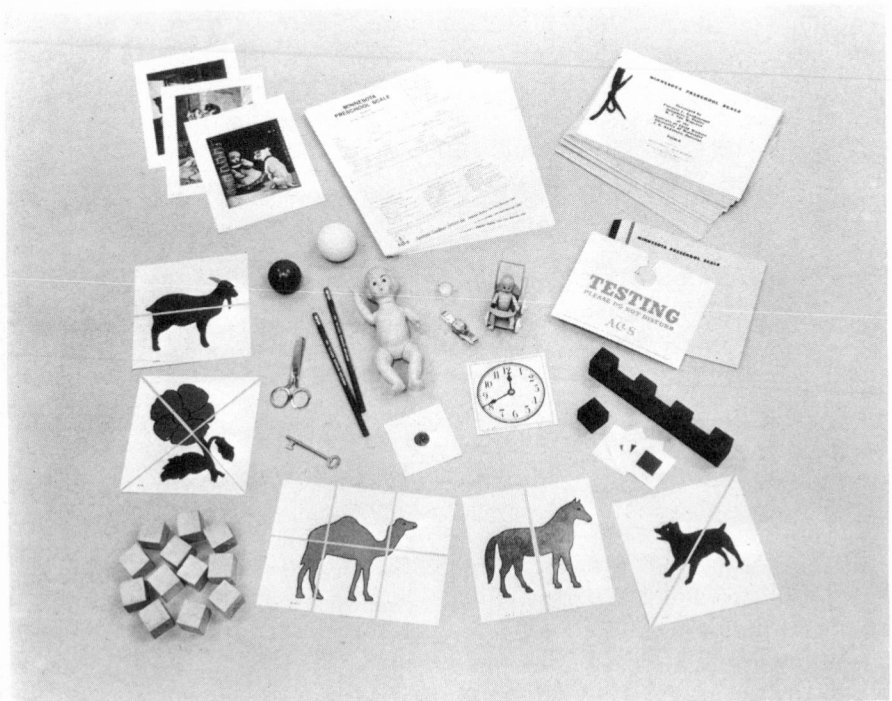

Figure 12-5.   Test materials used in the Minnesota Preschool Scale. *(Reproduced by permission of Educational Test Bureau, Minneapolis.)*

Many of the items are similar to those at the lower age levels of the Stanford-Binet. The instrument is largely a power test with no emphasis on speed, and the items are little concerned with motor skills. Tests at this age level which depend on speed and motor skills are probably poorer measures.

The Minnesota scale was standardized on a group of 900 children ranging in age from 1½ to 6 years. Equivalent-form reliabilities of the total scale vary from .80 to .94. There are some reasons to believe that the Minnesota scale is not an entirely adequate measure below the age of three. Although scores for children above three tend to correlate highly with Stanford-Binet scores obtained later, the correlation for children below the age of three is only .21. Also, clinical experience indicates that some of the test materials are not sufficiently interesting to hold the attention of children below the age of three. Two other preschool tests are the Intelligence Test for Young Children (Valentine, 1945) and the Merrill Palmer Scale (Stutsman, 1931).

THE NATURE OF "GENERAL INTELLIGENCE"

It has been shown that in spite of the separable factors that underlie tests of human ability there is a common ground among ability functions that can be reliably and usefully measured. The "verbal" intelligence tests, both individual and group, generally correlate highly enough with one another for us to speak of their common characteristics. If a marked difference in test scores is found between two kinds of people with one of the tests, the difference would most likely be reflected in the others. The wide use of intelligence tests during the last half century has shown a number of things about the underlying process:

1. Intelligence cannot at present be measured in children below the age of two years and not very well below the age of five or six years. Earlier in the chapter the difficulties of constructing tests for infants and preschool children were discussed. Perhaps the next decade will show an improvement in the early measurement of general ability.
2. The concept of general intelligence is more meaningful with children than adults. Although the evidence on this point is somewhat conflicting, it seems that abilities are more "general" in children. Comparative factor analyses of children and adults tend to show that there is more of a tendency toward one general factor in children. Some of the factors which are found in adult populations are difficult to find at all in children. This may be due in part

to the fact that different test materials have to be used with children than with adults. However, the weight of the argument is that abilities are more "general" in children. The factorial diversity of abilities in adults is probably due to different life experiences and different kinds of school and vocational training. It makes more sense to urge general intelligence tests with children than adults.

3. Intelligence as measured by current "verbal" tests is partly due to heredity and partly due to environment. The most telling arguments for this position come from the studies of resemblance between family members in intelligence. Conrad and Jones (1940) administered intelligence tests to over two hundred families in rural New England. They found that for children above the age of five years, intelligence of parents and children correlates .49. Numerous other studies have found correlations very close to .50. Conrad and Jones also found a correlation of .49 between siblings (between brothers, between sisters, or between brothers and sisters). Roberts (1941) pointed out that a correlation of .50 between siblings is what would be expected from multifactor inheritance. It is possible that the correlations which have been found between family members could be due to environment rather than heredity. Family members tend to share the same environment, talk about topics in common, and have similar kinds of schooling. Environment may explain part of the resemblance, but studies of twins make it apparent that this is not a complete explanation. Correlations between the intelligence test scores of fraternal twins (dizygotic) are usually higher than between siblings, ordinarily ranging from .50 to .70. Correlations between identical twins (monozygotic) are usually around .90—almost as high as the reliability of the tests! Fraternal twins can have very different genetic structures, but the genetic structures of identical twins are exactly alike. This leaves little doubt that at least a portion, and apparently a sizable portion, of intelligence is due to inheritance.

4. After the age of about six years, the individual's intelligence tends to remain stable with respect to his age group. That is, the superior people at one age level tend to be the superior people at other age levels (see Figure 12-6 for evidence on this point). The relationship is far from perfect, and isolated individuals may show drastic changes over a period of years.

5. There are definite group differences in intelligence test scores. Lower scores on the average are made by people of low socioeconomic status, people living in rural areas, people living in the Southern or Southwestern part of the United States, immigrants

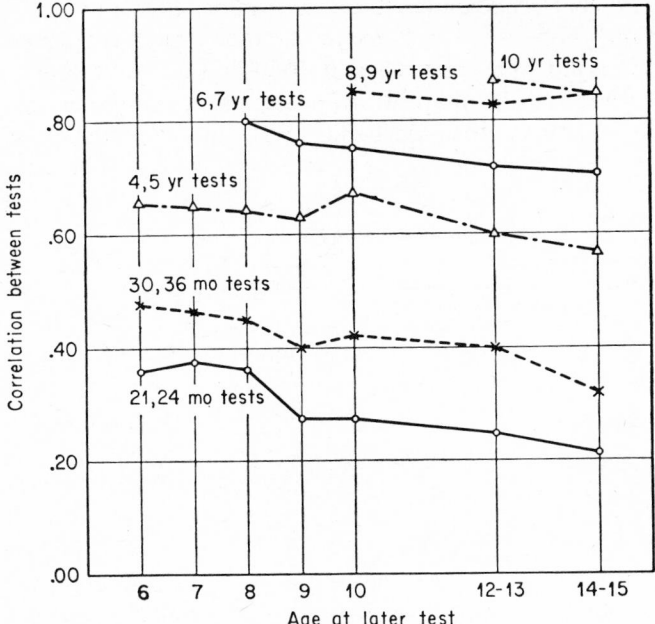

Figure 12-6. Effect of age at initial testing and test-retest interval on prediction of later Stanford-Binet IQ from earlier test. *(Adapted from Honzik, McFarlane, & Allen, 1948.)*

from southern Europe, and Indians and Negroes. The interpretation of differences of this kind places a large strain on the logical foundation of intelligence tests. As was discussed previously in this chapter, the traditional measures of intelligence are constructed in such a way as to favor certain groups. The question is whether or not the subgroups which tend to make lower scores would make high scores if afforded the advantages of the wider culture. There is some evidence to show that they would. It was found (Klineberg, 1935) that the longer Southern Negro children who migrate to New York have been in the city environment, the higher scores they make. Another point that should be considered is that even though some subgroups score lower on the average than others, at least some high-scoring individuals can be found in each. The whole question of ethnic and socioeconomic differences is highly charged with emotion in both professional and lay circles and is a point about which much more information needs to be obtained.

6.   Many different kinds of attainment involve intelligence as measured

by traditional "verbal" instruments. In particular, intelligence is one of the major factors in successful schoolwork. Numerous correlations of .50 and above between particular tests and school grades were cited in this chapter. Intelligence test scores differentiate occupational groups (see Table 12-2). However, it should

Table 12-2   AGCT standard scores of occupational groups in the Second World War (Adapted from Stewart, 1947.)

Occupational Groups	Percentile				
	10	25	50	75	90
Accountant	114	121	129	136	143
Teacher	110	117	124	132	140
Lawyer	112	118	124	132	141
Bookkeeper, general	108	114	122	129	138
Chief clerk	107	114	122	131	141
Draftsman	99	109	120	127	137
Postal clerk	100	109	119	126	136
Clerk, general	97	108	117	125	133
Radio repairman	97	108	117	125	136
Salesman	94	107	115	125	133
Store manager	91	104	115	124	133
Toolmaker	92	101	112	123	129
Stock clerk	85	99	110	120	127
Machinist	86	99	110	120	127
Policeman	86	96	109	118	128
Electrician	83	96	109	118	124
Meatcutter	80	94	108	117	126
Sheet metalworker	82	95	107	117	126
Machine operator	77	89	103	114	123
Automobile mechanic	75	89	102	114	122
Carpenter, general	73	86	101	113	123
Baker	69	83	99	113	123
Truck driver, heavy	71	83	98	111	120
Cook	67	79	96	111	120
Laborer	65	76	93	108	119
Barber	66	79	93	109	120
Miner	67	75	87	103	119
Farm worker	61	70	86	103	115
Lumberjack	60	70	85	100	116

be noted that there is considerable overlap among most groups. Comparing the extremes in Table 12-2, the top 10 per cent of lumberjacks score higher than the lower 10 per cent of accountants. Scores on intelligence tests are predictive of success on many but not all jobs (see Table 12-3). The fact that the correlations between test scores and job success are near zero in some cases does not necessarily mean that intelligence is not important for the job. The dispersion of intellectual ability usually is narrowed considerably in most jobs by the individual's gravitating toward a job at which he can work comfortably and by the selection procedures that are used in industrial settings. Also, it is important to note that the variability of intelligence test scores is higher for lower-level than for higher-level jobs. This indicates that, as would be expected, intelligence is a more important determiner of success in high-level occupations. The individual's ability to succeed is determined by his intelligence and by a host of other things as well: abilities not measured by intelligence tests, interests, personality traits, and just plain luck.

Table 12-3   Median validity coefficients of intelligence tests for various occupational groups in the prediction of job proficiency *(Adapted from Ghiselli & Brown, 1948, p. 577. Reproduced by permission of the American Psychological Association.)*

Occupational Group	Median Validity Coefficient	Number of Validity Coefficients
Clerical workers	.35	85
Supervisors	.40	9
Salesmen	.33	4
Salesclerks	−.09	18
Protective service	.25	6
Skilled workers	.55	6
Semiskilled workers	.20	45
Unskilled workers	.08	13

USING TESTS OF GENERAL ABILITY IN SCHOOLS

At a number of places so far in this book, it has been emphasized that tests are useful only to the extent that they help in making decisions. Tests of general ability are potentially useful in helping to make decisions about (1) grade placement, (2) ability grouping within grades, (3) special instruction, (4) counseling, (5) vocational guidance, and (6) planning for higher education. Some of the important principles for using tests of general ability in these ways are described as follows:

CHOICE OF TESTS. In this chapter, numerous different types of tests have been described. Which ones should be used for helping to make particular kinds of decisions? There are some rules that partially answer the question.

Most schools employ standardized tests of achievement. As has been mentioned in a number of places in the book, tests of general ability tend to correlate highly with achievement tests. Consequently, tests of general ability should be used only if they *add* something to what can be obtained from achievement tests alone. Tests of general ability (at least the good ones) definitely add something with children from five to about ten years of age. In those years, the child is still getting used to school, and he has not had enough "book learning" for achievement tests to accurately mirror what he may accomplish later. Because most tests of general ability, particularly at the earlier age levels, are relatively more concerned with "abstract" ability, they are more prognostic of later achievement than are achievement tests given in the primary grades.

Because the abstractness of many measures of general ability is an asset in dealing with children from five to ten years old, the more abstract the test, the better. At those age levels, the Stanford-Binet and the WISC are semi-independent of school learning, which is why they are highly recommended. The fact that the Lorge-Thorndike series provides for routinely obtaining a reliable nonverbal IQ score is considered an advantage. It can be expected that in order to add something to what can be obtained from routinely administered achievement tests, tests of general ability will become even more abstract. One step in this direction is to employ more items concerning figural relations, such as those illustrated earlier in this chapter.

The decisions about whether to use group or individual tests in general and about when to use one rather than the other are relatively easy to make. The individual tests are simply far too expensive to be given routinely to all children. Testing one child requires about half a day's time from an expert test examiner. Even if schools could afford this much time from highly paid individuals, in many cases expert examiners would not be available when needed. Consequently, most schools will have to rely on one of the group tests of the general ability for routine testing of students. The individual tests are necessary, and worth the expense, when the child constitutes a problem in some sense.

For several reasons, tests of general ability are more valuable in the elementary grades than in high school. One reason is that, as was argued previously, young children's abilities are more general; therefore, one general measure will tell much about the child. Beginning with the teens, it is advisable to use one of the multifactor batteries when possible. Another reason is that much of the need for a test of general ability no longer exists by the time the student is well along in high school. The major value of such tests is in getting students off to a good start in school, and by the time the student is in high school, much of the "good" or "evil" has already been done. A third reason is that tests of general ability for teen-agers and average adults (in contrast to some of those for young children) overlap considerably with tests of school achievement. The degree of overlap is less when the intelligence test emphasizes abstract abilities, rather than the more specific types of knowledge covered by achievement tests. (Abstract items for measuring intelligence were illustrated earlier in the chapter, e.g., those involving figural relations.) If the expense is not too much for schools to bear, it is wise to employ both comprehensive achievement tests and a relatively abstract measure of general intelligence. Even if the school cannot afford to administer intelligence tests routinely to all students, there are many instances in which valuable additional information about particular students can be obtained from intelligence tests.

COUNSELING AND GUIDANCE. Tests of general ability would be worthwhile if for no other reason than the important part they play with problem children. In a typical problem, the first-grade child is overactive, runs around the room rather than working on exercises, will not follow instructions, and is apparently incapable of doing first-grade work. The teacher suffers it for a month and then tells the principal something has to be done. The principal contacts a school psychologist, who administers the Stanford-Binet as one part of the clinical work-up. What the test shows has an important bearing on the child. If his score is very high, he may be restless out of boredom and need more challenging fare. If he is near average, he may have emotional problems centered in the home, or he may be poorly disciplined. If his score is very low, he may be totally unable to master the first grade and be causing trouble because he is frustrated and angry. Regardless of what the tests show, they supply one important type of information to help in making decisions about problem children.

Individually administered tests are particularly helpful in dealing with problem children. Many children who are too disturbed to perform well in class or on achievement tests often show high ability when carefully drawn out by the expert examiner. Also the individual testing situation provides the examiner with many opportunities to observe the emotional behavior of the child, his habits, and his methods of approach to problem-solving situations.

CURRICULUM MANAGEMENT.   Some school systems use tests of general ability to decide when children may be admitted to the first grade. If children score high enough, they can be admitted when they are only 5½ years old or even younger. Although the practice is controversial, the merit probably outweighs the potential dangers involved. Children of the same chronological age are not of the same mental age. Basing grade placement on chronological age is, if anything, less logical than basing it on mental age obtained from a good test.

An even more controversial practice is to place children in ability groups within particular grades. There are both very good and very bad things to be said about the practice. On the bad side the practice potentially can (1) make the slow learners feel inferior, (2) place an unhealthy emphasis on intelligence, and (3) deprive all students of the opportunity to learn about other children in general rather than only those of their own level of ability. On the good side, ability grouping potentially can (1) let every student learn at his own pace without either dragging along or being dragged along by the others, (2) let slow learners work with students of their own level of ability, and (3) simplify the teacher's work by giving him students who can do, and are interested in, much the same materials. No attempt will be made here to reach a final decision as to whether the potentially good features of ability grouping outweigh the potentially bad ones; but, should ability groups be used, tests of general ability are very helpful. Up to about the fourth or fifth grade, tests of general ability offer the best measures currently available for grouping children in terms of ability. After that point, standardized achievement tests do as well or better.

CLASSROOM INSTRUCTION.   To the child, "school" means the day-to-day interactions with his teacher and with fellow students. How can, and should, tests of general ability interact with that all important (for the child) microcosmos? Some argue that teachers and students would be better off it IQ tests had not been invented, and there is some truth in the arguments. On the negative side, teachers often display a naïve faith in the tests. They forget that they are man-made and only as good as men know how to make them at the present time.

Teachers must be careful not to let the IQ become an index of value or moral goodness. Good character, sportsmanship, pleasantness of personality, and most other desirable personal attributes *are not* related to measures of general ability. If the teacher wants to single out a student who is in need of special attention and consideration, it should be the child with a low IQ. School will always be an uphill fight for him, and he will have to settle for less in life than his brighter schoolmates can expect. If the teacher has any energy left from trying to love them all, that last ounce of affection and concern should go to the child who needs it most.

Tests of general ability give the teacher an approximate idea of what to expect from each child. If the child has a very high score, he can be expected to perform well beyond the average. If he has a very low score, he may need special instruction. However, teachers must remember that *general* measures are just that—they do not indicate the particular ways in which the child is more and less bright. If the child makes a very high score, he probably can perform well in most school topics. If he makes a very low score, he probably will have trouble in most school topics. However, most children are not at the extremes, and for them tests of general ability leave many unanswered questions. Although all abilities tend to go together, there are definite exceptions. Consequently, one child may show an average IQ but be high in mathematical ability and low in other respects, and many other patterns of ability are possible. Teachers should look for the particular abilities of the child rather than rely solely on one index of general ability.

Tests of general ability do not necessarily measure creative potential. Although students who make low scores seldom become creative adults, there is far from a one-to-one correspondence between IQ and creativity for above-average students. Some students with very high IQs do not grow to be creative adults, and some students with only moderately high IQs produce truly creative works. (Chapter 14 will discuss measures of creativity.) Tests of general ability are primarily useful for predicting how well children will do in school.

In using tests of general ability to predict success in school, teachers must remember that such tests are primarily useful for predicting and making decisions about the *next step*. A test of general ability given to a five-year-old is highly predictive of how well he will perform in the first several grades. A test of general ability given at the beginning of junior high is quite predictive of progress during the ensuing several years. However, tests of general ability *are not* highly predictive of performance years hence. For example, the correlation between measures of general ability given to five-year-olds and successful performance in college is nil.

Although the mental abilities of children change quite slowly, they do change. Mental abilities of children are not highly "crystallized." The child who appears only average at age six may appear superior at age eighteen. The child who appears above average at age seven may appear below average as an adult. Children grow at different rates, both physically and mentally, and it is no more sensible to expect a test of general ability given at age six to be an infallible judge of adult ability than it would be to expect a measure of height at that age to be an infallible judge of how tall the adult will be. As is true of all tests, more faith should be placed in the extremes. The child who obtains a score typical of mental defectives is probably always going to have trouble. The child whose score is typical of only the top 1 per cent of the population is probably going to do quite well in school. In between it is rather hazardous to make long-range forecasts with tests of general ability. Rather, the results of such tests should be considered primarily as good indications of how well children can perform during the ensuing several years.

SUMMARY

The purpose of intelligence tests is to measure *abstract* ability, which is distinct from actual accomplishment in school as evidenced in achievement tests and teacher-made examinations. The potential usefulness of measures of abstract ability is that they could forecast how well some children might do if their home and school environments were improved. Also, they point to children who are, in a sense, performing better in school than they "should," children who either are highly motivated to achieve or who overly impress teachers with their accomplishments. These two types of children are often spoken of as "underachievers" and "overachievers," respectively. It is very important to know about both types (regardless of what is done about them), and potentially, intelligence tests can help spot these children.

Unfortunately it is not possible to measure abstract ability entirely apart from actual achievement in school. Many of the items on intelligence tests and achievement tests are very similar, and the two types of tests correlate highly. However, in those few cases where large differences are found between scores on the two types of tests, this can provide very important diagnostic information.

The content of most tests of intelligence largely was determined by the intuitions of the test constructors, plus statistical analyses of test data. In spite of their intuitive beginnings, all the tests tend to share some common properties. They all capitalize on several factors of intellect, particularly verbal comprehension. The dominant factors in the tests tend to be the ones that are most involved in successful performance in elementary and secondary school. Because of the similarity of their content, all the tests tend to correlate rather highly with one another, and choices among them for particular uses often must be made on practical grounds.

In schools, intelligence tests have many uses if they are employed wisely. Teachers must realize that intelligence tests are not intended to measure what students have actually accomplished, and they are not perfect predictors of future accomplishment. The value of intelligence tests is in providing clues about underachievers and overachievers. It is particularly important for teachers to realize that the IQ is not the only important aspect of intellectual potential and personal worth. The IQ does not (1) indicate special abilities, (2) provide a sure index of creativity, or (3) strongly relate to personality and character.

SUGGESTED ADDITIONAL READINGS

Anastasi, A. *Psychological testing.* (3rd ed.) New York: Macmillan, 1968, chaps. 8–11.

Bayley, N. A new look at the curve of intelligence. In A. Anastasi (Ed.), *Testing problems in perspective.* Washington: American Council on Education, 1966, pp. 384–399.

Gesell, A., Halverson, H. M., Thompson, H., Ilg, F. L., Castner, B. M., Ames, L. B., and Amatruda, C. S. *The first five years of life: A guide to the study of the pre-school child.* New York: Harper & Row, 1940.

Hollingsworth, L. S. *Children above 180 IQ.* Yonkers, N.Y.: World, 1942.

Peterson, J. *Early conceptions and tests of intelligence.* Yonkers, N.Y.: World, 1926.

Pinneau, S. R. *Changes in intelligence quotient.* Boston: Houghton Mifflin, 1961.

Thorndike, R. L. *The concepts of over- and under-achievement.* New York: Teachers College, 1963.

Thorndike, R. L., and Hagen, E. *Measurement and evaluation in psychology and education.* (3rd ed.) New York: Wiley, 1969, chap. 10.

chapter 13

SPECIAL ABILITIES

There are many human attributes to measure other than the kinds of abilities which were discussed in the previous two chapters. There we talked about the components of intelligence or intellectual ability, which are usually thought of as the "higher processes," the most prized of abilities. However, individual differences are as easily found, and sometimes as important to study, in sensory, motor, mechanical, and artistic abilities. Individual differences in these regards are important to consider with respect to structuring educational experiences for individual students, vocational guidance in high school, educational research, and many other matters that are important to classroom teachers.

In order to understand fully an individual's potentialities and liabilities, much must be learned about him in addition to his intellectual capabilities. Two persons could make the same score on a general intelligence test and yet be very different in other important ways. Similarly, for all the factors which were described in Chapter 11, two persons could have exactly the same profile of scores and differ importantly in terms of other abilities. One student might be underweight and frail, the other an excellent physical specimen. This would make quite a difference in athletic activities, and because young boys are so concerned with physical prowess, the difference would be important in relation to the social adjustment of the two boys. One student might have a flair for mechanical work, and another might have little interest or ability. This difference would be important to a high school counselor in helping students choose future vocations. Two students with about the same over-all scholastic aptitude might differ in that one would have intense interests in graphic art and show a creative touch in art work, as compared with little artistic aptitude on the part of the other. The difference might be important in the school adjustment of the two students and in their plans after high school. Even if a student's basic scholastic aptitude is above average for his class, he might have a strong disadvantage because of a hearing deficit. The deficit would require special methods of instruction for the student, and would make it difficult for him to study and play as a normal child. These are only a few of the ways in which the "special" abilities interact with the "intellectual" abilities to influence school progress, social adjustment, and future careers.

VISION

The popular practice of talking about "good" and "poor" eyesight does considerable injustice to the complexity of visual functions. There are a number of separable and only partially related kinds of "good" vision. A primary distinction must be made between near acuity and far acuity. Near acuity concerns how well the individual can discern visual forms within 1 or 2 feet of his eyes. Far acuity concerns how well the individual can discern visual forms placed 20 or more feet away. A third component of "good" vision is depth perception, the ability to judge the proximity of objects to one another. Another component is the ability to distinguish colors. Although it is commonplace to think of color blindness as a unitary characteristic, there are different kinds of color blindness. Also, the ability to distinguish colors is partly a matter of degree rather than an all-or-none attribute.

Good near acuity and far acuity (obtained with glasses if need be) are absolutely essential to adequate classroom performance. The child with poor far acuity will have difficulty in many ways, including (1) discerning material on the chalk board or on other visual displays, (2) following the hand signals of teachers in art and music exercises, and (3) watching the ball in play activities. The child with poor near acuity will be crippled in dealing with any kind of written material. He cannot read because he literally cannot see the printed words. Also, he will have difficulty in learning to write well, because, being unable to see what he himself tries to write, he will have difficulty in correcting his spelling errors and poor penmanship.

WALL CHARTS.   The most familiar measure of visual ability is the ordinary wall chart, which nearly everyone has encountered in applying for a driver's license or taking a physical examination. The Snellen chart is used extensively for that purpose. It consists of rows of letters, each row containing smaller letters than the one above it. The chart is placed 20 feet from the student. If he can read the row of letters that the average student can, he is said to have 20/20 vision. If he needs to stand 20 feet from the chart to read the row that the average student can read from 40 feet, he is said to have 20/40 vision.

Although the Snellen chart is an adequate device for detecting gross deficiencies in visual acuity, it has a number of disadvantages. Like all the wall charts, it tests only far acuity. A schoolchild could have excellent far acuity and still have crippling visual defects of other kinds. Some alphabetical letters are easier to distinguish than others, and this is not taken into account when using the Snellen chart. Also, the rows of letters are easy to remember, and the test can often be "faked" by the person who has some prior knowledge of the chart. The amount of light on wall charts should be carefully controlled, but in much practical work this is given little consideration. When controlled conditions are obtained, the reliabilities of the Snellen and other wall charts are satisfactorily high. One study (Studies in Visual Acuity, 1948) reports a reliability coeffecient of .88 for the Snellen chart.

COLOR VISION.   One of the oldest tests for color vision is the Holmgren Woolens. The subject is given different colors of yarn and asked to sort the ones that are alike. It is a crude test which serves only to distinguish persons who are very deficient in color vision. A more systematic measure can be obtained with the Ishihara color plates (Stoelting Co.). The plates are composed of small patches of color. The person who has good color vision can see a number on the plate formed by patches of a particular color. The color-deficient person either does not see the number or sees a different number. More recent color-vision tests are the Farnsworth Dichotomous Test for Color Blindness (D. Farnsworth, 1947), the Farnsworth-Munsell 100 Hue Test (D. Farnsworth, 1957), and the Illuminant-Stable Color Vision Test (Freeman & Zaccaria, 1948). In order to keep color-vision tests adequately standardized, they must be used in the same illumination and protected from fading or soilage.

MULTIPLE-COMPONENT TESTS OF VISION.   In recent years, devices have been constructed which test a number of different aspects of vision. The three best-known instruments are the Ortho-Rater (Bausch and Lomb), the Sight Screener (American Optical Company), and the Telebinocular (Keystone View Company). Each of these instruments tests near vision, far vision, depth perception, color discrimination, and control of the eye muscles. In general, the multiple-component instruments represent a considerable advance over the older, single-component tests. Despite their advances, the instruments employed for testing multiple components are no more expensive than television sets and require only a small amount of special instruction to operate. Consequently, many schools can afford to have the instruments available to employ with all children, or at least with those who have difficulty with schoolwork.

AUDITION

The sense of hearing is also composed of a number of different functions. Only auditory acuity will be treated here—the ability to detect faint sounds. Auditory acuity is, itself, complex: The person who can hear well at one tone level may be nearly deaf at higher or lower frequencies. Because of their relevance to musical aptitude, some of the other auditory functions will be considered in a later section.

The older tests of auditory acuity employed sound sources, like whispered speech or the ticking of a clock. In the whispered-speech test, the examiner stands some distance from the subject and whispers a number of words. The subject tries to say what each word is in turn. The examiner walks farther and farther from the subject to determine the distance at which the whispered words can be heard. Although tests of this kind are adequate for detecting gross losses of hearing, they have a number of defects. It is difficult to standardize both the loudness and clarity of whispered speech. One examiner will inevitably whisper a bit louder and/or clearer than another, in spite of the best efforts at standardization. Such tests measure auditory acuity within a narrow range of the tone, or frequency, continuum. The person who can hear whispered speech might not be able to hear sound at a different frequency, such as the sound of a ticking clock. The difference in the acoustical properties of testing rooms and the problem of ruling out extraneous noises add to the difficulty of standardizing this type of test.

A number of instruments have been developed for measuring auditory acuity at different points on the frequency continuum. These are called pure-tone audiometers (see Davis, 1947; Watson & Tolan, 1949). Earphones are used to test one ear at a time. The standard procedure is to gradually raise the sound intensity until the subject indicates that he can hear the tone. Then, starting with a sound that the subject can hear well, the intensity is lowered to a point where it can no longer be heard. The procedure is repeated at different frequency levels. The resulting data can be plotted as a profile of auditory acuity (see Figure 13-1).

Pure-tone audiometers are now available for group testing. Earphones are given to all the subjects. Standard answer sheets are used for the subjects to indicate whether or not they hear the tone at different intensities. It is not possible to determine the individual's auditory acuity as finely in the group testing situation. The individual who shows a marked loss in any frequency range on the group test should, if possible, be given the individual test to determine more accurately the nature of his hearing deficiency.

A short case history will help show the nature and importance of hearing

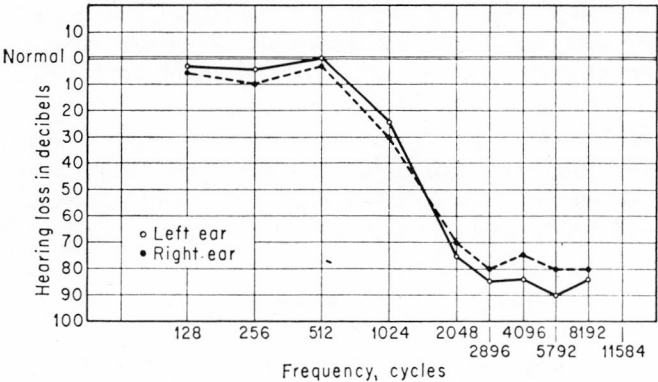

Figure 13-1. Audiogram of a child with severe high-tone deafness. *(Adapted from Watson & Tolan, 1949.)*

deficits. The teacher has difficulty in understanding the rather unusual behavior of Billy Aiken. Some of his symptoms are (1) he often fails to reply when asked questions; (2) he makes no attempt to find out what is going on in the classroom; (3) he mutters to himself but seldom talks to other children; (4) when other children talk to him, he usually smiles but looks embarrassed and does not reply; and (5) although he is seemingly bright in some ways, his over-all performance in class is well below average. The school guidance counselor suggests that Billy might have a hearing loss, and he requests the parents to have a thorough audiometric examination. The tests show that Billy has a severe hearing loss, particularly in the frequency range of human speech, and that the loss cannot be corrected by medicine or surgery. Billy must wear a hearing aid permanently in order to have normal auditory acuity. To help Billy in the classroom, the teacher provides remedial instruction in areas where Billy is behind the class, and engineers classroom activities in such a way as to help Billy develop confidence and learn to enjoy social participation. The guidance counselor talks with Billy's parents about ways to help in his remedial instruction and ways to encourage his social participation.

PRACTICAL USES FOR SENSORY TESTS

The individual with a visual or hearing defect is at a definite disadvantage in many performance situations. This is particularly true for the young school child who is handicapped. It is sometimes found that poor vision or hearing is responsible for apparent dullness. The child who cannot see the chalk board or cannot hear the teacher will learn very little regardless of his latent capacity for learning. Reading difficulties can often be traced to visual defects. In order to speak correctly, the child must imitate the speech of others. He cannot imitate what he cannot hear. The child with poor auditory acuity has difficulty learning to read by the use of phonics. To do well on most tests, the child must be able to hear the instructions and to read the test content. As is common practice in many school programs, children should be systematically tested at different age levels for auditory and visual acuity.

Even the sophisticated adult is often unaware that he has a visual or auditory defect. It often happens that individuals who wear glasses for the first time are surprised that the world "looks that way." Persons with poor far acuity often take it for granted that everyone sees objects more than 50 feet away as "big blurs." Consequently, the individual cannot be relied upon to detect his own sensory difficulty and seek help. He is likely to blame his inability to perform well on dumbness rather than on a visual or hearing loss.

Sensory ability is necessary for many different occupations. The classic example is the baseball umpire's dependence on "good eyesight." Color discrimination is paramount to the interior decorator, the tailor, and the artist. A moderate level of auditory acuity is necessary for most jobs, particularly if it is required to talk with others or to follow spoken instructions. However, there are few jobs in which high-level sensory ability is the primary attribute. Even jobs that would seem to depend heavily on sensory acuity usually require only average ability. A typical example is that of a sonar operator who uses a sound echoing device to detect hostile submarines. It was found that up to a certain point auditory acuity is a "must" for the job; but above the level of average hearing, auditory acuity is not a predictor of good and poor sonar operators.

Sensory disabilities are often prominently involved in adjustment problems. It is not uncommon for the student who is partially cut off from his environment because of a sensory disability to become withdrawn, depressed, and resentful. Sensory tests can be used to detect difficulties in audition and vision. Correction or compensation for the sensory disability often leads to an improvement in the student's personal relations.

MECHANICAL APTITUDE

Mechanical ability is popularly thought of as concerning the making and fixing of things as distinct from clerical, sales, administrative, and professional work. We generally speak of mechanical ability in relation to trades and various levels of skilled work. There is no fine dividing line between mechanical occupations and those that are not mechanical. Some occupations that most of us would classify as mechanical are plumber, carpenter, automobile mechanic, and television repairman.

Most teachers have little direct contact with mechanical aptitude tests. They mainly are of importance in the vocational guidance of high school students who are considering one of the skilled trades as a life pursuit. It is seldom the case that the school itself will have and use many of the tests required. Rather, such tests usually are administered by industrial or governmental agencies for selecting promising applicants for specialized programs of training. School counselors, and teachers in general, often are called on to help advise students about such vocational choices, and it is wise for them to learn something about the nature and use of mechanical aptitude tests.

There is no one type of test function which underlies mechanical work to the same extent that the general intelligence tests relate to schoolwork. In order to satisfactorily predict a particular mechanical job, a range of different kinds of tests must be used in a battery. Different combinations of tests are usually needed for different jobs. Some of the kinds of tests that have proved useful in the prediction of mechanical work and in vocational guidance are described in the following sections.

INTELLECTUAL ABILITY.   Because an individual is involved in making and fixing things, it does not mean that intelligence is an unimportant attribute. When it is possible to do so, either a battery of the major intellectual factors or at least a general intelligence test should be tried as a predictor. The spatial and perceptual factors are very useful in predicting many mechanical jobs. Some tests embodying these functions will be considered in a later discussion. However, it is important also to consider the verbal, numerical, and reasoning factors as well in the prediction of mechanical work. Because the "verbal" intelligence tests are mainly composed of these factors, a good intelligence test is often one of the best predictors of job success (see Table 13-1).

Intelligence tests tend to be more predictive of how well the individual does in job training than how well he performs subsequently on the job. This is probably because the training phase requires more abstract ability. In many cases the training program involves classroomlike procedures, reading of materials, and the learning of machine operations. These are the kinds of things that intelligence tests predict best. Predictor tests usually correlate higher with performance in training than with later job performance because, as a rule, performance is more reliably measured in the former than in the latter. Progress in training is usually graded

Table 13-1   Correlations of ability test scores with measures of job performance
(*Adapted from Ghiselli, 1949.*)

Test	Type of Job				
	Clerical	Protective Service	Skilled Trade	Semi-skilled	Unskilled
General intelligence	.36	.28	.45	.20	.16
Arithmetic	.42	−.12	. . .	.15	
Number comparison	.28	.25	. . .	.15	.15
Spatial relations	.06	. . .	.45	.30	.27
Mechanical principles	. . .	. . .	.45	.25	
Finger dexterity	.22	.20	.21	.30	.05

more carefully. There is more of an opportunity to observe the worker, and, in many cases, tests are used to assess progress in training.

Intelligence tests tend to be more predictive of success in high-skill rather than low-skill jobs. That is, validities are usually higher for such jobs as electrical technicians and complex machine operators than they are for jobs like truck drivers and furniture movers. The difference in validity is probably due to the increased importance of abstract ability in more highly skilled work. In selecting people for unskilled work, the problem is to set up minimum standards of intelligence rather than to seek persons of high intelligence (see Table 13-2).

MOTOR DEXTERITY.   It has long been recognized that the person who works well with his head does not necessarily work well with his hands. Accomplishments like shaping a fine piece of pottery, hitting a home run, and operating complex machinery have little to do with intelligence or with formal school training.

Among the oldest motor tests are the pegboards, designed to measure arm, hand, and finger dexterity. A typical example is the Stromberg Dexterity Test (Stromberg, 1951; see Figure 13-2). The first part of the test requires the subject to place sixty cylindrical blocks into holes as fast as he can. In the second part, the blocks are removed, turned over, and put back in the holes. Another widely used test is the Crawford Small Parts Dexterity Test (Crawford & Crawford, 1956; see Figure 13-3). In the first part of the test, the subject uses tweezers to place pins in holes and then places a small collar over each pin. In the second part, small screws are put in place with a screwdriver.

Some tests are designed specifically to test how well the individual can work with tools and small mechanical parts. A typical test of this

Table 13-2   Minimum mental ages for jobs (*From Beckman, 1930.*)

Mental Age, Years	Boys	Girls
5	Dishwasher	Sewer (simple patterns)
		Vegetable parer
6	Mixer of cement	Mangle operator
	Freight handler	Crocheter (open mesh)
7	Painter (rough work)	Cross stitcher
	Shoe repairer (simple tasks)	Hand-iron operator
8	Haircutting and shaving	Scarf-loom operator
	Gardener	Dressmaker (not including pattern work)
9	Foot-power printing-press operator	Fancy-basket maker
	Mattress and pillow maker	Cook (simpler dishes)
10	Sign painter	Sweater-machine operator
	Painter (shellacking and varnishing)	Launderer
11	Storekeeper	Librarian's assistant
	Greenhouse attendant	Power sealer in cannery

kind is the Bennett Hand-tool Dexterity Test (Bennett, 1947; see Figure 13-4). The test requires the subject to remove and replace nuts and bolts as quickly as possible.

More complex tests involving hand, arm, and leg coordination have been

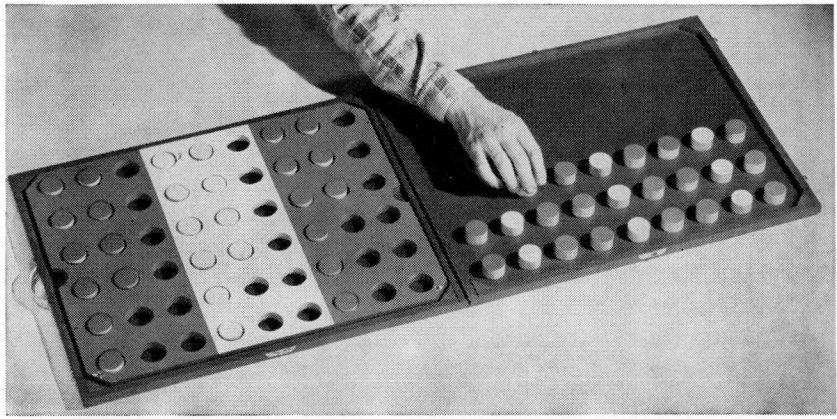

Figure 13-2. Stromberg Dexterity Test. *(Courtesy of The Psychological Corporation.)*

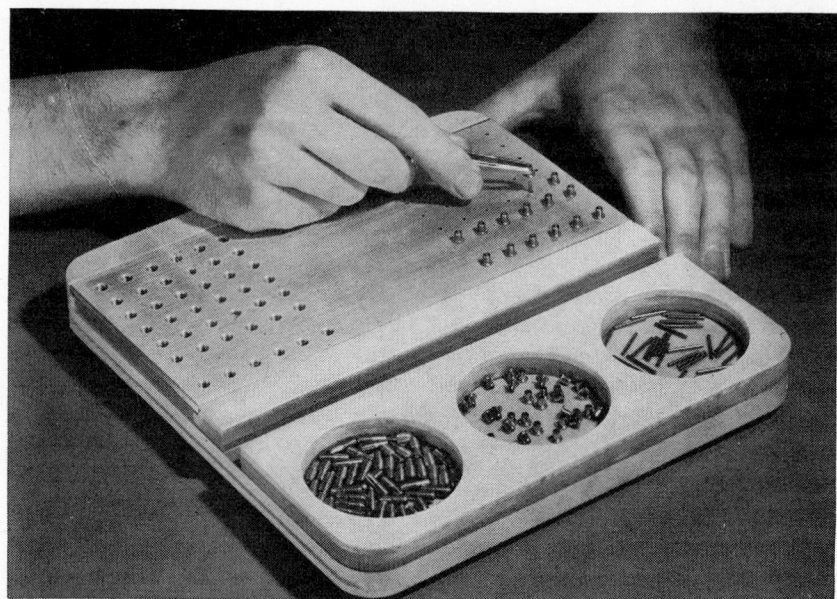

Figure 13-3.   Crawford Small Parts Dexterity Test. *(Courtesy of The Psychological Corporation.)*

Figure 13-4.   Bennett Hand-tool Dexterity Test. *(Courtesy of The Psychological Corporation.)*

designed for particular jobs. One of the best known of these is the Complex Coordination Test (Melton, 1947), used for the selection of pilots by the Air Force (see Figure 13-5). The test is a partial replica of an airplane cockpit, complete with stick and rudder. Lights on a control panel simulate the maneuvers of an airplane. The subject must use stick and rudder to match the stimulus light, which is the counterpart in the test of coordinating stick and rudder as required by the situation in an airplane.

Figure 13-5. Complex Coordination Test. *(Courtesy of the U.S. Air Force.)*

Most tests of motor dexterity are highly dependent on speed. Consequently, they prove to be better predictors of jobs in which speed rather than quality is important. There are many jobs in which speed is only a minor consideration. The person who can saw a board quickly does not necessarily have the craftsmanship of a skilled cabinetmaker.

Motor dexterity tests have acceptably high reliabilities, usually over .80 and sometimes over .90. An important characteristic of motor tests is that they tend to correlate very little with one another. Slightly different manipulations of the same material often have little in common. For example, the two parts of the Crawford Small Parts Dexterity Test correlate, on the average, less than .50. A correlation of only .57 was found between the two parts of the Stromberg Dexterity Test. Correlations between different motor tests prove to be even smaller. Factor-analytic studies of motor dexterity tests have generally found few broad common factors. Tests in this area are characterized by specificity.

Because of the small overlap between motor dexterity tests, there are no general measures of motor ability such as the general intelligence tests supply for intellectual functions. Motor tests are then of relatively little use in vocational counseling. They are most legitimately used in industrial selection where the job is simple, requires a definite set of motor skills, and is highly dependent on speed. Among jobs of this kind are those in production line work, sewing machine operation, and packaging.

Motor dexterity tests show at best only moderate predictive validity for most situations in which they are used. However, if they are used in conjunction with other ability tests, they often add a small, but important, increment to the over-all validity of the battery. Motor tests tend to be more valid when they are made to resemble the actual machine or instrument which is featured on the job. Tests designed in this way are called job miniatures. If the job is that of lathe operator in a machine shop, the best motor test would employ a mock-up of a lathe with the same kinds of dials, handles, and controls that appear on the real lathe. During the Second World War, the Army Air Force used a variety of motor tests for the selection of pilot trainees. The Complex Coordination Test, which resembles most closely what the pilot actually does, generally proved to be one of the most valid instruments.

Motor skills, and tests to measure them, are not very important to the average classroom teacher. Primarily this is because motor skills are almost totally unrelated to scholastic aptitude as evidenced in school topics such as reading, mathematics, and social studies. Motor skills are important mainly for certain specialized activities in schools, such as athletics, art, and some of the vocational courses in high school.

SPATIAL AND PERCEPTUAL TESTS. A wide variety of mechanical work requires the spatial and perceptual factors which were described in Chapter 11. The automobile mechanic needs spatial orientation in his work. In a typical job situation he is lying under the automobile and must remove a nut from the engine above him. The nut is slanted at a 45-degree angle, and he must remove it with a wrench that has two joints. The mechanic must orient himself spatially to the complex of angles and movements in order to do such work. In draftsmanship, it is necessary to portray three-dimensional objects on two-dimensional pieces of paper. In some drawings the objects must be shown in tilted positions or partially assembled. It takes spatial ability, both spatial orientation and visualization, to work as a draftsman and at many other jobs.

One of the best-known spatial tests for mechanical aptitude is the Revised Minnesota Paper Form Board Test (Likert & Quasha, 1948). It is a useful predictor of grades in shop courses, supervisors' ratings of workmanship, objective production records, and many other measures of mechanical performance (see Figure 13-6).

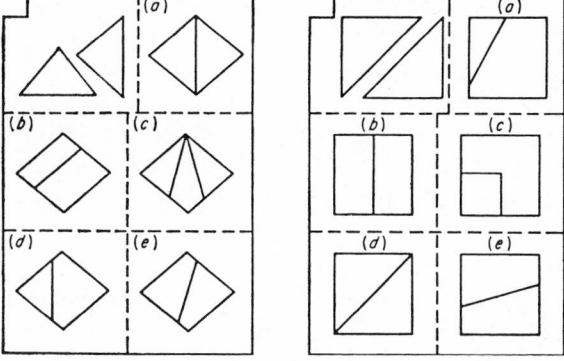

Figure 13-6. Sample items from the Revised Minnesota Paper Form Board Test. For each item, the subject must choose the figure which would result if the pieces in the first section were assembled. *(Reproduced by permission. Copyright 1941, renewed 1969 by The Psychological Corporation, New York. All rights reserved.)*

Perceptual ability is required in a variety of jobs. The perceptual speed factor has been used most often as a predictor, but it is likely that the other perceptual factors will eventually find their place in vocational guidance and job selection. The individual who sits by a fast-moving conveyor belt and looks for flaws in manufactured products uses perceptual ability. Any job in which it is necessary to detect aspects of a visual scene requires perceptual ability to some extent.

Examples of perceptual tests can be found in some of the multifactor batteries, which were discussed in Chapter 11. Some tests designed specifically for industrial selection will be described in the section on clerical aptitude.

MECHANICAL COMPREHENSION. Among the most successful tests of mechanical aptitude are those designed to measure the mastery of mechanical principles, or the ability to reason with mechanical problems. In a typical problem, a motorist must remove a boulder which blocks the road. He finds a long, stout pole to do the job. He must then decide whether to use the pole as a pry or as a lever. He can construct a lever by balancing the pole on a rock placed between the boulder and himself (the lever exerts more force than a pry). After deciding to use the lever action with the rock as a balancer (a fulcrum), he must then decide where to place the balancer (rock) and how to best exert his strength against the pole. As another example, a hoist is being built to lift tree trunks into the bed of a truck. A system of gears and chains is set up to transfer the power from an electric motor to the hoist. It must be decided how large the different gears should be to give the desired power to the hoist.

The two problems above are typical of those found in mechanical comprehension tests. Tests of this kind tend to range over several ability factors. Because of the paucity of factor-analytic studies of mechanical comprehension tests, it is not always possible to say just what a particular test measures. Some of them emphasize the spatial factors, which are prominently involved in many tests of mechanical aptitude. Other functions which appear in these tests are numerical computation, various aspects of the reasoning factors, and familiarity with tools and machinery. Examples of mechanical comprehension tests are the Bennett Mechanical Comprehension Test (Bennett, 1948, see Figure 13-7), the Mechanical Reasoning Test of the DAT (discussed in Chapter 11), and the SRA Mechanical Aptitude Test (Richardson, Bellows, Henry, and Company, 1950).

MECHANICAL INFORMATION. One of the most useful measures for the selection of skilled and semiskilled workers is a test of information, or knowledge, about tools and machinery. For example, a set of questions like the following would be useful in the selection of automobile mechanics:

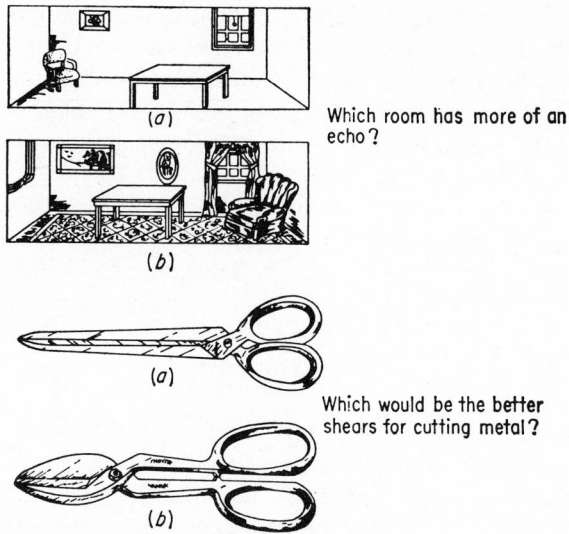

Which room has more of an echo?

Which would be the better shears for cutting metal?

Figure 13-7.   Sample items from the Bennett Mechanical Comprehension Test, Form AA. *(Reproduced by permission. Copyright 1940, renewed 1967 by The Psychological Corporation, New York. All rights reserved.)*

1.   What is a torque converter?

2.   What is a ratchet?

3.   Where is the "needle valve" in an automobile?

4.   What source of power is used to run the generator in most automobiles?

5.   How do you recognize "preignition"?

Information tests can be constructed either to measure general knowledge of mechanical work or to measure knowledge of one particular job. It is usually the case that a test constructed specifically for one job, such as for television repairmen, will be more predictive than a test of knowledge in general about mechanical work. However, the test which is constructed specifically for one job is likely to be useful only for selecting personnel for that job or for closely related jobs. Also, because of the specific knowledge which the instrument measures, it is usually of little use in vocational guidance, where it is usually necessary to measure broad functions rather than highly specialized information. A more general measure of mechanical knowledge is often useful in vocational guidance.

ANALYSIS OF MECHANICAL APTITUDE TESTS. A sufficient personnel-selection program usually requires a careful study of the particular industrial setting. The diversity of psychological functions which is required by different jobs makes it necessary to try out a range of tests to find the ones that will work well in practice. Also, it is often necessary to invent and construct tests for particular jobs.

Few of the mechanical aptitude tests have been studied as extensively as the tests of intellectual ability. Consequently, it is usually necessary to perform considerable research in the job setting to determine the utility of particular tests. In few cases have norms for the tests been obtained on a sufficiently representative sample to use them as dependable guides. It is generally more meaningful to obtain local norms for particular personnel selection or school programs.

Mechanical aptitude tests are fairly easy to standardize and make reliable. Reliabilities in many cases approach those of the better aptitude and achievement tests. Mechanical aptitude tests have modest validity for many different jobs, the amount varying considerably with the job. The seemingly small validities for some jobs should be regarded from a number of standpoints. Primarily there is the possibility that formal abilities such as those measured in psychological tests have little to do with job success. Another possibility is that the criterion of job success, the assessment, is unreliable and consequently cannot be predicted. If the assessment is determined only from the sketchy impressions of foremen and managers, it is seldom very reliable. Because of the unreliability inherent in most job assessments, mechanical aptitude tests are often considerably more valid than apparent from the correlation coefficients. The third point to consider is that the modest to low individual validities should not obscure the fact that a combination of several tests in a battery will often produce reasonably good predictive efficiency.

CLERICAL AND STENOGRAPHIC APTITUDES

CLERICAL APTITUDE. Clerical aptitude, as it will be discussed here, concerns the office clerk—the individual who deals with files, ledgers, accounts, and correspondence. The term "clerk" is much more general than this particular usage, referring variously to grocery clerk, department store clerk, and even court clerk. Perceptual speed tests have a special importance in the prediction of clerical performance. Perceptual speed is involved in chores like proofreading letters, searching for particular accounts in a long list, and alphabetizing names.

66273894 _____ 66273984
527384578 _____ 527384578
New York World _____ New York World
Cargill Grain Co. _____ Cargil Grain Co.

If the two names or numbers of a pair are exactly alike, make a check mark on the line between them.

Figure 13-8.   Sample items from the Minnesota Clerical Test. *(Reproduced by permission. Copyright 1933, The Psychological Corporation, New York. All rights reserved.)*

A typical test which emphasizes perceptual speed is the Minnesota Clerical Test (Andrew, Patterson, & Longstaff, 1946). The test is divided into two separately timed parts, Number Comparison and Name Comparison (see Figure 13-8). Retest reliabilities range from .85 to .91. Extensive validation research shows correlations ranging up to .60 between the Minnesota Clerical Test and business school and job performance criteria.

Perceptual speed is a necessary component of many clerical jobs, but other functions should be tested as well. Verbal comprehension is a desirable attribute, especially a knowledge of spelling and grammar. Clerical work often involves routine arithmetical operations, and therefore, a numerical computation test is likely to be a useful selection instrument. If the clerical job requires the use of accounting machines or other equipment, some of the motor dexterity tests may be of use. The DAT (Chapter 11) measures not only perceptual speed but also a variety of verbal and arithmetic abilities; hence, it probably would serve well in the selection of office clerks. The General Clerical Test (Psychological Corporation, 1950) is a short battery designed to cover the major functions required in clerical work. Scores on nine subtests are combined to form clerical, numerical, and verbal scores.

STENOGRAPHIC ABILITY.   The selection of stenographers is best made on the basis of specific job requirements. Typing and shorthand ability are the major requirements in most stenographic jobs. Therefore, achievement tests in these skills offer a sound basis for the selection of stenographers (for typical tests see Bisbee, 1934; Maxwell, 1950). Here, as in many other testing problems, the needs of a selection program are not always the same as those of the vocational guidance situation. In vocational guidance, before the individual has had an opportunity to test himself in specialized training or on the job, some prediction must be made as to how well he will perform. Although an insufficient amount of research has been done on the aptitude for stenographic work to allow us to speak with certainty, the most promising attributes seem to be the motor skills involved in typing, measures of verbal comprehension and language usage, and interest in stenographic work.

ARTISTIC APTITUDE

The nature of art and artistic ability has been a matter of interest to psychologists for well over a hundred years, but in spite of this long interest, the measurement of artistic ability lags behind the testing of other ability functions. This is due in part to practical considerations. There has always been a more urgent need for intellectual and vocational tests than for tests of artistic ability. Research on classifying men in the Armed Forces, testing children in school, and selecting men in industry has won financial support because of the immediate gains to be expected. Although the study of artistic ability offers some practical advantages, it never has promised a sufficient commercial market to merit strenuous test construction efforts.

Another reason that tests of artistic ability lag behind is the intrinsic complexity of the functions to be measured. In this area, it is very difficult to distinguish aptitude from achievement. The accomplished musician or painter can be judged by what he currently does. But it is difficult to find the underlying aptitudes that give one child an advantage over another in reaching eventual artistic accomplishment.

Good art is largely a matter of time and place. Chinese music sounds cacophonous to us, and no doubt much of our music seems strange to them. Some primitive music centers almost entirely on the drum and other percussion instruments. Complex rhythmic patterns used are too elusive for the "civilized" ear. We would miss the esthetic appreciation that the primitive has for his music as much as he would be baffled by the symphony orchestra. The delicate sensitivites of a Japanese poem are lost on an occidental audience. We might cite many other examples to show that art is a matter of values. Different people have different values, and values change over the ages.

Different abilities are involved in the production of art and in the appreciation of art. The music critic may not be a musician at all; the art historian may have never painted. Different kinds of art work require different abilities.

The measurement of artistic aptitude evolves into several components. For producing works of art there are probably some underlying abilities that cut across different times and different cultures. In graphic art work, the ability to make line drawings, to combine colors, and to achieve properties of "balance" are required in most paintings. In musical ability there are the basic sensory skills of tonal memory, sense of pitch, and recognition of rhythms, which to some extent cut across different kinds of musical production.

Another attribute which can be tested is the appreciation of art forms. Appreciation is dependent on the values in a particular culture and on the individual's knowledge and acceptance of those values. Finally, tests can be made of how well the individual can produce particular art forms; such achievement is dependent both on his initial aptitude and on the training that he has had.

MUSICAL APTITUDE

SEASHORE MEASURES.   One of the oldest and most widely used musical tests is the Seashore Measures of Musical Talents (C. E. Seashore, Lewis, & Saetveit, 1960). The test stimuli are reproduced on phonograph records which can be used for the testing of moderate-sized groups of subjects. The battery includes the following subtests:

1. *Pitch discrimination.*   The subject is asked whether the second of two tones is higher or lower than the first. The items are made progressively more difficult by decreasing the difference in pitch between the pairs of tones.
2. *Loudness discrimination.*   The subject judges which of two tones is louder.
3. *Time discrimination.*   One tone is presented for a larger period of time than another. The subject judges which of the two tones is longer.
4. *Rhythm judgment.*   The subject judges whether two rhythmic patterns are the same or different.
5. *Timbre judgment.*   The subject judges whether or not two tones are of the same musical quality.
6. *Tonal memory.*   Two series of notes are played. In the second series one of the notes is altered. The subject judges which of the notes is different.

Scores on the subtests correlate near zero on the average with intelligence tests. The subtest scores are partly independent, with median intercorrelations ranging from .48 to .25 for different samples. Split-half reliability estimates for the subtests range from .62 to .88. Rhythm and timbre are the least reliable. If, as is often done, the six subtests are added to form one general measure, high reliability can be expected for the test. Except for large differences in scores, the subtests are not sufficiently reliable for considering differential aptitudes within the test.

Scores on the Seashore test are affected very little by age. Similar norms are found for elementary school, high school, and adult populations. Although the research results are somewhat contradictory, it seems that scores are affected only slightly by musical training. These two findings taken together suggest that the Seashore subtests measure some basic aptitudinal functions which are possibly inherited. The larger question is whether the aptitudinal functions involved in the tests are of any importance in predicting musical accomplishment.

An insufficient amount of research has been done with the Seashore test to speak with firmness about its predictive utility. Modest to small correlations have been found with grades in music classes and with teachers' ratings of musical ability. The test differentiates moderately well between students who complete specialized musical training and those who drop out. It is reasonable to think that at the level of specialized music training most of the persons with poor ability in the Seashore type of measures will have already been eliminated.

A number of persons have argued that the Seashore measures are not very similar to the skills that are involved in the actual production of music. The Seashore subtests measure certain types of sensory discrimination which might be necessary for musical ability but not sufficient. Potentially, where the Seashore test would have its most important value would be in helping parents decide whether their children would profit from extensive musical training. This would save considerable money and would keep the neighbors from having to hear little Susan grind away for years at an instrument she will never master. At present the Seashore test is difficult to administer below the age of ten, and the predictive validity of the test at younger ages is not known.

WING TEST. The Wing Standardized Tests of Musical Intelligence (Wing, 1960) were designed to stay as close as possible to the skills involved in musical production and appreciation. Like the Seashore test, the Wing test uses phonograph recordings. The following seven functions are tested:

1. *Chord analysis.* Judging the number of notes in a chord
2. *Pitch change.* Judging the direction of change of notes in a repeated chord
3. *Memory.* Judging which note is changed in a repeated melodic phrase

4. *Rhythmic accent.*   Judging which performance of a musical phrase has the better rhythmic pattern
5. *Harmony.*   Judging which of two harmonies is better for a particular melody
6. *Intensity.*   Judging which of two pieces has the more appropriate pattern of dynamics, or emphasis
7. *Phrasing.*   Judging which of two versions has the more appropriate phrasing

The first three subtests measure complex sensory abilities. The other four concern the esthetic value of different compositions. The subtest scores are added to form one general measure of musical aptitude.

The Wing test has received favorable response from teachers of music, who feel that the test covers many of the skills that are important in musical training. Little is known about how well the test can predict available criteria. The author reports correlations of .60 and above between the test and teachers' ratings of musical ability in three small groups. It is possible that the Wing test will prove to be a better differentiator of musical talent at higher levels of ability than the Seashore battery. The Wing test might then be useful in the guidance and selection of students who want to go on from some initial musical instruction to more advanced training.

GORDON MUSICAL APTITUDE PROFILE.   A more recently developed test which appears to be quite promising as a predictor of later musical performance is the Gordon Musical Aptitude Profile (Gordon, 1965). The test is presented on tape and consists of seven subtests. The first four subtests deal with melody, harmony, tempo, and meter, respectively. The student must decide whether the second of two musical phrases is the same as, or different from, the first. In the last three subtests, the pupil is to decide which of two musical selections is better. The selections on each of the three subtests differ in terms of phrasing, balance, and tempo, respectively.

The reliability coefficients for the Gordon profile are very acceptable— e.g., in the .70s for the seven separate subscores and .90 to .95 for the composite score. Validity data reported by the author are, on the whole, quite encouraging. For example, in a carefully designed longitudinal study, fourth- and fifth-grade students who had no prior formal musical training were tested with the Gordon profile. They subsequently received training on a musical instrument and were evaluated at the end of one, two, and three years of training. One of the criterion measures involved recording a student's performance and presenting it to be judged anonymously.

Correlations between composite score and judged performance were .53 the first year, .69 the second year, and .68 the third year. Other research will need to be carried out on the validity of the instrument; however, initial findings suggest that the Gordon profile is a notable addition to existing tests of musical aptitude.

There are a number of other tests based on phonographically recorded tones and musical phrases. The Drake Musical Memory Test (Drake, 1934) emphasizes the memory component, which appears in only one subtest of the Seashore and Wing batteries. The Drake memory test is different in that the items concern short musical melodies instead of groups of tones. The subject must determine whether two melodies are the same, and if not, whether the change has been made in the key, the timing, or in specified notes. The Kwalwasser-Dykema Music Tests (Kwalwasser & Dykema, 1930) comprise a battery of ten subtests. Six of the subtests are similar to those on the Seashore. The subtests cover much the same ground as the Seashore, plus the ability to read musical notation and some components of musical appreciation.

ANALYSIS OF MUSICAL APTITUDE TESTS.   Not enough research has been done to say how well the current tests work. A particular problem is the dearth of adequate criteria of musical accomplishment. School grades in the history, techniques, and general knowledge of music are the most reliable indices. But these are not the same as artistry in musical production. Judgment of the actual mastery of musical instruments must necessarily be based on the impressions of teachers and other persons, and impressions of this kind usually have only modest reliability. Even if there are some difficulties in validating the instruments, much more research should be done to determine how well they work.

The tests which were discussed in the previous sections are all, strictly speaking, tests of appreciation. That is, the subject is not actually required to play an instrument but only to listen and judge what he hears. However, some of the complex judgments involved seem to underlie the skills that are needed in musical production. It is likely that other types of tests could be used in conjunction with the conventional measures to obtain a better estimate of musical ability. Motor skills are involved in playing most musical instruments, the piano being an outstanding example. Motor tests might be profitably used in the prediction of musical accomplishment. Although intelligence tests correlate very little with the available musical tests, this does not mean that they would be of no use in predicting musical accomplishment. It would be expected that intelligence and, more generally, the factors which underlie differential aptitude tests, would be useful in the prediction of course grades in musical curricula and in special music schools.

It is likely that an individual's interest in musical work will be as predictive of later success as tests of the ability type. Two such interest tests are the Farnsworth Scales (P. R. Farnsworth, 1949) and the Seashore-Hevner Tests for Attitude toward Music (R. H. Seashore & Hevner, 1933). The small amount of research that has been done indicates some promise for tests of musical interest.

GRAPHIC ART APTITUDE

McADORY TEST. The field of graphic art testing has been dominated by a particular type of item in which a masterpiece is compared with one or more altered versions of the same work. One of the oldest tests of this kind is the McAdory Art Test (McAdory, 1929). The test contains pictures of seventy-two works of art and covers a wide variety of contemporary art forms, ranging from pictures of furniture and automobiles to works of art in museums. Four versions of each work are given; these differ in shape, arrangement, shading, and use of color. The subject is required to rank-order the four versions in terms of his preferences.

Items for the McAdory test were selected on the basis of the judgments of experts, including teachers, critics, and artists. Items were retained only if at least 64 per cent of the judges agreed on the ranking of the four versions. A primary weakness of the test is its dependence on contemporary art values. For example, it is likely that preferences in furniture, automobile designs, and even paintings have changed since the test was constructed. The test was described in order to provide historical perspective for modern tests of artistic aptitude.

MEIER TEST. The Meier Art Judgment Test (Meier, 1942) is by far the most widely used test of art appreciation. It also uses the altered-version type of item. The test differs from the McAdory in that only one alternative version is given for each original art work, and the items concern relatively timeless art masterpieces. The items are all in black and white. The altered version of each masterpiece is meant to destroy the esthetic organization. In a typical altered version, one figure is moved to the side in such a way as to change the balance of the painting (see Figure 13-9).

The initial selection of items was made on the basis of expert judgments. Items on which there was high agreement among twenty-five experts were retained. The items were further pared down in terms of internal consistency statistics. Only those items showing a high correlation with the total score were placed in the final form.

Split-half reliabilities for the Meier test range from .70 to .84 in relatively homogeneous groups of subjects. Scores correlate only negligibly with

Figure 13-9. Illustrative items from the Meier Art Judgment Test. *(Reproduced by permission of Norman C. Meier.)*

traditional measures of intelligence. Only a small amount of research has been done to determine how well the test predicts available criteria. It has been shown that the test differentiates art students from non-art students and differentiates art students from one another in terms of the amount of training they have had. A correlation of .46 was found with the grades of fifty art students. Correlations ranging from .40 to .69 were found with ratings of creative art talent.

A more recently developed test (Meier, 1963) is the Meier Aesthetic Perception Test. The test is comprised of fifty items, each of which presents four slightly different versions of a work of art. (Figure 13-10 illustrates one of the items.) The examinee's task is to rank the four versions in order of preference from the one which is most pleasing, aesthetically, to the one which is least pleasing. This ranking procedure has the potential of providing finer differentiations between people than are provided by the binary-choice type of item employed on the earlier test by Meier.

The subject matter of the items consists of sculpture, painting, and abstract compositions selected to be representative generally of world art, from ancient to contemporary. This breadth of content represents a second

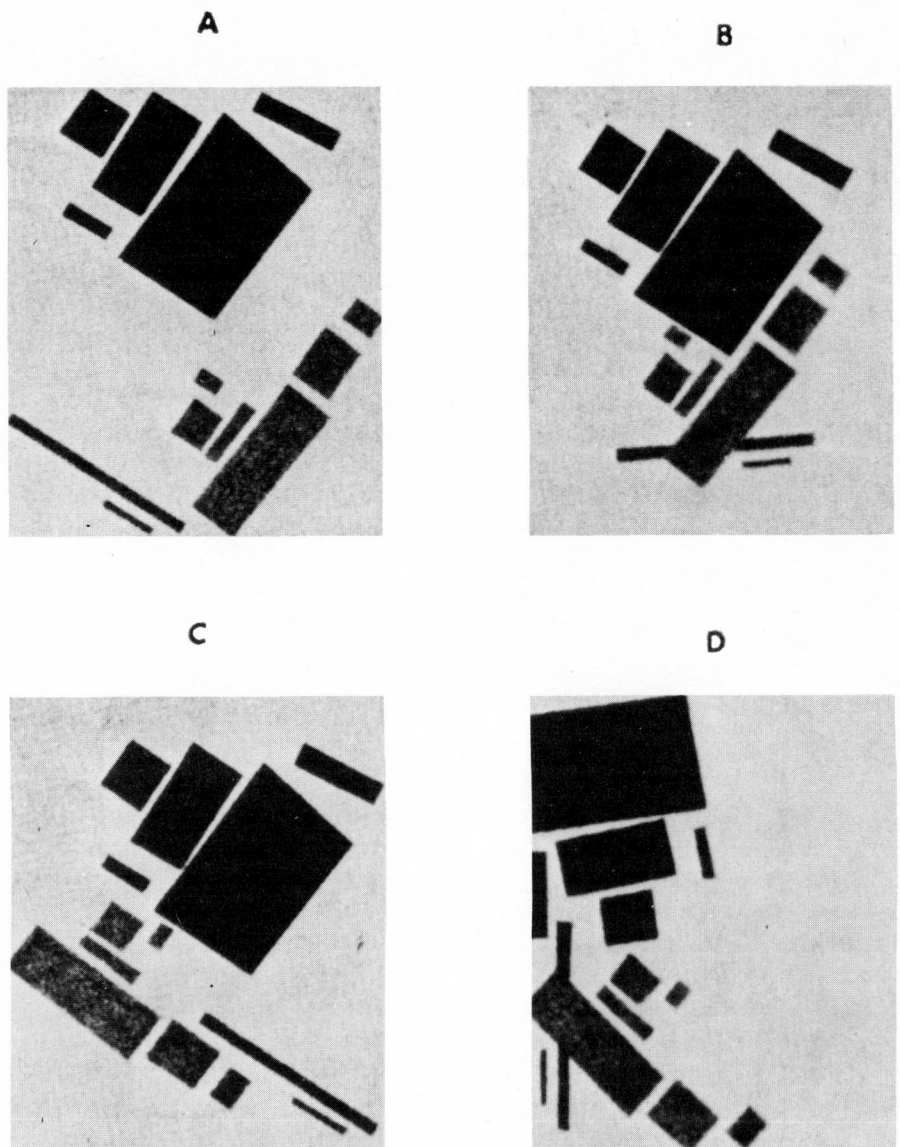

Figure 13-10.   Illustrative item from Meier Aesthetic Perception Test. *(Reproduced by permission of Norman C. Meier.)*

advantage of the newer test over the older one. The four versions in each item may differ in terms of unity, proportion, form, design, or the degree to which all these form a satisfying whole. As in the Meier Art Judgment Test, the items were tested on representative groups of artists and non-artists. Although only a small amount of data has been gathered on the predictive validity of the test, significant mean differences have been found among groups of artists, college art students, and high school art students.

GRAVES TEST. The Graves Design Judgment Test (Graves, 1948) consists entirely of abstract designs, which makes it as independent as possible of traditional and contemporary art values (Figure 13-11). Each test item consists of either two or three versions of the same basic design. The altered version or versions were constructed to violate accepted aesthetic principles. The judgments of art teachers and art students were

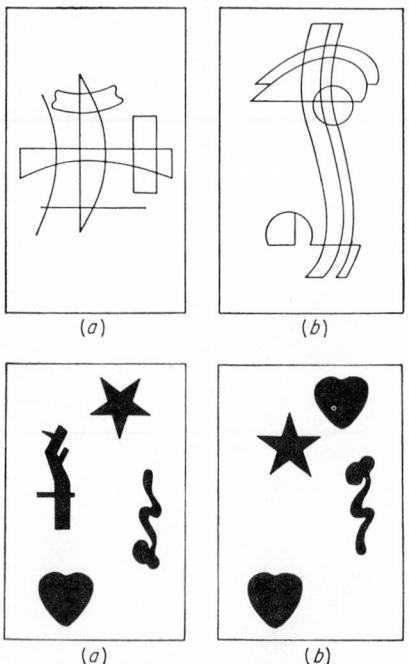

Figure 13-11. Illustrative items from the Graves Design Judgment Test. *(Reproduced by permission. Copyright 1946 by The Psychological Corporation, New York. All rights reserved.)*

used to select the best 90 items from an original list of 150. Split-half reliability estimates range from .81 to .93. Although the Graves test gives promise of being a useful measure, only a small amount of empirical work has been done with the instrument.

WORK-SAMPLE TESTS.   A number of tests have been designed to measure how well individuals can actually produce graphic art works. Typical of these is the Horn Art Aptitude Inventory (Horn, 1953), which includes the following subtests (see Figure 13-12):

1. *Scribble exercise.*   Making outline drawings of twenty objects
2. *Doodle exercise.*   Making abstract compositions out of simple geometrical forms
3. *Imagery.*   Working from a given set of lines to a completed composition

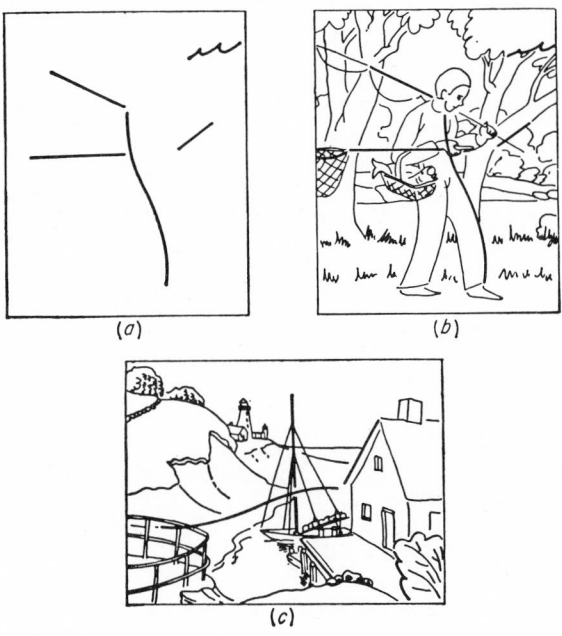

Figure 13-12.   Sample item from the imagery test of the Horn Art Aptitude Inventory. The subject is shown only the lines in rectangle *a*, from which he is to make a drawing. Examples of completed drawings are shown in *b* and *c*. *(From Horn & Smith, 1945, p. 351; reproduced by permission of the American Psychological Association.)*

Other tests which are concerned largely with the production of works of art are the Knauber Art Ability Test (Knauber, 1935) and the Lewerenz Tests in Fundamental Abilities of Visual Art (Lewerenz, 1927).

The work-sample tests must rely on the judgments of graders. Product scales are used in which a particular drawing is compared with a standard set. Sample drawings are available for each score level. The grader gives a score in accordance with the apparent nearness in quality of the subject's drawings to that of the product-scale examples. In spite of the apparent subjectivity of the scoring system, moderately high reliabilities are reported for tests of the work-sample type. Current evidence indicates that the work-sample tests predict course grades as well as the appreciation tests and that they do a better job of predicting teachers' ratings of creative ability.

ANALYSIS OF GRAPHIC ART TESTS.   The difficulties of defining and measuring musical aptitude are magnified in the measurement of graphic art aptitude. Since the graphic arts are more dependent on fashion, criteria of accomplishment are weaker; hence the underlying aptitudes are more difficult to determine. Unlike the sensory discrimination functions in musical aptitude, the current measures of graphic art aptitude appear to depend heavily on training. Consequently, they are of less value in the early guidance of prospective art students, where all tests of art aptitude would seem to have their most promising use.

Current tests are biased toward certain cultural groups. For example, it was found that much lower scores on the McAdory test are made by Navajo Indian children than by children in New York City, in spite of the fact that the Navajo culture has a highly developed art form of its own. The available tests appear in most cases to be clever and well designed, but the paucity of research which characterizes the testing of artistic abilities leaves many questions about how well the tests work in practice. Perhaps future factor-analytic studies of graphic art tests will lead to a better knowledge of the underlying functions and how they can best be measured.

Both musical and graphic art aptitude tests have a limited but important place in school testing programs. Rather than rely solely on such tests, it is better to let children try their hand at music and art so that it can be seen directly how well they actually perform. However, such actual classroom performance is not entirely predictive of how well the child might perform if his interests were increased or if he received more intensive training. Tests of musical and artistic aptitude can help fill that gap.

SUMMARY

In addition to the *intellectual* abilities which were discussed in the previous two chapters, there are many types of *special* abilities which interact with success in school and later success in vocational activities. The sensory abilities, particularly vision and audition, place limitations on how well students can perform in school. If children cannot see the chalk board or hear what the teacher says, they will perform poorly regardless of their intellectual potential. Teachers should be alert to possible sensory deficits in children, and tests of vision and audition should be periodically administered to all children.

Motor skills have little to do with scholastic aptitude, and different motor skills tend to correlate very little with one another. The motor skills involved in typing are different from the motor skills involved in repairing watches, and both are different from the motor skills required to fly airplanes. Motor skills are important primarily for certain vocational activities, particularly for those that heavily depend on speed of response, e.g., typists and operators of complex machines.

Mechanical aptitude concerns the making and repairing of apparatus, such as is involved in the work of the boat builder, airplane mechanic, and television repairman. Underlying mechanical aptitudes for a particular type of work are (1) at least a modest level of general intelligence, (2) motor skills relating to the particular activities, (3) perceptual and spatial abilities, (4) information about tools and machinery, and (5) above all, a strong interest in the particular line of work. Tests of mechanical aptitude are important only in the later years of high school when students are seeking advice about future vocational activities.

Although all will agree that it is important to promote artistic abilities in children, it has proved very difficult to develop valid predictor tests. This is partly because of the great complexity of artistic abilities and partly because artistic accomplishment is so much a matter of time and place. Tests for musical aptitude rely mainly on sensory abilities which relate to the memory, discrimination, and judgment of tones and chords. Such sensory abilities probably set a limit on how well students can perform in musical pursuits, but a high level of performance in such tests does not guarantee that students can reach a high level of musical virtuosity.

Tests of graphic art aptitude are even less informative than tests of musical aptitude. This is because (at least in these times) accomplishment in graphic art is so difficult to define. Most tests of graphic art aptitude require students to differentiate "good" from "less good" paintings and designs; others require students to produce line drawings.

Although tests of musical and graphic art aptitude have a place in elementary and secondary school, they should not be relied on as the sole guide as to whether students will profit from intensive training in artistic pursuits. Rather, it is best to let all children try their hands at artistic pursuits, bring out some appreciation and skill in even the least apt student, and let students find out for themselves and show others which of them has the propensity for high-fever accomplishment.

SUGGESTED ADDITIONAL READINGS

Anastasi, A. *Psychological testing.* (3rd ed.) New York: Macmillan, 1968, chaps. 14, 16.

Cronbach, L. J. *Essentials of psychological testing.* (3rd ed.) New York: Harper & Row, 1970, chaps. 11–13.

Super, D. E., and Crites, J. O. *Appraising vocational fitness by means of psychological tests.* New York: Harper & Row, 1962.

Thorndike, R. L., and Hagen, E. *Measurement and evaluation in psychology and education.* (3rd ed.) New York: Wiley, 1969, chap. 11.

chapter 14

CREATIVITY

Years ago one of the shibboleths in education was dealing with "the whole child," which was supplanted later with concerns over "why Johnny can't read." In these days much concern is being expressed over how to make Johnny more creative.

In the previous three chapters we discussed the types of abilities that are essential to success in schoolwork and in later vocational success. But so far we have not discussed the abilities which are involved in truly creative work, as evidenced in the work of leading scientists, scholars, and artists. What types of children grow into creative adults? What types of instruments can be used to measure creativity? What can the teacher do to promote the creative potentials of all children? In spite of the obvious importance of these questions, firm answers are not yet available. Considerable theorizing and research have been done on creativity, and some of the results are quite promising, but much more needs to be done before we can speak with certainty about the circumstances that surround and promote human creativity. This chapter will discuss some of the factors which are currently thought to determine creativity.

WHAT IS CREATIVITY? In spite of the widespread use of the term, people seldom stop to state what they mean by creativity. Implicit in most discussions is the notion of *creative products;* that is, before it is meaningful to talk about the creativity of individuals, we must talk about the creativity of some of their productions. We first look at what the person has done (whatever it may be) and then judge the creativity of the accomplishment. Until some products are available to be judged, it is rather meaningless to argue about the creative abilities of particular individuals.

If creative products are essential to judge creative ability, what types of products meet the standards. Sheer "goodness" is usually not enough to have a person's works labeled as creative. For example, most of us would not use the word "creative" to describe (1) a well-performed surgical operation, (2) the solution of a mathematical problem, or (3) the construction of an excellent piece of furniture. In describing these accomplishments, we would more likely use terms such as "highly skilled" or "knowledgeable."

In essence, the word "creative" concerns the *invention* of something, the production of something that is new, rather than the accumulation of skills or the exercise of book-learned knowledge. Creativity concerns what people *add* to the store of knowledge which was on hand before they came upon the scene. Of course, the "inventions" of children more often than not are rediscoveries of existing pieces of knowledge; but if this knowledge is not available to them from books, class discussion, and other sources, such rediscoveries constitute genuinely creative acts. Also, children sometimes are creative in the sense of actually adding to the existing store of knowledge.

Conceivably, creativity could be manifested in anything one did; however, here we will be concerned primarily with creativity as manifested in (1) scientific research, including the social and biological as well as the physical sciences; (2) scholarly work, such as in philosophy and history; and (3) artistic productions. We are not sure that the traits that make for creative ability in one of these three areas would lead to success in the others, and it may be that different types of home and school environments are necessary to nurture creative people for the three areas. Current research evidence indicates that there is enough common ground among different types of creativity to talk about traits that tend to make for creativity in general and environments that help promote creativity in general. Research on these matters is summarized in Taylor, 1964a, 1964b.

TRAITS RELATING TO CREATIVITY

What are some of the characteristics that denote the creative student? Because, as was said previously, it is necessary to witness creative products in order to judge creativeness, it is difficult to judge the creative ability of students, particularly that of students in the elementary grades. Few obviously creative products come from children. We may regard some of their products as clever or unusual, but seldom do they make a real imprint on the world. The line between the fool and the genius is indeed often quite fine. Consequently, to tell whether or not a student is actually creative often results in considerable guesswork. In children, creativity is best judged by the tendency to be original in many ways and on many occasions rather than by a few obviously creative productions of a kind that we associate with adult creativity. For example, the child who has creative potential as a scientist is not likely to manifest his creativity by actually producing an important new law of physics but rather by showing unusual insight into the implications of simple physical principles and by having many clever (for his age) ideas about how such principles relate to daily life. Similarly, the child who has creative potential as a writer is not likely to manifest his gift by writing a best-selling novel but rather by showing an unusual sensitivity to the meaning and use of words in themes and poems.

In discussing the characteristics that often go along with creativity, it will be necessary to talk about a "type" of student. Of course, "types" are only handy fictions that facilitate discussion. It is important to keep in mind that many creative students will be exceptions to the rule. Some will have none of the characteristics which will be discussed, and the majority will "go in opposite directions" on at least one of them. The following characteristics are currently *thought* to typify creative students *as a group.*

GENERAL ABILITY. How well do creative children score on tests of general ability, such as those discussed in Chapter 12? Some suggest, or apparently assume, that children who score only average, or even below average, may possess outstanding creative ability. All the evidence indicates that this is definitely a misconception. Although *all* children who perform well on tests of general ability are not creative, it is incorrect to leap from this observation to the conclusion that some children who do poorly on tests of general ability are quite creative. By any standard one chooses to apply, those children who are judged to be creative, as a group, score moderately high on tests of general ability. Most creative children are in the top 10 or 15 per cent on intelligence tests. Almost never does one find a child who is average, or below average, on tests of general ability whose products strongly indicate creative potential.

The real question is why only *some* of the children with high IQs are creative. Rather than make a distinction between the intelligent and the creative, it is more appropriate to make a distinction between the intelligent but not creative and the intelligent and creative. Apparently, to be creative it is necessary to have a moderately high level of ability as represented by conventional tests of general ability, but beyond that point such tests are not indicative of creative potential.

One of the difficulties in untangling the difference between intelligence and creativity is that the so-called intelligence tests have usurped a name that has broad connotations. As was stated in Chapter 12, tests of general ability relate to the *understanding* of subject matters; they do not necessarily relate to *invention* and *discovery.*

SUCCESS IN SCHOOL. Another misconception is that many creative children do only average or even quite poorly in schoolwork. The research evidence strongly suggests that this is not true. The studies show that those children who are judged to be creative, as a group, perform rather well in school. They may not make all A's, but it would be quite rare to find a creative child who did not generally do at least B work. Although creative children are often bored by the routines of schoolwork and are distracted by their own special interests, they usually have sufficient energy and general ability to carry them to at least moderate success in the classroom.

INTROSPECTIVENESS. Creative children typically like to think, and they enjoy having some time to be alone with their thoughts. They are not always the happy extroverts which, for some reason, we tend to cultivate. They may appear absentminded and distracted; and, of all sins, they do not always listen when the teacher talks. Because of their introspectiveness, creative children are seldom voted "most liked" by their peers, and they may not enjoy the same social life in and out of school as do their less creative classmates.

ADJUSTMENT. By ordinary standards (which perhaps we should revise) the creative child is often not as well adjusted as his noncreative peers. The creative child tends to be different in many ways. His searching mind goes far beyond that of his peers, and quite often beyond that of his teachers. In a sense, he knows too much—too much to take the "childishness" of his peers seriously, and too much to take seriously all that the teacher says and does. The creative child is in much the same position that the college graduate would be in if he were required to sit in a fourth-grade class and take it all seriously. He would be rather maladjusted in his surroundings.

In addition to a tendency to be somewhat isolated socially, creative children tend to possess some other personality characteristics. One of these is that they are not strongly influenced by the values and standards of others. They typically consider their own values to be best and will stick to them regardless of what others think. They often maintain a cynical view of what the teacher and the students value, which serves to isolate them from the group.

Another characteristic of many creative children is that they are very flexible in their ideas. They can change their minds quite readily, without feeling a strong need to have a "pat answer." They are always exploring new ways of looking at issues and are not very disturbed if one point of view proves to be faulty. In contrast, most intelligent but noncreative children look for, and want, "pat answers" and are disturbed by finding that a seemingly well-established point of view must be abandoned. To the creative child, thinking is like a game of chess, in which the game itself is enjoyable, and long periods of contemplation before each move are savored. To the noncreative child, thinking is, at best, a means to an end. He is happiest when the issue is settled and done, and glad that he has to think no more. The noncreative child wants to learn "how to do it," "what the facts are," and "how the problems are to be solved." The creative child has a less passive (and, in a sense, less disciplined) intellect. He dwells on what he considers to be intrinsically interesting, goes off on fascinating tangents, and soars above the mental level of the issue at hand. These are more reasons why he is different, and being so different he is likely to be labeled as odd, unfriendly, and troublesome.

Creative children usually have a great deal of faith in their own ideas. Because they actually do more thinking, and do it better than the people around them, they soon learn to trust their own ideas. In the classroom this often appears to be unreasonable stubbornness.

There is a type of teacher (rare, we hope) who is concerned primarily with convincing students of his own vast store of knowledge. Such an inflexible fellow is disturbed by the creative child who thinks that his ideas are better than those of the teacher. This is why the creative child is seldom made teacher's pet. When asked to rate the likability of their students, teachers typically prefer intelligent but noncreative children to intelligent and creative children.

HOME ENVIRONMENTS.   Creative children tend to come from unusual home environments—unusual in the sense that, by common standards, they are often bad. Studies of highly creative adults indicate that, as a group, few of them came from "ordinary" physical and social environments. Many creative children come from broken homes or from homes where either there is constant strife between parents or the relationship is cold.

Some of the other ways in which the home lives of creative children tend to be unusual are (1) having a mother who spends much time away from home in vocational or avocational pursuits, (2) being rejected by one or both parents, (3) having a father who is poorly adjusted as a man and as a family member, (4) frequently moving from city to city and/or from school to school, and (5) living with foster parents or with only one parent.

Of course no one creative child has all the bad features of home environment mentioned above, and because we are talking about group trends, many creative children do come from stable, happy homes. However, there is a tendency for there to be something unsavory about the home environment.

There is apparently some truth in the saying that "genius is born of misery." Hopefully, this is not necessarily so, but too many creative people come from unhappy beginnings to deny that the saying has some validity. Perhaps many creative children withdraw somewhat to escape the unpleasant features of their environments. They find pleasure in thought and fantasy that they do not find in their outside worlds. Thinking then becomes a habit which they carry with them all their lives. Conversely, it it may be that many children who are intelligent but not creative are absorbed by the pleasant features of their external worlds; therefore, there is no need for, and little enjoyment from, retreating into their own thoughts. If these things are so (and, admittedly, there is much conjecturing here), some way must be found for using methods of training to bring out the creative potential in all children rather than depending on "misery" to bring out the best in some of them. Some suggestions about how this can be done will be made later in this chapter.

MEASURING CREATIVITY

The measurement of creativity is still in its infancy. Consequently, the measures shown in this section are illustrative only of the efforts which are currently being made. Some of the published tests designed to measure creativity are discussed in Appendix D.

GENERAL ABILITY.   It must be remembered that even though all the students who make relatively high scores on intelligence tests are not creative, the converse does not hold: almost none of the students who make low scores on tests of general ability will prove to be creative. Up to a point, then, tests of general ability are among the best predictors of creative ability. The question is not whether creative students need relatively high IQs, but rather, what they need *in addition* to high IQs.

PERSONALITY CHARACTERISTICS.   Personality characteristics are among the most important determiners of creative ability. Some of the traits which apparently relate to creativity are (1) introversion, (2) flexibility of opinions, (3) intellectual self-confidence, (4) self-willed independence, and (5) immense energy for intellectual tasks. Some of the methods which are used to measure these personality characteristics are (1) teacher's observations and ratings, (2) self-reports from students, (3) projective tests, and (4) biographical inventories concerning past accomplishments, hobbies, and participation in intellectual pursuits. More about all these methods of attempting to measure personality characteristics will be said in Chapter 16. These methods of measuring personality characteristics relating to creativity are far short of perfection, but they do provide very useful information about the likelihood of a particular student's possessing creative talent.

DIVERGENT THINKING.   Guilford's conceptions regarding the "structure of intellect" were discussed in Chapter 11. One of the most important distinctions in those conceptions is that between *convergent* and *divergent* types of thinking. Convergent thinking is at issue whenever the student must seek a correct solution for a stated problem, such as (1) obtaining the correct solution to an algebra problem, (2) memorizing the multiplication table, (3) learning the definition of a technical term in biology, (4) learning how to find documents in the card catalogue of a library, and (5) learning how to diagnose mechanical problems presented in vocational courses. In all such instances, and others in which convergent thinking is the main issue, there is either only one correct solution or a very restricted class of correct solutions.

In contrast to convergent thinking, divergent thinking consists of going off in new directions rather than seeking the correct solution to a stated problem. Out of their factorial research on the structure of the intellect, Guilford and his associates have produced a number of tests designed to tap the many different facets of the operation of divergent production. These tests are known collectively as the Southern California Tests of Divergent Production and are discussed in Appendix D. In the following paragraphs, we shall discuss several aspects of divergent thinking which are thought generally to be basic to creativeness. A number of the Southern California tests will be mentioned as examples, as well as those of another battery, the Torrance Tests of Creative Thinking. Although the Torrance tests are similar in many respects to the Southern California tests, they were developed not from factor-analytic research but as part of an educational research program relating to stimulating creativity in the classroom (Torrance, 1959, 1962). This battery is discussed more completely in Appendix D.

UNUSUAL USES.   Supposedly, one aspect of creativity is the ability to see new and unusual uses for old objects and methods. This is illustrated by the pilot who, in a pioneering oceanic flight, thought of filling the wings of his plane with Ping-Pong balls to keep the craft afloat in case of engine failure over open water. Most of us noncreative folk could look at a Ping-Pong ball for hours and not think of such a clever usage. Of course, one such clever idea does not make a person creative. The creative person is forever seeing clever, unusual uses for common objects and methods.

Test items can be composed to measure students' abilities to see unusual uses for objects and methods. For example, students can be asked "What are some uses that can be made of empty tin cans?" Both the number and quality of answers are important. The noncreative student will think of "carry water," "plant flowers," "hold marbles," and then be at a loss to provide more answers. The really creative child will produce a flood of answers, including not only many of the ordinary uses mentioned above, but also such clever ones as "cut out the tops and bottoms and weld them together to make a stove chimney," "put them in the ground to make golf cups," and "cut holes in the bottom and use them to spread grass seeds." Similar items can be composed relating to screwdrivers, paper clips, bottle caps, and many others.

One of the Southern California Tests of Divergent Production is made up of precisely the type of items we have been discussing. The test entitled Alternate Uses calls upon the examinee to list possible uses for a specified object other than its common use. The student must then list as many uses as he can think of for such everyday objects as a coat hanger or a newspaper. Another such item appears in the Torrance Tests of Creative Thinking, where the student is also presented with the task of giving unusual uses for a familiar object.

CONSEQUENCES.   One facet of creativity is the ability to see the many consequences that would follow from a particular action or event. For example, what would some of the effects be if the average temperature of the earth were raised by 10 degrees? Some obvious consequences would be that less heating would be needed in homes, there would be less need for winter clothing, and people could swim most of the year. Some more unusual (and perhaps creative) responses would be that the polar ice cap would melt and flood many coastal cities, Eskimos would have to change their way of life drastically, and many new regions could be opened up to farming. Many other such items can be composed to measure the ability to visualize consequences. Both the Guilford tests and the Torrance battery include a test of this aspect of divergent thinking. For example, in the Guilford test one is posed with the hypothetical question, "What would be the results if people no longer needed or wanted sleep?" The responses are scored in terms of both the total number of obvious consequences given and the total number of original responses.

ORIGINAL RESPONSES TO SPECIFIC EVENTS.   One of the characteristics of many creative children is that they are often able to produce quite clever slogans, captions for cartoons, and endings to stories. In these instances, creative children manifest the inventive side of verbal ability, which goes beyond the passive aspect that is traditionally measured in tests of vocabulary and reading comprehension. Some illustrative items are as follows:

The student is asked to invent a clever title for the picture of a sleepy child standing near a worn-out tire. Noncreative students would give titles like "Off to bed," "Who is going to blow out the candle?" and "School in the morning." The creative child is likely to think of something quite clever, such as "Time to retire."

In another type of item students are asked to supply clever endings to a sentence or a short narrative. Following is an example.

John walked through the snow and up the porch steps. After fumbling for the key and not finding it, he pushed against the door and found it was unlocked. Inside no one greeted him, and when he called "I'm home," no one answered. With his eyes fixed on the light coming from an upstairs bedroom, he slowly climbed the stairs. As he reached the top stair, he stopped suddenly and said "Oh, my goodness, ——."

Noncreative children would complete the story with endings like "I forgot to let the dog in the house," "I meant to mail that letter," or "There is a ghost." More creative children would provide endings like "I took a bus home and left the family sitting in the car in front of my office," or "I don't live in a two story house." Many other such items can be constructed to test the creative ability to supply unusually clever verbal responses. Such clever responses represent another type of divergent thinking.

FLUENCY.   Apparently, one aspect of creativity is the sheer fluency with which words, ideas, and solutions to problems are produced. One aspect of fluency was considered in Chapter 11: verbal fluency, which concerns the rapid production of words. A part of the Southern California Tests of Divergent Production is the Christensen-Guilford Fluency Tests, in which the examinee must write words as rapidly as possible to meet certain specific conditions. For example, one task calls for examinees to produce as many words beginning with a specified letter as possible in two minutes. Although word fluency is only moderately well correlated with measures of general ability, it apparently does go along, to some extent, with measures of creativity.

Another type of fluency, one that is apparently related to creativity, is the ability to produce rapidly words in specific categories or words that bear specified relationships to one another. In the former case, for example, the subject is asked to produce quickly the names of objects that roll on wheels or the names of creatures that live in water. In the latter case the student might be asked to produce words that mean much the same as a given word, e.g., synonyms for "intelligent," such as "smart," "bright," and "clever." The Christensen-Guilford Fluency Tests present just such tasks, including one in which the examinee must construct four-word sentences, each word to begin with a given letter. The more different sentences he can construct, the higher the score. An example of such a problem might be "K _____ u _____ y _____ i _____," from which such sentences as "Keep unruly youngsters inside" or "Kill ugly yellow insects" could be made.

Another aspect of fluency is ideational fluency. Not only do creative children have better ideas, but they also have many more of them. Ideational fluency can be measured by counting the number of ideas and solutions which students produce. This can be done with respect to the tasks mentioned above: unusual uses, consequences, and original responses. Besides scoring for cleverness, simple counts are also made of the number of responses produced.

In addition to scoring other types of creativity measures for the fluency of ideas, items can be constructed specifically for that purpose. An example is as follows:

> Imagine that you own a company which produces bicycles and that you want to make many improvements in your product. What changes would you make in your bicycles? What would you do to make them better? During the next five minutes, write down as many improvements as you can. Try to give good ideas, and give as many of them as you can.

The number of different improvements listed would be one index of ideational fluency. Activity 4 of the Torrance Tests of Creative Thinking involves ways of improving a given toy so that children will have more fun playing with it.

Apparently, the various kinds of fluency are very important for some types of creativity. Creative people typically have floods of ideas, most of which are impractical but a few of which are highly ingenious. Sometimes creative people are unable to evaluate the "good" and "bad" among their own ideas. This is why some creative people work better with a partner or as a member of a team. They are the "idea men" who must be supplemented by others who can carefully evaluate, experiment with, and test their ideas.

In recognition of the fact that critical evaluation is a necessary part of the creative process, several tests to measure this aptitude have been developed. These tests, such as the Watson-Glaser Critical Thinking Appraisal and the Ship Destination Test, emphasize the general reasoning factor. (A discussion of these tests may be found in Appendix D.)

It is a mistake to judge the creative abilities of either adults or children by the number of unworkable ideas which they produce, but rather they should be judged by the number of ideas that do work. Because of the typical fluency of creative people, along with their good ideas, they are bound to produce many "whacky" ones as well.

Perhaps one of the reasons why more people are not creative is that they are not willing to let themselves be fluent, not willing to let themselves go mentally and produce a flood of ideas. Because many of these ideas are bound to appear silly to ourselves and others, we often stifle our thought processes rather than endure self-ridicule or the ridicule of others. To be creative, a flood of ideas must be produced, and the bad ones must be accepted as a natural part of the process. More about this will be said in a later section when we discuss what can be done in the classroom to promote creativity.

INGENIOUS SOLUTIONS TO PROBLEMS. Creativity concerns not only having many new and unusual ideas but also thinking of very clever ways to solve ordinary problems that occur in daily life. One such ingenious solution to a problem was shown long ago in the construction of a church in New Orleans. The water level in the ground was so high and the ground so soft that any ordinary foundation for the church would have soon collapsed. The solution: Hundreds of bales of cotton were buried in the mud, and the foundation was laid over these. The church to this day literally floats on bales of cotton.

Although it takes a skillful person, and takes him much time, test items can be composed to measure the ability to produce or recognize ingenious solutions to problems. An example is as follows:

> A truck is rushing medical supplies to a flooded town. Ten miles from the city, the truck driver discovers that his truck is about 1 inch too tall to go under a railroad overpass. There are no roads nearby that will allow him to go around the overpass. Every minute is important. What should he do?

The clever student will see that an excellent solution is to let some air out of the tires and then drive on.

By its nature most people would think that creativity could not be measured with multiple-choice items. Creativity concerns the *invention* of something. In contrast, multiple-choice items usually concern the *recognition* of correct answers. However, if the alternative responses contain only a key word or some letters in key words in the solution, multiple-choice items actually can measure inventiveness. An example is as follows:

A farmer living in a remote region finds that a 2-foot length of pipe has burst in the series of pipes that carries water from the pump to the house and barn. It is urgent that he get the water flowing again. He uses a wrench to remove the burst section of pipe. He looks in his tool shed and finds only one piece of pipe of the right length and diameter. On inspecting the piece of pipe he finds that both ends are threaded clockwise, which means that the turning motion that would be required to screw the pipe in at one end would be the opposite of the direction of turning that would be required to screw the pipe in at the other end. If he turns the pipe clockwise with his wrench, the pipe will screw in at one end but not the other, and vice versa if he turns the pipe counter-clockwise. He has no other pipe and no special tools for rethreading pipe, nor does he have welding equipment or any material sufficiently strong to bind one end of the pipe. A key word involved in a temporary solution to the problem is

a. frozen
b. halfway
c. bury
d. upside down
e. burn

The alternative answers give the student few clues, and, consequently, he must think of good solutions and see if any of the key terms apply. In the example above, only one term, "halfway," has been found to involve a good solution. The solution is to screw the pipe in tightly at one end, then, pressing together the unattached ends, unscrew halfway, which, in the process, will leave both ends halfway screwed into their respective attachments. The arrangement might leak slightly, but it would offer a clever temporary solution, better than any that can be obtained involving any of the other key terms.

To provide even fewer cues to students, only the first letter of one or more key terms can be placed in the alternatives. An example is as follows:

In a factory a hole has developed in a large steel container which is used to carry hot water from one vat to another. The container is part of an elaborate system of wheels and cables which is used to do the job. It may take several weeks to get a new container installed. The foreman tries to cover the hole with a steel disk, but because of vibration from the machinery, the disk keeps slipping away from the hole. Since the water is so hot, glue will not work, and no equipment is available to weld or bolt the disk over the hole. The disk can be held over the hole with a

a. t_____
b. p_____
c. h_____
d. s_____
e. m_____

The best solution involves the letter "m." A magnet placed on the bottom of the container under the hole would hold the steel disk firmly above.

CREATIVE PRODUCTIONS.   One of the most straightforward, and in many ways the best, method of testing for creative potential is to give the student an issue or problem and ask him to produce creative responses. Tests of creativity in the arts can be made using designs, parts of figures, and splotches of color. Starting from these bare beginnings, the student must create something on his own. For example, one of the Torrance Tests of Creative Thinking involves using a brightly colored curved shape as the starting point for drawing an unusual picture that "tells an interesting and exciting story." Another of the Torrance tests, Picture Completion, utilizes the same technique as the Horn Art Aptitude Inventory, discussed in Chapter 13; however, the product is scored in terms of fluency, flexibility, originality, and elaboration, rather than artistic ability. The Southern California Tests of Divergent Production also make use of this approach to measuring creativity. In a test called Making Objects, the examinee must draw specified objects using only a set of given figures. A sample item from this test is shown in Figure 14-1. A similar test, Sketches, presents the examinee with a page of identical figures (e.g., circles) from which he must make as many different sketches as he can.

Productions can also be used to test literary creativity. Students can be given the first two lines of a poem and asked to go on from that point to a finished product, or they can be given the first paragraph of a story and asked to complete it.

Productions can be used to measure scientific and scholarly creativity. For example, a problem that could be used with high school students in science courses is as follows:

Design and describe a vehicle for transporting people and supplies on the moon. Consider (1) the type of power supply needed, (2) the fuel that would be used, (3) the type of "wheels" that would be used, (4) special gadgets that would be needed for operating on the moon's surface, and (5) any other properties that you consider relevant.

Given these simple figures, make the objects named in the squares.

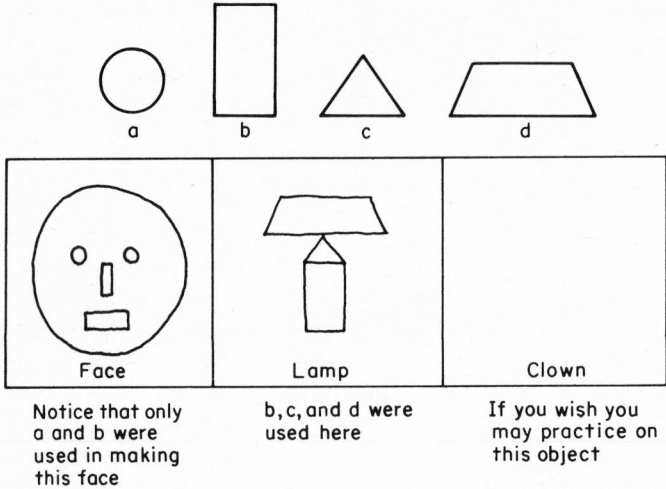

Figure 14-1. Sample item from one of the Southern California Tests of Divergent Production, Making Objects. *(Reproduced by permission of Sheridan Psychological Services, Inc.)*

A problem that could be used with students in the elementary grades is as follows:

> Suppose that we were going to build a new school and you were asked to design it. You would like for the school to be very modern and to contain many new ideas. What are some of the things that you would put in your school?

Relatively noncreative students will give such answers as "pretty flowers," "a better ball diamond," and "more chairs in the lunch room." More creative students will give answers such as "blinds run by motors that keep just the right amount of light coming in," "sliding walls that let you make rooms bigger or smaller," "little televisions on each desk where the teacher can show exercises, and it will tell you if you have the right answers," and "tape recorders so you can talk into them and then see if you are pronouncing correctly."

In using productions to test for creative ability, it is good if students are given plenty of time to respond. It would be best if students were allowed at least several days to write down their ideas. However, a problem that is often encountered in letting students wait so long to respond is that they will get their "creative" ideas from parents, older siblings, friends, or books. Even if it often is not feasible to give several days' time, students should be given as much time as possible in the classroom. For example, a fifth-grade student should be given at least one hour to respond to the question above relating to a new school.

If it were not for one salient difficulty, the production methods would be used quite widely in measuring creative ability. The difficulty is "How do you score the responses?" One part of the problem is that of finding scorers who can recognize creative answers when they see them. How can we score the productions of students who are more creative than we are? Actually this is not so much of a problem with students in the elementary grades. What would be creative responses for most of them are not beyond the mental comprehension of most teachers. It does get to be a problem with high school and college students, where some of the complex ideas creative students have are beyond the understanding of many teachers. Fortunately, it is not always necessary to be highly creative to recognize creative products. Even though we might not be clever enough to make the drawing, compose the poem, or design the school, we usually can recognize clever productions when we see them.

In most commercially distributed tests relating to productions, product scales are used for scoring. Expert judges score many different productions. From these, standard examples are chosen to represent different levels of performance. Productions of students are then scored by comparing them with the standard samples. This still involves an element of subjectivity, but carefully constructed product scales often have high reliability.

Another problem that is encountered in the scoring of productions is the sheer labor involved. Scoring each is like scoring a difficult essay question. If it were not for the vast amount of time needed to score responses, production items would probably be used quite widely to measure creative ability.

PERCEPTUAL TESTS. In addition to the types of measures mentioned previously, it currently is thought that some types of perceptual measures actually relate to creativity. We often talk about creative thinking as though there were some connection with perception. For example, in discussing creative processes, we talk about the ability to "see through" arguments, the ability to "focus" on important issues, and the ability not to be "distracted" by irrelevant cues. Not enough research has been done to know for sure whether creativity actually relates to perceptual processes, but some of the evidence is sufficiently interesting to encourage more research.

One type of perceptual problem that is thought to be related to creativity is illustrated in Figure 14-2. In each of the two items, the figure on the left is embedded in one or more of the complex figures on the right. In order to mark the correct figure, it is necessary to "*see through*" the maze of distracting lines and competing figures within the complex pattern. There is some evidence to suggest a relationship between this type of perceptual ability and the ability to see through irrelevancies in scientific problems. This and other types of perceptual abilities may relate to some extent to creativity.

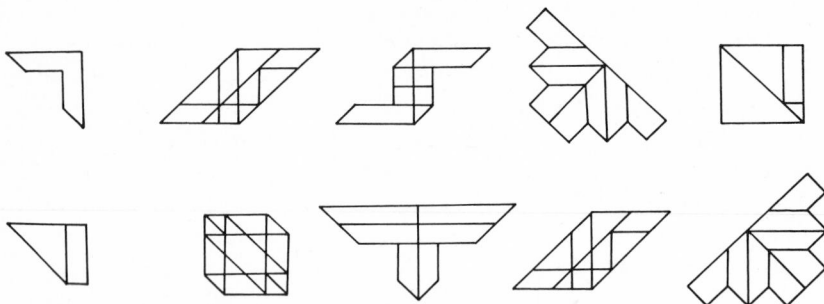

Figure 14-2. Two items concerning the ability to detect embedded figures. *(Reproduced by permission of Science Research Associates, Inc.)*

RECOGNIZING AND PROMOTING CREATIVITY IN THE CLASSROOM

In this chapter, examples were given of recently developed commercially distributed tests for the measurement of creativity. Others are discussed in Appendix D. Although such instruments show much promise, they should be considered largely experimental at the present time. Some interesting evidence regarding predictive validity is available for some of the tests, but a great deal more evidence in that regard will need to be obtained before the tests can be trusted to measure what they are purported to measure. Also, before tests of creativity can be routinely employed in educational research and practice, it will be necessary to obtain much more carefully constructed norms than are available for any of the instruments currently in use. Until these and other steps are taken to obtain well-standardized, valid measures of different aspects of creativity, the available tests should be confined primarily to research programs and to very limited roles in educational evaluation and counseling.

The caution stated here should not be taken to mean that teachers can or should do nothing toward detecting and fostering creativity in the classroom. Most of the types of measures discussed in the last section, e.g., measures of consequences and unusual uses, can be constructed and used by teachers. Such teacher-made tests can be used as exercises to promote creativity among students, as well as to provide hints about students who are either outstandingly creative or quite limited in that regard.

It is especially important that outstandingly creative students be recognized at an early age and that creative thinking be encouraged in young children. Evidently, by the teens, or perhaps even much younger, the creative abilities are crystallized. Either they have it by then or they never will. Consequently, if anything is to be done in the school and home to encourage creative thinking and work (and this is a commonly held value), it should be started with first graders. The study of creativity is still too new for us to say with certainty what should be done, nor can we list specific techniques of instruction that are sure to work. There are, however, some general practices and points of view which probably will help to bring out the best creative potentials of all students.

TOLERATE THE CHILD WHO IS DIFFERENT. Admittedly it is difficult to change our attitudes, but unless we do, we may be rejecting many creative students. As was stated previously, creative children tend to be different, if for no other reason than because they are so insightful. We tend to favor conforming students who memorize what we tell them and what is in the text. We favor the happy-go-lucky, all-American-boy type; and because some creative students are shy, and they sometimes enjoy sitting and thinking, we are sure that something is wrong with them. Of course we all worry about, and want to do something about, the child who is highly withdrawn and is autistic to the point of mental illness. Except for these extremes, we should not consider introversive, contemplative children as necessarily "sick." In a sense they may be better adjusted, or at least dedicated to a higher purpose, than the outgoing but vacuous "life of the party."

TOLERATE NEW POINTS OF VIEW. It is strange that among teachers, who are supposedly dedicated to critical thought, there is sometimes a tendency to react negatively to students who say (even if they say it politely) "I think there is a better reason" or "In my opinion, ..." As teachers we are all too prone to encourage students to depend on us to do the thinking, to give good grades and encouragement when students parrot our points of view, and to make it difficult for the student who has his own ideas. If we really want to promote creative thinking, we must learn to tolerate and encourage students to form their own opinions.

ENCOURAGE THINKING. We do not do nearly enough to encourage students to think on their own. We spend much time convincing students that there is a "right" answer or method and much time having students memorize what other people think. Of course there is a lot that students must memorize as a foundation for later knowledge, and in many cases the ideas of students are not as good as those in the book or those the teacher holds. But in addition to insisting that students learn the fundamentals, we should do everything that we can to encourage them to think on their own, to criticize, to invent, and to look for better reasons and methods.

The types of measures mentioned in the preceding section are useful, not only to index creative abilities, but also to provide guides regarding how to construct exercises for promoting the creative abilities of all students. For example, a class problem can be focused on "unusual uses." The teacher could instruct students as follows: "The problem for this week is to get some good ideas for using coat hangers. Let's think all week about what clever things we can do with coat hangers. On Friday we will report our ideas." Then each day of the week the teacher could maintain interest by reporting several ingenious uses that had been proposed for coat hangers.

Students can be encouraged to think of the consequences that would follow from particular actions and events. One set of instructions would be as follows: "The number of people in our country is growing rapidly. The population may double in the next fifty years. What are some of the problems that this will cause? How will that change the way of life of people in our country? What can be done to handle the problems that will arise? Think about the problem for several days, and then you can write down your ideas." As is true with all such "think" exercises, the teacher will have to prime the thinking processes of students by mentioning some ideas and problems of his own and sustain interest by bringing up several new ideas each day.

Exercises can be formulated which encourage students to think of ingenious solutions to problems, e.g., to put out forest fires, to help the blind move about, to translate foreign languages, and many others. Students can be encouraged to exercise their creative abilities to the full in their own productions—drawings, poems, short stories, essays, experiments, and theories.

In these and many other ways students can be encouraged to be creative and enjoy doing it. The teacher should measure the success of each day, not only by "How much did I teach them?" but also by "How much did I encourage them to think for themselves?"

SUMMARY

Beyond the ability to master school topics, some students possess creative talents which, if properly nourished, will allow them to make important contributions to society. Unfortunately, at the present time we are only beginning to develop methods for measuring creative ability. Studies of creative students and adults suggest a number of characteristics relating to creativity. Creative people tend to score relatively well on intelligence tests, and they tend to make at least moderately good grades in school. Creative people tend to be different—they tend to come from unusual home and social environments, and they differ from other students in the ways in which they approach intellectual problems. Some of the mental characteristics which currently are thought to distinguish creative students are (1) strong drive for intellectual accomplishment, (2) ability to see unusual aspects of problems and unusual solutions, (3) floods of ideas, and (4) ability to visualize the consequences of particular courses of action.

Because creative students tend to be different and are not always willing to agree with what other students and the teacher think, they are seldom highly popular. Consequently, it often takes a special effort on the part of teachers to appreciate the talents and energies of creative students. In addition to ensuring that all students obtain a good grounding in core topics, teachers can promote creativity in all students by encouraging them to give critical reactions, to seek new answers, and to think for themselves.

SUGGESTED ADDITIONAL READINGS

Crutchfield, R. D. Creative thinking in children: Its teaching and testing. In *Intelligence: Perspectives 1965*. New York: Harcourt, Brace & World, 1966, pp. 33–64.

Golann, S. E. Psychological study of creativity. *Psychol. Bull.*, 1963, **60**, 548–565.

Mackinnon, D. W. The nature and nurture of creative talent. *Am. Psychologist*, 1962, **17**, 484–495.

Taylor, C. W. (Ed.) *Creativity: Progress and potential*. New York: Wiley, 1964. (a)

Taylor, C. W. (Ed.) *Widening horizons in creativity*. New York: Wiley, 1964. (b)

Torrance, E. P. *Guiding creative talent*. Englewood Cliffs, N.J.: Prentice-Hall, 1962.

PART V

PREDICTION AND TRAIT MEASUREMENT: INTERESTS, ATTITUDES, AND PERSONALITY

Most of the discussion so far in this book has concerned the measurement of various types of ability: teacher-made tests, achievement tests, and aptitude tests. The major emphasis of the book has been purposefully set in that direction. However, there is another realm of measurement, one that is also very important and has its own special methods and problems. This other realm consists of the "noncognitive" attributes, which are sometimes lumped together under the overly general name of "personality."

A primary distinction should be made between measures of "maximum performance" and measures of "typical performance." Most of the measures discussed in previous chapters deal with how well an individual can perform when he tries his best. This is the case, for example, with measures of spelling ability and arithmetic reasoning. In contrast, some of the measures which will be discussed in this section are not obviously concerned with "maximum performance" (or ability), but rather with how the student *usually* acts. A test of courtesy offers a good example of why the distinction is necessary. A good test of courtesy should not depend mainly on knowledge of courtesy or on how courteous a student could be if he tried. Almost everyone knows how to be courteous, and people are differentiated in this respect by what they actually do in daily life. Consequently, it would be a poor test of courtesy to ask a student questions about what constitutes courteous behavior; rather, what is needed is some indication of the student's typical behavior in situations where courtesy is at stake.

Many other examples could be given of traits that concern typical performance rather than maximum performance. For example, a measure of interest in music should concern what the student typically does. All students know how to *act* interested in music: attend concerts, read books on music, turn the radio to "good music," etc. What is at stake is the student's daily behavior with respect to music. Does he actually attend concerts, etc.? The same is true of many other measures. They concern what people typically do in daily life rather than how well they can perform in situations requiring maximum performance.

Three major types of typical performance will be considered in this section: measures of interests, attitudes, and personality characteristics. Although these three kinds of measures will be more extensively spelled out in the following two chapters, it would be wise to stop for a moment here and give partial definitions of each.

There are no sharp dividing lines between the three types of measures to be discussed in this section. For some types of measures, it is difficult to decide whether they would be more appropriately placed in one category rather than another, e.g., interests or attitudes. However, because the three types of measures are used for somewhat different purposes and tend to involve different types of problems, it is important to distinguish them as well as possible.

Interests concern preferences for particular types of activities. Thus, if a student says that he enjoys playing baseball, giving speeches, and repairing mechanical devices, these would be classified as interests. The main standardized measures of interests concern preferences for activities related to vocations, and, consequently, they are of major importance for the vocational counseling of high school students. Other measures of interests relate to activities in school and are useful to teachers in structuring school activities.

Attitudes concern how students feel about things external to themselves. Different measures of attitudes differ largely in terms of the "things" on which they focus. Some of the typical studies of attitudes concern feelings about (1) racial and ethnic groups, (2) world problems, (3) social behavior, and (4) classroom practices.

The category of "personality" is somewhat more difficult to define. Principally, it refers to relatively enduring traits of individuals which determine their social behavior. Thus the category applies to traits such as shyness, aggressiveness, moodiness, and friendliness.

Before we move on to discuss particular measures of typical performance, a proper emotional tone should be set by admitting that measures of these kinds are not as effective as we would like. The development of effective measures of ability, of all the kinds discussed in previous chapters, has been quite encouraging. We already have much proved "hardware," and there is every indication that even better tests of ability can be constructed in the future.

Although there are numerous exceptions to the rule, generally it has proved somewhat more difficult to develop measures of typical performance than measures of maximum performance. This part of the book will discuss various approaches to measuring typical performance, problems encountered in the use of such approaches, and proposed methods of overcoming those problems. Following are some of the approaches that traditionally have been used in the attempt to measure interests, attitudes, and personality characteristics.

1. Self-report. By far the most widely used approach has been to ask the individual what his interests, attitudes, and personality characteristics are. Often many questions are used for this purpose, and they are carefully selected and combined on the basis of much research; but even so, the basic nature of the data is not altered. The data concern what the individual knows about himself and is willing to relate. Although problems of subjectivity and honesty are potentially inherent in dealing with data of this kind, later it will be shown that such problems are not nearly as severe as one might think.

2. Observation. Another approach to the measurement of typical performance is through observation. For example, rather than relying on the student to faithfully relate his own characteristics, a description can be obtained from the teacher. Although observation is useful in many situations, it often suffers because of the shortcomings of the observer, chief among which are (1) insufficient experience with students, (2) experience only in restricted circumstances, (3) wide differences in ability of observers, and (4) improper inferences about the meaning of what is observed. Methods will be discussed for obtaining the most valid information possible from observations of students.

3. Projection. A third approach is to try to interpret the free productions of students in composing themes, describing situations, and responding to pictures. For example, if the themes of a particular student frequently concern family strife, it is perhaps reasonable to conjecture that something is wrong in the student's own home. In such a situation it is said that the student is "projecting" his own problems into his themes. Many special instruments have been used for studying projection, particularly in relation to the measurement of personality characteristics. The major difficulty with most presently used projective tests is that they are highly dependent on the intuition of the examiner. Not only do these tests require the use of a highly trained tester, but the validity of particular findings depends on the skills of the tester being used. Suggestions will be given regarding the teacher's informal use of projective devices. Also, principles will be described whereby projective tests could be more highly standardized than they are at present.

4. Objective measures.   Eventually, it is hoped that interests, attitudes, and (particularly) personality attributes can be measured in part by objective tests which are similar in their properties to the objective measures of ability currently in use. There is suggestive evidence to indicate that some of the supposed measures of ability actually relate to personality characteristics. For example, as will be discussed more fully later, there are indications that some measures of perceptual ability relate to personality. Numerous other suggestive findings have related objective test results to personality characteristics. Although it is probably true that we shall continue to employ self-report, observation, and projective instruments for the measurement of typical performance, there is now some hope that these can be augmented by objective measures of abilities relating to personality characteristics, such as measures of physiological processes and perception. Measures of all these kinds will be amply discussed and illustrated in Chapters 15 and 16.

chapter 15

ATTITUDES AND INTERESTS

Teachers necessarily are very much concerned with the attitudes and interests of their students. Although some would deny it, teachers inevitably find themselves in the business of "selling" certain points of view, among which are patriotism, courtesy, sportsmanship, and a valuing of "good" art, scientific accomplishment, and scholarly productions. Undoubtedly we are in favor of these and many other things, and we try to sell these points of view to our students. Also, teachers are influenced by the attitudes and interests of their students. Much of our classroom activity is devoted to making topics more interesting. For this reason, we use films, contests, demonstrations—many things to excite the interests of students. If students value scholarly accomplishment and have positive attitudes toward education, it is relatively easy to start them on the road to becoming educated men; but it is very difficult if their attitudes in this respect are poor. In these and many other ways, teachers are concerned about the feelings of their students; and in order to deal effectively with these matters, it is important to know how best to measure attitudes and interests.

PSYCHOMETRIC APPROACHES TO MEASURING SELF-REPORT

Regardless of whether data concerning self-report are in relation to measures of interests, attitudes, or personality characteristics, a number of types of items can be used. Before discussing commercially distributed inventories of interests and attitudes, we shall consider some of the possible psychometric approaches to their measurement. These methods can be used on teacher-made instruments as well as in commercially distributed scales. With some practice, teachers will find that they can construct such measures for the particular purpose at hand. For example, teachers may find it helpful to obtain periodic measures of their students' interests in study topics, recreational activities, hobbies, and many other areas. Some of the most prominently used methods are described below.

ABSOLUTE RESPONSES.   One of the simplest techniques for studying self-report is to obtain "absolute responses" to a list of statements or activities. This can take the form of either ratings of agreement or disagreement with statements or ratings of liking or disliking of activities. An example is as follows:

		Dislike	Like
1.	Reading in front of the class	_____	_____
2.	Reading silently in class	_____	_____
3.	Reading my assignments at home	_____	_____

Instead of only a two-point (like-dislike) scale, a multipoint scale may be used. The following is a sample scale:

1. Always dislike
2. Usually dislike
3. Sometimes dislike
4. Sometimes like
5. Usually like
6. Always like

Either students are asked to write in the appropriate number, or, better, they can mark the appropriate number as follows:

		A-D	U-D	S-D	S-L	U-L	A-L
1.	Writing themes	1	2	3	4	5	6
2.	Writing book reports	1	2	3	4	5	6

Of course, with younger children one would not be able to use a five- or six-point scale such as the one above. Two- or three-point scales are all that can be used reliably in a group testing situation in the elementary grades. Students above about the fourth or fifth grade usually have no major difficulty employing multipoint scales. However, it behooves the teacher to explore the extent to which students in his class can deal meaningfully with scales that vary on more than two or three points.

Convenience dictates the wide use of absolute responses in self-report measures of interests, attitudes, and personality characteristics. It is rather easy to make a list of the things to be rated, and the absolute responses can be quickly made by students. Data obtained from the method also are relatively easy to analyze. To find the predominant interests of a class or larger group of students, all that is necessary is to obtain the percentage of "like" responses, or, if a multipoint scale is used, the average rating of each item.

In spite of the convenience and wide use of the absolute response technique, it has some potential faults. One fault is that the responses are affected by test-taking habits. Purely apart from the content involved, some students will mark "like" most of the time, and others will mark "dislike" most of the time. On multipoint scales some students will tend to mark toward the extremes of the scale, and others will mark mainly near the center of the scale. Such test-taking habits make the results somewhat difficult to interpret.

Unless practical considerations require the use of absolute responses, it generally is better to employ one of the types of "relative responses." With relative responses, the student chooses one from a list of things, marks which of two activities he likes more, or ranks activities from the one liked most to the one liked least. Several methods for obtaining relative responses are described in the following sections.

MULTIPLE CHOICE.   One of the simplest methods of obtaining relative responses is to have the student choose from a list the activity which he likes most. Examples are:

1. I most like to read about
    a.   scientific inventions
    b.   animals
    c.   explorers
    d.   life in foreign countries

2. My favorite class project would be
    a.   keeping goldfish
    b.   collecting rocks
    c.   making a science exhibit
    d.   working on a class newspaper

Although the multiple-choice item often is quite useful for studying interests and other types of self-report, it also has several potential disadvantages. One is that it gives no information about second, third, etc., choices. This is particularly disadvantageous when, as is often the case, there are many activities involved. If these are placed in one long list, and the student marks only the one that he likes most, this provides only meager information about the student's interests. When the list is long, one compromise is to break it into a number of multiple-choice items with only four or five activities in each. The difficulty with this method is that the apparent preference for an activity is very much related to the other alternatives in the particular item. If, for example, "keeping goldfish" is included with three very popular activities, it would appear to be very low in interest value. If it were included with three unpopular activities, the results would make it seem that "keeping goldfish" were highly popular. In order to learn more about students' interests, and in order to escape the difficulties encountered when breaking a longer list into a number of multiple-choice items, it is better to have students rank the members of the list from "like most" to "like least."

RANKING.   Interests can be measured by having students rank activities from "most like" to "least like" as in the following example:

	Reading topic	Rank
a.	Birds of North America	_____
b.	Exploring the Arctic	_____
c.	Life in Portugal	_____
d.	Wild West Stories	_____
e.	Planting a Garden	_____
f.	Murder at Midnight	_____
g.	Cartoon Comics	_____
h.	American Poetry	_____
i.	Lives of Great Men	_____
j.	How to Win Friends	_____

The students are instructed to look through the list, find the topic that sounds most appealing, and place a 1 in the appropriate space on the right; then write a 2 by the next most appealing, and so on until the appropriate number is written by the least-preferred topic.

The dominant interests of a group of students can be determined by calculating the average rank given to each activity. For example, it might be found that adventure topics (e.g., Exploring the Arctic) are ranked high and that intellectual topics (e.g., Lives of Great Men) are ranked low. Such findings would not only help the teacher understand the present interests of students for different topics but also indicate the directions in which reading habits might be improved.

A major caution in the use of ranking is that it is best to have no more than ten, or at most fifteen, "things" in the list, the number varying with the age of the student. Very long lists require a great deal of time to rank, and students often get quite confused in the clerical problems involved.

PAIR COMPARISONS.   Even more detailed relative responses than those obtained from multiple-choice or ranking techniques can be obtained from the method of pair comparisons. In this method, students are presented with all possible pairs of the things being studied and are required to mark the more preferred member of each pair. An example is as follows:

Pair 1: Birds of North America —————— Exploring the Arctic ——————
Pair 2: Birds of North America —————— Life in Portugal   ——————
Pair 3: Birds of North America —————— Wild West Stories   ——————

Only a part of the total list is shown above. The complete list for the ten reading topics shown previously would require a total of forty-five pairs. For each pair, the student marks either the space on the right or the space on the left to indicate his preference. The results can be analyzed by counting the number of marks for each topic in all the responses by one student, and then averaging these over all the students in a class or larger group.

The major advantage of the pair-comparisons technique is that it provides highly detailed and reliable results. However, because of the labor involved in administering, responding to, and scoring pair comparisons, the method is not frequently employed by teachers. It is described here because it is sometimes used by educational and psychological specialists in research investigations of interests and attitudes. Consequently, it is good for teachers to know something about the method in order to understand research results.

VOCATIONAL INTEREST INVENTORIES

The major commercially distributed inventories relate to occupational interests. They are used primarily in the vocational guidance of high school students. Most of these inventories are well standardized only for students in the junior and senior years of high school. The inventories are useful primarily in career counseling of students rather than for other purposes in education. Interest inventories that measure preferences for activities in daily life are also available. This latter type of inventory can easily be constructed by teachers for the particular purpose at hand. For example, an inventory can be constructed to study the preferences of students for different types of reading material or for different types of athletic activities. A commercially distributed test of interests that is aimed at daily activities in the classroom and is useful for many purposes will be discussed later. First, though, let us consider some of the prominent interest inventories for vocational guidance.

Interests were defined earlier as stated preferences for activities. As the word "stated" emphasizes, interest inventories depend on the individual's honest and accurate reporting of what he likes to do. At the outset some justification needs to be given for using interest inventories. The common-sense approach to learning about interests would be simply to ask the individual what occupations he prefers. If the individual already knows that he wants to be a physician, sea captain, or fireman, it would be a waste of time to have him record his preferences on a printed form. The purpose in administering tests is to gain some new information about people.

There is a considerable amount of evidence to show that stated preferences for occupations are unrealistic. This is particularly so among adolescents and young adults, with whom interest inventories are most needed. Young people usually are quite unaware of the specific activities which are entailed in different occupations. The individual's stated preferences for occupations are often prompted by glamorized stereotypes. The physician is remembered as the heroic figure who performs the miraculous operation while the gallery looks down in silent awe. The sea captain is seen holding steadfast to the helm against the stormy onslaught of the sea. The fireman is pictured descending the ladder with the rescued maiden on his shoulder. All these images are of course very unrealistic. Few physicians do surgery at all. They must spend many hours in unheroic activities such as reading medical texts, writing reports, and calming the fears of anxious patients. The sea captain has scant opportunity to steer the ship because of the modern electronic gadgetry which automatically navigates. The captain usually is a sea-going businessman, ambassador to passengers and clients, who must be concerned with such matters as bookkeeping, personnel management, and correspondence. No one considers what the fireman does in the larger portion of his time—tending equipment, collecting funds for charities, and helping rescue cats from inaccessible perches.

The purpose of the interest inventory is to ask the individual about his preferences for a wide range of relatively specific activities such as mending a clock, preparing written reports, and talking to groups of people. From these a diagnosis is made of the occupations which most closely match the interests of the individual. A fundamental assumption in the use of interest inventories is that people in different occupations have at least partially different interests. Otherwise there would be no way in which interest tests could be used successfully to advise people to consider one occupation rather than another.

THE STRONG INTEREST INVENTORY.   One of the earliest and still most widely used measures of interests is the Vocational Interest Blank (SVIB), developed by E. K. Strong, Jr. Originally published in 1927, it has undergone continuing research and revision. The current edition of the SVIB is an extensive revision by a group of Strong's disciples (Strong & Campbell, 1966). Separate forms are available for men and women. However, the blank for women has not been developed as fully as that for men, nor has it been successful in differentiating between the interests of occupational groups. The SVIB for men employs 399 questions about relatively specific activities. On most of the items, the student indicates his preference by marking one of three categories: "like," "indifferent," or "dislike." Some illustrative items from the men's form are as follows:[1]

Buying merchandise for a store	L	I	D
Adjusting a carburetor	L	I	D
Interviewing men for a job	L	I	D

Responses to the SVIB can be scored in terms of fifty-four occupations and five nonoccupational scales (Academic Achievement, Masculinity-Femininity, Occupational Introversion-Extroversion, Occupational Level, and Specialization Level) for men and thirty-two occupations for women. A separate scoring key is available for each occupation and for each nonoccupational scale. The scoring keys were developed from the responses to the SVIB made by successful persons in each of the occupational groups. Each scoring key is composed in such a way as to differentiate the people in a particular profession from people in general. The nonoccupational scales differentiate between the interests of broader groups. For instance, the Specialization Level scale differentiates men who would enjoy advanced study of a type involving narrow specialization. It was orginally developed by comparing the responses of medical specialists with the responses of physicians in general. This procedure for developing scoring keys is referred to as *criterion keying.*

Each scoring key consists of a set of weights to be applied to the item responses. The weights range from $+1$ to -1. A positive weight means that people in the profession—say, in accounting—mark "like" to the item more frequently than people in general. A negative weight means that accountants mark the "like" category less frequently than people in general. If an item does not differentiate a profession from people in general, it receives a zero weight. A considerable amount of research was required to obtain the occupational keys, and new scoring keys for other occupations are gradually being developed.

[1]Reproduced by permission of Stanford University Press.

An individual's responses are scored on either some or all of the professions. The scores can be converted to standard scores (with a mean of 50 and a standard deviation of 10) or to a grading system ranging from A to C. The resulting profile of scores is used to interpret the individual's interests. People usually express high interest in a number of related professions, such as mathematician, engineer, and chemist.

THE KUDER INTEREST INVENTORY. The Kuder Preference Record—Vocational (Kuder, 1956) and the SVIB are the two most widely used interest inventories. They present an interesting contrast in procedures of test development. Whereas on the SVIB the student considers each activity individually, the Kuder inventory presents items in triads. The student picks from three activities the one that he likes most and the one that he likes least. Three illustrative item triads are as follows:[2]

Exercise in a gymnasium	_____
Go fishing	_____
Play baseball	_____
Visit an art gallery	_____
Browse in a library	_____
Visit a museum	_____
Collect autographs	_____
Collect coins	_____
Collect butterflies	_____

Instead of scoring the form in terms of numerous separate occupations, scores are given in ten general areas: outdoor, mechanical, computational, scientific, persuasive, artistic, literary, musical, social service, and clerical. The ten categories were derived by item-analysis procedures, much the same as factor analysis would obtain. Unlike the SVIB, the ten interest areas on the Kuder inventory were not related in any direct way with the responses of people in specific occupations. The interpretation of an interest profile from the Kuder inventory is largely dependent on the judgment of the counselor in regard to the interests that are involved in different occupations.

Although the Strong and the Kuder inventories started out on different tracks, recent developments have brought them closer together. A number of broad interest areas have been developed for the SVIB by factor-analytic studies. Scores on these can be obtained in addition to those for specific occupations. Research done since the Kuder inventory was pub-

[2]From *Kuder Preference Record, Vocational* Form C. © 1948, G. Frederic Kuder. Reprinted by permission of the publisher, Science Research Associates, Inc.

lished shows that the original logical method of analyzing interests leads to good predictions for certain occupations and poor predictions for others. Consequently, another version of the Kuder inventory, the Kuder Occupational Interest Survey (OIS), has been developed; this inventory expresses individual scores in terms of correlations between the responses of the subject and the characteristic responses of people in different occupations. Thus, as in the case of the SVIB, criterion-keying procedures were developed for scoring responses, but without the use of a reference group of people in general. Kuder (1966) reports that the OIS scoring system achieved fewer errors of classification than a system involving a general reference group in a study conducted with thirty occupational and academic fields. However, because of the recency of the development of the OIS, not as many interpretive data are yet available for the OIS as for both the Kuder—Vocational and the SVIB.

INTERESTS AND ACCOMPLISHMENT.   Because a person is interested in certain activities, such as those relating to engineering, it does not necessarily mean that he has the capacity for accomplishment in that field. The relationship between interests and ability is particularly tenuous in children and young adolescents. The child who professes an interest in athletic activities, for example, may have little athletic ability, and similarly for artistic and scientific pursuits. However, there is an increasing congruence between interests and ability as the individual matures. It is very difficult for a person to maintain an interest in activities in which he constantly performs poorly. As the child matures, his interests gradually shift to the things that he can do at least relatively well.

STABILITY OF INTERESTS.   Without some stability over time, scores on interest inventories would be of little use in advising people on vocational choices. Interests are notoriously unstable in children and adolescents. They begin to stabilize in the late teens and remain remarkably stable throughout adulthood. Strong (1955) found retest correlations in the .70s and .80s over intervals as long as twenty-two years. This is both a credit to the SVIB and strong evidence that interests are relatively enduring characteristics of human adults.

INTEREST INVENTORIES IN VOCATIONAL GUIDANCE.   Interest inventories are second only to intelligence tests as aids to vocational guidance. Interests are, at least theoretically, very important to consider in choosing occupations. If an individual really likes a particular type of work, he often can succeed in spite of only a moderate amount of aptitude. No matter how much initial aptitude a person has, he can fail in a line of work through inattention and lack of effort.

In vocational guidance, interest inventories are used for two related purposes: to predict satisfaction in the work and to predict successful performance. The criterion keying on the Strong inventory provides some supporting evidence that interest tests can predict future satisfaction on the job. Another type of evidence is that follow-up studies of individuals who completed the SVIB in college show a strong tendency for people to enter occupations similar to their expressed interests (Strong & Campbell, 1966). Both these pieces of evidence also tend to support the hypothesis that interests are predictive, at least to some extent, of job performance. Strong has gathered more direct evidence to show that interest scores are predictive of performance in some occupations. For example, there is a relationship between the amount of interest shown on the key for insurance agents and the amount of insurance which agents sell.

Even though interests are, at least theoretically, very important to consider in choosing occupations, it does not necessarily follow that the available instruments are maximally effective measures of interests. As is true in most areas of testing, a great deal more research is needed.

It is unfortunate that interest tests cannot be used as successfully in the selection of people for particular jobs as they can in vocational guidance. It has been shown repeatedly that interest tests can be faked to a marked extent. If people are told to mark the Kuder or the Strong inventory as a successful engineer or physician would, they will obtain profiles similar to the profession in question.

People usually give honest responses in a vocational-guidance situation. They are there for information and advice, and there is little to gain by faking an interest inventory one way or the other. If, as is usually the case, the vocational-guidance facility is not connected with personnel-selection programs, there is no way in which test scores can lower the individual's chances of getting a particular job. When an individual applies for a job, he is seldom as desirous of learning about himself as he is of obtaining the position. If he is being interviewed for a job as an electrician, he knows that it behooves him to answer "yes" to an interest item such as, "Do you like to repair electric motors?" The small amount of success that interest inventories have in personnel-selection programs should not detract from their important place in vocational guidance.

In sum, interest inventories provide an extremely useful adjunct to vocational guidance. They do a reasonably good job of predicting future choices of schooling, completion of courses of training, entrance into occupations, satisfaction in occupations, longevity in occupations, and successful performance in different occupations. The available instruments are far from perfect, but they are definitely an additional useful source of information for vocational guidance.

A CASE HISTORY.   How interest inventories are helpful in vocational guidance is illustrated by the case of Martin Batson. Since he was in elementary school, he had always assumed that some day he would be a physician in general practice like his father. Now that he is in the twelfth grade and considering what college to attend, he wonders whether he will like, and succeed in, premedical training in college. The high school counselor suggests that preparatory to discussing college training, it probably would prove helpful to obtain information from tests. The counselor already has available Martin's school grades and the results from achievement tests that periodically had been administered over the years. In addition, he has Martin take the Differential Aptitude Tests (discussed in Chapter 11) and the Kuder Preference Record—Vocational. The results from the interest inventory provided both the counselor and Martin with some helpful information. Martin's raw scores on the Kuder were converted to a nine-point scale, with 9 representing the highest possible interest score, 1 representing the lowest possible interest score, and 5 representing an average interest score. Martin's scaled scores were then compared with the scores of physicians and surgeons in general. The following results were obtained:

Interest Area	Martin's Scores	Physicians' Scores
Mechanical	7	6
Computational	7	4
Scientific	9	7
Persuasive	4	3
Artistic	6	5
Literary	6	5
Musical	5	5
Social service	4	5
Clerical	3	3

Two points stood out in comparing the two profiles. Martin had higher interests in scientific and computational areas than did physicians in general. Seeing this finding, the counselor asked Martin whether or not he had ever considered a career in one of the basic sciences, such as physics or chemistry, rather than in medical practice. Martin said that he had always enjoyed science courses very much and had thought that these interests could be satisfied in medical practice.

A study of Martin's grades and scores on achievement and ability tests provided other clues. His over-all ability and achievement were quite high, particularly in mathematical areas. His course grades and achievement test scores were particularly high in science topics. In discussing these facts, Martin began to wonder whether he actually would be happy as a physician. The counselor gave Martin some literature to read about medical practice and about scientific careers. Also, he suggested that Martin get in touch with professors at a local university to find out about the differences in requirements in the premedical curricula as opposed to the basic science curricula. After digesting this information and discussing the matter with his family and friends, Martin came back to tell the counselor that he had decided to major in physics in college.

MEASURING INTERESTS RELATING TO DAILY CLASSROOM ACTIVITY

The same types of items that are employed for the measurement of interests in vocational inventories can be used to measure the interest of relatively young children in a wide variety of activities in the classroom. As was illustrated in the section on psychometric approaches to the measurement of self-report, teachers can employ various types of items to measure interests in recreational pursuits, reading materials, approaches to learning, and many other activities that are pertinent to daily life in the classroom. As is true in all areas of educational measurement, teachers will need to pay heed to the principles of constructing and using such measures discussed in this book. Also, as is typically the case, teachers will need practice in employing various types of items for the measurement of interests. In addition to the interest inventories which teachers construct or use with their own students, some commercially distributed interest inventories are available for essentially the same purpose. One of these commercially distributed interest inventories for use with elementary school children will be discussed in the following section.

AN INTEREST INVENTORY FOR ELEMENTARY SCHOOL CHILDREN. An especially well-constructed inventory of interests for use with children in the intermediate grades (4 to 7) is entitled What I Like to Do (Bonsall, Meyers, & Thorpe, 1954). The inventory is designed to yield an interest pattern for each student in eight activity areas—art, music, social studies, active play, quiet play, manual arts, home arts, and science. In each of

294 items, the student is presented with a specific activity and is asked to indicate whether he would or would not like to engage in that activity. A third choice gives the student the option of saying that he would neither like nor dislike engaging in the activity. Some sample items from the art interest area are:[3]

	No	?	Yes

Would you like to . . .

1. Paint pictures with watercolors

2. Take pictures with a camera

3. Go to see an art exhibit

4. Model things out of clay

5. Design new clothes

6. Read about the lives of great artists

A student's score for each interest area is the sum of his "yes" responses. The eight scores are then recorded on a profile chart from which percentile equivalents for each of the areas may be read. (See Figure 15-1 for a sample profile.) The percentile norms were computed for boys and girls separately in each of grades 4, 5, and 6 from data gathered on a national standardization sample of about thirty-eight hundred pupils. (Separate norms are not currently available for grade 7; grade 6 norms are to be used with seventh-graders.) Thus, if a sixth-grade boy's highest score is equivalent to a percentile of 90 in science, this indicates that he responded positively to more science-related activities than 90 out of every 100 sixth-grade boys nationally. This might lead the teacher to try to find ways to support and encourage the student's unusually high interest through classroom activities.

Content validity is claimed for What I Like to Do on the basis of the fact that items were accumulated as a result of an investigation of the literature on children's interests in specific areas. They were reviewed and evaluated by a number of judges representative of school administrators, teachers, guidance workers, child psychologists, and authors of children's books. Internal-consistency reliability coefficients for the profile are predominantly in the .80s, with the art interest scores showing the lowest reliabilities across all grades (median = .77) and the science score showing the highest coefficients (median = .96). The authors point out that interests of students in the intermediate grades are not highly

[3]From What I Like to Do by Louis P. Thorpe, Charles E. Meyers, and Marcella Ryser Bonsall. Copyright, 1954, Science Research Associates, Inc. Reprinted by permission.

PERCENTILES	A	B	C	D	E	F	G	H
	ART	MUSIC	SOCIAL STUDIES	ACTIVE PLAY	QUIET PLAY	MANUAL ARTS	HOME ARTS	SCIENCE
	10	*6*	*30*	*27*	*21*	*12*	*7*	*60*
—99—	26	25	42	38	31	26	29	62
—95—	21	21	41	36	28	24	23	61
—90—	19	18	38	34	26	22	20	60
—80—	16	16	33	32	24	19	16	56
—70—	15	13	30	30	21	16	12	50
—60—	13	11	27	27	20	14	11	45
—50—	12	10	24	26	18	12	9	39
—40—	10	8	21	24	16	10	7	32
—30—	9	6	17	22	14	8	5	27
—20—	7	4	14	19	12	6	3	19
—10—	4	2	9	15	8	4	1	11
— 5—	2	1	6	12	6	2	0	5
— 1—	0	0	1	6	1	0		0

Figure 15-1. Sample profile for a sixth-grade boy on the *What I Like to Do,* Profile Folder —An Inventory of Children's Interests. © 1954, Science Research Associates, Inc. Reprinted by permission.

stable and that long-range predictions from these interest scores are therefore not warranted.

The scores are said to be of the most use to the classroom teacher in current planning and in suggesting possible approaches to working with children who constitute a problem in one way or another. For example, the profiles of shy children might be helpful to the teacher in learning of special interests that could serve to draw them into group activities. Finding out the special interests of rambunctious children might serve to suggest ways in which their excessive energy could be channeled constructively. In assigning children to class projects, results of What I Like to Do might also be of help. For example, in a project on the colonial period in American history, those with a marked interest in music could work on a report on the music of the period. Perhaps they could even perform a typical song. Likewise, those who are highly interested in art could work on a series of pictures depicting modes of dress or historically significant events. Pupils interested in science could work on a report dealing with medicine or the inventions of the period, while those interested in social studies could report on government and economic life.

A model town might be constructed by those evidencing interest in manual arts.

How the interest inventory might be useful in working with the difficulties that particular students have in the classroom is illustrated by the following case study. Debbie, whose difficulties in learning to read had affected her attitude toward all schoolwork, caused concern to all her teachers by her tendency to give up on any task as soon as she encountered the slightest difficulty. She often expressed her frustration by disrupting the group activities in the classroom. None of the scores on her interest profile, shown in Figure 15-2, was above the 40th percentile. As might be expected, she had marked "no" for almost every activity which involved reading or learning. The teacher searched through Debbie's responses to the inventory to find those few activities in which interest was indicated. Two of these were "taking care of children" and "decorating the bulletin board." After a few days, Debbie's teacher had worked out a plan for taking advantage of Debbie's limited interests. She had arranged with the kindergarten teacher for Debbie to be a helper thirty minutes each day. Three days a week she read stories to them, and on the

PERCENTILES	A	B	C	D	E	F	G	H
	ART	MUSIC	SOCIAL STUDIES	ACTIVE PLAY	QUIET PLAY	MANUAL ARTS	HOME ARTS	SCIENCE
	15	15	6	21	16	4	17	4
−99−	28	29	42	39	32	26	30	62
−95−	25	27	40	36	30	22	29	60
−90−	23	25	37	34	28	19	28	58
−80−	20	22	33	30	26	16	25	52
−70−	19	20	29	28	24	13	23	46
−60−	17	18	26	26	22	11	21	40
−50−	16	16	23	24	20	9	19	35
−40−	15	15	20	22	18	8	17	31
−30−	14	13	17	20	16	6	15	26
−20−	12	10	14	18	14	4	12	19
−10−	10	8	10	15	10	2	8	10
− 5−	8	4	6	12	8	1	5	5
− 1−	4	2	2	7	2	0	0	0

Figure 15-2. Sample profile for a fifth-grade girl on the *What I Like to Do*, Profile Folder —An Inventory of Children's Interests. © 1954, Science Research Associates, Inc. Reprinted by permission.

other two days she helped to arrange their art work on the bulletin board and to design bulletin-board displays. In her own classroom, Debbie was often assigned to put together a bulletin-board display illustrating units on which the class was working. She had to decide what were important features to illustrate and then compose captions for pictures. With her new responsibilities, Debbie's attitude in her own classroom became more cooperative. Helping to "teach" others seemed to improve Debbie's willingness to concentrate on her own academic work, and her performance gradually improved. Her classmates' obvious appreciation of her bulletin-board displays bolstered her confidence in her own abilities and provided a constructive outlet for her attention-getting behavior.

A supplementary teacher's handbook which accompanies the What I Like to Do inventory presents numerous suggestions for using the results in curriculum planning, individual guidance, and parent-teacher conferences. Parents are often concerned about their children's development and want to know ways in which they can work with the school. Inventory results can provide a basis for suggesting to a child's parents means by which they can encourage and support his intellectual development. Thus, the What I Like to Do inventory can serve not only as a general planning device for the teacher but also as a diagnostic instrument for aid in student guidance.

MEASUREMENT OF ATTITUDES

Attitudes are predispositions to react negatively or positively, in some degree, toward a class of objects, ideas, institutions, or people. A student is displaying an attitude toward Negroes when he says, "I don't want to be in an 'integrated' school." A worker is displaying an attitude toward labor unions when he says, "Our best friend is the union." A high school student displays an attitude toward higher education when he says, "College isn't worth the effort." The attitude is obvious when a fourth-grade boy says, "I hate school." Such feelings are important, and important to learn about, because, in large measure, they determine what people actually do. If students hold positive attitudes, e.g., toward higher education, it is relatively easy to lead them toward desirable goals. In contrast, if attitudes are negative, it is very difficult. In order to obtain the cooperation of students in moving toward socially approved goals, it is necessary to study their attitudes and, if they are bad, find ways to improve them.

Whereas there are numerous commercially distributed measures of interests, such is not the case with measures of attitudes. This is because while measures of interests are very important in making practical decisions about people in school settings and in relation to vocational pursuits, most measures of attitudes have been used only in psychological and educational research. As an example of the use of measures of attitudes in psychological research, let us consider an experiment concerning the effectiveness of different methods of persuading people to change their attitudes toward various health practices, e.g., dental care. The types of persuasive communications under investigation concern (1) rational arguments, (2) "scare" tactics, and (3) testimony by prominent people. A control group would be included which was given no communication. In this experiment it would, of course, be necessary to measure attitudes toward dental care before the results of the different types of experimental treatments could be determined. In this case, and in many other instances in which measures of attitude are employed in basic research, there are no commercially distributed measures available; consequently, investigators would have to construct their own instruments.

An example of an investigation of attitudes in education would be one in which, as an incidental part of a project concerning different teaching methods, measures are made of the attitudes of students toward their own teachers. Aside from the educational value of different instructional approaches, the pleasant and unpleasant aspects of any particular program conceivably might "rub off" on the image of the teacher. Because of the particular types of attitudes that would be of interest in the investigation, the experimenters would have to construct their own measure of attitudes rather than use commercially distributed instruments.

Although commercially distributed instruments are not available to fill many of the needs for measuring attitudes in educational research and practice, such measures can often be borrowed from other investigations. Measures of attitudes for many purposes are reported regularly in the research literature in psychology and education. (Some sources for obtaining such reports are mentioned in Chapter 17.) By writing to the author of a research report, one frequently can obtain copies of a measure of attitudes and his permission to employ the particular measure in research.

The three major methods for studying attitudes are (1) observation, (2) self-report, and (3) projective techniques. Each of these will be discussed in turn.

OBSERVATION.   In some cases, the attitudes of students are so obvious that no refined methods of measurement are needed. For example, if in a particular high school, many capable students make no effort to go to college, it is obvious that attitudes toward higher education are not as favorable as they should be. As another example, if all the students in a particular high school course grumble about the instructor, the negative attitudes toward the instructor are easy to see.

The reason that observation is not always used to measure attitudes is that in many cases there is very little to observe. For example, before students reach the point of making decisions about college, it would be very difficult to determine through observations attitudes toward higher education. Sometimes we are interested in studying attitudes toward ideas or institutions for which there would be little, if anything, to observe directly. For example, it would not be possible to "observe" students' attitudes toward the United Nations, except in terms of incidental things they might say. Another reason why it is not always possible to rely on observation is that we are often concerned with fine distinctions between attitudes of a kind that are too subtle to be manifested in overt behavior. For example, even among students who elect to go to college, there still are very important differences in attitudes toward higher education. For these reasons, self-report and projective techniques are used as a supplement to observation.

SELF-REPORT. The methods and types of items for measuring self-report discussed earlier in this chapter can be employed for the measurement of attitudes as well as for the measurement of interests and personality. Most self-report forms for the measurement of attitudes employ some version of the "absolute-response" techniques rather than one of the "relative-response" techniques. Interests are properly measured in terms of relative responses because, primarily, we want to learn what activities interest students "more" and what activities interest them "less." Absolute-response methods are preferable with attitudes because it is necessary to learn how favorable students are, in an absolute sense, toward the particular attitudinal object.

The simplest, and in many ways the best, method of measuring attitudes through self-report is to present the student with a list of statements embodying various degrees of positive and negative feelings. He is asked to indicate his agreement or disagreement with each, either as a dichotomous response or in the form of a rating scale. An example concerning attitudes toward college education is as follows:

1. SA: Strongly agree
2. A: Agree
3. AS: Agree slightly
3. DS: Disagree slightly
2. D: Disagree
1. SD: Strongly disagree
1. A college education is essential for any type of high-level job.

	SD	D	DS	AS	A	SA
	1	2	3	4	5	6

		SD	D	DS	AS	A	SA
2.	A college education makes you a broader, more world-wise person.	1	2	3	4	5	6
3.	It is better to study on your own rather than go to college.	1	2	3	4	5	6
4.	People can do very well in life without going to college.	1	2	3	4	5	6
5.	College is only for snobs who want to act like they are better than other people.	1	2	3	4	5	6
6.	College provides you with many new ideas and interests.	1	2	3	4	5	6

In practice, such a scale would probably contain at least ten statements. Numerous statements are needed for two reasons. First, to reduce the "chance" influence (measurement error), it is good to have quite a number of items to "add over." Second, it is necessary to have numerous statements so that, in addition to learning about over-all attitudes, it is possible to learn the particular ways in which students react negatively and positively. It would, for example, be important to learn whether a student's over-all favorable attitudes toward college are due mainly to vocational aims or cultural enhancement.

The simplest way to analyze the results of a scale such as that shown above is to add the numbers corresponding to the positions on the scale. Thus, if a student marks "strongly agree" to the first statement, this is added to the corresponding numbers for the marks made on other statements. For negative statements, the scale should be reversed before ratings are added. That is, "strongly agree" should be counted 1 rather than 6, "agree" should be counted 2 rather than 5, and so on. After the negative statements are reversed in this way, all statements can be added and then averaged. A sample result might be an average rating of 5.2 for one student, showing that his over-all attitude toward college is highly favorable.

The use of statements, such as those shown above, provides a technique for the measurement of many different kinds of attitudes. By composing the proper kinds of statements, scales can be constructed to measure attitudes toward educational goals, institutions, government policy, religions, ethnic and racial groups, and many others.

Another method of measuring attitudes is with the Semantic Differential (Nunnally, 1967, pp. 514–558). With this method, the "thing" being studied, e.g., college education, is rated with respect to sets of bipolar adjectives. An example is as follows:

College education

Worthless	____:____:____:____:____:____:____	Valuable
Wise	____:____:____:____:____:____:____	Foolish
Unpleasant	____:____:____:____:____:____:____	Pleasant
Good	____:____:____:____:____:____:____	Bad
Friendly	____:____:____:____:____:____:____	Unfriendly

Each pair of bipolar adjectives is called a *scale*. The "thing" to be rated is called the *concept*. The usual practice is to present each concept on a separate page and list the scales immediately beneath the concept. A typical study employs from ten to twenty scales and from eight to about fifteen concepts.

Convenience is one of the great advantages of the Semantic Differential. Rather than study only one attitudinal object, e.g., college education, it is possible to study a dozen or more attitudinal objects at the same time. It is a simple matter to compose the scales and have them reproduced. Subjects can rate as many as twenty concepts on as many as twenty scales in less than an hour's time.

There are two important types of analyses to be made of Semantic Differential results. First, it is useful to obtain over-all "favorableness" averages for each student. For this, a mark in the space on the extreme left is counted as 1, the first space to the right 2, the next space to the right 3, and so on to 7 for the space on the extreme right. If the more positive adjective is on the left rather than the right, the scoring is reversed, e.g., 1 is given to a mark on the extreme right. The scores are then added and averaged over all scales in which one adjective is obviously more "favorable" than the other member of the pair. The result is an over-all favorableness rating. These average results would be expected to correlate highly with the average results obtained from making agree-disagree responses to statements like those shown previously.

A second important way to analyze Semantic Differential results in addition to obtaining average "favorableness" ratings is by obtaining profiles. This is done by finding the average rating given by a group of students to each concept on each scale. The average results can then be plotted to form a profile, or "picture," of the results. In Figure 15-3, some illustrative results are shown from a study by the author (Nunnally, 1961). Two hundred members of the general public were asked to rate concepts concerning mental illness and, for purposes of comparison, concepts relating to normal people. The figure shows the profiles of average ratings of three concepts: Neurotic man, Old man, and Me (self-rating). Comparisons of the profiles show many interesting differences in attitudes toward the three concepts.

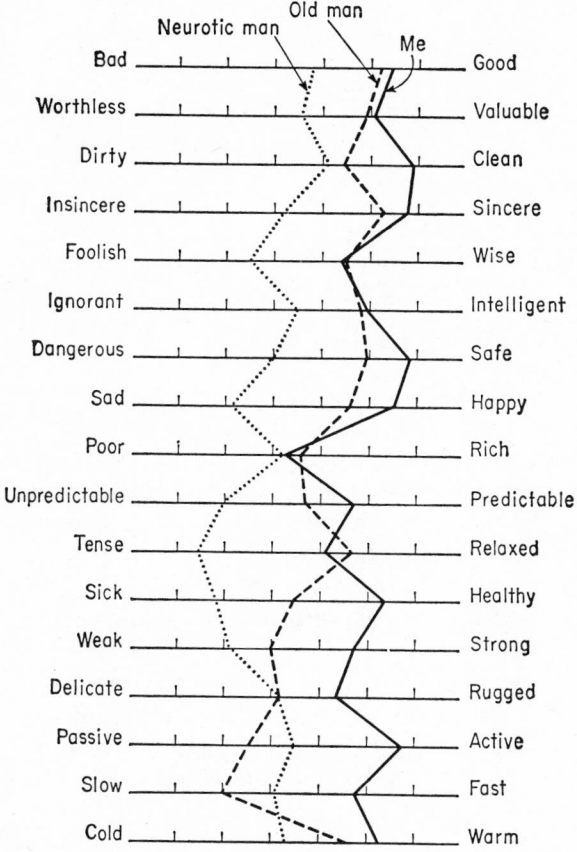

Figure 15-3. Semantic Differential profiles for the concepts Me (——), Old man (- - -), and Neurotic man (. . .). Each point represents the mean rating of 200 subjects.

A third important type of attitude scale is that developed by Bogardus (1933). The scale is useful only for studying attitudes toward various national, racial, and ethnic groups. The scale items concern the desired *social distance* from the members of a particular group. A typical scale is as follows:

Japanese
1. To close kinship by marriage   _____
2. To my club as personal friends   _____
3. To my street as neighbors   _____
4. To employment in my occupation   _____
5. To citizenship in my country   _____
6. As visitors only in my country   _____
7. Would exclude from my country   _____

The student marks those items which correspond to his desired "nearness" to the type of people, Japanese, in the example above. The social-distance scale should be useful to teachers in learning the feelings of students toward the different national, racial, and ethnic groups that they read about and discuss in class.

PROJECTIVE TECHNIQUES. The major use of projective techniques is for the measurement of personality characteristics, and, consequently, the topic will be discussed more fully in the next chapter. However, because projective techniques also are sometimes used to measure attitudes, brief mention will be made of how the techniques are used for that purpose.

A projective technique consists essentially of a relatively unstructured situation to which students can respond in a variety of ways. The way in which a student responds often is indicative of his attitudes toward the people, institutions, and ideas involved in the situation. Projective techniques for the measurement of attitudes usually employ either pictures to be interpreted or stories to be completed. Examples of both of these are given as follows:

Unstructured pictures could be used to measure attitudes toward Negroes. A picture shows a white man and a Negro standing on a street corner. The white man apparently is frowning as he says something to the Negro. The student is shown the picture and asked to tell what is going on. The responses that students give often are quite indicative of their attitudes toward Negroes. Following is the type of response that would indicate a very negative attitude toward Negroes:

The white man says, "You stole my money, and I want it back." The Negro says, "I ain't got your money, and I will kill you if you say that I have." He has a razor in his pocket.

A much more favorable attitude toward Negroes would be indicated by the following response:

> The white man says, "I wish these darn buses would come on time." The Negro man says, "You must have been waiting a long time. My wife will be here in a few minutes, and I will give you a ride home."

Instead of using pictures, attitudes toward Negroes could be measured with the use of incomplete stories. For example, students could be asked to complete the following:

> A white man and a Negro man are standing on the corner of a busy street. The white man turns, frowns, and says . . . .

A similar approach could be used to measure attitudes toward teachers. An example is:

> The teacher sees Johnny take a dime from Susan's desk. She knows that the money does not belong to him. At lunch time, the teacher asks Johnny to wait until the class is gone. Then she says to Johnny. . . .

A negative attitude toward teachers would be exemplified by a response like:

> "You are a dirty little thief. I am going to call the police and they will fix you for this. I am going to tell all the children what you are."

A more positive attitude toward teachers would be exemplified by:

> "You must have wanted the dime very much to take it from Susan's desk. Do you really need the money? Tell me, and maybe I can help."

Several cautions should be heeded in using projective techniques to measure attitudes. The interpretation of projective techniques is more of an art than a science. There are no purely objective ways to score the results of most projective techniques. Rather, the "measure" depends very much on the intuition of the examiner.

When used by experts, projective techniques often are able to uncover attitudes that could not be detected in other ways. However, to be able to do this requires much study and practice. Few teachers have the skills needed to make fine interpretations of projective techniques, and, consequently, they should be very cautious in using them. However, in a sense, teachers cannot "avoid" using projective techniques, because most reports and themes are partly that. For example, if in many of the themes written by a particular student, foreigners are pictured as dirty, mean, and dishonest, the attitude is clear. Whether the teacher purposefully uses projective techniques or only picks up projected attitudes in themes, definite interpretations should be made only if the evidence is very strong, and only if it occurs repeatedly. Fine distinctions among attitudes and "deep" interpretations of attitudes with projective techniques should be made only by qualified psychologists and educational specialists.

ATTITUDES IN CLASS. One of the principal uses by teachers of attitude scales is to measure what students feel about a particular unit of instruction—the text, the subject matter, and the teacher. Although students are not infallible judges of the quality of particular units of instruction, they often provide the only source of evaluation. It is difficult for school administrators and fellow teachers to evaluate how well a teacher is conducting his class. There are some bits of reliable information to help in making such evaluations, but too often impressions are formed on the basis of unreliable hearsay or a chance occurrence. Besides the teacher, only students actually "live through" the unit of instruction, and only they have a realistic basis for judging the quality of the instruction.

Apart from the difficulties that some have with clearly wording items, teachers should have little trouble in constructing scales to measure attitudes of students toward units of instruction. A sample set of instructions and a partial list of items that would be useful with high school students are as follows:

> You are to rate your feelings about this course, including your feelings about the teacher, the text, the exercises, and the topic. The results will be helpful to your teacher only if you are as frank as possible. Give praise where you think it is deserved, and do not hesitate to be critical when you think something could be improved. With the following scale, you are to rate this course in comparison to other courses you have had.
>
> 5. Exceptionally good
> 4. Above average
> 3. Average
> 2. Below average
> 1. Exceptionally bad
>
> If you feel that a particular aspect of the course is "below average," place 2 in the space to the right. If you feel that another aspect of the course is

"exceptionally good," place 5 in the space to the right. In this way, write in the number corresponding to each item.

1. The teacher's knowledge of the topic _____
2. Interestingness of lectures _____
3. Teacher's attention to problems of particular students _____
4. Teacher's encouragement of students to think on their own _____
5. Interestingness of the textbook _____
6. Clearness of the textbook _____
7. Subject-matter coverage of the textbook _____
8. Interestingness of the topic _____
9. Importance of the topic for your over-all education _____
10. Content of tests _____
11. Fairness of grading _____
12. Over-all evaluation of your experience in this course _____

At the end of the list of items, space should be provided for students to give additional comments. The simplest way to analyze the attitude ratings is to find the average rating by the class for each item.

Several principles must be heeded in order to validly construct, administer, and interpret student ratings of instruction. In order to obtain honest answers from students, frankness must be emphasized. It is difficult for teachers to be coldly objective about their own instruction, and it is difficult for them not to show this concern to their students. The responses will actually represent students' true feelings only if the attitude scale is administered in a matter-of-fact manner.

In order to obtain cooperation from students, anonymity is essential. It is too much to expect that students will criticize their teacher if their names are clearly visible on the inventory. Not only is it essential that no names or identifying marks be placed on the inventory, but it is much better if the forms are marked and stacked on a desk while the teacher is out of the room.

The first time that a teacher applies a scale of attitudes toward instruction, he quite likely will be pleasantly surprised. Although it is sometimes hard to believe, students, as a group, tend to be overly kindhearted toward their teachers. At least they tend to be in making attitude ratings of instruction. Students, as a group, tend to make more "above average" than "below average" ratings of all their teachers and all their courses. Because of this "error of leniency" it is necessary to make certain comparative interpretations of results. Comparisons can be made by the teacher of ratings given in previous classes and/or in courses relating to different topics. If large differences are found between these different sets of ratings, it provides hints about the quality of instruction.

Some schools either require, or suggest, that all teachers regularly apply attitude scales relating to instruction (which tends to traumatize some teachers). The ratings can be collected and analyzed by some "neutral" party, someone not directly connected with the school administration. This way, norms can be obtained for the school as a whole and for different types of classes. After the results are analyzed, the teacher's ratings are returned, and by this method, his anonymity is protected. This gives the teacher both an opportunity to see the ratings made by his own students and to compare them with norms for the school, or school system, as a whole. Although it sometimes hurts our vanity a bit to do it, attitude ratings by students provide extremely useful information about how to improve our instruction.

SUMMARY

Teachers necessarily are very much concerned with the attitudes and interests of their students, and, consequently, it is important to know something about related methods of measurement. In schools two types of interests are important: (1) interests in activities relating to vocational pursuits and (2) interests in activities within the classroom. The former is important in the vocational counseling of high school students. The latter is important in helping teachers to structure classroom exercises and projects.

Interests are measured almost exclusively with self-report techniques, for which a number of methods are available. The major reason why measures of vocational interests are needed is that students seldom are aware of the specific skills and activities which different professions require. The available evidence indicates that interest inventories work well as aids to vocational counseling. Teachers can easily construct their own self-report instruments for measuring interests in classroom activities.

Attitudes concern feelings about different types of people, ethics, and ways of life. Because much of education is intended to promote "healthy" attitudes, it is important to know how to measure attitudes. Although self-report techniques most frequently are used to measure attitudes, projective techniques and observational methods also can be employed. By employing these techniques, teachers can learn something about the impact of school and home on students. Also, in reading about educational research, teachers will see frequent mention made of studies of students' attitudes.

One important use of attitude measurement is in obtaining reactions of students to particular units of instruction. Teachers can easily construct self-report forms for that purpose. Students (at least those at the high school level) tend to be fairly good judges of the caliber of instruction, texts, exercises, examinations, and other aspects of their school; and attitudes of students toward instruction provide teachers with many helpful hints about how to most effectively conduct their classes.

SUGGESTED ADDITIONAL READINGS

Edwards, A. L. *Techniques of attitude scale construction.* New York: Appleton-Century-Crofts, 1957.

Guilford, J. P. *Personality.* New York: McGraw-Hill, 1959, chaps. 7, 9.

Nunnally, J. C. *Psychometric theory.* New York: McGraw-Hill, 1967, chap. 14.

Osgood, C. E. Studies on the generality of affective meaning systems. *Am. Psychologist,* 1962, **17,** 10–28.

Shaw, M. E., and Wright, J. M. *Scales for the measurement of attitudes.* New York: McGraw-Hill, 1967.

chapter 16

MEASUREMENT OF PERSONALITY

Mr. Martin tells a fellow teacher, "Jimmy Bartox has plenty of ability, but he makes low grades because of his disturbed personality." The principal is considering shifting Mrs. Blum from the first to the seventh grade because he doubts that she has the personality required to deal with young children. Jack Madden is the best-liked student in the twelfth grade because, as everyone says, he has such a good personality. In these and many other ways, personality attributes relate importantly to the joys and pains of everyday events in school. It need not be argued that educational decisions would be considerably improved by the employment of valid measures of personality attributes.

One of the impediments to discussing the measurement of personality is that there are so many different kinds of attributes that are included under the name. Some people even include interests and attitudes in this category, which we chose to discuss separately. One use of the word is in saying that a person has a *lot* of personality, meaning that he possesses all the social graces. Personality is often defined negatively as the nonability or noncognitive functions. Any test that is not clearly a measure of aptitude or achievement is called a personality test. One often hears elegantly vague definitions, such as "personality is the total functioning individual interacting with his environment." Retreating from this last definition, let us come down to earth and talk about some of the different kinds of attributes which can properly be said to constitute personality and which are, at least potentially, susceptible to measurement.

1. Character. Character concerns the extent to which students adhere to widely accepted standards of ethical and moral behavior. At one extreme are juvenile delinquents, and at the other extreme are students who are admired for their personal integrity. Some traits which are involved in character are honesty, sportsmanship, politeness, considerateness of others, and respect for widely held social values.

2. Social traits. This category concerns the characteristic behavior of an individual with respect to other people, excluding those traits that would more properly be subsumed under character. Typical social traits are shyness, moodiness, humor, talkativeness, and dominance. This is the category of attributes that is most frequently called personality. Of course social traits are not entirely independent of character. However, they are far from perfectly related. For example, a dishonest student might be either shy or aggressive, hyperactive or placid, or friendly or hostile.

3. Situational adjustment. This category refers to the realistically good and bad aspects of a student's home and school environment. It should be understood that some people are maladjusted, at least temporarily, by unsavory aspects of their current environments rather than because of more enduring aspects of their "permanent" personalities. For example, if a student comes from a home which is fraught with hostility and discord, he may appear quite unhappy and maladjusted. As another example, if a student is receiving the brunt of a teacher's own frustrations and embitterment, it is only to be expected that the student will be maladjusted in that situation. Some other factors which relate to situational adjustment are poverty, death in the family, frequent moves, crowded schools, unfit teachers, and physical disability.

4. Mental illness. If a student is extremely disturbed personally and/or if he is extremely disturbing to others, he is said to be mentally ill. For example, within limits, shyness is a normal social trait, but when it gets to the point that a student will hide in a closet for fear of others, it is said to be mental illness. Mental illness should not be taken to subsume some mysterious "disease in the mind." At the present time, we are not sure how mental illness gets started or what keeps it going. For the discussion in this chapter, it will be sufficient to think of mental illness as referring only to behaviors which are so extreme that everyone feels that "something needs to be done about the student."

Specialists in the measurement of personality characteristics have been accused of assuming that each person has a fixed set of personality characteristics, either inherited or stamped for life on the child at a rather early age. Regardless of the nature-nurture argument concerning the development of personality characteristics, and regardless of the long-range effects on personality of the early years of development, the science of measuring personality characteristics need make no assumptions about the fixity of personality traits. People's personality characteristics do change, but they seldom change overnight. Even if people's personality characteristics did change rather rapidly, that would not prevent the measurement of personality characteristics at one point in time. For example, the actual shyness of a fourth-grade student might be mirrored in a measure of personality; if the student no longer is shy by the time he reaches high school, that still does not change the fact that he actually was shy earlier or that the measure of personality administered earlier was valid. If and when people's personality characteristics do change, measures of personality should reflect the change as well as the standing at any point in time. Consequently, although changes in personality over time are interesting to investigate, the fact that such changes occur does not argue against the use of measures of personality to index the traits of students at any one point in time.

The general public seems to be both fascinated and afraid in relation to measures of personality characteristics. They are fascinated in the sense that they will eagerly latch on to any supposed shred of evidence regarding their own personality characteristics, such as might be provided by an inadequate questionnaire on marital happiness in a magazine, hints about personality characteristics found in a fortune cookie, or the homemade tests of amateur psychologists. That people are afraid of personality measures is mirrored in the unfair criticisms leveled against them. To criticize them as only semivalid is proper; to criticize them as inherently malicious in purpose is not proper. Admittedly, there have been abuses of personality measurement, but that should not hinder progress toward the long-range goal of adequately measuring personality characteristics for the sake of the individual as well as for the sake of society as a whole.

Most of the instruments to be discussed in this chapter are not frequently employed by classroom teachers; rather, they are often used by school psychologists in studying problem students, and they are used by specialists in research on the educational process. In order to communicate effectively with school psychologists and in order to understand educational research, it is very important for teachers to have a working knowledge of methods for measuring personality. The three major methods which are currently being used to measure personality are (1) self-report, (2) projective techniques, and (3) observational methods. Each of these will be discussed in turn.

SELF-REPORT METHODS

Self-report is one of the basic tools in the diagnosis of illness. The physician asks, "Where does it hurt?" "How is your appetite?" The patient volunteers information like, "I don't sleep so well," and "I am all out of pep." The self-report technique has carried over into psychiatry and clinical psychology. The questions are different, but the method is the same. The psychiatrist asks the patient whether he has nightmares or feels uncomfortable in a crowd; he inquires how the patient gets along with parents and friends. Over the years it has become apparent that certain questions are more successful than others in detecting maladjustment. These have become almost standard for all interviews, used along with questions that have particular relevance to a case. It is an easy jump from a list of standard questions to a test: all that is necessary is to write the questions down and have the subject indicate his agreement or disagreement with each. This is exactly how the first personality inventories were developed.

The first self-description inventory that achieved prominence was Woodworth's Personal Data Sheet (Woodworth, 1918). The inventory was developed as a means of weeding out emotionally unstable persons from the United States Army. A standard, time-saving procedure was needed because of the shortage of trained interviewers. The inventory contains 116 questions concerning neurotic tendencies, 10 of which are as follows:

Are you troubled with dreams about your work?
Do you often have the feeling of suffocating?
Have you ever had fits of dizziness?
Did you ever have convulsions?
Did you have a happy childhood?
Have you ever seen a vision?
Did you ever have a strong desire to commit suicide?
Can you stand the sight of blood?
Are you troubled by the idea that people are watching you on the street?
Does it make you uneasy to sit in a small room with the door shut?

The questions were obtained from a search of the psychiatric literature and from conferences with psychiatrists. A neurotic-tendency score is obtained for each person by adding the number of "neurotic" responses.

The personal data sheet was not considered to be a test in the strict sense of the word. Persons who gave more than thirty or forty "neurotic" responses were brought in for detailed psychiatric interviews. Although little direct evidence for validity was obtained, people who worked with the personal data sheet during the First World War were generally satisfied with the inventory as an aid to psychiatric screening. After the First World War an interest developed in the construction of tests of all kinds, personality inventories included. Most of the inventories were modeled directly after the personal data sheet, to the extent of using many of the same items.

PROBLEM CHECKLISTS. A widely used type of personality inventory for elementary and high school students is the problem checklist. Such inventories present long lists of typical problems at school, in the home, and among friends. Students either mark those problems that apply to them or they rate the extent to which each is a problem. A typical checklist is the STS Junior Inventory (Remmers & Bauernfeind, 1968) which samples problems in four areas designated as *about me and my school, about myself, getting along with others,* and *things in general.* Some items from the inventory are:

> I want to learn how to read better.
> I wish I had more "pep."
> I need more friends.
> I am too nervous.

For each item students rate whether it represents a "big," "middle-sized," "little," or "no" problem. The inventory is for children in grades 4 to 8. A companion checklist (Remmers & Shimberg, 1967) is available for students in grades 7 to 12.

The STS Junior Inventory, and most other checklists, provide area scores, e.g., getting along with others. However, rather than depend heavily on such scores, it is wiser to look at the particular problems which each student checks. These will provide many hints about the problem areas for each student.

A short case history will help to show how the results of a problem checklist provided valuable information about a seventh-grade student. A guidance counselor administers one of the problem checklists to all students as part of a school-wide testing program. Wade Martin checks many more problems than does the average student. In studying his responses, the guidance counselor sees that Wade has indicated many problems in the home and particularly with respect to his parents. The guidance counselor talks with Wade to see if he actually has a burden of personal problems. Wade seems depressed, and he has many unkind things to say about his "new mother." The guidance counselor has a talk with Wade's parents, which confirms the problems indicated on the checklist. Two years after the death of Wade's mother, the father remarried, and the new wife is much younger and different in many other ways from Wade's mother. The parents say that Wade always has been a sensitive boy and that the remarriage had a very depressing effect on him. The parents are eager to do whatever they can to help, but they have had very little success in dealing with Wade. The guidance counselor suggests that both Wade and his parents obtain counseling at a nearby psychological clinic.

MINNESOTA MULTIPHASIC PERSONALITY INVENTORY (MMPI). A self-description inventory which is frequently employed by guidance counselors and school psychologists in dealing with problem students at the high school level is the Minnesota Multiphasic Personality Inventory (Hathaway & McKinley, 1951). The MMPI represents the apex of research and detailed test construction in the area of adjustment inventories. Research on the instrument has gone on for twenty years now, and hundreds of journal articles have been devoted to its construction, refinement, and use. The MMPI is intended to measure the relative presence or absence of eight forms of mental illness, five of which are listed below. Two related items are shown for each type of mental illness. A plus sign means that persons who have the illness are likely to agree with the item; a negative sign means that they are likely to disagree.

Hypochondriasis (Hs). Overconcern with body functions and imagined illness.

Related items:

I do not tire quickly. (−)
The top of my head sometimes feels tender. (+)

Depression (D). This is used in the conventional sense to imply strong feelings of blueness, despondence, and worthlessness.

Related items:

I am easily awakened by noise. (+)
I sometimes keep on at a thing until others lose their patience with me. (+)

Hysteria (Hy). The development of physical disorders such as blindness, paralysis, and vomiting as an escape from emotional problems.

Related items:

I am likely not to speak to people until they speak to me. (+)
I get mad easily and then get over it soon. (+)

Psychopathic deviate (Pd). An individual who lacks "conscience," who has little regard for the feelings of others, and who gets into trouble frequently.

Related items:

My family does not like the work I have chosen. (+)
What others think of me does not bother me. (+)

Paranoia (Pa).   Extreme suspiciousness to the point of imagining elaborate plots.

Related items:

I am sure I am being talked about.   (+)
Someone has control over my mind.   (+)

The results of the MMPI can be plotted as a profile showing scores on the scales[1] (see Figure 16-1 for illustrative profiles). It is seldom found that a person scores high (the maladjusted direction) on only one of the scales. Typically, the maladjustment spreads across several of the scales.

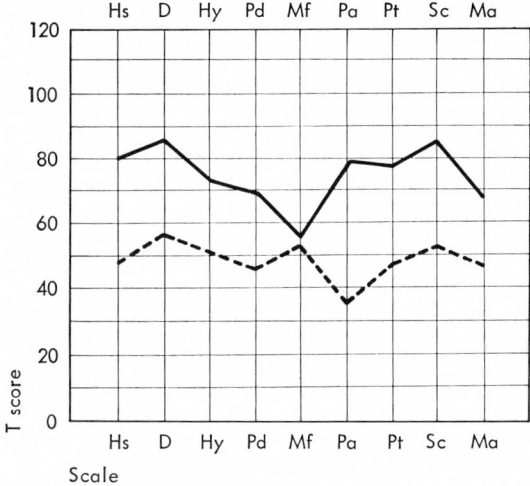

Figure 16-1. MMPI profiles for a normal adult (- - -) and for a "typical psychotic" (——). Adapted from H. G. Gough, Minnesota Multiphasic Personality Inventory. In A. Weider (Ed.), *Contributions Toward Medical Psychology*, Vol. II. Copyright 1953, The Ronald Press Company, New York.

Some of the scales correlate substantially with the others, which is to be expected because mental illness seldom occurs as one specific pattern of traits. It is usually the case that the patient has a mixture of different kinds of mental illness.

In order to interpret the MMPI profile, complex pattern scoring methods have been devised. Even with these, it is necessary to have an experienced clinical psychologist interpret the results. As is true of many

---

[1]The three other scales for mental illnesses are Psychasthenia (*Pt.* strong fears), Schizophrenia (*Sc,* bizarre thoughts), and Hypomania (*Ma,* overactivity). A ninth scale is included to measure Masculinity-Femininity *(Mf),* the balance of male versus female interests.

clinical methods, a complex lore has developed about the meaning of different kinds of MMPI profiles, some of which has only slight grounding in empirical fact.

The MMPI proved useful in diagnosing the problems of Ellen Cartwright. Although she had always been thought of as a problem student, in the eleventh grade her behavior became so deviant as to require immediate attention. She broke every rule in school, dressed oddly, and had many arguments with other students. The last straw was when she openly lit a cigarette in English class. The MMPI showed an extremely sick pattern, with particularly high scores on the psychopathic-deviate and paranoia scales. The school psychologist urged the parents to consult a psychiatrist. Ellen missed a year from school while she was under treatment. After returning to school, her behavior grew worse, and again she was removed from school. After another year at home, her behavior became so bizarre that it was necessary to place her in a mental hospital.

MULTIFACTOR BATTERIES. An extensive effort has been under way to chart the major factors arising from self-description inventories. The hope is to find a limited number of traits that account for the scores obtained from diverse inventories. A series of studies by Guilford and his associates laid the groundwork in this field. He first collected thirty-five statements which were purported by different authorities to be primary aspects of introversion-extraversion. These were made into an inventory and administered to groups of subjects. A factor analysis of the items produced five factors instead of the single continuum along which introversion-extraversion is commonly judged. Successive factor analyses were performed on new sets of items until thirteen factors were found in all. The ten most prominent factors appear in the Guilford-Zimmerman Temperament Survey (Guilford & Zimmerman, 1955). The factor names and descriptions are as follows:

G, *General activity.* High energy, quickness of action, liking for speed, and efficiency

R, *Restraint.* Deliberate, serious-minded, persistent

A, *Ascendance.* Leadership, initiative, persuasiveness

S, *Sociability.* Having many friends and liking social activities

E, *Emotional stability.* Composure, cheerfulness, evenness of moods

O, *Objectivity.* Freedom from suspiciousness, from hypersensitivity, and from getting into trouble

F, *Friendliness.* Respect for others, acceptance of domination, toleration of hostility

T, *Thoughtfulness.* Reflective, meditative, observing of self and others

P, *Personal relations.*   Tolerance of people, faith in social institutions, freedom from faultfinding and from self-pity

M, *Masculinity.*   Interested in masculine activities, hard-boiled, not easily disgusted, versus (for femininity) romantic and emotionally expressive

Multifactor batteries for the measurement of personality characteristics may eventually prove useful in school counseling programs and other practical aspects of school management. Presently, such batteries are used almost exclusively in basic research, for example, in research on the relationships between personality characteristics of students and the effectiveness of different methods of instruction.

EVALUATION OF SELF-REPORT INVENTORIES.   It is not necessary to be an expert in educational measurement to see that major problems are encountered in using self-report inventories as measuring instruments. Some of the major reasons why this is so are as follows:

1.   Reliability.   Self-report inventories are usually not as reliable as most tests of achievement and aptitude. Most of the commercially distributed tests of achievement and aptitude have reliability coefficients of .90 or higher. Very few of the self-report inventories reach this high level of reliability, and many of them dip below .80. This means that the scores of students might change considerably from day to day, which makes the interpretation of results somewhat difficult. The reliabilities of self-report inventories are seldom so low as to render them useless, but it usually can be expected that "chance" will play a larger part in them than it typically does in tests of aptitude and achievement.

When personality inventories have low reliabilities, this is usually caused by the employment of only a relatively small number of items. This is frequently the case on the multifactor inventories, some very bad examples of which employ less than ten items to measure some of the factors. Item by item, personality inventories tend to be about as reliable as measures of various types of abilities. For example, a measure of shyness containing twenty agree-disagree items is usually approximately as reliable as a measure of spelling in which the student must agree or disagree as to whether each of twenty words is correctly spelled. Thus, the less-than-optimal reliabilities of some personality tests are usually due to poor practices of test construction rather than to the inherent unreliability of items relating to personality traits. As was mentioned in Chapter 4, it is very unsafe to make important decisions about students on the basis of measuring instruments that have reliabilities less than .90. This principle holds as much for personality tests as it does for measures of aptitude and achievement. For example, if on a measure of general adjustment it was decided to refer a student to a psychological clinic, such a decision would be extremely unwise unless the measure of adjustment had a reliability of at least .90. (Even then, some of the factors to be mentioned later should be considered.) An inspection of test catalogues for commercially distributed tests of personality indicates that the available instruments vary quite widely in terms of reliabilities. One should inspect these reliabilities before selecting an instrument for use with students and before interpreting test results.

2.   Validity.   It is extremely difficult to determine the validity of most self-report inventories. Whereas achievement tests and aptitude tests can be straightforwardly, if laboriously, validated as assessments and predictors, respectively, it requires a complex type of *construct validation* to determine the worth of most self-report inventories. (At this point, it might be helpful to review briefly the three types of validity discussed in Chapter 2.) For example, in order to determine the construct validity of the "friendliness" factor on the Guilford-Zimmerman Temperament Survey, it would be necessary to show correlations with many other indices of friendliness, e.g., ratings by friends, observations of behavior, and many others. Construct validation is so complex and requires so much time and energy that very little of it has been undertaken purposely. However, it must be recognized that much, if not most, construct validation occurs incidentally as a function of the wide use of an instrument. This is the case with the MMPI, discussed previously. The MMPI has been used to compare so many different kinds of people in so many psychological experiments that mountains of evidence regarding construct validity have been obtained incidentally.

For lack of empirical evidence, most self-report inventories have had to rely on *face validity,* which means, essentially, that the items look as if they measure what they are purported to. In some instances, this is not an unreasonable assumption. For example, if on a problem checklist a student marks many problems directly concerning adjustment at home, it is reasonable to surmise that there actually is something wrong in his home environment (if the student is reporting accurately). Although face validity may be the best that can be mustered for many types of personality tests at the present time, it is hoped that the future will see much more work done on construct validation. Such work is in process for some of the better-established measures of personality characteristics.

3. Language difficulties. The validity of self-description inventories depends to a considerable extent on the clarity with which items are phrased. Consider, for example, a typical item such as "Do you usually lead the discussion in group situations?" Respondents must interpret what is meant by "usually"—60 per cent of the time, 75 per cent of the time, or 90 per cent of the time. Does the word "lead" mean to talk the most, make the most important points, or have the final say? Does the phrase "group situation" pertain only to formal groups such as club meetings, or does it include casual discussions among friends? This may be over-doing the difficulties of communicating social traits, but it illustrates the need for language clarity in the phrasing of self-description items.

In addition to the difficulty of wording items clearly, test constructors must be careful in describing the traits measured by inventories. This is true both of the inventories derived by factor analysis and those which are constructed on a "rational" basis. Some of the trait names appearing on current inventories are esoteric and confusing, such as "rathymia," and "adventurous cyclothemia." A school psychologist who uses self-description inventories must know the meaning of the traits being measured before the results can be put to any valid use. The problem is not confined to self-description inventories. Aptitude factors like verbal comprehension and perceptual speed might be misunderstood by the test user, but there is more of a problem in communicating the meaning of personality factors.

A serious consequence of the difficulty of naming and explaining personality traits such as those found in the multifactor inventories is that different inventories which purport to measure the same trait may have little in common. Correlations are sometimes very low between different inventories used to measure a trait such as introversion. Consequently, whether or not a person is said to be introverted depends on the inventory which is used.

4. The acceptability influence. A potentially important problem in the use of self-description inventories is related to people's tendency to place themselves in the best light rather than give truthful responses. There is a strong drive in all of us to appear socially acceptable and acceptable to ourselves. Acceptability in our society means being intelligent, courageous, courteous, kind, dominant, and so on. It is extremely difficult for an individual to admit to himself that he is ignorant, cowardly, rude, mean, or submissive. It is even more difficult for an individual to admit such failings publicly. People in general tend to describe themselves in rosy terms to an extent that lowers the diagnostic value of self-description inventories.

The strength of the acceptability influence in self-description inventories depends on the degree to which the item alternatives differ in social acceptability and in terms of the punishments which result from not appearing socially acceptable. There is some variance in acceptability among the alternatives in attitude, opinion, and interest inventories, but not nearly so much as is involved in most self-description inventories. The punishment received for not appearing socially acceptable is either embarrassment or failure to obtain a sought-after job or position.

The acceptability influence is less strong when respondents mark inventories in private, when they do not put their names on the forms, when assurance is given that all results will be kept confidential, and when the inventory is unconnected with selection procedures of any kind. This is the situation that prevails in most research studies, and it is in research studies that self-description inventories have their most valid use. Also, students are frequently quite honest in confessing their personal difficulties when they think it might lead to some type of help. For example, the sixth-grade student who is miserable in his home environment might frankly indicate this on a problem checklist if he thought that this would encourage the teacher and other school personnel to lend a helping hand. Also, when students seek guidance for personal problems or for career planning, they are usually motivated to tell the truth on personality inventories in order to receive proper advice and assistance.

In spite of the obvious fact that most personality inventories can be "faked" if the student wants them to be, there is surprisingly little evidence that this occurs in practice. What probably happens is that the average individual tends to paint himself in a somewhat unrealistically rosy light, but the *variance* in scores still validly represents individual differences in the trait in question. For example, on a scale of dominance-submission administered to boys, the average boy probably would picture himself as somewhat more dominant than he actually is. However, there still would be considerable variance in scores, ranging from those of boys who picture themselves as extremely dominant to those of boys who picture themselves as moderately submissive. In spite of the slight bias in the mean score, the variance in scores still would validly represent individual differences in the trait in question.

Even with the aforementioned problems in the employment of self-report inventories, they represent by far the best means available for the measurement of personality characteristics. There are mountains of circumstantial evidence to indicate that many of them are at least semi-valid. For example, numerous measures of the trait of anxiety have demonstrated considerable construct validity. They all correlate highly with one another, and they show similar changes in experiments. Also, if one compares the extremes on any of the well-established measures of anxiety, it will be found in many ways that the high-anxiety group really is more anxious than the low-anxiety group. In spite of the many years of research devoted to developing supposedly better measures of personality than those afforded by self-report inventories, nothing has succeeded so far, and nothing is on the horizon that even potentially might take their place.

PROJECTIVE TECHNIQUES

The projective techniques offer an approach to the measurement of personality which is interestingly different from that of the self-description inventories. Whereas the self-description inventories require the subject to describe himself, the projective techniques require the subject to describe or interpret objects other than himself. The projective techniques are based on the hypothesis that an individual's responses to an "unstructured" stimulus are influenced by his needs, motives, fears, expectations, and concerns.

If there is an agreed-on public meaning for a stimulus, it is referred to as a structured stimulus. If there is no agreed-on public meaning for a stimulus, and in consequence there is considerable latitude for individual interpretation, it is referred to as an unstructured stimulus. A structured stimulus is compared with an unstructured stimulus in Figure 16-2. First, what do you see in picture a? Nearly everyone will say that it is a house. A few people might call it a school or even a jail, but people will generally

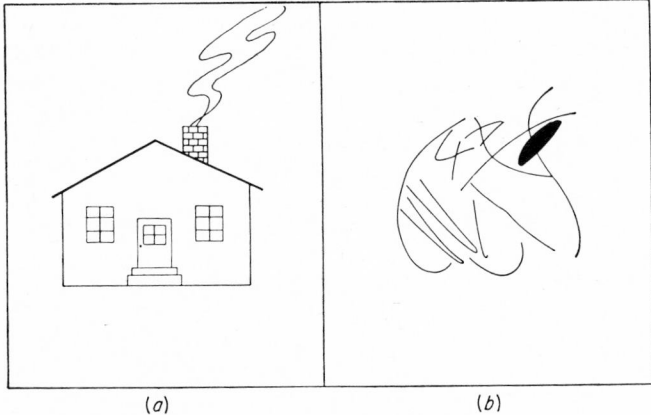

(a)   (b)

Figure 16-2. Comparison of a relatively structured stimulus (a) with a relatively unstructured stimulus (b).

agree that it is a dwelling of some kind. The shape of a house is a highly structured stimulus. Now what do you see in picture *b*? There is no accepted common meaning for that stimulus pattern. It might be interpreted as a thunderstorm, a dog, or an artist's palette.

There is a considerable body of evidence to show that interpretations of relatively unstructured stimuli are related to moods, needs, and expectations. Studies of the effect of food deprivation show that hungry subjects more frequently interpret ambiguous drawings as representing food than do nonhungry subjects. In one study a completely blank screen was used, and subjects were led to believe that faint images were being presented. It was found that the number of food responses increased as the interval of food deprivation lengthened. Other studies show that perception is influenced by values, social taboos, and personal conflicts. An experience common to most of us is the misreading of printed material in a way that indicates our concerns of the moment. For example, the student who worries over an examination coming the next day is likely to see in a hasty glance at the evening paper that "The police will give the examination tomorrow," whereas a careful reading will show that "The police will give the explanation tomorrow."

If the individual interprets picture *b* in Figure 16-2 as a thunderstorm rather than as a dog, this may indicate something about him personally. However, it is one thing to say that a response is significant and quite another thing to say just what it indicates about the person.

The instruments which will be discussed in this section are primarily based on the interpretation of personality charactistics from responses to relatively unstructured stimuli. The ultimate in unstructured stimuli is found in one of the pictures in the Thematic Apperception Test (TAT). The subject is asked to make up a story about a completely blank card. Other stimuli are structured to some extent to obtain information about particular needs and concerns. For example, in an instrument used to study attitudes, a picture which shows a white person and a Negro talking can be used. The stimulus is structured to that extent and in that manner in order to learn about attitudes toward Negroes.

In schools, projective techniques should be employed only by clinical psychologists and by school psychologists who have had intensive training in the use of the methods. Because of the need for a highly trained examiner, and because of the time required to administer and interpret many of the instruments, projective techniques usually are employed only with those students who show signs of having severe emotional problems.

RORSCHACH TECHNIQUE. By far the most widely used projective technique is the Rorschach (Beck, 1945, 1949, 1952). It was developed during and after the First World War by Hermann Rorschach, a Swiss psychiatrist. He experimented with different ink blots to find a set which would provide the most insight into the nature of mental disorder. The ten ink blots which he settled on are still in use. An ink blot like those used in the test is shown in Figure 16-3. Five of the ink blot cards are made in shades of black and gray only. Two of the remaining cards contain bright patches of red in addition to shades of gray. The three remaining cards employ various colors.

Figure 16-3. An ink blot of the type used in the Rorschach test.

The Rorschach, like the other projective devices, should be administered only by a highly trained examiner. The results will depend very much on the examiner's skill. The usual procedure followed in administering the Rorschach is to talk with the respondent for a while to gain rapport, seat him with his back to the examiner, and then introduce the task with approximately the following instructions: "People see all sorts of things in these ink blot pictures; now tell me what you see, what it might be for you, what it makes you think of." The respondent is allowed to give as many interpretations as he likes. If he gives only one response and apparently tries to give no more, the examiner suggests that he look for other things, saying something like, "People usually see more than one thing." A typical series of responses to one card would be for the subject to report, "It all looks like a bat," and "This part looks like a vase." After look-ing at the card for a few more seconds, he might give as his final response, "This little bit looks like a nose."

Before interpreting the Rorschach, the examiner applies numerous scoring systems to the responses. Responses are scored in terms of "con-tent," the types of objects which are seen. Some of the content categories are human, animal, anatomical, sex, food, and clothing. Responses are scored in terms of the extent to which they are ones that people in general tend to give rather than ones that are highly idiosyncratic. Responses are scored in terms of the extent to which various factors influenced the per-ceptions, such as the coloring of the blot, the outline of the form, and others. Also responses are scored in terms of the amount of the blot that is involved, e.g., whether the student weaves the whole blot into one interpretation or makes separate interpretations of different parts of the blot.

Rorschach responses are interpreted in terms of psychoanalytic and other "depth" psychologies. The response summary alone is only a part of the material used in the interpretation. The trained examiner takes note of many complex relationships among content, location, and determi-nants. Thus, the movement response "children playing ball" might be interpreted quite differently from "men playing ball" in terms of the other responses in the record. A response that would be interpreted one way for a man is often interpreted differently for a woman. If a person who has never finished high school gives numerous anatomical content responses, it might be taken as an indication of morbid thoughts. If a college student gives many anatomical responses, it might be interpreted as interest in and familiarity with biology.

Some of the responses of a very depressed female student in the tenth grade will illustrate the features that go into an interpretation of Ror-schach responses. In the classroom the girl shows obvious signs of per-sonal maladjustment. Although she is from a prosperous home, she shows very little concern for neatness and often has dirt on her hands and face. She is overweight, cries at the slightest provocation, and is extremely dependent on anyone who will show her affection. The Rorschach record shows signs of deep depression and provides some clues about the basis of the problem. She gives only fourteen responses to the ten cards, which is far fewer than normal. She responds slowly and seeks approval from the examiner for her responses. Most of her responses fall in the category of "poor perceptions." She gives mostly uncommon responses and ones that give little indication of creative imagination. There are many indica-tions of gloomy mood including content concerning death, storms, and garbage. A clue to the depressive reaction is found in the sexual content of the responses. In portions of blots where such responses are very seldom given by people in general she sees underwear, a girl in bed, and a man in a bathing suit. On cards where portions of the blot quite frequently are perceived either as sex objects or sex symbols, she is highly embarrassed and apparently looks for some time to find "safe" parts of the blots to interpret. The sexual aspects of the depression are brought out in subsequent therapeutic sessions with a clinical psychologist. It is found that because she is not pretty and feels unloved, she has engaged in numerous acts of sexual promiscuity in the hope that such would gain her the affection of boys. Coming from a highly religious home and having rather strict parents, she becomes increasingly ashamed of herself and fearful that her parents will learn the truth. The responses to the Rorschach had shown the nature of the problem and had provided clues that were useful in treatment.

The interpretation of Rorschach responses is an extremely complex task. Although there are reasonably clear-cut rules for scoring individual responses, there are only general standards and examples to direct the final interpretation. The interpretation depends heavily on the subjective impression of the examiner. It takes about two years of practice, usually working in close collaboration with experienced examiners, to become proficient at interpreting Rorschach responses.

THE THEMATIC APPRECEPTION TEST (TAT).   The TAT, developed by Murray (1943) and his associates, consists of pictures of people in various settings. One of the pictures is shown in Figure 16-4. Some of the pictures are more suited to young rather than older people, and some are more suited to males than females. The pictures are structured in such a way as to elicit responses concerning relationships between various social roles and responses relating to different emotions. The pictures are unstructured in the sense that a wide variety of interpretations can be given about the feelings and actions of the persons shown.

The subject is told to make up a story about each picture in turn. The instructions are approximately as follows: "I am going to show you some pictures. I want you to tell me a story about what is going on in each picture. What led up to it, and what will the outcome be?" The responses are either written down verbatim or a phonographic recording is made.

No formal scoring system is used by the majority of TAT examiners. The examiner interprets the responses in terms of his knowledge of personality and his experience with the instrument. Some interpretations are of a common-sense kind with which most examiners would agree. If a male student imputes unfriendly motives and actions to all the female characters, it strongly suggests that he is having troubled relations with women in real-life situations. If all the stories end in disappointment,

Figure 16-4. One of the pictures used in the Thematic Apperception Test. *(Reproduced by permission of Harvard University Press.)*

embarrassment, and failure, it is likely that the student feels defeated and depressed. If the stories are lacking in passion and violence, even in pictures where strong emotion is the evident theme, it indicates that the subject is suppressing his own emotions. If any one type of social interaction, such as adultery, is seen in numerous pictures and in pictures where there is little to suggest it, this indicates that the subject is overly concerned about a particular issue. Although there is no standard procedure of interpretation, responses to the TAT pictures provide many hints about the subject's concerns, his conception of himself, and the way he views his human environment.

The original set of pictures developed by Murray and his coworkers is only one of many such sets of pictures that presently are in use. The Murray pictures sometimes are used in diagnosing the problems of high school students. More appropriate sets of pictures are available for younger students (Symonds, 1948) and even for small children (Bellak & Bellak, 1955). Special sets of pictures have been composed for Negroes, Indians, and other racial and ethnic groups. Pictures of the TAT kind have been used to study anti-Semitism, family relations, attitudes toward military life, and many others.

OTHER PROJECTIVE TECHNIQUES. In addition to the Rorschach and the TAT, there are numerous procedures for evaluating personality which are best thought of as projective techniques. Almost anything that can be described, completed, or interpreted serves to some extent as a projective test. We tend to read our concerns and expectations into everything we do.

An old technique for learning about personality is to have an individual associate words. Various lists of words have been employed to get at particular kinds of reactions. The usual practice is to place certain emotionally tinged words among relatively neutral terms. The following list of words would be useful in studying the home and school adjustment of adolescents:

1.	Hair	_____	11.	Paper	_____
2.	Mother	_____	12.	Shoe	_____
3.	Home	_____	13.	Fight	_____
4.	Desk	_____	14.	String	_____
5.	Book	_____	15.	Sister	_____
6.	Father	_____	16.	Cake	_____
7.	School	_____	17.	Body	_____
8.	Love	_____	18.	Me	_____
9.	Tree	_____	19.	Brother	_____
10.	Hate	_____	20.	Friend	_____

The words are read to the subject one at a time. He is asked to give the first word that comes into mind. The examiner records the responses and notes the time taken to respond. There are several ways in which the results are interpreted. The words which are associated often indicate the subject's attitudes toward persons and activities. In obvious cases where, for example, the association to "father" is "spanking" and the association to "hate" is "father," there is the strong suggestion of a negative reaction to the father. Equally revealing as the associated words are the emotional reactions to the initial terms. If the subject takes a relatively long time to respond or gives signs of being embarrassed, a strong emotional reaction is suggested. Thus, even though the subject eventually supplies an innocuous association for "father," such as "hat," the long time taken to respond would suggest "blocking" and underlying conflict. A third type of information used in the interpretation is the tendency to give unusual associations. For example, most persons will associate "table" with "chair" or respond with some other related item of furniture. It is unusual to find the response "tiger" to "chair," and when numerous such associations are made, it might be related to mental illness.

A technique which is similar to word association is the use of incomplete sentences. Examples are as follows:

1. I dislike most to _____
2. I wish that I had never _____
3. Most people are _____
4. I become embarrassed _____
5. The people I like most _____

The usual procedure is to have subjects write their responses, permitting the testing of a number of persons at one time. The sentences can be structured to provide information on different areas of adjustment. No effort is made to time the responses. Consequently, the subject has time to make up whatever responses he chooses. The responses are analyzed similarly to those on the TAT. That is, the moods, motives, solutions, and expectations portrayed in the responses are interpreted with respect to the subject's personality.

A method which is especially useful with children is to employ play materials as a projective device. Children betray their feelings quite readily in play activities of all kinds, and almost any set of play materials serves as a "test." Dolls and puppets are used most often for this purpose. The situation can be structured by, for example, naming the dolls "mother," "father," "little brother," "me," and so on. Also the environment for the dolls can be structured to some extent by having present toy implements, such as a baby bottle, a toilet, a bed, doll clothing, and others. The child is encouraged to play with the material in whatever way he chooses. A revealing set of actions would be for the child to place the doll for "mother" and "little brother" with their faces to the wall while "father" gives the bottle to "me." Play activity of this kind is usually very rich in suggestions about the feelings and concerns of children.

Artistic productions can be used as projective devices. These may be almost completely unstructured like finger painting, or they may be structured to the point of asking for the drawing of a man. The advantage of the relatively unstructured task is that it is often not perceived as a test. A widely used procedure is to furnish clay to children and let them make whatever they like. The product can be analyzed for the symbolism apparent or simply in terms of the actions imputed to the clay figures. If the child makes a clay image of himself, it is important to note whether the bodily parts are in proper proportion. An oversized nose or excessively small arms might offer suggestions about the child's concept of himself. Children often manifest strong emotions in artistic productions that they would not talk about openly. For example, a disturbed child might make a clay figure of mother, then run over her with the toy car, tear off the arms, and finally throw her in the wastebasket.

EVALUATION OF PROJECTIVE TECHNIQUES. Some adherents of projective techniques feel that their instruments lay open the depths of personality to observation. Rather sweeping generalizations often are made about the response to an unstructured stimulus. Before the reader becomes alarmed about his own personality as it might be mirrored in the projective techniques, a look should be taken at the factual basis for the instruments. Some of the major points to consider are as follows:

1. Reliability. The ordinary measures of reliability are difficult to obtain with projective tests. If, as on the Rorschach, component scores are obtained prior to the interpretation, the reliability of these can be studied by split-half, equivalent-form, and other techniques. The reliabilities of single components on the Rorschach are less than those obtained with most tests of human ability but not so low as to render the indices unusable. There are two reasons why the reliability of projective techniques cannot be determined from component scores. First, most of the projective devices employ few, if any, scores for separate responses. Second, even if separate responses are scored, the interpretation is the final test result, not the initial scores. Consequently, it is necessary to test the reliability of interpretations from the test.

Whereas it is expected and usually necessary that scores on most tests remain stable over moderate periods of time, it is not necessarily expected with the results of projective techniques. If the scores made by students on an intelligence test fluctuate markedly over a period of six months or even several years, the use of the instrument would be seriously impaired. However, it is to be expected that some of the personality attributes mirrored in the projective techniques should sometimes change substantially in relatively short periods of time. For example, the Rorschach or TAT responses of an individual would likely change from the beginning to the end of a successful psychotherapy. Instruments like the TAT are probably affected to some extent by day-to-day changes in moods and by good and bad turns of events. Consequently, it is difficult to untangle the expected changes in responses from the measurement error inherent in the testing procedures.

It is doubtful that any one test can make the sweeping observations about personalities which are often claimed. Different techniques probably have different strong and weak points as personality measures. Because an instrument is shown to be reliable, it does not necessarily mean that it is valid for any purpose; but if it can be shown that interpretations regarding certain kinds of traits are unreliable, it means that they cannot be valid in any sense. Systematic studies of the reliability with which different projective techniques lead to interpretations of various personality characteristics would help define techniques in terms of what they measure, at least reliably, and would narrow the field of investigation for subsequent studies of validity.

2. Validity. Projective techniques must be classified as trait measures by default. It is difficult to argue that the projective techniques are assessments of personality. For example, if an individual calls an ink blot a butterfly, there is no reason to believe that this response represents anything about his personality unless evidence is provided to prove that such is the case. Consequently, the validity of projective techniques can be determined only by correlating interpretations with important behaviors outside the testing situation.

In comparison to the many applications of projective techniques, there are few studies of predictive validity. Consequently, no firm statements can be made concerning the validity of projective techniques as a group or about the validity of particular instruments. One of the problems is finding important variables for the projective testers to predict. The contrasted-groups study has been used most often to validate projective techniques. In a typical study an examiner is given the Rorschach records of both normal persons and individuals who are diagnosed as schizophrenic. The examiner must decide from the test results alone whether each person is from the normal or the schizophrenic group. Studies of this kind indicate that the Rorschach and the TAT are moderately successful in differentiating normal persons from the mentally ill. However, it should be pointed out that this is a very weak test of validity. The instruments are often used to make fine distinctions between people in the normal range and to differentiate among types of mental illness.

One of the difficulties in validating and improving the projective techniques is an unwillingness on the part of some devotees to subject their instruments to empirical investigation. A kind of cultism which encourages faith in the instruments rather than a healthy scientific skepticism has arisen among some projective testers. They would like other people to accept their projective devices and the elaborate interpretations which they make as self-evidently valid. It is encouraging to see that many exponents of projective techniques are aware of the need for empirical investigations and are busily performing the necessary research.

3. Standardization. A test was defined earlier as a standardized situation which provides the individual with a score. Do the projective techniques meet the requirements? In comparison to most tests, the projective techniques are relatively unstandardized. Although efforts are made to standardize the presentation of material to the subject, there are inevitable differences in the approaches used by different examiners. Much apparently depends on the way the examiner acts and the kind of person he is. With an instrument like the Rorschach, some examiners typically obtain more responses than other examiners, and women examiners sometimes obtain responses different from those obtained by male examiners.

The final results of projective techniques, the descriptions of individual personalities, are highly dependent on the intuitive judgment of the examiner. Not only are examiners unable to catalogue all the rules which they use in reaching interpretations, but they are probably not aware of many cues which they employ. The examiner is not a person who simply administers the test and as such plays a minor role in the result. The examiner is part of the projective technique and inseparable from the test materials. Some examiners are undoubtedly more effective than others in deriving personality descriptions. Consequently, the validity of the technique is interwoven with the ability of the examiner who uses it. Some efforts have been made to more fully standardize projective techniques, particularly the Rorschach (Holzman, 1959).

4. Special advantages. One of the foremost advantages of projective techniques is that most of them are difficult to fake. The subject is usually unaware of how his responses will be interpreted. The person who tries to distort responses often gives himself away. It was mentioned earlier in connection with the word-association technique that an effort to cover up unpleasant feelings can usually be detected by the relatively long time taken to respond. There are many other ways in which the experienced examiner can detect what the subject tries to hide. Even professional testers find it difficult to distort their own responses to projective techniques.

An advantage which is shared by most of the projective techniques is that they can be administered to persons of all ages, ethnic groups, and intelligence levels. The instructions are very simple and, in most cases, neither reading nor writing is required. The projective techniques are particularly applicable to children. Children who are unable or unwilling to discuss their problems directly usually react to the projective techniques as though they were games.

5. Summary evaluation. The projective techniques are ingenious efforts to measure personality variables. Many of the interpretations that arise from them appeal to common sense and fit in with psychological theory also. Unfortunately, the techniques are relatively unstandardized, and it is difficult to determine how well they work. Some projective testers have made unwisely sweeping claims for particular instruments. The techniques are often said to measure the "whole personality" and the "total behavior pattern." It is doubtful that activities so circumscribed as responding to ten ink blots or making up stories about particular pictures will lead to such broad conclusions about the complexities of human personalities. The indicated directions for future research are to standardize the projective techniques and to determine the kinds of personality attributes which each measures most effectively.

OBSERVATION OF BEHAVIOR

Rather than infer personality characteristics from paper-and-pencil or projective tests, another approach is to observe people as they actually behave. As a simple example, a disturbed child can be observed as he plays with a group of children. If the observations can be reliably recorded and scored, they can be used as personality measures. The advantage of observational testing is that it has a real-life quality not shared by conventional testing instruments.

Many everyday decisions about people are, of course, reached by a form of observational analysis. The football coach observes the freshman quarterback to see how well he passes, kicks, and runs with the ball. The new bank teller is judged in terms of his promptness, accuracy in maintaining accounts, and courteousness to customers. The new cook is judged by her cakes and pies and by the neatness of the kitchen. The following sections will discuss some of the ways in which behavioral observation can be used to measure personality traits.

RATINGS.   Ratings are used very widely as a means to record behavioral observation. This is frequently done in the elementary grades as an adjunct to the report card. Figure 16-5 shows a typical set of scales used on report cards. Figure 16-6 shows a set of rating scales that could be used with high school and college students.

Ratings are often said to be more objective than self-description inventories. It is certainly true that other people are less sensitive in recording a student's shortcomings than he himself would be. However, there are numerous pitfalls that beset ratings, and only after these have been guarded against will ratings provide a valid picture of personality.

One of the most common faults of ratings is due to lack of information

	Shows Satisfactory Growth	Needs Improvement
Takes pride in his work and completes it	_____	_____
Responds courteously and cheerfully to school regulations	_____	_____
Works well by himself	_____	_____
Shows self-control	_____	_____
Respects the rights and property of others	_____	_____
Pays courteous attention while others are speaking	_____	_____
Works well with others	_____	_____
Takes pride in class accomplishments and school activities	_____	_____
Makes good use of his time	_____	_____

Figure 16-5. Typical rating scale used on report cards.

about students being rated. In the elementary grades, teachers usually have a great deal of first-hand experience with their students, at least in that one setting. In high school, teachers may see students only during a small portion of the day, and, consequently, they are not sufficiently familiar with students to make valid ratings.

Even if teachers are in close proximity to students over a long period

	Much below average	Below average	Average	Above average	Much above average
Courtesy					
Intelligence					
Moral character					
Personal appearance					
Health					
Ambitiousness					
Friendliness					
Creative ability					
General knowledge					
Writing skill					
Emotional stability					
Diligence					

Figure 16-6. A typical set of rating scales.

of time, they still may not have sufficient evidence for making valid ratings. Typically, teachers are most familiar with the extremes. The very "good" and the very "poor," the very "healthy" and the very "sick" stand out; and teachers usually can make valid ratings about their personalities. The majority of students, however, do nothing either so good or so bad as to make their personalities clear, and, consequently, relatively unreliable ratings are made of them.

Even when teachers have extensive experience with students in their particular classroom setting, they may know little about how they behave in other classes, at play, and at home. The first step in obtaining valid ratings is to ensure that teachers have both an extensive acquaintance with students and that they have witnessed behavior in situations relevant to the traits being rated.

In addition to lack of information about students, ratings typically suffer from a number of other faults. One of these is personal bias toward students. It is difficult not to give better ratings to students whom we personally like than to students whom we do not know very well or whom we do not like. Another source of error is to rate all students generally high or generally low. Some teachers have a positive bias, tending to rate all students above average. Others teachers have a negative bias, tending to rate all students below average. Then, obviously, whether a student is rated as having a good rather than a bad personality depends on the happenstance of which teacher makes the ratings.

A form of bias called the "halo error" consists of giving all bad, all average, or all good ratings to students. Rather than think differentially about the strong and weak points in students, it is tempting to think of them as being all bad or all good. Consequently, teachers are prone to rate a student in much the same way on different rating-scale items even when that is not the true picture. For example, even if a student works well with others, and follows instructions, it does not necessarily mean that he is happy or has good health habits.

A number of things can be done to improve ratings. One, which was mentioned previously, is to provide more and better opportunities to observe students. In this connection, it would be better to have ratings made by only those teachers who see the students during a considerable portion of the school day. Also, ratings are usually more valid if they are made near the end of the term rather than in the early "get-acquainted" weeks of the term. A second way to improve ratings is to train teachers for the task. They should be told about the various types of errors that occur and given extensive practice in making ratings. Third, when possible to do so, substantially more valid ratings are obtained by averaging those given by two or more teachers. This tends to iron out the biases of individual teachers and greatly reduces the chance element.

CIRCUMSTANCES OF OBSERVATION. In discussing observations of behavior, it is very important to consider the circumstances in which they are made. Most commonly, observations are made in daily life as part of activities in school situations. For example, as was discussed previously, rating scales are frequently used to measure observations that result from the daily interactions of teachers and students. In this circumstance, the teacher is indexing his actual observations from real life. In other circumstances, however, observations are based on planned encounters rather than on accumulated experience. One such planned encounter is the interview, in which, for example, a parent and child are interviewed with respect to participation in an accelerated program of study in mathematics which occurs during the summer months. In addition to other information that has been obtained about the child, such as results from measures of scholastic aptitude and achievement, the teacher wants to learn about the student's personal and social adjustment. In this particular instance, the teacher has had very little contact with the student and wants to get to know him better. Consequently, the interview is arranged. The teacher's impressions from the interview are that the parent is pushing the child too hard in schoolwork and that the child is painfully shy about performing in unfamiliar circumstances. For these reasons, the teacher suggests that the child might profit more from engaging in normal summer recreational activities than from participating in the special program of instruction. But is the teacher correct? Has the teacher really learned enough from the interview to reach such definite conclusions about the student and the dispositions of the parent?

Although the teacher in the aforementioned circumstance may have reached wise decisions on the basis of an interview, that probably would have been the exception rather than the rule. Information obtained about personal and social adjustment from brief interviews is notoriously unreliable and seldom valid. (Research findings on the reliability and validity of interviews are summarized in Guilford, 1959, chap. 7.) It is very surprising that people who criticize self-report inventories for the measurement of personality characteristics frequently put undue faith in what can be learned from a brief interview. If the person conducting the interview has already had a considerable amount of direct experience in daily life with the student and if he has other important types of information about him, an interview might help round out the over-all impressions. However, if a brief interview is the only source, or almost the only source, of the information available about the student, impressions gained during the interview should be considered highly tentative.

Whereas interviews usually are not valid for indexing general traits of personality, such as aggressiveness, sociability, and others, they are frequently helpful in obtaining specific pieces of information about students. During the previously mentioned interview with a child and his parent concerning his participation in a summer program of instruction, for example, it might be found that the parents are required to be out of town all summer long, which of course would make it unfeasible for the child to participate in the program. Or it might be learned in the interview that the child is going to require surgery which would keep him out of school during approximately half the time that the special program of instruction is to take place. Obviously, to the extent that such specific items of information can be obtained during an interview, the interview is well worth the effort. However, such specific items of information tend to be particular to the persons being interviewed, and consequently they do not lend themselves to rating scales or other standardized scales relating to personal and social behavior. Whereas interviews generally are not valid devices for gaining information relative to general social and personal traits, they are frequently useful for obtaining the aforementioned particular types of information about students, parents, and other persons.

Ratings based on observations in daily life and ratings based on interviews constitute the end points of a continuum regarding the circumstances in which observations are made. Ratings based on observations in daily life are just that: they are not systematically engineered in any way. At the other extreme, the interview is quite intentional and prearranged, and the purpose is usually clear to both the person conducting the interview and the person being interviewed. In between these two extremes are many gradations of semistructured situations in which observations can be made about students. Examples in school situations are legion. We teachers frequently give students roles to carry out partly because the role is necessary in some instructional situation and partly to provide us with an opportunity to observe how students perform in different capacities. For example, a student who appears to have leadership qualities is given responsibility for keeping track of athletic equipment. If the student does a good job in that regard, our judgment is supported that the student does have qualities of leadership. In a somewhat more structured situation, students in vocational curricula are given real-life problems concerning the repair of electronic equipment. If they perform well in that regard, we are impressed with their skill and dedication to their work.

One could think of many other examples of observational circumstances that range between the two extremes of observations in daily life and interviews. In all such circumstances, however, one should pay heed to the cautions mentioned previously regarding the fallibility of observations in all situations and the problems inherent in making ratings based on observations. In many cases, such observational methods constitute the major approach available for estimating people's characteristic social behavior, but they should always be held as tentative and supported wherever possible by self-report measures, concrete evidence of social behavior, and other clues regarding personality traits.

PEER RATINGS. In addition to having ratings made by teachers, for some purposes it is useful to have students rate one another. Just as teachers frequently have a special advantage in making ratings about students, so do students have certain advantages in rating one another. Students are frequently aware of traits in their fellow students that are largely hidden to the teacher. Whereas it may escape the attention of the teacher that a particular student is dishonest in a number of ways, this is not likely to escape the attention of fellow students. With many other personality traits, students frequently have opportunities to make observations that are largely hidden to teachers and other adults. For these reasons, peer ratings frequently provide valuable information about personality traits in addition to information obtained from observations by teachers, self-report methods, and other methods of indexing personality traits. Such ratings are particularly helpful to the teacher in understanding the social problems of students. One method of obtaining peer ratings is called the "guess who" technique. Some sample items are as follows:

Name

Guess who is the best-liked boy in class. _____

Guess who is the best baseball player in class. _____

Guess who follows directions best. _____

Guess who starts the most arguments. _____

Guess who is the most generous boy. _____

Guess who is the most selfish boy. _____

A simple way to analyze the results of "guess who" items is to count the number of times each student's name is placed in each blank. This might show that Fred Cincwich is nominated by over half the class as "best-liked boy in class" and that Maurey Lawson is nominated by over half the class as "starts the most arguments." Such findings would provide many clues as to how students react to one another and would provide the teacher with valuable information for helping individual students.

Another type of peer rating is obtained by having students select those students that they would most like as friends or would most like as partners in particular activities. The results from a set of choices can be plotted as a diagram, or sociogram, as it is called, showing the pattern of choices. A sample sociogram is shown in Figure 16-7. The sociogram provides a handy picture of the pattern of choices. The one in Figure 16-7 shows, for example, that student 3 is an isolate, being chosen by none of the students. Students 5, 8, 11, and 12 form a closely knit clique. Student 12 is especially popular in that group, receiving the first-choice nominations of the other three members. Many other interesting relations can be seen in the pattern of choices.

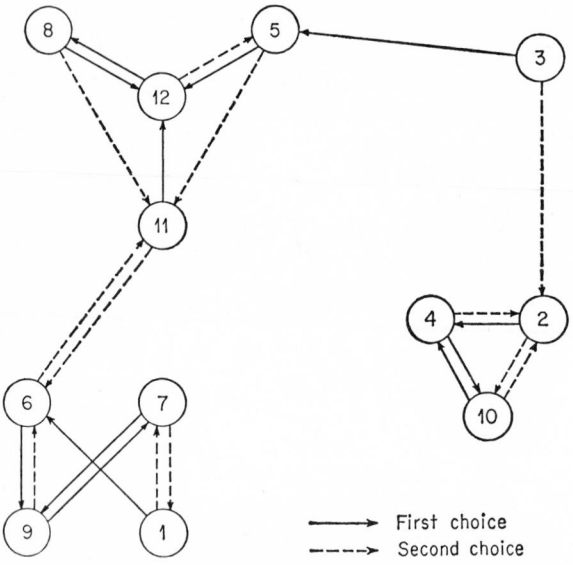

Figure 16-7. Sociogram showing the choices for work partners in a group of twelve students.

Sociometric information like that depicted in Figure 16-7 provides teachers with many suggestions for arranging daily classroom activities. The sociometric evidence might provide some surprising information for the teacher. He might not realize that one student is as popular as he is and that another student is an isolate. This information and other information obtained from peer ratings could be used to structure daily classroom activities. For example, if possible, it would be wise to place an isolate in a special group with at least one of the two persons that he prefers most. It would be wise to place student 3, depicted in Figure 16-7, in a special group with either student 5 or student 2. As another example, because of the popularity of student 12, his help could be useful in promoting worthwhile projects in the classroom. As another example, teachers would want to give special attention to students who are chosen very little as friends or work partners by other members of the class. The teacher would want to learn more about the social characteristics of the student that have led him to be rejected by his classmates. By employing self-report inventories, making observations of the student each day, and gathering other information about him, the teacher might find ways of making him better accepted by his classmates. These are only some of the ways in which peer ratings can be used to provide information about the structure of likes and dislikes among students in a classroom and to suggest ways of organizing subgroups in the classroom for particular instructional or recreational activities.

There are two major principles to follow in obtaining peer ratings. First, the ratings must be simple and directly understandable to the students. It would, for example, be quite inappropriate to seek ratings for such abstract traits as extroversion or neurotic tendency. The language should be kept simple, and the ratings should pertain directly to the student's world. The second principle is that ratings should be entirely anonymous. Students should be told that no one else in the class will see their ratings. Anonymity is necessary both to protect the feelings of students who receive "bad" ratings and to elicit honest responses from all students.

BEHAVIORAL TESTS. Another method of behavioral observation consists in collecting objective products of activity in lifelike situations. Such tests concern what an individual actually does rather than ratings of his behavior. One of the earliest and still the best-known use of behavioral tests was that of Hartshorne and May (Hartshorne, May, & Shuttleworth, 1930) of the Character Education Inquiry. They wanted to measure traits in school children, such as honesty, truthfulness, cooperativeness, and self-control. Rather than use conventional tests or ratings to measure these characteristics, they chose to observe the actual behavior of children with respect to the traits. The observations were conducted in the normal routine of school activities, in athletics, recreation, and classroom work.

Observations were made with respect to each trait in such a way as to provide an objective score. For example, one of the measures of cheating was obtained by allowing students to grade their own papers and noting the number of alterations of answers. Tests like vocabulary and arithmetic reasoning were administered in the classroom. The tests were collected and a duplicate copy made of each. The original unscored papers were returned to students along with a list of the correct answers. Children scored their own papers and either gave themselves the correct grade or altered answers to improve their standings. Scores reported by students were then compared with the scores students actually attained, as measured by the duplicate test copies. The amount of discrepancy between the two scores provided a measure of cheating.

Another of the Hartshorne and May tests concerned the trait of charity. Each child was given an attractive kit, including ten articles such as pencil sharpener, eraser, and ruler. After the children had examined the materials for some time, they were allowed to give away some or all of the items to "less fortunate children." The children were not coerced to donate, and the donations were made anonymously. Each child was provided with a large envelope in which to put his donation, and the donations were dropped into a common box. Unknown to the children, envelopes had been marked in such a way as to identify the donations of each child. The number of articles donated served as a measure of charity.

When behavioral tests of the kind originated by Hartshorne and May can be used, they have a number of attractive advantages. The use of actual behavioral products frees the measurement procedure from the subjectivity of rating scales. If observations can be made in natural situations where the subject is unaware that he is being tested in any sense, the results are probably more valid.

Other than the Hartshorne and May studies, there have been few attempts to develop systematic behavioral tests, although much the same thing is done informally in many evaluational efforts. The major uses of behavioral tests have been with children. This is because children are easier to find in group situations or easier to place in group situations without having them suspect an ulterior purpose. Also, the behavioral products of children are usually simpler and more easily measured than complex adult interactions. Behavioral tests are sometimes used with kindergarten and nursery school groups. Either the examiner can take notes on the children's behavior surreptitiously while in their presence, or he can view them through a one-way-vision screen. He may note the number of times a child offers a toy to others, the number of times he asks for adult help, and other relevant behavior. In order to get at more complex responses, it is sometimes necessary to use both direct recording of actions and ratings of behavior to measure such traits as responsiveness and tendency to withdraw.

Obviously, individual teachers are not likely to employ the aforementioned types of highly structured behavioral tests with their students. Such behavioral tests are useful mainly in educational research conducted by experts in that regard. Teachers should know about such behavioral tests in order to interpret the results of research properly.

THE TEACHER'S USE OF PERSONALITY MEASUREMENT

In the foregoing discussion of various types of personality measures, suggestions were made regarding the proper outlook and activity of teachers with respect to different types of measurement methods. Here those points will be summarized, and additional considerations will be discussed with respect to the teacher's role in personality measurement. First, measures of personality are not as refined as measures of aptitude and achievement, or even as trustworthy as most measures of interests and attitudes. Personality measures are far from worthless in most cases, however, and frequently provide very helpful information about students, but there is no use fooling ourselves into believing that at the present time the measurement of personality is an exact science. If teachers become involved in the use and interpretation of personality measures, they should impart to students, parents, and others a cautionary note regarding the possibilities of overly interpreting test results, e.g., a low score that a student obtains on a self-report measure of adjustment.

Second, teachers are more responsible for the intellectual development of their students than for their personality development. Whereas it is expected that teachers will play a leading role in guiding students to intellectual achievement, it is usually expected that the home environment will be all-important in guiding the child in his personal and social development. Teachers are rightly concerned with both cognitive and noncognitive characteristics, but their more legitimate role is in relation to the cognitive functions.

A third consideration, and one that is related to the second, is that teachers are usually much more expert at constructing, employing, and interpreting the results of measures of aptitude and achievement than they are at performing these operations with personality measures. For example, whereas any experienced fourth-grade teacher should be able to make intelligent decisions about the effectiveness of a particular achievement test, the same fourth-grade teacher might have little expert knowledge with respect to the employment and interpretation of a particular projective technique.

Whereas teachers should be highly familiar with methods for constructing and validating standardized achievement tests, teachers are not necessarily expert with respect to the construction and validation of self-report measures of personal adjustment. Teachers usually do not construct, administer, interpret, or make decisions based on personality tests. Rather, these matters are usually left to one or more types of specialists in the field of personality measurement. Guidance teachers in schools frequently employ various measures of personality with respect to "problem students." School psychologists frequently administer personality tests in relation to the counseling of students and parents about adjustment problems in the school, vocational choices, and decisions about future schooling. Educational researchers frequently employ personality tests in relation to many different types of research, e.g., in correlating personality tests with various types of school performance. Because teachers frequently work cooperatively with such specialists and because they need to understand what the work of these specialists means, they should be familiar with the best available techniques of personality measurement, their relative advantages and disadvantages, and the cautions that should be applied in interpreting results.

SUMMARY

There is no doubt that personality traits are very important things to consider in making decisions about everyday classroom activity as well as in making many other types of educational decisions. In spite of the urgent need, at the present time only approximate methods of personality measurement are available. The three approaches most frequently used are self-report inventories, projective techniques, and observation.

On the face of it, one would think that self-report inventories should provide valuable measures of personality. The individual "accompanies himself" wherever he goes and is in a position to observe himself in many types of social interactions. However, such self-report inventories involve a number of outstanding problems, among which are (1) people sometimes are not highly aware of their own personality characteristics, at least not in terms of how they would be judged by others; (2) most self-report inventories are rather transparent, and although there is no evidence that students in general tend to distort their responses strongly, they usually could do so if they tried; and (3) a number of technical problems are encountered in the use of personality inventories, such as "response sets" and lack of clarity in the meaning of items. In spite of the foregoing and other problems inherent in the use of self-report inventories, they constitute the best general tool presently available for measuring personality traits, and at the present time there is no approach even conceivably available to replace self-report measures.

The advantage of projective techniques (at least potentially) is that they can go beyond what the individual knows about himself and is willing to report. The difficulties with projective techniques are that (1) they require an expert examiner, (2) some examiners are much better than others at interpreting the results, and (3) they are prohibitively time-consuming and expensive for routine testing in schools. Presently, some efforts are being made to develop better-standardized and more easily employed projective tests, and eventually these may add materially to the available methods.

The use of observation to study personality has a real-life quality not shared by self-report inventories and projective techniques. Rating scales are used frequently to measure personality characteristics, and if certain cautions are heeded, they usually possess at least modest validity. If teachers make ratings of students, they must beware of several types of artifacts that tend to lower the validity. Also, if any faith is to be placed in the results, it must be ensured that teachers actually have sufficient acquaintance with students in situations relating to the particular traits being rated. A valuable addition to having teachers rate students is to have students rate one another. In many ways, students are far better acquainted with one another, particularly with their own feelings about one another, than the teacher ever could be.

Although teachers are rightfully concerned about the personality characteristics of their students, they should be very cautious in constructing, employing, and interpreting measures of personality. Teachers have more responsibility for the cognitive development of children than for their social and personal development. Also, teachers simply are much more expert in employing measures of cognitive attributes than they are in employing measures of personality attributes. Most frequently, personality tests are employed by various types of specialists, such as guidance teachers, school psychologists, and experts in educational research. In order to understand the activities of these specialists, it is important for teachers to be familiar with the best methods currently available for the measurement of personality attributes.

SUGGESTED ADDITIONAL READINGS

Anastasi, A. *Psychological testing.* (3rd ed.) New York: Macmillan, 1968, chaps. 17–20.

Cronbach, L. J. *Essentials of psychological testing.* (3rd ed.) New York: Harper & Row, 1970, chaps. 16–19.

Guilford, J. P. *Personality.* New York: McGraw-Hill, 1959.

Nunnally, J. C. *Psychometric theory.* New York: McGraw-Hill, 1967, chap. 13.

Thorndike, R. L., and Hagen, E. *Measurement and evaluation in psychology and education.* (3rd ed.) New York: Wiley, 1969, chaps. 12–15.

PART VI

DEVELOPMENT OF TESTING PROGRAMS

It is only natural to expect that by the time the reader has reached this point in *Educational Measurement and Evaluation*, he is becoming somewhat overburdened with facts and principles concerning the use of tests. Also, he is probably growing a little weary of the topic and is happy to see that only one chapter remains. What remains to be done is to try to tie together some of the most important principles in the book and relate those to the practical problems of obtaining and using tests. An effort will be made to do this in the final chapter.

chapter 17

DEVELOPMENT OF TESTING PROGRAMS

Even though by now the reader has, we hope, learned a great deal about the facts and principles of educational measurement, there still are some important things which he may not know. What tests should be used in a comprehensive testing program in elementary school? When should tests be given? Where do you obtain information about particular tests? Who makes decisions about which tests to use, and who administers the tests? How do you obtain the cooperation of teachers and parents in the proper use of tests? These are some of the questions with which this chapter is concerned.

SCHOOL-WIDE PROGRAMS

It is important to distinguish between the tests that teachers either construct or purchase for use with their own classes and those which are regularly administered throughout the school. For testing their own students, teachers usually have considerable autonomy in selecting or constructing tests and in deciding how they will be used. Also, teachers usually feel relatively free to alter their methods of test construction and to change their schedule of testing. In contrast, tests used in a school-wide program are usually selected by specialists in the particular school system with the help and advice of teachers and school administrators. Once tests are selected, they usually are employed at regular intervals throughout the school or school system. Because it disrupts the testing program to change tests from year to year, or to change the times of testing, school-wide programs should be carefully planned in advance so that such changes are minimal.

Looked at purely from the standpoint of measurement theory, there is no end to the number and kinds of tests that *should* be used. Potentially, any test administered at any point in time can provide valuable information to help in making educational decisions. There are, however, some practical considerations that militate against the use of many, many tests. Obviously, it takes time to find, order, use, score, and interpret tests.

Although one test for one student, e.g., a measure of intelligence, may cost as little as 25 cents, many tests given to many students can place a strain on the school budget. Between the first grade and high school graduation, students spend literally hundreds of hours taking tests of one form or another; and to the extent that it is possible, any unnecessary new testing should be discouraged.

The following sections will describe some of the major aspects of an acceptable testing program. Only some of the most prominent types of measures will be mentioned, e.g., intelligence tests and achievement tests. The many types of measures not mentioned are usually employed at the discretion of the individual school, or individual teacher, and at times that best fit their particular needs.

GROUP TESTS OF READING READINESS.   One could make a good argument that all schooling is concerned primarily with development of skills in the understanding and use of language. Certainly this is the case in the primary grades, where learning to read is all-important. Without at least a modicum of skill in understanding and using language, the student cannot hope to master content areas such as biology, history, geography, and others. Because of the central importance of learning to read in the primary grades, it is worthwhile to administer a good measure of reading readiness to all students. Tests of reading readiness were discussed in Chapter 10; a variety of commercially distributed tests for that purpose are outlined in Appendix D.

Most frequently, tests of reading readiness are administered during the first several weeks of the first grade, which provides the teacher with information about sectioning of students, giving special attention to students who will have difficulty in learning to read, and, generally, structuring teaching activities. Also, tests of reading readiness are frequently employed in kindergarten, either with all children or with children who appear to be behind their age group in cognitive skills. When applied in this way, tests of reading readiness frequently suggest forms of training for students before they enter the first grade or suggest delays in entering the first grade. Tests of reading readiness have proved highly effective for all the aforementioned purposes.

GROUP TESTS OF INTELLIGENCE.   Group tests of intelligence are most useful in the lower elementary grades, and they decline in usefulness from that point on. (The decline in usefulness is not so much a reflection on the tests as it is a credit to the usefulness of "competing" sources of information, particularly that from school grades and from achievement tests.) The cornerstone of a school-wide testing program should be the administration of one of the better group tests of intelligence to *all* students at some point in the primary grades. If tests of reading readiness are not employed for first graders, it would be wise to administer a group test of intelligence at that time. A better procedure is to employ a test of reading readiness at the beginning of the first grade and then employ a group test of intelligence in either the second or third grade. This will supply the teacher and the school with valuable information about what to expect from each child. In terms of the total amount of information supplied about a child at a particular point in time, this undoubtedly is the most valuable test the child will ever take. Rather than administer the test the first or second day of school, it is best to wait ten days to two weeks. This will give the child time to "settle down," learn to follow instructions, and get used to the classroom setting. Most group tests of intelligence can be administered by the teacher in his own classroom.

In addition to administering a group test of intelligence in the primary grades, it is wise to obtain group measures every other year, up through at least the seventh or ninth grade. As a very minimum, group tests should be given at least at one point in the middle of elementary school, say at the beginning of the fourth grade. It is hoped it was made quite clear at numerous points in the book that it is dangerous to assume that abilities remain absolutely stable over long periods of time. Ability tests are good predictors of school progress during the one or two years following the test administration; but they often are rather poor predictors of performance five or more years later. Consequently, there is no substitute for repeated testing with some of the most important types of measures.

Whether or not group tests of intelligence continue to be used beyond elementary school depends largely on what other tests are employed, which is a point that will be considered in a later section. If multifactor batteries of aptitude tests are not employed, it would be wise to employ measures of general intelligence at two points in high school, most probably at the beginning of the ninth and eleventh grades.

INDIVIDUAL TESTS OF INTELLIGENCE. Nearly all the experts would agree that for testing young children, the individual measures are preferred. Most experienced examiners can obtain a very reliable indication of intelligence from even the shy or obstreperous child. Why, then, are individual measures not made on all children? The answer is very simple: They are far too costly. It takes an expert about half a day to administer, score, and interpret an individual test. In terms of cost, this would mean about $25 to $50 for each child. Few schools can afford the luxury of individual testing of intelligence.

Individual testing should be done only for those children who make exceptional scores on the group measures, either exceptionally high or exceptionally low. These are the children who probably will need special attention and instruction, and it is important to document carefully the extent to which they are exceptional. Typically, it would be expected that no more than one child out of a beginning first-grade class of twenty-five would ever need individual testing. In addition to routinely administering individual tests to all those children who make exceptional scores on group measures, individual measures are frequently employed by school psychologists and guidance counselors with respect to any problem child. Regardless of whatever else may lie behind the problem, intelligence is one of the most important things to consider. When it is possible to employ them, individual measures are preferred for use with problem children.

MULTIFACTOR APTITUDE BATTERIES. In spite of the fact that there definitely are important subdivisions (factors) of intelligence, very little use is currently made of multifactor batteries, at least not until the eleventh or twelfth grade. At the earlier years of elementary and secondary school, the measures of general intelligence still dominate the scene and will probably continue to do so for some time to come.

The major reasons why multifactor batteries are not used more frequently are (1) good batteries are not available for students below the age of about fifteen, (2) the batteries would be too time-consuming and expensive for most schools to employ, and (3) the quantity of information obtained from the tests would be difficult for most teachers to interpret properly.

Multifactor batteries are presently used largely for students in the last two years of high school. At this level they are preferable to measures of general intelligence. The multifactor batteries are helpful in (1) understanding the problems that students have with particular school topics, (2) advising students on courses of study in high school, (3) giving vocational guidance, and (4) planning for higher education.

COMPREHENSIVE ACHIEVEMENT TESTS. Equally important to the use of intelligence tests with primary-grade students is the routine use of comprehensive measures of achievement. (As will be remembered from Chapter 9, comprehensive measures contain material relating to all, or most, of the topics in particular grades.) A comprehensive battery should be given to every student, every year, at least up through the elementary grades, and preferably on through high school. (The battery should be given near the end of the school year. The test manual usually states the proper time for testing.) The test results not only provide a valuable supplement to teacher-made tests, but they also are helpful in determining how well the class as a whole is doing. Now that the yearly, or other periodic, application of comprehensive achievement tests has become routine in most schools, it is hard to see how we previously did without them.

ACHIEVEMENT TESTS FOR SPECIAL TOPICS. Whereas most schools periodically apply comprehensive achievement tests, there is considerable variability among schools in the use of achievement tests for special topics. Most widely used are special tests for reading achievement in the primary grades. Such special tests are needed because (1) some comprehensive achievement tests do not fully cover the range of reading skills and (2) the once-a-year comprehensive tests do not come frequently enough to provide the teacher with on-the-spot information about how well students are progressing.

When the school can afford to do so, it is good practice to administer special achievement tests for reading skills several times each year for children in at least the first four grades. Also, special achievement tests are available for many other topics, e.g., mathematics, and to the extent that the school can afford the money and the time to use them, they provide very helpful supplements to teacher-made tests.

Achievement tests for special topics come into their own again in secondary school, particularly in the tenth through the twelfth grades. At these levels, the curriculum usually encompasses a wide variety of special topics, e.g., trigonometry and chemistry, and consequently it becomes difficult to represent adequately all areas of study in one comprehensive measure. For such topics as chemistry and trigonometry, special achievement tests provide very useful information. Particularly valuable are the end-of-term examinations, which are useful not only in assigning grades to students but also in gauging the over-all impact of the unit of instruction.

DIAGNOSTIC ACHIEVEMENT TESTS. It will be remembered from Chapter 10 that a diagnostic achievement test is intended to "look inside" the child's scholastic work habits in a particular area of instruction. True diagnostic tests are limited almost exclusively to reading and mathematics and to the first eight grades. Diagnostic tests would be used more frequently if better ones were available and if the present ones were less difficult to administer and score. Most schools use diagnostic measures only for those children who have real difficulty in mastering either reading or mathematics. In these cases, diagnostic measures often provide valuable clues about faulty work habits.

INTEREST INVENTORIES. Interest inventories relating to vocational preferences are seldom regularly administered to all students at any grade level. Because interests relating to vocational activities tend to stabilize only near the end of high school, interest inventories are used primarily for vocational and career guidance of students at that level. In those high schools where a guidance counselor is available, interest inventories are frequently administered to students who seek help in planning their futures. In addition to the use of inventories relating to vocational interests, teachers often construct or borrow inventories relating to daily activities to help in making decisions about schoolwork and recreation.

PERSONALITY TESTS. Only self-report inventories are widely used in schools, and schools vary considerably in terms of the amount of use made of them. Some schools do not routinely use personality inventories, and others apply them to all students at regular intervals. At the elementary school level, the routine use of one of the problem checklists (of the kind described in Chapter 16) would probably be worth the time and expense involved. For students in secondary school, a variety of self-report measures are available. At those levels, personality inventories are used mainly as part of the diagnosis and treatment of students who have special interpersonal and scholastic problems. They usually are, and should be, applied and interpreted only by qualified school psychologists and guidance counselors.

Projective techniques often are used by guidance counselors and school psychologists with students who give strong indications of having severe personal problems. Because they are very time-consuming techniques to apply, and because they require a highly trained examiner, they probably will continue to be applied in only very special cases.

OTHER MEASURES. Above are listed the major types of instruments that are found in school-wide testing programs. In addition, most of the other types of measures described in this book are potentially useful to the individual teacher or as part of a school program. For example, either the school as a whole or individual teachers may want to employ one of the measures of students' attitudes toward instruction, peer ratings, or tests of musical aptitude.

Some of the types of measures described in this book are not frequently employed in school-wide programs and not frequently used by individual teachers, such as measures of motor skills, creativity, and some measures of attitudes and personality. But it is important for teachers to understand all these measures because they often are used in educational research.

Teachers are, or at least should be, very much concerned with the results of educational research, and they cannot understand these results unless they understand the measures used in research.

WHO DOES WHAT

As is the case with many enterprises, it is easy for each of us to adopt the misconception that a testing program is started and managed by "someone else," some vaguely defined "expert" who will run the whole show. In fact, a thorough program of testing must have its roots directly in the classroom, and many people must cooperate to ensure that the program is a success.

It is not always possible to say exactly "who does what" in particular testing programs. Job titles do not always convey the specific functions of people. For example, although we can talk about the part that school psychologists *usually* play in testing programs, it might not apply at all in particular school systems. However, there is enough in common among different school systems to talk about the roles usually played by different professional workers.

SCHOOL PSYCHOLOGISTS. School psychologists usually have doctoral degrees, either the Ph.D. or the Ed.D. Usually they are well trained in general psychology, learning theory, clinical psychology, and, above all, in educational and psychological measurement. In a school system, they usually are the highest experts available on measurement problems. There are not enough school psychologists to fill all the needs, and it may be a long time before enough are available. Consequently, it is seldom that a school psychologist will work exclusively in one school. Rather, he will often operate centrally from the school board and be directly responsible to the superintendent of schools.

If a standard testing program is used throughout a school system, the school psychologist will have a lot to say about the instruments which will be used and how they will be used. If each school originates its own testing program, the school psychologist usually will be consulted. In addition to playing an important part in the management of testing programs, the school psychologist participates in the diagnosis and treatment of problem children. He might, for example, be asked to examine a third-grade boy who is far behind in reading ability. School psychologists usually are skilled in the use of individual tests of intelligence and projective tests of personality, and they often are required to use these in diagnosing problem cases. Individual testing of problem students and holding conferences with teachers and parents about the results occupy much of the school psychologists' time. In addition, they usually are called on for expert advice about any problem relating to educational measurement.

GUIDANCE COUNSELORS.   In some cases the boundary between school psychologists and guidance counselors is quite blurred, but there are some characteristics that usually distinguish the two. It is rare that guidance counselors hold doctoral degrees. Instead they are likely to hold master's degrees in guidance counseling. Many colleges and universities now offer special graduate level programs for that purpose. Unfortunately, many of the persons who now are called guidance counselors either have no advanced degree or do not have an advanced degree in guidance counseling. As is true of school psychologists, there are not nearly enough well-trained guidance counselors to fill the many needs, and it is often the case that some well-meaning, but untrained, teacher will assume the title in a particular school.

In contrast to the school psychologist, the guidance counselor almost always works exclusively in one school. Whereas school psychologists seldom teach regular courses, ordinarily guidance counselors do teach within the school. Usually they are given some reduction in teaching load to allow them time to perform their special duties.

Guidance counselors function much the same within a particular school as school psychologists do throughout a school system. Although they seldom are truly expert in problems of educational measurement, they often have had advanced course work in the area. Within a school, the guidance counselor is regarded as the local advisor on testing. Usually he reads about new tests and new developments in testing and is familiar with sources for obtaining information about tests. If a uniform testing program is established throughout a school system, the guidance counselor generally coordinates the testing program in the school with that in the system as a whole. If there is no uniform program throughout the school system, and, if, as is often the case, no school psychologist is available, the guidance counselor may have major responsibility for originating and managing a program in a particular school.

Guidance counselors usually spend a considerable amount of time dealing with problem children. Guidance counselors are, or at least should be, familiar with the use and interpretation of various types of individually administered tests—intelligence tests, diagnostic reading tests, projective tests, and others. In elementary school, they often teach, or supervise the teaching of, special remedial classes. Also, they often consult with teachers about problem students and have interviews with parents and other interested persons.

At the high school level, the guidance counselor has somewhat different functions. He is often the official disciplinarian as well as the person who typically works with any other type of problem student. In addition, he helps students plan their high school curriculum and counsels them about their vocational and future academic plans. For these purposes, he often uses interest inventories and tests of special aptitudes.

SCHOOL ADMINISTRATORS. Principals, school superintendents, and other administrators are involved to a greater or lesser degree in testing programs depending on the extent to which well-trained school psychologists and/or guidance counselors are available. If such specialists are available, administrators usually do, and should, rely heavily on their advice about matters relating to educational measurement. When specialists are not available, it necessarily will be the case that administrators will play leading parts in the selection and use of standardized tests. Administrators vary in expertise about educational measurement all the way from having considerable graduate-level training to having no formal course work on the topic. All school administrators should have at least enough grounding in educational measurement to understand why certain tests are used in school programs and what they are intended to measure.

TEACHERS. Even if teachers had no say about how testing programs were constituted, they would need to have a good grounding in educational measurement. They would need this not only to measure effectively the day-to-day progress of their students in class but also to interpret the results of school-wide testing programs. The individual teacher is the ultimate recipient and user of tests given in a school-wide program, and if he does not understand the purpose and nature of the tests, everything goes to waste.

Actually teachers should, and usually are, prominently involved in the establishment of school-wide programs. These days teachers are becoming more sophisticated in the technical aspects of educational measurement, and they can help make decisions about which tests to use and how to use them. In addition, teachers have a better opportunity than anyone else to judge how helpful particular tests are in making educational decisions. The teacher can tell whether or not a remedial reading test helped locate the difficulties of a particular child, whether a personality inventory helped find the troubles of another, whether a particular achievement test adequately sampled mathematics problems, and so on.

Before selecting particular tests, school psychologists and guidance counselors usually seek the advice of teachers about the adequacy of the measures. A good way to do this is to have a committee composed of teachers, school administrators, guidance counselors, and school psychologists to make decisions about various aspects of a testing program. Also, if they are available in the community, it is wise to obtain the advice of psychologists and educational specialists from colleges and universities. The pooled wisdom of the group will usually lead to a well-conceived testing program, and the committee can continually look for methods to improve the program. Also, if representatives from all the major professional groups are involved in making decisions about a testing program, they will tend to be cooperative in helping to make the program effective.

In addition to participating in school-wide testing programs, of course, teachers develop and/or apply many types of tests on their own. Cardinal examples are the tests that teachers employ for measuring progress in a unit of instruction—periodic exercises, tests to measure large portions of the unit, and end-of-term examinations in the particular topic. Although specially constructed measures of attitudes, interests, and sociometric relationships are not used as much as they should be, they can help teachers improve the learning environment of the classroom. How such measures can be developed and employed by the classroom teacher was discussed in Chapters 15 and 16. For example, early in the term, measures of interpersonal attraction among students (obtained from peer ratings) could be used to group students for special activities in such a way as to promote harmony and to ensure that students who are not very well liked in general will find themselves in more accepting social atmospheres.

SOURCES OF INFORMATION

When starting a school-wide testing program, where do you obtain information about tests? If a particular test is recommended by a friend, how do you determine whether or not the test is any good? If you would like to examine a particular test, where can you obtain a copy? These and other questions relating to sources of information about tests will be discussed in this section.

It is hoped that this book will, in part, serve as a source of information about particular tests. The book is not primarily intended as a reference source for all tests available or as a source of critical reviews for tests. However, many tests have been used in previous pages to illustrate principles of educational measurement, and readers might want to adopt some of these in their own classroom or school-wide testing programs. The author has tried to illustrate principles of testing with instruments that he considers to be generally good, and other tests are described in Appendix D, but this discussion should not be relied upon as an infallible guide. Literally thousands of tests are available; therefore, any author is bound to be somewhat limited in the range of his acquaintance with particular tests. Rather than rely exclusively on textbooks for information about particular tests and kinds of tests, it also is wise to consult the sources of information mentioned in the following sections.

MENTAL MEASUREMENT YEARBOOKS. By far the most valuable sources of information about tests are the six *Mental Measurement Yearbooks* prepared by Oscar Buros (e.g., Buros, 1965). The *Yearbooks* contain detailed information on thousands of tests covering not only all the major types of instruments but also such specialized instruments as tests of Hebrew aptitude. The major parts of the *Yearbooks* are concerned with critical reviews of tests by experts. The number of reviewers used for each test is determined by the wideness with which the test is employed. The reviewers give detailed, critical information and opinions about each test, pointing out specific advantages and disadvantages. Following is a portion of the review by Prof. John E. Milholland (Buros, 1959, pp. 350–351) of the Lorge-Thorndike Intelligence Tests:

> This test is admirable for the clarity with which its objective is stated and for the restraint exercised in the claims for what it will do. It is frankly labeled an intelligence test, and we are told that it is a test of abstract intelligence, defined as "the ability to work with ideas and the relationships among ideas." There is, of course, no precise objective criterion for this definition, so one is forced to rely upon indirect evidence, inspection of the items, and the professional reputation of the authors for the assessment of this kind of validity. All three lines of evidence are confirmatory.
>
> The suggestions made in the manual for the use of the results are reasonable and practical and do not rely upon exorbitant claims for what the test is measuring. The authors recommend administering both the verbal and nonverbal batteries in grades for which both are available, and state that "the functions are sufficiently similar so that, for most pupils, it will be appropriate to average the IQ's from the two batteries to yield a single more comprehensive and more reliable estimate of intellectual ability. However, in about 25 per cent of cases, the two forms will yield IQ's differing by as much as 15 points. In these cases, the difference may have practical significance in relation to a pupil's reading level, school achievement, or vocational planning."
>
> With the possible exception of the Word Knowledge and Arithmetic Reasoning, the subtest titles simply describe the types of items they contain. This should certainly reduce any temptation to try to interpret subtest scores, and, in keeping with this point of view, the authors present no subtest norms.

Later in his review, Professor Milholland says:

> The examiner's manuals seem to be especially well adapted for use by class-room teachers. They contain directions for administration, suggestions for using the test, and tables of norms. The two paragraphs explaining the standard error of measurement should probably be expanded. As they stand, these paragraphs might be more confusing than helpful to a great many teachers.

For each test reviewed, the *Yearbooks* provide many other useful items of information, including (1) test publisher, (2) grade levels for which the test is appropriate, (3) prices of testing materials, and (4) any special features. In addition to the reviews, the *Yearbooks* contain many references to research articles and books relating to particular tests and to measurement problems in general. Anyone who deals extensively with tests should obtain a copy of the most recent *Mental Measurements Yearbook*.

TESTS IN PRINT.   A very useful companion book to the *Yearbooks* is *Tests in Print* (Buros, 1961), which is essentially a list of all the tests that could be found in an extensive search of the *Yearbooks,* test catalogues, professional journals, and other sources. In the list are 2,126 tests presently in print and 841 tests which are out of print. The major advantage of the book is that it tells you where to obtain critical reviews and detailed information about each test. Many of the references are to reviews in the first five *Yearbooks;* others are to professional journals, publisher's manuals, and books. In addition to serving as a master source of references for tests, the book supplies a number of kinds of pertinent information about each test including (1) publisher, (2) age and grade levels for which it is appropriate, (3) number and types of forms available, (4) names of subtests, and (5) any special features. *Tests in Print* is the place to start to find the tests available in a particular area, e.g., achievement tests for Latin, and for finding detailed information and critical reviews about particular tests. Like the *Yearbooks, Tests in Print* is a "must" for anyone who deals extensively with standardized tests.

TEST PUBLISHERS.   Other important sources of information are test publishers. The commercial concerns most widely engaged in publishing tests are listed in Appendix A. Each major publisher has, and usually will mail on request, a catalogue of tests which lists all the tests available, accompanied by pertinent information such as price, grade levels for which test is appropriate, testing time, and number of forms that can be had. To learn more about particular tests listed in the catalogue, teachers can obtain a "specimen set" of test material and a testing manual. The combined cost of these is seldom more than $2.

By inspecting the specimen set of test materials, teachers can judge whether or not the material is appropriate for the measurement problem at hand. The test manual usually provides detailed information about how the test was constructed, standardized, and validated. Also, test manuals usually provide norms, directions for administering and scoring, and suggestions for interpreting the results.

It is too much to expect that commercial distributors of tests will be completely unbiased in describing their wares. They are in the business of selling tests, and it is quite natural to expect that they will make their tests sound as attractive as possible. Most testing concerns are relatively honest in mentioning some of the limitations of their tests, but it is hard for them to be as dispassionately critical as an expert reviewer might be. That is why it is essential to consult expert critical reviews in the *Yearbooks* and elsewhere before finally deciding to adopt a particular test.

Test manuals vary greatly in the care with which directions are spelled out and in the amount and quality of research evidence presented. It is hoped that the principles stated in this book will help teachers evaluate the claims and evidence presented in test manuals.

PROFESSIONAL JOURNALS. Because the *Mental Measurements Yearbooks* have, on the average, appeared only about every four years, it has been difficult to obtain critical reviews and detailed information about new tests. The only way to obtain such information about recently developed tests is through research and review articles in professional journals in psychology and education. Most teachers will not have the inclination to regularly pursue the technical fare of these professional journals, but if they want up-to-date information about new tests, that is the only major resource. Research evidence on tests is reported in a number of journals, particularly in the *Journal of Consulting Psychology, Journal of Counseling, Personnel and Guidance Journal, Educational and Psychological Measurement,* and *Journal of Educational Research.* Two master guides can be used in the search for articles relating to particular tests. For psychological journals, *Psychological Abstracts* provides a rather complete listing of articles in different areas, and a short summary is provided for each. For journals in the field of education, the *Educational Index* provides a very wide listing of journal articles. Using these sources, one could, for example, find references to articles dealing with research on achievement tests or intelligence tests.

SOME OF THE MOST IMPORTANT USES OF TESTS

Throughout the book, it has been emphasized that tests should be used only if they help in making educational decisions. The word "decision" is used broadly in relation to changes of curriculum for all or some of the students, changes in plans by parents about the study practices and future education of their children, grade placement and promotion of students, changes in self-conceptions of students about their own abilities and personality characteristics, and many others. If tests are employed only because it is fashionable to do so, and if test results actually do not influence educational decisions, then it is foolish of the school to waste the time and money involved. In each chapter, efforts have been made to show how particular kinds of tests can be helpful in making particular kinds of decisions, and it would be redundant to rehash all that material here; but it might be helpful to summarize some of the most important kinds of decisions for which tests are helpful.

ADMINISTRATIVE DECISIONS. In every school, the principal's office needs test results to help in making decisions about students. Typical of the decisions that must be made is one involving the grade placement for a transfer student. The student may have moved from a far-away state in which the schools operate quite differently from those in the new region. In what grade should the student be placed? Does he need remedial work in some topics, or is he capable of moving on to advanced work in other topics? Another type of administrative decision is that of determining whether or not an apparently slow learner should be removed from the regular school curriculum and given special schooling. It would be very difficult to make such decisions without the information obtained from teacher-made tests and commercially distributed tests of achievement and aptitude.

DECISIONS IN COUNSELING. Tests are the mainstay of those who specialize in counseling and guidance work. If a child is having difficulty in keeping up with his class, is it because of a lack of aptitude or because of other factors? Should the parents be consulted, and if so, what should they be told? Tests of intelligence, diagnostic achievement tests, and results from teacher-made tests would help considerably in making those decisions.

In high school, many students seek counseling because they are having personal problems or because they are unsure of what they should study now and what they will want to do after they graduate. Personality tests and tests of interests and special aptitudes help both the counselor and the student in discussing the particular problem.

DECISIONS IN RESEARCH.   Whole schools and individual teachers are constantly conducting informal experiments about the effectiveness of different approaches to education. Mrs. Brown tries a new approach to teaching algebra. Does it work? The only way to tell is to compare teacher-made and standardized achievement test results of students who learn by the new method with students who learn by the old method.

In addition to the many kinds of informal experiments that teachers conduct on their own instructional practices, psychologists and educational specialists conduct many systematic studies in school settings. They want to make decisions about the effectiveness of teaching machines in the learning of foreign languages, the differences in attitudes toward higher education engendered by different types of curricula, the impact of the classroom on the personal and social development of children, and many others. It would be all but impossible to validly conduct such research were it not for the availability of many types of tests.

CLASSROOM DECISIONS.   Perhaps most important of all, many types of tests are directly helpful to teachers in making day-to-day decisions about what goes on in the classroom. Is the class behind in learning number skills, and should proportionately more time be devoted to that topic? Should Lewis Martin be given extra homework in spelling? Should Joe Stevens be allowed to skip the fifth grade? Would it be wise to suggest to Anne Jackson's parents that she do remedial work in summer school? In these and in countless other decisions teachers are aided materially by the results from their own tests and standardized tests provided by outside agencies.

A PHILOSOPHY OF MEASUREMENT

In this final section it is important to consider the proper attitudes to hold toward the use of tests in making educational decisions. Although standardized tests are becoming widely accepted by both educational experts and the public at large, there still are many who criticize their use. The major criticisms are of two kinds. The first is that the wide use of tests leads to "unfair" educational practices, and the second is that tests are poor measurement devices.

Regarding the first point, critics will say that tests serve to "brand" students, unfairly segregate them into ability groupings, restrict the ranges within which students are allowed to grow and change, and encourage unhealthy feelings of superiority and inferiority in children. These criticisms are potentially correct, but it must be firmly kept in mind that it is not the tests, per se, that bring about such unfortunate consequences but rather the improper use of test results. Tests are intended to supply *information,* and it is not the fault of the tests or the people who construct them if that information is unwisely used. When important decisions are to be made, it would be foolish to ignore any worthwhile source of information; and tests usually rank high in the importance of the information which they supply.

Part of the feeling that tests are "unfair" springs from the cherished concept in our society that "all men are created equal." We all are (or should be) equal in the social and legal sense, but we are not equal in our abilities and personality characteristics. To ignore such differences would deprive help to those students who need special attention; would cause chaos in planning the future education and careers of students; and would deprive teachers, parents, and students themselves of information which they badly need.

The criticisms that tests are poor measurement devices take several forms. One of these is to challenge the ability of any paper-and-pencil device to get at the "real" understanding of school subjects. These critics often point to specific items on tests that are concerned with trivia or that are so poorly formulated that even the most knowledgeable student is likely to get the wrong answer. Of course, it is a challenge to measure the more important aspect of learning, but many examples have been shown in this book of how it can be done.

Critics also point to those instances in which aptitude tests (such as tests of intelligence) greatly underestimate how well students will perform. The affection that all of us hold for the underdog makes us feel good when we hear of the lad who is judged to be below average by an intelligence test but who manages to graduate from college with a Phi Beta Kappa key. Such instances are quite rare, and all concerned should realize the improbability of such events before time, money, and hope are invested in them.

Tests are neither perfect measures of current achievement and personality, nor perfect predictors of later adjustment and accomplishment; but they are by far the best indicators available. Whenever the validity of tests is compared with what would be relied on if tests were not available, e.g., impressions of teachers, the tests clearly do better. Tests are here to stay, and they are growing in importance each year. The only proper attitude is to want to make tests better and better and better.

SUGGESTED ADDITIONAL READINGS

Hill, G. E., and Scott, J. D. *School testing program inventory.* Athens, Ohio: Ohio University, Center for Educational Service, 1960.

Kent Area Guidance Council. *A proposed 12-year testing program.* Columbus, Ohio: State Department of Education, 1959.

Stanley, J. C. *Measurement in today's schools.* (4th ed.) Englewood Cliffs, N.J.: Prentice-Hall, 1964, chap. 10.

Thorndike, R. L., and Hagen, E. *Measurement and evaluation in psychology and education.* (3rd ed.) New York: Wiley, 1969, chap. 16.

appendix A

MAJOR PUBLISHERS OF PSYCHOLOGICAL AND EDUCATIONAL TESTS

American Guidance Service, Inc., Publishers Building, Circle Pines, Minn. 55014

The Bobbs-Merrill Company, Inc., Test Division, 4300 West 62nd St., Indianapolis, Ind. 46206

Bureau of Educational Measurements, Kansas State Teachers College, Emporia, Kans. 66801

Bureau of Educational Research and Service, State University of Iowa, Iowa City, Iowa 52240

California Test Bureau, Del Monte Research Park, Monterey, Calif. 93940

Consulting Psychologists Press, Inc., 577 College Ave., Palo Alto, Calif. 94306

Cooperative Test Division, Educational Testing Service, Princeton, N.J. 08540

Educational Test Bureau, 720 Washington Ave., S.E., Minneapolis, Minn. 55414

Harcourt Brace Jovanovich, Inc., 757 Third Ave., New York, N.Y. 10017

Houghton Mifflin Company, 110 Tremont St., Boston, Mass. 02107

Industrial Relations Center, University of Chicago, 1225 East 60th St., Chicago, Ill. 60637

Institute for Personality and Ability Testing, 1602 Coronado Dr., Champaign, Ill. 61822

Ohio Scholarship Tests, State Department of Education, 751 Northwest Blvd., Columbus, Ohio 43212

The Psychological Corporation, 304 East 45th St., New York, N.Y. 10017

Psychological Test Specialists, Box 1441, Missoula, Mont. 59804

Psychometric Affiliates, Brookport, Ill. 62010

Scholastic Testing Service, Inc., 480 Meyer Rd., Bensenville, Ill. 60106

Science Research Associates, Inc., 259 East Erie St., Chicago, Ill. 60611

Sheridan Psychological Services, P.O. Box 837, Beverly Hills, Calif. 90213

C. H. Stoelting Company, 424 North Holman Ave., Chicago, Ill. 60611

Teachers College Press, Columbia University, 525 West 120th St., New York, N.Y.
  10027
University Bookstore, Purdue University, 360 State St., West Lafayette, Ind. 47906
University of London Press, Ltd., St. Paul's House, Warwick Lane, London EC4,
  England
Western Psychological Services, 12035 Wilshire Blvd., Los Angeles, Calif. 90025

appendix B

PROPORTIONS OF THE AREA IN VARIOUS SECTIONS OF THE NORMAL DISTRIBUTION*

	Z Standard Score (x/σ) (1)	Area Between (2)	Area Beyond (3)
+ and −	0.00	0.0000	1.0000
	0.05	.0392	.9602
	0.10	.0796	.9204
	0.15	.1192	.8808
	0.20	.1586	.8414
+ and −	0.25	.1974	.8026
	0.30	.2358	.7642
	0.35	.2736	.7264
	0.40	.3108	.6892
	0.45	.3472	.6528
+ and −	0.50	.3830	.6170
	0.55	.4176	.5824
	0.60	.4514	.5486
	0.65	.4844	.5156
	0.70	.5160	.4840

*If, for example, in a normal distribution of test scores, you want to estimate the number of persons who make scores between plus one standard deviation of the mean and minus one standard deviation of the mean, you would look opposite 1.00 in the first column at the proportion in the second column. There it is seen that the proportion is .6826 or, in other words, approximately 68 per cent. This means that approximately 32 per cent of the individuals make scores either greater than one standard deviation above the mean or less than one standard deviation below the mean. If you want to determine the proportions of people who lie within or beyond certain standard score units above the mean only or below the mean only, the proportions in columns 2 and 3 should be halved.

	Z Standard score (χ/σ) (1)	Area Between (2)	Area Beyond (3)
+ and −	0.75	.5468	.4532
	0.80	.5762	.4238
	0.85	.6046	.3954
	0.90	.6318	.3682
	0.95	.6578	.3422
+ and −	1.00	.6826	.3174
	1.05	.7062	.2938
	1.10	.7286	.2714
	1.15	.7498	.2502
	1.20	.7698	.2302
+ and −	1.25	.7888	.2112
	1.30	.8064	.1936
	1.35	.8230	.1770
	1.40	.8384	.1616
	1.45	.8530	.1470
+ and −	1.50	.8664	.1336
	1.55	.8788	.1212
	1.60	.8904	.1096
	1.65	.9019	.0990
	1.70	.9108	.0892
+ and −	1.75	.9198	.0802
	1.80	.9282	.0718
	1.85	.9356	.0644
	1.90	.9426	.0574
	1.95	.9488	.0512
+ and −	2.00	.9544	.0456
	2.05	.9596	.0404
	2.10	.9642	.0358
	2.15	.9684	.0316
	2.20	.9722	.0278
+ and −	2.25	.9756	.0244
	2.30	.9786	.0214
	2.35	.9812	.0188
	2.40	.9836	.0164
	2.45	.9858	.0142

	Z Standard score (X/σ) (1)	Area Between (2)	Area Beyond (3)
+ and −	2.50	.9876	.0124
	2.55	.9892	.0108
	2.60	.9906	.0094
	2.65	.9920	.0080
	2.70	.9930	.0070
+ and −	2.80	.9948	.0052
	2.90	.9962	.0038
	3.00	.9973	.0027
	3.10	.99806	.00194
	3.20	.99862	.00138
+ and −	3.40	.99932	.00068
	3.60	.99968	.00032
	3.80	.999856	.000144
	4.00	.9999366	.0000634
	4.50	.9999932	.0000068
	5.00	.9999942	.00000058
	6.00	.999999998	.000000002

appendix C

STATISTICAL APPENDIX

CONTENTS

1. Corrections for attenuation. Because of the measurement error inherent in all tests, correlations among tests are less than they would otherwise be. To the extent to which correlations are lowered in this manner, it is said that they are "attenuated" by unreliability. The more reliable the tests, the less the attenuation; the less reliable the tests, the more the attenuation. According to the theory, completely unreliable tests could not possibly correlate other than zero with any other measures (except for the departures from zero correlation that would occur as a function of sampling errors). If in examining a correlation the reliability of one or both tests is known, the theory of measurement error allows us to estimate what the correlation would be if the reliability of one or both of the measures were increased.

A simple formula allows us to estimate what the correlation would be if measurement error were entirely removed from one of the two measures, that is, if one of the measures were made perfectly reliable. The formula is

$$\bar{r}_{12} = \frac{r_{12}}{\sqrt{r_{11}}}$$

where r_{12} = obtained correlation between tests 1 and 2

r_{11} = reliability of test 1

$\bar{r}_{12}$ = estimated correlation between tests 1 and 2 if test 1 (but not test 2) were made perfectly reliable

To illustrate the use of the formula, assume that a vocabulary test (test 1) correlates .48 with a mathematics test (test 2). A prior study of the reliability of test 1, say comparing alternate forms of the test, produces a reliability coefficient of .64. At this point assume that we have no information about the reliability of test 2. Correction for the attenuation due to the measurement error in test 1 is made as follows:

$$\bar{r}_{12} = \frac{.48}{\sqrt{.64}}$$

$$= \frac{.48}{.8}$$

$$= .60$$

The estimate is that if test 1 were made perfectly reliable the correlation of .48 would, in another study, increase to .60.

In the above formula we only considered the unreliability in one test. Of course, the second test also would not be perfectly reliable. Let us say in this case that the reliability is known to be .81. The following formula allows us to estimate the correlation that would be obtained if both tests were made perfectly reliable:

$$\bar{r}_{12} = \frac{r_{12}}{\sqrt{r_{11}}\sqrt{r_{22}}}$$

Substituting the figures from the example we find:

$$\bar{r}_{12} = \frac{.48}{\sqrt{.64}\sqrt{.81}}$$

$$= \frac{.48}{.8 \times .9}$$

$$= \frac{.48}{.72}$$

$$= .67$$

If both tests were made perfectly reliable, the formula estimates that the correlation between the two tests would, in a subsequent study, be .67 instead of .48.

These formulas are useful for estimating the "true" relationships between variables, that is, if measurement error were not attenuating the relationships. One place in which the formulas are useful is in examining the correlation between a predictor test t and its criterion c. Say in this case t is a test to select college freshmen and c is grades in college. Because of the measurement error in c, the correlation of t with c underestimates how well the test actually works. Consequently, it is justifiable to make the correction for the unreliability in c by dividing the correlation between t and c by the square root of the reliability of c. However, in this instance, it would not be as directly meaningful to make the double correction for attenuation by correcting for both t and c. That correction would offer only a promissory note as to how well the test would work if it were made perfectly reliable.

Of course, perfect reliability is only a handy fiction, and to make estimates on the basis of that assumption is only useful to guide our thinking relative to the usefulness of tests. A more down to earth problem is to estimate how much a correlation would increase if the reliability were increased by any particular amount. A formula for doing this is as follows:

$$\bar{r}_{12} = \frac{r_{12}\sqrt{r'_{11}}\sqrt{r'_{22}}}{\sqrt{r_{11}}\ \sqrt{r_{22}}}$$

where r_{11} and r_{22} = original reliabilities of the two tests
  r'_{11} and r'_{22} = new reliabilities
  r_{12} = original correlation
  $\bar{r}_{12}$ = estimated correlation after the reliabilities are
    increased

Assume *(a)* that the original correlation between the two tests is .36, *(b)* that the original reliabilities of the two tests are .64 and .49, and *(c)* after improving the two tests (for example, by making them longer), the reliabilities increase, respectively, to .81 and .64. Then the estimate of the correlation that would be obtained from the more reliable measures is as follows:

$$\bar{r}_{12} = \frac{.36\sqrt{.81}\sqrt{.64}}{\sqrt{.64}\sqrt{.49}}$$

$$= .46$$

The formula also can be used to estimate how the correlation would change if both of the reliabilities were decreased (for example, by shortening the tests) or if one of the reliabilities were increased and the other were decreased.

2. Correlation and regression formulas. In the text, the basic formula for the correlation coefficient was stated in terms of standard scores as follows:

$$r_{12} = \frac{\Sigma Z_1 Z_2}{N}$$

where Z_1 = standard scores on one test
Z_2 = standard scores on another test
N = number of people in the study

In using the formula, one simply multiplies standard scores for each person on the two tests, sums these for all persons in the study, and divides by the number of persons in the study.

Although the correlation coefficient ultimately concerns the relationship between two sets of standard scores, it is more convenient to compute the correlation from either deviation scores or raw scores. Essentially what these formulas do is to convert scores to standard-score form in the context of the calculations rather than require a prior transformation to standard-score form. The following formula can be used to compute the correlation from deviation scores:

$$r_{12} = \frac{\Sigma x_1 x_2}{\sqrt{\Sigma x_1^2}\sqrt{\Sigma x_2^2}}$$

where x_1 = deviation scores on one test
x_2 = deviation scores on another test

With this formula, one first multiplies the deviation scores for each person on the two tests and sums these over the number of people involved in the study. Then one squares the score for each person on test 1 and sums the squared scores over people; the same is done for scores on the second test. These quantities are then inserted into their proper places in the formula.

Actually, if an automatic calculator is available, it is easiest to compute correlations from raw scores, using the following formula:

$$r_{12} = \frac{N\Sigma X_1 X_2 - \Sigma X_1 \Sigma X_2}{\sqrt{N\Sigma X_1^2 - (\Sigma X_1)^2}\sqrt{N\Sigma X_2^2 - (\Sigma X_2)^2}}$$

where X_1 = raw scores on one test

$X_2 =$ raw scores on another test

$N =$ number of people

Although the above formula may look complex, actually it is a straightforward extension of the more simple appearing standard-score formula. Again it should be emphasized that all these formulas supply the same numerical results. They are different computational approaches to obtaining the same statistic.

After the correlation coefficient is computed, it is possible to obtain a best-fit line that most effectively summarizes the relationship between the two variables being studied. Examples of such best-fit lines are shown in Figures 4-1 and 4-2. If variables are expressed in standard-score form, the equation for determining the best-fit line is as follows:

$$Z'_2 = r_{12} Z_1$$

where $Z_1 =$ scores on the predictor variable

$Z'_2 =$ estimated scores on the variable being predicted

$r_{12} =$ correlation between the two variables

Suppose that the correlation between two tests is .50. To estimate scores on one test from the other, standard scores are multiplied by .50. For example, if a student has a standard score of 2.00 on one test, the estimate is that he has a standard score of 1.00 on the other test. If a student has a standard score of -1.00 on one test, the estimate is that he has a standard score of $-.50$ on the other test. Because when the best-fit line is plotted for sets of standard scores the line must go through the origin, it is necessary to obtain only one other point to draw the best-fit line.

If the variables are expressed in deviation-score form rather than standard-score form, the equation for the best-fit line is as follows:

$$x'_2 = r_{12} \frac{\sigma_2}{\sigma_1} x_1$$

where $x'_2 =$ estimates of deviation scores

$x_1 =$ deviation scores on the predictor variable

σ_1 and $\sigma_2 =$ standard deviations of the variables

If variables are plotted in terms of raw scores, the regression equation is as follows:

$$X'_2 = r_{12} \frac{\sigma_2}{\sigma_1} (X_1 - M_1) + M_2$$

where $X'_2 =$ estimates of raw scores

$X_1 =$ raw scores on the predictor variable

M_1 and $M_2 =$ means of the variables

3. Internal-consistency measures of reliability. When an alternate form of a test is not available, very useful estimates of the reliability can be obtained from formulas concerning the internal consistency of the test items. If a test is reliable, all the items should tend to measure the same thing and should correlate positively with one another. The higher items correlate with one another, the more reliable the test. To say it another way, if the items within a test correlate highly with one another, the whole test should correlate highly with an alternate form. By making several reasonable assumptions, good estimates can be made of how highly a test would correlate with an alternate form. The basic formula is as follows:

$$r_{11} = \frac{n}{n-1}\left(1 - \frac{\Sigma pq}{\sigma_1{}^2}\right)$$

where $r_{11} =$ reliability of the test

$n =$ number of items in the test

$\sigma_1{}^2 =$ squared standard deviation of the test

$p =$ proportion of students passing each item

$q =$ proportion of students failing each item

In computing the reliability, the major computational chore is to multiply the proportion of students passing each item by the proportion of students failing each item. For example, if .40 of the students pass the first item and .60 fail the first item, the product is .24. These products are computed and summed over all the test items. After this quantity is obtained, it is a simple matter to obtain the other terms for the formula.

The formula above is called the *Kuder-Richardson formula 20.* It should be emphasized that what KR-20 does is to estimate the correlation between an existing test and a hypothetical alternate form. Usually the estimate is very good. When alternate forms are available, the actual correlation usually corresponds closely to the estimate given by KR-20.

As mentioned previously, KR-20 is employed when tests are scored dichotomously, e.g., when there are "yes" or "no" answers and answers that are either correct or incorrect. In many cases it is necessary to estimate the reliability of tests composed of items that are scorable on more than two points, such as six-point rating scales concerning attitudes. When items are scorable on more than two points, the internal-consistency reliability is estimated by a different equation from KR-20, as follows:

$$r_{11} = \frac{n}{n-1}\left(1 - \frac{\Sigma \sigma_i^2}{\sigma_1^2}\right)$$

where r_{11} = reliability of the test
n = number of items in the test
σ_1^2 = squared deviation of the test
$\Sigma \sigma_i^2$ = sum of squared standard deviations of item scores

The above equation is referred to as *coefficient alpha*. It is based on exactly the same logic as KR-20. Actually, KR-20 is a special computation of coefficient alpha in the case where items are scored dichotomously.

Coefficient alpha would be applied, for example, in an eleven-question essay examination in which each item is scored on a six-point scale. In performing statistical analyses of test results, it is found that standard deviations on the items range from .75 to 1.25, with the sum of squared standard deviations being 10.0. The squared standard deviation of total test scores is 30.0. When these statistics are entered into the above formula for coefficient alpha, the result is a reliability estimate of .73.

Although in Chapter 4 it was said that the ideal measure of reliability in most instances is obtained from the correlation of alternate forms of a test, the measures of reliability based on internal consistency provide very useful information. Unless a trait is being investigated that tends to change markedly over relatively short periods of time, e.g., moods, measures of reliability based on internal consistency are usually very close in value to those based on alternate forms of a test. To the extent that the two kinds of measures are different, measures based on internal consistency tend to be somewhat higher. This is because measures based on internal consistency do not take account of measurement error that occurs because of changes in people from week to week and month to month. For this reason, measures based on internal consistency provide upper limits to the results usually obtained from alternate forms. For example, if by the former type of reliability measurement one obtains a coefficient of .85, the expectation is that the measure of reliability obtained from alternate forms will be either .85 or somewhat less. Because measures of internal consistency usually provide an upper limit to the reliability obtained from alternate forms, the former type of measure provides very early evidence as to whether a test will be reliable when measured by alternate forms. If the internal-consistency reliability is very low (e.g., .50 or lower), then it is hopeless to find a high reliability as measured by alternate forms. This important type of information would lead the test constructor either to modify his original instrument or to develop an entirely different type of test.

4.   Measurement error—effects on score distributions.   It will be recalled that measurement error has two effects on scores. First, it introduces a source of bias, scores above the mean being biased upward and scores below the mean being biased downward. Second, it introduces a zone of uncertainty, or error, for each score. It is helpful to obtain unbiased estimates of "true" scores and to assert confidence zones about those estimates. Unbiased estimates of true scores can be obtained as follows:

$$x'_t = r_{11}x_1$$

where x'_t = estimated true scores
$\quad x_1$ = deviation scores on the test
$\quad r_{11}$ = test reliability

If an individual has a test deviation score of 10 and the reliability of the test is .90, the best estimate of his "true" score is 9. If another individual has a test deviation score of -20, his estimated "true" score is -18. What the formula above does is to regress scores back toward the mean. The further out scores are in either direction, the more (in an absolute sense) they are pulled back toward the mean.

It should be clear that the formula above does not change the relative ordering of students. The top student with respect to obtained scores will remain the top with respect to estimated true scores, and the bottom student on obtained scores will remain there on estimated true scores. Because the relative ordering of students is not changed, it rightly can be asked why the formula serves any useful purpose. It is useful primarily for asserting the center of confidence bands, which we now will consider.

Although the formula above provides an estimate of "true" scores, it gives no indication of the amount of error entailed in the estimate. If we gave people many forms of the same test, their scores would vary somewhat from day to day. It would be expected that the scores for each would range about some typical value, that typical value being the estimated true score for the student. How widely scores range about the true score is an indication of the amount of measurement error. One way to gauge the amount of error would be to compute the standard deviation of obtained scores for each person. The larger the standard deviation, the more measurement error there would be. The standard deviation would be zero only if the test were perfectly reliable. Of course, it is not possible to measure the amount of error exactly in this way because we never administer numerous forms of the same test to people. However, by making some reasonable assumptions, an estimate can be made of the standard deviation of scores that would be obtained. The formula is as follows:

$$\sigma_{\text{meas}} = \sigma_1 \sqrt{1 - r_{11}}$$

where σ_{meas} = standard error of measurement
σ_1 = test standard deviation
r_{11} = reliability of test 1

The *standard error of measurement* (SEM) is a special kind of standard deviation which indicates the amount of error in a test due to unreliability. Illustrating the computations, if a test has a standard deviation of 10 and a reliability of .90, the computations would be as follows:

$$\sigma_{\text{meas}} = 10 \sqrt{1 - .90}$$
$$= 10 \times 3.16$$
$$= 3.16$$

In other words, if we actually gave a person numerous comparable forms of the test, the expected standard deviation of scores (SEM) would be 3.16 score units.

The formulas for estimating true scores and for obtaining the SEM can be brought together in an illustration of how confidence bands are set. Previously it was shown that with a test reliability of .90 the estimated true scores corresponding to obtained scores of 10 and -20, respectively, are 9 and -18. These estimated true scores would serve as the centers of confidence bands. In the previous example of a test with a standard deviation of 10 and a reliability of .90, the SEM was 3.16. By marking off points above and below estimated true scores corresponding to numbers of SEMs, odds can be set regarding the probabilities of obtained scores on comparable forms exceeding specified limits. Conventionally we work with a confidence band extending two SEMs above and two SEMs below estimated true scores. For the person with an estimated true score of 9, the confidence band extends from 2.68 to 15.32. For the person with an estimated true score of -18, the confidence band would extend from -24.32 to -11.68. Because it is not possible to obtain fractional scores on most tests, these numbers would be rounded, and the confidence bands would extend from 3 to 15 and from -24 to -12, respectively.

Because the SEM is a special kind of standard deviation, odds corresponding to confidence zones can be found in the proportions of area under various regions of the normal curve shown in Appendix B. There it will be found that approximately 95 per cent of the cases lie between plus two and minus two standard deviations about the mean. In other words, by asserting the confidence band as ranging from two SEMs below to two SEMs above the estimated true score, we develop a zone which allows us to feel "95 per cent sure." In other words, if the individual were administered 100 comparable forms of the test, the expectation is that only 5 times out of 100 would obtained scores be either greater or less than the limits of the confidence band.

Although it has been emphasized that obtained scores are biased and it is best to regress scores toward the group mean, in practice it is sometimes difficult to know exactly how this is to be done. The problem is that sometimes we are not sure what mean should be the pivotal point for regressing scores. For example, if someone tells me that he tested a child and found an IQ of 110, what should I use as the mean toward which the score is to be regressed? Should I use the over-all mean of 100 found in the test standardization? Yes, that is the best thing to do *if* you have no other information about the child. But suppose I learn that the child comes from a school in which the average IQ is 115. Should I still regress the score toward a mean of 100? No, now that I have obtained additional information about the child, I should not blindly follow the original statistical rules for regressing scores. More sensible would be to consider the score as probably *lower* than the true score rather than higher. Admittedly this becomes a rather complex problem, but there is no way of avoiding the fact that additional information changes the estimates one makes about measurement error. Two general rules can be stated. First, if you have no other information about a child, regress the obtained score toward the mean of the standardization sample, e.g., toward an IQ of 100. If you do have additional information about a child which allocates him to a definite subgroup of the population, temper your judgment of the need to regress the score toward the mean of the standardization sample. It would be difficult to give exact statistical rules for how to do this, but the additional information about the child should be considered in making judgments about his score.

Fortunately, the knotty conceptual problems above are not met in classroom stituations. There it is eminently sensible to regress scores toward the mean of all the students in a particular class. There it is safe to bet that, on any kind of test, high scores tend to be biased upward and low scores biased downward. There the teacher has a well-defined group in which the measurement error concepts and formulas clearly apply.

5. Median—computational procedures. As was stated in the text, strictly speaking the median is defined only for an unusual circumstance. By its definition, the median is the point on the test continuum which separates the top 50 per cent from the bottom 50 per cent of the students. Obviously then a particular score, e.g., 18, could be the median only if half of the students score 19 or higher and half of the students score 17 or lower. In other words, it would not be possible to obtain the median in the strict sense if anyone scores exactly at the median, 18 in the example above. Usually it will be the case that numerous students will make the score corresponding to the median. An example was in the text where to declare a "whole" score the median would be misleading. Consequently, it is necessary to transform the "whole" score corresponding to the median to a fractional score which more nearly fits the definition of the measure. The computational procedures can be illustrated with the following distribution of test scores.

Score	Number of students
24	1
23	3
22	2
21	4
20	3
19	1
18	6
17	4
16	4
15	3
14	1
13	3
12	1
11	1
10	1

The computation of the median begins by determining the number of students in the distribution, which in the example above is 38. This is then divided by 2, giving 19. One then counts up from the bottom to find the score made by the 19th student, which in this case is 18. This might be used as the approximate median, but it is only an approximation because six students make scores of 18.

The best way to consider the problem is to think of a score of 18 as lying in a band from 17.5 to 18.5 and to think of the median as lying somewhere in that band. How far up in the band the median lies depends on the proportion of the students making the score (18) that must be counted in order to include 50 per cent (here, 19) of the students. In this case it is necessary to count only one of the six students who make scores of 18. Consequently, one-sixth is added to the lower bound of the category (17.5). This gives a median of 17.67. Admittedly those computations would not be employed unless the problem were important. However, because teachers will see frequent mention of the median with respect to commercially distributed tests and research reports, they need to know how the measure is computed.

6. Sampling error of correlation coefficients.   In the text it was emphasized that sampling error is involved in obtaining any correlation coefficient. This is because correlations usually are obtained from only a sample of all the students that conceivably could be studied. For example, if the correlation between an intelligence test and an achievement test is obtained on 50 students, this is only a tiny fraction of all the students in the county on whom the correlation conceivably could be computed. Consequently, it is not safe to regard any correlation as an exact value but rather as lying in a confidence band extending above and below the obtained value. The width of the confidence band is inversely proportional to the number of students in the study. If only 10 students are in the study, it is hard to place any confidence at all in the correlation. If 100 students are in the study, the zone of uncertainty about the correlation is much less. If 10,000 students are used to compute the correlation coefficient and these actually have been sampled from the population, the zone of uncertainty is so small that, for all practical purposes, the obtained correlation can be taken as almost identical to the value that would be obtained if the whole population were studied.

How to obtain confidence bands can be illustrated with the situation in which the population correlation actually is zero. That is, if all the students in the country were measured in order to compute the correlation, the actual value would be found to be zero. What would happen if we sampled only 100 students instead of measuring the whole population? Would the correlation in that sample be exactly zero? If we drew different samples of 100 students, would all the correlations be exactly zero? No, they would range about zero, some of them being positive and some of them being negative. This would happen because of the chance factors involved in drawing samples of students. Expected in this instance would be an approximate normal distribution of correlations, with the mean at zero. How widely sample correlations ranged about zero would depend on the number of students in each sample. With only 10 students, the standard deviation of sample correlations would be very large; with 100 students, the standard deviation would be smaller; with 10,000 students the standard deviation would be so small that it could be overlooked altogether.

A standard deviation of sample values is called a *standard error*. After the standard error is obtained, it can be used to set confidence zones for interpreting correlations. First, we will show how a standard error is obtained and then show how it is used to set confidence zones. A standard error for the correlation coefficient can be computed as follows:

$$\sigma_r = \frac{1}{\sqrt{N-1}}$$

where σ_r = standard error of a correlation coefficient
N = number of students being studied

Suppose that a correlation is obtained on 101 students (to pick a convenient number). The standard error would be:

$$\sigma_r = \frac{1}{\sqrt{101-1}}$$

$$= .10$$

In other words, with an N of 101, the estimated standard deviation of sample correlations (in a population where the true value is zero) is .10.

Suppose that with an N of 101 a correlation of .40 is obtained. A confidence zone could be set by marking off correlation points so many standard errors above and so many standard errors below the obtained correlation. Frequently we employ a confidence zone of two standard errors above and below the obtained correlation. In Appendix B it is shown that approximately 95 per cent of the cases lie within two standard deviations (standard errors here) of the mean. Here the confidence band would extend from correlation values of .20 to .60. The meaning is that we can feel 95 per cent sure that the real correlation lies somewhere between .20 and .60.

Suppose with a sample of 101 students the obtained correlation is only .15. Then the confidence band extends from —.05 to .35. In other words, in different samples, 5 times out of 100 the correlation might be less than —.05 or greater than .35. When the confidence band crosses zero, it means that it is not safe to conclude that the real correlation is other than zero. In that instance we say that the correlation is "not statistically significant" and withhold judgment about the correlation until more students are studied.

Here we have illustrated the sampling error of correlations only in the simplest case. More complex procedures are required to study the sampling error of the difference between two correlations obtained on different samples, of the difference between two correlations obtained with the same sample, and others. Also, the reader should be warned that the formula given above for the standard error of the correlation is only an approximation. Although it works fairly well in many instances, more exact formulas are available. For more exact estimates of standard errors and for a more complete discussion of how to take account of sampling error, the reader should consult texts on statistics. Some good texts on statistics are listed in the Suggested Additional Readings at the ends of Chapters 3 and 4.

More important for teachers than to know all the statistical procedures concerning the sampling error of correlations is to adopt appropriate attitudes toward correlations reported in the research literature and correlations computed in school settings. First, it is important to realize that there is some sampling error connected with any correlation coefficient. Second, it is wise to be suspicious of correlations unless they are based on a relatively large number of students. Usually, unless at least one hundred students are being studied, there is so much sampling error that the real value of the correlation is highly in doubt. Third, it is important to realize that statistical procedures are available for asserting confidence bands for correlations, and when the need arises, the necessary statistics can be obtained from available texts.

7. Effects of test length on reliability. As was mentioned at a number of places in the text, when the number of items in a test is increased, the reliability tends to increase. By making some reasonable assumptions, a formula can be obtained to estimate how much the reliability will increase as a function of the increase in test length. The formula is as follows:

$$r_{nn} = \frac{nr_{11}}{1 + (n - 1)r_{11}}$$

where r_{nn} = estimated reliability of a test n times as long as the original test

r_{11} = reliability of the original test

n = number of times the test is lengthened

If the reliability of a twenty-item test is .70 and if forty similar items are added to the original twenty, the estimate of the reliability of the sixty-item test is as follows:

$$r_{nn} = \frac{3(.70)}{1 + (3 - 1).70}$$

$$= \frac{2.1}{2.4}$$

$$= .88$$

Whereas the twenty-item test has a reliability of .70, the estimate is that the reliability will increase to .88 by adding forty items (by making the eventual test three times as long as the original).

This general formula can be used both to estimate how much the reliability will increase if more items are added to a test and also to estimate how many items will be required to reach a specified level of reliability. Thus, if a test has a reliability of .75, and a reliability of .90 is needed, these two values can be entered in the formula (substituting .90 for r_{nn}), and the solution will estimate the number of times the test must be lengthened.

It should be pointed out that in the formula n need not be a whole number. It can be a fractional number. For example, the formula can be used to estimate the increase in reliability obtained from adding twenty more items to a forty-item test. In this case n would be 1.5.

The formula also can be used to estimate the reliability of a shortened test. In some instances it is helpful to have a shorter version of a test to use for rough screening purposes. If the reliability of the longer test is known, it is helpful to have an estimate of the reliability of the shorter version. This can be accomplished by making n the ratio of the number of items in the shorter test to the number of items in the longer test. For example, if the number of items in the longer test is forty and the number of items in the shorter test is twenty, then an n of .5 is entered in the formula.

The general formula takes on a simple appearance in the special case where it is necessary to estimate the reliability of a test doubled in length:

$$r_{11} = \frac{2r_{hh}}{1 + r_{hh}}$$

where r_{hh} = reliability of half the eventual items
r_{11} = reliability of the total (twice as many) items

This version of the formula is particularly useful in studying the reliability of a test by the split-half method. As was mentioned in the text, one way to measure reliability is to split the items within a test into two parts and correlate scores obtained on the two parts. The most popular procedure is to obtain separate scores on the odd- and even-numbered items. The two scores are then correlated. However, a correction must be made to obtain the reliability of the whole test, not just of the half tests. The formula above provides the necessary correction. For example, if the correlation of the split halves is .80, the correction is as follows:

$$r_{11} = \frac{2(.80)}{1 + .80} = \frac{1.60}{1.80} = .89$$

What the formula does is to estimate how much the total collection of items would correlate with another collection of similar items of the same size.

A caution should be heeded in applying the above formulas. The formulas assume that the items to be added (or taken away) are similar to those in the original test (or those in the remaining collection after the test is shortened). If the items to be added or taken away are grossly different from the original or remaining (in a shortened test) items, the formulas give misleading results. For example, in lengthening a test, this would occur if the new items were either much easier or much harder than the original ones, or if the new items concerned different factors of ability or personality. Although it is useful to keep these assumptions in mind, it seldom is the case that they are grossly violated in actual work with tests. Consequently, the formulas usually supply very good estimates of the effect on reliability of either lengthening or shortening tests.

8. Standard deviation—computational approaches. In the text, the basic formula for the standard deviation was given as follows:

$$\sigma = \sqrt{\frac{\Sigma x^2}{N}}$$

where σ = standard deviation of the test
x = deviation scores on the test
N = number of students

To compute the standard deviation, the first step is to subtract the mean from all raw scores. The resulting deviation scores are then squared and summed. The sum is divided by the number of scores. The square root of this quantity is the standard deviation.

Although it is easier to discuss the standard deviation in terms of deviation scores, if an automatic calculator is available, it is easier to compute the standard deviation from raw scores as follows:

$$\sigma = \sqrt{\frac{\Sigma X^2}{N} - \left(\frac{\Sigma X}{N}\right)^2}$$

Several tips are helpful in thinking about and in computing the standard deviation. First, the standard deviation obtained from the raw-score formula above is not changed if a constant is either added to or subtracted from all the scores. Consequently, it is permissible to add or subtract a constant from all the numbers before entering them in the raw-score formula. Suppose that the lowest test score is 40, then the computation of the standard deviation would be simplified by first subtracting 40 from each score. The resulting numbers would be easier to work with in calculating the standard deviation. This rule can also be used to get rid of negative numbers. If points are subtracted for making certain types of errors, some test scores are likely to be negative. These negative numbers can be avoided by adding a positive quantity equal to the largest negative score to each of the scores. This will not change the standard deviation.

Another tip is that if all the scores are multiplied by a constant, the standard deviation is multiplied by the same constant. For example, if all the scores are multiplied by two, the standard deviation obtained from the raw-score formula will be twice as large as that which would have been obtained from the original numbers. This fact allows us to throw out decimal points in the computation of the standard deviation. For example, if we have scores like 2.3, 1.6, and 3.8, these can be converted to 23, 16, and 38. The obtained standard deviation can then be divided by 10.

Of course, there is no point in obtaining the standard deviation of a set of standard scores. By definition, a set of standard scores has a standard deviation of 1.00.

9.   Transformations of objective test results to point scales.   In order to provide a uniform basis for combining results from objective tests with those from essay tests, it was suggested in the text that a point scale be used. Illustrations were given of the use of a five-point scale for grading essay examinations, term papers, and others. Such a five-point scale can easily be applied to all evaluational material except for objective test results. In grading objective tests it is necessary to specify grade levels in terms of percentages of items correct. For example, an illustration was given where 85 per cent of the items correct was considered as an A grade, 72 per cent correct as a B grade, etc.

The figure on the following page illustrates how percentage-correct grades on objective tests can be transformed to a point scale. To construct such a figure, first mark off on the baseline the percentages of items that correspond to various grade levels on the objective test. On the five-point scale, 1.0 means a totally failing grade. Corresponding to that on the objective test would be the per cent of items correct that a student could obtain purely by guessing, which is one divided by the number of alternatives for each item. In the figure it is assumed that multiple-choice ques-

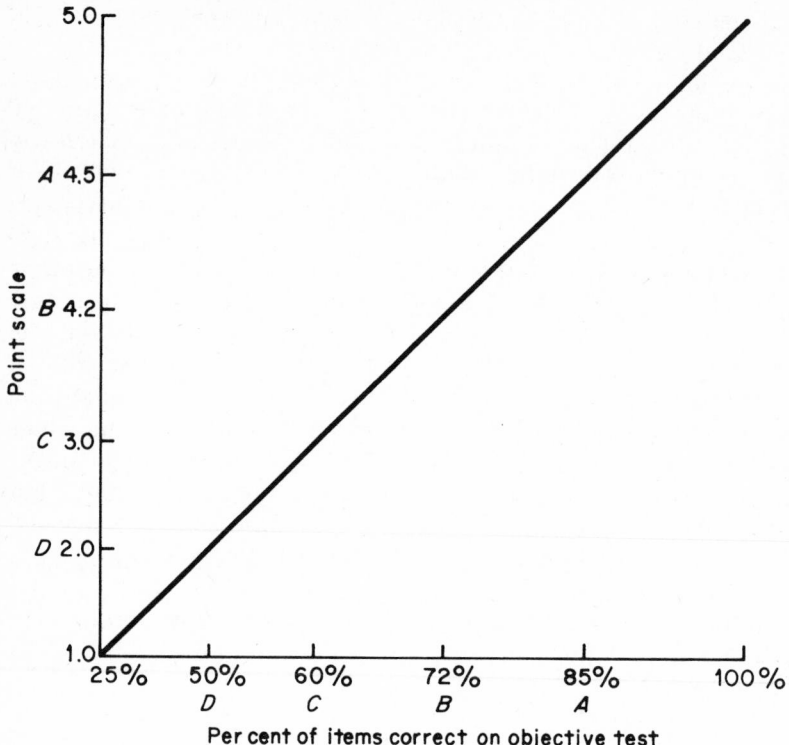

Per cent of items correct on objective test

tions are used with four alternative answers for each question. Consequently, a percentage correct of 25 should correspond to a score of 1.0 on the five-point scale. Sometimes one finds a percentage-correct score of less than that which would be expected by chance, in which case it is probably wisest to give that student the lowest possible score on the point scale, here 1.0.

At the upper end of the objective test continuum, 100 per cent correct logically corresponds to the highest possible score on the point scale, in this example 5.0. It is important to note that in the figure, distances between grade levels are not all equal. For example, C and B are separated by twelve units (3.0, 3.1, etc., to 4.1), but B and A are separated by only three units (4.2, 4.3, and 4.4). To more accurately translate percentage scores to point scores, on the point-score continuum the correct number of units should be made to separate the grade levels. For example, the distance on the vertical scale of the graph from B to A should be divided into three equal segments. The lower bound of the first segment would be 4.2, the lower bound of the second segment 4.3, and the lower bound of the third segment would be 4.4. Similarly, the distance from C to A would be divided into twelve equal segments.

After the graph is completed, it is a simple matter to translate percentage-correct scores directly to a point scale. For example, it can be seen that a percentage correct score of 55 corresponds to a point score of 2.5.

Although it may seem like a lot of work to construct a graph for translating percentage-correct scores to point scores, once the graph is constructed it can be used over and over as long as the same standards of grading are used on both scales. Of course, if after some experience with the graph it is decided to change grading standards on one or both scales, it would be necessary to construct a new graph.

10.   Transformations of score distributions.   A problem that is often encountered in using psychological tests is that of transforming an obtained set of raw scores to a set with a particular mean and standard deviation. For example, it might be found that the mean of the obtained raw test scores is 40 and that the standard deviation is 5. In order to compare scores on the test with scores on another test, or in order to place the scores in an easily interpretable form, it might be desirable to transform the raw scores in such a way that the new scores have a mean of 50 and a standard deviation of 10. Transformations of this kind can be performed with the following formula:

$$X_t = \frac{\sigma_t}{\sigma_o} X_o - \left(\frac{\sigma_t}{\sigma_o} M_o - M_t \right)$$

where X_t = scores on the transformed scale
X_o = scores on the obtained scale: raw scores
M_o, M_t = means of X_o and X_t, respectively
σ_o, σ_t = standard deviations of X_o and X_t, respectively

The formula can be applied to the problem illustrated above as follows:

$$X_t = {}^{10}\!\!/_5 X_o - ({}^{10}\!\!/_5 \, 40 - 50)$$
$$= 2X_o - 30$$

By this transformation a raw score of 40 would be transformed to a score of 50, and a raw score of 25 would be transformed to a score of 20. Because the formula is a linear transformation, it does not change the shape of the score distribution.

11. Reliability of difference scores. As was mentioned in Chapter 4, one is frequently concerned about the reliability of an observed difference between two test scores. This is the case when comparing scores of two students on a test. A second problem arises when comparing scores of the same student on two different tests in a battery. A third problem occurs when comparing the score of one student with the average score for the class as a whole or some other reference group. In each case, however, one is concerned with the reliability of differences in scores rather than with the reliability of scores considered separately. The problems that arise with each one of these matters will be discussed in turn.

As an example to guide discussion of the first problem mentioned above, consider the instance in which we are comparing the scores of two students on the mathematics section of a comprehensive achievement test battery. Norms for the test are expressed in terms of a mean of 50 and a standard deviation of 10. It is observed that John obtains a score of 70 (two standard deviations above the mean of the normative sample) and Fred obtains a score of 60. Without further consideration, it is tempting to reach the conclusion that John is well ahead of Fred in mathematical achievement. However, such observed differences may be due entirely to the unreliability inherent in tests rather than to real differences in ability. The standard error of measurement (SEM), which concerns the zone of error surrounding a particular test score, was discussed previously. When one is comparing differences in test scores, one must take account of the measurement error inherent in both of the scores. The first problem discussed above is that of comparing the scores of two students on the same test. That problem is very simple to handle. To obtain an SEM for the difference score in that case, all one needs to do is to multiply the SEM for either score by the square root of 2. It will be remembered from the previous discussion of the SEM that any test has an SEM that holds for all subjects who take the test. Consequently, the SEMs for John and Fred in the example above are the same. However, when one compares the two scores, the SEM is larger, namely, by a factor of the square root of 2. Thus, if the SEM were 10 for individual scores, the SEM for comparing differences of scores for two people on the same test would be approximately 14. Then if differences in scores were not at least twice as large as that amount (28), one could place very little confidence in the observed difference. Rather, one should pass off the apparent difference as probably being due to measurement error.

The second case mentioned above concerned comparing scores of the same student on two tests, say, tests of reading achievement and mathematics. If the score on reading is higher than that on mathematics, one might conclude that the person is achieving better in the former topic than the latter. However, one would have to assess this difference for measurement errors. This case differs from the first in three important ways. First, in many instances the errors of measurement for the same person on two tests are systematically related. Thus, a student may take two tests of achievement on a day when he is in a good mood and is feeling well, and he may be tested in an environment that favors making high scores. These forms of good fortune would extend to all the tests taken on that day, and his scores on all tests would be somewhat higher than if he had taken the tests at another time and in other circumstances. There are no simple formulas that can be used to untangle such dependence of measurement errors on one another. Consequently, only an approximate formula will be given. However, the formula is conservative, in the sense that it would usually overestimate rather than underestimate the SEM for that situation.

Another way in which the second case would differ from the first is that the means and standard deviations of the two tests might not be the same. Formulas can be derived for the SEM of difference scores in that case, but it is far simpler to convert scores on the two tests to some standard form, e.g., a mean of zero and a standard deviation of 1.0 or a mean of 500 and a standard deviation of 100. It is usually the case that commercially distributed tests have scores reported in some standard form.

The third way in which the second case differs from the first is that the SEMs for the two tests would probably not be exactly the same. This would be the case if the two tests differed in reliability, e.g., if one had a reliability of .93 and the other had a reliability of .84.

With the foregoing considerations in mind, a formula for the SEM for differences in two scores (SEMD) for the same person on two tests is given as follows:

$$\text{SEMD} = \sqrt{(\text{SEM}-1)^2 + (\text{SEM}-2)^2}$$

where SEM$-$1 $=$ SEM of the first test
    SEM$-$2 $=$ SEM of the second test

After finding the SEMs in the usual way, these would be substituted into the above formula. For example, if one SEM was 3 and the other was 4, then the SEMD would be 5.

The third case concerning the reliability of difference scores is much easier to handle from a statistical point of view than the second one. This is the case in which one is comparing the score of one individual on a test with the average score of a group of individuals. This would occur, for example, in comparing the score of one student on an achievement test for spelling with the average score of students in the class. There is one source of measurement error in the score for the student and another source of measurement error in the average score for the class. However, if there are as many as twenty students in the class, the measurement error for the group averages out to a point of practical insignificance. Therefore, one can forget that source of measurement error and simply use the SEM for the one student's score.

As important as determining the SEMD, or more important, is estimating the reliability of difference scores. In essence what one does in examining difference scores is to subtract the score on one test from the score on another test. (In the following discussion it will be assumed that both sets of test scores are in some standard form, i.e., have the same mean and standard deviation.) This reliability coefficient (r_{dif}) provides a general index of the extent to which observed differences in scores are reliable or are due to measurement error instead. A formula for that purpose is as follows:

$$r_{dif} = \frac{r_{11} + r_{22} - 2r_{12}}{2(1 - r_{12})}$$

Thus, if the reliability of the first test is .80, the reliability of the second test is .90, and the correlation between the two tests is .60, r_{dif} would be .62.

The above example illustrates a problem that frequently comes up when working with difference scores: Difference scores are often much less reliable than scores on the two tests. There are two reasons why this is true. First, the difference score contains a double dose of error, one from each test. Second, by subtracting one set of scores from the other, one removes the part that is common to the two (as evidenced in the correlation between the two tests, r_{12}). The higher the correlation between the two tests, the lower the reliability of difference scores. In the example above, the reliabilities of the two tests are in the neighborhood of those found on many commercially distributed tests, and correlations as high as .60 between tests are not rare. Consequently, one can see that in the typical case, difference scores have only very modest reliability (.62 in the example above). This example should lend caution in placing faith in any differences in scores that are not quite large, i.e., separated by at least two SEMDs.

Of course, if reliabilities of the two tests are high and the correlation between the tests is low, difference scores are highly reliable. One can readily see from inspecting the formula above that if the correlation between the two tests is zero, r_{dif} is the average of r_{11} and r_{22}.

appendix D

COMMERCIALLY DISTRIBUTED TESTS

SECTION 1: COMPREHENSIVE ACHIEVEMENT TEST BATTERIES

California Achievement Tests, 1957 edition (with 1963 norms)
California Test Bureau
Levels: Lower primary, grades 1–2 (110 minutes)
         Upper primary, grades 2.5–4.5 (145 minutes)
         Elementary, grades 4–6 (175 minutes)
         Junior high level, grades 7–9 (190 minutes)
         Advanced, grades 9–14 (190 minutes)

The test reports two scores in each of the three basic skill areas of reading, arithmetic, and language. Although the manual describes methods for obtaining diagnostic information about pupils, such information is based on a relatively small number of items in many cases. At the primary and elementary levels, the test provides a good coverage of the three basic skill areas. At the junior high and advanced levels, the test does not provide enough information about achievement in content areas. Although items with respect to content areas are included, scores are not obtainable for different content areas. Because of the emphasis on core skills rather than content areas, the test is recommended mainly for students at the primary and elementary levels.

Cooperative Primary Tests
Educational Testing Service
Levels: End of grade 1 to grade 3
Testing time: 210 minutes (five sessions)

This attractively presented battery consists of five subtests designed to measure concepts and developments considered basic to future development in the core areas of elementary education. The subtests are listening, ord analysis, mathematics, reading, and writing skills. The test items are said to emphasize understanding and thinking rather than memorization. Great care has been taken not only to make the test materials visually appealing to young children but also to facilitate the process of test administration with this age group, thus increasing the chances of obtaining valid responses. A ten-item pilot test is included to give the pupils practice with the format of the items and the kinds of questions to come. Reliability coefficients (internal-consistency and alternate-form) are acceptably high. Validity data, other than for content validity, are lacking. Since the manual encourages the use of the test scores for predicting future scholastic accomplishment, it is important that data on the predictive usefulness of the battery be reported as soon as possible.

Essential High School Content Battery
Harcourt Brace Jovanovich, Inc.
Levels: Grades 10–12
Testing time: 225 minutes (five sessions)

The battery covers four fields: mathematics, science, social studies, and English. In general, the test appears to have been carefully designed and constructed. Although over-all scores on the test should provide good indications of students' progress, some of the subtest reliabilities are rather low, and it is hazardous to seek diagnostic information from differences in scores within the test. Because of its content, the test is probably a more useful measure for students in general or college preparatory curricula than for students in technical and commercial curricula.

Iowa Tests of Basic Skills (ITBS)
Houghton Mifflin Company
Levels: Grades 3–9 (multilevel format) go to (2) p. 10
Testing time: 315 minutes (four sessions)

This is a very thorough battery of tests. Content areas are not covered; rather, the tests are aimed at the core skills of reading, language, arithmetic, and study skills. The battery provides fifteen scores: vocabulary (1), language (5), reading comprehension (1), study skills (4), arithmetic (3), and total score. A modern math supplement is available in addition to, or in place of, the arithmetic skills test. Reliabilities of all subtests are good. An unusual feature is that norms are provided for the beginning, middle, and end of the school-year periods. Special percentile norms are available for geographic regions, Catholic schools, and large-city schools. The manuals provide very clear instructions for administering and using the tests. Apparently the tests were very carefully designed and constructed. Unless there is a need to test for content areas, the battery provides an excellent measure of core skills.

The Iowa Tests of Educational Development
Science Research Associates, Inc.
Levels: Grades 9–12
Testing time: 405–540 minutes (two days or nine class periods)

The battery provides nine scores: understanding of basic social concepts, general background in the natural sciences, correctness and appropriateness of expression, ability to do quantitative thinking, ability to interpret reading materials in the social sciences, ability to interpret reading materials in the natural sciences, ability to interpret literary materials, general vocabulary, and uses of sources of information. Unquestionably the battery provides excellent measures of achievement at the secondary level. The tests were carefully designed and composed, and norms are based on large, representative samples of students. A revision with completely new content was published in 1970. The manuals are clearly written and provide much information useful to teachers. The test publisher provides a scoring service which gives not only results for individual pupils but also statistical summaries of results from each school and item-analysis data. The battery exemplifies achievement measurement at its best.

Metropolitan Achievement Tests, 1970 edition
Harcourt Brace Jovanovich, Inc.
Levels: Primary I, grade 1.5 (115 minutes)
          Primary II, grade 2 (125 minutes)
          Elementary, grades 3–4 (177 minutes)
          Intermediate, grades 5–6 (267 minutes)
          Advanced, grades 7–9 (277 minutes)
          High school, grades 9–12 (316 minutes)

The content of this battery is outlined in detail in Chapter 9. At the younger levels the test concerns primarily core skills; at higher levels tests are also included for content areas. The test can be recommended on many points, including (1) careful design of content and construction of items, (2) clear and frank manuals, and (3) practicality of administration and scoring.

Sequential Tests of Educational Progress (STEP)
Educational Testing Service
Levels: Level 4, grades 4–6

Level 3, grades 7–9
Level 2, grades 10–12
Level 1, grades 13–14
Testing time: 640 minutes

At each level the battery contains six tests: (1) reading, (2) writing, (3) mathematics, (4) science, (5) social studies, and (6) listening. All the tests are composed of multiple-choice items. The most noteworthy feature of the STEP is that the test items are aimed more at the over-all goals of instruction than at the mastery of particular topics. The items concern principally how well students can use their school training to seek answers and to solve problems. Some of the items are very cleverly composed. Whereas on the one hand it can be argued that by aiming at the major end products of education, the STEP is more uniformly fair to students in different schools, on the other hand it may be hard for some schools to see how their instruction is directly related to the items. Because it emphasizes end products of education rather than obvious course content, the STEP is a significant departure from the other major comprehensive batteries. Aside from the nature of the item content, the STEP shares many of the features of other major achievement test batteries, including careful standardization, high reliability, and detailed reporting of norms.

SRA Achievement Series
Science Research Associates, Inc.
Levels: Grades 1–2 (270–300 minutes)
              Grades 2–4 (300 minutes)
              Grades 3–4 (340 minutes)
              Grades 4–9, multilevel (370 minutes)

The battery provides measures of vocabulary, reading comprehension, language, arithmetic, and, in the multilevel edition, study skills, social studies, and science. At the two upper levels, tests are long and provide broad coverage of material relating to core areas of instruction. One noteworthy feature is that on the test for grades 1 to 4, part of the reading comprehension material concerns concepts essential to reading, which is much like the content found on reading-readiness tests. The tests at each age level are somewhat more difficult than those found on other achievement test batteries. Consequently, they will be appealing to schools that have above-average students, but they would serve rather poorly to provide diagnostic information about slow learners. The items were apparently very carefully constructed. Reliabilities of individual tests are good. Because of the generally high correlations between subtests, most of the information from the test is given in one total score. The manuals for the tests are very clear and detailed.

Stanford Achievement Tests, 1964 revision
Harcourt Brace Jovanovich, Inc.
Levels: Primary I, grades 1.5–2.5 (160 minutes)
         Primary II, grades 2.5–3.9 (235 minutes)
         Intermediate I, grades 4–5.5 (230–300 minutes)
         Intermediate II, grades 5.5–6.9 (219–303 minutes)
         Advanced, grades 7–9.9 (201–287 minutes)

In terms of content and item type, this is one of the more conservative achievement batteries. At all levels, spelling and arithmetic are tested, and the verbal skills are emphasized in sections on paragraph meaning, word study skills, and language. For the younger pupils there is considerable attention to phonics; for older pupils there are many items devoted to concepts taught in general science, social studies, and advanced arithmetic classes. Above grade 3 the individual tests are available separately and thus may be used by teachers as content-area tests. All the tests are well constructed, and they have been improved during a series of revisions. The test manual is very good. Some may feel that the tests for content areas are too heavily oriented toward simple factual information. A companion battery of tests is available at the high school level.

Tests of Academic Progress (TAP)
Houghton Mifflin Company
Levels: Grades 9–12 (multilevel)
Testing time: 6 hours (three half-day sessions)

TAP provides tests in six basic areas of instruction: social studies, composition, science, reading, mathematics, and literature. The manuals for administering, scoring, and interpreting the test results are especially detailed and complete. Over-all, TAP is a flexible, well-constructed, carefully normed battery of tests which should prove useful in many high school testing programs.

SECTION 2: READING TESTS

Durrell-Sullivan Reading Capacity and Achievement Tests
Harcourt Brace Jovanovich, Inc.
Levels: Primary, grades 2.5–4.5 (55–65 minutes)
         Intermediate, grades 3–6 (75–95 minutes)

Five scores are obtained: (1) word meaning, (2) paragraph meaning, (3) spelling, (4) written recall, and (5) total score. A noteworthy feature of the test is that part of the materials are given orally by the teacher, and the remainder is read by the student. This provides information about discrepancies between ability to comprehend oral and written language. In general this is a good test and is useful primarily for measuring over-all achievement in reading, but it also provides some diagnostic clues about difficulties of particular students.

Gates-MacGinitie Reading Tests
The Psychological Corporation
Levels: Grade 1
          Grade 2
          Grade 3
          Grades 4–6
          Grades 7–9
Testing time: 40–50 minutes

This battery of tests for assessing group and individual achievement in reading is a revision of the 1958 Gates Reading Tests. At the levels for grades 1 to 3 the basic test consists of two parts, vocabulary and comprehension. A short supplementary test is also available for grades 2 and 3 to measure speed and accuracy. The basic tests for grades 4 and above measure speed, vocabulary, and comprehension. Split-half and alternate-form reliabilities are reported and are satisfactorily high. The battery is generally well constructed and standardized. Students in the normative sample were also administered the Lorge-Thorndike Intelligence Tests, and tables are provided to aid in interpretation of reading scores relative to intelligence test scores.

Iowa Silent Reading Tests, new edition
Harcourt Brace Jovanovich, Inc.
Levels: Elementary, grades 4–8
          Advanced, grades 9–14
Testing time: 50–60 minutes

At both levels the following scores are obtained: (1) rate of comprehension, (2) directed reading, (3) word meaning, (4) paragraph comprehension, (5) sentence meaning, and (6) location of information. The advanced battery contains a seventh test, poetry comprehension. Although in general the tests are good, they are all speeded; therefore, speed of reading and comprehension are emphasized. The tests would probably give a faulty picture of the performance of a student who reads well but slowly. Otherwise they are well constructed and standardized.

Kelley-Green Reading Comprehension Test
Harcourt Brace Jovanovich, Inc.
Levels: Grades 9–13
Testing time: 65–75 minutes

The test obtains scores for four types of reading skills: (1) selecting the central idea, (2) reading carefully and skimming for details, (3) drawing inferences from what is read, and (4) remembering details. Good norms are provided for high school levels.

Nelson-Denny Reading Test, Revised Edition
Houghton Mifflin Company
Levels: Grades 9–16
          Adults
Testing time: 35–40 minutes

The test provides four scores: (1) vocabulary, (2) paragraph comprehension, (3) reading rate, and (4) total score. A noteworthy feature of the test is that it is easily administered and scored. To provide sufficient ceiling for use with superior students and adults, the administrative procedure is modified by shortening the working time. Percentile and grade-equivalent norms are provided for grades 9 to 16, and special adult norms are available for use with superior students and with adults in efficient-reading classes or in business reading programs. The test is too brief to provide truly diagnostic information about reading difficulties. Its primary use is for a relatively quick appraisal of over-all reading skill.

Primary Reading Profiles
Houghton Mifflin Company
Levels: End of grade 1 to beginning of grade 2
          End of grade 2 to beginning of grade 3
Testing time: 90 minutes

See Chapter 10 for a discussion of this test. Norms were established to be comparable to the norms provided with the Iowa Tests of Basic Skills and the Lorge-Thorndike Intelligence Tests.

Reading Comprehension: Cooperative English Tests, 1960 edition
Educational Testing Service

Levels: Grades 9–12
              Grades 13–14
Testing time: 45 minutes

The test provides scores for (1) vocabulary, (2) speed of comprehension, (3) level of comprehension, and (4) total reading comprehension. Extensive research with this test demonstrates that it is a good predictor of school achievement. One of the best features of the test is that it attempts to measure subtle aspects of reading comprehension that are not measured by some other tests. This is one of the best reading achievement tests for high school students.

SECTION 3: TESTS FOR SPECIAL TOPICS

Content Evaluation Series
Houghton Mifflin Company

This series gathers together a number of independently developed standardized end-of-year tests designed to assess student progress in individual subject areas in junior and senior high school. Each test can be administered during a single class period. The following tests are included in the series:

The Language Arts Tests (Grades 7–9).   The Language Ability Test and the Composition Test both seek to measure achievement in language usage. The Literature Test deals with the student's familiarity with the principal types of literature and with his basic understanding of, and feeling for, poetry, fiction, nonfiction, and drama.

The Mathematics Test (Grades 7–9).   The test measures knowledge of mathematical facts, ability to perform operations, and understanding of basic mathematical principles with emphasis on their applications in a variety of situations.

The Science Tests (Grades 8–9).   Two tests, the Physical Science Test and the Earth Science Test, seek to measure the student's familiarity with the vocabulary of each specific area and his grasp of concepts basic to that area of science.

Modern Geometry Test (Grades 10–12).   Objective test items emphasizing higher-level concepts in high school geometry are presented to assess the student's mastery of the subject.

Modern Economics Test (Grades 10–12).   The test is designed for students enrolled in full-semester courses in economics and covers the national income, monetary and fiscal policy, the price system, and international economics and economic development.

The Office Information and Skills Test (Grade 12).   Four subtests measure knowledge and skills required of clerical employees in most business offices. The tests are (1) the Office Information Questionnaire (filing, communication, clerical routine, machine operation, desirable work habits), (2) the Timed Typewriting Test, (3) the Error Location and Correction Test (proofreading and correction of errors in a letter), and (4) the Transcription Test (transcription of dictation into final typewritten copy).

Cooperative English Tests
Educational Testing Service
Levels: Grades 9–12
              Superior grade 12; college freshmen and sophomores
Testing time: 50 minutes

This is a well-presented, carefully constructed pair of tests for measuring two fundamental areas. The tests are Reading Comprehension and English Expression. The test scores may be interpreted separately or combined to yield a total English score. The Reading Comprehension test has been described above in the section on reading tests. The English Expression test consists of two parts, Effectiveness and Mechanics. Effectiveness tests the ability to recognize and select a word or phrase which precisely conveys the intended meaning of a sentence. Mechanics measures the ability to recognize errors in usage, spelling, punctuation, and capitalization.

Cooperative Mathematics Tests
Educational Testing Service

This series consists of a wide range of tests suitable for use at the junior high or high school level. Most of the tests can be administered in a single class period. The tests in the series are Arithmetic (basic concepts, grades 7 to 9), Structure of the Number System (grades 7 and 8), Algebra I (concepts and skills up to quadratic equations), Algebra II (concepts and skills at the end of a second course in algebra), Algebra III (for use in advanced secondary school or college algebra courses), Geometry (Part I, standard course in Euclidean geometry; Part II, advanced understanding of geometry, proof, and spatial reasoning), Trigonometry (functional and numerical trigonometry), Analytic Geometry, Calculus (Part I, algebraic functions with emphasis on differential calculus; Part II, transcendental functions with emphasis on integral calculus).

Cooperative Science Tests
Educational Testing Service

Five tests are included in this series. Each test can be administered in one or two class periods. The tests are General Science (grades 7 to 9), Advanced General Science (grade 9 and superior grade 8), Biology (grades 10 to 12), Chemistry (grades 10 to 12), and Physics (grades 10 to 12).

Cooperative Social Studies Tests
Educational Testing Service
Testing time: About 40 minutes

The series includes seven tests of social studies topics generally taught in junior high and high schools across the country. The emphasis in each test is upon factual information and concepts generally considered to be basic to the specific area of social studies. The tests in the series are American History (grades 7 and 8; emphasis on the period from 1865 to the present), Problems of Democracy (grades 10 to 12; items concerning political questions, foreign policy issues, urban problems, economic affairs), American Government (grades 10 to 12; United States Constitution and the federal government), Modern European History (grades 10 to 12; covers the period from 1450 to the present), and World History (grades 10 to 12; emphasizes European history and the period since 1800).

Diagnostic Tests in English Composition
The Bobbs-Merrill Company, Inc.
Levels: Grades 7–12
Testing time: About 25 minutes for each test

The four subtests deal with common mistakes in English composition frequently made by students. Scores are obtained for performance in capitalization, punctuation, grammar, and sentence structure. Four alternate forms are available for each subtest, thus allowing the teacher to use the diagnostic tests more than once with the same class, e.g., as a pretest prior to reviewing grammar rules and again later as a posttest after instruction. A special record sheet is provided which permits the teacher to determine quickly the specific rules on which the class as a whole or individual students are having difficulty.

Diagnostic Tests and Self-helps in Arithmetic
California Test Bureau
Levels: Grades 3–12

This series consists of four screening tests and twenty-three diagnostic tests and self-help exercises. The screening tests concern whole numbers, fractions, decimals, and arithmetic operations, respectively. They are designed to identify weaknesses in the student's ability to perform basic arithmetic processes. When these weaknesses have been identified, the students are to be administered the diagnostic tests that follow. Each of the diagnostic tests is accompanied by a self-help exercise to aid the student in strengthening his skills and understanding his errors. The tests may be used individually or with groups. They may be administered at the beginning of the year to aid the teacher in planning review work, during the year when individuals seem to be having difficulty, or as practice exercises for improving skills. A limitation of the tests is that they do not incorporate the modern math approach to teaching arithmetic and thus may not be appropriate for use in many schools, particularly in the lower grades.

MLA-Cooperative Foreign Language Tests
Educational Testing Service
Levels: M—first two years of language study in high school or first two
                semesters of language study in college
              L—third and fourth years of language study in high school or
                third and fourth semesters of language in college
Testing time: 105–145 minutes

The series includes tests of competence in five languages—French, German, Italian, Russian, and Spanish. Separate measures are provided of skills in listening, speaking, reading, and writing. The listening and speaking tests involve use of a tape recording, thus providing more standardized testing conditions. Developed in conjunction with the Modern Language Association of America, the current edition of the tests was prepared after a number of years of experience with earlier forms.

SECTION 4: TESTS OF FIRST-GRADE READINESS

Metropolitan Readiness Tests
Harcourt Brace Jovanovich, Inc.
Level: Beginning first graders
Testing time: 60 minutes (three sessions)

Tests which measure readiness for first-grade instruction have much in common with intelligence tests for the primary grades, and the Metropolitan Readiness Tests are no exception. Correlation with scores on the Pintner-Cunningham Primary Tests is .76. The authors cite a number of characteristics thought to be important for success in first grade, e.g., comprehension and use of oral language, visual perception and discrimination, auditory discrimination, richness of verbal concepts, knowledge of numerical and quantitative relationships, and sensorimotor abilities of the kind required in handwriting. The six subtests are designed to measure these characteristics and to yield a total score indicative of the pupil's over-all level of readiness for coping with first-grade work. A seventh, optional subtest is provided, in which the child is instructed merely to draw a picture of a man. The drawing is judged according to specific criteria and is placed into a category on the basis of the degree of perceptual development and motor control exhibited. These tests appear to be very carefully constructed. Reliability coefficients are in the .90s. Scores have been found to be predictive of end-of-year scores on the Stanford Achievement Tests. The Metropolitan Readiness Tests should provide the first-grade teacher with some very useful information about the range of mental maturity in his class and may point up particular learning problems of individual pupils.

Murphy-Durrell Reading Readiness Analysis
Harcourt Brace Jovanovich, Inc.
Level: Beginning first grade
Testing time: Approximately 90 minutes (two sessions)

The Murphy-Durrell test is an outgrowth of an earlier edition and has been refined as the result of more than a decade of research. The primary emphasis is on analysis of a pupil's current stage of development in the abilities which must be mastered in learning to read. Scores are obtained on three subtests and may be combined into a total reading-readiness score. The Phonemes Test tests the ability to identify sounds in spoken words after brief instruction. The Letter Names Test measures the pupil's familiarity with capital and lowercase letters. A rather unique feature is the Learning Rate Test, which measures the number of printed words a child can recognize one hour following standardized formal instruction. Unfortunately, the value of this last subtest has not been established. Its correlation with later reading achievement level is lowest of any of the scores, and it appears to be measuring something quite different from the other two subtests. Split-half reliabilities are in the .90s; however, it would be desirable to have test-retest reliability coefficients because of the difficulties involved in maintaining the attention of children at this age and because of the high degree of dependence on the teacher's ability to enunciate clearly on the Phonemes Test. Not enough validity data are reported to establish clearly the predictive usefulness of the Murphy-Durrell analysis.

SECTION 5: TESTS TO MEASURE SCHOLASTIC APTITUDE

Academic Promise Tests (APT)
The Psychological Corporation
Levels: Grades 6–9
Testing time: Two hours

The APT are, in part, an outgrowth of the Differential Aptitude Tests (see Chapter 11). The objective of the battery is to provide more information than typically is available from scholastic aptitude or mental-maturity tests, but without attempting to measure all the diverse areas tested with the DAT. The four tests and their particular emphases are verbal (analogies), numerical (quantitative concepts), abstract reasoning (figure classification), and language usage (grammar, spelling, and punctuation). A score for each test and three scores resulting from combining subtest scores are obtained. Alternate-form reliability coefficients range from .81 to .90 for the individual tests and from .88 to .94 for the combined scores. Extensive and detailed validity data are presented with respect to prediction of course grades and scores on a number of achievement tests. In sum, the APT appear to be a carefully constructed and well-researched battery of tests which should be useful in educational guidance, sectioning, and placement at the junior high school level.

The American College Testing Program Examination (ACT)
American College Testing Program
Levels: Grade 12 and junior college students preparing to transfer to
               four-year colleges
Testing time: 210 minutes

The ACT was launched in 1959 and has served as a healthy competitor to the SAT (discussed below) for use in predicting scholastic achievement at the college level. The test is administered on four Saturdays during the year (in February, April, June, and November) at participating colleges and centers established by the publisher. The test renders five scores: English usage, mathematics usage, social studies reading, natural sciences reading, and a composite score. Individual students serve as the customers of the ACT program, and hence scores are sent directly to them as well as to their high schools. The reporting service of the ACT also sends the individual's scores to three colleges which he designates at the time of application. A special feature of the reporting service is that colleges which participate in the research services of the American College Testing Program also receive predicted grade-point averages on each prospective student for each subject area tested and over-all. This prediction service is efficient and has proved extremely valuable to colleges.

College Entrance Examination Board Scholastic Aptitude Test (SAT)
Educational Testing Service
Level: Candidates for college entrance
Testing time: 210 minutes

The SAT has come to be one of the more familiar and relied-upon tests used by colleges in selecting the most promising students from among all those who apply for admission. It continues to be the leading test for this purpose nationally, although the ACT may be used more in parts of the South and the Middle West. The SAT is administered one to five times annually (January, March, May, July, December) at centers established by the publisher. The test measures general verbal and mathematical comprehension. The verbal score is based upon antonyms, sentence completion, analogies, and reading comprehension items. The mathematical score involves word problems and data-sufficiency items. The test is very carefully constructed and has many alternative forms. Studies have found that test-score gains from coaching are negligible, although two administrations effect a gain of approximately twenty points on both sections. A wealth of normative data and detailed information concerning the test is available to aid the test user. The scoring and reporting service associated with the admissions program of the CEEB is both prompt and reliable. Scores are reported to the student's high school and to three colleges or universities of his choice. He may have results forwarded to additional institutions for a small fee. A list of the candidates who select an institution as first, second, or third choice at each national test administration is sent immediately to the institution. Other features with regard to the SAT include forms for use by the handicapped and the establishment of overseas administration centers.

Concept Mastery Test
The Psychological Corporation
Levels: Grades 15–16
               Graduate students and applicants for executive and research
               positions
Testing time: 45 minutes

This test is a by-product of Terman's extensive studies of gifted children and of those same children as adults. It is a high-level verbal test for adults and is intended to give an indication of a person's ability to deal with abstract concepts. Two types of items are employed: (1) synonym-antonym items and (2) analogies. The test has shown good validity for predicting success in university courses, but more research is needed before it can be widely used with advanced students and for predicting criteria of job success. However, it is excellent for its initial purpose of measuring at a high level and over a wide range the ability to understand verbal concepts and abstractions.

Cooperative School and College Ability Tests (SCAT)
Educational Testing Service, Cooperative Test Division
Levels: Grades 4–6
               Grades 6–8
               Grades 8–10
               Grades 10–12
               Grades 12–14
               Grades 15–16
Testing time: 95 minutes

At all levels the test yields three scores: (1) verbal, (2) quantitative, and (3) total. Although the total score provides most of the information obtainable from the test, if students score very differently on the verbal and quantitative portions, this indicates areas of unevenness in educational development. Generally the test is well constructed and standardized. The manual provides clear instructions for administering and interpreting the test. The major fault that some may find with the test is that it strongly emphasizes school-learned material rather than more abstract aspects of intelligence.

Graduate Record Examinations Aptitude Test (GRE)
Educational Testing Service

Levels: Grades 16–17
Testing time: 170 minutes

The Graduate Record Examinations have come to be used widely by colleges and universities for selecting candidates for admission to graduate school. In addition to this more obvious use, they are employed for such things as evaluating applicants for scholarships and fellowships and as a part of comprehensive examinations for undergraduate degrees. The GRE consists of (1) an aptitude test yielding verbal and quantitative scores, (2) advanced tests for twenty specialized curriculum areas, and (3) area tests covering social science, natural science, and the humanities.

There are two programs for administering the GRE: the National Program for Graduate School Selection and the Institutional Testing Program. The national program is administered five times annually (November, January, March, April, and July) at centers established by the publisher. It includes the aptitude test and one of the advanced tests selected by the candidate according to the individual college requirement. Under the institutional program, the colleges and graduate schools themselves may administer the GRE at any time except on dates when the national program is scheduled. The institutional program provides not only the aptitude and advanced tests but also the area tests, which measure general understanding of basic concepts and their application rather than the recall of specific facts.

The tests have been revised regularly and appear to be well constructed and standardized. They can be recommended in terms of normative data, satisfactory reliability, and generally good validity; but, as with all tests of higher-level scholastic aptitude, local studies of the predictive validity of the GRE are highly recommended.

Miller Analogies Test
The Psychological Corporation
Level: Candidates for graduate school
Testing time: 55 minutes

The Miller Analogies Test is a well-constructed, convenient, single-score test of high-level verbal ability. It has been used extensively for many years and subjected to a considerable amount of research. The evidence indicates that the test measures abilities which are related to general intellectual performance, and thus it has been found useful in selecting people for high-level business positions as well as in predicting graduate school grades.

The test is restricted in its distribution to prevent coaching and to protect its security, and it is administered only at licensed centers. Scoring and reporting are handled by the local center. At the time of testing, the examinee may request to have his scores reported to three institutions or companies. Scores are released to the individual as well. The brief yet comprehensive manual includes a discussion of factors which cause the test to be more effective in some situations than in others. Norms are given for eighteen academic and five industrial groups.

SECTION 6: GROUP TESTS OF GENERAL INTELLIGENCE

California Test of Mental Maturity, 1963 revision
California Test Bureau
Levels: Kindergarten to entering grade 1
          Grades 1–3
          Grades 4–6
          Grades 7–9
          Grades 9–12
          Grades 12–16
          Adults
Testing time: 58–93 minutes

The chief claim for validity of the CTMM is that the original test was designed to correlate with the Stanford-Binet. The test provides three main scores (language total, nonlanguage total, and over-all total) and scores for each of five subtests (logical reasoning, spatial relationship, numerical reasoning, verbal concepts, and memory). This is an excellent test of general intelligence and has real value for comparing an individual's verbal and nonverbal abilities. However, caution should be exercised in using scores on the individual subtests until more data are available on their validity for educational selection, prediction, and guidance at each of the age and grade levels.

Chicago Nonverbal Examination
The Psychological Corporation
Levels: Age six to adult
Testing time: 40 minutes

The test consists entirely of pictorial and symbolic material that requires little, if any, language usage. It can be administered either with oral instruction or, for those who have a severe language deficit, entirely by pantomime. Separate norms are provided for both types of administration. Although tests of this type are not the best measures of general intelligence for most purposes, they have an important place with specific types of students. They are particularly useful with children who have a severe language handicap, such as the deaf and children who have recently emigrated from other countries. Also, nonlanguage tests of this type are useful with children in this country who have led culturally impoverished lives.

Cognitive Abilities Test (CAT)
Houghton Mifflin Company
Levels: Kindergarten to grade 1
          Grades 2–3
Testing time: Approximately 60 minutes (four sessions)

The CAT, published in 1968, is the primary level of the Lorge-Thorndike Intelligence Tests (see Chapter 12). It is a nonreading battery, administered orally to groups of fifteen or fewer students at a time. The four subtests designed to measure the development of "generalized thinking skills" in young children are oral vocabulary, relational concepts (size, position, quantity), multimental (categorizing and classifying objects), and quantitative concepts. The deviation IQs and other scores are linked normatively with the Lorge-Thorndike series to provide comparable scores for a pupil over different points in time. Split-half reliabilities are all around .90; however, validity data are lacking. It does appear, though, that the CAT can be used reliably to differentiate broad levels of cognitive development in kindergarten and the primary grades.

Henmon-Nelson Tests of Mental Ability, revised edition
Houghton Mifflin Company
Levels: Grades 3–6
          Grades 6–9
          Grades 9–12
          Grades 13–17
Testing time: 35–45 minutes

The test provides only one total score for grades 3 to 12 but three scores (quantitative, verbal, and total) for grades 13 to 17. Although it is a short test, it correlates well with longer tests of general intelligence and with achievement tests. The test is concerned mainly with verbal ability (as most tests of general intelligence are). Good norms are available for the test, and test reliabilities are high. The test provides a reasonably good, quick estimate of scholastic aptitude.

Kuhlman-Anderson Intelligence Tests, 7th edition
Personnel Press, Inc.
Levels: Kindergarten
          Grade 1
          Grade 2
          Grades 3–4
          Grades 4–5
          Grades 5–7
          Grades 7–9
          Grades 9–12
Testing time: 25–60 minutes

The seventh edition of this test involves primarily a revision of the test used at grades 4 to 7. At all levels the test places a strong emphasis on verbal comprehension. A single IQ is obtained from numerous separate subtests. At the fourth-grade level and above, scores are also given for verbal and quantitative performance. The two portions correlate so highly that little information can be obtained from comparing scores on the two parts. At all levels the test provides a good, rapid estimate of scholastic aptitude.

Otis-Lennon Mental Ability Test
Harcourt Brace Jovanovich, Inc.
Levels: Kindergarten, beginning grade 1 (30–35 minutes)
          Grades 1.5–3 (55–60 minutes)
          Grades 4–6 (45–50 minutes)
          Grades 7–9 (45–50 minutes)
          Grades 10–12 (45–50 minutes)

This test is a revision of the Otis Quick-scoring Ability Tests, one of the pioneering group tests of intelligence, itself an outgrowth of the Army Alpha Examination used in classifying World War I recruits. The Otis-Lennon closely resembles the earlier forms of the test in stressing verbal comprehension. Pictorial items are used exclusively for levels below grade 4. A single total-score IQ is obtained. Alternate-form reliability coefficients range from .81 for age five to .94 for age fourteen, with a median of .92. Validity data for the Otis-Lennon appear in the Technical Handbook. The Manual for Administration provides an instructive discussion of interpretation of the test results. Norms are provided for deviation IQs, percentiles, and mental ages.

Pintner General Ability Tests, Nonlanguage Series
Harcourt Brace Jovanovich, Inc.

Levels: Grades 4–9
Testing time: 50–60 minutes

Like other nonlanguage tests, this one requires no reading and no spoken or written language. The test is primarily useful for children with a severe language handicap.

Pintner General Ability Tests, Verbal Series
Harcourt Brace Jovanovich, Inc.
Levels: Primary, kindergarten to grade 2 (25 minutes)
Elementary, grades 2–4 (45 minutes)
Intermediate, grades 4–8 (45 minutes)
Advanced, grades 9–12 and above (55 minutes)

At all levels this test has many points in common with other group measures of general intelligence, including a very heavy emphasis on verbal ability. Generally the test is well constructed and standardized.

Progressive Matrices
H. K. Lewis and Co., Ltd. (American distributor: The Psychological Corporation)
Levels: Standard Progressive Matrices, age six and over (60 minutes)
Coloured Progressive Matrices, ages seven to eleven and mental patients and the elderly (30 minutes)
Advanced Progressive Matrices, age eleven and over (50 minutes)

These tests rely solely on perceptual tasks to measure intellectual functioning. The tasks or matrices consist of designs which require completion. The subject chooses his answer from among multiple-choice options. An answer which fits may (1) complete a pattern, (2) complete an analogy, (3) systematically alter a pattern, (4) introduce systematic permutations, or (5) systematically resolve figures into parts. The advanced test consists of two sets, the first of which may be used alone as a rough screening device or as a practice set. Set 2 may be used without a time limit as a "test of intellectual capacity" or with a time limit as a "test of intellectual efficiency." Although much more research is needed before the matrices should be regarded as precise measures of intelligence, they can be quite helpful as screening devices for groups where estimates of levels of intelligence need to be determined. Since the tests are easy to administer and no verbal responses are required, they should be particularly useful with individuals who have communications disorders or handicaps, such as the deaf or cerebral-palsied.

SRA Tests of Educational Ability, 1962 edition
Science Research Associates, Inc.
Levels: Grades 4–6 (52 minutes)
          Grades 6–9 (67 minutes)
          Grades 9–12 (45 minutes)

The test attempts to measure three different aspects of scholastic aptitude: (1) language, (2) reasoning, and (3) quantitative. However, not
enough items are included to provide reliable measures of these three
aspects, and it is much better to interpret only a total score for the three
subtests. As an over-all measure of general intelligence, the test should
take its place with other good measures of that kind.

Terman-McNemar Test of Mental Ability
Harcourt Brace Jovanovich, Inc.
Levels: Grades 7–13
Testing time: 40–45 minutes

This test has many of the characteristics of other verbal tests of intelligence. It is concerned mainly with verbal comprehension. The test was
very carefully designed and constructed.

SECTION 7: TESTS FOR ASSESSING CREATIVITY AND REASONING

Although the tests described in this section are commercially available
and hold promise for tapping abilities not measured by tests of intelligence or scholastic aptitude, they should still be considered largely experimental. More research, especially with regard to predictive validity,
is needed before they should be used widely in applied settings. For the
present, these tests should be confined primarily to research programs
and to limited roles in educational evaluation and counseling.

Remote Associates Test (RAT)
Houghton Mifflin Company
Levels: Grades 9–12
          College students and adults
Testing time: 40 minutes

The authors of the RAT define the creative process as one of "seeing
relationships between seemingly mutually remote ideas and forming them
into new combinations which are either useful or meet specified criteria."

The test items require the examinee to form such new combinations with items of the following form: "rat, blue, cottage." The task is to supply a fourth word which could serve as a specific kind of associative link between the three stimulus words. The answer in this example would be "cheese." In taking an "associative" approach to the measurement of creativity, the RAT provides an interesting contrast to those tests which emphasize divergent production (see Chapter 14). Validity studies have been conducted in industrial research and development laboratories, graduate schools, and college classrooms; however, the data must be considered only suggestive at this stage. Alternate-form reliability is reported to be about .81. Norms are available only for the high school level.

Ship Destination Test
Sheridan Psychological Services
Levels: Grade 9 and over
Testing time: 20 minutes

This imaginative test is described to the subject in terms of conditions affecting a ship in traveling from one point to another. He is required to perform a series of easy additions and subtractions on each item. The numbers to be added or subtracted are determined by a set of rules. The rules are different for each set of three items and grow progressively more complex. Studies have shown that this test is a good measure of general reasoning ability. The manual is well constructed and provides a substantial amount of relevant data to aid in using the test.

Southern California Tests of Divergent Production
Sheridan Psychological Services
Levels: Vary with the individual test, but generally ranging from grades
          6 to 16 and adults
Testing time: 10–30 minutes, depending on the individual test

These tests resulted from the research program carried on for many years by Guilford and his associates on the structure of the intellect. These intriguing tests are deceptively simple but appear to have good construct validity. Other such tests in this series are still being developed and may be published over the coming years. A listing of the tests follows:

Alternate Uses.   Involves listing possible uses for a specified object, other than its common use.

Christensen-Guilford Fluency Tests.   A battery measuring four types of verbal fluency (word, ideational, associational, and expressional).

Consequences.   Items requiring the subject to list what the results might be if some unusual situation came to pass; scored in terms of ideational fluency and originality.

Decorations.   Involves outline drawings of common objects to be decorated with as many different designs as possible and measures the "ability to add meaningful details."

Making Objects.   Measures "figural expressional fluency" by having the subject draw specified objects using only a set of given figures.

Match Problems.   Measures "originality in dealing with concrete visual material" and involves having a subject remove a certain number of matchsticks, leaving a specified number of squares or triangles.

Possible Jobs.   Requires the subject to list possible jobs symbolized by a given object and measures the "ability to suggest alternative deductions."

Sketches.   Requires the subject to make as many different sketches as possible by elaborating on each of a set of identical figures.

Torrance Tests of Creative Thinking
Personnel Press, Inc.
Levels: Kindergarten through graduate school

These tests are divided into two batteries: (1) a verbal battery consisting of seven tasks and (2) a pictorial battery consisting of three tasks. In the verbal battery, the subject performs such activities as telling all the things that would happen if a certain improbable situation were true, making a list of unusual uses for a common object, and improving a given toy so that children will have more fun playing with it. In the pictorial battery, the activities involve drawing pictures using various shapes and lines provided by the examiner as starting points. Unusual ideas are stressed rather than artistic quality. Detailed scoring guides are provided in the manual. Scores are expressed in terms of factors labeled "fluency," "originality," and "elaboration."

Watson-Glaser Critical Thinking Appraisal, 1963 revision (with 1952 norms)
Harcourt Brace Jovanovich, Inc.
Levels: Grades 9–16 and adults
Testing time: 50–60 minutes

Five subtests measure different aspects of critical thinking: (1) drawing inferences, (2) recognizing assumptions, (3) drawing appropriate deductions, (4) interpreting data, and (5) evaluating arguments. Some items employ content which is abstract and noncontroversial, while others involve issues of a controversial nature which typically provoke emotional and prejudiced responses from many individuals. Those interested in studying the effect of emotion or prejudice on critical thinking are advised in the manual to select for themselves the items which are likely to be pertinent to their own group. While this test can be useful for such things as selection in school and industry and evaluation of the effectiveness of instruction, the scores should be used cautiously as the test has not been standardized thoroughly enough to permit their use in any absolute way.

SECTION 8: INTEREST INVENTORIES

Brainard Occupational Preference Inventory
The Psychological Corporation
Levels: Grades 8–12
Testing time: 30 minutes

Covered in the inventory are six broad occupational fields: (1) commercial, (2) mechanical, (3) professional, (4) esthetic, (5) scientific, and (6) personal service (for girls) or agriculture (for boys). The inventory is simple to administer and score. Although designed primarily for use with high school students, it may also be used with adults who have limited educational and vocational backgrounds. At the present time, no evidence on the validity is available.

Kuder General Interest Survey
Science Research Associates, Inc.
Levels: Grades 6–12
Testing time: 30–40 minutes

Developed as a revision and downward extension of the Kuder Preference Record—Vocational, the General Interest Survey requires only a sixth-grade reading vocabulary and thus is useful at the junior high school level. Scores are obtained for ten rather general areas: outdoor, mechanical, computational, scientific, persuasive, artistic, literary, musical, social service, and clerical. Separate profiles are used to plot scores for grades 6 to 8 and grades 9 to 12. Research has shown that scores obtained on the General Interest Survey correlate very highly with scores on the Kuder Vocational, which suggests that the two might be used interchangeably.

Kuder Preference Record—Occupational
Science Research Associates, Inc.
Levels: Grades 11–16
          Adults
Testing time: 30–40 minutes

This is one of three interest inventories by Kuder. All three share the same type of test item and test format. The purpose of this inventory is to provide scores for fifty specific occupations. The average reliability of the occupational scores is only about .60, which is too low for use in counseling students. The instrument needs to be further standardized and validated for use in high school counseling programs.

Kuder Preference Record—Personal
Science Research Associates, Inc.
Levels: Grades 9–16
          Adults
Testing time: 40–45 minutes

The purpose of this interest inventory is to measure five personal characteristics that are potentially important for occupational choice: (1) being an active participant in group activities, (2) being in familiar and stable situations, (3) dealing with abstract ideas, (4) avoiding conflict, and (5) leading and directing others. Potentially, this inventory could serve as a supplement to the occupational and vocational forms, principally the latter. There has been neither enough research evidence about the instrument nor enough practical experience with it to enable us to know how helpful it will be in high school counseling.

Kuder Preference Record—Vocational
Science Research Associates, Inc.
Levels: Grades 9–16
          Adults
Testing time: 40–50 minutes

See discussion in Chapter 15. For many years this has been one of the most widely used interest inventories in high school and college counseling programs. In contrast to the occupational form, this form provides scores in nine broad vocational areas rather than for many separate occupations. A masculinity-femininity score is also obtained. The instrument is well designed and standardized. The ten scales each have moderately high reliability. Although not enough evidence is available about validity, the instrument is judged to be useful by many high school and college counselors.

Strong Vocational Interest Blank for Men, revised
Consulting Psychologist's Press
Levels: Age seventeen and over
Testing time: 30–60 minutes

See discussion in Chapter 15. This is by far the most widely used interest inventory. It provides scores for numerous separate occupations as well as a number of global interest scores. Considerable research has been done with the inventory. Results show that most of the occupational scores are sufficiently reliable, that scores are predictive of occupations that students enter some years after taking the test, and that some scales differentiate between successful and unsuccessful people in occupations. The instrument is very useful in counseling high school students and college students about future schooling and careers.

Strong Vocational Interest Blank for Women, revised
Consulting Psychologist's Press
Levels: Age seventeen and older
Testing time: 30–60 minutes

This inventory for women is very similar to the form for men. It provides scores on thirty occupations. Not nearly as much research has been done with this form as with the form for men. Because of the similar methods used in constructing both instruments, it is expected that the form for women will prove to be useful in high school and college counseling.

SECTION 9: PERSONALITY AND ADJUSTMENT INVENTORIES

Bell Adjustment Inventory
Consulting Psychologist's Press
Levels: Grades 7–16
            Adults
Testing time: 35 minutes

The student form provides scores in six areas of adjustment; (1) home, (2) health, (3) submissiveness, (4) emotionality, (5) hostility, and (6) masculinity-femininity. The adult form is scored for five areas: (1) home, (2) health, (3) social, (4) emotional, and (5) occupational. This inventory suffers from all the difficulties that others do. It is dependent almost entirely on the individual's awareness of his personal problems and his willingness to relate them. This inventory is useful primarily for the rough screening of students who may need help with personal problems. It has been used for many years in conjunction with high school counseling programs.

California Test of Personality, 1953 revision
California Test Bureau
Levels: Kindergarten to grade 3
          Grades 4–8
          Grades 7–10
          Grades 9–16
          Adults
Testing time: 60 minutes

This is one of the few inventories that attempts to measure personality characteristics of young children. Scores are provided with respect to twelve personality characteristics, e.g., school relations, sense of personal worth, and withdrawing tendencies. Also available is a total adjustment score and two subtotal scores relating, respectively, to social and personal adjustment. Scores on the individual scales are far too unreliable for use. Consequently, only the total adjustment scores and the two subtotal scores should be used. Although there are some legitimate uses of personality inventories, there are so many problems in developing valid measures, and so much still is unknown about the meaning of responses to personality inventories with young children that this and other inventories should be used with extreme caution. Inventories for young children should be administered and interpreted only by well-trained counselors.

Gordon Personal Profile
Harcourt Brace Jovanovich, Inc.
Levels: Grades 9–16
          Adults
Testing time: 15–20 minutes

The inventory provides five scores: (1) ascendancy, (2) responsibility, (3) emotional stability, (4) sociability, and (5) total adjustment score. Not enough research evidence and practical experience are available to enable us to say how useful the inventory will be.

Guilford-Zimmerman Temperament Survey
Sheridan Psychological Services
Levels: Grades 9–16
                Adults
Testing time: 50 minutes

This inventory arose from extensive factor-analytic investigations of items typically appearing on personality inventories. Scores are provided for ten personality factors. Although generally this is a well-constructed instrument, it may provide more information than can be interpreted by counselors. Research evidence still is lacking regarding its validity. This inventory may be useful in the hands of highly trained and experienced counselors but would probably prove difficult for less well-trained and experienced counselors to use.

Heston Personal Adjustment Inventory
Harcourt Brace Jovanovich, Inc.
Levels: Grades 9–16
                Adults
Testing time: 40–55 minutes

The inventory provides six scores: (1) analytical thinking, (2) sociability, (3) home adjustment, (4) emotional stability, (5) confidence, and (6) personal relations. It was apparently well constructed and standardized.

Minnesota Multiphasic Personality Inventory (MMPI)
The Psychological Corporation
Levels: Age sixteen and over
Testing time: 30–90 minutes

See discussion in Chapter 16. The purpose of the inventory is to detect tendencies toward nine different forms of mental illness. The instrument is widely used by clinical psychologists and school psychologists. Considerable professional training and experience are required to interpret the results. Consequently, it is not wise to employ this inventory unless highly trained personnel are available. A new group form is available which permits all fourteen of the regular scores to be obtained from the first 399 items; items used for research only are grouped as numbers 400 to 566.

Mooney Problem Checklist, 1950 revision
The Psychological Corporation
Levels: Grades 7–9
        Grades 9–12
        Grades 13–16
        Adults
Testing time: 30–50 minutes

This is an old and very sensible instrument. Rather than purporting to be a test, in the formal sense of the word, it is intended to be used as a screening device for students with personal problems typical of those which bother some students. The items were obtained from written statements of problems by over four thousand students and from other sources. The problems concern social relations, home adjustment, health, financial difficulties, sexual problems, religious difficulties, and others. In using the checklist, it is as important to study the particular kinds of problems indicated as it is to observe the number of problems checked. Wisely used, this checklist (and the two to be described next) have an important place in school counseling programs.

STS Junior Inventory
Scholastic Testing Service, Inc.
Levels: Grades 4–8
Testing time: about 45 minutes

The inventory is similar in item content to the Mooney Problem Checklist. Problems are sampled from four areas: (1) "about myself," (2) "about me and my school," (3) "getting along with others," and (4) "things in general." The good things said about the Mooney inventory also apply to this one. It probably is the best adjustment inventory available for students in elementary school.

STS Youth Inventory
Scholastic Testing Service, Inc.
Levels: Grades 7–12
Testing time: about 35 minutes

This is an extension of the Junior Inventory for older students. What was said about the Junior Inventory holds with equal force in regard to this form.

REFERENCES

Allport, G. W., and Allport, F. H. *The A-S Reaction Study: Revised manual.* Boston: Houghton Mifflin, 1939.

American Educational Research Association and National Council on Measurements Used in Education, Committee on Test Standards. *Technical recommendations for achievement tests.* Washington: National Education Association, 1955.

American Psychological Association. *Technical recommendations for psychological tests and diagnostic techniques.* Washington: American Psychological Association, 1954. (Also in *Psychol. Bull.,* 1954, **51,** No. 2, Part 2.)

Anastasi, A. *Psychological testing.* (3rd ed.) New York: Macmillan, 1968.

Andrew, D. M., Patterson, D. G., and Longstaff, H. P. *Minnesota Clerical Test: Manual.* New York: Psychological Corporation, 1946.

Bayley, N. The California First-year Mental Scale. *Univ. of Calif. Syllabus Serv.,* 1933, No. 243.

Bayley, N. A new look at the curve of intelligence. In A. Anastasi (Ed.), *Testing problems in perspective.* Washington: American Council on Education, 1966.

Bayley, N. *Bayley Scales of Infant Development.* New York: Psychological Corporation, 1968.

Bean, K. L. *Construction of educational and personnel tests.* New York: McGraw-Hill, 1953.

Beck, S. J. *Rorschach's test.* New York: Grune & Stratton, 1945, 1949, 1952, 3 vols.

Beckman, A. S. Minimum intelligence levels for several occupations. *Personnel J.,* 1930, **9,** 309–313.

Bellak, L., and Bellak, S. S. *Children's Apperception Test.* New York: C. P. S. Company, 1955.

Bennett, G. K. *Hand-tool Dexterity Test: Manual.* New York: Psychological Corporation, 1947.

Bennett, G. K. *Bennett Mechanical Comprehension Test, Form AA: Manual.* New York: Psychological Corporation, 1948.

Bennett, G. K., Seashore, H. G., and Wesman, A. G. *Differential Aptitude Tests: Manual.* (4th ed.) New York: Psychological Corporation, 1966.

Binet, A., and Simon, T. Méthodes nouvelles pour le dianostic du niveau intellectuel des anormaux. *Année Psychol.,* 1905, **11,** 191–244.

Bisbee, F. V. *Bisbee Junior and Senior Shorthand Tests.* Bloomington, Ill.: Public School, 1934. (Now Bobbs-Merrill.)

Blommers, P., and Lindquist, E. F. *Elementary statistical methods in psychology and education.* Boston: Houghton Mifflin, 1960.

Bloom, B. S. (Ed.) *Taxonomy of educational objectives. Handbook I: Cognitive domain.* New York: Longmans, 1956.

Bogardus, E. A social distance scale. *Sociol. Soc. Res.,* 1933, **17,** 265–271.

Bond, E. A. Tenth grade abilities and achievements. *Teachers Coll. Contrib. Educ.,* 1940, No. 813.

Bonsall, M., Meyers, C. E., and Thorpe, L. P. *What I Like to Do: Examiner manual.* Chicago: Science Research, 1954.

Buros, O. K. *Tests in print.* Highland Park, N.J.: Gryphon Press, 1961.

Buros, O. K. *The sixth mental measurements yearbook.* Highland Park, N.J.: Gryphon Press, 1965. (First yearbook, 1938; second, 1940; third, 1949; fourth, 1953; fifth, 1959.)

Buswell, G. T., and John, L. *Diagnostic Test for Fundamental Processes in Arithmetic: Manual of directions.* Indianapolis: Public School, 1925. (Now Bobbs-Merrill.)

Caldwell, O. W., and Courtis, S. A. *Then & now in education: 1845–1923.* Yonkers, N.Y.: World, 1924.

Cattell, P. *The measurement of intelligence of infants and young children.* New York: Psychological Corporation, 1947.

Coffman, W. E., and Kurfman, D. A. A comparison of two methods of reading essay examinations. *Am. Educ. Res. J.,* 1968, **5,** 99–107.

Conrad, H. S., and Jones, H. E. A second study of familial resemblance in intelligence: Environmental and genetic implications of parent-child and sibling correlations in the total sample. *39th Yearb., Nat. Soc. Stud. Educ.,* 1940, Part 2, 97–141.

Crawford, J. E., and Crawford, D. M. *Small Parts Dexterity Test: Manual.* (Rev. ed.) New York: Psychological Corporation, 1956.

Cronbach, L. J. *Essentials of psychological testing.* (3rd ed.) New York: Harper & Row, 1970.

Crutchfield, R. D. Creative thinking in children: Its teaching and testing. In *Intelligence: Perspectives 1965.* New York: Harcourt, Brace & World, 1966, pp. 33–64.

Cureton, E. E. Validity. In E. F. Lindquist (Ed.), *Educational measurement.* Washington: American Council on Education, 1951.

Davis, H. (Ed.) *Hearing and deafness.* New York: Murray Hill Books, 1947.

Diederich, P. G. Factors in the judgment of writing ability. *Educ. Testing Serv. Res. Bull. 61–65.* Princeton, N.J.: Educational Testing Service, 1961.

Drake, R. M. *Musical Memory Test: Manual.* Bloomington, Ill.: Public School, 1934. (Now distributed by Science Research.)

DuBois, P. H. A test-dominated society: China, 1115 B.C.–1905 A.D. *Proc. 1964 Invitational Conf. on Testing Problems.* Princeton, N.J.: Educational Testing Service, 1965, pp. 3–11.

Durost, W. N. (Ed.) *Metropolitan Achievement Tests.* New York: Harcourt, Brace & World, 1960.

Ebel, R. L. Writing the test item. In E. F. Lindquist (Ed.), *Educational measurement.* Washington: American Council on Education, 1951, chap. 7.

Ebel, R. L. *Measuring educational achievement.* Englewood Cliffs, N.J.: Prentice-Hall, 1965.

Edwards, A. L. The relationship between the judged desirability of a trait and the probability that the trait will be endorsed. *J. Appl. Psychol.,* 1953, **37,** 90–93.

Edwards, A. L. *Techniques of attitude scale construction.* New York: Appleton-Century-Crofts, 1957.

Eells, W. C. Reliability of repeated grading of essay type questions. *J. Educ. Psychol.,* 1930, **21,** 48–52.

Escalona, S. The use of infant tests for predictive purposes. In W. E. Martin and C. B. Stendler (Eds.), *Readings in child development.* New York: Harcourt, Brace, & World, 1954, pp. 95–103.

Farnsworth, D. *The Farnsworth Dichotomous Test for Color Blindness: Manual.* New York: Psychological Corporation, 1947.

Farnsworth, D. *The Farnsworth-Munsell 100 Hue Test for the Examination of Color Discrimination: Manual.* (Rev. ed.) New York: Psychological Corporation, 1957.

Farnsworth, P. R. Rating scales for musical interests. *J. Psychol.,* 1949, **28,** 245–253.

Flanagan, J. C. Units, scores, and norms. In E. F. Lindquist (Ed.), *Educational measurement.* Washington: American Council on Education, 1951.

Freeman, E., and Zaccaria, M. A. An illuminant-stable color-vision test, II. *J. Optical Soc. America,* 1948, **38,** 971–976.

French, J. W. The description of aptitude and achievement tests in terms of rotated factors. *Psychometric Monogr.,* 1951, No. 5.

French, W. *Behavioral goals of general education in high school.* New York: Russell Sage, 1957.

Furst, E. J. *Constructing evaluation instruments.* New York: McKay, 1958.

Garrett, H. E. *Elementary statistics.* (2nd ed.) New York: McKay, 1962.

Gerberich, J. R. *Specimen objective test items.* New York: Longmans, 1956.

Gerberich, J. R., Greene, H. A., and Jorgensen, A. N. *Measurement and evaluation in the modern school.* New York: McKay, 1962.

Gesell, A., and Amatruda, C. S. *Gesell Developmental Schedules.* New York: Psychological Corporation, 1949.

Gesell, A., Halverson, H. M., Thompson, H., Ilg, F. L., Castner, B. M., Ames, L. B., and Amatruda, C. S. *The first five years of life: A guide to the study of the preschool child.* New York: Harper & Row, 1940.

Ghiselli, E. E. The validity of commonly employed occupational tests. *Univ. of Calif. Publ. Psychol.,* 1949, **5,** 253–287.

Ghiselli, E. E., and Brown, C. W. The effectiveness of intelligence tests in the selection of workers. *J. Appl. Psychol.,* 1948, **32,** 575–580.

Gilliland, A. R. *Northwestern Intelligence Tests. Test A, for infants 4–12 weeks old.* Boston: Houghton Mifflin, 1949.

Godshalk, F. I., Swineford, F., and Coffman, W. E. *The measurement of writing ability*. New York: College Entrance Examination Board, 1966.

Golann, S. E. Psychological study of creativity. *Psychol. Bull.*, 1963, **60**, 548–565.

Goodenough, F. L. *Mental testing*. New York: Rinehart, 1949.

Goodenough, F. L., and Van Wagenen, M. J. *Minnesota Preschool Scale: Forms A and F*. (Rev. ed.) Minneapolis: Educational Test Bureau, 1940.

Gordon, E. *Musical Aptitude Profile*. Boston: Houghton Mifflin, 1965.

Goslin, D. A. *The search for ability: Standardized testing in social perspective*. New York: Russell Sage, 1963.

Goslin, D. A. *Teachers and testing*. New York: Russell Sage, 1967.

Gough, H. G. Minnesota Multiphasic Personality Inventory. In A. Weider (Ed.), *Contributions toward medical psychology*. New York: Ronald, 1953, vol. 2.

Graves, M. *Design Judgment Test: Manual*. New York: Psychological Corporation, 1948.

Gray, W. S. *Standardized Oral Reading Paragraphs*. Indianapolis: Public School, 1915. (Now Bobbs-Merrill.)

Guilford, J. P. *Psychometric methods*. (2nd ed.) New York: McGraw-Hill, 1954.

Guilford, J. P. *Personality*. New York: McGraw-Hill, 1959.

Guilford, J. P. Factorial angles to psychology. *Psychol. Rev.*, 1961, **68**, 1–20.

Guilford, J. P. *Fundamental statistics in psychology and education*. (4th ed.) New York: McGraw-Hill, 1965.

Guilford, J. P. *The nature of human intelligence*. New York: McGraw-Hill, 1967.

Guilford, J. P., and Zimmerman, W. S. *The Guilford-Zimmerman Temperament Survey: Manual*. Beverly Hills, Calif.: Sheridan Supply, 1955.

Hartshorne, H., May, M. A., and Shuttleworth, F. K. *Studies in the organization of character*. New York: Macmillan, 1930.

Hathaway, S. R., and McKinley, J. C. *Minnesota Multiphasic Personality Inventory*. (Rev. ed.) New York: Psychological Corporation, 1951.

Hill, G. E., and Scott, J. D. *School testing program inventory*. Athens, Ohio: Ohio University, Center for Educational Service, 1960.

Hollingsworth, L. S. *Children above 180 IQ*. Yonkers, N.Y.: World, 1942.

Holzman, W. H. Objective scoring of projective tests. In B. M. Bass and I. A. Berg (Eds.), *Objective approaches to personality assessment*. Princeton, N.J.: Van Nostrand, 1959.

Honzik, M., McFarlane, J., and Allen, L. The stability of mental test performance between two and eighteen years. *J. Expl. Educ.*, 1948, **17**, 309–324.

Horn, C. C. *Horn Art Aptitude Inventory: Manual*. Chicago: Stoelting, 1953.

Horn, C. C., and Smith, L. F. The Horn Art Aptitude Inventory. *J. Appl. Psychol.*, 1945, **29**, 350–355.

Kearney, N. C. *Elementary school objectives*. New York: Russell Sage, 1953.

Kent Area Guidance Council. *A proposed 12-year testing program*. Columbus, Ohio: State Department of Education, 1959.

Klineberg, O. *Negro intelligence and selective migration.* New York: Columbia, 1935.

Knauber, A. J. *Knauber Art Ability Test: Examiner's manual.* Cincinnati, Ohio: Author, 1935.

Krathwohl, D. R., Bloom, B. S., and Masia, B. B. *Taxonomy of educational objectives. The classification of educational goals. Handbook II: Affective domain.* New York: McKay, 1964.

Kuder, G. F. *Kuder Preference Record—Vocational.* Chicago: Science Research, 1956.

Kuder, G. F. *Kuder Occupational Interest Survey: General manual.* Chicago: Science Research, 1966.

Kwalwasser, J., and Dykema, P. W. *Kwalwasser-Dykema Music Tests: Manual of directions.* New York: Carl Fischer, 1930.

Lewerenz, A. S. *Tests in Fundamental Abilities of Visual Art: Manual of directions.* Los Angeles: California Test Bureau, 1927.

Likert, R., and Quasha, W. H. *Revised Minnesota Paper Form Board Test: Manual.* New York: Psychological Corporation, 1948.

Lindquist, E. F., and Hieronymus, A. N. *Iowa Tests of Basic Skills: Manual for administrators, supervisors, and counselors.* Boston: Houghton Mifflin, 1964.

Lordahl, D. S. *Modern statistics for behavioral sciences.* New York: Ronald, 1967.

Lorge, I. The fundamental nature of measurement. In E. F. Lindquist (Ed.), *Educational measurement.* Washington: American Council on Education, 1951.

Lorge, I., Thorndike, R. L., and Hagen, E. *The Lorge-Thorndike Intelligence Tests* (multileveled). Boston: Houghton Mifflin, 1964.

Lyman, H. B. *Test scores and what they mean.* Englewood Cliffs, N.J.: Prentice-Hall, 1963.

McAdory, M. *The McAdory Art Test: Manual.* New York: Teachers College, 1929.

Mackinnon, D. W. The nature and nurture of creative talent. *Am. Psychologist,* 1962, **17,** 484–495.

Marshall, J. C. Composition errors and essay examination grades reexamined. *Am. Educl. Res. J.,* 1967, **4,** 375–386.

Maxwell, W. C. *International Typewriting Tests.* Minneapolis: Educational Test Bureau, 1950.

Meier, N. C. *The Meier Art Tests: I. Art Judgment: Examiner's manual.* Iowa City: University of Iowa, Bureau of Educational Research Service, 1942.

Meier, N. C. *The Meier Art Tests: II. Aesthetic Perception: Examiner's manual.* Iowa City: University of Iowa, Bureau of Educational Research Service, 1963.

Melton, A. W. (Ed.) Apparatus Tests: *AAF Aviation Psychol. Prog. Res. Rep.,* No. 4. Washington: GPO, 1947.

Michaelis, J., Grossman, R., and Scott, L. *New designs for the elementary school curriculum.* New York: McGraw-Hill, 1967.

Miller, G. A. *Psychology: The science of mental life.* New York: Harper & Row, 1962.

Murray, H. A. *Thematic Apperception Test.* Cambridge, Mass.: Harvard, 1943.

National Society for the Study of Education. The measurement of understanding. *45th Yearb. Nat. Soc. Stud. Educ.,* Part I. Chicago: University of Chicago Press, 1946.

Noll, V. H. *Introduction to educational measurement.* (2nd ed.) Boston: Houghton Mifflin, 1965.

Nunnally, J. C. *Popular conceptions of mental health: Their development and change.* New York: Holt, 1961.

Nunnally, J. C. *Psychometric theory.* New York: McGraw-Hill, 1967.

Nunnally, J. C. *Introduction to psychological measurement.* New York: McGraw-Hill, 1970.

Nunnally, J. C., and Flaugher, R. F. Correlates of semantic habits. *J. Pers.,* 1963, **31,** 192–202.

Osgood, C. E. Studies on the generality of affective meaning systems. *Am. Psychologist,* 1962, **17,** 10–28.

Osgood, C. E., Suci, G. J., and Tannenbaum, P. *The measurement of meaning.* Urbana: University of Illinois Press, 1957.

Peterson, J. *Early conceptions and tests of intelligence.* Yonkers, N.Y.: World, 1926.

Pinneau, S. R. *Changes in intelligence quotient.* Boston: Houghton Mifflin, 1961.

Pintner, R., Cunningham, B., and Durost, W. *Pintner-Cunningham Primary Test: Directions for administering, scoring, and interpreting.* New York: Harcourt, Brace & World, 1966.

Psychological Corporation. *General Clerical Test: Manual.* New York: Author, 1950.

Ragan, W. B. *Modern elementary curriculum.* (3rd ed.) New York: Holt, 1966.

Remmers, H. H., and Bauernfeind, R. H. *STS Junior Inventory.* Bensenville, Ill.: Scholastic Testing Service, 1968.

Remmers, H. H., and Shimberg, B. *STS Youth Inventory.* Bensenville, Ill.: Scholastic Testing Service, 1967.

Richardson, Bellows, Henry, and Company, Inc. *SRA Mechanical Aptitudes: Manual.* Chicago: Science Research, 1950.

Roberts, J. A. F. Resemblances in intelligence between sibs selected from a complete sample of an urban population. *Proc. Internat. Genet. Congr.,* 1941, **7,** 252.

Scannell, D. P., and Marshall, J. C. The effect of selected composition errors on grades assigned essay examinations. *Am. Educl. Res. J.,* 1966, **3,** 125–130.

Science Research Associates. *SRA Achievement Series interpretive guide.* Chicago: Author, 1968.

Seashore, C. E., Lewis, D., and Saetveit, J. G. *Seashore Measures of Musical Talents.* (Rev. ed.) New York: Psychological Corporation, 1960.

Seashore, H. G. Methods of expressing test scores. *Test Serv. Bull.,* No. 48. New York: Psychological Corporation, 1955.

Seashore, R. H., and Hevner, K. A. A time-saving device for the construction of attitude scales. *J. Soc. Psychol.,* 1933, **4,** 366–372.

Shaw, M. E., and Wright, J. M. *Scales for the measurement of attitudes.* New York: McGraw-Hill, 1967.

Smith, E. R., and Tyler, R. W. *Appraising and recording student progress.* New York: Harper, 1942.

Spearman, C. E. *The abilities of man.* New York: Macmillan, 1927.

Stalnaker, J. M. The essay type of examination. In E. F. Lindquist (Ed.), *Educational measurement.* Washington: American Council on Education, 1951, chap. 13.

Stanley, J. C. *Measurement in today's schools.* (4th ed.) Englewood Cliffs, N.J.: Prentice-Hall, 1964.

Stewart, N. A.G.C.T. scores of army personnel grouped by occupations. *Occupations,* 1947, **26,** 5–41.

Strang, R. *How to report pupil progress.* Chicago: Science Research, 1955.

Stromberg, E. L. *Stromberg Dexterity Test: Preliminary manual.* New York: Psychological Corporation, 1951.

Strong, E. K. *Vocational interests 18 years after college.* Minneapolis: University of Minnesota Press, 1955.

Strong, E. K., and Campbell, D. P. *Manual for Strong Vocational Interest Blanks.* Stanford, Calif.: Stanford University Press, 1966.

Stroud, J. B., Hieronymous, A. N., and McKee, P. *Primary Reading Profiles, Level 2.* Boston: Houghton Mifflin, 1967.

Studies in visual acuity. *Personnel Res. Sec. Rep.* 742. AGO, 1948, 161.

Stutsman, R. *Mental measurement of preschool children.* Yonkers, N.Y.: World, 1931.

Super, D. E., and Crites, J. O. *Appraising vocational fitness by means of psychological tests.* New York: Harper & Row, 1962.

Symonds, P. M. *Symonds Picture-story Test.* New York: Teachers College, 1948.

Taylor, C. W. (Ed.) *Creativity: Progress and potential.* New York: Wiley, 1964. (a)

Taylor, C. W. (Ed.) *Widening horizons in creativity.* New York: Wiley, 1964. (b)

Terman, L. M., and Merrill, M. *Stanford-Binet Intelligence Scale.* Boston: Houghton Mifflin, 1960.

Thomas, R. M. *Judging student progress.* (Rev. ed.) New York: Longmans, 1960.

Thorndike, R. L. Reliability. In E. F. Lindquist (Ed.), *Educational measurement.* Washington: American Council on Education, 1951.

Thorndike, R. L. *The concepts of over- and under-achievement.* New York: Teachers College, 1963.

Thorndike, R. L., and Hagen, E. *Measurement and evaluation in psychology and education.* (3rd ed.) New York: Wiley, 1969.

Thurstone, L. L. A factorial study of perception. *Psychometric Monogr.,* 1944, No. 4.

Tiegs, E. W., and Clark, W. W. *California Achievement Tests*. Monterey, Calif.: California Test Bureau, 1950, 1957.

Torrance, E. P. Current research on the nature of creative talent. *J. Couns. Psychol.,* 1959, **6,** 309–316.

Torrance, E. P. *Guiding creative talent*. Englewood Cliffs, N.J.: Prentice-Hall, 1962.

Valentine, C. W. *Intelligence tests for young children*. London: Methuen, 1945.

Vaughn, K. W. Planning the objective test. In E. F. Lindquist (Ed.), *Educational measurement*. Washington: American Council on Education, 1951, chap. 6.

Wason, P. Response to affirmative and negative binary statements. *Brit. J. Psychol.,* 1961, **52,** 133–142.

Waters, L. K. Effect of perceived scoring formula on some aspects of test performance. *Educl. Psychol. Meas.,* 1967, **27,** 1005–1010.

Watson, L. A., and Tolan, T. *Hearing tests and hearing instruments*. Baltimore: Williams & Wilkins, 1949.

Wechsler, D. *Wechsler Intelligence Scale for Children: Manual*. New York: Psychological Corporation, 1949.

Wechsler, D. *Manual for the Wechsler Adult Intelligence Scale*. New York: Psychological Corporation, 1955.

Wechsler, D. *Wechsler Preschool and Primary Scale of Intelligence*. New York: Psychological Corporation, 1967.

Wing, H. D. *Wing Standardized Tests of Musical Intelligence*. (Rev. ed.) London: National Foundation for Educational Research in London and Wales, 1960.

Wood, D. A. *Test construction*. Columbus, Ohio: Merrill, 1960.

Woodworth, R. S. *Personal Data Sheet*. Chicago: Stoelting, 1918.

Wrinkle, W. L. *Improving marking and reporting practices in elementary and secondary schools*. New York: Rhinehart, 1956.

Zern, D. Effects of variations in question phrasing on true-false answers by grade-school children. *Psychol. Rep.,* 1967, **20,** 527–533.

name index

subject index